OFFSHORE ENERGY LAW

This book examines the regulatory, environmental, financial, socio-legal and safety aspects that shape offshore energy infrastructure projects and their operation.

The marine environment holds vast resources to provide energy solutions for humankind. The sustainable development of such offshore energy resources is one of the most pressing challenges posed by the energy transition.

However, and despite the pivotal role offshore energy is to play in the future, the interaction, synergies and conflicts arising between these regulatory, socio-legal, environmental and financial dimensions of offshore energy are often not discussed within the energy law scholarship. This book aims to fill this evident gap in existing energy law research to distil critical legal lessons from traditional offshore energy sectors to encourage best practice regulation of offshore energy net zero industries.

Offshore Energy Law provides a functional analysis that covers the life cycle of offshore energy developments, including renewable and hydrocarbons, within the broader context of the energy crisis and energy transition debates. Written and edited by leading global offshore energy experts, the book brings together a global and sectoral comparative perspective to central offshore energy topics such as licensing, socio-legal challenges and opportunities, safety and ecological governance, and the use of marine/maritime spatial planning.

Global Energy Law and Policy: Volume 11

Global Energy Law and Policy

Series Editors
Peter D Cameron
Pieter Bekker
Volker Roeben
Leonie Reins
Crina Baltag

Energy policy and energy law are undergoing rapid global transformation, characterised by the push in favour of decarbonisation. The 2015 Sustainable Development Goals, the Paris Agreement and COP26 on international climate and energy action have forged a consensus for a pathway to a universal just transition towards a low-carbon economy for all states and all societies.

This series publishes conceptual work that help academics, legal practitioners and decision-makers to make sense of these transformational changes. The perspective of the series is global. It welcomes contributions on international law, regional law (for example, from the EU, US and ASEAN regions), and the domestic law of all states with emphasis on comparative works that identify horizontal trends, and including transnational law. The series' scope is comprehensive, embracing both public and commercial law on energy in all forms and sources and throughout the energy life-cycle from extraction, production, operation, consumption and waste management/decommissioning. The series is a forum for innovative interdisciplinary work that uses the insights of cognate disciplines to achieve a better understanding of energy law and policy in the 21st century.

Recent titles in this series:

Decarbonisation and the Energy Industry
edited by Tade Oyewumni, Penelope Crossley, Frédéric Gilles Sourgens and Kim Talus

The Global Energy Transition: Law, Policy and Economics for Energy in the 21st Century
edited by Peter D Cameron, Xiaoyi Mu and Volker Roeben

The Law and Governance of Mining and Minerals: A Global Perspective
by Ana Elizabeth Bastida

National Climate Change Acts: The Emergence, Form and Nature of National Framework Climate Legislation
edited by Thomas L Muinzer

Governing the Extractive Sector: Regulating the Foreign Conduct of International Mining Firms
by Jeffrey Bone

Stability and Legitimate Expectations in International Energy Investments
by Rahmi Kopar

Land Law and the Extractive Industries: Challenges and Opportunities in Africa
by Victoria R Nalule

China's Global Energy Expansion: A Regulatory Assessment
by Xiaohan Gong

Critical Minerals, Sustainability, and the Energy Transition in the Global South: A Justice Perspective
by Susan Nakanwagi

International Investment Law and the Energy Transition
edited by Rahmi Kopar and Volker Roeben

Offshore Energy Law: Challenges and Opportunities for Renewables and Hydrocarbons
edited by Ignacio Herrera Anchustegui, Madeline Taylor, Eduardo G Pereira and Eddy Wifa

Offshore Energy Law

Challenges and Opportunities for Renewables and Hydrocarbons

Edited by
Ignacio Herrera Anchustegui
Madeline Taylor
Eduardo G Pereira
and
Eddy Wifa

•HART•
OXFORD • LONDON • NEW YORK • NEW DELHI • SYDNEY

HART PUBLISHING

Bloomsbury Publishing Plc

Kemp House, Chawley Park, Cumnor Hill, Oxford, OX2 9PH, UK

1385 Broadway, New York, NY 10018, USA

Bloomsbury Publishing Ireland Limited, 29 Earlsfort Terrace, Dublin 2, D02 AY28, Ireland

HART PUBLISHING, the Hart/Stag logo, BLOOMSBURY and the Diana logo are trademarks of Bloomsbury Publishing Plc

First published in Great Britain 2025

A catalogue record for this book is available from the British Library.

A catalogue record for this book is available from the Library of Congress.

Library of Congress Control Number: 2025933504

ISBN: HB: 978-1-50996-439-0
ePDF: 978-1-50996-441-3
ePub: 978-1-50996-440-6

Typeset by Compuscript Ltd, Shannon

For product safety related questions contact productsafety@bloomsbury.com

To find out more about our authors and books visit www.hartpublishing.co.uk. Here you will find extracts, author information, details of forthcoming events and the option to sign up for our newsletters.

FOREWORD

As states continue to evolve non-hydrocarbon energy resources as part of the necessary energy transition in light of the 2015 Paris Agreement, there is rising interest in utilising the offshore environment for the generation of energy. Such a concept is not new. For more than seven decades, pioneered in the US Gulf of Mexico and perfected in the North Sea, private entities, state-owned oil companies, and a combination of the two, have developed the rich subsea hydrocarbon deposits. In developing these offshore resources, many technological innovations, work practices, and safety systems have been developed. Concomitant, economic fortunes for both individuals and states have been realised on the back of the development of oil and gas resources offshore.

States such as Norway have developed not only a thriving petroleum export industry, complete with a critical role in the provision of gas to European States, but also associated industries within the economy. In the early 1970s, commencing with the third licensing round, Norway utilised the 10 oil commandments (Commandment number three: 'new business activity shall be developed with a basis in petroleum'), building on existing national strengths such as shipbuilding to develop new industries, including concrete and steel platform construction, and development of new technologies for such construction. Other states have not been so lucky, such as Australia, which disregarded two parliamentary inquiries in the 1990s which recommended 'local content provisions' to aid in the development of Australian industry as the North West Shelf Petroleum province was developed. Today Australia gets another chance as it embarks on the development of offshore renewable energy assets while implementing the 'Future Made in Australia' policy and legislation to ensure benefit to Australian businesses and communities.

Landmark accidents and incidents in offshore environments, including the *Sea Gem* drilling disaster, the *Ekofisk Bravo* blowout, *Alexander Kielland* flotel capsize, the horrific Piper Alpha platform catastrophe, and the Deepwater Horizon disaster, have provided painful memories, as well as milestones in technological, legislative, process, and safety development. It is these lessons that the burgeoning offshore renewable energy industry can capture, learn from, and incorporate into legal processes and instruments.

Today we reap the rewards of the offshore petroleum pioneers and titans that came before the offshore renewable energy industry. Technologies, safety systems, policies, and legislative and regulatory frameworks that govern offshore renewable energy production have had their origins in the hydrocarbon industry. All that has occurred before and has been learnt before will not be in vain. Its application to the offshore renewable energy industry will ensure that deaths are minimised, the environment is protected, and other marine users are considered.

Once upon a time it would have been almost heretical to have a book dedicated only to legal aspects of offshore energy law. Certainly, the inclusion of legal aspects of offshore energy has long been included in tomes dedicated to offshore energy, especially from the engineering and science disciplines. But law? A decade ago, unlikely, where traditional thinking would be that the regulation of offshore renewable energy was a part of either the regulation on onshore energy extended to the offshore zone, or as part of the study of offshore wind generation in general.

It is clear that offshore energy law has come into its own. This book, with contributions by offshore law masters such as Paterson and Herrera Anchustegui, joined by newcomers such as Wifa and Shapovalova, as well as the plethora of other talented academics, has earned its place as an essential read in both offshore renewable energy regulation. It is also a masterful insight into how one activity can provide regulatory insight and guidance for another, seemingly unrelated activity to guide development and assure the integrity and harmony of regulatory activities.

As this book considers offshore energy law research in the context of the energy transition, the reference to and consideration of petroleum law, regulation and policy, and the development of such in harsh marine environments, will ensure that a sound, measured and safe legal framework will evolve in a manner that can preserve life, protect precious environmental resources, and abide by every evolving rule of International Law.

This is a book that I would have (and should have) contributed to, and it is certainly one that will have a prominent place in my bookshelf. I commend both the authors of the individual chapters, and the editors, for their efforts in completing such a seminal tome.

Professor Tina Soliman-Hunter
November 2024

TABLE OF CONTENTS

LIST OF CONTRIBUTORS

Ignacio Herrera Anchustegui is Professor, Faculty of Law, University of Bergen, Norway. Leader of the Research Group for Climate, Energy and Environmental Law of the University of Bergen, and member of the Bergen Offshore Wind Centre (BOW).

Madeline Taylor is Associate Professor, Macquarie Law School, Australian Research Council EC Fellow, and Co-Lead of the Transforming Energy Markets Research Centre, Macquarie University.

Eduardo G Pereira is Professor at the Siberian Federal University and Research Fellow at the University of São Paulo.

Eddy Wifa is Senior Lecturer, Centre for Energy Law, and Convener, Global South Law Research Network, School of Law University of Aberdeen, UK.

Angelo Goethals is Doctoral Researcher (PhairywinD, ETF Funded), Faculty of Law and Criminology, University of Ghent, Belgium.

Frank Maes is Professor Emeritus, Faculty of Law and Criminology, University of Ghent, Belgium.

Frederik Vandendriessche is Professor, Faculty of Law and Criminology, University of Ghent, Belgium, Lawyer, Stibbe, Brussels, Belgium.

Daria Shapovalova is Senior Lecturer in Energy Law, University of Aberdeen. Director of the Aberdeen University Centre for Energy Law. Coordinator of the Just Transition Lab at the University of Aberdeen. Chair of the Scottish Arctic Network.

Pedi Obani is Associate Professor, School of Law, University of Bradford, United Kingdom. UK Research and Innovation Future Leaders Fellow.

Solomon N Obulor is Solicitor specialising in commercial and contract law at the City of Edinburgh Council, United Kingdom.

Joy A Debski is Lecturer in Law at the Robert Gordon University, United Kingdom.

Nnennaya J Nwali is PhD researcher at the University of Aberdeen, United Kingdom.

John Paterson is Professor, Centre for Energy Law, School of Law, University of Aberdeen, UK.

Cătălin-Gabriel Stănescu is Associate Professor, Department of Law, Syddansk Universitet, Denmark.

Cristian Rubanovici is Legal Advisor, Poul Schmith/Kammeradvokaten.

Diana Rodrigues Prado de Castro is Brazilian Counsel of the Rio de Janeiro tax practice of Tauil & Chequer in association with Mayer Brown. Master in Public Finance, Taxation and Development by Rio de Janeiro State University (UERJ).

João Oliveira is Senior Corporate Energy Lawyer, Projects, Operations & Procurement. BP plc.

Elena I Athwal is SJD Candidate in international energy and environmental law at the College of Law, Hamad Bin Khalifa University (HBKU), and Research Fellow for the UNESCO Chair of Environmental Law and Sustainable Development in Doha, Qatar.

Opeyemi Omotuyi is Barrister and Solicitor of the Supreme Court of Nigeria and Lecturer in the Department of Private Law, Federal University Oye-Ekiti.

Reg Fowler is Acting General Counsel, Calyx Global Inc. and Senior Legal Consultant, Viridor Waste Limited.

Cameron Kelly is General Counsel at the Australian Renewable Energy Agency (ARENA) and Advisor to the New South Wales Government on the delivery of the Electricity Infrastructure Investment Roadmap.

Keith B Hall is the Nesser Family Chair in Energy Law, Campanile Charities Professor of Energy Law at Louisiana State University Law School, where he also serves as Director of the Mineral Law Institute.

Knut Høivik is Associate Professor, Faculty of Law, University of Bergen, Norway. Member of Research Group for Climate, Energy and Environmental Law of the University of Bergen.

Heidi Eikenes Seglem is Lead Counsel, Equinor ASA.

Sondre Dyrland is Associate Professor, Scandinavian Institute of Maritime Law, Department of Energy and Resources Law, Faculty of Law, University of Oslo, Norway.

Camilla Grytten is Partner, Advokatfirmaet Schjødt AS. Member of the Norwegian Bar Association's Energy, Hydropower and Oil and Gas Law Committee.

Rüdiger Tscherning is Associate Professor, Faculty of Law & Research Fellow, School of Public Policy, University of Calgary, Canada; Associate Professor II, Faculty of Law, University of Bergen, Norway.

Ana Carolina Marins de Carvalho is Associate at Mattos Filho Advogados (Brazil), and founder of Mentes de Energia, a study group focused on the oil and gas industry, in partnership with the Brazilian Petroleum, Gas and Biofuels Institute (IBP).

Aurelia Reid is Attorney at Law at Griffin Chambers in Port of Spain, Trinidad & Tobago.

Constantinos Yiallourides is Senior Lecturer of Public International Law, School of Law, Macquarie University, Sydney, research leader in law of the sea, British Institute of International and Comparative Law, London, and a practicing consultant in international law.

PART I

Offshore Energy: Fostering Environmental Stewardship and Community Collaboration

1

Introduction to Offshore Energy Law: Challenges and Opportunities for Renewables and Hydrocarbons

MADELINE TAYLOR, EDDY WIFA, EDUARDO G PEREIRA AND IGNACIO HERRERA ANCHUSTEGUI*

1. Introduction

The success of the global energy transition hinges on the effective development of offshore energy resources. While offshore hydrocarbons have been explored and extracted for over a century, the offshore renewable industry is still nascent yet rapidly expanding. At first a Northern European phenomenon, as of 2023, offshore wind installed capacity has expanded globally, reaching 75 GW with an annual growth rate of 24 per cent, led by China.[1] Offshore renewable expansion will continue in different regions, resorting to various energy technologies. For example, global offshore wind capacity is projected to increase up to 410 GW by 2033,[2] while tidal and offshore hydrogen production projects are starting to become a reality. This rapid offshore renewable energy expansion at sea is linked to climate change issues and onshore conflicts, well-illustrated by the 'not-in-my-backyard' phenomenon. The commitment to triple global renewable energy capacity requires ramping up offshore low-carbon energy technologies to limit global warming to $1.5^{\circ C}$.[3]

However, despite the rise of offshore low-carbon energy industries, conventional offshore energy development remains critical in multiple jurisdictions. For example, oil

* We acknowledge the Traditional Custodians of the lands and waters where this book was conceived and written. We pay our respects to Elders past, present, and emerging, and recognise their ongoing connection to land, sea, and community. We also extend this respect to all First Nations peoples across the world honouring their rich cultures, knowledge systems, and histories that have existed for thousands of years.

All websites were last accessed on 10 October 2024.

[1] Wood Mackenzie, 'China leads global wind turbine manufacturers' market share in 2023' (Woodmac, 1 May 2024), www.woodmac.com/press-releases/2024-press-releases/global-wind-oem-marketshare/.

[2] GWEC, 'Global Offshore Wind Report 2023' (GWEC, 2024), gwec.net/gwecs-global-offshore-wind-report-2023/.

[3] COP28, 'Global Renewables and Energy Efficiency Pledge' (COP28, 2023) www.cop28.com/en/global-renewables-and-energy-efficiency-pledge.

and gas production contributes to 15 per cent of the Norwegian GDP, 10 per cent of the Brazilian GDP, and 3 per cent of the Australian GDP.[4] New offshore jurisdictions such as Guyana and Suriname are also appearing, making large offshore hydrocarbon discoveries in recent years, bringing rapid socio-economic transformations and environmental and climate responsibilities. In addition to hydrocarbon's role in the current energy scenario in which oil production is projected to peak in 2030,[5] existing conventional offshore oil and gas infrastructure and offshore energy expertise will play a critical role in the global energy transition.

For instance, existing oil and gas infrastructure may be utilised to support low-carbon energy forms, like offshore hydrogen production or even transport. If oil and gas platforms are repurposed, offshore wind to hydrogen production is projected to attract a price of USD 7/kg by 2030 and 1/kg by 2050.[6] Furthermore, offshore sector-coupling and projects combining hydrocarbons with renewable energy are being developed to promote the energy transition as well as the decarbonisation of the oil and gas industry, exemplified by the currently operating Norwegian Hywind Tampen project,[7] and the Scottish Green Volt project licensed in April 2024.[8] These offshore oil and gas electrification activities have a clear link to climate ambitions set by states and energy companies. The objective is to ensure the climate compatibility of offshore petroleum projects. As an example, the UK North Sea Transition Authority has committed to a 50 per cent reduction in upstream offshore petroleum emissions by 2030 under the North Sea Transition Deal. This initiative will require petroleum proponents 'where reasonable' to participate in regional low-carbon power schemes or invest in standalone low-carbon power solutions.[9]

The energy transition is having an unprecedented impact on the offshore energy landscape, which currently, unlike only a few years ago, integrates a complex interplay of established and emerging industries, underscoring the urgent need to identify synergies between conventional and renewable energy sectors. While decarbonisation will drive a new suite of legal instruments, markets, and tools in energy law, comparative analyses of both conventional and low-carbon energy industries and their respective regulatory frameworks remain underexamined in existing energy law scholarship.

As proposed by the contributors in this *Offshore Energy Law* book, regulatory lessons must be distilled from existing conventional offshore energy operations for the future development of decarbonised energy and electricity sectors. Increasing offshore energy development creates growing demands on marine spaces and natural resources, sparking concern amongst policymakers, regulators, and communities – partly prompted by

[4] These States are some of the analysed jurisdictions throughout this book. See Statista, 'Share of GDP attributed to oil and gas production in select countries worldwide in 2023' (Statista, 2023) www.statista.com/statistics/1451878/share-gdp-oil-and-gas-production-select-countries-globally/.

[5] International Energy Agency (IEA), 'Slowing demand growth and surging supply put global oil markets on course for major surplus this decade' (IEA, 12 June 2024) www.iea.org/news/slowing-demand-growth-and-surging-supply-put-global-oil-markets-on-course-for-major-surplus-this-decade.

[6] Bloomberg NEF, 'Offshore Wind-to-Hydrogen Sounds A Starting Gun' (Bloomberg NEF, 30 June 2021) about.bnef.com/blog/offshore-wind-to-hydrogen-sounds-a-starting-gun/.

[7] Equinor, 'Hywind Tampen' (2024) www.equinor.com/energy/hywind-tampen.

[8] GreenVolt, 'The Future of Floating Wind' (2024) greenvoltoffshorewind.com.

[9] Tom Wheeler and NSTA, *Stewardship Principles for Electrification* (2023) www.nstauthority.co.uk/media/9061/nsta-industry-electrification-letter-05042023.pdf.

the 'fight for space' and new interactions between new stakeholders.[10] Such concerns indicate potential legal lacunas in existing offshore hydrocarbon and renewable regulatory frameworks. Transplanting and applying existing regulatory paradigms alone will not be sufficient to satisfy the ongoing requirements of new and emerging offshore low-carbon energy sources, particularly concerning offshore carbon capture and storage, an increasingly important technology to achieve Geological Net Zero.[11] This *Offshore Energy Law* book analyses the different and diverging dimensions of offshore energy development against the backdrop of the global race to decarbonise. It delves into multidisciplinary opportunities for reform in energy law and policy, which will shape how offshore energy is harnessed, transported, and exploited.

The collection of chapters within this book explores the complex challenges and opportunities shaping and governing energy infrastructure projects and their operations from environmental, financial, socio-legal, safety, and commercial lifecycle perspectives. These essential dimensions of energy development are often overlooked within the existing energy law literature, as, for example, environmental and social aspects of energy development are frequently confined to environmental law. At other times, the literature focuses on either public or private law aspects, but not both. This work aims to critically and comparatively analyse these environmental, socio-legal, financial, safety, and commercial lifecycle offshore energy perspectives. It studies and probes key functions in the offshore energy regulatory realm, such as offshore energy licensing, safety, ecological governance, and marine/maritime spatial planning. The analyses presented throughout the book aim to provide valuable insights into both commercial operations and legal frameworks. As the energy transition accelerates, the book also addresses critical societal issues and opportunities, focusing on the impact on non-industry stakeholders. The book also applies a socio-legal lens on the energy transition to explore aspects of energy justice, the just transition, and the social contract, highlighting the importance of inclusivity and equity in shaping the future of offshore energy.

This book is structured in three parts: *Part I – Offshore Energy: Fostering Environmental Stewardship and Community Collaboration*; *Part II – Offshore Energy: Business and Financing*; and *Part III – Offshore Energy: Complex Infrastructure and Overarching Conclusions*. In this first introductory chapter, we outline the array of research explored throughout this book within the context of the offshore energy transition. Each chapter addresses distinct aspects of offshore energy transitions, from offshore energy project design to decommissioning, as well as including the topic discussion in its social, environmental, financial, or legal context.

Our aim with this *Offshore Energy Law* book is to chart the future directions of energy law research in the context of the offshore energy transition by delineating principles and legal typologies to guide development and assess decarbonisation measures, regulatory practices, and commercial trends. The chapters presented reveal that the offshore energy transformation is more than the deployment of technological solutions. It hinges on the tactical integration, responsive cooperation, and commercial

[10] Olivia Woolley, 'Trouble on the Horizon? Addressing Place-based Values in Planning for Offshore Wind Energy' (2010) 22 *Journal of Environmental Law* 223–50.
[11] Myles Allen et al, 'Net Zero: Science, Origins, and Implications' (2022) 47 *Annual Review of Environment and Resources* 849–87.

adaption of all stakeholders in the energy supply chain, underpinned by robust and adaptive technology-neutral regulations. Regulators hold an increasing responsibility to ensure that offshore energy resource development meets both existing and emerging sustainability objectives and obligations. This book aims to offer a regulatory roadmap to achieving these pivotal goals.

2. Part I – Offshore Energy: Fostering Environmental Stewardship and Community Collaboration

Defining and mitigating diverse socio-legal risks are fundamental requirements for a successful offshore energy transition.[12] As recognised by The United Nations Climate Change Conference (COP28) Agreement, a just, orderly, and equitable energy transition[13] must underscore the global tripling of renewable energy capacity by 2030.[14] Yet, how to balance social impacts and risks to deliver sustained benefits to communities remains a pervasive question amongst energy policymakers. Part I of this book directly addresses this critical dilemma by exploring avenues for policy and regulatory reform to achieve socially responsive and nature-positive net zero offshore energy transformations. The chapter contributions within Part I present a cutting-edge technology-neutral examination of regulatory regimes in over seven different jurisdictions, offering timely lessons for regulatory reform. In so doing, the chapters in Part I of this book provide an analysis of the various conflicts and tensions that may arise in the development of both offshore oil and gas and offshore renewable-like wind energy. It debunks the erroneous assumption that the sea is endless and therefore, holds unlimited space for offshore energy development and other activities. These relational tensions are analysed with the view of encouraging a more sustainable offshore energy development.

Mapping marine spaces raises crucial legal questions on how to balance environmental risk mitigation with the evolving demands and liabilities of multi-sector operations. **Goethals, Maes and Vandendriessche** in '*Multiple use in the North Sea: evolving towards a new legal framework? – A case study based on the Belgian and Dutch examples*' in chapter two examine multiple offshore energy infrastructure uses while balancing environmental protection in the North Sea. **Goethals, Maes and Vandendriessche** provide both a comprehensive and analytical account of the priorities for developing offshore wind, whilst still providing flexibility for multi-sector development, as the analyses relate to the multiple uses of offshore wind zones. The chapter engages with questions about the liabilities of the parties involved, the environmental assessments and permits,

[12] Benjamin K Sovacool, Heike Brugger, Iska Brunzema, Alicja Dańkowska, Devon Wemyss, Anne-Lorène Vernay, Regina Betz, Flor Avelino, Tessa de Geus, Agata Dembek, Elisabeth Duetschke, Sabine Hielscher, Marfuga Iskandarova, Leticia Müller, Jörg Musiolik, Adélie Ranville, Joachim Schleich, Agata Stasik, Marta Strumińska-Kutra, Christian Winzer, Julia Wittmayer and Karoline S Rogge, 'Social innovation supports inclusive and accelerated energy transitions with appropriate governance' (2023) 289 *Communications Earth and Environment* 1–11.

[13] UNFCC, 'COP28 Agreement Signals "Beginning of the End" of the Fossil Fuel Era' (2023) unfccc.int/news/cop28-agreement-signals-beginning-of-the-end-of-the-fossil-fuel-era.

[14] IRENA, 'Tripling renewable power and doubling energy efficiency by 2030: Crucial steps towards 1.5°C' (2023) www.irena.org/Digital-Report/Tripling-renewable-power-and-doubling-energy-efficiency-by-2030.

the concessions and conditions, and safety zones. The chapter analyses the multi-use regime in both a regional EU and jurisdictional perspective, comparing the Belgian and Dutch legal frameworks. However, it would appear that there is a limited legal obligation to enforce this, which could create challenges in its adoption. In contrast, the Dutch system follows a top-down approach with active stakeholder participation, where the government decides which shared-use activities are permitted. In the Dutch model, multiple uses are clearly identified and monitored due to the structured nature of the regime. The chapter acknowledges the complexity of multi-use and coexistence within offshore energy zones. It also recognises the need for further risk assessments of potential multiple uses and the risks that could arise in this connection.

In chapter three, **Wifa, Shapovalova and Obani** in '*Balancing Environmental Protection with Offshore Wind and Petroleum Development Two Peas in a Pod?*' offer a detailed analysis of the regulatory framework for mitigating environmental and ecological risks on the UK continental shelf, examining both offshore wind and offshore petroleum developments. Considering the North Sea's status as the 'energy jewel' of the United Kingdom, owing to its decades of offshore oil and gas exploration, energy transition has equally given rise to a growing number of offshore wind energy projects. On the surface, the UK regulatory regime appears to be somewhat mature following decades of oil and gas exploration. The conducted research reveals, however, the fragmented nature of the regime and the inherent limitations of international and national legislation that need to be balanced between environmental risks and maximisation of economic recovery from offshore energy developments. The chapter engages with various regulatory mechanisms aimed at mitigating these environmental and ecological risks. Here, regimes such as Strategic Environmental Assessment; Marine Spatial Planning, Environmental Impact Assessments, and others are critically discussed. In reconciling the maximisation of offshore energy resources and the protection of the environment, the chapter raises some concerns about the implementation of the regime and its fragmentation. In particular, the authors highlight that, in their view, the discussions leave the overall impression that similar errors are being made in the context of transitioning from petroleum to renewable energy despite decades of experience. In some ways, these shortcomings reveal that the regime is also fraught with inherent limitations, such as the potential for conflict of interests and the political economy of speed. All of these are extensively discussed in the chapter.

Developing critical minerals offshore is a salient debate in energy law literature. This debate hinges on legal complexities surrounding deep-sea mining beyond national waters, coupled with technical and feasibility challenges, and environmental concerns. Following considerable research, the Norwegian Offshore Directorate has invited applications for the first seabed minerals development licensing round.[15] Conversely, Africa has not engaged with the United Nations International Seabed Authority to commence the process for potential exploration permits for offshore critical minerals development. Deep seabed mining licensing is expected to increase alignment with the International Energy Agency's projection of a sevenfold increase for critical minerals by 2050 to develop critical and rare-earth minerals as key components in net zero

[15] Norwegian Offshore Directorate, 'The Minerals we Need' (2024) www.sodir.no/en/whats-new/news/general-news/2024/the-minerals-we-need/.

energy technologies.[16] **Obulor, Debski and Nwali**, in '*Avoiding (Offshore) Renewable and Critical Mineral-Based Resource Curse in Africa: The Role of a Continent-wide Legal Regime*' in chapter four explore the role of offshore critical minerals in supporting offshore renewable energy technological development in the African energy transition. Drawing parallels with the regulatory failures for offshore petroleum development creating the conditions for the Resource Curse[17] phenomena in Africa, the authors critically examine the emergence of a 'new colonialism'[18] forecast in offshore minerals development. They extend the Resource Curse concept to encapsulate a new 'Critical Minerals-Based Resource Curse' by highlighting the similar risks associated with short-term economic rental returns with offshore mineral exploitation without considering intergenerational equity. By probing the African Integrated Maritime Strategy 2050,[19] the chapter offers a critical intervention in the African Just Energy transition literature by calling for a strategy for local content regulatory requirements for potential offshore critical minerals development to counter the development of a Critical-Minerals Based Curse. The authors call for a regulatory pivot with the Just Transition at the heart of a future developed African Offshore Critical Minerals Strategy. This approach aims to move Africa beyond the status of a 'rentier state'[20] to foster 'in-country' sustained value creation.

Extending the focus on the importance of establishing robust protections for individuals involved in the energy transition, **Wifa and Paterson**, in chapter five, examine '*Health and Safety Regulation in the United Kingdom's Offshore Hydrocarbon and Wind Energy Industries: Similarities, Differences, Reforms*'. This chapter analyses the regulatory frameworks governing health and safety risks for traditional offshore petroleum compared with offshore wind industries in the UK. The UK is often recognised as a global leader in offshore wind development, boasting its position as the second largest offshore wind market with 13.9 GW of offshore wind capacity representing a fourfold increase between 2012–2024.[21] An ambitious target of reaching 50 GW of offshore wind capacity by 2030, including 5 GW from floating wind projects has been set for the UK.[22] The permitting and auction process to develop offshore wind in the UK has rapidly advanced to meet such ambitious goals. However, comparatively, the health and safety regulatory framework for offshore wind lags considerably behind. **Wifa and Paterson** highlight this regulatory inertia in developing health and safety regulations for the offshore wind sector by tracing the legal evolution of the UK's offshore petroleum health and safety regime since 1971, highlighting critical moments such as the Piper Alpha disaster. The authors comparatively critique the current UK

[16] International Energy Agency, *Mineral Requirements for Clean Energy Transitions* (2024).
[17] Richard M Auty, *Sustaining Development in Mineral Economies: The Resource Curse Thesis* (Routledge, 1993) 4.
[18] Mark Curtis, 'New Colonialism: Britain's Scramble for Africa's Energy and Mineral Resources' (WaronWant, 2016), waronwant.org/sites/default/files/TheNewColonialism.pdf?_ga=1.163857279.1562019882.1468355472.
[19] African Union, *2050 Africa's Integrated Maritime Strategy 2050 AIM Strategy* (2012).
[20] Hossein Mahdavy, 'The Pattern and Problems of Economic Development in Rentier States: The Case of Iran' in MA Cook (ed), *Studies in the Economic History of Middle East* (Oxford University Press, 1970).
[21] Great Britain and Northern Ireland, 'Offshore Wind' (2024) www.great.gov.uk/international/content/investment/sectors/offshore-wind/.
[22] ibid.

offshore wind safety approach, which mirrors the petroleum sector's 'goal-setting' to reduce risks to As Low As Reasonably Practicable (ALARP). **Wifa and Paterson** call for a proactive and well-defined offshore wind safety regulatory framework. They propose drawing on lessons learned from the fourth phase of offshore petroleum safety regulations and advocate for a specific offshore wind safety case regime to better address the unique risks of the rapidly growing UK offshore wind industry.

Finally, drawing on the common social contract thread throughout Part I, **Taylor** in chapter six entitled '*Beyond Social Licence to Operate: Charting "Social Gaps" and the Social Contract in the Emerging Australian Offshore Wind Sector*' crafts an engaging chapter analysing Australia's emerging offshore wind sector and probing its current regulatory framework. The first feasibility offshore wind licences in Australia were granted in 2024. However, the mapping, declaration, and licensing of Australia's six offshore wind zones have not been without social conflicts. **Taylor** directly examines these social concerns by providing a unique reframing of the 'social gaps' framework, systematically applied to highlight principles of regulatory reform addressing democratic deficits, legal conditions, and place protections. Importantly, the chapter examines the protection and recognition of Sea Country and Native Title rights following the Tipakalippa decision,[23] which redefined consultation requirements for Native Title rights in offshore energy development. Drawing lessons from regulatory and policy-mature offshore wind jurisdictions, including Denmark and Belgium, the chapter provides important considerations to reduce community conflict and establish Social Impact Assessments for offshore wind in Australia. The chapter concludes by highlighting the need for Marine Spatial Planning to map and mitigate 'social gaps', by harnessing regulatory strategies from established offshore wind jurisdictions. This socio-legal platform is crucial for Australia to realise its offshore wind ambitions.

Overall, *Part I – Offshore Energy: Fostering Environmental Stewardship and Community Collaboration* illustrates the tension between expediting offshore energy development, creating best practice regulation, maintaining environmental standards, and a sustained social contract. Part I aims to provide a unique contribution to existing offshore energy transition literature by moving beyond conceptualisations of the social licence to operate to examine the concept of the social contract. The energy transition social contract extends beyond transactions between energy proponents and communities and reevaluates the critical tripartite relationship among the State, energy proponents, and communities in delivering net-zero energy systems. This relational trilemma aims to foster socially responsive regulatory frameworks to consider social impacts, risks, and benefits at each offshore energy development lifecycle stage. All chapters in Part I focus on embedding elements of the social contract and environmental protection within various legal regimes and regulatory instruments, addressing the ever-evolving puzzle of achieving a just and environmentally sustainable energy transition. In doing so, it presents pioneering socio-legal and environmentally responsible reconceptualisations, regulatory strategies, and reform agendas for transitioning offshore energy sectors. These interventions are crucial to navigating adaptive complex socio-legal requirements and boundaries against the

[23] *Santos NA Barossa Pty Ltd v Tipakalippa* [2022] FCAFC 193.

global backdrop of addressing the ever-evolving puzzle of achieving a just and environmentally sustainable energy transition.

3. Part II – Offshore Energy: Business and Financing

Part II provides a dynamic collection of chapters exploring the essential foundational underpinnings for a successful energy transition – specifically, access to and investment in offshore energy. According to the IEA, global investment in renewable energy has doubled in comparison to fossil fuels in 2024,[24] with total global investment in clean energy reaching $2 billion. A critical issue for negotiation at COP29 is the need to attract public and private capital to create 'bankability' for energy transition assets. At this pivotal policy moment, Part II brings contributions centred around the importance of the State in facilitating capital flowers, implementing taxation incentives, structuring project finance, local content, and other financing trends, opportunities, and hurdles in a variety of jurisdictions and regions. However, it also discusses the role of corporate strategies and private capital and its relation to public policies.

The offshore energy sector stands at a critical juncture, balancing the established hydrocarbon industry with the burgeoning offshore wind sector while assuring sustained access to finance is a crucial topic critical to underpinning all activity. Chapter seven, '*A Double-Edged Sword: Alignments and Conflicts in the International, Regional, and Domestic Governance of Offshore Energy Projects*' by **Stanescu and Rubanovici**, delves into the complex interplay between international, regional, and domestic governance frameworks that shape the development of offshore energy projects, with a particular focus on the emerging opportunities and challenges in offshore wind investment. The analysis begins with an examination of the multilayered legal landscape governing offshore energy, from international conventions like UNCLOS and the Paris Agreement, to regional accords such as the OSPAR Convention, and finally to domestic regulations. This intricate web of governance creates both alignments and conflicts in areas such as resource allocation, environmental protection, and investment safeguards. The interaction between these various levels of regulation is analysed, highlighting instances of harmony and tension between global commitments and national economic priorities.

Building on the theme of complex regulatory conflicts moving from conventional offshore petroleum to emerging sectors including low-carbon hydrogen, **Castro** in chapter eight examines the '*Energy Transition and Tax Considerations for oil, gas, wind projects and carbon taxation for Offshore Energy–Focus on Brazilian experience*'. The chapter canvases Brazil's energy transition and taxation. Unlike many other nations, Brazil's energy grid is predominantly made up of hydroelectric power, which accounts for more than 60 per cent of the total, with natural gas, solar, and wind power contributing around 20 per cent. This distinct energy profile distinguishes Brazil from global standards, with a far reduced reliance on coal but still substantial dependence on oil and its derivatives. **Castro** dives into Brazil's attempts to produce low-carbon hydrogen,

[24] Orlando Jenkinson, 'World investing twice as much in renewables as fossil fuels – IEA' (2024) www.windpowermonthly.com/article/1875763/world-investing-twice-renewables-fossil-fuels-%E2%80%93-iea.

emphasising the country's potential to be a key worldwide player in this industry. Brazil is predicted to be a prominent supplier of green hydrogen by 2030, with more than $30 billion in hydrogen projects approved. To promote the growth of a green hydrogen economy, the Brazilian government established the National Hydrogen Program and approved the Low-Carbon Hydrogen Act. Offshore wind energy is another area of study, with Brazil having enormous potential in this field. The chapter addresses several recent legislative changes, including the recent Brazilian Tax Reform, adopted by Constitutional Amendment No. 132/2023, which marks a watershed event by expressly including environmental protection into the tax system. It establishes a dual-modal Value Added Tax system, comprised of the Contribution on Goods and Services (CBS) and the Tax on Goods and Services (IBS), as well as an Excise Tax (IS) for regulatory reasons. This reform seeks to build a more sustainable tax structure that is responsive to environmental concerns, including preferential taxation for biofuels and low-carbon hydrogen. However, the chapter identifies a conundrum in the new tax regime. While it provides incentives for low-carbon emission measures, it may boost taxes on oil and gas activity. The proposed Excise Tax, which might be paid on oil extraction regardless of destination, has the potential to dramatically damage the sector's competitiveness as well as the overall Brazilian economy. The chapter forecasts that this new tax would cost the oil and gas sector R$7 billion (US$1.5 billion) annually.

Continuing the theme of financing the offshore energy transition, the evolving offshore energy investor landscape is highlighted in chapter nine on '*Risk vs Rewards between oil, gas and wind investments: dealing with business, finance and economic issues and how to attract invest in these industries*' by **Oliveira**. The increasing comfort of financiers with offshore wind projects over the past decade is traced in this chapter, evidenced by higher leverage ratios, declining interest rate spreads, and the growing use of project finance structures. By examining the alignments and conflicts in governance, analysing financing trends, and proposing innovative models for project development, this chapter aims to provide a thorough understanding of the challenges and opportunities in the offshore energy sector, with a particular emphasis on accelerating sustainable offshore wind development in emerging markets. Building upon this foundation, the analysis delves deeper into the nuanced challenges and opportunities presented in the offshore energy sector, mainly those related to the transition from traditional hydrocarbon extraction to renewable wind power. The study extends to offshore energy projects' technical and operational aspects, highlighting the similarities and differences between oil and gas installations and offshore wind farms. This includes examining the evolving technologies in both sectors, from advanced drilling techniques and subsea production systems in oil and gas to increasingly larger and more efficient wind turbines. The chapter concludes by synthesising central lessons and offering insights into the prospects of offshore energy investment, particularly in the Global South.

Local content provisions for net-zero energy projects are increasingly recognised as pivotal to balancing sustained economic and social benefits with energy development. In the UK, local content requirements within the offshore wind Contract for Difference scheme mandate that offshore wind proponents demonstrate local procurement and development plans. This requirement has been widely acknowledged as creating a successful and sustainable supply chain. **Athwal, Pereira, Omotuyi, and Herrera Anchustegui** in chapter ten on '*Building local capacity and expertise via local content* *rules and transferring skills and knowledge between offshore developments*' provide a novel analysis of local content dynamics and legal approaches from offshore oil and gas, applicable to offshore wind. Drawing on mature petroleum jurisdictions and emerging offshore wind markets in Brazil, Nigeria, Norway, and the UK, this pragmatic chapter offers timely recommendations to facilitate a just transition while ensuring sustainable economic benefits for the regions assessed. This chapter outlines three key reform measures to redefine or re-think local content boundaries for transitioning offshore energy infrastructure, especially in developing countries. First, embedding local content in national petroleum infrastructure rehabilitation and decommissioning. Second, enhancing local workforce skill and knowledge transfer programmes. Finally, fostering robust community engagement and stakeholder collaboration to establish comprehensive workforce data before implementing local capacity requirements.

The shift from hydrocarbon dependence to renewable energy sources has the potential to redraw the map of global energy politics. The role of international cooperation and competition in developing offshore energy resources is critical, including the potential for cross-border projects and shared infrastructure. A detailed case study approach is employed by **Fowler** in chapter eleven entitled '*The Prospects for Offshore Wind Investment in the Global South– Lessons from the Offshore Oil & Gas Sector?*' which illustrates the practical application of the concepts discussed. This includes an in-depth look at successful offshore wind projects in mature markets like the North Sea, as well as nascent developments in emerging economies. These case studies provide valuable insights into the diverse approaches to project development, financing, and risk mitigation across different regulatory and economic contexts. The analysis also addresses the critical issue of grid integration and energy storage, which are particularly pertinent to the large-scale deployment of offshore wind. The challenges of connecting remote offshore installations to onshore grids and balancing intermittent wind power with baseload demand are explored, along with potential solutions such as energy storage technologies and hybrid systems that combine wind power with other energy sources. The analysis concludes with a forward-looking assessment of the offshore energy sector's trajectory. This includes projections for the growth of offshore wind capacity globally, the expected evolution of financing structures and investment patterns, and the potential emergence of new technologies such as floating wind turbines and ocean energy systems. The analysis also considers the long-term future of offshore oil and gas assets, including possibilities for repurposing infrastructure for renewable energy or carbon capture and storage projects.

The discussion in Part II then shifts to the financing trends, opportunities, and hurdles facing offshore energy projects in chapter twelve '*Offshore Energy Financing: Trends, Opportunities and Hurdles*' by **Kelly**. Drawing comparisons between traditional oil and gas investments and the rapidly evolving offshore wind sector, the unique risk profiles and bankability considerations of the transitioning offshore energy sector are explored. The capital-intensive nature of these projects, requiring significant upfront investments and long payback periods, necessitates innovative financing approaches and careful risk mitigation strategies. A key focus of the chapter discussion is the potential application of investor-state agreement models from the offshore oil and gas sector to offshore wind projects, particularly in developing countries. The adaptation of Production Sharing Agreements (PSAs) and other contractual structures used in the hydrocarbon industry is examined in the chapter as a potential solution to address the specific challenges faced by offshore wind developments in emerging markets. This includes issues such as regulatory uncertainties, grid connection challenges, and the lack of creditworthy power purchasers. **Kelly** proposes and evaluates a symbiotic model that pairs offshore wind projects with energy-intensive industrial facilities as anchor customers. This innovative approach aims to provide guaranteed power offtake whilst enabling industrial development powered by clean energy, potentially unlocking significant opportunities in regions like Africa and Latin America.

The interplay between technological innovation, policy frameworks, market dynamics, and environmental imperatives is consistently highlighted throughout *Part II – Offshore Energy: Business and Financing*. By providing this multifaceted analysis, Part II aims to equip policymakers, investors, and industry stakeholders with the insights needed to navigate the complex and rapidly evolving landscape of offshore energy development. The ultimate goal is to foster a transition that balances energy security, economic growth, and environmental sustainability in the offshore realm.

4. Part III – Offshore Energy: Complex Infrastructure and Overarching Conclusions

This final Part III of the *Offshore Energy Law* book focuses on Complex Offshore Energy Infrastructure and the overarching conclusions derived from the contributions to this volume. Part III, therefore, discusses how the energy transition is transforming the way regulatory frameworks address structural issues. Technological progress and the juxtaposition of offshore energy exploitation and other activities at sea have made the development of projects more complex and integrated. A combination of stakeholder interests and space optimisation challenges establish regulatory regimes that, more often than not, are ill-equipped to tackle integrated energy solutions. In addition, Part III on structural offshore energy issues, illustrates that there are several other subjects than substantive law in a transforming offshore energy landscape that also need to be revisited. An underlying theme is that of the revision of powers, competencies, and tasks attributed to energy regulators such as project complexity, the energy transition, and the way more active use of sea spaces challenges established areas of competence and expertise in the public sector.

A common theme for Part III is the complex interplay between existing and future infrastructure to optimise energy production, as well as mitigating the carbon footprint from offshore hydrocarbon projects. This is the case for efforts made to electrify oil and gas operations and/or combine them with carbon capture and, therefore, address (and reduce) scope one and two[25] greenhouse gas emissions prompted by States' international and national obligations and company-driven climate targets. This interaction between different infrastructures is already present in international waters, such as the linkage

[25] For more on the different 'scopes', see: United States Environmental Protection Agency (EPA), 'Scopes 1, 2 and 3 Emissions Inventorying and Guidance', www.epa.gov/climateleadership/scopes-1-2-and-3-emissions-inventorying-and-guidance.

between different offshore energy sources as part of the same projects. Examples are the Norwegian Hywind Tampen[26] or the Scottish Green Volt[27] projects, which combine floating offshore wind with offshore oil and gas production, and the Sealhyfe pilot hydrogen production project powered by BW Ideol's floating wind turbine, Floatgen.[28] An important issue is whether these operations constitute the same or separate projects when it comes to the application of the law,[29] which is explored by the contributions in this part of the book, highlighting the complexity of combining energy solutions and overlapping regulatory regimes. This Part III also integrates elements related to the energy transition and the energy-climate nexus by including a set of contributions dealing with the end-of-life of offshore infrastructure and circular and sustainable trends in decommissioning, and the relationship between oil and gas activity and carbon capture, use, and storage projects.

One of the most important and mature offshore petroleum developers, the United States, offers a salient example of the complexities of pivoting to offshore wind and other offshore clean energy technological developments. The American offshore petroleum sector commenced exploitation in 1896 and its regulation represents one of the most widely adopted petroleum licensing systems and one of America's most successful legal exports. Yet, the American offshore wind sector remains largely underdeveloped, consisting of just two operating offshore wind projects producing a total capacity of 42 megawatts and 18 projects in the permitting phase. Against this low watermark, the Biden Administration is ambitiously targeting 30 GW of offshore wind capacity by 2030. In chapter thirteen, '*From a Mature Offshore Oil & Gas Sector to an Embryonic Alternative Energy Sector: The US Experience*', **Hall** explores issues related to federalism and regulatory boundaries between federal and state permitting and regulation of offshore energy development. The chapter delves into the complexities of American legal doctrines and governance complexities of offshore petroleum, creating regulatory failures in some instances, including the Deepwater Horizon incident of 2010. The discussion shifts to examine the immature offshore wind sector, carbon sequestration, and other forms of emerging offshore energy technologies such as floating, tidal, and wave energy and the potential legal duplication between state and federal

[26] The first medium-sized offshore floating wind park powers two oil and gas fields in Norwegian waters, not being connected to the national grid. It started operating in 2023 and received state aid from the Norwegian government for its development. See Equinor, 'Hywind Tampen' (2024) www.equinor.com/energy/hywind-tampen, and Ignacio Herrera Anchustegui, 'Is Hywind Tampen's State Aid Approval a Kickstart for the Norwegian Offshore Wind Industry? Decision 017/20/COL Hywind Tampen, EFTA Surveillance Authority' (2020) 19 *European State Aid Law Quarterly: EStAL* 225.

[27] Green Volt involves 35 floating wind turbines that will supply power to offshore oil and gas facilities as well as the onshore grid. See more: Green Volt, 'The first commercial-scale floating offshore windfarm in Europe' (Green Volt, 2024) greenvoltoffshorewind.com/. The Marine Licence for this project was awarded by Marine Scotland on 19 April 2024. For more, see Marine Scotland, 'Green Volt Offshore Windfarm' (Marine Scotland, 2024) marine.gov.scot/ml/green-volt-offshore-windfarm.

[28] In November 2023, the hydrogen production capacity was returned onshore after 14 months of testing and being able to produce up to 400 kilograms of hydrogen a day and being the first offshore hydrogen project. Lhyfe, 'Lhyfe Reviews the Results of the Sealhyfe Project: The World's First Offshore Hydrogen Production Pilot, Objectives Met and Progression to an Unprecedented Level of Operational Excellence' (Lhyfe, 26 January 2024) www.lhyfe.com/press/lhyfe-reviews-the-results-of-the-sealhyfe-project-the-worlds-first-offshore-hydrogen-production-pilot-objectives-met-and-progression-to-an-unprecedented-level-of-operational-excellence/.

[29] Ignacio Herrera Anchustegui and Rudiger Tscherning, 'Offshore oil and gas infrastructure electrification and offshore wind: a legal exploration' (2024) 17 *The Journal of World Energy Law & Business* 35.

legal permitting regimes to explore for and develop these technologies offshore. The chapter provides critical pragmatic examples of opposition to offshore renewable energy projects, notably highlighting recent litigation in Massachusetts based on offshore wind visibility and commercial fishermen alleging turbine interference. Citing a powerful array of broader offshore energy transition challenges, such as inflation, supply chain distributions, and the need for clear regulatory permitting procedures, **Hall** concludes by serving a significant and stark series of warnings for the future viability of the US offshore energy transition.

Two chapters are devoted to illustrating the complex interface of sector-coupling between energy generation forms and the regulatory impact this has on both project design, for the developers, and project regulation, for the offshore energy authorities. In chapter fourteen, '*Coupling of Petroleum, Offshore Wind, and CCS: Scopes, Interfaces, And Coordination of Licensing Regimes – The Norwegian Experience*', **Høivik, Seglem, Dyrland and Grytten** discuss how the energy transition is affecting how Norwegian authorities and commercial actors approach the decarbonisation of the country's oil and gas activity while they adapt and reutilise existing petroleum infrastructure. As put forward by the authors, the coupling between oil and gas production, offshore wind, and carbon capture projects is prompted by action against climate change to mitigate its consequences, as well as adjusting infrastructure to adapt to new energy realities. Using Norway as a background, the chapter shows how these industries and activities, primarily under different licensing regimes and even sometimes under the scrutiny of different governmental entities, may be combined in practice and in law to create a sum larger than its infrastructural parts. However, the combination of projects and infrastructure tests the boundaries of the more traditional and 'silo' regimes, creating regulatory challenges for those energy law regulatory systems not designed for such coupling.

In another variation of energy infrastructure coupling, **Tscherning** analyses the integration of offshore wind energy with hydrogen electrolysis on repurposed oil and gas installations in chapter fifteen, '*Three Parts to the New Offshore Economy: Integrating Offshore Wind Energy with Hydrogen Electrolysis on Repurposed Oil and Gas Installations*'. This contribution explores the future role of combining offshore wind with renewable hydrogen production in Atlantic Canada. The chapter discusses the possibility of repurposing existing oil and gas installations for hydrogen electrolysis, maximising the potential of hydrocarbon infrastructure that is likely to be phased out as an alternative to decommissioning of installations. **Tscherning** notes that while these aspirations are no longer science fiction, important legal challenges are associated with these repurposing and sector-coupling energy infrastructure projects. Legislators and regulators face significant hurdles when developing a regulatory framework for novel energy production schemes, especially when different energy production methods are interconnected. **Tscherning** concludes by evaluating various regulatory risks and challenges related to liability, ownership, transfer of assets, and licensing rights, while highlighting opportunities. The author advises legislators to consider the interplay between existing offshore oil and gas regimes and new offshore renewable energy frameworks to facilitate sector integration.

The end of life of offshore infrastructure is starting to become a more important theme as offshore energy installations begin to be decommissioned as a result of either the field that they exploit being depleted or near depleted, or the assets themselves being too old to be safely and efficiently operated. In chapter sixteen, '*Circular Economy in the Decommissioning of Oil and Gas Platforms: Costs, Legislation, and Importance for Energy Transition*', **Pereira, Marins de Carvalho and Reid** discuss the global trends and emerging themes around such decommissioning. With over 12,000 offshore oil and gas installations around the world reaching the end of their operative lifetime, project operators and authorities need to prepare for the cessation and eventual decommissioning of these assets. Decommissioning is a complex engineering operation that involves large investments, raises important environmental considerations, and risks related to the unsuccessful completion of decommissioning projects and associated liabilities for operators and, ultimately, also the state. Through an analysis of current decommissioning trends and data, the authors highlight lessons that ought to be learned from the oil and gas industry in the offshore renewable energy world. Among these, the importance of developing a robust offshore decommissioning framework as a pending issue for several jurisdictions is highlighted, as well as the role of law in promoting more circular and value-enhancing decommissioning processes by allowing for and even requiring more sustainable decommissioning practices, such as demanding the use of the waste hierarchy approach or, even more creatively, utilising platforms, or their parts for photovoltaic farms or hydrogen production or transport.

The location of projects and associated infrastructure is inevitably linked to the availability of resources. While examples of joint development of hydrocarbons exist around the globe, **Yiallourides** in chapter seventeen conducts an in-depth discussion of the legal complexity arising from such cross-border projects in areas with overlapping maritime claims in '*Joint Development in the Energy Transition: From Joint Petroleum Zones to Joint CO_2 Storage Zones*'. In this thought-provoking and forward-thinking chapter, Yiallourides uses existing solutions for the peaceful and shared exploitation of hydrocarbon reservoirs between countries as inspiration, even if the maritime borders have not been mutually agreed upon and defined for carbon capture and storage projects. In his assessment, it is put forward that the established concept of joint development zones – and the intricate and ad hoc nature of these international agreements – may be used to similar ends for carbon capture projects that may or may not use depleted or out-of-production offshore oil and gas reservoirs. However, technological differences, legal developments, and challenges require tailoring standard joint development zone provisions for these yet-to-be-come projects.

This edited book concludes *Part III – Offshore Energy: Complex Infrastructure and Overarching Conclusions* with chapter eighteen, '*On the Future of Offshore Energy*', by **Herrera Anchustegui, Pereira, Wifa and Taylor**, in which they draw common themes and conclusions arising from the contributions and aim to put forward a research and regulatory agenda for offshore energy.

2

Multiple Use in the North Sea: Evolving Towards a New Legal Framework? – A Case Study Based on the Belgian and Dutch Examples

ANGELO GOETHALS, FRANK MAES
AND FREDERIK VANDENDRIESSCHE

1. Introduction, Aim and Structure

The Belgian Part of the North Sea (BPNS) and, by extension, the North Sea in general are increasingly being used for the realisation of offshore wind farms (OWFs). Given that space in the North Sea is limited and given the accelerated and extensive plans to realise wind energy projects,[1] this creates tensions with other use options (eg fisheries, aquaculture, tourism, navigation, etc). For this reason, more and more voices are being heard that call for more flexibility as it comes to multiple use in the offshore wind zones. Until now, little attention has been paid to the legal questions that multiple use can raise.[2] These questions relate to, for example, liability of the various parties involved, the power of initiative, the environmental assessments and permits (integration or not), the concession conditions, the entry conditions and safety zones. In this chapter the authors examine the concept of multiple use, the different types of multiple use applications in the BPNS and the different ways in which multiple use can be regulated in the offshore energy zones. Multiple use will be explored from a Belgian and Dutch perspective, being the current state of play on the matter in the BPNS and the Dutch Part of the North Sea (DPNS). This chapter contains an overview of various models to which multiple

[1] ilvo.vlaanderen.be/nl/dossiers/ruimte-op-zee.

[2] See Edward L Miles, 'Concepts, Approaches, and Applications in Sea Use Planning and Management' (1989) 20 *Ocean Development & International Law* 213, 232; Geir Ulfstein, 'The Conflict between Petroleum Production, Navigation and Fisheries in International Law' (1988) 19 *Ocean Development & International Law* 229, 229; Lawrence Juda, 'The European Union and the Marine Strategy Framework Directive: Continuing the Development of European Ocean Use Management' (2010) 41 *Ocean Development & International Law* 34, 44; Ceciel Nieuwenhout, *Regulating Offshore Electricity Infrastructure in the North Sea – Towards a New Legal Framework* (Groningen University, 2020) 196–98.

use with the offshore energy zones can be subjected. The Belgian legal framework is quite concise and does not facilitate the large roll-out of multiple use in the BPNS, more particularly in the demarcated energy zones. The current legal framework in Belgium does not actively encourage multiple use, but does not forbid it either. The Dutch model starts from a more central approach and therefore has more tools to develop multiple use in the DPNS, as will be demonstrated in this chapter. The question posed in this chapter is whether the Belgian, Dutch or another model is the most effective for developing multiple use in the BPNS.

This chapter starts with an introduction of the EU's Integrated Maritime Policy (IMP) and the EU Maritime Spatial Planning (MSP) policy (section 2). It continues with an introduction to the concept of multiple use, as well as other associated concepts and various applications (sections 3 and 4). The core of this chapter is to map out some legal models that can be used to give legal substance to multiple use in offshore energy zones (section 5(B)). This chapter also attempts to make a comparison of the current practices regarding multiple use in both Belgian and Dutch offshore renewable energy zones to highlight possible best practices (section 5(C)). Finally, some recommendations are made to stimulate the implementation of multiple use in the future (section 6).

2. From Integrated Maritime Policy to Maritime Spatial Planning and Coexistence

The EU's Integrated Maritime Policy (IMP) aims 'to foster coordinated and coherent decision-making to maximise the sustainable development, economic growth and social cohesion of Member States, and notably the coastal, insular and outermost regions in the Union, as well as maritime sectors, through coherent maritime-related policies and relevant international cooperation'.[3] The IMP essentially focuses on the identification and coordination of the different interests (based on the various policy areas) that the different stakeholders have within the sea areas under the jurisdiction of the EU Member States.[4] In the context of the IMP, maritime spatial planning plays an essential role. According to the Maritime Spatial Planning Directive, MSP is defined as 'a process by which the relevant Member State's authorities analyze and organise human activities in marine areas to achieve ecological, economic and social objectives'.[5] Each EU Member State must define and implement MSP, taking into account economic, social and environmental aspects with the aim of supporting sustainable development and growth in the maritime sector, through an ecosystem-based approach, but also with the aim to promote the coexistence of relevant activities and uses (energy at sea, maritime

[3] Directive 2014/89/EU establishing a framework for maritime spatial planning, OJ L 28 August 2014, vol 257, art 3(1).

[4] T Paramana, M Dassenakis, N Bassan, C Dallangelo, P Campostrini, S Raicevich, F Ronchi, G Giorgi, A Murillas-Maza, MC Uyarra, N Papadopoulou, C Smith, K Jarni, Š Koren Bačovnik, K Klančnik, M Pavičić, S Skejić, O Vidjak, JF Cadiou, L López-López, I Alvarez, L Giannoudi, N Streftaris and P Pagkou, 'Achieving coherence between the Marine Strategy Framework Directive and the Maritime Spatial Planning Directive' (2023) 155 *Marine Policy* 1, 2.

[5] Directive 2014/89/EU art 3(2); Ellen Peccue, Kris Hostens and Frank Maes, 'Governance analysis of MPAs in the Belgian part of the North Sea' (2016) *Marine Policy* 265, 268–69.

transport, fisheries and aquaculture, preservation, protection and improvement of the environment, promotion of sustainable tourism and the sustainable extraction of raw material).[6] Coexistence implies that different sectors can coexist within the same zone designated in the MSP, with the aim, among other things, of aligning the different interests and policies with each other. This is also related to the fact that there are many activities that also take up a lot of space (for example renewable energy production), so that the exclusivity of a certain zone can potentially cause tensions between the various stakeholders. From this it can be deduced that MSP is inherently linked to multiple use. The effect of this largely depends on the discretion of the Member States and the emphasis they wish to place. To date, it can be noted that in EU Member States the coexistence of different uses is limited and the main emphasis is on the monotonous distribution of uses in the designated zones.[7]

3. Defining Multiple Use, Associated Concepts and the Growth and Importance of a Multiple Use Policy

This section builds on the research conducted by Schupp et al,[8] as well as the research conducted in the H2020 projects MUSES (Multi-Use in European Seas)[9] and UNITED (Multi-Use offshore platforms demonstrators for boosting cost-effective and eco-friendly production in sustainable marine activities).[10] The notions 'multiple use' and 'multi-use' of ocean or marine spaces are used and are considered as synonyms.[11] In this contribution, the notion 'multiple use' is used.

Zaucha et al define multiple use as 'the joint use of resources in close geographic proximity by either a single user or multiple users. It is an umbrella term that covers a multitude of use combination in the marine realm and represents a radical change from the concept of exclusive resource rights to the inclusive sharing of resources and space

[6] Directive 2014/89/EU arts 4–5; Zacharoula Kyriazi, Frank Maes and Steven Degraer, 'Coexistence dilemmas in European marine spatial planning practices. The case of marine renewables and marine protected areas' (2016) 97 *Energy Policy* 391, 392; maritime-spatial-planning.ec.europa.eu/co existence-activities-and-multi-use.

[7] See inter alia Elizabeth T Methratta, 'Food for Thought – Monitoring fisheries resources at offshore wind farms: BACI vs. BAG designs' (2020) 77 *ICES Journal of Marine Sciences* 890, 890–91; Michael Roach, Andy Revill and Magnus J Johnson, 'Co-existence in practice: a collaborative study of the effects of the Westermost Rough offshore wind development on the size distribution and catch rates of a commercially important lobster (Homarus Gammarus) population' (2022) 79 *ICES Journal of Marine Sciences* 1175, 1175–76; Nathalie A Steins, Jeroen A Veraart, Judith EM Klostermann and Marnix Poelman, 'Combining offshore wind farms, nature conservation and seafood: Lessons from a Dutch community of practice' (2021) 126 *Marine Policy* 1, 1–2; Maximilian Felix Schupp et al, 'Fishing within offshore wind farms in the North Sea: Stakeholder perspective for multi-use from Scotland and Germany' (2021) 279 *Journal of Environmental Management* 1, 1–2; Henrice M Jansen et al, 'The feasibility of offshore aquaculture and its potential for multi-use in the North Sea' (2016) 24 *Aquaculture International* 735, 736–37.

[8] Maximilian Felix Schupp et al, 'Toward a Common Understanding of Ocean Multi-Use' (2019) 6 (165) *Frontiers in Marine Science* 1, 1–12.

[9] Jacek Zaucha et al, *Analytical Framework (AF) – Analysing Multi-Use (MU) in the European Sea Basins* (MUSES-project 2017); muses-project.com/.

[10] www.h2020united.eu/about; Schupp et al (n 8) 1, 3.

[11] In Dutch, the legislation refers to the notions 'meervoudig ruimtegebruik op zee', 'meervoudig gebruik van windparken op zee' or 'medegebruik van windparken'.

by one or more users'.[12] According to Zaucha et al, a user must be understood as the 'individual, group or entity that intentionally benefits from a given resource. If a business creates a separate legal entity to exploit an additional resource, this entity is then considered another user.'[13] In this context, Zaucha et al describe a 'resource' as 'a good or service that represents a value to one or more users. Such a resource can be biotic (e.g. fish stocks) or abiotic (e.g. ocean space) and can be exploited through either direct (e.g. fishing) or indirect (e.g. nature conservation) uses.'[14] The primary user can be a windfarm operator, whereas the additional user can be, for example, a company specialised in aquaculture. The notion 'use' as 'a distinct and intentional activity, through which a direct (e.g. profit) or indirect (e.g. nature conservation) benefit is drawn by one or more users. For the purpose of this definition, a clear distinction is made between different types of uses.'[15] The different types of uses will be discussed later in chapter four.

In the last two decades, the development of offshore renewable energy projects, especially offshore wind energy, has increased exponentially which implies a significant reduction of other potential uses in those specific areas.[16] This is mainly related to the fact that the infrastructure related to the effective functioning of the OWFs must be protected against calamities. For example, with the designation of the Princess Elisabeth Zone (PEZ), Belgium created a new zone for renewable energy production at Noordhinder-Noord, Noordhinder-Zuid and the Fairybank with the intention of tripling the installed capacity of offshore wind energy in the BPNS.[17] Under Belgian law, a safety zone of 500 meters is demarcated around the OWFs, which implies that no vessel may enter the safety zone in order to prevent damage (intentional or unintentional) to the infrastructure.[18] There are some exceptions to this, such as for warships, ships in use of marine safety systems, ships belonging to the concessionaires of on behalf of the concessionaire of the OWFs or permit holders for the cables, ships used for scientific research (subject to permission from the concessionaire and in accordance with the permit regulations), maintenance ships for cables and the pipelines, means for aquaculture and fisheries, ships in distress, for the safety of life at sea and properties and the case of force majeure.[19] Given the size of the zones concerned, as well as the designated safety zone, the impact on other activities should certainly not be underestimated. Multiple

[12] www.h2020united.eu/about; Zaucha et al (n 9) 14.

[13] ibid.

[14] ibid.

[15] ibid.

[16] For example: fisheries, aquaculture, shipping lanes, or even tourism activities.

[17] Royal Decree of 22 May 2019 establishing the marine spatial plan for the period from 2020 to 2026 in the Belgian marine areas, *Belgian Official Journal* 2 July 2019, art 8; Frank Maes, 'Het nieuw Belgisch marien ruimtelijk plan voor de periode 2020–2026' (2020) 4 *Tijdschrift voor Milieurecht* 416, 418; Tobe Steel, 'Regering mikt op verdrievoudiging windenergie op zee' (2021) *De Tijd*, see www.tijd.be/ondernemen/milieu-energie/regering-mikt-op-verdrievoudiging-windenergie-op-zee/10339099.html. On the website of the Belgian TSO, Elia, the different infrastructure projects can be consulted: www.elia.be/en/infrastructure-and-projects/infrastructure-projects/princess-elisabeth-island.

[18] Belgium has designated a safety zone in accordance with Article 60, paras 4 and 5 of UNCLOS; Frank Maes, 'Hernieuwbare energie op zee en scheepvaart: het Belgisch marien ruimtelijk plan' in An Cliquet and Frank Maes (eds), *Recht door zee: Hedendaags internationaal zee- en maritiem recht. Liber amicorum Eddy Somers* (Maklu, 2015) 69–72; Royal Decree of 4 February 2020 establishing safety zones in the maritime areas under Belgian jurisdiction, *Belgian Official Journal* 27 February 2020, art 3.

[19] Royal Decree of 4 February 2020 establishing safety zones in the maritime areas under Belgian jurisdiction, *Belgian Official Journal* 27 February 2020, art 9.

use is therefore becoming increasingly essential, as it seeks to mitigate the exclusivity of the allocation of certain zones and therefore a more balanced approach for the different stakeholders who want to develop (or prevent) activities in the limited space available in the BPNS (see below).

In the context of the elaboration of the (Belgian) North Sea Vision 2050 (*Noordzeevisie 2050*), three working groups were established, one of which was dedicated to 'multiple use'. The contribution of that working group led to the elaboration of some non-binding policy objectives on multiple use for the BPNS.[20] In this policy document, the objective is formulated that multiple use within the BPNS will be the rule by 2050.[21] This policy document was taken into account when elaborating the Belgian Marine Spatial Plan (BMSP) 2020–2026, through the clear designation of zones for pilot projects whereby multiple use should be supported.[22] These zones for pilot projects aim to stimulate industrial and commercial activities outside the designated offshore energy zones.[23] The first approved project zone is the cultivation of various aquaculture products, mainly mussels and seaweed by the same operator. This zone and the regulations pertaining to it will not be discussed as such in this contribution, as it does not relate to the zones that are the subject of the offshore domain concessions, which is the central theme of this contribution. With regard to the zones designated for the generation of renewable energy, there is no clear reference in the regulations to the notion of multiple use, whereas multiple use is indeed formulated as a policy objective in the North Sea Vision 2050. Two relevant forms of multiple use of space in the energy zones that are put forward in the BMSP 2020–2026 are aquaculture and passive fisheries (see below).[24] However, other forms of multiple use with the exception of passive fishing and aquaculture, are not allowed within the energy zones concerned.[25]

4. Different Types of Multiple Use According to Belgian Law in the Offshore Energy Zones

In this chapter, the different types of multiple use which are possible in the Belgian energy zones, according to Belgian legislation, are identified. As will be illustrated,

[20] Philippe De Backer, *Noordzee 2050* (Think Tank North Sea, 2017) 10, www.health.belgium.be/nl/langetermijnvisie-noordzee-2050#anchor-33317.

[21] Maes (n 17) 422; De Backer (n 20) 31–32.

[22] Royal Decree of 22 May 2019 establishing the marine spatial plan for the period from 2020 to 2026 in the Belgian marine areas, *Belgian Official Journal* art 19, §2.

[23] The Royal Decree of 22 July 2019 introduced a procedure for user permits in zones for commercial and industrial activities, based on a number of criteria (both social, economical and geographical). Royal Decree of 22 July 2019 establishing the procedure for obtaining a user permit for the zones for commercial and industrial activities in the marine areas under the jurisdiction of Belgium, *Belgian Official Journal* 20 September 2019, art 3.

[24] Royal Decree of 22 May 2019 establishing the marine spatial plan for the period from 2020 to 2026 in the Belgian marine areas, *Belgian Official Journal* 2 July 2019, art 14.

[25] Passive fishing includes longline fishing, jig fishing, handline method, fishing with standing nets and the fishery with pots and baskets. In terms of aquaculture, this could include farming mussels (Edulis project), oysters and scallops within the relevant energy zones. In addition to aquaculture for food, aquaculture can also be done for the purpose of coastal protection, blue biotechnology, nature restoration, etc, ilvo.vlaanderen.be/nl/dossiers/aquacultuur-op-zee. Activities that are prohibited include, for example bottom-disturbing (fishing) activities, diving, hydrogen production, etc.

under current Belgian law, in addition to nature protection,[26] three forms of multiple use are possible in the Belgian energy zones, namely (1) aquaculture, (2) passive fisheries and (3) electricity storage.[27]

Aquaculture is allowed in the two energy zones (namely the already realised energy zone and the PEZ). Passive fisheries are only allowed in the PEZ.[28] With regard to aquaculture, a distinction must be made. In the already realised energy zone, in order to deploy aquaculture three conditions need to be fulfilled. First, a permission from the concession holder is required. Second, It must be further demonstrated that aquaculture reduces the eutrophication level within the concession zone and, third, the concession or licensing minister can, where necessary, safeguard a control zone within the demarcated zone, as a reference for the situation without aquaculture activities.[29] In the area of the PEZ which is not subject to a Natura 2000 authorisation, there is, first, a need to demonstrate that aquaculture reduces the eutrophication level within the concession zone and, second, the concession or licensing minister can, where necessary, safeguard a control zone within the demarcated zone, as a reference for the situation without aquaculture activity.[30] In the PEZ, it is clear that permission from the concession holder is no longer a requirement for aquaculture. This therefore implies a shift of decision-making authority from the concessionaire to third parties that wish to engage in aquaculture. The same goes for the area in the PEZ which is subject to a Natura 2000-authorisation. In those specific areas, a Natura 2000-authorisation is required, before engaging in aquaculture.[31]

To date, there are no practical examples of energy storage in the BPNS.[32] The Belgian Electricity Act provides for the possibility of granting offshore domain concessions for energy storage from hydropower.[33] These installations were called energy-atolls (*energie-atollen*), but were never realised due to the high cost and a lack of support mechanisms,

[26] The literature sometimes raises the question of whether nature can be regarded as a user. Since this discussion goes beyond the scope of this contribution, it will not be discussed further. It is important to know that there is a school of thought that states that nature can also be regarded as a user, while there is also a school of thought that states that nature is not a user.

[27] In the preparatory studies of the BMSP 2020–2026, it is not clear how these forms of multiple use were arrived at and which parameters were applied. During the preparations, it is clear that the aim is to achieve as much homogeneity as possible and to mitigate negative interference as much as possible with the main objective of the energy zones concerned, namely the generation of renewable energy. Furthermore, the choice may have to do with the (relative) economic and technical maturity of these user functions. With regard to passive fisheries and aquaculture, the reason can be found in a possible compensation for the fishing industry, since large fishing areas are lost due to the designation of energy zones in the BPNS. Royal Decree of 22 May 2019 establishing the marine spatial plan for the period from 2020 to 2026 in the Belgian marine areas, *Belgian Official Journal* 2 July 2019, Annex II; Maes (n 17) 430–31.

[28] Royal Decree of 22 May 2019 establishing the marine spatial plan for the period from 2020 to 2026 in the Belgian marine areas, *Belgian Official Journal* 2 July 2019, art 14, §4.

[29] ibid art 14, §1.

[30] ibid art 14, §2.

[31] ibid art 14, §3.

[32] Wim De Preter, 'Waterstof uit de zee komt eraan' *De Tijd* (21 August 2021) www.tijd.be/de-tijd-vooruit/innovatie/waterstof-uit-de-zee-komt-eraan/10327222.html; Steven Degraer, Robin Brabant, Bob Rumes and Laurence Vigin, *Environmental Impacts of Offshore Wind Farms in the Belgian Part of the North Sea* (Royal Belgian Institute of Natural Sciences, 2023) 14; Maëlig Gaborieau, Ozlem Ceyhan Yilmaz and Katherine Dykes, 'Economic impact assessment of Hydrogen generated from Offshore Wind: A case study for Belgium' (2023) *Journal of Physics: Conference Series* 1, 10.

[33] Act of 29 April 1999 on the organization of the electricity market, *Belgian Official Journal* 11 May 1999, art 6/1 (Hereafter: Electricity Act).

resulting in limited interest from the industry.[34] There were two zones designated for hydro-electric energy storage in the BMSP 2014–2020.[35] The BMSP 2020–2026 no longer contains specific designated zones for hydro-electric energy storage, but still contains a possibility to designate such an area within the new offshore wind concessions zones or to examine under which conditions these installations can be built in the marine protected areas (MPAs).[36] When energy storage takes place within the concession zones, it can be considered as a form of multiple use. Where it used to be limited to installations for hydroelectric energy storage, the concept 'installations for energy storage' is mentioned in the current legal framework, which can be interpreted in a broader technological and regulatory sense. This can therefore also include power-to-x (P2X) installations and batteries. P2X means that the renewable energy created by the OWFs (in this case) is converted into for example energy carriers such as hydrogen and renewable fuels, which enables seasonal storage, system flexibility, and other associated benefits.[37] It must of course be emphasised that these applications are still in an experimental phase and that their effectiveness has not yet been proven, given the capacity losses, the high costs and the great need for scarce raw materials.

5. Regulating Multiple Use in Energy Zones

A. Introduction

This section examines which (theoretical) multiple use models are conceivable and what the advantages and disadvantages of these models are.[38] In doing so, the focus lies on multiple use within the demarcated energy zones in the MSPs. Multiple use in other designated zones is only discussed if this offers added value for the research into multiple use in energy zones. Furthermore, the current legislative frameworks in Belgium and the Netherlands are taken as benchmarks for these theoretical models.

B. Legal Models

i. Compulsory

a. Top-down

In the top-down approach, it is assumed that the government determines the desired direction in which multiple use should develop within the zones designated for

[34] Maes (n 17) 429; Memorie van toelichting, Wetsontwerp houdende diverse bepalingen inzake energie, *Parl. St.* Kamer, 2013–2014, nr. 3511/001, 4; Frank Maes, 'Ruimtelijke planning op zee in België: van plan naar proces en een nieuw plan' (2016) 4 *Tijdschrift voor Milieurecht* 415, 422.

[35] Royal Decree of 20 March 2014 establishing the marine spatial plan, *Belgian Official Journal* 28 March 2014, art 8, §5.

[36] Maes (n 17) 430.

[37] Ioannis Kountouris, Lissy Langer, Rasmus Bramstoft, Marie Münster and Dogan Keles, 'Power-to-X in energy hubs: A Danish case study of renewable fuel production' (2023) 175 *Energy Policy* 1, 1.

[38] It should be noted that many intermediate applications are possible in practice and that these theoretical models should not be interpreted too dogmatically.

offshore energy.[39] It goes without saying that this model provides more clarity for the developers of OWFs and offers more legal certainty for multiple use parties. However, much depends on the practical application of this model, since it also allows for different gradations. For example, it is possible that the concessionaire of the OWF can still grant a sub-concession and therefore has control over the practical application of multiple use. The other scenario is also possible, in which the government issues a separate user permit / concession to the other users of the demarcated zone, albeit in consultation with the active concession holder, but with or without their approval.

A disadvantage of the top-down model is that attention must be given to ensure that all actors are sufficiently involved in order to prevent tension and incidents. This is not an obvious task, the responsibility of which rests with the governmental authorities. The OWF operator can be less flexible if they do not feel involved in the policy decisions. Another disadvantage of this model is that the OWF developers will be more reluctant to participate in the tender, as they have to implement the necessary safety margins (both physical and financial) in the development of the OWF. In addition, the government's lack of expertise and insight into the practical implementation of multiple use also plays as a disadvantage for this model, since it is possible that the most efficient and effective envisaged application of multiple use is not applied to that specific area.

b. Bottom-up

Another approach within the compulsory spectrum is a bottom-up approach, in which the legislator obliges the developers or concession holders to work out multiple uses in their demarcated zones: the government sets out minimum thresholds, but leaves the main choices to the developer.[40] This is based on the idea that it is up to the developer to determine what activities are possible in conjunction with their activity and where they can take place. The main advantage of this scenario is the active involvement of the primary user of the energy zone, namely the OWF-developer. Multiple use is in this model clearly an obligation, so there is no choice as to whether or not to proceed with multiple use. It is important to note that this model only makes sense if certain conditions are met. For example, it is necessary that the (most) relevant stakeholders are involved (as in the top-down approach, discussed above). This promotes support and ensures checks and balances. For this reason, the bottom-up model seems quite complex, since it is not self-evident to involve various actors in a balanced way without maintaining control as a government. It is also important that the government monitors compliance with the developers' own obligations, so that consistent application of the plans is respected. This model also shares the inconvenience of the fact that wind developers in principle do not have the know-how to carry out activities other than generating wind energy. This complicates the developer's prospects, but can be

[39] This model more or less coincides with rule-based regulation approach; Julia Black, Martyn Hopper and Christa Band, 'Making a success of Principles-based regulation' (2007) 1 *Law and Financial Markets Review* 191, 198; John Braithwaite, 'Rules and Principles: A Theory of Legal Certainty' (2002) 27 *Australian Journal of Legal Philosophy* 47, 50–52.

[40] This implies that the distinction between top-down and bottom-up becomes more blurred; Black et al (n 39) 198; Braithwaite (n 39) 50–52.

accommodated by forming all kinds of consortia with other actors involved (such as companies specialised in aquaculture).

ii. Forbidding Multiple Use

A first scenario is the prohibition of other activities in the zones intended for offshore energy production. In this scenario, energy projects must absolutely prevail over other activities and therefore exclude other activities than energy production. The rationale behind this is based on the right of the coastal state under UNCLOS to establish safety zones of 500 meters (as in Belgium and The Netherlands) around installations, structures or artificial islands.[41] This implies that it is practically impossible to develop all kinds of activities within certain zones.[42]

Another reason for opting for a ban on multiple use has to do with the insurability of ancillary activities in these zones, since the risk of calamities then increases drastically and insurance companies are less experienced in insuring offshore multiple use activities, which is so far a very small market.[43] The advantage of such a scenario is that the risk of calamities is minimised because other activities are in principle forbidden or are only allowed to a limited extent and under strict conditions.

Another advantage of this model is that by banning other activities, such as fisheries, nature is less negatively disturbed and biodiversity can be improved or restored.[44] This system also allows the wind farm operator not to be accountable to other users within the specific energy zone and not to supervise the other activities. The disadvantage of this scenario is that, by definition, there is little or no room for multiple use for other stakeholders.

iii. Freedom of the Operator

In this second scenario, the will of the concession holder (generally also the operator) prevails in the area covered by their concession. The operators are often reluctant to foresee multiple use, even more so because they want to physically safeguard their investments (and associated assets). After all, the risks of calamities appear to be higher when other activities are also taking place in the area. Insurability and investment

[41] UNCLOS, art 60(5).

[42] Royal Decree of 4 February 2020 establishing safety zones in the marine areas under Belgian jurisdiction, *Belgian Official Journal* 27 February 2020, art 3; Angelo Goethals et al, 'Energy (including cables and pipes)' in Steven Dauwe, Thomas Verleye, Hans Pirlet, Chantal Martens, Matthias Sandra, Fien De Raedemaecker, Lisa Devriese, Ann-Katrien Lescrauwaet, Maxime Depoorter, Ine Moulaert and Jan Mees (eds), *Knowledge Guide Coast and Sea 2022 – Compendium for Coast and Sea* (VLIZ, 2022) 88; Steven Degraer, Robin Brabant, Bob Rumes and Laurence Vigin, *Environmental Impacts of Offshore Wind Farms in the Belgian Part of the North Sea: Empirical Evidence Inspiring Priority Monitoring, Research and Management* (Royal Belgian Institute of Natural Sciences, 2020) 16.

[43] Elisa Ciravegna, Luc van Hoof, Christian Frier, Frank Maes, Hanna Barbara Rasmussen, Anemoon Soete and Sander Willem Kors van den Burg. 'The hidden costs of multi-use at sea' (2024) 161 *Marine Policy* 106017, 6–7.

[44] This seems to be in line with the ecosystem-based approach as prescribed in arts 1, 3 of the MSFD and art 5 of the MSP Directive. These provisions state that when drawing up marine strategies and MSPs, the ecosystem-based approach must be taken into account as much as possible in relation to other human activities within the zones involved.

prospects can be affected in this way and it must be clear from the outset what risks can be run.[45] For example, the curtailing/redispatching of offshore electricity production due to external factors (eg calamities[46]) should be avoided at all times, because otherwise the return on investment (ROI) can be negatively impacted. Consequentially, if the will of the concession holders prevails, multiple use will often be of little use since they cannot derive any direct benefit from this.[47]

A disadvantage of this model is that the operator does not have the necessary know-how to develop such activities, or to allow these types of additional activities. Under the current framework, multiple use is allowed in the BPNS in the concession zones that fall under the management of Parkwind (being Belwind and Nobelwind), but these applications are merely pilot projects and as such have not been rolled out on a large or commercial scale. For this reason, it is very difficult to draw general conclusions from these pilot case studies. Moreover, due to the increase of biodiversity in and around these energy zones,[48] it cannot be ruled out that environmental law will interfere with the issue of the necessary permits, since certain activities (such as aquaculture) can have a potential negative impact on the current conservation status (ie 'the sum of the influences acting on a natural habitat and its typical species that may affect its long-term natural distribution, structure and functions as well as the long term survival of its typical species within the territory referred to in Article 2').[49] For example, in the Baltic Sea, where the waters are more shallow and where there are semi-closed brackish bodies of water, the water suffers from critical levels of eutrophication and in these waters nutrients, which can sometimes be necessary to cultivate aquaculture, can have a negative local impact.[50] Some activities, such as aquaculture, can be hindered due

[45] Multiple risks are envisaged. For more information about the risks and risk mitigation, read Gerrit van der Want, *Risk Mitigation Multi-Use Offshore Wind Farms* (TKI WIND OP ZEE, 2021) 7; Erwin Van Iperen and Cees van der Tak, *Veiligheidsstudie offshore windpark 'Eldepasco'* (MARIN, 2009) 94; Bob Rumes et al, *Milieueffectenbeoordeling van het NORTHER offshore windmolenpark ten zuidoosten van de Thorntonbank – Onderzoek van de aanvraag van de n.v. Norther voor een vergunning en de machtiging voor de bouw en de exploitatie van een windmolenpark in de zeegebieden onder de rechtsbevoegdheid van België (Milieueffectenbeoordeling (MEB))*, (Koninklijk Belgisch Instituut voor Natuurwetenschappen: Beheerseenheid van het Mathematisch Model van de Noordzee, 2011) 63.

[46] For example, a ship may become adrift due to technical problems and damage the infrastructure, making rapid intervention necessary. This may also require curtailing the OWFs. Furthermore, it is also possible that certain activities can damage the underwater infrastructure, such as cables (intentionally or unintentionally), which can entail a serious cost for the operators (in terms of loss of revenues). These risks also complicate the insurability of many activities.

[47] This should be nuanced however, since it is possible that the operator implements multiple use itself with a profitable business model.

[48] Degraer et al (n 42) 102; Steven Degraer, Robin Brabant, Bob Rumes and Laurence Vigin, *Environmental impacts of offshore wind farms in the Belgian part of the North Sea – Attraction, avoidance and habitat use at various spatial scales* (Royal Belgian Institute of Natural Sciences (RBINS), 2021) 104; Steven Degraer, Robin Brabant, Bob Rumes and Laurence Vigin, *Environmental impacts of offshore wind farms in the Belgian part of the North Sea – Getting ready for offshore wind farm expansion in the North Sea*, (Royal Belgian Institute of Natural Sciences (RBINS), 2022) 106.

[49] Council Directive 92/43/EEC of 21 May 1992 on the conservation of natural habitats and of wild fauna and flora, OJ L 22 July 2022, vol 206, art 1(e); James S Diana, 'Aquaculture Production and Biodiversity Conservation' (2009) 59 *BioScience* 27, 30–31; Helen Glenn and Hannah White, 'Legal Traditions, Environmental Awareness and a Modern Industry: Comparative Legal Analysis and Marine Aquaculture' (2007) 38 *Ocean Development & International Law* 71, 89.

[50] Niko Soininen, Antti Belinskij, Jukka Similä and Raine Kortet, 'Too important to fail? Evaluating legal adaptive capacity for increasing coastal and marine aquaculture production in EU-Finland' (2019) 110

to the presence of MPAs or Natura 2000 sites in the BPNS.[51] When, for example, in the BPNS there is the intention to engage in aquaculture in a Natura 2000-site, then a Natura 2000-authorisation is required. This can lead to a different (ie more stringent) outcome disadvantaging aquaculture by the presence of SACs and SPAs. After all, it is not *a priori* excluded that aquaculture can be cultivated, but the assessment is stricter. The main advantage under this system is related to the fact that the windfarm operator can (in line with permitting procedures and their own risk profile/assessment) determine what type of multiple use can be developed in its concession zone and how intensively it can be applied.

iv. Multiple Use as One of the Award Criteria for a Concession (eg PEZ)

The model in which multiple use is linked to the award criteria for domain concessions implies that the participant in the tender can/must formulate to what extent and how multiple use can or will be developed in the concessions they are tendering for. In addition to the evaluation of the other award criteria, the granting government will include the aspects of multiple use in its considerations. This means that other criteria, which normally will be given more weight in the decision, will play a more decisive role. By including multiple use in the award criteria, the participant is at least made aware of the government's interest to also deploy multiple use in those renewable energy zones.

However, if multiple use is not considered feasible by the participating developers, the concession can still be awarded to them. This system has thus the advantage that the developers are actively involved in the implementation of various user functions within the respective energy zones and that they consider it when designing the setup of the OWFs. Another advantage is that the permits for these other activities could (in theory) be granted together with the user permit for the operation and construction of the OWF, which eliminates an administrative burden. It should be emphasised that this is not automatic.[52] What is worth mentioning is that, according to current Belgian law, activities with the same purpose (for example generating offshore wind energy and generating offshore solar energy) can be subject to one integrated environmental impact assessment and one integrated environmental impact report if the Scientific Service Management Unit of the Mathematical Model of the North Sea (MUMM) deems it desirable and decides to do so.[53] After all, this does not mean that it concerns one and the same permit, but it does concern a streamlining of the procedure. However, when

Marine Policy 5; Harri Helminen and Tuija Honkane, 'The role of aquaculture in the eutropication process of the Archipelago Sea SW Finland' (2002) 28 *Internationale Vereinigung für Theoretische und Angewandte Limnologie: Verhandlungen* 1176, 1176–79.

[51] Jansen et al (n 7) 741.

[52] This implies that the application for a permit and/or authorisation for a specific activity can be integrated with the application for a permit and authorisation for the construction and exploitation of an OWF. This does not mean that there must be an explicit integration of both activities in the application.

[53] Act of 11 December 2022 for the protection of the marine environment and for the organization of marine spatial planning in the Belgian sea areas, *Belgian Official Journal* 16 December 2022, art 19 §2 *J°* art 20 §2 (hereafter: MEPA 2022).

it concerns an activity with a purpose other than, for example, the generation of electricity, such as aquaculture, then an integrated EIA and EIR are not possible according to current Belgian law. This is an important side note, since it can be expected that for the same permit application there would be some kind of streamlining with regard to the environmental impact assessment and report. After all, it is recommended that the Belgian framework must be amended in order to create a smoother integration for both activities. This has the advantage that a (certain) administrative burden is removed, without detracting from the fact that an environmental impact assessment is indeed carried out.

A possible disadvantage is that the directing role will once again lie with the OWF developer, which means that there is less room for third parties to also use the energy zone. Nevertheless, this has to do with setting priorities such as renewable energy deployment, as long as it does not exclude other legitimate uses (such as passive fishing). Furthermore, it is most likely not the core expertise of the OWF-developer to conduct such activities, which might also complicate the development of multiple use in that energy zone. This does not always have to be the case, since in Belgium, for example, the (former) operator of certain wind farms in the BPNS, namely Parkwind, was part of the Colruyt Group, which has accumulated expertise in aquaculture over the years.[54] It is important that such a system is well-developed and that there is some kind of oversight that allows other potential actors to participate in a fair manner and that follows-up the commitments of the OWF-developer.

v. Freedom for the OWF-Operators and Third Parties

This model implies that there are no restrictions and no explicit obligations to implement multiple use in the demarcated energy zones. In this model, it is presumed that not only the OWF-operator but anyone who has the necessary permits/authorisations can develop all kinds of activities in the demarcated energy zones, without the concession holder having any control over this.

The advantage of this model is that there are no restrictions on the form of the activities as well as the location of the activities. This is also the main disadvantage, since the unlimited possibilities also entail enormous risks. There is, for example, the safety risk for OWFs, but also the possibility of carrying out certain activities in zones that are actually not well suited for these activities. Such a model can only be usefully applied on the condition that there is really sufficient space, which is not the case in such a small area as the BPNS, where space is limited.

It should also be noted that the total freedom model does not automatically imply that just anything is allowed. After all, it is to be expected that activities will still be subject to a permit or an authorisation, which means that there is not an absolute freedom. In any case, it seems unavoidable that while granting these permits, the government will have to take these other interests into account, such as interests of the concession holders of the OWFs, environmental considerations, etc.

[54] www.blauwecluster.be/projecten/united.

C. Assessment of the Belgian and Dutch Approach

i. Belgium

The North Sea Vision 2050 presented a clear picture of how the concept of multiple use should be implemented by Belgium in 2050. The North Sea Vision 2050 was published in 2018. This document presents the long-term strategy outlining the main principles for establishing the ground rules of good governance for the BPNS until 2050. This long-term strategy states that multi-use should become the rule in the BPNS by 2050.[55]

When elaborating on the BMSP, one could somewhat assume that multiple use would play a key role, since multiple use was one of the three central points in the North Sea Vision 2050. Nothing could be further from the truth, since the BMSP did not propose any legal innovations with regard to multiple use, making the 2020–2026 BMSP essentially business as usual in that regard. The concept of multi-use has been integrated in the Royal Decree of 2019 on user permits, but this does not relate to the entire BPNS, but only to a few zones for commercial and industrial activities (see above) and not for energy zones.

Figure 1 Relationship between various legislative acts

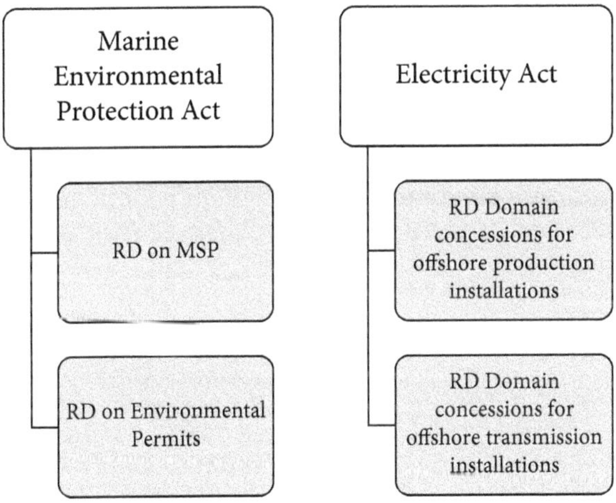

Source: Authors' own.

The Marine Environmental Protection Act (MEPA) of 1999 and more specifically the provisions with regard to MSP in the Act do not contain rules regarding to multiple use, but do not exclude multiple use either. In other words, multiple use could be made possible under the MEPA 1999, but the Act as such did not directly facilitate the application of multiple use. The new MEPA 2022 does not contain much innovation in terms of multiple use. As under the MEPA 1999, the MSP should include an analysis of the current uses of the sea areas and the uses that can be carried out together with

[55] This document is not a binding instrument, but a mere policy instrument.

the current use and which uses cannot be carried out together[56] In relation to this, the concept of multiple use has not been explicitly implemented in the MEPA 2022.

Multiple use is often associated with MSP, which has to do with the fact that the MSP divides the sea areas into various zones in which certain activities are allowed, whether or not exclusively. Such an approach *de facto* results in multiple use (eg the whole Belgian sea area) on a meso-scale. However, if within a specific zone, for example in an energy zone, other activities (eg aquaculture, tourism, etc) than the generation and transmission of energy are carried out, then this can be regarded as multiple use on a micro-scale.

Before 2012, spatial planning in the BPNS took place on an ad hoc basis.[57] MSP based on a holistic approach was only introduced in 2012 by amending the MEPA 1991 and was intended to enable spatial planning in the marine areas under Belgian jurisdiction.[58] Belgium was one of the frontrunners with regard to MSP, for two main reasons. The first reason is that the surface of the BPNS is very small (ie 0.5 per cent of the total surface of the North Sea), with a large number of activities which might potentially lead to conflicts. This implied that the necessity for better planning was urgent, and it was more achievable to initiate a MSP. The second reason relates to the fact that there is a lot of scientific knowhow about the BPNS, which is considered to be the driving force of the BMSP. Moreover, it probably was an advantage that, in a pretty early stage, a minister for the North Sea was assigned.[59] As a result, the first BMSP was adopted in 2014 and builds further on the Masterplan North Sea (In Dutch: Masterplan Noordzee) of 2003–2005, which only covered certain areas of the BPNS and was characterised by limited legal certainty.[60] The findings from the North Sea Vision 2050 were taken into account to a certain extent when the BMSP 2020–2026 was elaborated. In this context, a zone was designated in which various research and innovation projects must be given priority over other activities and in which multiple use must be used as much as possible.[61]

[56] Explanatory Memorandum, Draft act for the protection of the Marine Environment and for the organization of marine spatial planning in the Belgian sea areas, *Parliamentary Piece* Chamber 2021–2022, 47; MEPA 2022, art 24.

[57] Maes (n 34) 415.

[58] Act of 20 July 2012 amending the Act of 20 January 1999 for the protection of the marine environment in marine areas under the jurisdiction of Belgium, as regards the organization of marine spatial planning, Belgian *Official Journal* 11 September 2012; Ann-Katrien Lescrauwaet, Jan Mees, Patrick Roose, Gert Verreet and Jesse Verhalle, 'Integrated Maritime Policy' in Dauwe et al (n 42) 262; The procedure for adopting the MSP is included in the Royal Decree of 13 November 2012 on the establishment of an advisory commission and the procedure for adopting a marine spatial plan in the Belgian marine areas, *Belgian Official Journal* 28 November 2012.

[59] Maes (n 17) 415; Peccue et al (n 5) 268–70.

[60] The Masterplan North Sea consisted of two phases. The first phase (2003) had an economic angle (sand and gravel extraction and exploitation of renewable energy at sea) and was based on the Act of 22 April 1999 on the exclusive economic zone of Belgium in the North, whereas the second phase (2005) had an environmental angle (marine protected areas, SACs and SPCs, etc) and was based on the MEPA of 1999; Act of 22 April 199 on the Exclusive Economic Zone of Belgium in the North Sea, *Belgian Official Journal* 10 July 1999; Act of 20 January 1999 for the protection of the marine environment in the maritime areas under the jurisdiction of Belgium, *Belgian Official Journal* 12 March 1999; Royal Decree of 20 March 2014 establishing the marine spatial plan, *Belgian Official Journal* 28 March 2014; Frank Maes and Jan Seys, 'Ruimtelijke planning op zee: waar België goed in is' (2014) 39 *VLIZ – De Grote Rede* 15, 18–19; Peccue et al (n 5) 268–70.

[61] Royal Decree of 22 May 2019 establishing the marine spatial plan for the period from 2020 to 2026 in the Belgian marine areas, *Belgian Official Journal* 2 July 2019, art 19, §2; Maes (n 17) 428.

In addition, the BMSP 2020–2026 includes five zones in which various commercial or industrial activities are permitted on the condition that if they have a potential impact on the nature conservation areas a Natura 2000 permit will be required and the activities have to be compatible with military activities.[62] Such activities can be aquaculture, RES-projects, energy storage and desalination, among others.[63] Here too, multiple use should be stimulated as much as possible.[64]

According to Belgian law, a distinction is made between domain concessions granted with regard to the first OWFs (Mermaid, Seastar, Belwind, Nobelwind, Northwester 2, Northwind, Rentel, C-Power and Norther) and the OWFs that will be built in the PEZ, at Noordhinder-Noord, Noordhinder-Zuid and the Fairybank. The first group of OWFs were subject to article 6 of the Electricity Act, which did not contain any provision with regard to multiple use.[65]

The OWFs planned to be built in the PEZ in the future are subject to another provision in the Electricity Act, which foresees that the Royal Decree establishing the specific rules for these domain concessions must contain rules with regard to the activities that the holder of the domain concession can develop in addition to the production of electricity from RES in the relevant site.[66] With the introduction of article 6/3 in the Electricity Act through the Act of 12 May 2019 amending the Act of 29 April 1999, the concept of multiple use was legally anchored in the Electricity Act. However, this has not been formulated as a hard obligation, but only obliges the government to develop a regulation that offers the possibility of multiple use. The substantive meaning of this stipulation can therefore be classified as particularly conditional, since it only imposes the obligation for the government to regulate in the Royal Decree the activities that the concessionaire can carry out in addition to its normal activities.[67] This still means that there is no obligation to apply multiple use and certainly no right for non-concession holders to claim multiple use.

ii. *The Netherlands*

Much like in Belgium, the Dutch government is gradually starting to focus on multiple use in the Dutch part of the North Sea (DPNS).[68] In the Netherlands, two forms of multiple use are distinguished, namely passage and shared use. The aim of the Dutch government is to keep as many wind energy areas as possible navigable, albeit under

[62] Royal Decree of 22 May 2019 establishing the marine spatial plan for the period from 2020 to 2026 in the Belgian marine areas, *Belgian Official Journal* 2 July 2019, art 23.

[63] Maes (n 17) 428.

[64] Maes (n 17) 433; Royal Decree of 22 July 2019 establishing the procedure for obtaining a user permit for the zones for commercial and industrial activities in the sea areas under the jurisdiction of Belgium, *Belgian Official Journal* 20 September 2019.

[65] Electricity Act, art 6.

[66] Electricity Act, art 6/3.

[67] Electricity Act, art 6/3 §3, 7°.

[68] An important difference with Belgium is that the OWFs in the DPNS are generally located further apart and less densely concentrated. This is due to the fact that the DPNS is much larger than the BPNS (10% of the total surface of the North Sea compared to the Belgian 0.5%), which obviously means that there is more room to build OWFs and less densely concentrated OWFs. Despite a much larger sea area, the Dutch government also recognises that space is scarce and that efforts must be made to combine several spatial functions. windopzee.nl/onderwerpen/wind-zee/landingspagina-0/meervoudig-gebruik/.

certain conditions. Moreover, the Dutch government emphasises that passage and shared use are often mutually exclusive. It is therefore very important to set priorities. Vessels up to 46 meters can use the passageways (ie fishing vessels and recreational craft can use the passageways). Shared use is the other form of the multiple use and entails ecological development, passive fisheries, aquaculture and other forms of sustainable energy production.[69]

In the Netherlands, the Water Act provides the legal basis for the Water Decree, which sets out the main points that the national water plan must comply with.[70] The national water plan encompasses the entire Dutch kingdom and includes both the inland waters as well as the sea areas over which the Netherlands can exercise jurisdiction.[71] The North Sea Programme that is part of the National Water Plain contains, among other things, the rules and policy objectives related to the Dutch MSP.[72] The implementation programme of the North Sea Programme provides for the stimulation of pilot projects for multiple use, large-scale experimentation with sustainable multiple use of OWFs and the setting up of a monitoring programme in order to map out the ecological effects of (large-scale) multiple use.[73]

In the North Sea Programme 2022–2027, a policy and assessment framework for shared use of OWFs was elaborated.[74] Since April 2018, the OWFs Luchterduinen, Princess Amalia and Egmond aan Zee have been set up for passage and shared use by a decree in which some nuance was applied to the established safety zones around the OWFs.[75] This means that under certain conditions shared use and passage must be possible. In practice, shared use often relates to passive fisheries.[76]

In addition to the MSP-provisions in the Netherlands, the Offshore Wind Energy Act of 2015 introduced the concept of 'plot-decision', which is defined as a 'decision in which a site and a route for connection are designated'.[77] In a plot decision, the

[69] Trawl fishing is, for example, not allowed, windopzee.nl/onderwerpen/wind-zee/landingspagina-0/meervoudig-gebruik/.

[70] Act of 29 January 2009 containing rules regarding the management and use of water system, *Dutch Official Journal* 12 March 2009, art 4.1–4.3 (hereafter Water Act); Decree of 30 November 2009 containing rules regarding the management and use of water systems, *Dutch Official Journal* 18 December 2009, art 4.5a (hereafter Water Decree).

[71] Nieuwenhout (n 2) 98; Ministerie van Infrastructuur en Waterstaat, Ministerie van Landbouw, Natuur en Voedselkwaliteit, Ministerie van Binnenlandse Zaken en Koninkrijkrelaties, *Het nationale waterbeleid en de uitvoering in de rijkswateren – Nationaal Water Programma – 2022-2027* (Rijksoverheid, 2022) 132.

[72] Ministerie van Infrastructuur en Waterstaat, Ministerie van Landbouw, Natuur en Voedselveiligheid, Ministerie van Economische Zaken en Klimaat and Ministerie van Binnenlandse Zaken en Koninkrijkrelaties, *Programma Noordzee 2022–2027* (Rijksoverheid, 2022) 7.

[73] Rozanne Spijkerboer, Chistian Zuidema, Tim Busscher and Jos Arts, 'The performance of marine spatial planning in coordinating offshore wind energy with other sea-uses: The case of the Dutch North Sea' (2020) 115 *Marine Policy* 1, 2; Ministerie van Infrastructuur en Waterstaat et al (n 72) 96.

[74] Ministerie van Infrastructuur en Waterstaat et al (n 72) 124.

[75] Decree of the Minister of Infrastructure and Water Management of 16 April 2018, no. RWS-2018/13729 establishing a policy rule for the establishment of a safety zone for offshore wind farms (Policy rule establishing a safety zone for offshore wind farms), *Government Journal* 26 April 2018.

[76] zoek.officielebekendmakingen.nl/stcrt-2018-22895; zoek.officielebekendmakingen.nl/stcrt-2018-22909.html; zoek.officielebekendmakingen.nl/stcrt-2018-23769.html.

[77] Rozanne Spijkerboer, Chistian Zuidema, Tim Busscher and Jos Arts, 'Unravelling institutional work patterns: Planning offshore wind farms in contested space' (2021) 40 *Environmental Innovation and Societal Transitions* 249, 254; Act of 24 June 2015 containing rules regarding offshore wind energy, *Dutch Official Journal* 30 June 2015 (Offshore Wind Energy Act) art 1.

preconditions for the construction and exploitation of an OWF are laid down, which can therefore also include provisions with regard to shared use and passage.[78] The fundamental principles with regard to shared use in specific energy zones are laid down in an Area Passport Guide (In Dutch: *Handreiking Gebiedspaspoort*).[79] These area passport guides indicate per offshore wind zone which type of activity is preferred for shared use (also called co-location), based on area-specific characteristics and based on the most favourable prospects. When it seems there is no need for a shared use of the activity specified in the area passport guide, the area can be released for another type of activity in a shared use context. This means that the preferences established in the area passport guides are not carved in stone. From that perspective, the compulsory character of the area passport guides can be nuanced, since it can be qualified as a guideline.[80] Moreover, a top-down approach does not necessarily mean that the government simply imposes everything unilaterally in area passports. As a matter of fact, this is done in consultation with other stakeholders (such as environmental organisations, professional associations and wind farm developers).[81] A first area passport guide was published in 2020 and relates to the Borssele OWF.[82] The area passports guides of the OWFs Hollandse Kust (South, North and West), Ijmuiden Ver and North of the Wadden Islands are being developed. The area passport guides with regard to the OWFs Luchterduinen, Offshore Windpark Egmond aan Zee and Princess Amalia Windpark allow vessels up to 24 meters (LOA) with an Automatic Identification System (AIS) sailing in their passage lanes during day time. Shared use in these wind farms has so far been limited to pilot projects, partly in view of the limited space, such as a trial of fishing with baskets and tubs for crabs and lobsters in the Princess Amalia Wind Farm. Sport fishing with a rod is also allowed (keeping a distance of 50 meters from the turbines and 500 meters from the converter stations).[83] A permit is also required to exercise various user functions.

iii. Comparative Discussion

The current Belgian framework for the existing OWFs foresees that multiple use can be applied in the energy zones, but this is not a legal obligation (see above). This creates the risk that multiple use will not be adopted. The directing role rests with the concessionaire of the OWF, which means that little effort is put into the multiple use of the energy zone involved, since the main priority is safeguarding the assets. In other words, most of the concession holders have little incentives to facilitate multiple use in their respective zones, because they and their investors aim to avoid the

[78] Hans Erik Woldendorp, 'Wind uit een andere hoek – De nieuwe Wet windenergie op zee' (2015) 4 *Vastgoedrecht* 1.

[79] Ministerie van Binnenlandse Zaken en Koninkrijkrelaties, *Handreiking gebiedspaspoort Borssele*, (Noordzeeloket.nl, 2020) 2, www.noordzeeloket.nl/functies-gebruik/windenergie/doorvaart-medegebruik/borssele/.

[80] Ministerie van Binnenlandse Zaken en Koninkrijkrelaties (n 79) 2.

[81] ibid 3; Overlegorgaan Fysieke Leefomgeving, *Onderhandelaarsakkoord voor de Noordzee* (Rijksoverheid, 2020) 19–21.

[82] Ministerie van Binnenlandse Zaken en Koninkrijkrelaties (n 79) 2.

[83] windopzee.nl/onderwerpen/wind-zee/landingspagina-0/meervoudig-gebruik/.

risks for calamities at the maximum. Aquaculture is allowed, under certain conditions (see above nr. 6) in the existing and future concession zones, despite the fact that there is a safety zone applicable for those respective zones. Except for aquaculture and passive fisheries, other applications of multiple use are not allowed in those respective zones.

With the 'legal anchoring' of multiple use in article 6/3 of the Belgian Electricity Act, the OWFs to be developed in the PEZ in the future can be subject to multiple use. It is, however, highly unlikely that providing or facilitating multiple use in the tender proposal might have a significant impact in the decision to grant the domain concession. It remains to be seen how the new Royal Decree on the domain concessions will further elaborate this aspect. Furthermore, it is also impossible to deduce in advance which forms of multiple use should be preferred within the specific zones, especially given the lack of expertise of the OWF-developer regarding multiple use. Finally, it is not clear whether the package deal aspect will also relate to permits required to carry out certain ancillary activities within the respective zones. It is advisable to re-evaluate this and to look at a rather more targeted approach that is more in line with the North Sea Vision 2050. It was expected that the new Royal Decree on domain concessions would include the sustainability criterion, which also includes the aspect of multiple use, as an award criterion for the future tender of the OWFs in the PEZ. However, the recent decision of the Federal Government shows that this idea has been abandoned and it is therefore a guess as to how and if multiple use of space will be part of the future tendering procedure.[84]

The Dutch approach is based on a top-down approach with active stakeholder participation, in which the government determines in advance which activities with regard to shared use and passage are possible in certain energy zones, based on the present characteristics of that specific area. In the OWFs, such as Borssele, the basic rules for passage and shared use will apply. The multiple use choices will in principle be subject to customisation depending on the OWF (not the operators). These choices are based on the policy frameworks referred to above. The advantage of this approach is that multiple use is clearly identified and monitored very closely. The disadvantage is that there is a risk that the innovative options available to OWF-operators cannot always be implemented, given the restrictions set by the central authority. In other words, options that might be more efficient or effective would not always be listed by the central authority or could potentially be ranked less favourably. Another disadvantage is that it can also deter wind farm operators from participating in the tender procedure. In comparison with the Belgian approach, for example, passage is not an issue, given the density of (existing and future) OWFs and the (somewhat more rigid nature of the) safety zones that have been established around the Belgian OWFs. Whether this approach is the most suitable, given the disadvantages associated with the top-down approach, remains to be seen in practice. However, it should be noted that proper consultation with various stakeholders when drawing up an area passport guide is essential in order to deal with these perceived disadvantages.[85]

[84] The documentation study was completed in February 2024.

[85] Ministerie van Binnenlandse Zaken en Koninkrijkrelaties (n 79) 3; Noordzeeakkoord, art 4.16.

Table 1 Comparative summary of the Belgian approach vs. the Dutch approach

Belgian approach	**Dutch approach**
Limited to aquaculture, passive fishing and energy storage.	The practice of using area passports opens the door for various uses.
Bottom-up approach.	Top-down approach.
Priority is safeguarding the assets.	Will of the central government prevails. Clearly identified and monitored very closely.
Will of OWF concession holder often prevails.	Risk that not the most innovative options are implemented.

Source: Authors' own.

6. Conclusions and Recommendations

It follows from the foregoing that various (theoretical) models are conceivable with which multiple use can be achieved in the zones that are demarcated for the generation of renewable energy. Each model has advantages and disadvantages, making it difficult to make an absolute value judgement. Various factors can play a role in the choice of model, such as the technological and economic state of the art of the activity that one wishes to carry out.

In practice, it is often the case that there is a combination of different theoretical models outlined above. From a legal point of view, the Dutch model offers the most legal certainty for wind farm developers and companies interested in carrying out certain activities in addition to generating renewable energy from wind. By applying area passports, the Dutch government imposes which forms of multiple use of space are the most desirable, taking into account all kinds of (local) factors. This is preceded by a lot of preliminary research, which in a sense makes it easier for those involved. After all, wind farm developers can already take into account the other possible uses that can take place in the energy zones involved when designing their OWFs. Moreover, companies that are interested in carrying out certain activities towards energy generation can already check what a viable business case is for them.

The Belgian model only allows for a few forms of multiple use, such as energy storage, aquaculture and passive fishing. This model also offers legal certainty to a certain extent, since the rules are sufficiently clear. However, unlike the North Sea Vision 2050, the current legislative framework does not implement the idea that multiple use should be the rule by 2050. The idea of including multiple use as an award criterion (under the sustainability criterion) in the new Royal Decree on domain concessions was also omitted in the most recent principle decision by the federal government. This is somewhat regrettable, but undoubtedly follows from the fact that the zones designated for the generation of renewable energy must be fully used for the generation of renewable energy (which is essential to succeed in the energy transition). From a legal point of view, it is advisable to adopt a wait-and-see attitude and to see how the forms of shared use evolve from a technological and economic point of view, in order to then develop a more legally secure framework. This will of course have the disadvantage that the new wind farms in the PEZ will already be developed, without taking possible other uses into account. From that point of view, an area passport based on the Dutch model is an interesting option that could be considered. In the current legal framework, a provision should facilitate the integration of the environmental impact assessment for another activity with an impact other than energy generation in order to reduce the administrative burden of preparing separate environmental impact assessments. It is strange that an integrated environmental impact assessment is permitted for similar activities, but not for different activities, even though the effects are still cumulated in practice. Scientific research should be carried out into the technical, the insurance and the economic feasibility of certain forms of multiple use in order to gain a good picture of what is possible within the energy zones concerned. Research should be conducted into the risk assessment of potential multiple use damage and the interrelationship between the density of the wind turbines and the different forms of multiple use, as not every OWF takes the same approach when it comes to density of offshore wind turbines. Mapping the risks and how these risks can be mitigated is essential for making sure that the activities can be insured at all.

3

Balancing Environmental Protection with Offshore Wind and Petroleum Development: Two Peas in a Pod?

EDDY WIFA, DARIA SHAPOVALOVA AND PEDI OBANI

1. Introduction

The UK has a rich history of oil and gas production since the first discovery in the North Sea in 1969. However, despite an established oil and gas industry, the shift to cleaner energy sources has led to the growth of the offshore wind energy industry as explained below. The maturity of the UK Continental Shelf makes for a more challenging operating environment and raises concerns about energy security and the future of the oil and gas workforce, largely concentrated in the North-East of Scotland. It also raises concerns regarding the balance between energy security and environmental conservation coupled with climate change.

In 2015, the Government adopted the strategy to 'maximise the economic recovery' from the North Sea, making it a legally binding objective for the oil and gas regulator.[1] This was later updated to incorporate the legally mandated Net Zero target albeit without a clear mechanism for climate assessment or procedural steps to follow in the event of a conflict between economic and climate interests.[2] The policy direction for the oil and gas industry in the UK, as of July 2024, remains uncertain following the recent change of government through a general election. The previous Conservative Government was supportive of more frequent oil and gas licensing rounds, initiating the Offshore Petroleum Licensing Bill[3] and expressed strong commitment to maximising production in the UK Continental shelf.[4] The incumbent Labour party has so far

[1] Infrastructure Act 2015, s 41 amending the Petroleum Act 1998, s 9A. See further Greg Gordon, John Paterson and Uisdean Vass, 'The Wood Review and Maximising Economic Recovery upon the UKCS' in Greg Gordon, John Paterson and Emre Üşenmez (eds), *UK Oil and Gas Law: Current Practice and Emerging Trends : Volume I: Resource Management and Regulatory Law*, 3rd edn (Edinburgh University Press, 2018).

[2] Daria Shapovalova, 'Climate Change and Oil and Gas Production Regulation: An Impossible Reconciliation?' (2023) 26(4) *Journal of International Economic Law* 817.

[3] Offshore Petroleum Licensing Bill, HC Bill (Session 2023–24) [49], bills.parliament.uk/bills/3504.

[4] UK Government, 'Powering Up Britain: Energy Security Plan' (2023) 2, 13, www.gov.uk/government/publications/powering-up-britain#:~:text=We%20will%20move%20towards%20energy,will%20play%20in%20that%20transition.

pledged to rule out new oil and gas exploration and create a State energy company with a portfolio in green energy.[5] The expectation is that offshore wind will continue to be a major driver of the party's green revolution strategy.

The UK has the highest wind energy potential in Europe; as the leader in offshore energy development, it has been dubbed the 'Saudi Arabia of Wind Energy'.[6] Offshore wind is centre stage in the UK energy policy with the Labour Government's ambitious targets for quadrupling offshore wind to 55 GW and an additional 5 GW from floating turbines.[7]

The Government is under the obligation not only to meet the 2050 Net Zero target, but also to set five-yearly carbon budgets and develop policies and programmes to meet them.[8] Various policies and measures to support investment in offshore wind feature heavily in this process.[9] This is notwithstanding the pressure on the UK's energy security from recent crisis such as COVID-19 and the Russia-Ukraine war that raised concerns about the previous Government's commitment to climate action and renewables, and in many ways led to tensions between the speedy transition to renewable energy and the continuous exploration of oil and gas.[10] Although the UK has oil and gas reserves, the production peaked in 1999 and the UK has been a net importer of oil and gas since 2004. With natural gas imports to the UK coming primarily from Norway, the share of Russian oil and gas imports was not high. However, high reliance on gas for both electricity production and heating meant that supply and price were significantly affected by the knock-on effects of the fallout in the global gas market. With both industries operating in the United Kingdom Continental Shelf (UKCS), it is relevant to explore the environmental risk and synergies. The construction, operation and decommissioning of these offshore installations have a variety of impacts on the marine environment that could not only displace marine species but also impact on their growth and development.

This chapter employs doctrinal and functional analysis between the environmental considerations of both offshore wind and oil and gas regulations to 'describe the roles they are designed to preform and are actually performing, drawing on explanatory theories and heuristics'.[11] The chapter provides an original and rigorous exploration of

[5] Peter Walker, 'Labour Confirms Plans to Block All New North Sea Oil and Gas Projects' *The Guardian* (28 May 2023) www.theguardian.com/politics/2023/may/28/labour-confirms-plans-to-block-all-new-north-sea-oil-and-gas-projects.

[6] Godfrey Boyle, 'Offshore Wind: The Potential to Contribute a Quarter of UK Electricity by 2024' (2007) 32(2) *Wind Engineering* 65.

[7] Lara Williams, 'UK Offshore Wind Power's Potential Needs Labour's Love, Too' (*Bloomberg*, Opinion, 15 July 2024) www.bloomberg.com/opinion/articles/2024-07-15/uk-offshore-wind-market-potential-needs-labour-s-attention. For more on offshore wind As a national critical infrastructure in the UK, see John Paterson, 'Offshore Wind Licensing in the United Kingdom' in Ignacio Herrera Anchustegui and Tina Soliman Hunter (eds), *Offshore Wind Licensing* (Edward Elgar, 2024).

[8] Climate Change Act 2008, ss 1, 4, 12, 13.

[9] UK Government, 'Carbon Budget Delivery Plan' (2023) www.gov.uk/government/publications/carbon-budget-delivery-plan.

[10] UK Parliament, 'Accelerating the Transition from Fossil Fuels and Securing Energy Supplies' Fourth Report of Session 2022–2023, publications.parliament.uk/pa/cm5803/cmselect/cmenvaud/109/report.html. See also Shapovalova (n 2) 817.

[11] Eloise Scotford, 'The Status of Environmental Principles in Environmental Law' in Douglas Fisher (ed), *Research Handbook on Fundamental Concepts of Environmental Law* (Edward Elgar, 2022) 386.

the environmental and ecological functionality of both industries, particularly in relation to the marine ecosystem and the conflict of other users of the sea. We examine the law through the lens of ecological governance, building on and updating Woolley's work on critical assessment of the UK's offshore energy development.[12] While acknowledging that there are some differences in environmental impacts of developing wind and petroleum offshore, particularly in relation to oil spills, we recognise the increasing synergies between both offshore energy developments and their impacts on the marine ecosystem.[13] These include coastal supporting infrastructure, reuse of fixed oil platforms, electrification of platforms with offshore wind, and the use of fixed bottom structures,[14] which have similar cumulative environmental consequences. While research on comparative environmental impact of both offshore wind and offshore petroleum are quite limited, on the direct and indirect impacts to biodiversity and selected ecosystems, this chapter reflects on these synergies and tensions engaging with a variety of theoretical framings of ecological governance to interrogate the limits of environmental law.

The chapter is divided into six parts. Following this introduction, the second section explores environmental impacts of offshore energy development, both renewable and fossil fuel-based. The third section examines the governance and regulation of planning, licensing and leasing regime for offshore energy in the UK. In the fourth section, we critically examine project-specific environmental impact assessment (EIA) tools while section five provides a critical reflection on the suitability of these tools and the overall regulatory regime for ecological governance of the marine environment, emphasising fragmentation and lack of overall coherence. Conclusions are drawn in section six.

2. Adverse Environmental and Ecological Impacts of Offshore Petroleum and Wind Energy Development and Conflicts with Other Sea Uses

Both petroleum and offshore wind developments produce impacts on the surrounding environment. During the construction and development stage, these impacts are quite similar.[15] In this section, we engage with the environmental impacts of both oil and gas and wind offshore. While synergies exist between both energy production systems,[16] the impacts and environmental implications of wind compared to oil and gas

[12] Olivia Woolley, 'Ecological Governance for Offshore Wind Energy in United Kingdom Waters: Has an Effective Legal Framework been established for Preventing Ecologically Harmful Development?' (2015) 30 *The International Journal on Marine and Coastal Law* 765.

[13] Nathan Jones and Liba Pejchar, 'Comparing the Ecological Impact of Wind and Oil and Gas Developments: A Landscape Scale Assessment' (2013) 8(11) *PLOS ONE* 1.

[14] James Schneider and Marc Senders, 'Foundation Design: A Comparison of Offshore Oil and Gas Platforms with Offshore Wind Turbines' (2010) 44(1) *Marine Technology Society Journal* 32–50; Erika Nogueira, Rafael Marais and Amara Pereira, 'Offshore Wind Power Potential in Brazil: Complementarity and Synergies' (2023) 16(16) *Energies* 5912.

[15] Schneider and Senders (n 14).

[16] Jorun Marvik, Eirik Oyslebo and Magnus Korpas, 'Electrification of Offshore Petroleum Installation with Offshore Wind Integration' (2013) 50 *Renewable Energy* 558–64.

developments differ significantly, and thus in many respects require different regulatory tools and approaches.

For both petroleum and offshore wind energy infrastructure, environmental assessments are conducted at a high-level during planning and leasing and at a more detailed project-level – during the project authorisation process. Consequently, the analysis in this chapter focuses primarily on the regulatory tools used to prevent environmental harm and greenhouse gas emissions from marine energy. Although offshore wind is renewable and less polluting than fossil fuels, its development comes with environmental impacts.

Both offshore petroleum and offshore wind energy development have been undertaken under the erroneous assumption that the offshore environment provides a limitless opportunity and space. The reality is that the very large areas required for offshore wind energy development compete and conflict with other users of the marine space.[17] The space conflict occurs in a lesser way with the offshore oil and gas installations as while they do not require such large spaces, the attached safety zones which have to be strictly observed.

Uses of the sea that offshore energy development conflicts with include navigation for trade, public transport, leisure, fisheries, defence and aviation and other energy installations.[18] Article 60(1) of the United Nations Convention of the Law of the Sea (UNCLOS) provides that Coastal States have the exclusive right to construct and to authorise and regulate the construction and operation of artificial islands and installations and structures which includes offshore wind energy installations.[19] However, it recognises the exception to this rights where interference may be caused to the use of recognised sea lanes essential to international navigation.[20] This requirement has been transposed into the UK domestic law.[21]

There can often be significant opposition to offshore wind energy development due to the visual impacts particularly when the development is visible from the coastline.[22] That said, individuals and communities see offshore developments in their complexity beyond the visual impacts and there is evidence of increasing desire for deliberative approaches in decision-making for all forms of energy development.[23]

[17] Paul Todd, 'Marine Renewable Energy and Public Rights' (2012) 36(3) *Marine Policy* 667.

[18] David Toke, 'The UK Offshore Wind Power Programme: A Sea-Change in UK Energy Policy?' (2011) 39 *Energy Policy* 526, 531.

[19] United Nations Convention on the Law of the Sea (signed 10 December 1982, entered into force 16 November 1994) 1833 UNTS 3 (UNCLOS), art 60(1).

[20] UNCLOS 1982, art 60(7).

[21] Electricity Act 1989, s 36B; See also Department for Energy and Climate Change (DECC), 'Guidance Note on the New Process for Varying Consents Granted under s 36 of the Electricity Act 1989 for the Generating Stations in England & Wales' (July 2013), www.gov.uk/government/uploads/system/uploads/attachment_data/file/252014/DECC_varying_consents.pdf; Energy Act 2004, s 99.

[22] Drew Bush and Porter Hoagland, 'Public Opinion and the Environmental, Economic and Aesthetic Impacts of Offshore Wind' (2016) 120 *OCM* 70–79. For instance, this informed the case instituted by Donald Trump who argued that the offshore wind farm was visible from his golf course and would obstruct the beauty and view of the course. However, the UK Court unanimously ruled against him and ordered that permission be granted for the development of the wind farm. The BBC, 'Donald Trump Loses Wind Farm Legal Challenge', www.bbc.co.uk/news/uk-scotland-north-east-orkney-shetland-35106581.

[23] Marine Scotland, 'A two way Conversation with the People of Scotland on the Social Impact of Offshore Renewables' (2022) www.gov.scot/binaries/content/documents/govscot/publications/research-and-analysis/2022/06/two-way-conversation-people-scotland-social-impact-offshore-renewables/documents/marine-scotland-two-way-conversation-people-scotland-social-impact-offshore-renewables/marine-scotland-two-way-conversation-people-scotland-social-impact-offshore-renewables/govscot%3Adocument/marine-scotland-

Offshore wind energy developments also conflict with other activities such as dredging, offshore oil and gas production installations, military activities, or radars and aviation.[24] There can further be significant effects on fisheries and other sea-based economic activities.[25] To resolve this conflict in the wind industry, the Fishing Liaison with Offshore Wind and Wet Renewable Group (FLOWW) was formed in 2002.[26] Despite much progress in this area, there are still reports of what the fishing industry calls a 'spatial squeeze' due to offshore wind and marine protected areas.[27]

There are also concerns over the electromagnetic and chemical effects of offshore wind energy installations. This is because during deployment and routine operational services, including decommissioning, there is the potential risk of chemical spills from associated marine vessels and equipment, particularly in pieces of machinery that use hydraulic fluids.[28] Electromagnetic fields can also impact marine inhabitants although research data in this area is limited to date.[29]

While climate impacts of offshore wind are limited, offshore petroleum production activities contribute to climate change at all stages – from exploration and extraction to the final burning of the produced product. Oil and gas installations or wind farms, depending on where they are located, can damage sea-bed habitats, affect areas of importance for critical life stage areas (eg breeding) of marine species,[30] obstruct migration routes and in some cases endanger the lives of birds.[31] These concerns are further complicated by a high degree of uncertainty and insufficient data regarding the environmental effects of offshore wind farms, particularly as a result of ambient noise underwater and electromagnetic fields from cables in the sea-bed.[32] The effect of such

two-way-conversation-people-scotland-social-impact-offshore-renewables.pdf; Daria Shapovalova et al, 'Measuring Just Transition: Indicators and Scenarios for a Just Transition in Aberdeen and Aberdeenshire' (*Just Transition Lab*, 2023) doi.org/10.57064/2164/22364.

[24] Andrej Abramic et al, 'Site Selection Within the Maritime Spatial Planning: Insights from Use-Cases on Aquaculture, Offshore Wind Energy and Aggregates Extraction' (2024) 251 *Ocean and Costal management* 107051.

[25] Similarly, studies have shown that offshore wind farm sites could also be beneficial to the growth and development of the UK Aquaculture industry. This is believed to aid the maximisation of the value of the UK sea. See SEAFISH Project, 'Commentary Benefits of Alternative Energy: Suitability of Offshore Wind Farm as Aquaculture Site', www.seafish.org/media/Publications/10517_Seafish_aquaculture_windfarms.pdf. See also Prince Owusu Bonsu et al, 'Co-Location of Fisheries and Offshore Wind Farms: Current Practices and Enabling Conditions in the North Sea' (2024) 159 *Marine Policy* 105941.

[26] The Crown Estate, 'FLOWW Best Practice Guidance for Offshore Renewable Development: Recommendation for Fisheries Liaison' (January 2014) www.thecrownestate.co.uk/media/1775/ei-km-in-pc-fishing-012014-floww-best-practice-guidance-for-offshore-renewables-developments-recommendations-for-fisheries-liaison.pdf.

[27] ABPmer, 'Spatial Squeeze in Fisheries' Final Report, ABPmer Report No. R. 3900 (National Federation of Fishermen's Organisations and Scottish Fishermen's Association 2022) www.sff.co.uk/news/spatial-squeeze-report.

[28] US Department of the Interior Bureau of Ocean Energy Management Office of Renewable Energy Programs, 'Environmental Risks, Fate and Effects of Chemicals Associated with Turbines on the Atlantic Outer-Continental Shelf' (November 2013) espis.boem.gov/final%20reports/5330.pdf.

[29] See eg Petra Harsanyi et al, 'The Effects of Anthropogenic Electromagnetic Fields (EMF) on Early Development of Two Commercially Important Crustaceans, European Lobsters, Homarus Gammarus (L.) and Edible Crab, Cancer Pagurus (L.)' (2022) *Journal of Marine Science Engineering* 564.

[30] Paul Thomson et al, 'Framework for Assessing Impacts of Pile-Driving Noise from Offshore Wind Farm Construction on a Harbour Seal Population' (2013) 43 *Environmental Impact Assessment Review* 73.

[31] Kaoshan Dai et al, 'Environmental Issues Associated with Wind Energy – A Review' (2015) 75 *Renewable Energy* 911–21.

[32] Malte Busch and Stefan Garthe, 'Approaching Population Thresholds in Presence of Uncertainty: Assessing Displacement of Seabirds from Offshore Wind Farm' (2016) 56 *EIAR* 31.

uncertainty is that the cumulative effects of multiple large-scale offshore wind farms on marine ecosystems in all aspects are unascertained due to its comparative immaturity with petroleum.

Petroleum production has unique environmental impacts which require careful management, from noise pollution during seismic exploration to impacts from decommissioning. Generally, such harm can be divided into routine or operational and accidental. Former includes 'spills from pipelines, chemical and oil spills associated with drilling activities, oil contaminated drill cuttings, produced water, unloading of oil, human-generated waste such as sewerage and rubbish, and chemical spills from maintenance activities (such as pipeline cleaning)'.[33] These emissions are expected but should be minimised, controlled, and monitored through regulation. While accidents for offshore wind carry risk largely to personnel safety,[34] oil and gas accidents can also have catastrophic environmental consequences with risks of large-scale oil spills such as *Deepwater Horizon* and *Ixtoc 1*, both caused by well blowouts.[35]

The highlighted micro and macro environmental implications of siting and operating both offshore wind and offshore oil and gas infrastructure reflects the need for a proactive approach characterised by research and comprehensive assessments of possible impacts, to identify and propose mitigation measures. Therefore, the legal and regulatory tools are discussed below starting with the processes of planning and licensing, to project authorisation and monitoring.

3. The UK Offshore Wind and Petroleum Planning, Licensing and Leasing

The legal regimes for planning, leasing, and licensing offshore energy development are informed by the division of powers between the Scottish and the UK Governments, where the former is responsible for much of the renewable energy projects in Scottish waters, and the latter for all matters relating to oil and gas. In this section we examine the regulatory processes related to the licensing and leasing for offshore energy development in the UK. We review the relevant regulators and regulatory tools for environmental protection, including Strategic Environmental Assessment and Marine Spatial Planning including protected areas. The focus here is on the processes in place

[33] Luke Havemann, and Tina Hunter, 'Environmental Law and Regulation on the UKCS' in Gordon, Paterson and Üşenmez (n 1) 339–90.

[34] A 2023 report showed a 94% increase in safety incidents in offshore wind compared to 2022. See G+ Global Offshore Wind, G+ Global Offshore Wind Health and Safety Organisation 2023 incident data report, www.gplusoffshorewind.com/?a=1538335. Also, offshore wind has a 3–4 times higher injury rate compared to oil and gas. See David Rowell, David McMillan and James Carroll, 'Offshore wind H&S: A Review and Analysis' (2024) 189 *Renewable and Sustainable Energy Reviews* 113928. See also Eddy Wifa and Tina Hunter, 'Mitigating Occupational Health and Safety Risks in the Proposed Australian Offshore Wind Energy Industry: Lessons from the Safety Case Regime' (2022) 49(1) *Journal of Energy and Natural Resources Law* 83.

[35] Tina Soliman Hunter, 'The Role of Science, Technology and Engineering in the Regulation of Arctic Oil Spills: An Interdisciplinary Approach' (University of Aberdeen Working Paper Series 000/19, 2019). www.abdn.ac.uk/law/documents/000.19%20-%20Hunter.pdf.

to assess and minimise impacts when deciding where and how the energy development will be taking place and before any concrete project plans materialise.

A. Powers and Regulators for Offshore Energy Leasing, and Licensing in the UK

Although the Scottish Government has devolved responsibility for the majority of activities within its territorial sea limits (12 nautical miles), certain matters, including oil and gas, are reserved with Westminster. In the exclusive economic zone (between 12 to 200 nm) the UK Government additionally has powers over planning and nature conservation.[36] The energy matters are more generally reserved to Westminster, with a few exceptions. Thus, the Scottish Government has powers under planning and environmental regulation for onshore energy infrastructure, which includes renewable energy and any potential onshore oil and gas. Therefore, issues pertaining to onshore energy infrastructure and all offshore renewable infrastructure are executively devolved, meaning the Scottish Government 'administers the activity but has no powers to change the legislation',[37] and is responsible for offshore renewable installations licensing, impact assessments, safety zones and decommissioning in Scottish waters.[38]

These devolution arrangements dictate the complex structure of planning and licensing for offshore energy in the UK. While the oil and gas planning and licensing is conducted by the UK Government, regardless of the location; the offshore wind development licensing process depends on which administration it falls under.

For oil and gas the UK Government's North Sea Transition Authority (NSTA, formerly Oil and Gas Authority) is the main regulator operating independently from the Government Department of Energy Security and Net Zero (DESNZ).[39] NSTA announces and holds licensing rounds and is responsible for issuing licences for offshore oil, gas, and carbon capture and storage. NSTA grants exploration and production licences and consents for drilling or any well operations.[40] Once an economic discovery is made, a Field Development Plan must be approved by the NSTA for all new developments and extensions for existing fields. After Plan approval, a further consent from the NSTA is required for production, flaring and venting operations. The Office of Petroleum Regulator for Environment and Decommissioning (OPRED) is part of the DESNZ responsible for administering environmental regulations on offshore oil and gas operations. OPRED further plays a role in safety regulation, forming the competent safety authority together with the HSE (Health and Safety Executive).

[36] The Scottish Government, 'Scottish Marine Bill Strategic Environmental Assessment (SEA): Environmental Report' (2008) www.gov.scot/binaries/content/documents/govscot/publications/factsheet/2020/10/marine-scotland-act-2010/documents/strategic-environmental-assessment-sea/strategic-environmental-assessment-sea/govscot%3Adocument/Scottish%2BMarine%2BBill%2BStrategic%2BEnvironmental%2BAssessment.pdf.

[37] Scotland Act 2016, ss 47–49; see also ibid.

[38] Scotland Act 2016, s 62.

[39] NSTA, 'OGA Framework Document' (2016) www.nstauthority.co.uk/news-publications/oga-framework-document/.

[40] NSTA, 'Licensing and Consents', www.nstauthority.co.uk/regulatory-information/licensing-and-consents/overview/.

Offshore wind energy in the UK is made available to developers through a process called leasing rounds.[41] The DESNZ undertakes a Strategic Environmental Assessment (SEA) of UK waters to identify which areas can best support offshore wind energy development.[42] This information is then transmitted to the Crown Estate UK or Crown Estate Scotland, which exercise ownership over the seabed and grant leases to developers for such area of the seabed to be used for offshore wind farm development subject to relevant statutory consents.[43] For this, the developers are requested to prepare and submit for development, consent for projects over 100MW of generation capacity in size to the Planning Inspectorate.[44] In Scotland, all applications for marine projects are submitted to Marine Scotland.[45] These applications will include details of project design, an EIA, Habitats Risk Assessment and evidence that the developer has carried out detailed consultation with stakeholders on the project as it progresses.[46] These processes are examined closely in section 4 below.

For oil and gas, the first licensing round took place in 1964.[47] Since then there have been 33 licensing rounds held as of June 2024.[48] The rounds take place every one to three years periodically, and, as discussed above, the attempts by the past Government to make these annual are not likely to be successful.

For offshore wind, the UK officially launched its Round 1 in 2001 as a demonstration round, though the first commercial offshore wind farm was installed in 2000 near shore in Blyth Harbour, North East England.[49] Round 2 launched in 2003 and was larger and further out to sea.[50] Round 3 in 2010 was made up of nine zones and was set to generate as much as 13GW of electricity.[51] The fourth offshore wind licensing round was concluded in 2023.[52] With the growth of the industry, the wind farms are to be located in much deeper waters with greater environmental risks.[53] It has become increasingly

[41] BVG Associates, 'Guide to an Offshore Windfarm: Updated and Extended' (The Crown Estate and the Offshore Renewable Energy Catapult, 2019) www.thecrownestate.co.uk/media/2860/guide-to-offshore-wind-farm-2019.pdf.

[42] UK Offshore Energy Strategic Environmental Impact Assessment 4 (OESEA4), www.gov.uk/government/consultations/uk-offshore-energy-strategic-environmental-assessment-4-oesea4.

[43] Department of Energy Security and Net Zero, Offshore Petroleum Regulator for Environment and Decommissioning and Department for Business, Energy & Industrial Strategy, 'Offshore Energy Strategic Environmental Assessment (SEA): An Overview of the SEA Process', www.gov.uk/guidance/offshore-energy-strategic-environmental-assessment-sea-an-overview-of-the-sea-process.

[44] The Crown Estate, 'Marine: Offshore Wind', www.thecrownestate.co.uk/our-business/marine/offshore-wind.

[45] Marine Directorate, 'Sectoral Marine Plan for Offshore Wind Energy' (2020) www.gov.scot/publications/sectoral-marine-plan-offshore-wind-energy/.

[46] BVG Associates (n 41).

[47] Oil and Gas Authority, 'Oil and Gas: Licensing Rounds' (2013) www.gov.uk/guidance/oil-and-gas-licensing-rounds.

[48] For a detailed review of the UK oil and gas licensing process see Greg Gordon, 'Petroleum Licensing' in Gordon, Paterson and Üşenmez (n 1).

[49] BVG Associates (n 41).

[50] IRENA-GWEC, 'United Kingdom (including Scotland)' www.irena.org/-/media/Files/IRENA/Agency/Publication/2013/GWEC/GWEC_UK.pdf?la=en&hash=E8BEE8160570AB71ED71D93D515C50883C14C2D5.

[51] ibid.

[52] The Crown Estate, 'Offshore Wind Leading Round 4', www.thecrownestate.co.uk/our-business/marine/Round4.

[53] British Wind Energy Association (BWEA), 'What does the Round 3 Announcement Mean? Briefing Note on Offshore Wind Energy' (2009) csmres.co.uk/cs.public.upd/article-downloads/Round%203%20Briefing%20from%20BWEA_a6293.pdf.

necessary to reduce conflict with other users of the sea, especially in a crowded offshore environment.[54]

A relatively new development signalling increasing synergy of offshore petroleum and wind development is the creation of offshore wind leasing rounds specifically targeting projects that would help mitigate emissions from oil and gas production. In Scotland, the Innovation and Targeted Oil and Gas (INTOG) leasing round allows developers to apply for licences for 'IN' – small scale, innovative projects, of less than 100MW, and 'TOG' – projects connected directly to oil and gas infrastructure, to provide electricity and reduce the carbon emissions associated with production.[55] During 2022–2023, 13 projects were offered agreements under this scheme, with the final option agreement being subject to inclusion into Sectoral Marine Plan for INTOG, still in development.[56]

B. Strategic Environmental Assessment for Energy Licensing

Before a licensing round takes place, for offshore petroleum or wind, the Government needs to demonstrate that it conducted a Strategic Environmental Assessment (SEA).[57] The most recent, fourth SEA (OESEA4) was published in September 2022, taking into account the new policy objectives, marine spatial planning, oil and gas licensing, and offshore renewables.[58]

The requirement stems from European EU legislation which is not binding in the UK post-Brexit but many environmental directives and regulations have been already incorporated into the UK law. The EU Directive 2001/42/EC required Member States to adopt laws that mandate the assessment of such plans and programmes that are likely to have significant environmental effects.[59] In England, Strategic Environmental Assessments are implemented through the Environmental Assessment of Plans and Programmes (England) Regulations 2004 and in Scotland by the Environmental Assessment (Scotland) Act 2005.

The SEA process involves several stages of screening, scoping and consultation, after which an environmental report is produced identifying significant environmental effects of the proposed plan or programme and reasonable alternatives.[60] These

[54] Anne-Mitchell Slater, 'Marine Spatial Planning: Implications for the Marine Environment Through Examination of Darwin Mounds and the James River "Toxic" Fleet cases' (2004) 16 *ELM* 287–95.

[55] Crown Estate Scotland, 'INTOG Leasing Round', www.crownestatescotland.com/scotlands-property/offshore-wind/intog-leasing-round.

[56] ibid, see section 3(C).

[57] Environmental Assessment of Plans and Programmes Regulations 2004, SI 2004/1633.

[58] BEIS, 'UK Offshore Energy Strategic Environmental Assessment: OESEA4' (2022) assets.publishing.service.gov.uk/government/uploads/system/uploads/attachment_data/file/1061670/OESEA4_Environmental_Report.pdf. Prior to publication, the OESEA4 has undergone consultation, where the issue of no planned reduction in production has been raised by multiple respondents. The Government responded with reference to the Climate Compatibility Checkpoint and the North Sea Transition Deal. See 'UK Offshore Energy Strategic Environmental Assessment: Government response to OESEA4 Public Consultation' (September 2022).

[59] Directive 2001/42/EC, arts 2 and 3.

[60] John Phylip-Jones and Thomas Fischer, 'Strategic Environmental Assessment (SEA) for Wind Energy Planning: Lessons from the United Kingdom and Germany' (2015) 50 *Environmental Impact Assessment Review* 203. See also The European Commission, 'Strategic Environmental Assessment' ec.europa.eu/environment/eia/sea-legalcontext.htm.

issues are all taken into consideration before adoption and in conducting post-adoption monitoring.[61] The SEA process facilitates the consideration of cumulative effects, offers measures to mitigate any potential adverse environmental effects, promotes transparency, improves the consultation process and provides a rigorous system for including environmental factors in decision making.[62]

Although the SEA appears laudable, it is criticised for merely being a procedural law which 'does not place any substantive obligations for environmental protection on decision makers'.[63] In some cases the SEA is seen to have had little direct or measurable influence on decisions,[64] Despite the above criticisms, SEA still remains an effective tool in ensuring a balance between environmental protection and offshore wind energy development if adequately utilised.

A contentious point regarding SEA and environmental assessments for licensing rounds in general is the consideration of climate impacts, particularly for oil and gas developments. In October 2023, two judicial claims challenged the scope of OESEA4 in relation to an oil and gas licensing round, on the basis that it did not consider Scope 3 emissions and failed to properly assess reasonable alternatives.[65] Although the High Court rejected the claimants arguments using the EIA process and the *Finch* case as analogy,[66] given the latest Supreme Court decision in *Finch*, future similar challenges might have a different result.[67]

The crux of the issue lies in an apparent inconsistency between the Government Policy of Maximising Economic Recovery (MER) and Net Zero. Following the decline in production of petroleum on the UK Continental Shelf, the Government adopted the MER Strategy, making it a legally binding objective for the licensing authority.[68] In 2021, the Government incorporated the Net Zero target into the strategy, albeit without a clear mechanism for climate assessment or procedural steps to follow in an event of a conflict between economic and climate interests.[69] The North Sea Transition Deal, announced in March 2021, details non-binding industry and Government commitments to the decarbonisation of North Sea production, development of new industrial sectors (eg hydrogen), and support for the workforce. The potential incompatibility of the MER Strategy with the Net Zero commitment led to the development of the

[61] Tim Bean et al, 'A Review of the Tools used for Marine Monitoring in the UK: Combining Historic and Contemporary Methods with Modeling and Socioeconomics to Fulfil Legislative Needs and Scientific Ambitions' (2017) 4 *Marine Ecosystem Ecology* 263.

[62] Scottish Government Guidance on Strategic Environmental Assessment (2013) www.gov.scot/publications/strategic-environmental-assessment-guidance/.

[63] Woolley (n 12) 77; Jane Holder, *Environmental Assessment: The Regulation of Decision Making* (Oxford University Press, 2006) 235.

[64] Monica Tetlow and Marie Hanusch, 'Strategic Environmental Assessment: The State of the Art' (2012) 30(1) *Journal of Impact Assessment and Project Appraisal* 15–24.

[65] *Greenpeace LTD v Secretary of State for Energy Security and Net Zero, Uplift v Secretary of State for Energy Security and Net Zero* [2023] EWHC 2608 (Admin).

[66] ibid [97]–[116].

[67] *R (on the application of Finch on behalf of the Weald Action Group) v Surrey County Council and others* [2024] UKSC 20. See analysis in section 4(A) below.

[68] Infrastructure Act 2015, s 41, amending the Petroleum Act 1998, s 9A. See further Greg Gordon, John Paterson and Uisdean Vass, 'The Wood Review and Maximising Economic Recovery upon the UKCS' in Gordon, Paterson and Üşenmez (n 1).

[69] NSTA (n 40).

Climate Compatibility Checkpoint for new petroleum licences in the UK. The initial Checkpoint draft presented an ambitious six-point test for consultation,[70] but the final version contained only three tests without an apparent threshold for passing or any requirement to pass all three.[71] As presented, the Checkpoint is a procedural and a non-statutory requirement and has so far been applied to the 33rd offshore oil and gas licensing round.[72]

C. Marine Spatial Planning and Protected Areas

Marine spatial planning (MSP) is 'a public process of analysing and allocating the spatial and temporal distribution of human activities in marine areas to achieve ecological, economic and social objectives that usually have been specified through a political process'.[73] The notion is borne out of the realisation that the 'problems of the ocean'[74] are caused by conflict with several users of the sea and need to be adequately considered and resolved.[75] The expectation is that in using an 'ecosystem-based approach',[76] MSP can serve as an effective environmental protection tool capable of identifying the cumulative effects of human activities that can be maintained within natural carrying capacities and will not impair the functionality of the ecosystem.[77] MSP should be designed to encompass all policies, programmes and activities affecting the seas enabling planners to form an overview of the uses of the sea and their impacts.[78]

[70] BEIS, 'Designing a Climate Compatibility Checkpoint for Future Oil and Gas Licensing in the UK Continental Shelf: Consultation Document' (December 2021) www.gov.uk/government/consultations/designing-a-climate-compatibility-checkpoint-for-future-oil-and-gas-licensing-in-the-uk-continental-shelf. Discussion here is based on Daria Shapovalova and Tavis Potts, *Climate Change: UK Test for New Oil and Gas Fields' Impact on Emissions Targets is not Fit for Purpose* (13 October 2022, the Conversation) theconversation.com/climate-change-uk-test-for-new-oil-and-gas-fields-impact-on-emissions-targets-is-not-fit-for-purpose-191803.

[71] BEIS, 'Climate Compatibility Checkpoint Design' (September 2022) www.gov.uk/government/publications/climate-compatibility-checkpoint-design.

[72] Shapovalova (n 2).

[73] UNESCO Intergovernmental Oceanographic Commission, Marine Spatial Planning, www.ioc.unesco.org/en/marine-spatial-planning.

[74] UNCLOS preamble.

[75] Charles Ehler and Fanny Douvere, 'Visions for a Sea Change, Report of the First International Workshop on Marine Spatial Planning, UNESCO' (2007) 5 www.belspo.be/belspo/northsea/publ/sea%20change%20vision%20.pdf.

[76] This has been defined by the OSPAR and Helsinki Commissions as 'the comprehensive integrated management of human activities based on the best available scientific knowledge about the ecosystem and its dynamics, in order to identify and take action on influences which are critical to the health of marine ecosystems, thereby achieving sustainable use of ecosystem goods and services and maintenance of ecosystem integrity'. It is worth noting that this approach is largely guided by the precautionary principle is decision making. See para 5 of the 'Statement on the Ecosystem Approach to the Management of Human Activities', First Joint Ministerial Meeting of the Helsinki and OSPAR Commissions, Bremen, 25–26 June 2003, helcom.fi/wp-content/uploads/2019/10/First-Joint-Ministerial-Meeting-of-the-Helsinki-and-OSPAR-Commissions.pdf. See also, Rena Long, 'Legal Aspects of Ecosystem-Marine Management in Europe' (2012) 26(1) *Ocean Yearbook* 417.

[77] Dorota Pyc, 'The Role of Law in Marine Spatial Planning' in Jacek Zaucha and Kira Gee (eds), *Marine Spatial Planning: Past, Present and Future* (Palgrave, 2019). See also Woolley (n 12) 778.

[78] Ehler and Douvere (n 75) 16.

In the UK, this process is governed by the Marine and Coastal Access Act 2009 and the Marine (Scotland) Act 2010 for the Scottish territorial sea. MSP can help mitigate adverse effects of offshore energy developments by highlighting areas that should be preserved to protect their environmental sensitivity and identifying possibilities for co-locating marine activities so as to avoid possible conflict and reduce pressure on the marine environment.[79] There is not a mandatory requirement to follow the MSP as decision-makers have the discretion to depart from the plan policies.[80] Furthermore, there is 'lack of evidence of a causal relationship between the marine plan policies and the decisions in adopted marine plan areas'.[81]

The MSP process in the UK is quite elaborate. In England, there are 11 marine plan areas and in Scotland, a National MSP, 11 regional and a Sectoral Marine Plan for Offshore Wind.[82] The marine planning process to cover all English waters was complete only in 2021,[83] as the process has been perceived as 'more complex to develop than was perhaps anticipated' due (amongst other things) to extensive engagement requirements.[84] Scotland's National Marine Plan was adopted by the Scottish Parliament in 2015 and there is a requirement to review and report on the implementation of the Plan every three years.[85] The Scottish Regional Marine Plans are being prepared by Marine Planning Partnerships, and as of July 2024, three have been adopted.[86]

In relation to offshore energy projects, the Marine and Coastal Access Act serves several functions including the creation of the UK Government's Marine Management Organisation, marine planning and licensing (other than oil and gas),[87] and the establishment and management of Marine Conservation Zones (MCZ).[88] Licences in MCZs have to comply with the Conservation of the Offshore Marine Habitats and Species Regulations 2017. There is no outright prohibition of activities, including oil and gas in MCZs or in their proximity, but the Marine Management Organisation can adopt byelaws for specific MCZs to limit disturbances including movements of vessels, killing or disturbance of animals, and interference with the seabed.[89] Even where projects are

[79] Anne-Michelle Slater, 'What is Marine Spatial Planning' (2012) 14 *Environmental Law Review* 2.

[80] Anne-Michelle Slater and Jim Claydon, 'Marine Spatial Planning in the UK: A Review of the Progress and Effectiveness of the Plans and Their Policies' (2020) 22(2) *Environmental Law Review* 85.

[81] ibid.

[82] Marine Management Organisation, 'Marine Plan Areas in England' (2014) assets.publishing.service.gov.uk/media/5a7de4d4ed915d74e33eeb82/marine_plan_areas.pdf; Scottish Government, 'Marine Planning: Regional Boundaries' (2020) www.gov.scot/publications/marine-planning-regional-boundaries/.

[83] UK Government, 'Adoption of Marine Plans marks Big Step Forward for England's Seas' (23 June 2021) www.gov.uk/government/news/adoption-of-marine-plans-marks-big-step-forward-for-englands-seas.

[84] Slater (n 80).

[85] Marine Scotland, 'Scotland's National Marine Plan: A Single Framework for Managing Our Seas, The Scottish Government' (March 2015); 'National Marine Plan Review 2021: Three Year Report on the effectiveness of Scotland's National Marine Plan' marine.gov.scot/sites/default/files/national_marinc_plan_review_2021.pdf.

[86] Shetland, Clyde, and Orkney – see NatureScot, 'Marine Planning in Scotland', www.nature.scot/professional-advice/planning-and-development/marine-planning-scotland.

[87] Marine and Coastal Access Act 2009, s 77.

[88] JNCC, 'Marine Conservation Zones' jncc.gov.uk/our-work/marine-conservation-zones#management-of-offshore-mczs.

[89] Marine and Coastal Access Act 2009, s 129.

not located in an MCZ, environmental statements for new developments must include details of protected sites that 'do not overlap the location of the project but could be impacted'.[90]

There is discretion accorded to public authorities in relation to activities which might affect MCZs. They must exercise their functions 'in the manner which [they] consider best furthers the conservation objectives stated for the MCZ'; or if not possible – in a manner that 'least hinders the achievement of those objectives'.[91] Where there is a significant risk to MCZs, the relevant authority must be satisfied that with no reasonable alternatives, the public benefit outweighs the risk of environmental damage, and mitigating measures will be made.[92]

The relevant regulators and statutory consultees here are the Joint Nature Conservation Committee (JNCC) and its Scottish counterpart, NatureScot. Their duties include providing advice to the appropriate authorities on the development and implementation of policies for or affecting any nature conservation matter.[93] JNCC must be notified if any significant risk to MCZ is detected and may give advice and guidance as to a wide range of matters related to MCZ management.[94]

It is worth noting that the Conservation of Offshore Marine Habitats and Species Regulations 2017[95] provide a procedural order for the designation of protection areas, including Special Areas of Conservation (for the protection of certain habitats and marine species) and Special Protection Areas or SPAs (for the protection of wild birds).[96] The main requirements for assessments for the purposes of offshore oil and gas activities in these areas are still regulated by the 2001 Regulations,[97] but some activities (eg decommissioning) can be covered. 2017 Regulations provide for a licensing regime for such cases,[98] and DESNZ advises that operators work closely with OPRED and JNCC in such cases. The Scottish Government had been developing a similar scheme for Scottish waters but scrapped it after criticism from the fishing industry and coastal communities.[99] The consultation on the proposal attracted 2,458 substantive responses with 43 per cent of respondents expressing opposition to the introduction of

[90] BEIS OPRED, 'The Offshore Oil and Gas Exploration, Production, Unloading and Storage (Environmental Impact Assessment) Regulations 2020 – A Guide' (2021) assets.publishing.service.gov.uk/government/uploads/system/uploads/attachment_data/file/1005109/The_Offshore_Oil_and_Gas_Exploration__Production__Unloading_and_Storage__Environmental_Impact_Assessment__Regulations_2020_-_A_Guide__July_2021.pdf.

[91] Marine and Coastal Access Act 2009, s 125(2)–(3).

[92] Marine and Coastal Access Act 2009, s 126.

[93] Natural Environment and Rural Communities Act 2006, s 34; Natural Heritage (Scotland Act) 1991, s 3; Nature Scot, Managing Coasts and Seas, 'Oil and Gas', www.nature.scot/professional-advice/land-and-sea-management/managing-coasts-and-seas/oil-and-gas.

[94] Marine and Coastal Access Act 2009, s 127.

[95] Conservation of Offshore Marine Habitats and Species Regulations 2017, SI 2017/1013.

[96] Conservation of Offshore Marine Habitats and Species Regulations 2017, regs 11 and 12. See these discussed in more detail in section 4(B) below.

[97] See oil and gas exception in the Offshore Marine Habitats and Species Regulations 2017, reg 55(16)(f).

[98] Offshore Marine Habitats and Species Regulations 2017, reg 55.

[99] Philip Sim, 'Scottish Government Scraps Marine Conservation Plan' (*BBC News*, 29 June 2023) www.bbc.co.uk/news/uk-scotland-66053133.

the Highly Protected Marine Areas.[100] The main reasons for opposition revolve around the perceived lack of a scientific basis for their establishment, the arbitrary and disproportionate nature of the proposed policy, and the potential for serious socio-economic impacts on island and coastal communities.[101]

In 2015, Woolley noted that even though the introduction of the MSP regime in the UK espoused an ecosystem-based approach, there was a lack of near absolute constraints on developments on ecological grounds.[102] This is true to this day with a minor exception – in 2023, the UK Government established three zones as Highly Protected Marine Areas – 'areas of the sea that allow the protection and recovery of marine ecosystems by prohibiting extractive, destructive and depositional uses and allowing only non-damaging levels of other activities to the extent permitted by international law'.[103] This would presumably include a ban on both offshore wind and petroleum development in such zones. The aim is for regulators including the Marine Management Organisation to introduce appropriate management measures and an assessment in respect of each site as to whether any additional measures are needed to manage other activities that are not extractive, destructive, or depositional, based on the species and habitats found in the site.[104] These zones are the first to have the prohibition of energy development activities offshore, which demonstrates some move towards an ecological governance approach, albeit for a very limited area.

This section has demonstrated the growth and development of both offshore energy developments and despite being almost four decades apart, there are similarities in terms of how they both navigate the political economy of speed, albeit with different justifications. In both cases, there are difficulties in implementing measures that minimise both the macro and micro environmental consequences. Achieving an ecosystem-based approach is challenging with fragmented regulation and limited understanding of cumulative impacts of various marine activities. The length of time that it takes to produce regional MSPs and the fact that these are coming after so many licences are already awarded is further testament to this.

While some examples of synergies between offshore wind and petroleum leasing can be identified, such as the INTOG rounds, the tensions and conflict between the Government's MER strategy and its Net Zero objective have only resulted in fragmentation and inconsistencies as the policies and associated legislation are potentially promoting two counteracting functions. For both offshore wind and petroleum, the tensions remain as the environmental assessment measures are largely procedural and may have limited impact on the final decision. All of these reflect the imbalances between energy maximisation and environmental protection.

[100] Dawn Griesbach, Alison Platts and Jennifer Waterton Griesbach & Associates, 'Highly Protected Marine Areas (HPMAs): Analysis of Consultation Responses' (Scottish Government, November 2023) www.gov.scot/publications/highly-protected-marine-areas-hpmas-analysis-consultation-responses-final-report/documents/.

[101] EA Virtanen et al, 'Balancing Profitability of Energy Production, Societal Impact and Biodiversity in Offshore Wind Farm Design' (2022) 158 *Renewable Energy and Sustainable Energy Reviews* 112087.

[102] Woolley (n 12) 765–93.

[103] DEFRA, 'Consultation on Sites Proposed as Highly Protected Marine Areas' (2022) consult.defra.gov.uk/hpma/consultation-on-highly-protected-marine-areas/supporting_documents/Highly Protected Marine Areas consultation document.pdf.

[104] ibid 13.

4. Environmental Impact Assessment for Offshore Energy Development in the UK

At the level of specific project approval and authorisation, EIA is used in the UK to establish the potential environmental impacts of offshore energy development and to potentially prevent significant harm. During operations, an extensive legal framework regulates the activities by for example establishing appropriate discharge limits, monitoring systems and liability.[105] The aim is to strike an appropriate balance between development of offshore energy, whether oil and gas or wind, on the one hand and protection of the environment on the other.[106] Although the regulatory regime for mitigating the environmental impacts of offshore energy development is quite sophisticated, it remains fragmented, complex and often difficult for developers to navigate. In this section, we focus on the process of EIA that all developers must conduct prior to applying for production licence/consent.

A. The EIA Regulations for Offshore Petroleum and Wind

In contrast to the more high-level SEA, EIA applies to individual developments of offshore wind or oil and gas. EIA is also a procedural requirement and even if a significant risk of harm is found, the relevant legislation does not necessarily require application refusal. Similar to the SEA, the current form of EIA regulations in the UK result from implementing EU law. The process includes conducting the assessment and the preparation of an environmental report using the information obtained. This will be submitted along with the application for development consent to enable decision-makers to take into consideration such likely environmental impacts of the projects when reaching a decision. An EIA is mandatory for projects listed in Annex I of the EIA Directive, including 'extraction of petroleum and natural gas for commercial purposes where the amount extracted exceeds 500 tonnes/day in the case of petroleum and 500 000 cubic metres/day in the case of gas'.[107] For projects listed in Annex II, which include renewable energy projects, there is discretion as to whether an EIA is required with a case-by-case approach.[108]

In the UK, there are two separate EIA regimes for offshore wind and for oil and gas. Offshore wind EIA is governed by the Electricity Works (Environmental Impact Assessment) Regulations 2017[109] in England/Wales and in Scotland by the Electricity Works (Environmental Impact Assessment) (Scotland) Regulations 2017.[110] The Regulations generally require an assessment of generating plants over 50MW, though

[105] See Daria Shapovalova, 'Environmental and Planning Law' in Geoff Hewitt and Terrence C Daintith (eds), *United Kingdom Oil & Gas Law* (Sweet & Maxwell, 2022).
[106] Josep Lloret et al, 'Unravelling the Ecological Impact of Large-Scale Offshore Wind Farms in the Mediterranean' (2022) 824 *Science of the Total Environment* 153803.
[107] Directive 2011/92/EU amended in 2014 by Directive 2014/52/EU, Annex I, s 14.
[108] Directive 2011/92/EU amended in 2014 by Directive 2014/52/EU, art 4.
[109] Electricity Works (Environmental Impact Assessment) (England and Wales) Regulations 2017.
[110] Electricity Works (Environmental Impact Assessment) (Scotland) Regulations 2017.

the need for an EIA is determined on a case-by-case basis.[111] For oil and gas, the relevant regulations are the Offshore Oil and Gas Exploration, Production, Unloading and Storage (Environmental Impact Assessment) Regulations 2020[112] which require consideration of the environmental impacts of proposed offshore oil and gas projects.

For all energy development, the EIA process involves several stages including screening, scoping, consultation, and the preparation of the environmental statement (ES), which is then submitted to the Planning Authority for consideration[113] During this period, the opinion of the statutory and non-statutory consultees, planning authorities, the general public and other stakeholders are also relevant in the decision-making process. Once consent is granted, adequate monitoring is necessary, particularly where there are conditions attached to the consents.

The developer must ensure that the ES is prepared by competent experts and contains the required information including the description of the location of the project, and the project itself, its main characteristics and estimated residues, emissions, and waste it is likely to cause.[114] An ES must further include a description of the reasonable alternatives to the project (in terms of location, size, project design, technology) and reasons for the option chosen.[115] A further requirement is the provision of the baseline scenario, or the description of the current state of the environment and its likely evolution without the proposed project.[116] A detailed account of the likely significant effects of the project on the environment is required, including cumulative effects with other approved projects, impacts on climate, and risks to human health.[117] Although in the UK the consideration of social or economic impacts is not required by the regulations, developers often include some consideration of these impacts.[118] Finally, an ES must be accompanied by a non-technical summary, to allow the public to understand the impact of the proposed development without necessarily having the technical knowledge.

There are requirements for the proposed projects to undergo public consultation for at least 30 days and seek consultation of specific authorities.[119] Public notice must be given of the application for consent and the ES, including a publicly accessible website, and provision for requesting further copies by post or electronically. Where the project is likely to have transboundary impacts, a notice must be issued to the affected country, and a consultation organised if requested.[120]

[111] Ruth Stevenson, 'Environmental Impact Assessment for Offshore Wind Farms' 2.

[112] SI 2020/1947.

[113] Electricity Works (EIA) (England and Wales) Regulations, regs 10(1), 18(1), 13(1), 9(1).

[114] Oil and Gas EIA Regulations 2020, regs 8 and 10. For offshore wind – Electricity Works (EIA) (England and Wales) Regulations 2017, reg 17(1).

[115] Oil and Gas EIA Regulations 2020, Sch 6, s 2; Electricity Works (EIA) (England and Wales) Regulations 2017, Sch 4, s 1.

[116] ibid Sch 6, s 3. For offshore wind, see ibid Sch 4, s 2.

[117] ibid Sch 6, ss 4 and 5. See detailed review of oil and gas EIA regulations in Shapovalova (n 2).

[118] John Glasson et al, 'Guidance on Assessing the Socio-economic Impacts of Offshore Wind Farms' (Oxford Brookes University, 2020) doi.org/10.24384/ax1s-jr48; for oil and gas see Equinor, 'Rosebank Environmental Statement ES/2022/001' (2022) www.gov.uk/government/publications/rosebank-field-development.

[119] Oil and Gas EIA Regulations 2020, reg 12. For offshore wind = Electricity Works (EIA) (England and Wales) Regulations 2017, reg 25.

[120] Oil and Gas EIA Regulations 2020, reg 13. For offshore wind – Electricity Works (EIA) (Scotland) Regulations 2017, Part 10; Infrastructure Planning (Environmental Impact Assessment) Regulation 2017, s 32.

Any consent or authorisation may be subject to conditions designed to safeguard the environment.[121] For oil and gas, the OPRED 'would not normally expect to have to reject an ES submission, as any significant issues would either be resolved with the developer prior to the preparation of the environmental submission or resolved during the review process'.[122] The NSTA's decision on whether to grant consent is conditional on the Secretary of State's decision and must be made within a reasonable time of it.[123] The NSTA may choose not to grant consent even if the Secretary of State has agreed.[124] For offshore wind, the final decision on whether any offshore renewable energy project can be developed rests with the relevant planning authority, which will issue consent, that is, a Development Consent Order for major offshore renewable energy projects in the appropriate area if it is satisfied that the project should proceed.

Even where some procedural violations take place during the EIA process, unless they are material to the final decision, this is not likely to impact the final outcome, but rather warrant a resubmission rectifying any outstanding issues.[125]

A significant change to the EIA process, specifically on the consideration of Scope 3 emissions in oil and gas projects, has been recently brought by the UK Supreme Court decision in *Finch*.[126] While the Government's approach so far has been to only consider exploration and production emissions, the Court's decision establishes that emissions resulting from burning the produced oil and gas (regardless of where it occurs) – or Scope 3 emissions – have to also be considered. The scope of climate impacts in the EIA regulations has previously been interpreted by the developers and regulators to consider only upstream emissions. As mentioned above the regulations are based on the EU EIA Directive, which defines impacts broadly to include 'indirect, secondary, cumulative, transboundary, short-term, medium-term and long-term, permanent and temporary, positive and negative effects of the project'.[127]

There have been many attempts to incorporate downstream emissions into the UK regulators' decision-making process, including the Climate Checkpoint discussed in section 3(B). Several cases were brought by environmental NGOs challenging oil and gas licences on the grounds that Scope 3 emissions were not taken into account. Before the Supreme Court's decision, courts have sided with the Government in all these cases, including the lower courts' decisions in *Finch* and *Greenpeace Limited v The Advocate General*.[128] The Supreme Court engaged extensively with arguments around causality, impact of government policy, scope of the proposed project and concluded that for oil and gas projects, the Scope 3 assessment is required. The impact of this decision will

[121] Oil and Gas EIA Regulations 2020, reg14(2)d.

[122] BEIS OPRED (n 90).

[123] Oil and Gas EIA Regulations 2020, reg 15.

[124] ibid reg 15(4).

[125] See eg *Greenpeace Limited v the Advocate General* [2021] CSIH 53.

[126] *R (on the application of Finch on behalf of the Weald Action Group) v Surrey County Council and others* [2024] UKSC 20.

[127] Directive 2014/52/EU (16 April 2014) amending Directive 2011/92/EU on the Assessment of the Effects of Certain Public and Private Projects on the Environment OJ L 124, Annex IV section 4.

[128] *R (Finch) v Surrey County Council* [2021] PTSR 1160; *Greenpeace Limited v The Advocate General* [2021] CSIH 53.

be seen in pending cases challenging the approvals for the Jackdaw and Rosebank oil fields.[129] It might also have wider implication on planning and SEA process in the future.

Overall, the EIA, if used effectively, can assist in the identification of environmental risk from offshore oil and gas and wind as it provides environmental information that can help decision and policy makers to prevent adverse development.[130] Unfortunately, as with the SEA, the EIA places only procedural obligations on decision-makers and fails to provide concrete obligations on them for the protection of the environment.[131]

Woolley argues that the main concern regarding EIA is that the effects of human activities cannot be evaluated on the back of one-off assessments and final decisions made based on those evaluations.[132] Although the EIA's relevance in generating information about 'specific interventions into ecosystems, for the legitimacy of decisions cannot be emphasised enough',[133] its application has not been without challenges, and this will be discussed in section 5 of this chapter.

B. Habitats Regulation Assessment

Included in the ES, where relevant, must be the assessment of impacts on habitats and protected sites, derived from the Habitat Directives prior to Britain leaving the EU.[134] Following such an assessment, authorities shall 'agree to the plan or project only after having ascertained that it will not adversely affect the integrity of the site concerned and, if appropriate, after having obtained the opinion of the general public'.[135]

The responsibility for this in the UK's EEZ is placed on the Conservation of Offshore Marine Habitats and Species Regulations 2017[136] and in the territorial sea by the Conservation (Natural Habitats etc.) Regulations 1994.[137]

The objective of the Habitats Assessment is to promote the maintenance of biodiversity while giving economic, social and cultural requirements adequate consideration. It was for this reason that the Birds Directive was promulgated and the Natura 2000 Ecological Network for Protected Areas was created and designed to safeguard against plans and programmes that may have a significant environmental impact.[138] Unfortunately, there has been considerable difficulty in the implementation of the Birds Directive and Habitats Directive, particularly in 'assessing the usefulness

[129] *Greenpeace v North Sea Transition Authority*, pending case, climatecasechart.com/non-us-case/greenpeace-v-north-sea-transition-authority/. 'Uplift and Greenpeace Take Government to Court to Stop Rosebank Oil Field' (18 December 2023) www.greenpeace.org.uk/news/uplift-greenpeace-rosebank-legal-case/.

[130] Eddy Wifa, 'The Role of Environmental Impact Assessment in the Nigerian Oil and Gas Industry using the United Nation's Environmental Programme EIA on Ogoni as a Case Study – Lessons from some International Good Practices' (2014) 3 *International Energy Law Review* 117.

[131] Olivia Woolley, 'Developing a System of Ecological Governance: A Legal Framework for Determining Offshore Wind Energy's Role in the Formation and Implementation of an Ecologically Coherent Policy' (DPhil thesis, University College London, 2011) 228.

[132] ibid.

[133] ibid.

[134] Council Directive 92/43/EEC on the Conservation of Natural Habitats and of Wild Fauna and Flora.

[135] Habitats Directive, art 6(4).

[136] SI 2017/1013.

[137] SI 1994/2716.

[138] European Commission, 'Natura 2000', ec.europa.eu/environment/nature/natura2000/index_en.htm.

of the existing guidance and whether it remains fit-for-purpose' spanning 1600 pages.[139] Habitats Assessments can significantly aid the identification and mitigation of adverse impacts of offshore wind energy development on protected sites. In fact, some proposed offshore wind farms have been rejected because of their likely impacts on protected sites, for example the Navitus Bay wind park.[140] Regarding offshore oil and gas activities, the Offshore Petroleum Activities (Conservation of Habitats) Regulations 2001 implement the combined protections offered in the EU Wild Birds and Habitats Directives.[141] The main purpose of the Regulations is to provide additional protection to the so-called 'relevant sites' which include areas of conservation (SAC),[142] sites of Community importance,[143] candidate SACs[144] and sites designated under EU Directives, often referred to as European protected sites. SACs are 'sites that have been formally designated by the government of each country in whose territory the site lies.'[145] 116 of SACs have marine components covering approximately 14 per cent of UK waters, and 15 are in offshore waters (two of those are in Scotland).[146]

Where the Secretary of State considers that anything or an activity is likely to have a significant effect on a relevant site (whether individually or in combination with any other plan or project), they must make an appropriate assessment of the implications for the site in view of the site's conservation objectives.[147] While there is no exhaustive list of 'significant effects', the test of significance is where proposed activity 'could undermine the site's conservation objectives'.[148] The assessment of that risk (of 'significance') must be made in the light, amongst other things, of the characteristics and specific environmental conditions of the site concerned.

Whilst it is for the competent authority to make the assessment, the onus is on the applicant to provide the information necessary to secure an approval, which might

[139] HM Government, 'Report of the Habitats and Wild Birds Directive Implementation Review' (March 2012) assets.publishing.service.gov.uk/media/5a79926f40f0b642860d920f/pb13724-habitats-review-report.pdf.

[140] The Planning Inspectorate, 'Navitus Bay Wind Park: Examining Authority's Report of Findings and Conclusion and Recommendations to the Secretary of State for Energy and Climate Change' (11 June 2015) infrastructure.planninginspectorate.gov.uk/wp-content/ipc/uploads/projects/EN020022/EN020022-004883-Appendix%20O%20-%20Extracts%20from%20ExA%20Report%20on%20Navitus%20Bay%20DCO.pdf.

[141] SI 2001/1754.

[142] There are 'sites that have been formally designated by the government of each country in whose territory the site lies.' JNCC, 'Special Areas of Conservation Overview' jncc.gov.uk/our-work/special-areas-of-conservation-overview. There are 656 such sites in the UK, including 15 in offshore waters (2 of those are in Scotland).

[143] These are 'sites that were adopted by the European Commission before the end of the Transition Period following the UK's exit from the EU, but not yet formally designated by the government of each country.' There is only 1 such area in the UK according to JNCC, 'Special Areas of Conservation Overview', jncc.gov.uk/our-work/special-areas-of-conservation-overview.

[144] These are 'sites that were submitted to the European Commission, before the end of the Transition Period following the UK's exit from the EU, but not yet formally designated.' ibid JNCC.

[145] ibid JNCC.

[146] ibid.

[147] The Offshore Petroleum Activities (Conservation of Habitats) Regulations 2001, reg 5(1).

[148] NatureScot (2023), 'Habitats Regulations Appraisal of Local Development Plans – Guidance for planning authorities in Scotland', www.nature.scot/doc/habitats-regulations-appraisal-hra-local-development-plans-ldps-guidance-planning-authorities#Interpretation+of+a+'likely+significant+effect.

require additional research and assessment. In this process, the Secretary of State must consult and have regard to any representation by the JNCC; general public consultation is optional.[149] The assessment must take into account the effects of any associated infrastructure, so even if the development itself is not within a protected site, pipelines crossing a protected site require an assessment. This has been the case in environmental statements for Rosebank[150] and Cambo fields.[151] In the light of the conclusions of that assessment the Secretary of State shall, generally, approve the grant of any licence or consent, authorisation or approval 'only after having ascertained that nothing might be done and no activity that might be carried out … would have an adverse effect on the integrity of [the] site'.[152]

However, the Secretary of State may override the general prohibition in relation to projects: (1) to which there is no satisfactory alternative; and (2) which should be carried out for imperative reasons of overriding public interest of a social or economic nature.[153] There are stricter rules for exception where a relevant site hosts 'a priority natural habitat type or a priority species'.[154]

Thus, although governed by different regulations, the requirements and processes accorded to relevant protected sites are largely analogous. Putting in place additional assessment and safeguards, the regulations nevertheless do not rule out energy development activities in or near such sites, leaving the Government some discretion. A divergence would materialise in the consideration of decarbonisation or pursuing Net Zero as an 'overriding public interest' in authorising offshore wind farms. In the EU, the 'planning, construction and operation of plants and installations for the production of energy from renewable sources' as well as storage and grid connections 'shall be presumed as being in the overriding public interest and serving public health and safety' for the purposes of inter alia the Habitats Directive.[155] Practice in the UK indicates that climate change is indeed increasingly accepted as a matter of overriding public interest in offshore wind projects.[156]

[149] The Offshore Petroleum Activities (Conservation of Habitats) Regulations 2001, reg 5(2).

[150] Equinor, 'Rosebank: Environmental Statement ES/2022/001' (2022), assets.publishing.service.gov.uk/government/uploads/system/uploads/attachment_data/file/1097880/Rosebank_Environmental_Statement_-_Final_for_Submission_To_OPRED_Equinor_3rd_August_2022.pdf.

[151] Siccar Point Energy, 'Cambo Oil Field, UKCS Blocks 204/4a, 204/5a, 204/9a and 204/10a: Environmental Impact Assessment (EIA)' (2021) assets.publishing.service.gov.uk/government/uploads/system/uploads/attachment_data/file/991817/D-4261-2021_-_ES.pdf.

[152] The Offshore Petroleum Activities (Conservation of Habitats) Regulations 2001, reg 5(3); Shapovalova (n 105). The Inner House of the Court of Session has confirmed that the obligation only extends to designated sites, and not draft proposed sites: *The Royal Society for the Protection of Birds v Scottish Ministers* [2017] CSIH 31, [222]–[225].

[153] The Offshore Petroleum Activities (Conservation of Habitats) Regulations 2001, reg 6(1); the Conservation of Offshore Marine Habitats and Species Regulations 2017, reg 29(1).

[154] The Offshore Petroleum Activities (Conservation of Habitats) Regulations 2001, reg 6(2); The Conservation of Offshore Marine Habitats and Species Regulations 2017, reg 29(2).

[155] Regulation 2022/2577 (22 December 2022) Laying Down a Framework to Accelerate the Deployment of Renewable Energy L335/36, art 3(1).

[156] See eg West of Orkney Wind Farm Derogation Case (2023) 2, 48–55, marine.gov.scot/sites/default/files/west_of_orkney_windfarm_-_derogation_case.pdf; BEIS, 'Application for Development Consent for the Norfolk Boreas Offshore Wind Farm' (10 December 2021) 5.28–5.36, infrastructure.planninginspectorate.gov.uk/wp-content/ipc/uploads/projects/EN010087/EN010087-002917-NORB-Boreas-Decision-Letter.pdf.

5. Reconciling Maximising Offshore Energy Resources and Protection of the Environment: Criticisms of the Current UK Regulatory Strategy

The concerns raised in this section are an indication of the complexity of the marine environment and its multiple uses resulting in the prevalence of uncertainties that makes the regulation of the 'unknown' particularly challenging. However well-intentioned the regulatory regime might be, the resulting fragmented international, regional and national laws are challenging for developers to navigate and are not the most effective way of developing an ecological governance approach to marine governance.

This section highlights and analyses three particular difficulties in this regard: (i) the challenges of implementing the environmental governance regime, (ii) the potential for conflict of interest in the role of the Crown Estate, and (iii) the role of climate change and Net Zero in offshore energy governance.

Offshore energy will continue to make significant contributions to ensuring energy security, economic development, and combatting climate change. However, these developments can conflict with other sea users and marine protected areas, thereby causing severe negative impacts on species and marine mammals that inhabit the sea and rely on it for survival.[157] Although there are environmental regulations and assessments to mitigate such environmental effects, the regime is fragmented. This is because the environmental regulatory regime is based on a patchwork of national, regional and international regulations which are not cohesive and make it difficult for developers to comply.[158] On the complexity of legislation and guidance, the findings of the Habitats and Wild Birds Directives Implementation Review state that it 'can be difficult for competent authorities to navigate and is all the more daunting for developers [… reinforcing] a perception of inconsistency and lack of transparency in the process'.[159]

One reason for such complexity, as Pieraccini suggests, is that 'the high scientific uncertainty surrounding marine environment' particularly in the wider context of global environmental change challenges the design and implementation of effective marine conservation laws.[160] Despite this, Government is advised that through the effective application of the principles of ecological governance, the above challenges can be mitigated and balance can be achieved between offshore energy development and protection of the marine environment.[161] Achieving this will require a more holistic,

[157] Mark A Shields et al, 'Strategic Priorities for Assessing Ecological Impacts of Marine Renewable Energy Devices in the Pentland Firth (Scotland, UK)' (2009) 33(4) *Marine Policy* 635.

[158] Catherine Caine, 'The Dogger Bank Offshore Wind Farm Proposal: A Study of The Legal Mechanisms Employed in The Construction of an Offshore Wind Farm' (2014) 2 *NELR* 89, 123; HM Government, 'Report of the Habitats and Wild Birds Directives Implementation Review' (2012) 13, www.gov.uk/government/uploads/system/uploads/attachment_data/file/69513/pb13724-habitats-review-report.pdf.

[159] ibid HM Government.

[160] Margherita Pieraccini, 'Establishing an Ecological Coherent Network of Marine Protected Areas in English Waters: What Does the Designation of Marine and Coastal Access Act 2009 Add to the Picture?' (2013) 15 *Environmental Law Review* 104–20.

[161] In this sense ecological or environmental governance is the way individual or collective interests are managed in pursuance of public environmental good. See Nathan Bennett and Terre Satterfield, 'Environmental Governance: A Practical Framework to Guide Design, Evaluation and Analysis' (2017) 11(6) *Journal of the Society for Conservation*; Woolley (n 12) 765–93.

interconnected and comprehensive approach towards governance and decision-making that is in contrast to a mechanistic orientation.[162] In designing and applying an ecological governance regime, Woolley emphasises the need for collective decision-making and the role of Government and its institutions in this regard.[163] Furthermore, through strategic ecological planning, regulatory clarity and certainty and effective communication, there will be the establishment of an effective and comprehensive approach to governance that will 'steer markets and non-market actors towards behaviours that serve ecological ends'.[164]

Another criticism of the regime is that due to its fragmented nature, particularly regarding the consenting regime, the various stages and elements of the process operate in isolation which makes it uncoordinated and lacking integration.[165] For such a process that involves several parties functioning at different levels, there is also the possibility of neglect and delay.[166] As the process moves through the various levels and parties, the obligation for environmental protection is shuffled between them, giving the opportunity for some elements of environmental protection to be overlooked at each stage.[167] Therefore, there is less opportunity for a detailed and strategic consideration of the environmental impact of the development. This is exacerbated by the inefficient timing and questionable impact of some processes, as evidenced in the MSP and SEA examples. One would expect the MSP and SEA to be conducted before and directly impact the leasing and licensing process to ensure that environmental impacts are sufficiently accounted for, particularly in the cumulative context.

The current regime is plagued by ad hoc and weak implementation of the environmental regulatory requirements for offshore wind energy development.[168] This suggests that in some ways, the development of offshore wind energy receives much more political priority than the protection of the marine environment. The reason for this assertion is the fact that leasing and licensing rounds in the past were carried out in a rather ad hoc manner because there was limited 'legal regime for marine planning during the preparation of plans for the three licensing rounds'.[169] Also, SEA preceded the implementation of Rounds 2 and 3, which suggests that the Crown Estate leased areas for offshore wind development without reliance on the SEA.[170]

The Crown Estate in 2009, during the second leasing rounds, continued to lease areas for offshore wind energy development without 'receiving additional information from the second national SEA, OESEA2, which was released in 2010'.[171] In fact, during Round 3, there was no SEA for the Crown Estates' selection of zones for the construction

[162] Peter Robertson and Taehyon Choi, 'Ecological Governance: Organising Principles for an Emerging Era' (2010) 7 *PAR* 89; Lennart Lundqvist, *Sweden and Ecological Governance* (MUP, 2004).

[163] Woolley (n 12).

[164] Woolley (n 131) 115; Olivia Woolley, *Ecological Governance: Reappraising Law's Role in Protecting Ecosystem Functionality* (Cambridge University Press, 2014).

[165] Caine (n 158) 122.

[166] ibid.

[167] ibid.

[168] ibid 123.

[169] Woolley, *Ecological Governance* (n 164) 771.

[170] ibid.

[171] Caine (n 158) 89, 126.

of offshore wind farms.[172] Rather, in an ad hoc manner, it used its Geographic Information System to identity zones 'suitable' for offshore wind farm construction.[173] It is for this reason that Caine argues that 'regrettably the Crown Estate does not take extensive environmental considerations into their site leasing guidelines'.[174] It therefore means that plans for offshore wind energy development in the UK have been carried out without detailed and robust environmental scrutiny.[175]

Perhaps one reason for the Crown Estate's inconsistent approach in using SEA is borne out of the possible conflict between its primary commercial function and the protection of the environment. Therefore, the absence of external supervision or scrutiny in this regard and the pressure to maximise offshore wind energy suggests that the scales balancing offshore wind energy development and environmental protection are heavily tipped in favour of offshore wind development.

It is argued that such dual consideration is likely to conflict with the Crown Estate's statutory principal duty as a body corporate; with the duty to 'maintain and enhance' the value of the Crown's portfolio of property and rights by securing 'the best consideration in money or money's worth which in their opinion can be reasonably attained, having regard to all the circumstances of the case'.[176] This is to be with regard to good management practices.[177] Unfortunately, the phrase 'good management' is unclear and not defined in legislation.[178] It is based on this possible conflict that Woolley questions why 'key stages of decision-making by this primarily commercial body have been allowed to pass all licencing rounds without external scrutiny'.[179] She adds that this raises concerns over the 'commitment of successive UK governments to prevent exploitation of the offshore wind energy resources from causing ecological harm'.[180]

Furthermore, based on the fact that the developer has the responsibility to carry out the bulk of the environmental assessment, there is the concern that these assessments and environmental statements will be constructed to their benefit.[181] In fact, Holder observes how environmental statements have been constructed with special emphasis placed on the positive aspects of the development, with little weight paid to the real environmental problems that arise from the development.[182] One reason for this, as opined by Johnstone, is that 'scientists' are contracted by the developer to prepare the environmental statement thereby creating a situation where the result of the studies carried out is, more often than not, in favour of the developer.[183] The limited nature of

[172] The Crown Estate, 'Round 3 Site Selection' (2009) 4, www.thecrownestate.co.uk/media/5666/ei-round-3-offshore-wind-site-selection-summary.pdf.
[173] ibid.
[174] Caine (n 158) 89, 123.
[175] Woolley, *Ecological Governance* (n 164) 765, 771.
[176] Crown Estate Act 1961, ss 1(3) and 3(1).
[177] Woolley (n 12) 765, 770; House of Commons Treasury Committee, *The Management of the Crown Estate, 8th Report of Session 2009–2010*, vol 1 (The Stationery Office Limited London 2010) 10–11.
[178] ibid.
[179] Woolley, *Ecological Governance* (n 164) 765, 771.
[180] ibid.
[181] Caine (n 158) 89, 125.
[182] Jane Holder, *Environmental Assessment: The Regulation of Decision Making* (Oxford University Press, 2004) 267.
[183] Magnus Johnson and Dale Rodmell, 'Fisheries, the Environment and Offshore Wind Farms: Location, Location, Location' (2009) 4(1) *Food Ethics* 23–24.

the information required in the environmental statement has also been questioned.[184] For example, while there is some information on short and medium term impacts, they usually do not contain long term consequences.[185]

Finally, the climate change crisis and the legal and political commitments to Net Zero add further complexity in the ecological governance. For offshore wind, the decarbonisation benefit means that there are limited climate impacts to consider, and what is more, climate change mitigation can be used as a mitigating factor if significant impacts to protected sites are identified. At the same time, for oil and gas, while no such derogation is possible, the contradiction between the MER policy and Net Zero is manifesting in the creation of the Climate Compatibility Checkpoint and the recent inclusion of Scope 3 emissions into the EIA by the Supreme Court. However, the MER objective stands and given that the climate assessment requirements would be procedural rather than substantive requirements, the reconciliation is still left to the discretion of the regulator and the political approach of the Government in question.

The lack of clear threshold indicators further limits the prospects for accountability and ensuring tangible outcomes from the application of the Checkpoint. Moreso, one of the principles of the Checkpoint is that it must be evidence-based, using reliable data or credible projections. This could result in a bias against precaution in the absence of data on environmental risks of offshore oil and gas developments, further undermining environmental protection. The description of the other two key principles of the Checkpoint – transparent and simple – while prioritising the need for a clear, objective, and methodical process, further suggest a predominantly technocratic focus which is a limitation for effective environmental governance.

While one may understand that the nexus between environmental policy, sustainability and the offshore oil and gas and wind energy industry is fraught with difficulty and contention due to varying interests, the role of law in ensuring a balance between these interests is continuously tested. There must be persistent effort on the part of Government, industry and stakeholders to engage and find the appropriate balance and in fact prioritise the protection of the environment.

6. Conclusion

This chapter examined the environmental regulation of planning, licensing, and authorisation of offshore energy in the UK, focusing on both wind and petroleum. Analysing these two regimes together steps outside of the traditional approach but is necessary to reveal the interactions and tensions brought by the increased fragmentation and challenge of climate change. We start with setting out the environmental impacts both renewables and fossil fuels development can inflict on the marine environment and process with a functional analysis of the legal framework from planning to leasing,

[184] Stuart Bell, Donald McGillivray and Ole W Pedersen, *Environmental Law*, 8th edn (Oxford University Press, 2013) 476–77.

[185] More generally see Andreea Nita, Stacey Fineran and Laurentiu Rozylowicz, 'Researchers' Perspectives on the Main Strengths and Weaknesses of Environmental Impact Assessment (EIA) Procedures' (2022) 92 *Environmental Impact Assessment Review* 106690.

licensing and EIA. In this analysis we focused on the environmental protections and safeguards that are in place before the development takes place, revealing the inconsistencies between the functions of the policy and legislation and its operation and results. We also explored the implications of the devolved powers on the environmental governance process. Oil and gas developments have made a significant contribution to the UK's energy security in the past but today, with depleting basin and climate targets, the contribution of offshore wind to addressing both these challenges cannot be overstated. However, both activities come with environmental impacts and risks and this is particularly relevant when considering the co-location of both offshore energy sources.

Despite the seemingly robust yet fragmented environmental regulations aimed at reducing the impact of these offshore energy developments on the marine ecosystem, evidence in this chapter suggests that there is an inherent imbalance that is in many ways politically motivated. This is because from an ecological perspective, the planning system in the UK, particularly England and Wales, is based on a decision-making process whereby judgements are made through a consideration of economic, social and environmental interests, with the scale tilted in favour of development and economic interest. In some ways, it would appear that 'there is a manifest imbalance in that the benefits of environmental protection and conservation have to be demonstrated while the benefits of development are taken as axiomatic'.[186] As the challenge to balance energy security, affordability, sustainability and social acceptance remains ever so present, the limits of law are constantly tested.

[186] Woolley (n 131) 163; Richard Cowell and Susan Owens, 'Governance Space: Planning Reform and the Politics of Sustainability' (2006) 24(3) Environmental Planning 403–421.

4

Avoiding (Offshore) Renewable and Critical Mineral-Based Resource Curse in Africa: The Role of a Continent-wide Legal Regime

SOLOMON N OBULOR, JOY A DEBSKI AND NNENNAYA J NWALI

1. Introduction

Africa has ample (offshore) renewable energy and critical minerals, which are essential for developing renewable and low-carbon technologies to transition to a carbon-neutral economy. It is estimated that Africa accounts for about 30 per cent of the world's critical mineral reserves.[1] For instance, the Democratic Republic of Congo is estimated to hold 74 per cent of the world's cobalt supply, South Africa controls 90 per cent of global platinum reserves, and Nigeria has been identified as having a substantial quantity of various critical minerals.[2] Furthermore, the potential of offshore wind, hydropower, and solar energy in Africa is vast. For instance, it is reported that South Africa could produce up to 901 gigawatts (GW) of power from both floating and fixed seabed-mounted offshore wind.[3]

However, like traditional hydrocarbon and other non-renewable natural resources such as diamonds, gold, etc, there is a scrabble for both onshore and offshore renewable energy resources and critical minerals in Africa by the Global North. Curtis refers to this increasing contest as the 'New Colonialism' – a concept that depicts the plundering of Africa's natural resources, especially strategic energy and mineral resources by the Global North.[4] The resultant impact of the 'New Colonialism' on Africa's renewable

[1] James Boafo et al, 'The Race for Critical Minerals in Africa: A Blessing or Another Resource Curse?' (2024) 93 *Resource Policy*.

[2] NEITI, 'Solid Minerals Audit Report 2015' (2017) eiti.org/sites/default/files/attachments/neiti-sma-report-2015-full-011117_002.pdf; Fidele Niyagaba, 'How Africa Can Spark Bargaining Power Locked in Critical Minerals' *The Standard* (2024) www.standardmedia.co.ke/opinion/article/2001502653/how-africa-can-spark-bargaining-power-locked-in-critical-minerals.

[3] Alessandra Pardini, 'Seven Thoughts on Kickstarting Offshore Wind in South Africa' (2023) www.aoshearman.com/en/insights/perspectives-on-energy-transition-in-emerging-markets/seven-thoughts-on-kickstarting-offshore-wind-in-south-africa#1.

[4] Mark Curtis, 'New Colonialism: Britain's Scramble for Africa's Energy and Mineral Resources' (*WaronWant*, 2016).

energy and critical mineral development in the absence of a robust regulatory framework is the risk of a renewed Resource Curse in the context of the offshore energy and critical minerals transition, as will be discussed in this chapter.

The Natural Resources Curse, otherwise referred to as the Paradox of Plenty, describes the counter-intuitive relationship between resource abundance and socioeconomic development in many resource-rich countries.[5] This phenomenon is observed as 'economies with abundant natural resources (tending) to grow less rapidly than natural-resource-scarce economies'.[6]

The risk of a renewable energy/critical mineral-based resource curse in Africa is exacerbated by the fact that on a continent base, there are gaps in the policy and regulatory frameworks established to regulate the exploitation of offshore renewable resources and offshore critical minerals. For instance, the African Integrated Maritime Strategy 2050 (AIMS)[7] outlines the regulatory framework for the 'sustainable' exploitation of Africa's Maritime Domain (AMD) with the vision of wealth creation. Yet, the AIMS tends to prioritise trade-related marine activities and does not provide a clear regulatory strategy regarding the maximisation of marine non-living resources for the good of Africa and the protection of the marine ecosystem and coastal communities.[8]

Furthermore, despite the establishment of the African Critical Minerals Strategy Group (ACMSG), the proposed African Critical Minerals Strategy (ACMS), and the importance of critical minerals in the energy transition paradigm, the African Union (AU) has yet to enact a critical mineral strategy. Consequently, no strategy for building downstream capacity for processing critical minerals exists in Africa to promote local economic contributions.[9] This chapter argues that these gaps, examined in section 3 below, would deprive African countries of domestic value creation that comes with the development of mineral resources. This missed opportunity will inevitably exacerbate energy poverty in Africa and continue the narrative that African natural resources can create an economic, social, and environmental curse.

Given the need to develop Africa's offshore renewable energy resources and critical minerals, there is a need to examine whether the regulatory regimes governing the exploitation of these resources – particularly offshore marine resources such as wind and tidal energy, and critical minerals such as cobalt, nickel, copper, lithium, manganese, and platinum – are robust enough to ensure a just transition. The development of these resources is vital for clean energy technologies needed to accelerate the African and global energy transition, necessitating an effective regulatory approach to promote socio-economic growth and drive the industrialisation of Africa.

[5] Richard M Auty, *Sustaining Development in Mineral Economies: The Resource Curse Thesis* (Routledge, 1993) 4.

[6] Jeffrey D Sachs and Andrew M Warner, 'Natural Resource Abundance and Economic Growth' (1995) NBER Working Papers 5398.

[7] Namira Negm, 'Africa's Integrated Maritime Strategy 2050' (2012) au.int/sites/default/files/newsevents/workingdocuments/33832-wd-african_union_3-1.pdf.

[8] Eddy Wifa and Patrick Achor, 'Offshore wind development in Africa: An analysis of regional and national legal regimes' in Ignacio Herrera Anchustegui and Tina S Hunter (eds), *Offshore Wind Licensing* (Edward Elgar, 2024).

[9] Cullen S Hendrix, 'Building Downstream Capacity for Critical Minerals in Africa: Challenges and Opportunities' (2022) *Peterson Institute for International Economics Policy Brief* No 22-16.

The examination is important as the exploitation of both onshore and offshore hydrocarbon in Africa over the past few decades has not addressed energy poverty in Africa nor led to the industrialisation of the continent. Conversely, they have resulted in theorisation which is usually supported by empirical findings, casual observations and journalistic commentaries that the exploitation of non-renewable energy/natural resources in Africa is generally a curse given that such exploitations have hampered socio-economic growth and are associated with environmental damage. This resonates with the resource curse hypothesis.[10]

This chapter, therefore, examines the risk of offshore renewable and critical mineral-based resource curse in Africa in light of the energy transition by transplanting the general principles of the natural resource curse to the exploitation of offshore renewable energy and critical minerals. Furthermore, the chapter examines the role of a continent-wide policy and law in avoiding offshore renewable energy/critical mineral-based resource curse in Africa. As such, this chapter contributes to the discourse on (offshore) renewable energy/critical minerals-based resource curse in Africa in the light of the energy transition. This discourse is important for two main reasons. First, literature on (offshore) renewable energy/critical minerals-based resource curse in Africa is scarce as this is a new area of scholarship.[11] As such, the chapter would add to offshore renewable energy and critical mineral-based resource curse literature. Second, the chapter will make best practice recommendations that, when implemented, could help to avoid the resource curse materialising in the course of developing Africa's offshore renewable energy and critical minerals.

The chapter hypothesises that without robust regulatory frameworks for African renewable energy and critical minerals that African Union (AU) Member States would have to adapt into their national law, the likelihood of an offshore renewable energy/critical mineral-based resource curse in Africa is inevitable. The arguments presented in this chapter are supported by two-fold reasoning as discussed below.

First is the fact that mineral wealth from the exploitation of both onshore and offshore hydrocarbon and non-renewable natural resources such as diamonds, gold, coal, iron ore, and copper in many African resource-rich countries has not resulted in any socio-economic development or increased per capita gross domestic product (GDP) of these African energy/natural resource producers. The exploration of these natural resources has not ensured that citizens have access to energy in line with the United Nations Sustainable Development Goal 7. Rather, exploitation of natural resources has become a source of environmental degradation, deprived coastal communities livelihoods, and transformed the economies of these countries into a mono-cultural economy where state actors, government business partners, and the international mining companies are the sole beneficiaries.[12]

[10] Kwamina Panford, *Africa's Natural Resources and Underdevelopment: How Ghana's Petroleum Can Create Sustainable Economic Prosperity* (Palgrave Macmillan, 2017) 33.

[11] Alycia Leonard et al, 'The Resource Curse in Renewable Energy: A Framework for Risk Assessment' (2022) 41 *Energy Strategy Reviews*; Hendrix (n 9); Boafo et al (n 1).

[12] Michael Watts et al, 'Alienation and Militancy in the Niger Delta: A Response to CSIS on Petroleum, Politics and Democracy in Nigeria' (2003) *Foreign Policy in Focus*; Leif Wenar, 'Rights and the Resource Curse' (2008) 36(1) *Philosophy and Public Affairs* 4–5; Adeoye O Akinola, *Globalisation, Democracy and Oil Sector Reform in Nigeria: African Histories and Modernities* (Palgrave Macmillan, 2018) 5; IEA, 'Africa Energy Outlook 2022' (2023) www.iea.org/reports/africa-energy-outlook-2022/key-findings.

Second, resource curse literature in Africa has emphasised the role of regulatory frameworks and institutions that administer the extraction, processing, and management of rents from natural resources as the determinant factors that underpin how natural resource development can translate to socio-economic growth.[13]

The reason mineral wealth from hydrocarbon and non-renewable natural resources alike in Africa has not resulted in socioeconomic development is arguably due to the existence of a *rentier state* – rent-seeking behaviour on the part of governmental actors. This rent-seeking behaviour breeds corruption and mismanagement of natural resource wealth.[14] The *Rentier State* theory is attributable to Mahdavy and describes the impacts of rents on state-society relations and governance in the Iranian state before the Islamic Revolution in the 1970s which largely resulted from deficiencies or lack of regulatory frameworks.[15] Ross categorises claims that a *Rentier State* inhibits socio-economic development into two.[16] The first claim suggests that energy/natural resource wealth makes states less democratic, and the second is that energy/natural resource wealth causes governments to do a poorer job of promoting economic development. Again, these two claims resonate with the importance of law in curbing rentier states.

Following this introduction, the chapter first theoretically frames issues relating to deep-sea mining and the risk of offshore renewable and critical mineral-based resource curse in the light of energy transition by transplanting the natural resource curse hypothesis to offshore renewables and critical minerals' development, particularly issues relating to resource development impact on coastal communities. Second, the chapter integrates issues pertaining to the just transition and energy justice into the offshore renewable energy and critical mineral-based resource curse before undertaking a detailed analysis of AIMS 2050 that regulates the development of offshore renewable energy and critical minerals in Africa on a continent-base intending to identify gaps in the frameworks. Finally, the chapter concludes by recommending best practices that could close the identified gaps to ensure that offshore renewable energy and critical minerals' development in Africa do not hamper socioeconomic development that would continue the same natural resource curse narrative.

2. (Offshore) Renewable Energy and Critical Minerals-Based Resource Curse in Africa and Energy Transition

This section theoretically frames issues around renewable energy and critical mineral-based resource curse in Africa in light of energy transition against the backdrop of potential deep sea mining. It is noted that the deep sea may be host to offshore renewable energy and significant reserves of critical minerals. Developing these

[13] Uwafiokun Idemudia, 'The Resource Curse and the Decentralization of Oil Revenue: the Case of Nigeria' (2012) 35 *Journal of Cleaner Production* 184.

[14] Adeel Malik, 'Rethinking the Rentier Curse' in Giacomo Luciani (ed), *Combining Economic and Political Development: the Experience of MENA* (Brill, 2017).

[15] Hossein Mahdavy, 'The Pattern and Problems of Economic Development in Rentier States: The Case of Iran' in MA Cook (ed), *Studies in the Economic History of Middle East* (Oxford University Press, 1970).

[16] Michael L Ross, 'Does Oil Hinder Democracy?' (2001) 53(3) *World Politics* 330.

resources effectively and responsibly is essential to the energy transition.[17] As such, the examination of a curse or blessing conducted throughout this chapter becomes essential. First, section 2 of this chapter sets out the resource curse hypothesis. It then considers energy transition as a trigger of offshore renewable energy and critical minerals development, evaluates the risk of a resource curse resulting from the exploitation of seabed non-living resources, specifically, offshore renewable energy and critical minerals, and finally, integrates the concept of the just transition and energy justice into the analysis presented.

Before delving into the discourse, it is important to answer the question, what are critical minerals? Critical minerals are types of green minerals. They generally have two characteristics. These include their essential nature 'for (first) the functioning of modern technologies, economies, or national security, and (second) the risk that their supply chains could be disrupted.'[18] Despite these characteristics, their classification is based on geopolitical trading blocs, and regions and countries have utilised different parameters and definitions.[19] For instance, Australia has classified 47 minerals as critical based on four criteria – essential to modern technologies, economies, and national security; geological potential for resources; in demand from strategic international partners; and vulnerable to supply chain disruption. The classification consists of two mineral groupings – rare-earth elements and platinum-group elements.[20] The European Union and the United States of America have differing classification parameters.[21] However, the African region is yet to define and classify critical minerals.

A. The Natural Resource Curse Hypothesis

Empirical findings in political economy and legal literature demonstrate that the development of non-renewable energy and natural resources, especially oil and gas in the Global South (GS), has not translated into the socio-economic growth that was seen in the Global North (GN), especially coal exploitation during the eighteenth and nineteenth centuries which characterised the industrialisation of the GN.[22] In particular, in an African context, except for Botswana, a wide range of literature supports a popular theory that the exploitation of non-renewable energy/natural resources in Africa has generally been a curse, as it hampers socio-economic growth and is associated with environmental damage.

[17] Oliver Ashford et al, 'What We Know About Deep-sea Mining – and What We Don't' (2024) *World Resource Institute*.

[18] Boafo et al (n 1).

[19] Vlado Vivoda et al, 'A Critical Minerals Perspective on the Emergence of Geopolitical Trade Blocs' (2024) 89 *Resource Policy*.

[20] Australia's Critical Minerals List and Strategic Materials List, www.industry.gov.au/publications/australias-critical-minerals-list-and-strategic-materials-list.

[21] European Parliament, 'Critical Raw Materials for the EU: Enablers of Green and Digital Recovery' (2020) www.europarl.europa.eu/RegData/etudes/BRIE/2020/659426/EPRS_BRI(2020)659426_EN.pdf.

[22] Jeffrey A Frankel, 'The Natural Resource Curse: A Survey' (2010) National Bureau of Economic Research Working Paper No 15836 1–38, www.nber.org/papers/w15836; Gavin Wright, 'the Origin of American Industrial Success, 1878–1949' (1990) 80(4) *American Economic Review* 635; Alan Fernihough and Kevin Hjortshøj O'Rourke, 'Coal and the European Industrial Revolution' (2014) University of Oxford Discussion Papers in Economic and Social History No 12.

Nigeria is typically used as a prime example of this view.[23] This is for several reasons. First, earnings from the non-renewable energy/natural resource sector have not increased Nigeria's per capita GDP.[24] Second, earnings from energy and natural resource exploitation have not evidentially improved the well-being of Nigerians, as the majority of the populace live below the poverty line. In contrast, the earnings from these natural resources have enriched political actors.[25] Third, most Nigerians do not have access to energy in line with the United Nations Sustainable Development Goal 7.[26] Fourth, energy/natural resource development has become a source of environmental degradation. It deprives host communities of their means of livelihood, given that they mainly depend on the environment for sustenance.[27] Finally, dependence on the petroleum sector has transformed the Nigerian economy into a mono-cultural economy where state actors, government business partners, and international mining companies are the sole beneficiaries.[28] This resonates with the natural resource curse hypothesis.[29]

The natural resources curse was coined by Auty.[30] Auty's definition defied the conventional insight that abundant natural resources were a blessing that translated to economic prosperity and that countries with abundant natural resources were fortunate as such resources are assets and form parts of the country's natural stock of capital.[31] However, given its multidimensional manifestation, there is no one-size-fits-all definition of the resource curse.[32] This notwithstanding, the concept demographically denotes a paradoxical relationship in which many natural resource-rich countries experience stunted or negative economic growth compared to others without such natural resource endowment. Such economic growth is usually measured in terms of aggregate output per capita or gross domestic product.[33]

Various econometric instruments have been harnessed to explain why the exploitation of natural resources harms economic growth and the environment. Dutch disease, Nigerian disease, state fragile existentialism, and Peruvian disease are exponential tautologies used to define the natural resource curse to mean the observed negative impacts of energy and natural resource extraction on economic growth, democratic governance, stability and peace, social and environmental justice, and human rights in many energy/natural resource-producing countries.[34]

[23] Annegret Mähler, 'Nigeria: A Prime Example of the Resource Curse? Revisiting the Oil-Violence Link in the Niger Delta' (2010) German Institute of Global and Area Studies Working Paper No 120.

[24] Xavier Sala-i-Martin and Arvind Subramanian, 'Addressing the Natural Resource Curse: An Illustration from Nigeria' (2013) 22(1) *Journal of African Economies* 570–615.

[25] Wenar (n 12).

[26] IEA (n 12).

[27] Akinola (n 12).

[28] Watts et al (n 12).

[29] Panford (n 10).

[30] Auty (n 5).

[31] Graham A Davis and John E Tilton, 'Should Developing Countries Renounce Mining? A Perspective on the Debate' (2002) www.researchgate.net/publication/228584093_Should_developing_countries_renounce_mining_A_perspective_on_the_debate.

[32] Jeffrey D Sachs and Andrew M Warner, 'Natural Resources and Economic Development: The Curse of Natural Resources' (2001) 45 *European Economic Review* 83.

[33] Her Majesty's Treasury, 'Gross Domestic Product (GDP): What it Means and Why it Matters' (2017) www.gov.uk/government/news/gross-domestic-product-gdp-what-it-means-and-why-it-matters.

[34] Solomon Obulor, *Benefit-Sharing in Relation to Energy and Natural Resources Development: A Comparative Analysis of Impact and Benefit Agreements in Nigeria and Australia* (PhD thesis submitted to the University of Aberdeen, 2022).

Furthermore, another formulation used to explain the manifestation of the resource curse is the lack of cross-sectoral linkages and economic diversification in many resource-rich countries. Arguably, this is stated to be the root cause of the resource curse. This is because the lack of backward, lateral, and forward linkages between other sectors of the economy and the resource sector makes the country a 'rentier state' that only collects rent from international corporations that exploit the resources without any 'in-country value' addition through such exploitation.[35] To circumvent this, local content requirements in many countries, including African States have been developed.[36] These instrumentations intricately define the causal mechanism by which resources paradoxically undermine economic growth. The literature identifies four causal mechanisms: price fluctuations, Dutch Disease, enclave economies, and rent-seeking.[37] Overdependence on the resource sector is also a notable causal mechanism.

From a legal perspective, the resource curse could be examined in terms of sovereignty over resources, the role of the State in commercial exploitation, and the right to responsibly exploit resources, which are in tension with the maximisation of economic gains. However, the following explanation is in light of the two basic legal questions by Viñuales, namely: (i) who owns natural resources, and (ii) what legal consequences are attached to spoliation or misuse.[38] In this regard, the analysis focuses on international and African legal frameworks (rather than any specific domestic legal system) generally governing the ownership of energy resources. This is important given the position of Boudreaux et al that many of the so-called 'resource cursed' countries depend on ownership regimes 'originally established for colonial-era exploitation' where the natural resources in the colony are ostensibly owned and exploited for the benefit of the colonising state.[39]

Ownership as a legal concept originates from the historiography of property rights under Roman Law.[40] It may connote different things to different persons depending on context and might 'either be so simple as to need no explanation or so elusive as to defy definition'.[41] However, it essentially connotes the ultimate right to use a thing to the exclusion of others. Blackstone, for instance, views ownership as the 'sole and despotic dominium which one man claims and exercises over the external things of the world, in total exclusion of the right of any other individual in the universe'.[42]

[35] Tina Hunter, 'Law and Policy Frameworks for Local Content in the Development of Petroleum Resources: Norwegian and Australian Perspectives on Cross-Sectoral Linkages and Economic Diversification' (2014) 27(2–3) *Mineral Economics* 123; Valérie Marcel et al, 'A Local Content Decision Tree for Emerging Producers' (2016) *The Royal Institute of International Affairs* 3.

[36] Damilola S Olawuyi, 'Local Content Policies and Their Implications for International Investment Law' in Julien Chaisse et al (eds), *Handbook of International Investment Law and Policy* (Springer, 2019).

[37] Kathleen J Hancock and Benjamin K Sovacool, 'International Political Economy and Renewable Energy: Hydroelectric Power and the Resource Curse' (2018) 20 *International Studies Review*.

[38] Jorge E Viñuales, 'The "Resource Curse" – A Legal Perspective' (2010) 17 *Global Governance* 197–212.

[39] Karol Boudreaux et al, 'Reverse the Resource Curse: How Can Oil Help the Poor?' (2014) 92 *Foreign Affairs* 182.

[40] Eva Jakab, 'Land, Law and Exploitation of Natural Resources Property Rights in Ancient Rome' in P Erdkamp et al (eds), *Ownership and Exploitation of Land and Natural Resources in Roman World* (Oxford University Press, 2015).

[41] Barry Nicholas, *An Introduction to Roman Law* (Oxford University Press, 2008) 153.

[42] William Blackstone, *Commentaries on the Laws of England: A Facsimile of the First Edition of 1765–1769 Volume 2* (University of Chicago Press, 1979) 2.

Theoretically, ownership of natural resources could be explained through the absolute or qualified theory. However, some legal scholars and jurists recognise a third theory, the non-ownership theory.[43] These theories explain the type of ownership model prevalent in a country, that is, whether natural resource ownership will vest in the government or private individual.[44] This section does not engage in a discourse on the concept of property rights and theories of natural resource ownership. Instead, it analyses the ontology of natural resource ownership in the international and African context.

In relation to Viñuales' two questions discussed above, it is noted that 'ownership of natural resources in international law rests upon the legal concept of sovereignty'.[45] The point here is that natural resources located in a country's territory belong to the country. This was affirmed in the United Nations General Assembly Resolution 1803 (XVII) on Permanent Sovereignty over Natural Resources, which states in Article 1 that 'the right of peoples and nations to permanent sovereignty over their natural wealth and resources must be exercised in the interest of their national development and of the wellbeing of the people of the State concerned.' At the forefront of this principle is the interest of the people who are entitled to their wealth and natural resources in view of exercising their right to self-determination.

In Africa, peoples' right to their natural resources are asserted in the African Charter on Human and Peoples' Rights (the Charter). Article 21 is reproduced below for emphasis:

1. All peoples shall freely dispose of their wealth and natural resources. This right shall be exercised in the exclusive interest of the people. In no case shall a people be deprived of it.
2. In case of spoliation, the dispossessed people shall have the right to the lawful recovery of its property as well as to an adequate compensation.
3. The free disposal of wealth and natural resources shall be exercised without prejudice to the obligation of promoting international economic co-operation based on mutual respect, equitable exchange, and the principles of international law.
4. States parties to the present Charter shall individually and collectively exercise the right to free disposal of their wealth and natural resources with a view to strengthening African unity and solidarity.
5. States Parties to the present Charter shall undertake to eliminate all forms of foreign economic exploitation, particularly that practised by international monopolies so as to enable their peoples to fully benefit from the advantages derived from their national resources.

It is noted that Article 21(4) empowers countries to dispose of their natural resources. This legitimatises authoritarian leaders granting licences to corporations to exploit the resources to enrich themselves rather than strengthen 'African unity and solidarity'. This makes ownership of natural resources in Africa ambiguous, given that the emphasis is on people. As such, domestic law applies to spoliation. However, a discourse on a specific domestic legal system is beyond the scope of this chapter. In conclusion, the

[43] Lanre Aladeitan, 'Ownership of Oil, Gas, and Mineral Resources in Nigeria Legality and Legitimacy' (2013) 38(159) *Thurgood Marshall Law Review*.

[44] *Stephen County v Mid-Kansas Oil & Gas Co* (1923) 113 Tex 160, 167, 254 SW 290–292; *Brown v Humble Oil & Refining Co* (1935) Tex SC 83 SW (2d) 935–940.

[45] Viñuales (n 38).

resource curse describes the negative effect of natural resource abundance and development on economic growth and the environment.[46]

B. The Risk of Renewable Energy and Critical Mineral-Based Resource Curse in Africa

The resource curse hypothesis arguably applies to the abundance and development of offshore renewable energy and critical minerals. For instance, issues of ownership and spoliation of offshore renewable energy and critical minerals like subsoil resources are based on sovereignty, as previously discussed in this chapter. Furthermore, similar to the extraction of subsoil resources, offshore renewable energy and critical minerals development have adverse effects on the environment and socioeconomic development.[47] The International Energy Agency notes that the extraction of offshore renewable energy and critical minerals has significant environmental implications, including ecosystem impacts, water stress contamination and waste generation, which may be potentially hazardous.[48] In relation to critical minerals, cobalt exploitation in the Democratic Republic of Congo exemplifies this. Kara documents the negative impact of cobalt exploitation in the Congo Basin on the environment and in vulnerable communities, which is typical of the resource curse.[49]

The impact of offshore renewable energy and critical minerals' development on host or coastal communities, such as those related to offshore wind, wave, and tidal energy exploration, underpin the concept of the (un)just transition energy, which is examined in the following section. While specific African countries might have limited wave and tidal energy potential, coastal African states have significant offshore wind power potential. The strongest winds can be found in the northwest and northeast of southern Africa.[50] Offshore wind power has been found to have fewer negative impacts on humans and the environment than fossil fuels, however it is noted that offshore wind also has its own set of disadvantages and advantages including the potential to impact the marine ecology when developed in ecologically sensitive marine areas.[51]

Consequently, the chapter applies some of the resource curse hypothesis' causal mechanisms on developing offshore renewables and critical minerals to demonstrate the potential of an offshore renewable energy and critical mineral-based resource curse.

[46] Mahmood Ahmad et al, 'Policy Framework Considering Resource Curse, Renewable Energy Transition, and Institutional Issues: Fostering Sustainable Development and Sustainable Natural Resource Consumption Practices' (2023) 86 *Resources Policy*.

[47] Emmanuel Aramendia et al, 'Global Energy Consumption of the Mineral Mining Industry: Exploring the Historical Perspective and Future Pathways to 2060' (2023) 83 *Global Environmental Change*, doi.org/10.1016/j.gloenvcha.2023.102745.

[48] IEA, 'The Role of Critical Minerals in Clean Energy Transitions' (May 2021) www.iea.org/reports/the-role-of-critical-minerals-in-clean-energy-transitions.

[49] Siddharth Kara, *Cobalt Red: How the Blood of the Congo Powers our Lives* (St Martin's Press, 2023).

[50] African Development Bank, 'Assessing the Potential of Offshore Renewable Energy in Africa' (2021) www.afdb.org/sites/default/files/documents/publications/assessing_the_potential_of_offshore_renewable_energy_in_africa_report.pdf.

[51] Kehinde Adeyeye et al, 'Exploring the Environmental and Economic Impacts of Wind Energy: A Cost-Benefit Perspective' (2020) 27(8) *International Journal of Sustainable Development & World Ecology*.

The first is over-dependence on the resource sector. It is noted that the tendency of African countries to rely heavily on the offshore renewable and critical mineral sector for their socioeconomic development is very high. This is because many African countries are dependent on their extractive sectors, particularly petroleum, diamonds and gold and will simply switch from relying on the fossil fuel sector to offshore renewable energy and critical minerals development. A country is considered resource-dependent when it generates at least 8 per cent of its GDP and 40 per cent of its export earnings from an energy/natural resource sector.[52] As such, the risk of offshore renewable and critical mineral-based resource curse is high for African countries that are currently dependent on traditional extractive sectors.

The price of offshore renewable and critical minerals will likely fluctuate and given that African countries have not developed the downstream capacity to refine these resources into finished products, the resources like hydrocarbon would be sold as raw materials in the international market. The consequence is that it would lead to volatility, 'unstable and unpredictable income for the state, which may lead to overspending, followed by severe economic hardship or even debt default'.[53]

The Dutch Disease postulates that the inflow of massive capital due to a booming energy and natural resource export sector increases the relative price of non-tradable goods and services and leads to a real appreciation of a country's exchange rate and, as a result of rising wages, reallocation of some of the labour force to the resource sector.[54] The appreciation in the country's exchange rate reduces the international competitiveness of other tradable sectors like manufacturing and agriculture, which are overshadowed by commodity exports from the natural resources sector.[55] Thus, the country faces the risk of de-industrialisation – a shrinkage in the traded-manufacturing sector over time.[56] The potential that there will be a movement of capital and labour to offshore renewable energy and critical minerals sector is very high in Africa. This is supported by the fact that African petroleum-producing countries are already experiencing this.[57]

Finally, rent-seeking will equally manifest in the development of offshore renewable energy and critical minerals. This is especially so given that many African countries lack measures to constrain government actors from plundering the rent that would flow from offshore renewable energy and critical minerals. This position is supported by the fact that rent from developing petroleum and other subsoil resources in African petroleum-producing countries have been plundered – Nigeria is a prime example. For instance, it is estimated that Abacha looted over $3 to $5 billion from the Nigerian oil treasury within his five-year military regime.[58]

[52] Auty (n 5).

[53] Hancock and Sovacool (n 37).

[54] Paul Collier and Benedikt Goderis, 'Commodity Prices and Growth: An Empirical Investigation' (2012) 56 *European Economic Review*.

[55] Paul Cashin et al, 'Commodity Currencies and the Real Exchange Rate' (2004) 75 *Journal of Development Economics* 241.

[56] Reda Cherif, 'The Dutch Disease and the Technological Gap' (2013) 101 *Journal of Development Economics* 249.

[57] Sala-i-Martin and Subramanian (n 24).

[58] Enemaku Idachaba, 'Chronology of Major Political Events in the Abacha Era (1993–1998)' in Kunle Amuwo et al (eds), *Nigeria During the Abacha Years (1993–1998): The Domestic and International Politics of Democratisation* (French Institute for Research in Africa–Nigeria, 2001); Brennan Kraxberger, 'The Geography of Regime Survival: Abacha's Nigeria' (2004) 103(412) *African Affairs* 413–30.

Another prevalent issue associated with the natural resource curse is the lack of host community engagement in resource development decision-making and benefit-sharing.[59] This is already manifesting in the development of offshore renewable energy and critical minerals as host communities are not engaged. Sovacool's review of 332 worldwide case studies on renewable and climate change mitigation technologies highlights four primary forms of energy injustice: economic enclosure, such as privatisation and land grabbing; political exclusion, often affecting local stakeholders; ecological encroachment; and social entrenchment, which includes discrimination against indigenous populations and women, as well as issues such as modern slavery and murder.[60]

For instance, the allocation of resources in South Africa is predominantly driven by policy interventions established through the renewable energy independent power producer procurement programme, black economic empowerment policy and legislation and corporate social investment initiatives of the wind farms.[61] This approach is in no way different from the Nigerian resource allocation strategy for host communities,[62] where trusts established for communities affected by petroleum operations as prescribed by the Petroleum Industry Act 2021 are managed by persons subject to government and multinational corporations control, rather than members of the host communities.[63] A study on resource extraction and host community participation in South African and Germany demonstrates that some of the host communities in South Africa were unaware of the existence of a trust or how to access it.[64] This lack of awareness is a recurring barrier in the distribution of natural resource wealth and risk of this occurring in relation to offshore energy and critical development is high as the same set of government functionaries and multinational corporations would be involved.[65]

It is noteworthy that without a favourable community outlook on a project, disputes, and conflicts, will almost inevitably emerge over time. The Lake Turkana Wind Project (LTWP) is a good case study in which the host community contested the land title and it was held that the land title deeds were 'irregular and unlawful'.[66] The local Indigenous community had expressed longstanding grievances about this extensive wind energy initiative. They claimed that, among other issues, the project did not adhere to the appropriate free, prior, and informed consent procedures, failed to provide proper compensation for the land acquisition, and breached existing and previous land laws.

[59] Carole Brunet et al, 'The Three Paradoxes of the Energy Transition – Assessing Sustainability of Large-Scale Solar Photovoltaic through Multi-Level and Multi-Scalar Perspective in Rwanda' (2021) 288 *Journal of Cleaner Production*; Oleg Golubchikov and Kevin O'Sullivan, 'Energy Periphery: Uneven Development and the Precarious Geographies of Low-Carbon Transition' (2020) 211 *Energy and Buildings* 109818; Siddharth Sareen, 'Digitalisation and Social Inclusion in Multi-Scalar Smart Energy Transitions' (2021) 81 *Energy Research and Social Sciences*.

[60] Benjamin Sovacool, 'Who Are the Victims of Low-Carbon Transitions? Toward a Political Ecology of Climate Change Mitigation' (2021) 73 *Energy Research and Social Sciences*.

[61] Lisa Schulte and Bryan Robinson, 'Owning the Just Transition: Comparing Citizen Participation in South African and German Wind Farms' (2024) 19 *Contemporary Social Science* 117–34.

[62] Joy Anwulika Debski, *An Effective Multi-Stakeholder Strategy for Environmental Sustainability in Oil and Gas-Producing Areas* (PhD thesis submitted to Robert Gordon University, 2023).

[63] ibid.

[64] Lisa and Bryan (n 61) 75.

[65] Debski (n 62) 76.

[66] Business & Human Rights Resource Centre, 'Kenya: Court Rules That Lake Turkana Wind Power Acquired Community Land Unprocedurally' (2021) www.business-humanrights.org/en/latest-news/kenya-court-rules-that-lake-turkana-wind-power-acquired-community-land-unprocedurally/.

Five months after this 2021 ruling, LTWP asked for a review of the judgment on account of new evidence. On 22 May 2023, the Kenyan Environment and Land Court in Meru rejected the review application filed by the LTWP.[67] The rationale was that within the LTWP, all component projects were intended primarily for export, resulting in no direct benefits for the communities. Notably, the electricity produced via the LTWP would not benefit the communities. As it currently stands, LTWP, unfortunately, serves as an example of an investment that has neglected and even worsened the situation for Indigenous peoples.

C. The Just Transition and Energy Justice Applied to Renewable and Critical Mineral Development in Africa

As demonstrated above, offshore renewable energy and critical mineral development are inextricably linked to socio-economic impacts similar to the manifestation of the resource curse. As such, unless adequately regulated, renewable development as a result of the current energy transition paradigm will entrench or exacerbate the injustices that have trailed coastal communities, creating new 'sacrifice zones' under the guise of climate change prevention.[68] This realisation has propelled the concept of a 'just transition'.

The just transition concept originated from labour unions aimed at promoting the assurance of green jobs as a vital component of the transition to cleaner energy.[69] It has since gained considerable traction in scholarship, law, policy, and public discourse.[70] For instance, it is famously incorporated in the preamble of the Paris Agreement: '[parties] take into account the imperative of a just transition of the workforce and the creation of decent work and quality jobs in accordance with nationally defined development priorities'.[71] It is noteworthy that in the African continent, South Africa is the first country to have developed and adopted a 'just transition planning framework' which offers opportunities to address practical issues related to jobs, local economies, skills, social support, and governance.[72]

There is no agreed definition of the just transition, a feature some have decried as making it difficult to communicate and debate. Others, however, have accepted this on the basis that a just transition will attract different meanings for different places depending on their unique social, economic, cultural and political background.[73] Thus, the

[67] International Work Group for Indigenous Affairs, 'Indigenous Communities in Kenya Take Court Action Over Lake Turkana Wind Project' (*IWGIA*, 3 November 2023) www.iwgia.org/en/news/5342-indigenous-communities-kenya-court-proceedings-lake-turkana-wind-project.html.

[68] Xinxin Wang and Kevin Lo, 'Just Transition: A Conceptual Review' (2021) 82 *ERSS* 102291.

[69] Noel Healy and John Barry, 'Politicising Energy Justice and Energy System Transitions: Fossil Fuel Divestment and a "Just Transition"' (2017) 108 *Energy Policy* 451.

[70] Stephen Williams and Andréanne Doyon, 'The Energy Futures Lab: A Case Study of Justice in Energy Transitions' (2020) 37 *EIST* 290.

[71] UNFCCC, 'Adoption of the Paris Agreement' (Twenty-first session of the Conference of the Parties, UN Doc FCCC/CP/2015/L9/Rev.1, 2015) unfccc.int/sites/default/files/english_paris_agreement.pdf.

[72] Presidential Climate Commission, A Framework for a Just Transition in South Africa (2022) pccommissionflo.imgix.net/uploads/images/22_PAPER_Framework-for-a-Just-Transition_revised_242.pdf.

[73] Dimitris Stevis et al, 'Introduction: The Genealogy and Contemporary Politics of Just Transitions' in E Morena et al (eds), *Just Transitions: Social Justice in the Shift Towards a Low-Carbon World* (Pluto Press, 2020).

definition needs to remain flexible.[74] Harrahill and Douglas posit that 'differing conceptions of the just transition are possible, incorporating different visions of a "sustainable society" and the means of achieving it'.[75] Nonetheless, there is some consensus that, in its simplest form, the just transition is the application of human rights and social justice principles to the energy transition paradigm.[76] It is also defined as the mandate for societies to mitigate and adapt to climate change while reducing inequality and promoting justice.[77]

Indeed, the key value of the just transition concept is that it provides a space for negotiating trade-offs and balancing the competing concerns of the energy transition – energy security, access, climate change, and sustainability – otherwise known as the 'energy quadrilemma'. Creating a just energy transition encapsulated a broad range of stakeholders, risks, and benefits of each dimension, in a manner that ensures public support, legitimacy, and equity in burdens and benefits, creating broader consideration of issues, solutions, and social resilience. As Sandel puts it, 'a just society involves reasoning together about the good life'.[78] Thus, it posited that the 'just transition' provides the means through which actual transformative changes can be realised. Without the active, ongoing, and comprehensive consideration of justice during the decision-making, implementation and planning processes, policies, and solutions to these concerns will undoubtedly yield unintended social consequences.

Energy justice is a fundamental instrument and driver of the energy transition.[79] The just transition 'seeks to apply social justice principles to energy policy, energy production and systems, energy consumption, energy activism, energy security, and climate change'.[80] Consequently, it is relevant to examine the concept of energy justice which is often closely linked to just transition literature.

Five central tenets of energy justice are identified in the literature, namely distributive, procedural, recognition, restorative, and cosmopolitan justice. Distributive justice ensures the equitable sharing (or resharing) of the risks, costs, benefits, and burdens of blue economy activities in a manner that fosters social acceptance, community resilience, and universal community well-being over narrow vested interests.[81] The procedural justice tenet is concerned with the 'process' of making energy decisions and policy, and within that process, the fairness and transparency of decisions (including greater information disclosure and local knowledge mobilisation), the legitimacy and inclusivity of institutions involved in decision making, as well as the adequacy of legal protections.[82]

[74] Peter Howson et al, 'Asia-Pacific ClimateScapes: Exploring Opportunities, Challenges and Trade-Offs Toward Just Transitions for Decarbonisation' (2022) doi.org/10.5871/just-transitions-a-p/p-h-s-k.

[75] Kieran Harrahill and Owen Douglas, 'Framework development for "just transition" in coal producing jurisdictions' (2019) 134 *EP* 110990.

[76] Peter Howson et al, 'Asia-Pacific Climate Scapes: Exploring Opportunities, Challenges and Trade-Offs Toward Just Transitions for Decarbonisation' (2022) doi.org/10.5871/just-transitions-a-p/p-h-s-k.

[77] Elizabeth Eliis, 'A Just Transition to Climate-resilient Coastal Communities in Aotearoa New Zealand' (2021) 17 *Policy Quarterly*.

[78] Michael J Sandel, *Justice: What's the Right Thing to Do?* (Penguin Books Ltd, 2009) 261.

[79] John Morrissey, 'Coastal Communities, Blue Economy and the Climate Crisis: Framing Just Disruptions' (2023) 189 *TGJ* 283.

[80] Kirsten Jenkins, 'Energy justice: A Conceptual Review' (2016) 11 *Energy Research and Social Science*.

[81] Morrissey (n 79).

[82] Benjamin Sovacool et al, 'Energy Decisions Reframed as Justice and Ethical Concerns' (2016) 1 *NE*.

Recognition justice requires the identification and acknowledgement of unjust patterns of distribution and marginality in decision-making processes.[83] It also calls for the acknowledgement of divergent perspectives and experiences rooted in socio-cultural, ethnic, gender, and racial differences.[84] Restorative justice is concerned with repairing the harm done (to society and nature) rather than punishing the offenders.[85] It aims to acknowledge and redress harms done to communities, groups, the environment or other species, or the processes, decisions, conditions, or policies that have caused this harm or otherwise disenfranchised these groups.[86]

Cosmopolitan justice originates from the stoic idea of 'human beings as rational creatures with universal rights as citizens of the "cosmopolis"'.[87] It establishes that 'all human beings have equal moral worth, and our responsibilities do not just halt at borders'.[88] Instead, these ethical responsibilities apply everywhere, not only to members of one community or another but to all moral agents capable of understanding and acting on them.[89] As such, principles such as those from distributive and procedural (recognition and restorative justice) must apply universally to all human beings in all nations.[90]

The various tenets of justice do not exist in a vacuum; instead, they complement and reinforce each other.[91] For instance, distributive justice affects recognition since those receiving fewer resources are often marginalised; procedural justice ensures marginalised groups are recognised and included in decision-making; a lack of recognition can exacerbate existing injustices; and energy projects often burden communities and the environment, intertwining restorative and distributive justice.[92]

However, these justice dimensions can sometimes also conflict with each other. For instance, conflict can arise where 'an emphasis on participation serves to empower the powerful further to articulate at the expense of vulnerable groups.'[93] Energy interventions can inadvertently harm vulnerable groups; for example, the expansion of coal-fired power plants to alleviate energy poverty in India simultaneously led to an increase in coal mining, sometimes carried out by child labourers.[94]

The above highlights the complexity of energy justice and the just transition concept. The focus of both concepts in the African context must be on identifying, considering,

[83] Stephen Williams, and Andréanne Doyon, 'Justice in Energy Transitions' (2019) 31 *EIST* 144.
[84] Naomi Fraser, 'Social Justice in The Age of Identity Politics' in G Henderson, *Geographical Thought: A Praxis Perspective* (Taylor and Francis, 1999).
[85] Tony Marshall, *Restorative Justice: An Overview* (Crown Copyright, 1999) www.antoniocasella.eu/restorative/Marshall_1999-b.pdf; Mariah D Caballero et al, 'Energy Justice and Coastal Communities: The Case for Meaningful Marine Renewable Energy Development' (2023) 183 *RSER*.
[86] Morrissey (n 79) 99.
[87] Raphael Heffron et al, 'Resolving Society's Energy Trilemma Through the Energy Justice Metric' (2015) 87 *EP* 168.
[88] Darren McCauley et al, 'Energy Justice in the Transition to Low Carbon Energy Systems: Exploring Key Themes in Interdisciplinary Research' (2019) *AE*.
[89] Sovacool et al (n 82) 16.
[90] McCauley et al (n 88).
[91] R Gillard et al, 'Advancing an Energy Justice Perspective of Fuel Poverty: Household Vulnerability and Domestic Retrofit Policy in the UK' (2017) 29 *ERSS* 53.
[92] Margot Hurlbert and Jeremy Rayner, 'Reconciling Power, Relations, and Processes: The Role of Recognition in the Achievement of Energy Justice for Aboriginal People' (2018) 228 *AE* 1320.
[93] Aileen McHarg, 'Understanding the "Ethical Turn" in Energy Law and Policy' in Íñigo del Guayo et al (eds), *Energy Justice and Energy Law*, 1st edn (Oxford University Press, 2020).
[94] Benjamin Sovacool et al, 'New Frontiers and Conceptual Frameworks for Energy Justice' 1 (2017) *EP* 677.

and negotiating these trade-offs with vulnerable communities, groups, and regions to ensure fair and equitable outcomes. Therefore, the next section examines the role of law and policy in avoiding the (risk of) resource curse and injustice in light of the transition to carbon-neutral energy in Africa.

3. The Role of Policy and Law in Avoiding a Renewable Energy and Critical Mineral-Based Resource Curse in Africa

The impact of global and region-wide frameworks and cooperations in the energy sector on national laws to incorporate good governance and institutional quality; transparent and accountable management of resource wealth; environmental and social impacts of resource extraction monitoring; and engagement of citizens in resource development decision-making and benefit-sharing cannot be overemphasised. For instance, the impact of the 1982 United Nations Convention on the Law of the Sea on the national laws of the Member States is evident in the delimitation of maritime boundaries. Furthermore, the impact of the Renewable Energy Directive (2009/28/EC)[95] and Regulation (EU) 2024/1252[96] on regulating renewable energy and critical minerals in the European Union (EU) Member States has fundamentally shaped the EU energy transition. In relation to offshore renewable energy and critical minerals development in Africa, this chapter argues that regional cooperation 'facilitates large-scale renewable energy deployment and helps create economies of scale';[97] enhances the harnessing of Africa's offshore energy and critical minerals that could lead to the path of industrialisation;[98] enhances capacity-building; and ensures a just transition and energy justice.

Consequently, the question arises as to whether an Africa-wide policy regulating offshore renewable energy and critical mineral development would inform a change in resource development narratives. It is noteworthy that AIMS 2050 exists with the intent to regulate marine/offshore energy resources. Importantly, it is noted from the outset that this is a mere strategy, not a charter like the African Charter on Human and Peoples' Rights. The various African regions have also adopted policies to support renewable energy development.[99] Whilst many African-wide and regional frameworks

[95] Directive 2009/28/EC of the European Parliament and of the Council of 23 April 2009 on the promotion of the use of energy from renewable sources and amending and subsequently repealing Directives 2001/77/EC and 2003/30/EC (OJL 140).

[96] Regulation (EU) 2024/1252 of the European Parliament and of the Council of 11 April 2024 establishing a framework for ensuring a secure and sustainable supply of critical raw materials and amending Regulations (EU) No 168/2013, (EU) 2018/858, (EU) 2018/1724 and (EU) 2019/1020.

[97] IRENA, 'Africa 2030: Roadmap for a Renewable Energy Future (2015) www.irena.org/-/media/Files/IRENA/Agency/Publication/2015/IRENA_Africa_2030_REmap_2015_low-res.pdf?v=0331.

[98] Africa Natural Resources Management and Investment Centre, 'Approach Paper towards Preparation of an African Green Minerals Strategy' (2022) African development Bank www.afdb.org/sites/default/files/documents/publications/approach_paper_towards_preparation_of_an_african_green_minerals_strategy.pdf.

[99] IRENA, 'Sub-Saharan Africa: Policies and Finance for Renewable Energy Deployment' (2024) www.irena.org/-/media/Files/IRENA/Agency/Publication/2024/Jul/IRENA_SS_Africa_policies_finance_RE_2024.pdf.

exist,[100] the major challenge with these is the non-binding nature of the frameworks and, consequently, the inability to influence national policies.[101]

The African Natural Resources Management and Investment Centre within the African Development Bank and its partners in 2022 created an initiative to develop an African Green Minerals Strategy to proactively engage with the new conditions flowing from the energy transition and the establishment of the ACMSG in January 2024. However, the ACMSG is yet to create these conditions and there is no classification of critical minerals in Africa either in terms of the United Nations Framework Classification of Resources or other known parameters.[102]

Therefore, the AIMS 2050 and ACMSG propositions are analysed below to consider whether they could encourage the sustainable development of renewable energy and critical minerals in Africa to avoid the emergence of a renewable energy and critical mineral-based resource curse. After identifying gaps in the AIMS 2050 and ACMSG propositions, recommendations are provided to improve the AIMS and the proposed ACMS.

A. The 2050 Africa's Integrated Marine Strategy Framework (2050 AIMS) and the African Critical Minerals Strategy (ACMS)

The 2050 AIMS is a broadly designed framework intended for the sustainable exploitation and wealth creation associated with marine resources, including offshore energy, in Africa.[103] AIMS sets an ambitious 'plan of action for its operationalisation with a clearly defined vision and (supposedly) achievable goals, including specific desirable objectives, activities, and milestones towards attaining the Strategic End of Increased wealth creation in a stable and secured AMD' to achieve its purpose.[104] It encourages African stakeholders to 'rethink how to manage her inland, waterways, oceans and seas' because 'they are a key pillar for all African Union (AU) Members States' economic and social development and are vital in the fight against poverty and unemployment'.[105]

[100] In relation to the regional policies, it is noted that Southern Africa adopted the Renewable Energy and Energy Efficiency Strategy and Action Plan in 2017 after the establishment of the Southern African Development Community Centre for Renewable Energy and Energy Efficiency in 2015; the East African Community established the East African Centre of Excellence for Renewable Energy and Energy Efficiency in 2016; the Economic Community of Central African States adopted the Renewable Energy Roadmap and created the Centre for Renewable Energy and Energy Efficiency for Central Africa to coordinate renewable energy exploitation; West African states in 2013 adopted the Economic Community of West African States (ECOWAS) Renewable Energy Policy and established the ECOWAS Centre for Renewable Energy and Energy Efficiency; and finally, North African countries in conjunction with the other members of the League of Arab States have adopted the Arab Renewable Energy Framework and the Pan-Arab Sustainable Energy Strategy – 2030 which expanded the Pan-Arab Strategy for the Development of Renewable Energy 2010–2030.

[101] IRENA (n 99).

[102] Boafo et al (n 2); United Nations Framework Classification of Resources 2019, UNFC_ES61_Update_2019.pdf (unece.org). The African Ministerial Conference on the Environment, held between 14–16 August 2023, issued the Environmental aspects of critical African minerals in the clean energy transition.

[103] Article IV(18) 2050 AIMS.

[104] Article VII(21) 2050 AIMS.

[105] Article I(8) 2050 AIMS.

Notwithstanding that the 2050 AIMS is not a charter, from a legal standpoint it is contended that it is not robust enough given that it is, first, a mere strategy and, second, due to its silence on the issue of sustainable exploitation of offshore renewable energy despite identifying offshore renewable energy as one of the sectors with most growth potential and recognition of its importance for energy security in Africa.[106] Although it generally provides for marine space governance,[107] it is also noteworthy that the AIMS only sets an ambition for Member States to achieve given that its provisions are not binding.

In relation to marine space governance, the AIMS provides that AU Member States shall be encouraged to 'develop legal frameworks for coordinated State intervention at sea and inland waterways and subsequent action … harmonise national maritime laws and enhance bi-lateral and regional strategic synergies, including signing and ratification and accession by Member States of the relevant international maritime instruments'.[108] It is contended that while this provision is not specific to renewable energy, it applies to offshore renewable energy governance, given that offshore energy forms part of marine resources.

The implication of the above is that governance of offshore renewable energy and critical minerals in Africa is left to the discretion of coastal states, which would ordinarily be in accordance with Member States' national laws. Whilst this respects the doctrine of permanent sovereignty over natural resources, this is problematic as the intended uniform law would not be achieved given the lack of a common political and economic agenda on ocean exploitation in all AU Member States.[109] Furthermore, it is a given that many AU coastal Member States do not have robust national laws and institutions and have not also domesticated the abysmal applicable regional policies adopted by the respective African regions. As such, African countries would operate different regulatory regimes. The result is that many would serve as rentier states collecting rent from the resources without any linkage with the other sectors for in-country value addition.

Thus, it is contended that AIMS, like many other frameworks adopted by the AU, cannot achieve the anticipated uniform regulation of offshore renewable energy on the continent that can facilitate socio-economic growth.[110] As such, this chapter argues African States are treading on the path that gave rise to the resource curse in relation to the exploitation of non-renewable resources, and a renewable energy-based resource curse is inevitable.

African countries are major producers of some of the minerals classified as critical minerals in line with the United Nations Framework Classification of Resources and other known parameters. However, despite initiatives to produce a region-wide framework to regulate the exploitation of these minerals, there has been no success. The

[106] Article XIII(83) 2050 AIMS.

[107] Article XII(k)(i)(60) AIMS.

[108] Article XII(k)(i)(60) AIMS.

[109] Institute of Marine Sciences, University of Dares salaam, 'Development of Ocean Governance Strategy for Africa: Summary of Scoping Study and Gap Analysis' (2018) https://wedocs.unep.org/handle/20.500.11822/25703;jsessionid=5B76C47CF7206ACDD54FA13C26B4602C.

[110] Solomon N Obulor and Eddy L Wifa, 'Regional Cooperation and Mining Governance in Africa: An Assessment of the African Mining Vision 2009' in Victoria N Nalule (ed), *Mining and Governance in Africa* (Routledge, 2023).

implication is that governance of the exploitation of these critical minerals is exclusively left to the individual countries.[111]

The African Development Bank and its partners produced a guidebook in 2022 to help develop an African Green Minerals Strategy to assist in drafting an ACMS. However, the effort has not materialised.[112] It is noted that the African Ministerial Conference on the Environment in 2023 issued the environmental aspects of critical minerals in Africa in the clean energy transition, which recognised that 'effective governance serves as an enabler for sustainable mining of critical minerals and advocated for the development of an 'Africa region-wide response on critical minerals'.[113] Despite this recognition and advocacy, a strategy to govern offshore renewable energy and define critical mineral development on an African region base has yet to be produced. This implies that all of Africa's minerals relevant to the energy transition would be considered green minerals. The following section concludes and provides recommendations.

4. Conclusion and Recommendations

This chapter examines the risk of offshore renewable and critical mineral-based resource curses in Africa in light of the energy transition. It probes and compares the general principles of the traditional natural resource curse paradigms to the exploitation of offshore renewable energy and critical minerals. The chapter further examines the role of a continent-wide policy and law in avoiding offshore renewable energy/critical mineral-based resource curse in Africa. In examining the issues, the chapter integrates issues relating to the just transition and energy justice before undertaking an analysis of AIMS 2050 that regulates the development of offshore renewable energy and critical minerals in Africa to identify gaps. The chapter centrally argues that without robust regulatory frameworks specifically for African renewable energy and critical minerals development that African Union (AU) Member States would have to adapt into their national law, the likelihood of an offshore renewable energy and critical mineral-based resource curse in Africa is high.

The chapter suggests that the AU's AIMS 2050 and the ACMS are important regulatory regimes that could assist African countries in avoiding an offshore renewable energy and critical mineral-based resource curse. However, an examination of the AIMS 2050 and the ACMS demonstrates that AIMS 2050 in its present form lacks the capacity to correct the deficiencies associated with non-renewal energy resource regulatory regimes in most AU Member States. This is because the AIMS 2050 is not specific to renewable energy development but generic to marine resources and despite the establishment of the ACMSG and the effort of the African Development Bank to establish the ACMS, the ACMS is yet to be finalised.

In order to diminish the likelihood of an offshore renewable energy and critical minerals curse, the AU should adopt the 2050 AIM as a treaty to give it a binding

[111] Boafo et al (n 1) 37.
[112] Africa Natural Resources Management and Investment Centre (n 98) 118.
[113] AMCEN/19/EGM/4.

force and resolve the weakness identified or, alternatively, adopt a charter on (offshore) renewable energy and critical minerals similar to the EU's Renewable Energy Directive (2009/28/EC) and Regulation (EU) 2024/1252 in an African socio-cultural and legal context. Such a Directive could create a common framework for promoting energy from renewable sources. Similar to the EU Renewable Energy Directive, an African Directive could set mandatory national targets for the overall share of energy from renewable sources in gross final energy consumption and the share of energy from renewable sources in transport.

The AU should urgently classify critical minerals using similar parameters as Australia as those essential to modern technologies, economies, and national security; those which have geological potential for resources; those which are in demand from strategic international partners; and those which are vulnerable to supply chain disruption. This classification could be supplemented by a clear critical minerals strategy and a binding treaty or charter that ensures that African countries do not serve as mere rentier states but are engaged in the processing of the minerals to enhance in-country value addition.

5

Health and Safety Regulation in the United Kingdom's Offshore Hydrocarbon and Wind Energy Industries: Similarities, Differences, Reforms

EDDY WIFA AND JOHN PATERSON

1. Introduction

As a mature offshore oil and gas jurisdiction, the United Kingdom has had six decades to develop its approach to the regulation of occupational health and safety in a complex, high-risk industry operating in an unforgiving environment. It is, therefore, not surprising to find, first, that the regulatory regime in this regard is now in its fourth phase of development, and that each successive stage has been driven by lessons learned the hard way in the form of serious accidents and, second, that these developments have been the subject of considerable academic analysis and comment.[1] While by no means having such a long history, the offshore wind industry in the UK is now among the most significant globally – and is reaching a stage where decisions must be taken about the fate of early projects (repower, decommission, etc) and where ongoing exponential expansion is envisaged.

That the occupational health and safety dimension of this industry has not been the subject either of significant regulatory reform efforts or (until comparatively recently) of much in the way of academic consideration, may suggest that there is nothing here that gives rise to concerns of the sort that have at times been so obvious in the context of offshore oil and gas. It is true that offshore wind does not involve volatile substances. It is also true that there have been no serious accidents involving multiple deaths. Does this more benign appearance, however, mask more insidious problems? There have been, for

[1] For a detailed account of the evolution of offshore health and safety in the UKCS, see John Paterson, *Behind the Mask: Regulating Health and Safety in Britain's Offshore Oil and Gas Industry* (Dartmouth Publishing Company, 2000).

example, indications that the offshore wind industry has a relatively high rate of accidents, injury, and death.[2] Furthermore, academics and industry actors have questioned the apparent complacency of the regulator in suggesting that offshore wind does not pose particular risks or merit specific regulatory attention.[3] Finally, there are very ambitious plans for the increase in installed generating capacity, the development of floating infrastructure, and a considerable expansion in the workforce. As a consequence, this chapter argues that the time is ripe for a closer look at the way in which occupational health and safety is regulated in the UK's offshore wind industry, specifically with reference to the lessons that may be learned from the experience of the country's offshore oil and gas industry – not least in relation to the benefits offered by a comprehensive and systematic approach to risk assessment and management in the context of a safety case approach.

Far from this being a radical proposal, it can be demonstrated that this is an approach that enjoys support not only from workers and unions, but also from at least some among industry-leading companies.[4] Further, it can be argued that recent moves by the regulator may lead logically in time to this precise regulatory regime.[5]

The chapter is structured as follows. In section 2, the evolution of the regulatory regime for health and safety in the offshore oil and gas industry is traced, demonstrating that early complacency was rapidly exposed by a serious accident which gave rise to calls for more detailed prescriptive regulation. In due course, as might have been expected given the development of the Health and Safety at Work Act 1974, this prescriptive approach was also exposed as inadequate by a further serious accident. The enquiry which followed led to the development of a regime characterised by goal-setting regulations and the obligation for operators to produce installation-specific safety cases which have the virtue of requiring a systematic approach to the identification of hazards, the quantification of risks, and the putting in place of mitigating measures to reduce risk to a level as low as a reasonably practicable. That this last approach underpins the regulatory regime under the EU offshore safety directive suggests it enjoys relatively widespread confidence. With these observations in mind, section 3 goes on to consider health and safety in offshore wind in the UK. It first considers the way in which risk is perceived in this relatively new industry, noting

[2] The 2023 incident data report by G+ reveal that offshore wind accidents almost doubled from previous years, see www.gplusoffshorewind.com/work-programme/workstreams/statistics. Also, studies reveal that offshore wind incidents are four times higher than offshore oil and gas. For this see, David Rowell, David McMillian and James Carroll, 'Offshore Wind Health and Safety: Review and Analysis' (2024) 198 *(Part A) Renewable and Sustainable Energy Reviews* 113928.

[3] Union officials liken offshore wind to 'the wild west', see Energyvoice at /www.energyvoice.com/renewables-energy-transition/wind/uk-wind/553546/study-finds-offshore-wind-injury-rate-four-times-higher-than-oil-and-gas/. See also Eddy Wifa and Tina Soliman Hunter, 'Mitigating Occupational Health and Safety Risks in the Proposed Australian Offshore Wind Energy Industry: Lessons from the safety Case regime' (2022) 40(1) *Journal of Energy and Natural Resources* 83.

[4] Siemens have explored the use of safety cases on offshore wind farm projects. See risktec.tuv.com/wp-content/uploads/2018/10/Riskworld-24_LR.pdf.

[5] Health and Safety Executive (HSE) and Marine Coastguard Agency (MCA), 'Regulatory Expectations for Emergency Response Arrangements for Offshore Renewable Energy Industry', www.hse.gov.uk/offshore/assets/docs/is2-2019.pdf.

that while some see a benign situation characterised by well understood processes, others (and often those most directly involved) see a potentially high risk industry where even if the individual processes are well understood, better account needs to be taken of the impact of such factors as scale, location, and interaction with other users of the marine space. The section goes on to look in more detail at the specific risks involved and at what the available data indicate about the scale of the problem. Noting that there are indeed indications that the risks are higher than might appear to be the case at first glance, reasons for the situation are discussed before the current regulatory approach is reviewed. The section closes with a discussion of whether a safety case regime may indeed be emerging in offshore wind before conclusions are drawn in section 4.

2. Offshore Oil and Gas: Evolution of the Health and Safety Regime

A. Phase 1: Licence Condition and Industry Code of Practice (Apparent Self-Regulation, De Facto Prescription)

When it became apparent in the 1960s that hydrocarbons might be present beneath the UK's continental shelf, the government of the day moved very rapidly to put in place the legal and regulatory arrangements that would allow exploration to begin without delay. At that point, there were no rules with respect to the health and safety of workers, only a licence condition that the licensee should comply with such written instructions as the Minister may from time-to-time issue. Lacking any knowledge of what the nascent industry involved, it is perhaps not surprising that those instructions when they emerged contained nothing substantial that had been produced by the Ministry, but rather instructed licensees to comply with a code of practice that had then recently been introduced by the Institute of Petroleum.[6]

Commercial gas was first discovered in the UK sector of the North Sea in the summer of 1965 by the Sea Gem jack-up drilling rig. In the last days of that same year, the Sea Gem collapsed killing 13 men. An inquiry was set up (not without difficulty, given that it emerged the rig did not fall within any category that would have provided statutory authority in this regard) to determine the causes and to make recommendations for the future. This inquiry, chaired by a lawyer, curiously observed both that, given the novelty of the industry and the rapid pace of its development, it would be inapt and even dangerous to make generalisations, and that a regulatory regime with statutory authority (characterised, of course, by precisely such generalisations) should be established.[7]

[6] John Paterson, 'Health, Safety and Environmental Regulation in the United Kingdom in the Aftermath of the Macondo Disaster' (2016) 4(2) *L.S.U Journal of Energy and Natural Resources* 260.

[7] Ministry of Power (1967), *Report of the Inquiry into the Causes of the Accident to the Drilling Rig Sea Gem* (Cmnd. 3409).

B. Phase 2: Development of De Jure Detailed Prescriptive Regulations

Despite the clarity of the call and the readiness of the government to accept it, it would be four more years before legislation was passed in the form of the Mineral Workings (Offshore Installations) Act 1971. No doubt reflecting the difficulty involved in meeting the Inquiry's demands as a consequence of the rapidly evolving nature of the new industry, Parliament failed, however, to provide the level of detail requested by the Sea Gem inquiry, but established instead a framework statute, which delegated the job of writing more specific regulations to the Department of Energy. The latter finally completed this task only after the passage of a further nine years, meaning that many of the large early discoveries of oil were developed before the full regulatory arrangements for occupational health and safety were in place – a mismatch in speed that did not go unnoticed or uncriticised.[8]

This undesirable situation was compounded by the fact that simultaneously, in relation to health and safety in the workplace generally, the UK effectively rejected the precise regulatory approach recommended by the Sea Gem inquiry and given effect by the Mineral Workings 1971 Act and subsequent regulations. This significant step was taken following the publication in 1972 of the report of the Robens Committee which criticised efforts from the nineteenth century to date to regulate health and safety in every workplace via detailed prescriptive rules enforced by industry-specific regulators – noting, for example, that this approach produced large volumes of rules that could quickly go out of date, encouraged a compliance mentality that could actually increase risk, and gave rise to inconsistencies between industries.[9] The government accepted both the Committee's criticisms and its proposals for detailed rules to be replaced by general duties enforced by a specialist regulator. The passage of the Health and Safety at Work Act 1974 containing these duties, and the establishment of the Health and Safety Executive (HSE), thus marked an important change in the regulatory model for workplace health and safety in the country that had been at the forefront both of industrialisation and of factories legislation.[10] Despite the fact that the nascent offshore oil and gas industry thus risked being left behind were it not to be brought properly within the ambit of the 1974 Act, the government somehow contrived to make the situation even worse by simultaneously applying both the 1971 Act approach and the 1974 Act approach with all that this implied in terms of a mismatch, to say nothing of the risk of outright contradiction – in particular, the fact that the HSE would be encouraging employers to take responsibility for identifying and managing the risks created in their own specific workplaces under the 1974 Act while the Department of Energy was itself taking responsibility for identifying and managing those risks in the context of supposedly generalisable regulations under the 1971 Act.[11]

[8] Wesley Carson, *The Other Price of Britain's Oil: Safety and Control in the North Sea* (Martin Robertson, 1984) 84.

[9] Lord Robens, *Safety and Health at Work: Report of the Robens Committee* (Cmnd 5034, 1972).

[10] Wesley Carson, 'Some Sociological Aspects of Strict Liability and the Enforcement of Factory Legislation' (1970) 33(4) *Modern Law Review* 396–412.

[11] John Paterson, 'Health and Safety at Work Offshore' in Greg Gordon, John Paterson and Emre Üşenmez (eds), *UK Oil and Gas Law* (Edinburgh University Press, 2018) 284–338.

A chance to sort out this situation arose when, in response to a blowout on the Ekofisk Bravo platform in Norway in 1978, the government established a committee under the chairmanship of Dr JH Burgoyne, an engineer, to consider whether the UK's regulatory approach to offshore health and safety was fit for purpose. That the committee did not ultimately make any strong recommendations in this regard may perhaps be explained by the fact that at the point at which it reported in 1980, the final piece of regulation under the 1971 Act had only just been passed into law (a consequence no doubt of developing prescriptive rules for the rapidly evolving industry – as Robens' analysis would have predicted), meaning that there was an argument that the regime recommended by the Sea Gem inquiry in 1967 should be given the chance to prove itself. The possibly stronger argument for accepting the findings of the Robens Committee, and thus allowing the offshore workforce to enjoy precisely the same protections as their onshore counterparts under the 1974 Act, may have been overlooked in the context of reassurance from the offshore operators that even were an accident such as had befallen Ekofisk Bravo to occur in UK waters, their exemplary emergency response arrangements would be more than equal to the challenge.[12] The comprehensive failure of all of those arrangements in the context of the Piper Alpha disaster in July 1988, discussed in the next section, suggest that the industry reassurance was misguided, and that the Burgoyne Committee's indulgence of the 1971 Act regime was misplaced.

C. Phase 3: Goal-setting Regulations and the Safety Case

The main cause of the Piper Alpha disaster was a failure of the permit to work (PTW) system by which the dayshift should have communicated to the nightshift that maintenance on pipework had not been completed.[13] This led to the nightshift restarting operations involving that pipework which led to a leak of gas and an explosion and fire. This emergency was then compounded by a number of factors identified by Lord Cullen, the judge charged with identifying the causes of the disaster and making recommendations to ensure no reoccurrence.[14] First, neighbouring production platforms continued to pump hydrocarbons thus fuelling the fires on the Piper Alpha. Second, the Piper Alpha's Offshore Installation Manager 'took no initiative in an attempt to save life'.[15] Third, emergency systems designed to respond to and minimise the effects of such an accident were themselves disabled by the explosion. Fourth, both the platform's Stand-by Vessel, the Silver Pit, and a specialist fire-fighting vessel, the Tharos, which happened to be on station, proved ineffective. Lord Cullen reserved particular criticism for the platform's owners, a consortium led by Occidental Petroleum (Caledonia) Limited, stating that they displayed a superficial attitude to risk and were unprepared for an emergency of this scale. He was also critical of the Petroleum Engineering Division of the Department of Energy, which had regulatory responsibility for offshore health and safety at the relevant time, describing its inspections as being 'superficial to the

[12] JH Burgoyne, *Offshore Safety: Report of the Committee* (Cmnd 7866, 1980).
[13] Lord Cullen, *The Public Inquiry into the Piper Alpha Disaster* (Cm 1310, 1990) 191.
[14] Lord Cullen, *The Public Inquiry into the Piper Alpha Disaster* (Cm 1310, 1990).
[15] ibid.

point of being of little use as a test of safety on the platform' and not an effective means of assessing the management of safety.[16]

Such far-reaching criticisms easily explain the root and branch reform recommended by Lord Cullen – and accepted by the UK government without exception. Out went the detailed prescriptive regulatory approach under the 1971 Act; in came a goal-setting approach[17] of the sort implied by the 1974 Act. Regulatory responsibility was removed from the Department of Energy and given entirely to the Health and Safety Executive. The new approach was implemented via the Offshore Safety Act 1992, the Safety Case Regulations 1995, and a set of goal-setting regulations.

Under this new regime each operator was required to show, for each installation, that they had identified the hazards it faced, quantified the risks, and put in place mitigating measures to reduce those risks to a level that was as low as reasonably practicable. The obligation on each operator, therefore, was to make the case to the regulator that they could operate an installation safely, and the HSE would only permit them to do so insofar as they had accepted the relevant individual safety case. In accordance with Lord Cullen's recommendations, it was also emphasised that the safety case should be a 'living document', meaning that it should be updated on an ongoing basis to reflect the changing circumstances of the individual installation.

The industry itself was enthusiastic about the new regulatory approach, indicating that it represented tangible progress in relation to the health and safety of workers offshore. Others, however, perceived problems. First, the triennial resubmission of the safety case to the HSE appeared excessively bureaucratic and risked the creation of a gap between the physical operation of the installation and what could easily become a parallel paper exercise. Second, irrespective of the industry's warm welcome for Lord Cullen's recommendations, there was evidence that operators found it difficult to implement the requirement for quantitative risk assessment, meaning that they all too often farmed out this integral aspect of the development of a safety case to specialist contractors. Third, while the involvement of the workforce in the initial preparation of a safety case was to be applauded, their apparent absence from its ongoing maintenance – and therefore from the effort to ensure that it truly was a living document – was a matter of concern.[18]

Encouragingly, however, these criticisms did not go unaddressed. Rather, the Safety Case Regulations 2005 and associated guidance increased the period for resubmission to five years, emphasised the importance of operator ownership of risk assessment (reminding them that qualitative judgement would be sufficient in many cases), and required ongoing workforce involvement in the process of maintaining the safety case.[19]

[16] ibid.

[17] 'A goalsetting approach typically involves the setting of goals, outcomes, principles or standards, usually cast at a high level; a lack of prescription about how regulatees achieve these requirements; and requires regulatees to exercise judgement to predict what actions will achieve the regulatory objective'. See Department for Business, Energy and Industrial Strategy, 'Goal Based and Rule Based Approach to Regulation' (2018) BEIS Research Paper No. 8, assets.publishing.service.gov.uk/media/5b17b32eed915d2cb16267d9/regulation-goals-rules-based-approaches.pdf.

[18] Charles Woolfson, John Foster and Matthias Beck, *Paying for the Piper: Capital and Labour in Britain's Offshore Oil Industry* (Mansell, 1996).

[19] HSE, Guidance on Risk Assessment for Offshore Installations, Offshore Information Sheet No. 3/2006 (2006).

Notwithstanding these developments, it was not long before signs emerged that there could be no room for complacency regarding the adequacy of the safety case approach. While carrying out inspections with a view to understanding the causes for an increase in reports of unplanned releases of hydrocarbons, the HSE became concerned about the overall condition of some of the installations concerned. This led to the establishment of the so-called Key Programme 3 (KP3) initiative which focused on asset integrity offshore, which revealed examples of operators losing control of the maintenance management of safety critical infrastructure. While no precise reason was offered, the HSE noted an apparent increase in the influence of the financial function within operators at the expense of the engineering function.[20] More worryingly, it could be inferred from the KP3 findings that whatever the stated desire in terms of the safety case being a living document, this was not being achieved in every case. A similar inference could be drawn from what looked like contradictory conclusions in the report of the parliamentary select committee examining the UK's approach to offshore health and safety following the Macondo disaster in the Gulf of Mexico. Though MPs agreed with regulators that the UK's approach enjoyed benefits not apparent in that of the US (where the detailed prescriptive regulatory approach abandoned after Piper Alpha had persisted), they nevertheless also noted that the industry was too often reactive rather than proactive in relation to safety. Were every safety case genuinely to be a living document, that should not have been possible.[21]

D. Phase 4: Post-Macondo Development of the Safety Case

Though the reactive nature of the regime remains a concern in relation to the safety case, it is surely significant that this model formed the foundation for the EU's approach in the context of the Offshore Safety Directive introduced in the aftermath of the Macondo disaster.[22] The major hazard report which the Directive requires is essentially a safety case. It develops the original UK safety case version, however, by adding environmental hazards and risks to those relating to occupational health and safety. It is notable also that despite leaving the EU the UK has maintained this enhanced format for the safety case, with the competent authority responsible for its implementation, the Offshore Major Accident Regulator, involving collaboration between the HSE and the Offshore Regulator for Environment and Decommissioning (OPRED) under a Memorandum of Understanding.[23]

This brief review of the evolution of the UK's approach to health and safety in the offshore oil and gas industry reveals that there are clear risks in complacency, in believing that because nothing has gone wrong so far this situation will continue. It also demonstrates the limitations and the potential of different models of regulation. Though

[20] HSE, Key Programme 3: Asset Integrity Programme: A Report of the Offshore Division of the HSE's Hazardous Installations Directorate (2007).

[21] House of Commons Energy and Climate Change Committee, UK Deepwater Drilling – Implications of the Gulf of Mexico Oil Spill, Second Report of Session 2010–11, HC 450–451 (2011).

[22] European Parliament Offshore Safety Directive 2013/30/EU.

[23] Memorandum for the establishment of the Offshore Major Accident Regulator online at www.hse.gov.uk/agency-agreements-memoranda-of-understanding-concordats/assets/docs/opred-hse.pdf.

superficially attractive, a prescriptive approach, for example, implies that its rules encompass all possible future states of the world – a manifestly unrealistic assumption. By the same token, though apparently better adapted to complexity and uncertainty, the safety case approach requires ongoing commitment to ensure that it achieves the status of a living document – and this is something that the evidence mentioned above suggests is difficult to do. With these observations in mind, in the next section attention turns to the situation with regard to health and safety in the UK's offshore wind industry.

3. Health and Safety in Offshore Wind

A. The Perception of Risk in Offshore Wind

Despite the undoubted environmental credentials of offshore wind energy generation, the very considerable expansion of the industry planned for the coming years raises the question of whether the potential risks to the workforce have been adequately addressed. At first sight, this could appear to be a rhetorical question: majestically rotating windmills are a far cry from the all too obvious risks of producing offshore oil and gas. The stark differences in appearance can, however, be deceptive. Just because a technology is environmentally friendly does not mean that it poses no risks to workers. Such an easy dismissal of risk may have been evident in the 2006 Health and Safety Executive (HSE) Report for the UK Government's energy review, where it described offshore wind operations as 'a relatively simple operation' and concluded that the 'existing regulatory arrangements are sufficient to deal with an expansion of energy production from offshore wind, wave and tidal' and, therefore, capable of containing any health and safety risk arising therefrom.[24] The HSE Report was, however, criticised as oversimplistic, revealing a superficial knowledge and understanding of the industry, and failing to consider the risks and hazards associated with the entire lifecycle of offshore wind energy operations.[25] In 2009, the HSE admitted that 'given the large expansion planned in the wind turbine construction it can be expected that the potential for accidents will increase, some of which will involve workers and public'.[26]

This latter observation was proved the more accurate by a 2013 report into occupational safety and health in the wind energy sector carried out by the European Agency for Safety and Health at Work.[27] On the one hand, this went some way towards agreeing with the original HSE position insofar as it confirmed that '[m]any of the OSH risks faced by the industry are not new as such' but, on the other, it noted that these risks 'are found in new, different situations or combinations of situations that bring along

[24] Health and Safety Executive (HSE) (2006), 'The Health and Safety Risks and Regulatory Strategy Related to Energy Developments' 49, technokontrol.com/pdf/environment/energyreport.pdf.

[25] Peter Atkinson, 'Securing the Safety of Offshore Wind Workers' (2010) 11(3) *Renewable Energy Focus* 34–36.

[26] Health and Safety Executive, 'HSE Horizon Scanning Wind Energy' (2009).

[27] European Agency for Safety and Health at Work (2013), 'Occupational Safety and Health in the Wind Energy Sector: European Risk Observatory Report', osha.europa.eu/en/publications/reports/occupational-safety-and-health-in-the-wind-energy-sector. It is interesting to note that the majority of contributors to this report (six out of nine listed) were from the UK's Health and Safety Laboratory.

new, different challenges'.[28] In relation to offshore wind in particular, it noted that this 'introduces multiple hazards not experienced onshore'[29] and listed a range of hazards involving higher risk offshore than onshore wind, including: personnel transfers, diving, emergency evacuations, exposure to weather, structural failures, and crane lifts.[30] At the time of writing that report, however, a key challenge for the authors was a lack of OSH data and information, a situation it explained as a consequence of the relative youth of the industry, a focus on risks to the public, and confidentiality.[31]

The perception of offshore wind as essentially benign appears to lead to the sense that its operations are simple, and thus the attitude that no special regulatory measures are required.[32] By contrast, it can be persuasively argued that the offshore wind industry is a complex, hazardous, and fast developing industry whose health and safety risks may all too easily be underestimated. Paul Gipe, for example, suggests great care is necessary when describing wind as a benign source of energy because this could lead to complacency and ultimately fatalities among workers.[33] According to Chris Lawson, offshore wind energy is at least a medium risk industry and can be classified as high risk depending on the nature of the generation and the location offshore, 'as wind farms are developed further from shore, and correlatively the environmental conditions become more unpredictable and hostile, these risks will increase'.[34] In terms of what this could mean for regulation, Bud Hudspith, Unite the Unions Health and Safety adviser, has suggested that 'serious consideration should be given to operators developing a safety case approach as with the offshore oil and gas'.[35] He adds that 'if you have got other forms of activity that create additional risks, there could be a case for this type of legislation.'[36]

To gain an understanding of the significance of these observations and to consider whether calls for the regulatory approach adopted in the offshore oil and gas industry are well-founded, it is necessary next to look more closely at the hazards and risks affecting offshore wind operations.

B. Offshore Wind Occupational Health and Safety Risks

Some examples of hazards encountered during the development of an offshore wind farm include:

- falls from heights;
- mechanical hazards such as contact with moving parts;

[28] ibid 60.
[29] ibid 11.
[30] ibid 24–25.
[31] ibid 60.
[32] ibid.
[33] Paul Gipe (2012), 'Wind energy – The Breath of Life or the Kiss of Death: Contemporary Wind Mortality Rates' wind-works.org/wind-energy-the-breath-of-life-or-the-kiss-of-death-contemporary-wind-mortality-rates/. For updated data, see wind-works.org/wind-the-breath-of-life-or-the-kiss-of-death-analysis-of-wind-energy-fatalities/. See also Paul Gipe, *Wind Energy Comes of Age* (John Wiley & Sons Inc New York, 1995).
[34] Chris Wharburton, 'The Winds of Change: the regulation of a lower risk sector' (*Croner-i*, 23 August 2012).
[35] ibid.
[36] ibid.

- blade failures;
- ice throws;
- ship collision, personnel transfer accidents or men overboard which may occur during marine operations and transportation;
- electrical hazards; and
- fire or explosion of turbine or vessel.

Others might include issues relating to manual handling, ergonomics, the risk from working with dangerous substances, working in confined spaces, and exposure to noise and vibration.[37] While these hazards are not novel, the fact that they occur in a remote and unpredictable offshore environment makes them more challenging. And the further the industry moves from the shore, the more acute these issues become: emergency response will take longer and there may be interactions with a more diverse group of users of the marine space.

C. The Scale of the Problem

It is a question, however, whether the fears and concerns expressed by industry participants have been borne out by experience or whether the confidence of the HSE has been shown to be justified.

In this regard, it is instructive to consider the available statistics for accidents in the industry. The HSE might be expected to be the key source in this regard, but unfortunately it does not publish such data as the industry has not been allocated a Standard Industry Classification code. As such, accidents may be listed under other categories such as construction or electricity. Contrast this with the position in relation to offshore oil and gas where detailed reports are produced by the HSE annually.[38] Data must thus be gathered from industry sources, such as the G+ Global Offshore Wind Health and Safety Association, which brings together lead operators and owners.[39] With the caveat that this information comes from the industry, it does offer some grounds for optimism, especially in relation to the situation in the UK. Over the period from 2014 to 2020,

[37] European Agency for Safety and Health (EASH), Occupational Safety and Health in the Wind Energy Sector, 12 December 2013. osha.europa.eu/en/publications/occupational-safety-and-health-wind-energy-sector. Some of these hazards apply equally to the offshore oil and gas industry whilst others are specific to offshore wind. It is interesting to note, however, that when it comes to the reporting of dangerous occurrences under the Reporting of Injuries, Diseases and Dangerous Occurrences Regulations 2013, offshore wind farms are excluded from the definition of 'offshore workplaces' (reg 2, read in conjunction with The Health and Safety at Work etc. Act 1974 (Application outside Great Britain) Order 2013) despite the fact that some of the matters requiring to be reported could apply equally to them as to offshore oil and gas installations, including: collapses, 'the failure of equipment required to maintain a floating offshore installation', dropping objects, weather damage, collisions, subsidence or collapse of seabed, loss of stability or buoyancy, evacuation, falls into water (Sch 2, Pt 6). These issues, as defined in the 2013 Regulations, are not easily accommodated in other parts of Sch 2 and would seem to indicate a gap in the reporting requirements and perhaps something of a blind spot in relation to offshore wind.

[38] See eg Health and Safety Executive (HSE) Offshore Statistics and Regulatory Activity Report (2023), online at www.hse.gov.uk/offshore/assets/docs/hsr2023.pdf.

[39] G+ Global Offshore Wind Health and Safety Organisation, 2020 Incident data report, www.gplusoffshorewind.com/__data/assets/pdf_file/0010/853246/G-Plus-Global-Offshors-Wind-Health-and-Safety-Organisationjk.pdf.

while total hours worked across all G+ member[40] sites remained of the same order of magnitude, the total recordable injury rate (TRIR) fell from 6.03 to 3.75 and the lost time injury frequency (LTIF) fell from 1.86 to 1.70.[41] The UK, the jurisdiction with the largest presence in the G+ (with four times as many sites as the next largest, Germany), had a TRIR of 3.0 and an LTIF of 1.5.[42] During that period, it is interesting to note that the G+ identified the nacelle as 'the area with the greatest number of accumulated historical incidents', most of which occurred 'while personnel were undertaking routine maintenance tasks'.[43]

More data from G+ are less encouraging, however. First, it interesting to note that in the latest report there is only one example of information being presented broken down by jurisdiction, with the rest offered on an aggregated basis. It may be speculated that such an approach may make it easier to obtain data in the first place, but it can also be argued that it makes it more difficult to understand any movements in the figures on the basis of, say, legislative and regulatory interventions in a given jurisdiction. Second, for all that there has been a substantial increase in the total hours worked in the industry in the last year, this alone does not account for the increases in problems reported. For example, while medical treatment injuries rose 59 per cent, once the increase in hours worked is factored in, the rise is lower but still 15 per cent.[44] Similarly, lost workday injuries show an increase even after higher overall work hours are factored in and '[f]or the first time in G+'s reporting history these numbers include a fatality'.[45] Furthermore, the 2023 data from G+ has raised concerns as safety incidents have almost doubled from the previous year. The report revealed a 'recorded total of 1,679 incidents worldwide in 2023, up from the 867 recorded in 2022'. Thus, representing a 94 per cent increase. While these are global figures, the UK there were 503, up from 348 in 2022. Also, when compared with other renewable energy sectors, wind energy has the most incident frequency.[46]

Data such as these, however, only take us so far. What do they mean in terms of understanding whether offshore wind has problems with regard to occupational health and safety? Is it more or less dangerous than other industries? Even if available reports undoubtedly reveal accidents and injuries, are they out of line with what is observed elsewhere in the workplace? Most strikingly, in this regard, a recent comprehensive

[40] In Denmark, France, the Netherlands, Sweden, Taiwan, the UK, and the US.

[41] G+ (n 39) 6.

[42] Unfortunately, it is not possible to comment on the trend in the UK, as incident data are not disaggregated by member country in the equivalent 2014 report: G9 Offshore wind health and safety association, 2014 incident data report, www.gplusoffshorewind.com/__data/assets/pdf_file/0008/633572/g9-2014-incident-report.pdf. It would also be interesting to compare incident rates with those in the oil and gas industry, but this is not easy to do because while the G+ reports on the basis of incidents per 1,000,000 hours worked, the HSE reports on the basis of 100,000 full-time equivalent workers. See eg HSE, Offshore Statistics & Regulatory Activity Report 2020, November 2021, www.hse.gov.uk/offshore/assets/docs/hsr2020.pdf. Note also that whilst from 2013/14 until 2017 the HSE's annual report on offshore activity included offshore wind farms as well as oil and gas, the data were not disaggregated by industry. From 2018 onwards, the same annual reports do not include mention of offshore wind farms. These reports are available at www.hse.gov.uk/offshore/statistics/index.htm.

[43] G+ (n 39) 9.

[44] Global Offshore Wind Health and Safety Organisation (G+) incident Data Report (2023), online at www.gplusoffshorewind.com/work-programme/workstreams/statistics, p 6.

[45] ibid.

[46] Benjamin Savacool et al, 'Balancing Safety with Sustainability: Assessing the Risk of accidents for Modern Low-carbon Energy Systems' (2016) 112 (5) *Journal of Cleaner Production* 3952.

literature review by Rowell, McMillan and Caroll 'highlights that offshore wind is a high-risk industry and current injury rates are 3–4 times those of the oil and gas industry, indicating that there is huge potential for improvement' and that 'existing globally reported injury rates … do not include some serious incidents due to not being part of reporting groups'.[47] A careful analysis of the data is concerning but perhaps while offshore wind may not be particularly more dangerous than offshore oil and gas, the chapter argues that the complacency and limitations of the current regulatory approach is arguably a reason for higher incidents.

D. Offshore Wind as a High-Risk Industry

On the face of it, this is both very troubling and counter intuitive. How can an industry characterised by majestically turning wind turbines be so much more dangerous than that which extracts volatile hydrocarbons, increasingly from high-pressure and high-temperature reservoirs? A variety of reasons have been offered by those with firsthand experience of offshore wind. One is that the rapid expansion of offshore wind means that industry suffers from a significant persistent gap in the availability of skilled staff, and the involvement of relatively inexperienced workers in the processes of constructing and operating offshore wind farms increases the likelihood of accidents. In this regard, in the area of transportation generally and vessel transfer in particular, it has been suggested by the Chief Inspector of Marine Accidents, Steven Clinch, that the recruitment of staff from the fishing or leisure industries without recognising the specific challenges raised by offshore wind leads to increased health and safety risks.[48] He added that the:

> [S]kills gap is likely to grow as the renewable energy industry moves even further offshore in the future. As such, there is a clear potential for rise in the number and severity of accidents unless action is taken to ensure that vessels' crews have the necessary competencies needed to operate their crafts safely.[49]

In 2020 Trevor Johnson of the HSE Energy Division raised concerns that improvements in offshore wind health and safety had at best stalled if not reversed and he was particularly concerned that such reversal may continue.[50] Concerns such as these are by no means limited to those with a regulatory role but are also shared by at least some industry managers. Peter Finn, the EHS Manager for GE Energy, for example, suggested over a decade ago that as larger turbines are installed further offshore, more challenges would arise, especially regarding onsite accommodation, the need for better emergency response and the logistics of spare parts delivery, adding that overall the expansion would 'result in more turbines, more technicians, more transfers and thus an increased

[47] Rowell, McMillian and Carroll (n 2).

[48] Maritime Accident Investigation Branch – Accident Report No 23/2013 (2013), online at https://assets.publishing.service.gov.uk/media/547c6f44e5274a429000001b/W9IPReport_Web.pdf, p (i).

[49] ibid.

[50] Letter from Trevor John (HSE Energy Division) to Andy Goldsmith (International Marine Contracts Association) on 10th July 2020, online at imcaweb.blob.core.windows.net/wp-uploads/2020/08/UK-HSE-Letter-to-IMCA-Health-and-Safety-at-work-act-1974.pdf.

risk of incidents'.[51] The data reviewed above certainly suggest that his predictions were accurate.

Similarly, despite early recognition of the challenges raised for health and safety by the rapidly expanding offshore wind energy industry, there is evidence that the poor safety culture of some companies served to exacerbate the situation. In the words of Andrew Linington, a spokesman for Nautilus:

> Operators who apply high safety standards are losing out to companies that cut corners … [T]he situation is frighteningly similar to the boom in North Sea oil in the 1970s. Back then people were warning of poorly enforced standards, but it wasn't until 167 men died in the Piper Alpha disaster that anything was done to clean up the industry.[52]

Nor is this an inappropriate analogy. WG Carson, writing in 1981, suggested that an apparent willingness to accept an ongoing toll of injury and death among offshore oil and gas workers – in that case on the basis that it was the inevitable price of the use of cutting-edge technologies in a hostile environment – would only survive until there was a major disaster.[53] Piper Alpha proved him right. There may, of course, still be scepticism that the analogy really works; it is perhaps hard to imagine, after all, that any accident in the offshore wind sector could ever rival the devastation of Piper Alpha. On one hand, however, one need only consider the possible consequences of a collision accident involving a large vessel in the context of installation or maintenance operations. On the other, if there is evidence of a worryingly high rate of injury and even death, is it appropriate to suggest or at least imply that no strong action needs to be taken insofar as no single accident involves multiple deaths? And then there is the fact that, generally speaking, the regulatory reforms following Piper Alpha appeared to be effective to the point where the health and safety record of offshore hydrocarbons has become a key reference point for those in offshore wind who are worried by what they see closer to home. For example, Anne Marit Hanssen, the Environmental Health and Safety Manager for Statoil (now Equinor), noted – again more than a decade ago – that 'the number of serious incidents and accidents in the offshore wind industry are too high when compared with offshore oil and gas', and that there are significant lessons to be drawn from the oil and gas industry.[54]

Offshore wind is already a significant aspect of the UK's energy mix and is set, quite rightly, to become even more important in a relatively short space of time. It has the potential to play a key role in the country's efforts to balance the energy quadrilemma. It is important, however, that the price of the development of that industry is not paid in the currency of injury and death among the rapidly expanding workforce. It behoves policy makers and regulators to make decisions in this regard on the basis of reliable evidence rather than on well-meaning but ill-informed assumptions about the level of risk the offshore wind industry involves. Meeting this challenge requires that it first of

[51] OffshoreWind.biz, 'Denmark: Wind Energy Update Releases Offshore Wind Health and Safety Information Pack' (2012) www.offshorewind.biz/2012/08/16/denmark-wind-energy-update-releases-offshore-wind-health-and-safety-information-pack/.

[52] Will Crisp, 'Offshore Wind Farm "Wild West" of Renewable Energy, Union Warns' *The Guardian* (14 February 2014) www.theguardian.com/environment/2014/feb/14/offshore-windfarms-renewable-energy.

[53] Carson (n 8).

[54] OffshoreWind.biz (n 51).

all be acknowledged. Unfortunately, some industry stakeholders think the problem is exaggerated while others deny it.[55]

E. The Current Regulatory Approach for Offshore Wind Energy

This section examines the current regime for offshore wind health and safety, principally governed by the Health and Safety at Work etc Act 1974 and selected complementary regulations – the Construction (Design Management) Regulations 2015 and the Management of Health and Safety at Work Regulations 1999. It reveals a variety of regulatory gaps, including the absence of a permissioning regime and of independent third-party verification, as well as the overall complexity and fragmented nature of the regulatory architecture. Before discussing these problems further, it is instructive to consider how such a situation arose.

In a move perhaps reminiscent of the enthusiasm which greeted the onset of the offshore oil and gas industry on the UKCS in the 1960s, the Government set out on the road to the development of the offshore wind industry just over two decades ago without any apparent detailed consideration of what the regime for health and safety should look like. Rather than engage regulators, industry, and other stakeholders in the systematic design of a robust health and safety regulatory framework in this regard, it chose the much quicker option of simply transplanting the onshore wind health and safety approach offshore.[56] The implication is that there is little difference between the onshore and offshore wind health and safety regulatory regimes.[57] This is despite significantly higher level of risk offshore.[58] After the initial AOGB Order was passed in 2001, the first commercial offshore wind farm (North Hoyle) was constructed in 2003. This meant that the nascent but rapidly expanding offshore wind energy industry was reliant on the general duties under Health and Safety at Works Act 1974 and its subordinate regulations.[59]

These arrangements embody a generally goal-setting approach to health and safety risk which replaced the prescriptive approach which predated the Robens Committee Report, discussed above. On the one hand, this is encouraging insofar as responsibility for managing the risk to workers and others is placed in the hands of those who create it. On the other, especially given the experience of the offshore oil and gas industry, we may wonder whether more effort should have been expended to ensure that the particularities of this new industry in a challenging environment were sufficiently well understood to justify such a rapid reliance on existing regulatory arrangements. After all, the general duties imposed on employers (and others) in the 1974 Act may be read as underpinning

[55] Crisp (n 52).

[56] See now The Health and Safety at Work etc. Act 1974 (Application Outside Great Britain[AOGB]) Order 2013, www.legislation.gov.uk/uksi/2013/240/contents/made, which replaces earlier orders. See also HSE offshore Information Sheet 1/2013-Application of health and safety law offshore.

[57] RenewableUK, 'Offshore Wind and Marine Energy Health and Safety Guidance Note' (2014) 12, www.sgurrenergy.com/wp-content/uploads/2015/09/offshore-marine-h-s-guidelines-21840.pdf.

[58] Wifa and Soliman Hunter (n 3) 83.

[59] Management of Health and Safety At Work Regulations 1999 (MHSWR), Construction (Design And Management) Regulation 2007 (CDM), Reporting of Industrial Diseases And Dangerous Occurrences Regulations 2013 (RIDDOR), Supply of Machinery (Safety) Regulations Harmonised Standards, Provision And Use of Work Equipment Regulations 1998 (PUWER), Personal Protective Equipment Regulations 2002.

an essentially self-regulatory approach, which could all too easily lead to complacency, particularly in the absence of measures of regulatory scrutiny like a permissioning regime and independent third party independent verification as would be seen in the safety case regime discussed below. In this regard the general duties read as follows:

> Section 2(1) It shall be the duty of every employer to ensure, so far as is reasonably practicable, the health, safety and welfare at work of his employees.
>
> Section 3(1) It shall be the duty of every employer to conduct his undertaking in such a way as to ensure, so far as is reasonably practicable, that persons not in his employment who may be affected thereby are not thereby exposed to risks to their health and safety.

The following duty is also relevant for those who provide materials used in the workplace:

> Section 6(1) It shall be the duty of any person who designs, manufactures, imports or supplies any article for use at work … to ensure, so far as is reasonably practicable, that the article is so designed and constructed that it will be safe and without risks to health at all times when it is being set, used, cleaned or maintained by a person at work.

Thereafter, the Management of Health and Safety at Work Regulations 1999 set out how an employer must fulfil the duties contained in sections 2 and 3 of the 1974 Act:

> Reg 3(1) Every employer shall make a suitable and sufficient assessment of
>
> (a) the risks to the health and safety of his employees to which they are exposed whilst they are at work; and
>
> (b) the risks to the health and safety of persons not in his employment arising out of or in connection with the conduct by him of his undertaking,
>
> for the purpose of identifying the measures he needs to take to comply with the requirements and prohibitions imposed upon him by or under the relevant statutory provisions.

Much then depends upon what counts as reasonably practicable in any given situation. In this regard, complementary regulations and guidance from both the regulator and industry bodies may play an important role.[60] But just as legislation, regulation, and guidance in combination may offer some clarity to a duty holder, the regime becomes fragmented and may equally at times overwhelm and confuse. Perhaps it is such confusion that has led to concerns of lack of regulatory clarity and an increasing appetite for industry specific safety legislation like the oil and gas safety case regime.[61] This latter situation was the focus of a review of health and safety regulation generally by Professor Ragnar E Lofstedt in 2010. There he suggested that there was evidence which indicated that 'regulations are putting undue cost on business whilst doing little to improve health and safety outcomes'.[62] One reason for this, he suggested, was that 'the sheer mass of regulation is a key concern for many businesses. Although there is considerably less

[60] For example, RenewableUK (n 57) 12. This is intended to provide information on specific technical, legal or policy issues relevant to the core members of RenewableUK.

[61] Mathew Perry (EnergyVoice), 'Study Finds Offshore Wind injury rate four times higher than oil and gas' (2024), online at www.energyvoice.com/renewables-energy-transition/wind/uk-wind/553546/study-finds-offshore-wind-injury-rate-four-times-higher-than-oil-and-gas/.

[62] Ragnar Lofstedt, 'Reclaiming Health and Safety for All: An Independent Review of Health and Safety Legislation' (2011) www.gov.uk/government/uploads/system/uploads/attachment_data/file/66790/lofstedt-report.pdf.

regulation than 35 years ago, businesses still feel that they have to work through too many regulations or use health and safety consultants'.[63] This issue has also been highlighted specifically within the offshore wind industry. Peter Lloyd, for example, has noted that, in addition to legislation and regulations,

> a general managers' guide to health and safety at work could stretch to over 300 pages, the RenewableUK guidance on Offshore Wind and Marine Energy Health and Safety Guidance is 268 pages and the Trade Industry Organisation, G9, Guidance on one specific aspect, Working at Height in the Offshore Wind Industry extends to 143 pages.[64]

He thus recommended that the HSE should undertake a programme of sector-specific regulatory consolidation to simplify the regulatory framework.[65]

Following from the broad general duties under the 1974 Act, complementary regulations like the Construction Design and Management (CDM) Regulation 2015, the Control of Major Accident Hazards Regulations (COMAH) 1999 and the Management of Health and Safety at Work Regulations 1999 all provide for 'suitable and sufficient assessment'. To fulfil this requirement of 'suitable and sufficient assessment', the duty holder would prepare a safety management systems (SMS)/safety report and undertakes a Quantified Risk Assessments (QRA). While these are generally useful in identifying health and safety risks and providing measures to mitigate them, the heavy reliance on QRA method can be abused especially in the absence of a third-party verification. Professor Ragnar E Lofstedt, while admitting the significant contribution of QRA to risk management, added that in practice it has become 'a bureaucratic nightmare' where companies are producing and 'paying for lengthy documents at the expense of controlling the significant risk in the work place'.[66] In fact, Lord Cullen warns that QRA should be 'viewed with great caution and treated as only one parameter on an essentially judgemental exercise'.[67] Because the QRA is an arithmetic prediction of potential risks, the HSE views it as a 'mechanistic demonstration that risk has been reduced through such QRA calculation'.[68] Therefore, while accepting the use of QRA, Lord Cullen suggested other measures such as Formal Safety Assessments (FSA) that became a feature of the safety case regime that was adopted following the Piper Alpha disaster. If these limitations of the QRA regime that is a main feature of the offshore wind health and safety regime are anything to go by, the question then is, what regulatory lessons can be adopted from a more mature offshore oil and gas industry.

F. The Emergence of a Safety Case for Offshore Wind

Following the Piper Alpha disaster as discussed earlier in the chapter, the safety case regime was adopted as an industry specific legislation and was designed with various

[63] ibid.
[64] Peter Lloyd, 'Health and Safety of Offshore Wind Farm' in Chong Ng and Li Ran (eds), *Offshore Wind Farms: Technologies, Design and Operation* (Woodhead Publishing, 2016) 1.
[65] ibid.
[66] Lofstedt (n 62).
[67] Lord Cullen Report, 284 paras 17–49.
[68] Health and Safety Executive, 'Regulating Higher Hazards: Exploring the Issues' (2001) 9.

regulatory safeguards that foster compliance. Such regulatory safeguards like a permissioning regime and an independent third-party verification process saw a more enhanced role of the Health and Safety Regulator (HSE) during the licensing process. Unfortunately, this is absent under the current offshore wind energy regime under the 1974 Act and all complementary regulations. This section will provide a functional comparative analysis between the current offshore wind health and safety regime and the offshore oil and gas safety case regime. This analysis will reveal the regulatory strengths of the safety case regime that are worthy of transplantation to the offshore wind energy industry.

The Health and Safety at Work Act 1974 established the Health and Safety Executive (HSE) as the competent regulatory body that is responsible for ensuring compliance with the Act and other subsidiary regulation.[69] The HSE as a non-departmental body regulates health and safety risks in the workplace. It adopts a general regulatory approach in the form of goal setting 'which forms the backcloth to the regulatory arrangements to deal with more specific risks'.[70]

Its functions also include development of regulations and standards, carrying out research and providing information and advice.[71] Its specific duties include investigation of accidents, taking enforcement action where necessary and carrying out inspection of workplaces, installations and facilities.[72] While these are some of the general functions of the HSE, for offshore wind energy operations, these functions were carried out through its Field Operations Directorate ((FOD) but later transferred to the Energy Division.[73]

Under the offshore oil and gas safety case regime, the HSE has a more prominent and enhanced role during the licensing process through the acceptance of the safety case, without which the operator or duty is unable to operate. This is known as the permissioning regime or a permit system. One challenge with the current offshore wind regime is the absence of a permissioning regime as it applies under the safety case regime. A permissioning regime does not only require duty holders to demonstrate that risk is reduced ALARP, but it 'demands the active commitment of the duty holders in practice'.[74] A permissioning regime is one 'under which the start or continuation of particular work activities are conditioned upon a consent, license, letter or conclusion or acceptance of a safety case or safety report by the health and safety regulator'.[75] The permissoning regime as a measure of regulatory scrutiny has resource intensive requirements for both the regulator and duty holder, and is therefore only used in industries 'where there are or could be significant hazards which require a higher degree of regulatory control'.[76]

[69] Health and Safety at Work etc. Act 1974, s 10.
[70] Health and Safety Executive 'Offshore Health and Safety Strategy' (2010).
[71] RenewableUK (n 57).
[72] HSWA 1974, s 11.
[73] See hansard.parliament.uk/commons/2023-03-06/debates/DC1937BC-2733-44EE-A1D4-47A718DBA44B/OffshoreWindFarmsHealthAndSafety#:~:text=The%20HSE's%20energy%20division%20has,enforcement%20of%20high%2Drisk%20activities.
[74] Health and Safety Executive (n 68).
[75] Health and Safety Commission, 'Policy Statement: Our Approach to Permissioning Regimes' (2003).
[76] ibid.

In proposing the adoption of a 'permissioning regime', the HSE is guided by the following principles:

A

- There is a need to have regard to high, sustainable and broadly based levels of societal concern, either existing or likely, over potential risks of harm (eg high levels of public dread or aversion associated with hazards and vulnerability of those exposed to the hazard): and/or
- There is significant risk of multiple fatalities from a single (or linked series of) event(s); and/or
- There is significant risk of widespread and significant adverse effects on human health;

And

B

- The proposed regime adds proportionate value in terms of risk control and/or allows specific activities (with clear benefits to society) to proceed.[77]

It is for the reasons above that the permissioning regime is viewed as one that 'secures the systematic management of hazardous activities throughout the stages of design, construction, operation and decommissioning'.[78] Furthermore, it ensures that 'the risks are properly controlled, so securing public confidence in high levels of health and safety without compromising industry's ability to operate'.[79] This therefore implies that a permissioning regime does not only provide for proactive and comprehensive demonstration that risk is ALARP, but it equally provides an appropriate balance between safety and economic benefits. Based on the above considerations for the adoption of a permissioning regime, this chapter argues that like the oil and gas industry, the offshore industry absolutely satisfies the above requirements.

Despite the above strengths of the permissioning regime under the safety case, the HSE has been reluctant in adopting this approach in the offshore wind energy industry. Understandably, the permissioning regime is quite resource intensive and HSE is quite stretched at the moment with only four offshore wind inspectors compared to 120 in the offshore oil and gas industry.[80] Although notifications are adopted under section 6 of the Control of Major Accident Hazards Regulations 2015, this is largely inferior and insufficient when compared to the permissioning regime as it offers very little by way of regulatory scrutiny. All of these points point to not only the regulatory limitations of the current approach under the 1974 Act and complementary regulations, but the overall limited function of the regulator when compared with the offshore oil and gas industry.

The HSE in 2010 had an opportunity to reconsider its earlier view that offshore wind energy developments essentially raised no novel problems requiring specific action. In a

[77] ibid.
[78] ibid.
[79] ibid 4.
[80] Mathew Perry (EnergyVoice), 'Safety Concerns for Offshore Wind as HSE has only four inspectors' (2023) online at https://www.energyvoice.com/renewables-energy-transition/wind/uk-wind/536219/rmt-offshore-wind-hse-inspectors/.

report published that year, it acknowledged the complex and rapidly evolving nature of the offshore wind energy industry:

> The scale and speed of the changes catalysed by the drive towards a new energy economy will pose a significant challenge. As emerging technologies arrive in the market place, new players join the industry and smaller businesses play a greater role within it, some new hazards will supplement longer-standing ones associated with energy production and use. In addition, many familiar hazards will extend into new environments and new contexts. All these have the potential to impede the anticipated transformation of the UK's energy sector.[81]

On the regulatory approach, the HSE questioned the general nature of its 'one size fits all' solution as it combines and regulates emerging energy technologies including offshore wind.[82] On this regulatory approach, the HSE was not convinced of its fitness for purpose. In its Executive Senior Management Team Paper, it admitted that the 'present regulatory regime cannot cope with all the challenges posed by the emerging energy sectors'.[83] Although it acknowledged the current regulatory challenges, it was unclear as to what regulatory strategy to adopt. More particularly, it was unclear whether it should maintain the current regulatory strategy of a broad application of the HSWA 1974 and its subordinate regulations or 'reform a package specifically directed at EET [Emerging Energy Technologies] that would bring clarity to EET duty holders and an appropriate degree of consistency between onshore and offshore provinces'.[84]

It is evident, then, that the HSE recognises the challenges. In fact, Trevor Johnson, the then Principal Inspector for the HSE, wrote to offshore renewable energy trade bodies to express his concern '"that in some sectors of the wind energy industry, improvements in health and safety performance [have] at best stalled if not reversed'.[85] He added that 'in 2020, there have been a number of serious incidents both in the UK and elsewhere which could indicate that any reversal may continue'.

The HSE in its Health and Safety Executive Senior Management Team Paper recognised that the current broad application of the HSWA 1974 and its subordinate regulations are unable to cope with the challenges posed by emerging technologies, prominent amongst them being offshore wind farms.[86] Despite this recognition, the HSE does not appear willing to make any regulatory changes to its approach.

That said, however, there is one indication that the HSE may be moving somewhat in the direction of a safety case approach. This is evident in a document first published with the Maritime and Coastguard Agency in 2019 and updated in April 2024: Regulatory expectations for emergency response arrangements for the offshore renewable energy industry.[87]

[81] Health and Safety Executive 'Health and Safety in the New Energy Economy: Meeting the Challenge of Major Change' (2010).

[82] ibid.

[83] Health and Safety Executive, 'Senior Management Team Paper: An Update on Emerging Energy Technologies Programme' (7 April 2010) 4.

[84] ibid.

[85] Energy Voice, 'The future of Health and Safety in the Energy Transition' (2021) www.energyvoice.com/opinion/332998/the-future-of-health-and-safety-in-the-energy-transition/#:~:text=Her%20comments%20followed%20the%20publication,also%20to%20help%20all%20parties.

[86] Health and Safety Executive (n 83) 4.

[87] HSE and MCA, Offshore Information Sheet 02/2019, revised 02/04/2024, www.hse.gov.uk/offshore/assets/docs/is2-2019.pdf.

Of particular interest in this document is the section which sets out the principles to be adopted in the provision of the appropriate arrangements for emergency response, and especially the subsection on risk assessment. Here the regulators note that 'Each offshore renewable energy development is unique and therefore the organisation in control must carry out a suitable and sufficient assessment to determine the measures required for that site to ensure the relevant statutory provisions are met.' They continue 'The arrangements should be suitable for any foreseeable event of whatever nature with the potential to cause harm and to require the evacuation, escape, recovery and rescue of one or more persons and extent to occurrences for the potential for a *major accident hazard*.' After setting out in the issues to be considered in an assessment, the regulators remind duty holders that they 'should consider in detail all scenarios that could lead to evacuation, escape, recovery and rescue, taking into account factors such as rapid spread of fire and smoke, explosion, and toxic gas release' and note that 'performance acceptance criteria must be relevant for all stages of the structure's lifecycle'.[88]

Interestingly, the HSE and MCA state that 'duty holders can draw upon the experience of other offshore industries that have already developed emergency response performance standards'.[89] What is most striking about this is that in essence the regulators are asking duty holders to carry out the sort of process that is integral to the safety case seen in the offshore oil and gas industry albeit that in the case of offshore renewables this is essentially restricted to the situation where something has already gone wrong and thus an emergency response is required. Especially when the safety case under a permissioning regime was designed to proactively anticipate the risk throughout the entire life cycle of the project and not only in emergency situations. It would appear to be a very short step indeed from this to what looks like the logical conclusion that duty holders should carry out a similarly structured exercise which is focused first on reducing risks to a level that is as low as reasonably practicable and only second on ensuring that there is suitable emergency response in the event that any such risk crystallises. Regulators will no doubt object that this is in any case the obligation of the duty holder under relevant legislation and regulation. The question is, however, why a properly structured safety case approach should not be implemented to ensure that duty holders are meeting all of these obligations in an appropriately structured and coherent manner rather than piecemeal as would appear to be at least possible at present?

4. Conclusion

In conclusion, then, it is apparent first that the UK has devoted considerably more effort to the development of an adequate regulatory regime for health and safety in the offshore oil and gas industry than it has in relation to the equivalent in relation to offshore wind. This can, of course, be explained by the impact of serious accidents in the hydrocarbon industry both in UK waters and elsewhere on the thinking of policymakers and regulators. Growing evidence suggests, however, that the time may well have come for a more

[88] ibid 2.
[89] ibid.

thorough appraisal of the situation in relation to offshore wind. First, there is evidence that the HSE itself is aware that, as a key emerging energy technology which the UK plans to deploy at very significant scale, offshore wind may well tax the limits of a simple transfer of the onshore regime under the 1974 Act offshore. Second, there is growing statistical evidence that workers in the offshore wind industry are suffering injuries and accidents at a significantly greater rate than those in offshore oil and gas. While this may not necessarily mean that offshore wind is inherently more dangerous than oil and gas, it provides strong evidence to support a similar regulatory strategy.

So far, the HSE has not formally moved in the direction of a safety case regime in relation to offshore wind, but some in the industry think such a development may be inevitable.[90] Peter Lloyd, the Global Head of the Siemens Centre of Competence EHS Offshore, has suggested that with the current growth of the industry, and especially as personnel are being employed permanently offshore for long periods, 'it may become very difficult to justify that a principal duty holder could control risk without adopting such a process'.[91] Further, it is noteworthy that the HSE/MCA guidance in relation to emergency response may be read as pointing to the safety case as a logical conclusion.

There will undoubtedly be some hesitation in accepting this conclusion without further discussion: if even the regulator is not explicitly calling for it, why would the industry seek out an approach which looks more complex than current arrangements? To the contrary, however, it can be suggested that as the industry itself becomes more complex and significantly larger, moves further from shore, and interacts with a larger and more diverse range of other users of the marine space, a safety case approach can make things easier insofar as it provides a framework for a systematic identification of hazards, assessment of risks, and implementation of mitigating measures. Furthermore, it can provide a clear focal point for the interaction of relevant stakeholders so that the voices that need to be heard can be heard. Finally, in terms of providing reassurance about an increased regulatory burden, this chapter would very much endorse the idea of the 'proportionate' application of the safety case, ensuring that it is 'optimised' for offshore wind.[92]

[90] Perry (n 61).
[91] Peter O Lloyd, 'Health and Safety of Offshore Wind Farms' in Ng and Ran (n 64) 574–87, 586.
[92] RiskTecWorld (2013) online at risktec.tuv.com/wp-content/uploads/2018/10/Riskworld-24_LR.pdf.

6

Beyond Social Licence to Operate: Charting 'Social Gaps' and the Social Contract in the Emerging Australian Offshore Wind Sector

MADELINE TAYLOR*

1. Introduction

Nearly six decades since oil and gas development commenced offshore, Australia is entering its offshore wind era. Australia's decarbonisation strategy to date has largely targeted the deployment of onshore renewables to reach its target of 82 per cent renewable energy in the National Electricity Market (NEM) by 2030.[1] Renewable energy represents 39.4 per cent of the overall Australian electricity supply – all of which is entirely onshore.[2] Rooftop solar photovoltaic systems have emerged as the leading renewable energy technology following decades of attractive feed-in tariffs and subsi dies representing 11 per cent of overall Australian electricity generation[3] Australia's high solar and wind potential, coupled with its comparatively plentiful land base, has made onshore renewable energy the most technically and financially feasible decarbonisation choice.

Australia holds substantial offshore wind resources comparable to leading offshore wind regions, like the North Sea, with the ability to support an estimated 5,000 GW of power.[4] In 2021, Australia established its first offshore electricity regulatory framework,

*The author acknowledges the tradition of custodianship and law of the Country on which the Macquarie University campuses stand. She pays her respects to Elders past, present and emerging and to those who have cared and continue to care for Country and acknowledges that sovereignty was never ceded. The analysis within this chapter is current up to August 2024.

[1] As mandated by the Climate Change Act 2022 (Cth). (Cth) represents Commonwealth level legislation.

[2] Clean Energy Council. 'Clean Energy Australia' (2024) assets.cleanenergycouncil.org.au/documents/resources/reports/clean-energy-australia/Clean-Energy-Australia-2024.pdf, 9.

[3] Clean Energy Council. 'Clean Energy Australia' (2024) assets.cleanenergycouncil.org.au/documents/resources/reports/clean-energy-australia/Clean-Energy-Australia-2024.pdf.

[4] NOPSEMA, 'Offshore Wind Energy' (2021) www.nopsema.gov.au/sites/default/files/2021-11/Offshore%20wind%20energy%20brochure_0.pdf.

the Offshore Electricity Infrastructure Act 2021 (Cth) (OEI Act) to provide the foundations for an offshore wind sector.[5] Australia does not hold federal offshore wind targets or commitments. However, six priority assessment areas for offshore wind in Commonwealth offshore areas off Victoria,[6] New South Wales, Victoria, Tasmania, and Western Australia have been identified with at least 12 offshore wind farms likely to apply for preliminary feasibility licences.[7]

In 2022, Australia announced its first offshore wind priority area in Gippsland to commence its offshore wind development journey.[8] This first offshore wind zone attracted 37 feasibility licence applications, with six provisional feasibility licences awarded, representing 12 GW of electricity generation and illustrating the appetite for an emerging Australian offshore wind sector.[9] In 2024, the last of the six priority areas for offshore wind was declared in Bunbury, Western Australia, and Illawarra, New South Wales (NSW).[10] While there are several offshore wind projects currently in planning and pre-feasibility discussions, the first six feasibility licences were recently awarded in the Gippsland offshore wind zone representing a major step to developing the first offshore wind project in Australian waters.[11]

Enabling offshore wind requires more than a technological shift.[12] While offshore wind developers are generally located to encourage minimal or no visual and noise impacts compared to onshore wind, offshore wind also requires analysis of technical, social, economic, and legal factors to ensure its ongoing success.[13] The recent reduction of Victoria's second offshore wind zone, the Southern Ocean Wind Zone, in March 2024 represents the turning tide of public attitudes potentially putting Australia's future offshore wind plans at risk. The Southern Ocean Wind Zone, previously

[5] This includes wind-generated waves; tides; ocean currents; light or heat from the sun; rain; and the scope to extend the scope of the legislation to any other resource, event or circumstance prescribed by the regulations pursuant to the Offshore Electricity Infrastructure Act 2021 (Cth) Offshore Electricity Infrastructure Regulations 2022 (Cth).

[6] In the absence of a federal offshore wind policy or target, the state of Victoria has to date been the most ambitious in its offshore wind policy targeting 2 GW of offshore wind capacity by 2032, 4 GW by 2035, and 9 GW by 2040.

[7] The six identified offshore wind areas are: Gippsland, Victoria; Hunter, New South Wales; Southern Ocean, Victoria/South Australia; Illawarra, New South Wales; Bass Strait, Tasmania; and Perth/Bunbury, Western Australia. Australian Government, 'Wind Energy' (2024) www.globalaustralia.gov.au/industries/net-zero/wind-energy.

[8] Offshore Electricity Infrastructure (Declared Area OEI-01-2022) Declaration 2022 (Cth).

[9] Australian Government, Gippsland, 'Victoria declared offshore wind area' (2023) www.dcceew.gov.au/energy/renewable/offshore-wind/areas/gippsland.

[10] Australian Government, 'Indian Ocean off the Bunbury region, Western Australia proposed offshore wind area' (2024) www.dcceew.gov.au/energy/renewable/offshore-wind/areas/bunbury.

[11] The feasibility licences were granted or offered to: High Sea Wind Pty Ltd; Gippsland Skies Pty Ltd; Blue Mackerel North Pty Ltd; Kut-Wut Brataualung Pty Ltd; Ørsted Offshore Australia 1 Pty Ltd (Gippsland 01); and Star of the South Wind Farm Pty Ltd.

[12] Chloe S Fleming, Sarah Ball Gonyo, Amy Freitag and Theresa L Goedeke, 'Engaged minority or quiet majority? Social intentions and actions related to offshore wind energy development in the United States' (2022) 84 *Energy Research and Social science*, 102440; Hideaki Obane, Yu Nagai and Kenji Asano, 'Assessing the potential areas for developing offshore wind energy in Japanese territorial waters considering national zoning and possible social conflicts' (2021) 129 *Marine Policy*, 104514.

[13] Benjamin Sovacool, Hans Lindbow and Ole Odgaard, 'Is the Danish Wind Energy Model Replicable for Other Countries?' (2008) 21 *The Electricity Journal* 27–38.

mapped across the Victorian and South Australian marine space representing 14.6 GW, was reduced by 80 per cent due to vocal opposition concerning marine biodiversity protection lowering capacity to 2.9 GW. This chapter builds on the need to consider new 'renewable energy landscapes'[14] by probing regulations and policies in the new Australian offshore wind landscape and whether they are sufficient to engage with mitigating social gaps.

Defining and applying socio-legal conceptualisations to the emerging Australian offshore wind sector is critical to understanding risks, benefits, and opportunities for reform.[15] The experience of the onshore wind sector has proven the importance of attaining a social licence to operate (SLO) and broader social contract. In Victoria, the state which also hopes to lead Australia in offshore wind development, ambitious targets to reach 2 GW of offshore generation capacity by 2032, 4 GW by 2035, and 9 GW by 2040[16] has led to a recent shift in policy to accelerate onshore infrastructure supporting offshore wind within a new Development Facilitation Programme.[17] This programme will be similar to the EU Renewables Directive measures to accelerate renewable energy deployment by fast-tracking construction and removing the planning panel process including third-party appeal rights for communities in some circumstances[18] leading to heightened community concerns and may create a new SLO flashpoint in Australia.

This chapter aims to provide the first analysis of 'social gaps' within the emerging Australian offshore wind regulatory framework to create a foundation for the broader social contract between State, offshore wind proponents, and communities. In so doing, it outlines a comparative analysis of differing socio-legal approaches to addressing these social gaps across several mature offshore wind jurisdictions highlighting areas for legal reform within Australia's OEI Act regulatory framework.

The chapter is structured in six key parts. It begins by discussing the concepts of SLO and the social contract in Australia's offshore energy transition, introducing the 'social gap' framework. It then systematically applies the three key principles to close 'social gaps' by examining the need for reform to address democratic deficit; legal conditions; and place protections. Finally, the chapter concludes by highlighting the importance of addressing the tension between the regulatory aim of expediting offshore wind development and maintaining a sustained social contract alongside community objectives and benefits. The chapter exposes the urgency for a significant regulatory reappraisal of the current licensing and management plan assessment approach. As examined within this

[14] Dean Apostol, James Palmer, Martin Pasqualetti, Richard Smardon and Robert Sullivan (eds), *The Renewable Energy Landscape* (Routledge, 2016).

[15] Ignacio Herrera Anchustegui and Tina Soliman Hunter (eds), *Offshore Wind Licensing* (Edward Elgar Publishing, 2024); Madeline Taylor and Riley Taylor, 'Planning for Offshore Wind Energy: The Case for Marine Spatial Planning in Australia' (2022) *Oil, Gas & Energy Law* 1–23.

[16] Victorian Government, 'Offshore Wind Energy' (2024) www.energy.vic.gov.au/renewable-energy/offshore-wind-energy.

[17] Victorian Government, 'Development Facilitation Program' (2024) www.planning.vic.gov.au/planning-approvals/planning-enquiries-and-requests/development-facilitation-program#:~:text=The%20Development%20Facilitation%20Program%20%28DFP%29%20is%20an%20accelerated,people%20in%20jobs%20and%20create%20homes%20for%20people.

[18] Directive (EU) 2023/2413 of the European Parliament and of the Council, Article 44.

chapter, this points to a need for 'social gaps' to be understood, assessed, and addressed for Australia to reach its offshore wind ambitions.

2. From the Social Licence to Operate to the Social Contract: Addressing 'Social Gaps' in the Australian Offshore Energy Transition

The concept of the SLO in the context of onshore mining and energy development is not new. The SLO concept was coined in the late 1970s and holds its origins in addressing social fragmentation from onshore mining development. Fundamentally, the SLO is steeped in the acknowledgment of local community acceptance as critical to the long-term viability of development.[19] The SLO paradigm is authoritatively defined by Boutilier and Thomson as 'the ongoing acceptance and approval of an operation by those local communities affected by it and those stakeholders who can affect its profitability'.[20] As a new energy technology entrant in Australia, the offshore wind regulatory regime requires must address social gaps.[21]

In contrast to the legal licences[22] issued between the State and energy proponents to explore, develop, and eventually decommission operations, the SLO seeks to enable communities to co-design, influence decision-making, and potentially prescribe community 'conditions' for energy proponents to attain the SLO. Forrester et al acknowledge 'to ignore social licence is to risk project delays, project failure as some communities acquire de facto veto rights, increasing costs, and reputational risk that hinders the ability of a developer to attract skilled workers and even financial capital'.[23] In a socio-legal analysis of offshore energy development, 'contestation gives rise to the need for States and companies to attain a social licence, in addition to a legal State licence, to operate'.[24] This twin necessity for both legal licensing regimes and meeting SLO conditions is particularly evident when establishing new regulatory frameworks for emerging energy technological entrants, such as offshore wind.

To achieve ongoing acceptance and approval by communities and stakeholders, the pyramid structure of the SLO devised by Boutilier and Thomson is often cited. The SLO pyramid is illustrated in Figure 1 below by outlining four key levels

[19] Geoffrey Wood, Jędrzej Górski and Gokce Mete, *The Palgrave Handbook of Social License to Operate and Energy Transitions* (Springer, 2022).

[20] Robert Boutilier and Ian Thomson, 'Modelling and Measuring the Social License to Operate: Fruits of a Dialogue between Theory and Practice' (2011) www.socialicense.com/publications/Modelling%20and%20Measuring%20the%20SLO.pdf.

[21] Natasha Larkin, Chantel Carr and Natacha Klocker, 'Building an offshore wind sector in Australia: economic opportunities and constraints at the regional scale' (2024) 55 *Australian Geographer* 45–68.

[22] For a detailed discussion on offshore wind licensing systems and regulation please see Herrera Anchustegui and Soliman Hunter (n 15).

[23] Peter Forrester, Kent Howie and Alan Ross, 'Energy Superpower in Waiting: New Pipeline Development in Canada, Social Licence, and Recent Federal Energy Reforms' (2015) 53 *Alberta Law Review* 419, 426.

[24] Madeline Taylor and Tina Hunter, *Agricultural Land Use and Natural Gas Extraction Conflicts: A Global Socio-Legal Perspective* (Routledge, 2019) 4.

of SLO: (1) withheld/withdrawn; (2) acceptance; (3) approval; and (4) psychological identification. Community trust is established at level (3) associated with social approval with (4) psychological identification as the highest form of SLO.[25] Rather than adopting the SLO hierarchy, this chapter applies the 'social gaps' framework. The social gaps framework is critical to provide baseline social impacts and benefits before the upscaling of new energy technology entrants. In contrast, the SLO model is typically applied to incumbent and existing onshore and offshore energy developments and is often understood as a hierarchical process moving through each of the four levels.

Understanding 'social gaps' is particularly essential in developing new sectors facing technical complexities, unknown risks, and community empowerment moving beyond the SLO concept to create a tripartite social contract between the State, energy proponents, and communities. As argued by de Fontenelle, 'the social contract raises questions about the distribution of roles and responsibilities, the sharing of choices, and solidarity between actors … in setting the direction for the development of energy as a whole'.[26] Understanding these 'social gaps' is crucial to creating co-benefits and sustained benefits beyond communities and the offshore wind sector, as is the focus of the SLO concept, but amongst the trilateral relationship of the State, energy proponents, and communities in the social contract. These social gaps and comparative socio-legal approaches are analysed within this chapter relevant to Australia's offshore wind regulatory framework: (1) *Democratic deficits* in the OEI Act consultation provisions, the rights of Native Title holders in the Native Title Act 1993 (Cth); (2) *Legal conditions* relating to community cooperatives and social impact assessments; and (3) *Place protection* activated by social and environmental regulations within Marine Spatial Planning.

Figure 1 below outlines the three 'social gaps': democratic deficit; legal conditions; and place protection applied as preliminary conditions to achieve the stages of the SLO pyramid between proponents and communities, and ultimately, the social contract between the State, proponents, and communities.[27]

This chapter seeks to fill the evident gap in existing research examining Australia's offshore wind potential by providing a socio-legal lens. As confirmed by Pasqualetti et al to date '[t]he social barriers to renewable energy have been underappreciated and underexamined' in regulation, particularly in regards to offshore renewable energy.[28] In so doing, this chapter provides the first examination of social gaps in Australia's current offshore wind regulatory framework providing pragmatic recommendations for reform representing a foundation for Australia's offshore wind sector.

[25] Boutilier and Thomson (n 20) 2.

[26] Louis de Fontenelle, 'Energy Justice and the Social Contract Theory' in Raphael J Heffron and Louis de Fontenelle, *The Power of Energy Justice & The Social Contract* (Palgrave, 2024) 9–13.

[27] Justine Penneman, Astrid Buchmayr, Luc Van Ootegem and Elsy Verhofstadt, 'The evolution of the pre- and post-construction public opinions toward offshore wind energy on the Belgian coast' (2022) 66 *Journal of Environmental Planning and Management* 2536–55; Benjamin Walker, Bouke Wiersma and Etienne Bailey, 'Community benefits, framing and the social acceptance of offshore wind farms: An experimental study in England' (2014) 3 *Energy Research & Social Science* 46–54.

[28] Martin Pasqualetti, 'Social Barriers to Renewable Energy Landscapes' (2011) *Geographical Review* 101, 219.

Figure 1 Social Licence to Operate Pyramid, The Social Contract, and Preliminary 'Social Gaps' Framework

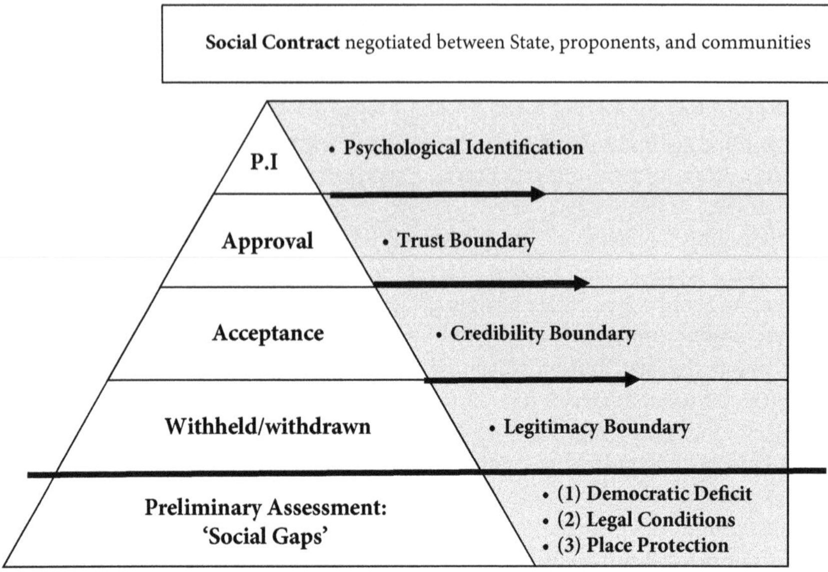

Source: Authors' own adapted from Joel Gehman, Lianne Lefsrud, and Stewart Fast, 'Social license to operate: Legitimacy by another name?' (2017) 60 *Canadian Public Administration*, 293–17, 296, onlinelibrary.wiley.com/doi/pdf/10.1111/capa.12218.

3. *Addressing Democratic Deficit:* Community Consultation and Empowerment

Community consultation literature examining offshore wind is 'fragmented' at best and focuses largely on mature offshore wind jurisdictions such as Belgium,[29] Denmark,[30] the UK[31] and the USA. As examined by Wiersma and Devine-Wright, an important yet often unacknowledged distinction exists between onshore and offshore consultation activities due to lower levels of public knowledge; differing visual impacts; marine spatial contexts; and different sets of stakeholders in decision-making.[32]

As originally highlighted in Arnstein's Ladder of Citizen Participation, participation requires redistribution of power to citizens and various levels of participation to the top ladder rung of citizen control whereby powers are afforded to community members.[33]

[29] Penneman, Buchmayr, Van Ootegem and Verhofstadt (n 27).
[30] Julia le Maitre, 'Price or public participation? Community benefits for onshore wind in Ireland, Denmark, Germany and the United Kingdom' (2024) 114 *Energy Research and Social Science* 103605.
[31] Walker, Wiersma and Bailey (n 27) 46–64.
[32] Bouke Wiersma and Patrick Devine-Wright, 'Public engagement with offshore renewable energy: a critical review' (2014) 5 *WIREs Climate Change* 493–507.
[33] Sherry R Arnstein, 'A Ladder of Citizen Participation' (2019) 85(1) *Journal of the American Planning Association* 24–34.

Consequently, citizen participation moves beyond consultation, which can be interpreted as tokenism, to citizen empowerment through community delegated power, control, partnership, and social contract. Community empowerment is not a panacea to ensure 'social gaps' addressed. However, a key pillar of any public resource system is diminishing competition and conflict with communities by managing and allocating resources in the public interest within the social contract paradigm for economic gain.[34] Despite this, no clear social impacts, benefits, and participation policy exists in the Australian offshore wind context and the existing OEI Framework requires consultation only rather than participation.[35]

Offshore energy development in Australia is regulated at a federal level where activities take place in Australian Commonwealth waters. Australian Commonwealth waters are defined as three nautical miles from the relevant state and territory coastline to 200 nautical miles from the coastline (the outer limit of the Exclusive Economic Zone) and the continental shelf extending beyond the 200 nm limit of the EEZ.[36] The OEI Act provides the framework for the grant of offshore licences in Commonwealth offshore areas meaning the seabed and subsoil beneath those areas: (a) the territorial sea of Australia; (b) the exclusive economic zone; but does not include the coastal waters of a State or the Northern Territory.[37] This starkly contrasts with onshore energy development which incorporates the 'cooperative federalism'[38] paradigm whereby states and territories regulate onshore energy development and licensing activities due to constitutional limitations.[39]

The definitions of 'communities' and 'consultation' are also absent within the OEI Act. However, the Australian Energy Infrastructure Commissioner (AEIC) recommends consultation with specific sectoral stakeholders, for example, fisheries, oil and gas, maritime defence, carbon capture, tourism and shipping, and the broader community hosting offshore wind and transmission infrastructure including First Nations communities.[40] The quantity and quality of community consultation are expected to vary on a project by project basis without any mandatory community stakeholders defined within the OEI framework.

The current OEI framework encompasses two key areas of wider community consultation at the federal level. First, during the Ministerial offshore wind zone declaration and second, during the exhibition of the management plan. In undertaking community consultation, the Australian government first conducts a preliminary

[34] Taylor and Hunter (n 24).

[35] It must be noted the OEI framework is currently incomplete with several regulations still under development including the environmental regulations supplementing the OEI Act. The latest draft regulation is the Offshore Electricity Infrastructure Amendment Regulations 2024 (Cth) which spans workplace health and safety, management plan requirements, consultation requirements amongst other requirements if enacted.

[36] Donne Wagemans, Christian Scholl and Veronique Vasseur, 'Facilitating the Energy Transition – The Governance Role of Local Renewable Energy Cooperatives' (2019) 12 *Energies* 4171.

[37] Offshore Electricity Infrastructure Act 2021 (Cth), s 8.

[38] Lee Godden and Anne Kallies, 'Governance of the Energy Market in Australia' in Michael Faure (ed), *Elgar Encyclopedia of Environmental Law* (Edward Elgar Publishing, 2021) 208.

[39] Commonwealth of Australia Constitution Acct 1977 (Cth).

[40] AIEC, 'Considerations for Offshore Wind Industry on Community Engagement' (2023) www.aeic.gov.au/sites/default/files/documents/2023-10/aeic-considerations-offshore-wind-industry-community-engagement.pdf, 7.

assessment and the relevant energy Minister declares a notice of proposal to declare a suitable area for offshore wind. The declared area is subject to public submission for at least 60 days[41] after which a proposed area is declared. In deciding on whether a declared area is suitable for offshore renewable energy infrastructure, pursuant to section 19 of the OEI Act, the Minister must have regard, amongst other matters,[42] to the potential impacts: (a) of the construction, installation, commissioning, operation, maintenance, or decommissioning of offshore renewable energy infrastructure in the area on other marine users and interests; and (b) any submissions as a result of public consultation and any other matters the minister considers relevant. Second, public exhibition and consultation on the proponent's management plan provide the second avenue for wider public engagement and participation pursuant to Division 2 of the OEI Act and Division 2 of the proposed draft Offshore Electricity Infrastructure Amendment Regulations 2024 (Cth)[43] amending the current Offshore Electricity Infrastructure Regulations 2022 (Cth).

The management plan and all other offshore wind licensing in Australia take place under a discretionary licensing system empowering the Minister to grant licences based on discretionary merit criteria.[44] The draft Offshore Electricity Infrastructure Amendment Regulations 2024 (Cth) requires proponents to provide a description of how the offshore infrastructure project is or will contribute to the Australian economy and local communities including in relation to regional development and job creation.[45] This proposed amendment may see the development of potential local content plans as part of the assessment process by the Minister to grant a commercial licence and will likely require further community consultation to identify local content opportunities. Once the commercial licence for an offshore wind project has been granted under section 42 of the OEI Act, no further opportunities for ongoing community consultation appear evident.

The OEI Act is consequently focused on providing community consultation through submissions in both the declaration and management plan stages, rather than engagement and participation from the community at the outset during the design and mapping phase of offshore wind zones. For example, public submissions are not invited until the pre-declaration phase whereby the Minister has declared a proposed offshore area. Following this submission process for a period of at least 60 days, the Minister may, but is not compelled to, amend the proposed offshore declared area.

Consultation is then required at the feasibility and planning stage in relation to planning and other environmental approvals with 'co-users of the licence area who

[41] Offshore Electricity Infrastructure Act 2021 (Cth), s 18.

[42] See Offshore Electricity Infrastructure Act 2021 (Cth), s 19 for the additional matters the Minister must have regard to.

[43] The Draft Regulations are modelled on Well Operations Management Plans for Offshore oil and gas development pursuant to the Offshore Petroleum and Greenhouse Gas Storage (Resource Management and Administration) Regulations 2011 (Cth).

[44] Herrera Anchustegui and Soliman Hunter (n 15).

[45] Offshore Electricity Infrastructure Amendment Regulations 2024 (Cth), proposed s 33(4)(d).

may be directly impacted by any potential offshore wind infrastructure projects'.[46] The methods, measures, and quality of what constitutes community consultation are not part of the offshore wind licensing merit criteria. This is because the basis of offshore wind licences as part of the Australian discretionary system is largely based on the technical and financial capability to undertake the proposed project, for the Minister to consider granting feasibility, commercial, research and development, or transmission and infrastructure licence.[47] The Minister *may* optionally consider community interests when considering whether a proposed project is in the national interest:

> The project's impact on, and contribution to, the Australian economy and local communities, including in relation to regional development, job creation, Australian industries, and the use of Australian goods and services.[48]

The project's impact and construction on local communities are currently not a mandatory consideration for the award of offshore wind feasibility or commercial licences by the State.

Within the Australian offshore wind licensing process, the key instrument for assessment in offshore wind licence applications is the management plan. The development and approval of a management plan is a condition for commercial licence awards,[49] which will cover the operation, management, health, safety, decommissioning, and environmental impact mitigation of the proposed project. A management plan will be required following the grant of a feasibility licence for the installation of any fixed and tethered infrastructure and a separate management plan for the management of the commercial project prior to an application for a commercial licence.[50] The outcomes of pre-management plan consultation and feedback received as part of the offshore wind zone declaration process are not mandatory considerations in the assessment and approval of the management plan.[51]

The Minister may also require a feasibility licenceholder seeking to apply for a commercial licence to undertake 'specified kinds of consultation'.[52] It is unclear whether communities will be consulted once a management plan is approved and during the commercial licence application phase, and whether consultation is required during the decommissioning phase of a project. In addition to the need for community consultation definitions and methodologies under the OEI Act, one critically important area of community engagement deficit is engagement with Australia's Aboriginal and Torres Strait Islander communities as examined in the remainder of section 3 of this chapter.

[46] AIEC, 'Considerations for Offshore Wind Industry on Community Engagement' (2023) www.aeic.gov.au/sites/default/files/documents/2023-10/aeic-considerations-offshore-wind-industry-community-engagement.pdf, 11.

[47] Offshore Electricity Infrastructure Act 2021 (Cth), Subdivision B.

[48] Offshore Electricity Infrastructure Regulations 2022 (Cth), s 26(4)(a).

[49] Offshore Electricity Infrastructure Act 2021 (Cth), ss 31(1)(a), 40 (1)(a).

[50] AIEC, 'Considerations for Offshore Wind Industry on Community Engagement' (2023) www.aeic.gov.au/sites/default/files/documents/2023-10/aeic-considerations-offshore-wind-industry-community-engagement.pdf, 11.

[51] Offshore Electricity Infrastructure Act 2021 (Cth), s 115(2)(f).

[52] Offshore Electricity Infrastructure Act 20211 (Cth), s 43.

A. Native Title Rights Offshore

In Australia, the protection and recognition of native title rights[53] and interests are recognised by the common law adopted within the Native Title Act 1993 (Cth) (NTA). First established in *Mabo v Queensland (No 2)*,[54] native title is the post-colonial recognition of rights and interests for Aboriginal and Torres Strait Islanders and the rejection of the myth of *terra nullius* – that is, that Australia was unoccupied or uninhabited at the time of British colonisation. Native title does not constitute the recognition of sovereignty in Aboriginal peoples. Unlike other Commonwealth states, such as Canada and New Zealand, Australia does not hold a treaty system. The native title regime does not recognise the existence of Aboriginal and Torres Strait Islander pre-existing laws and customs. In broad terms, the NTA seeks to enforce and protect native title rights by protecting these rights from extinguishment.[55] Native title is defined pursuant to section 223(1) of the NTA as:

> The communal, group, or individual rights and interests of Aboriginal peoples or Torres Strait Islanders in relation to land or *waters*, where:
>
> (a) the rights and interests are possessed under the traditional laws acknowledged, and the traditional customs observed, by the Aboriginal peoples or Torres Strait Islanders; and
>
> (b) the Aboriginal peoples or Torres Strait Islanders, by those laws and customs, have a connection with the land or waters; and
>
> (c) the rights and interests are recognised by the common law of Australia (emphasis added).

Offshore wind electricity infrastructure will be located onshore. Consequently, the interface between Sea Country and coastal management and Native Title land rights will be deeply interlinked. As argued by Hunter et al, as Native Title rights are linked from sea to land, a Cultural Licence to Operate framework is required 'for creating the ecosystem for an ethical, equitable, dynamic, and responsive system in which negotiations are customised at place'.[56] The Cultural Licence can be enforced where native title exclusive possession rights at sea or on land are afforded. Hunter et al recommend key principles to create a Cultural Licence to Operate and drive co-benefits for First Nations Communities including legislative requirements to create co-benefits for First Nations communities in the development of the Blue Economy.[57]

Native title recognition requires the establishment of laws and customs with the land or waters Aboriginal peoples, or Torres Strait Islanders, where native title rights over waters are recognised by the common law through court determination[58] or limited statutory water use rights. For example, fishing 'to satisfy their personal, domestic, or

[53] This chapter does not engage with First Nations concepts of Sea Country, Songlines, and other critically important First Nations concepts. Please see the research of Jodi Edwards and other First Nations Scholars for expert treatment of these concepts.

[54] (1992) 175 CLR 1.

[55] Native Title Act 1993 (Cth) Division 1.

[56] C Hunter, E Lee, W Wood, A Marsh and M Fischere, 'Cultural Licence to Operate in the Blue Economy' *Final Project Report* (Blue Economy Cooperative Research Centre, 2024), blueeconomycrc.com.au/wp-content/uploads/2024/05/BECRC_CLTO-Report_A4_S_e290524.pdf.

[57] ibid.

[58] Native Title court determinations are made pursuant to Native Title Act 1993 (Cth), s 255.

non-commercial communal needs, and in exercise or enjoyment of their native title rights and interests'[59] is a communal or group right vested in a body corporate and would be recognised as a native title right over waters.[60]

Native title rights over waters are non-exclusive. The case of *Commonwealth v Yarmirr*[61] recognised non-exclusive native title rights and interests within Australia's territorial sea extending to 12 nautical miles. This is because exclusive native title rights in the territorial sea would be inconsistent with the Crown's prerogative rights and sovereignty over its territorial sea pursuant to The United Nations Convention on the Law of the Sea 1982.[62] Beyond the territorial sea, section 6 of the NTA confirms its application to 'each external Territory, to the coastal sea of Australia and of each external Territory, and to any waters over which Australia asserts sovereign rights'. Native title in the EEZ is an area over which Australia asserts sovereign rights and could be recognised by the common law.[63] This principle was laid out by Justice Finn in *Akiba v Queensland (No 2)*[64] who further argued that native title could potentially extend rights over sea territories outside areas where Australia has not previously asserted sovereignty as:

> It would be anomalous and unprincipled, in my view, for the common law to require an Aboriginal or Islander society to be faithful to their laws and customs from the time sovereignty was first acquired … but to refuse to acknowledge a subsequent accretion to those rights and interests in an area not hitherto the subject of Australian territorial sovereignty.[65]

Munkara v Santos NA Barossa Pty Ltd (No 3)[66] recently confirmed intangible cultural heritage could be recognised in areas of Sea Country. *Munkara* concerned an injunction application to prevent the construction of a proposed offshore gas pipeline in the Barossa Gas Field which was alleged to impact spiritual connection to Sea Country by interrupting song lines or interfering with the travels of ancestral beings.[67] Although the injunction application was unsuccessful, the Federal Court acknowledged intangible cultural heritage through traditional cultural beliefs may be examined as potential environmental risks to be mapped and mitigated for the purpose of an offshore gas infrastructure petroleum environmental plan. Similar arguments may surface for offshore wind exploration and development activities, including subsea cabling infrastructure.

The uncertainty over native title rights beyond traditional and cultural water rights extending to commercial rights, like offshore wind development, is likely to remain.[68] As argued by Macpherson concerning onshore waters, there is likely limited potential for native title rights to extend to commercial water rights in the future 'because native

[59] Native Title Act 1993 (Cth), s 211(2)–(3).
[60] Native Title Act 1993 (Cth) 1993, s 224.
[61] (2001) 208 CLR 1.
[62] As reproduced in the Schedule to the Seas and Submerged Lands Act 1973 (Cth).
[63] Melissa Perry and Stephen Lloyd, *Australian Native Title Law*, 2nd edn (Thompson Reuters, 2018).
[64] (2010) 204 FCR 1.
[65] *Akiba v Queensland (No 2)* (2010) 204 FCR 1 [736]–[738].
[66] [2024] FCA 9.
[67] [2024] FCA 9 [71].
[68] Samantha Hepburn, 'Native Title Rights in the Territorial Sea and Beyond: Exclusivity and Commerce in the Akiba Decision' (2011) 34(1) *University of New South Wales Law Journal* 159–81.

title recognises traditional, or pre-sovereignty, interests. If indigenous rights to water are to be provided for in Australia for cultural and commercial purposes alike, this is most probably (and effectively) to be achieved alongside, but outside of, the limited native title recognition model'.[69] Further, section 223(1)(c) of the NTA does not allow water ownership as native title rights must be recognised by the common law which does not currently permit water ownership in its natural state.[70] As ownership cannot be conferred over Commonwealth marine waters, native title rights over offshore waters cannot be exclusive rights as that would be inconsistent with the legislative vesting of the right to control and use Commonwealth marine waters.

The fundamental hurdle remains for Traditional Owners to prove the content of pre-sovereignty traditional laws and customs over 200 years since colonisation in order for native title to be acknowledged. This continuality is a key component to acknowledging native title over land and water.[71] It is particularly difficult to provide the continuity of traditional laws and customs over offshore waters which have been used for defence, commercial, tourism, and other purposes. As famously argued by Marshall, *Aqua Nullius*[72] has unjustly been applied in Australia as an obstacle to the economic and commercial rights over land and waters. Statutory allocation of the right to use water for commercial purposes has been effectively argued by Macpherson in the onshore water context.[73] Such statutory allocation will be an important future research agenda for offshore wind and native title rights offshore.

Native title rights in offshore areas are also confirmed in the procedural and compensation rights for 'future acts'[74] being those that affect native title and set the standards for those dealings including compliance with the 'right to negotiate'. The right to negotiate represents a statutory right to negotiate in good faith to obtain an agreement between the proponent and Traditional Owners.[75] In relation to offshore energy activities, and specifically offshore wind, the OEI Act[76] recognises a strict offence whereby a licence holder or a person carrying out activities on behalf of a licence holder interferes with the exercise of native title rights and interests.[77] This strict offence holds the caveat of being breached where interference with native title rights is greater than is necessary

[69] Elizabeth Macpherson, *Indigenous Water Rights in Law and Regulation* (Cambridge University Press, 2019) 50.

[70] *ICM Agriculture v The Commonwealth* [2009] 240 CLR 140.

[71] *Mabo* (1992) 175 CLR 1, 60 (Brennan J).

[72] Virginia Marshall, *Overturning Aqua Nullius: Securing Aboriginal Water Rights* (Aboriginal Studies Press, 2017).

[73] Macpherson (n 70) 49–98.

[74] Native Title Act 1993 (Cth), s 24NA.

[75] Native Title Act 1993 (Cth), Pt 2, Div 3.

[76] The Underwater Cultural Heritage Act 2018 (Cth) and the Environment Protection and Biodiversity Conservation Act 1999 (Cth) will also likely be triggered as Aboriginal cultural heritage and Indigenous values may coincide with 'matters of national environmental significance' in World Heritage Properties. However, the interaction of the federal environmental regime, underwater cultural heritage, and native title is beyond the scope of this chapter. See Emily Gerrard, 'First Nations Clean Energy Network Summary of key legislation applying to offshore renewable development areas' (2023) assets.nationbuilder.com/fncen/pages/310/attachments/original/1691038043/Summary_of_key_legislation_applying_to_offshore_renewable_development_areas_August_2023.pdf?1691038043.

[77] Offshore Electricity Infrastructure Act 2021 (Cth), s 78(1)(c)(ii) and s 77.

for the reasonable exercise of rights within the relevant licence or the performance of licence obligations.

This raises the question of what can be considered 'reasonable' and 'necessary' when interfering with native title rights and interests offshore for the development of offshore electricity resources. Both terms are not defined within the OEI Act. Defining such interference and what is acceptable as reasonable will thus be critical during consultation and engagement with native titleholders before offshore wind development. Without adequate consultation, offshore energy developments may be stalled or face litigation, as has recently been experienced in offshore petroleum.

B. The *Tipakalippa* Decision: A Turning Point for Native Title Consultation in Offshore Energy Development?

The recent *Santos NA Barossa Pty Ltd v Tipakalippa*[78] decision provides a cautionary decision on offshore petroleum development over the failure to adequately consult with traditional owners. The case concerned a Munupi Senior Lawman and Tiwi Traditional Owner Dennis Tipakalippa who argued that the traditional owners of Sea Country in the area were not adequately consulted. The Tiwi Island traditional owners alleged NOPSEMA, the federal petroleum regulator, could not be 'reasonably satisfied' that the petroleum titleholder had carried out consultations with 'every relevant persons' in drilling environmental plans for the sinking of eight wells in Barossa gas field within the environmental plan process.[79]

The Federal Court of Australia helpfully defined consultation in the native title context as 'consultation, it is intended that the titleholder provide "sufficient information to allow" the affected authorities, organisations and individuals "to make an informed assessment of the possible consequences" of the proposed activity … It is also intended that the consultation be genuine, in that the affected authorities, organisations and individuals are required to be given a "reasonable period" for the consultation, that is, a reasonable time to identify the effect of the proposed activity on their functions, interests or activities'.[80] As the petroleum licence holder sent information to the native titleholders as 'an email with a package of information'[81] without any follow up consultation within a 'reasonable period', this rendered their consultation unsatisfactory.

Significantly, the decision was the first successful legal challenge to an offshore energy project due to consultation inadequacy. As a result, NOPSEMA's approval of the environmental plan was rendered invalid. Similar arguments may be raised in the offshore wind context where licence holders do not adequately consult native title holders, particularly in the context of their management plans which also require environmental impact assessments according to the OEI Act. Following the *Tipakalippa* decision, the federal

[78] [2022] FCAFC 193.

[79] As required by Division 2.2A of the Offshore Petroleum and Greenhouse Gas Storage (Environment) Regulations 2009 (Cth).

[80] [2022] FCAFC 193 [56].

[81] [2022] FCAFC 193 [94].

Australian government has recently launched a review of the offshore environment management framework for offshore petroleum to ensure it is 'fit for purpose in a decarbonising economy'[82] within the Protecting the Spirit of Sea Country Bill 2023 (Cth).

The Protecting the Spirit of Sea Country Bill 2023 (Cth) is currently being proposed to amend the Australian Offshore Petroleum and Greenhouse Gas Storage Act 2006 (Cth) and introduce the requirement for the free, prior, and informed consent of traditional owners as a condition of acceptance of an offshore petroleum or greenhouse gas storage environment plan.[83] If adopted, the Protecting the Spirit of Sea Country Bill is likely to provide targeted regulatory reform on clarifying consultation requirements for offshore petroleum and greenhouse gas storage regulatory approvals, pointing to the need for consultation reform in the OEI Act when engaging with Traditional Owners. The OEI Act must take into account the design and implementation of consultation specific to offshore electricity projects, particularly, offshore wind about culturally appropriate consultation with Aboriginal and Torres Strait Islander communities and clarifying potential effects of offshore wind operations including subsea cabling, transmission infrastructure onshore, and the co-location with traditional fishing grounds. The right to free, prior, and informed consent of traditional owners must also be critically inserted in the OEI Act to de-risk community engagement. Prescribing legal conditions to encourage community ownership and the mapping of social impacts and benefits is another critical pathway to ensuring a social contract in the offshore wind context as explored below in section 4 of this chapter.

4. *Creating Legal Conditions*: Citizens Cooperatives and Social Impact Assessments

The 'energy quadrilemma'[84] adds the fourth element of social dimensions to the traditional World Energy Trilemma Framework balance of energy security, energy equity and environmental sustainability.[85] In the offshore wind context, energy justice, representing the fourth energy quadrilemma pillar, has been applied to offshore wind to expose regulatory reform roadmaps, particularly concerning community benefit sharing.[86] Energy justice is concerned with creating just and equitable energy development decision-making by 'providing a guiding framework to create and recognise processes and functions governing diverse sectors and societal actors'.[87] Energy justice

[82] Australian Government, 'Offshore petroleum and greenhouse gas storage environmental management review' (2024) www.industry.gov.au/mining-oil-and-gas/oil-and-gas/offshore-oil-and-gas/offshore-petroleum-and-greenhouse-gas-storage-environmental-management-review.

[83] Protecting the Spirit of Sea Country Bill 2023 (Cth), s 782(2).

[84] Abdul Olabi, 'Energy Quadrilemma and the Future of Renewable Energy' (2016) 108 *Energy* 1, 2.

[85] World Energy Council, 'World Energy Trilemma Framework' (2023) www.worldenergy.org/transition-toolkit/world-energy-trilemma-index.

[86] Ignacio Herrera Anchustegui, 'Distributive justice, community benefits and renewable energy: the case of offshore wind projects' in Ruven Fleming, Kaisa Huhta and Leonie Reins, *Sustainable Energy Democracy and the Law* (Brill, 2021) 214–39.

[87] Madeline Taylor, Jordie Pettit, Takashi Sekiyama and Maciej Sokolowski, 'Justice-driven agrivoltaics: Facilitating agrivoltaics embedded in energy justice' (2023) 188 *Renewable and Sustainable Energy Reviews* 1–11, 2.

is often cited as comprising five key elements: distributive; procedural; recognition; cosmopolitanism; and restorative justice.[88] Building on the existing studies applying energy justice to offshore wind is the consideration of the principles of energy democracy acknowledging the 'increasing role of societal actors'[89] in the energy sector.

Energy democracy requires the exploration of alternative legal conditions to create active and ongoing community participation in energy development.[90] Such conditions may challenge existing energy systems requiring debate on the means of community engagement to explore innovative regulatory approaches and modes. For example, the EU has championed energy communities as part of larger reforms of its Clean Energy for All Europeans package in 2019 and again in 2023.[91] Developing energy community initiatives to empower energy communities remains largely unexplored in Australia. This represents a crucial opportunity to reform the OEI Act to integrate energy democracy into the Australian offshore wind sector. Section 4 of this chapter examines the potential of citizen cooperatives and social impact assessments as important tools and legal processes to create energy democracy in offshore wind development.

A. Enabling Citizens Cooperatives

Creating opportunities for community participation and ownership is a prevailing topic in energy law and democracy scholarship.[92] One mechanism for community ownership of energy projects is citizens cooperatives. Citizens cooperatives, as a sub-set of energy communities, stem from the socio-legal approach of forming a new 'commons' to allow for collective resource management.[93] As argued by Pappalardo, 'commons' resource management requires a resource material or immaterial), a community (commoners), and a practice of collective governance (communing).[94] Citizens cooperatives to manage and benefit from offshore wind 'commons' will require regulatory frameworks and potentially offshore wind licence conditions to allow 'commoners' to practice collective governance and potentially, ownership.

Citizens cooperatives are defined as 'autonomous associations of citizens who collaborate voluntarily to meet their common economic, social and cultural needs and aspirations through a system of businesses that are jointly owned and democratically controlled'.[95] Cooperatives are established based on the principles of democracy and

[88] Maciej Sokolowski and Madeline Taylor, 'Just energy business needed! How to achieve a just energy transition by engaging energy companies in reaching climate neutrality: (re)conceptualising energy law for energy corporations' (2023) *Journal of Energy and Natural Resources Law* 157–74.

[89] Kacper Szulecki, 'Conceptualizing energy democracy' (2018) 27 *Environmental Politics* 21, 23.

[90] Denise Fairchild and Al Weinrub, *Energy Democracy* (Springer, 2017).

[91] See Directive on common rules for the internal electricity market (EU/2019/944) and revised Directive (EU) 2023/2413 (Renewable Energy Directive).

[92] Frans HJM Coenen and Thomas Hoppe (eds), *Renewable Energy Communities and the Low Carbon Energy Transition in Europe* (Springer, 2022); Frédéric Wurtz, Gilles Debizet and Marta Pappalardo (eds), *Local Energy Communities Emergence, Places, Organizations, Decision Tools* (Taylor and Francis, 2022).

[93] Wurtz, Debizet and Pappalardo (n 93).

[94] Marta Pappalardo, 'Energy Communities and Commons' in Wurtz, Debizet and Pappalardo (n 93) 68.

[95] Romin Mauger, 'Making Sense of Changing Concepts for the Energy Transition' in Fleming, Huhta and Reins (n 87) 28–53.

transparency for their members typically stemming from the principle of one member equating to one vote in cooperative decision making.[96] Citizens cooperatives for onshore wind have been evident in Australia since Hepburn Wind was commissioned in 2005 representing the first community owned wind farm and currently providing 42 per cent of Hepburn Shire's energy needs.[97] Despite increasing attention on onshore energy citizens cooperatives,[98] existing studies do not explore the potential for offshore wind citizen cooperatives in Australia.

More mature offshore wind jurisdictions have taken a comparative citizen participation approach to offshore wind energy beyond traditional exhibition and public consultation requirements. Denmark provides one of the most prevalent examples of community ownership opportunities within offshore wind projects. Previously, section 13(1) of the Promotion of the Renewable Energy Act (DE) provided the option to purchase shares in an offshore wind project with guidance that each development is at least 20 per cent locally owned.[99] Although this particular participation scheme was repealed in 2020, this community ownership model stemmed from the Middelgruden offshore wind farm cooperative commissioned in 1996 with 50 per cent community ownership representing 8,000 members.[100]

The community ownership scheme was abolished in favour of community payment funds under the 'Renewable Energy Bonus' scheme representing an annual bonus payment for neighbours to wind turbines.[101] The 'Green Pool' scheme requires a one-time payment to the relevant municipal board(s) of DKK 165,000 per MW for offshore wind turbines.[102] Similar to the previous community ownership scheme, the 'Renewable Energy Bonus' and 'Green Pool' systems do not apply to wind turbines established 'following a call for tenders in an area designated for large offshore wind farms'.[103] While Denmark has recently moved away from actively requiring 'open door' offshore wind proponents to consider community ownership, the 'Renewable Energy Bonus' and 'Green Pool' scheme continue to represent an important mechanism for community benefits.

Belgium provides another interesting example of community cooperatives for offshore wind. The SeaCoop initiative provides a mechanism for citizen cooperatives to participate in offshore wind projects.[104] The SeaCoop movement is a direct result of other jurisdictions such as Denmark previously implementing mandatory community ownership of offshore wind schemes.[105] The model aims to restructure the dynamics

[96] Keith Taylor, *Governing the Wind Energy Commons* (West Virginia University Press, 2019); Charles Autry and Roland Hall, *The Law of Cooperatives* (American Bar Association, 2009).

[97] Hepburn Energy, 'About our co-operative' (2024) www.hepburnenergy.coop/about/.

[98] Cooperative Power, 'Home' (2024) www.cooperativepower.org.au/.

[99] Birgitte Egelund Olsen, 'Community Wind in Denmark' in Lars Holstenkamp and Jorg Radtke (eds), *Handbuch Energiewende und Partizipation* (Springer, 2017) 1033–35.

[100] State of Green, 'Middelgrunden Wind Turbine Cooperative' (2024) stateofgreen.com/en/solution-providers/middelgrunden-wind-turbine-cooperative/.

[101] Promotion of Renewable Energy Act (Denmark) LBK No 1791 of 2 September 2021, s 13.

[102] Promotion of Renewable Energy Act (Denmark) LBK No 1791 of 2 September 2021, s 14(4), para 4(2).

[103] Promotion of Renewable Energy Act (Denmark) LBK No 1791 of 2 September 2021, s 14(4), para 3.

[104] REScoop, 'Belgium leads the way in citizen participation for offshore wind energy' (2023) www.rescoop.eu/news-and-events/press/belgian-government-wants-significant-citizen-participation-in-offshore-wind-energy.

[105] Offshore Electricity Infrastructure Act 2021 (Cth), s 15, para 4.

between State, proponents, and communities, directly applicable to the three actors in the social contract paradigm. It advocates for the State to encourage and promote ownership and property rights in offshore wind projects through citizens cooperatives actively collaborating with offshore wind proponents. The SeaCoop will act as a point of contact for the 34 local offshore wind energy cooperatives that exist in Belgium to enable citizens to co-invest in offshore wind projects and gain guaranteed direct access to offshore wind energy produced. SeaCoop has a target for 20 per cent ownership of offshore wind farms to supply 20 per cent of electricity to citizens by actively participating in offshore wind tendering and establishing partnerships with offshore wind proponents to bid directly for an offshore wind licence.[106]

Expanding beyond traditional public consultation to integrate energy citizen communities and cooperative frameworks, as exemplified by SeaCoop, could signal the adoption of a similar tool in Australia's offshore wind landscape. A potential community ownership scheme offering ownership opportunities to coastal communities could form new and important merit criteria in the Australian discretionary offshore wind licensing assessment regime. While the Offshore Electricity Infrastructure Regulations 2022 (Cth) (OEI Regulations) provide the potential for the Minister to consider conflicts and measures to mitigate conflicts with uses and users of the licence area offshore,[107] this provision would exclude coastal communities onshore that do not directly engage in marine activities. An amendment to consider conflicts and measures to mitigate conflicts with proximate coastal communities as an additional 'user' in the licence area could trigger this provision. Such a measure to reduce conflict would be the offer of ownership stakes in an offshore project in a cooperative approach or a compensation scheme, similar to that of Denmark or Belgium.

B. Shaping Social Impact Assessments for Offshore Wind

In assessing and potentially offering community ownership or participation in offshore wind projects, the mapping and mitigation of social risks will be critical. Social Impact Assessment (SIA) processes aim to identify, mitigate, and continually monitor the social impacts to ensure social benefit throughout the lifecycle of projects. SIAs first arose in the 1970s as annexures to Environmental Impact Assessments (EIAs) as a 'process of managing social issues throughout the life of a project'.[108] The International Principles for Social Impact Assessments defines SIAs as 'the processes of analysing, monitoring and managing the intended and unintended social consequences, both positive and negative, of planned interventions (policies, programmes, plans, projects) and any social change processes invoked by those interventions. Its primary purpose is to bring about a more

[106] Act on the Organisation of the Electricity Market (*Wet betreffende de Organisatie van de Elektriciteitsmarkt*) 1999-04-29/42, art 6, with details provided in *Koninklijk besluit* (fn 20) 43557.

[107] Offshore Electricity Infrastructure Regulations 2022 (Cth), s 26(4).

[108] Frank Vanclay, 'Principles to Gain a Social Licence to Operate for Green Initiatives and Biodiversity Projects' (2017) 29 *Current Opinion in Environmental Sustainability* 48–56; Frank Vanclay, 'After 50 years of social impact assessment, is it still fit for purpose?' (2023) 72 *Current Sociology* 774–78, 774.

sustainable and equitable biophysical and human environment'.[109] This definition emphasises the need to analyse, and monitor social impacts and benefits throughout a particular project. The issues identified within an SIA must be combined with 'community engagement to deliver value to local communities and potentially mitigate social gaps'.[110]

Several countries require SIAs ranging from Australia to The Netherlands[111] as a legal requirement within national or state-level EIA regulatory frameworks. The UK government[112] is currently conducting a review of social impact assessment processes to deliver social value for communities as part of offshore wind development plans.[113] Imperiale and Vanclay argue a change is required from the project-based SIA framework to a community-based framework to enable the co-production of local community risks, well-being, and resilience to build a common vision and create an SIA Framework for Action.[114]

SIAs in Australia are typically conducted in three key phases as one component of the Environmental Impact Assessment and community consultation regulatory process. For example, in New South Wales (NSW), State Significant Developments[115] must undertake the SIA process. The three key steps of the SIA process are outlined by the New South Wales Social Impact Assessment Guideline: (1) SIA scoping takes place after the project development and scope have been submitted to the relevant regulatory authority as an initial assessment to inform the required SIA report; (2) assessment of identified SIA impacts and benefits with management measures resulting in an SIA report; (3) post-project approval by the regulator, the SIA report is verified and refined depending on the conditions of consent or approval for development to monitor and manage ongoing social impacts and benefits.[116]

[109] Frank Vanclay, 'Conceptualising Social Impacts' (2002) 22 *Environmental Impact Assessment Review* 183–211; Frank Vanclay, 'International Principles for Social Impact Assessment' (2003) 21 *Impact Assessment Project Appraisal* 6.

[110] IAIA, 'Social Impact Assessment Definition', www.iaia.org/wiki-details.php?ID=23#:~:text=Definition,processes%20invoked%20by%20those%20interventions.

[111] As assessed by the Netherlands Commission for Environmental Assessment. See NCEA, 'The NCEA' (2024) www.eia.nl/en/about-us/why-the-ncea'.

[112] Following previous research into social impacts of offshore wind farms in Scotland. See Marine Scotland, *A two way Conversation with the People of Scotland on the Social Impact of Offshore Renewables* (2022) www.gov.scot/binaries/content/documents/govscot/publications/research-and-analysis/2022/06/two-way-conversation-people-scotland-social-impact-offshore-renewables/documents/marine-scotland-two-way-conversation-people-scotland-social-impact-offshore-renewables/marine-scotland-two-way-conversation-people-scotland-social-impact-offshore-renewables/govscot%3Adocument/marine-scotland-two-way-conversation-people-scotland-social-impact-offshore-renewables.pdf.

[113] The Crown Estate, *The Crown Estate commissions new research on how to assess the social impact of marine activities* (2024) www.thecrownestate.co.uk/news/the-crown-estate-commissions-new-research-on-how-to-assess-the-social-impact.

[114] Angelo Jonas Imperiale and Frank Vanclay, 'From project-based to community-based social impact assessment: New social impact assessment pathways to build community resilience and enhance disaster risk reduction and climate action' (2024) 72 *Current Sociology* 601–788.

[115] State Significant Developments are defined pursuant to s 20 of the State Environmental Planning Policy (Planning Systems) 2021 (NSW) as 'Development for the purpose of electricity generating works or heat or their co-generation (using any energy source, including gas, coal, biofuel, distillate, waste, hydro, wave, solar or wind power) that – (a) has an estimated development cost of more than $30 million, or (b) has an estimated development cost of more than $10 million and is located in an environmentally sensitive area of State significance'. Consequently, offshore wind in coastal waters would be considered a State Significant Development and require a SIA.

[116] NSW Government, *Social Impact Assessment Guideline* (2023) www.planningportal.nsw.gov.au/sites/default/files/documents/2023/GD1944%20SIA%20Guideline_NEW%20VI_14_02_23.pdf.

One of the most critical outputs of the SIA takes place during the second step of the assessment of identified SIA impacts and benefits. This assessment results in a social baseline study using relevant social indicators to highlight the social context and capital of the particular communities. Benefit sharing opportunities are also typically the result of an SIA exercise to develop a strategy addressing local community concerns to provide tangible outputs such as social benefit funds.[117] In creating a value system to empower communities, the SIA process complements the management plan assessment of offshore wind proposals including their technical, economic, and environmental assessment and feasibility.[118]

SIA impacts as defined by Vanclay[119] and Burdge[120] include people's way of life; culture; community; political and decision-making systems; environment; health and wellbeing; fear and aspirations; and personal and property rights. SIAs are typically not detailed in planning and assessment regulation and are non-statutory instruments assessing the direct, indirect, cumulative, temporary, permanent, experienced, and perceived impacts of project development.[121] The monitoring and enforcement of SIAs are currently not expressly required in the OEI regime. There is increasing adoption of guidelines and proponents developing SIAs forming part of the EIA process for onshore energy development.[122]

Typically, at least five stakeholder interests are targeted for an SIA including community and stakeholder engagement; workforce management; housing and accommodation; local business and industry procurement; health, and community well-being.[123] Each of these stakeholder interests is critically important in the offshore wind context which has direct and indirect impacts on communities at different phases during the lifecycle of each project. For example, the feasibility licence stage of any energy development is often the most intensive during the construction phase requiring potential changes to communities in employment and housing. At the commercial offshore wind licence stage, the development of transmission and other infrastructure is essential. The five stakeholder interests must be considered when developing an SIA during each of these licensing stages.

The SIA processes for offshore renewable energy in Scotland were recently examined in the 2021–22 Marine Scotland Dialogue project, providing an interesting example of SIA value setting through community dialogues. The Marine Scotland

[117] Frank Vanclay, 'Benefit-sharing and enhancing outcomes for project-affected communities' in Frank Vanclay and Ana Maria Estees (eds), *Handbook of Social Impact Assessment and Management* (Edward Elgar Publishing, 2024) 426–43.

[118] ibid.

[119] Frank Vanclay, 'Conceptualising Social Impacts' (2002) 22 *Environmental Impact Assessment Review* 183–211; Frank Vanclay, 'International Principles for Social Impact Assessment' (2003) 21 *Impact Assessment Project Appraisal*.

[120] Rabel Burdge, *The Concepts, Process, and Methods of Social Impact Assessment* (University Press of Colorado, 2015).

[121] Queensland Government, 'Social Impact assessment Supplementary Material' (2023) eisdocs.dsdip.qld.gov.au/Social_Impact_Assessment/supplementary-technical-guidance-for-assessing-and-managing-social-impact-2023.pdf.

[122] Frank Vanclay and Henk A Necker, *The International Handbook of Social Impact Assessment* (Edward Elgar Publishing, 2003).

[123] Queensland Government, 'Social Impact Assessment' (2024) www.statedevelopment.qld.gov.au/coordinator-general/strong-and-sustainable-resource-communities/social-impact-assessment.

Dialogue created a conceptual framework based on social values to implement more meaningful SIAs for offshore renewable energy development in Scotland.[124] The conceptual framework was developed based on clusters of social values explored through dialogues between communities and experts across six locations in Scotland. Following two rounds of social impact dialogues with community members, the use of social value clusters at the different stages of SIA was suggested to reform the Scottish offshore renewable energy licensing system. The Marine Scotland Dialogue recommends four key SIA stages: (1) scoping requiring a public dialogue to practice key social value clusters; (2) the assessment of social impacts based on information on key social value clusters based on surveys; (3) consultation presenting information in terms of values and engaging in public dialogue; and (4) post-adoption to use social value clusters to address issues raised during the SIA process and providing ongoing surveys or dialogue. The recognition of a set of social value clusters matched with SIA monitoring mechanisms was also recommended to implement more effective and meaningful SIAs.

In Australia, SIAs are required for state significant developments or large resource projects in some Australian states and territories, including Queensland[125] and New South Wales,[126] offshore wind development in Commonwealth offshore areas in Australia currently does not require an SIA. Potential social impacts of offshore wind development during project feasibility, construction, operation, and decommissioning require specific SIA considerations beyond existing onshore renewable energy SIA guidelines. For example, offshore wind SIA guidelines could consider aesthetic and visual changes; construction impacts due to project-related traffic and road changes; social amenity issues associated with the construction of onshore substations and transmission lines; disruption or displacement of existing land uses due to construction and operation of project infrastructure; impacts to accommodation affordability; and impacts to existing local maritime industries.[127]

Importantly, the SIA process could be prescribed pursuant to Subdivision C of the OEI Regulations permitting the Minister to offer feasibility licences to proponents with 'conditions that would apply to the licence'.[128] This legal condition could include the completion of an SIA and the development of SIA guidelines requiring ongoing opportunities for energy democracy, for example, community leadership in disseminating SIA conditions such as community benefit schemes. SIA assessments can only be successful in the broader context of EIAs and spatial planning regimes. As explored in section 5 of this chapter, Australia currently lacks comprehensive location-specific data essential for accurately assessing the impacts and benefits of offshore wind. This data deficiency is due to the absence of federal Marine Spatial Planning (MSP) processes and dedicated EIA regulations for offshore wind projects.

[124] Marine Scotland (n 113).

[125] Strong and Sustainable Resource Communities Act 2017 (Qld).

[126] NSW Government, 'Social Impact Assessment Guideline' (2024) www.planningportal.nsw.gov.au/sites/default/files/documents/2023/GD1944%20SIA%20Guideline_NEW%20VI_14_02_23.pdf.

[127] Unwelt, 'Greater Gippsland Offshore Wind Project' (2022) www.planning.vic.gov.au/__data/assets/pdf_file/0031/658741/Attachment-7-GGOWP_Social-Risk-and-Opportunities.pdf.

[128] Offshore Electricity Infrastructure Regulations 2022 (Cth), s 27.

5. *Proactive Place Protection*: Marine Spatial Planning and Environmental Impact Assessments

EIAs for offshore wind projects are one of the most important avenues for the creation of sectoral and spatial planning proactively protecting sensitive marine areas and providing the conditions for offshore wind licensing. As discussed in section 3 of this chapter, the OEI Act currently provides the generic framework for EIAs at several stages prior to the grant of a commercial offshore electricity licence. Section 5 of this chapter is confined to an assessment of the OEI Act and the current guidance for management plans as the key framework for any EIAs informing and creating legal conditions for a proposed offshore wind project in Commonwealth waters.[129] An important aspect of licensing and concessions for offshore wind development conducive to mitigating social gaps is ensuring environmental issues are assessed and minimised. This is particularly important in addressing the third category of the 'social gap' to address proactive place protection, particularly Marine Spatial Planning (MSP), currently absent in Australia.

A. Marine Spatial Planning: Addressing Place Protection

MSP is defined as the 'public process of analysing and allocating the spatial and temporal distribution of human activities in marine areas to achieve ecological, economic and social objectives that are usually specified through a political process'.[130] MSP is applied in the offshore wind context in a variety of jurisdictions, with Belgium representing one of the most established MSP regimes. MSP is a spatial and temporal process to manage conflicts and impacts between marine uses and the environment. It moves beyond regulatory prohibitions, for example, by limiting fishing and underwater noise, and aims to minimise conflict through shared GIS-based mapping and data to promote effective co-location of marine sectors. Australia has previously engaged in regional MSP processes within the Great Barrier Reef Marine Park Act 1975 (Cth). This MSP process was restricted to the mapping and development of the Great Barrier Reef region only as a Marine Protected Area rather than to promote co-location with other sectors. Australia currently lacks a general MSP framework in Commonwealth offshore waters to plan and regulate offshore wind development.

Offshore wind spatial mapping can also lead to establishing areas where wind energy development is prohibited. Typically, offshore wind free areas are established due to the high sensitivity of ecological areas. For example, the EU Natura 2000[131] environmentally protected areas provide positive conservation measures and preventative measures,

[129] A proposal for offshore wind facilities and transmission onshore and development in coastal waters will also trigger state and territory planning laws which will assess impacts and provide planning permissions within their respective environmental assessment frameworks. No state or territory in Australia has provided guidance or legislative reform to accommodate offshore wind infrastructure and how its environmental assessment will be performed.

[130] Charles Ehler and Fanny Douvere, *Marine Spatial Planning: A Step-by-Step Approach Toward Ecosystem-Based Management* (Report, IOC/2009/MG/53 2009) 18.

[131] Pursuant to the Natura 2000, Habitats Directive 92/43/ECC and Birds Directive 79/409/ECC.

which may include offshore wind energy development being authorised on a case by case basis only.[132] For example, the Environment Protection and Biodiversity Conservation Act 1999 (Cth)(EPBCA) could declare and exclude biologically important areas for listed threatened species and ecological communities[133] in the Commonwealth marine environment as identified in marine bioregional plans and marine region profiles from offshore wind farm development.[134]

In the absence of MSP for offshore wind development in Australia, a case by case approach to the assessment of an EIS for offshore wind projects has led to calls for the establishment of Strategic Environmental Assessments (SEA).[135] SEAs are evident in several mature offshore wind jurisdictions, including the UK.[136] Wawryk argues for a SEA process in Australia to 'assess the environment of marine areas, identify competing interests in those areas, and provide information to help determine areas where offshore wind energy could be given priority over other users'.[137] A SEA regimen to gather ecological data differs from the self-assessment model currently evident within the OEI Act to an assessment of the relevant 'development envelope' and surrounding areas. The self-assessment method creates legal conditions for operation based on the current assessment period, rather than producing an environmental baseline to monitor cumulative impacts over time and promote sectoral co-location.[138] A SEA approach would likely take a regional approach to determine whether a proposed cluster of offshore wind projects could be developed in adherence to sustainable development principles.[139]

In creating an MSP process for Australia, several principles have been proposed building on Ehler's[140] framework adding the seventh principle on climate change mitigation:

1. 'an ecosystems-based approach underpinning sustainable development;
2. a process consistent with the requirements under relevant Commonwealth laws and international obligations regarding marine and environmental protections;

[132] European Commission, *Managing and protecting Natura 2000 sites* (2024) < environment.ec.europa.eu/topics/nature-and-biodiversity/natura-2000/managing-and-protecting-natura-2000-sites_en.

[133] See Australian Government, *Threatened species & ecological communities* (2024) www.dcceew.gov.au/environment/biodiversity/threatened.

[134] See Australian Government, *Key environmental factors for offshore windfarm environmental impact assessment under the Environment Protection and Biodiversity Conservation Act 1999* (2023) www.dcceew.gov.au/sites/default/files/documents/key-environmental-factors-offshore-windfarm-environmental-impact-assessment-under-EPBC-Act.pdf.

[135] Madeline Taylor, 'Marine Spatial Planning and Offshore Wind: Preliminary Principles for Australia' (2023) 11 *Renewable Energy Law and Policy Review* 48; Taylor and Taylor (n 15) 1–23.

[136] UK Government, 'Offshore Energy Strategic Environmental Assessment (SEA): An overview of the SEA process' (2023) www.gov.uk/guidance/offshore-energy-strategic-environmental-assessment-sea-an-overview-of-the-sea-process.

[137] Alex Wawryk, 'Legal Framework to Develop Offshore Wind in Australia' in Anton Ming-Zhi Gao and Chien-Te Fan, *The Development of a Comprehensive Legal Framework for the Promotion of Offshore Wind Power* (Kluwer Law International, 2017) 186.

[138] UK Government (n 137).

[139] Andrew Gill et al, 'Environmental Implications of Offshore Energy' 132, 133 in Katherine Yates and Corey Bradshaw (eds), *Offshore Energy and Marine Spatial Planning* (Routledge 2018).

[140] Charles N Ehler, 'Marine Spatial Planning: An idea whose time has come' in Yates and Bradshaw (n 140) 7.

3. a process consistent with policy objectives affecting the marine area to achieve sustainable development and preserve and potentially improve ecosystems by taking into account the benefits of best design principles of offshore wind;
4. a process that is participative and informed by data provided by consultees, stakeholders, regulators, and relevant experts;
5. a streamlined and efficient process, for example making effective use of existing GIS data and governance agencies;
6. adaptive and flexible monitoring and implementation processes by responsive scientific, economic, and environmental research programmes; and
7. prioritising climate change mitigation, adaptation, and decarbonisation in marine spatial planning without compromising environmental objectives'.[141]

The need to avoid conflicts is also cited in the OEI Act merit criteria whereby offshore electricity licences must be granted in the 'national interest'. Pursuant to section 26 of the Offshore Electricity Infrastructure Regulations 2022 (Cth), the expansive definition of what may constitute the 'national interest' includes '(e) conflicts that might arise with other uses or users of the licence area; and (f) any measures that are proposed to mitigate such conflicts'. Requiring conflict mitigation with other users and mitigation measures could create the justification of MSP processes in Australia to satisfy the criterion of the 'national interest'.

MSP may involve co-design processes with Traditional Owners. In the province of British Columbia Canada, the Marine Plan Partnership (MaPP) collaborative MSP process between 2007–2011 involved the collaboration between the provincial government and 17 First Nations Communities to develop plans for current and future marine uses in the Northern Shelf-Biodregion.[142] The MaPP process resulted in the creation of four sub-region plans. These plans were created in a 'nested planning process' through participatory leadership of First Nations communities to firstly scope their goals for ecological and social wellbeing. This involved a Community Coordinator establishing a marine planning committee of community members to represent traditional knowledge supported by the Marine Planners providing technical expertise.

The Indigenous-driven co-governance process of the MaPP is based on gathering Traditional Ecological Knowledge as the first mapping step to identify ecological and culturally significant areas. This process is highlighted by Diggon et al as enabling 'First Nations involvement throughout the design, the MaPP collaboration enhances the ongoing agency of First Nations and the successful inclusion of indigenous knowledge'.[143] Although the MaPP process did not take place at a federal level and resulted in non-binding guidelines, this process could be extended to incorporate federal waters to undertake a nested planning process in the currently proposed Canada Offshore Renewable Energy Regulations.[144]

[141] Taylor (n 136) 48–56.

[142] Steve Diggon, Caroline Butler, Aaron Heidt, John Bones, Russ Jones, and Craig Outhet, 'The Marine Plan Partnership: Indigenous community-based marine spatial planning' (2021) 132 *Marine Policy* 1–12.

[143] ibid.

[144] Canada Gazette, 'Canada Offshore Renewable Energy Regulations' (Index, Part I, Volume 158, Number 8).

B. Environmental Impact Assessments and Place-Based Values

Alongside MSP processes, EIAs represent another critical tool to ensure place-based values are protected. Management plans are required at the offshore wind feasibility licensing stage for up to seven years and must be approved before a proponent can apply for an offshore wind commercial licence of up to 40 years. Once a commercial licence is granted an updated management plan will be required for activities in relation to the construction, installation, commissioning, operating, maintenance, and decommissioning of the proposed licence area. The management plan must address a variety of matters listed in section 115 of the OEI Act including:

(a) how the licence holder is to carry out offshore infrastructure activities and other activities under the licence;
(b) any matters that the conditions of the licence require to be addressed in the management plan; and
(c) environmental management, including how the licence holder is to comply with any obligations under the *Environment Protection and Biodiversity Conservation Act 1999* (Cth)(EPBCA).

Where an offshore wind project is expected to have a 'significant impact' on a 'matter of national environmental significance', which includes Commonwealth marine areas,[145] the EPBCA is invoked.[146] Once the feasibility stage management plan is approved by the EPBCA, there is no further or updated environmental assessment required to the finalised management plan after a commercial licence is granted. The management plan must also address the maintenance and decommissioning of property, financial security, and the provision of records concerning work health and safety. The regulations regarding the detailed requirements for a management plan content inclusions and criteria for approval are contingent on finalisation of the OEI Amendment Regulations which are currently under revision.

Unlike offshore petroleum licences, EIAs for offshore wind are not undertaken in a streamlined approach by the Offshore Electricity Regulator. Rather, the environmental impact assessment process will be assessed by the federal Department of Climate Change, Energy, the Environment, and Water (DCCEEW) under the EPBCA.[147] The management plan must demonstrate 'environmental management' as assessed under the EPBCA to promote the ecologically sustainable development of offshore renewable energy.

Fundamentally, the OEI Act requires self-assessment by offshore wind proponents to refer themselves to the DCCEEW for their EIS assessment pursuant to the EPBCA. This assessment is required under the EPBCA and the management plan must

[145] Environment Protection and Biodiversity Act 1999 (Cth), s 24.

[146] A 'significant impact' is defined and determined by the relevant federal environmental minister taking into account matters within ss 67 and 75 of the EPBCA on a case by case basis. Bates defines 'significant impact' as '"significant" properly operates as a limitation to exclude impacts that are minor or negligible … the question of significance, however, is not expressed as a matter of objective fact that must exist before the minister can decide whether an action is a controlled action'. See Gerry Bates, *Environmental Law in Australia*, 10th edn (Lexis Nexis, 2019) 142.

[147] Environment Protection and Biodiversity Act 1999 (Cth), pts 7–9.

illustrate how the developer intends to comply with the relevant EPBCA provisions. The effectiveness of the approach will likely be limited based on the historically poorly defined 'significant impacts' and what such impacts could represent in the offshore wind context without existing baseline data. Uncertainty is likely to result due to the complex self-assessment procedure for offshore wind proponents. Consequently, the current EPBCA reforms as a result of the Samuels Review, including the establishment of a new independent national environmental protection agency, are likely to streamline project assessment decisions and post-approval following new National Environmental Standards.[148]

The uncertainty and complexity of offshore wind EIAs are heightened as the EPBCA currently does not apply a decarbonisation objective. When energy or infrastructure projects are proposed, the EPBCA assessment process does not take into account whether they are carbon-intensive or produce low or zero carbon. This gap in the existing EPBCA framework is evident in the decision by the federal environmental minister to veto[149] the Victorian State-owned Port of Hastings Corporations Victorian Renewable Energy Terminal application to build a terminal to ship wind turbine components. The proposed project involved dredging a channel for vessels to transport offshore wind turbine components through nearly 121 hectares of Ramsar protected wetlands as a 'Matter of National Environmental Significance' triggering the EPBCA. This dredging was deemed an unacceptable impact primarily on the ecological character of the Ramsar Wetland.

The Port of Hastings was chosen due to its deep water channels and its proximity to proposed offshore wind projects in the Gippsland region. Interestingly, the potential economic and social investment in the development of Port Hastings to support the offshore wind energy sector and the preparation of a Community Consultative Committee and Communications and Engagement Strategy was likely to provide 'significant benefit to the State of Victoria'.[150] These benefits were not sufficient to permit the development of the project. No appeal rights exist for a veto decision. However, the Victorian state government is likely to propose a similar infrastructure and shipping facility in an alternative location.

EIAs are critical instruments to assess offshore wind to identify and assess critical impacts and benefits and hence to acknowledge place-based protection concerns, mitigate environmental impacts and strengthen SLO. A dramatic shift is required in the balance of complexity and opportunities for EIAs as part of a broader MSP process and supplemented by SIAs as discussed in section 4(B) of this chapter. The OEI Act requires the broad 'one stop shop' management plan as a condition to the grant of offshore wind licences. Yet, the absence of a crucial decarbonisation objective within the Australian federal environmental assessment process has rendered the EPBCA inadequate for evaluating large-scale renewable energy projects like offshore wind.

[148] Australian Government, 'EPBC Act Reform' (2024) www.dcceew.gov.au/environment/epbc/epbc-act-reform.

[149] Environment Protection and Biodiversity Act 1999 (Cth), s 74B.

[150] Australian Government, 'Victorian Renewable Energy Terminal: Statement of Reasons for Decision that the Action is Clearly Unacceptable under the EPBC Act' (2023) epbcpublicportal.awe.gov.au/all-referrals/project-referral-summary/project-decision/?id=082e5d90-3366-ee11-9ae7-000d3a7943d3.

This deficiency belies the significant decarbonisation benefits associated with offshore wind, its supporting infrastructure, and manufacturing facilities. It remains to be seen whether the EPBCA review and Sustainable Oceans Plan, aimed at establishing Australia's first federal marine environment and ocean economy policy, will effectively address these deficiencies.[151] Acknowledging decarbonisation and place protection established in MSP and EIAs is crucial for addressing the third social gap pillar while facilitating the development of the necessary construction, operation, and maintenance facilities for Australia's offshore wind sector.

6. Conclusion

Since the development of the OEI Act in 2021, Australia's ambitions to progress offshore wind development have continued to accelerate, including the first awards of offshore wind feasibility licences. At this critical phase, the community reaction to offshore wind development has been complex and highly varied. This chapter outlines an agenda for regulatory and policy reform to foster understanding to mitigate 'social gaps' in Australia's emerging offshore wind sector. It focuses on mitigating three social gaps: democratic deficit, legal conditions, and place protection to accelerate the establishment of trust, ultimately creating a sustained social contract.

In doing so, this chapter has canvassed and highlighted the immaturity of the existing OEI Act and supporting regulations to meaningfully engage with communities. The evidence of social gaps is rising in community contestation and the reduction of offshore wind zones, such as the Southern Ocean Wind Zone. Understanding, assessing, and reforming the current regulatory approach to incorporate social impact and benefit objectives is critical not only to achieve offshore wind objectives in Australia but also to embrace the emergence of other critical offshore decarbonisation technologies, such as offshore renewable hydrogen. The UK is currently developing its offshore hydrogen framework, creating a clear signal of the potential for Australia to adopt a similar regulatory framework. However, acknowledging and mitigating 'social gaps' is an essential preliminary step in creating a socio-legal regulatory framework for offshore wind to facilitate a social contract for hybrid projects harnessing offshore wind for future renewable hydrogen projects.

The offshore wind regulatory landscape in Australia is rapidly evolving. Critically, several key supplementary regulations, particularly relating to management plan assessment, are yet to be formally enacted. This state of regulatory immaturity provides a salient opportunity to create guidance and reform regulation to ensure that 'social gaps' are addressed. There is no single silver bullet to build and maintain a social contract and the SLO. These are ever-changing locally specific and subjective state of acceptance and trust between State, industry, and communities.

However, as argued throughout this chapter, establishing a regulatory environment receptive to social gaps such as: (1) democratic deficits; (2) creating legal conditions;

[151] Australian Government, 'Sustainable Ocean Plan' (2024) www.dcceew.gov.au/environment/marine/sustainable-ocean-plan.

and (3) proactive place protection, offers a roadmap for reform to more effectively address social benefits in Australia's offshore wind journey ranging from safeguarding Sea Country, citizens cooperatives, SIAs and a broader MSP process. Australia's emerging offshore wind sector holds the important advantage of drawing on learning from early adopters and mature offshore wind jurisdictions. Australia must leverage these regulatory lessons to secure its ambitions as a leading and responsive offshore wind nation.

PART II

Offshore Energy: Business and Financing

7

A Double-Edged Sword: Alignments and Conflicts in the International, Regional, and Domestic Governance of Offshore Energy Projects

CĂTĂLIN-GABRIEL STĂNESCU AND CRISTIAN RUBANOVICI

1. Introduction

This chapter provides a detailed account of the intricate interactions between the international, regional, and local governance of offshore hydrocarbons and wind projects. It sheds light on the ongoing tension between favourable alignments and conflicting outcomes related to resource allocation, environmental protection, and investment protection mechanisms. The offshore energy sector is a crucial part of the global energy industry, encompassing hydrocarbons and renewable energy. Between 1947 and 2017, over 12,000 offshore oil and gas installations were established on the continental shelves of 53 countries.[1] As of July 2023, there were 231 operational units located in countries such as Saudi Arabia, Brazil, Mexico, Norway, and the US.[2] Technological advancements have made constructing larger platforms in deeper waters possible,[3] contributing to the industry's global prominence. By 2025, offshore oil production will account for approximately 28 per cent of the world's oil.[4] These installations boost output and help mitigate energy costs, create job opportunities, stimulate local industries, advance engineering endeavours, generate state revenues, and establish micro-ecosystems.[5] Nevertheless, concerns about the potential for pollution, exacerbated by incidents like

[1] Sean van Elden, Jessica J Meeuwi, Richard J Hobbs, and Jan M Hemmi, 'Offshore Oil and Gas Platforms as Novel Ecosystems: A Global Perspective' (2019) 6(548) *Frontiers in Marine Science* 1, doi:10.3389/fmars.2019.00548.

[2] OUCO, 'Offshore Oil Rigs: Some Important Facts You Should Know' (24 August 2023), ouco-industry.com/offshore-oil-rigs-some-important-facts-you-should-know/.

[3] ibid.

[4] MSI Pipe Protection Technologies, 'Benefits and Consequences of Offshore Drilling' msipipeprotection.com/benefits-and-consequences-of-offshore-drilling/.

[5] FIELDA, 'Why are Offshore Drilling Rigs Important Today?', fielda.com/blogs/why-are-offshore-drilling-rigs-important-today/. See also van Elden, Meeuwig, Hobbs and Hemmi (n 1) 3–6.

the Deepwater Horizon, as well as the costs and challenges of decommissioning, have precipitated international, regional, and national regulation.[6]

Offshore wind farms play an equally pivotal role despite being a relatively nascent industry compared to their fossil fuel counterparts. The inaugural offshore wind farm, Vindeby, commissioned in Denmark in 1991,[7] marked the inception of an industry that has rapidly evolved.[8] In January 2023, there were 260 operational offshore wind farms globally,[9] and the International Energy Association (IEA) forecasts[10] that the industry will attract up to USD 1 trillion in investments by 2040.[11] This investment will significantly impact global energy consumption, employment, and carbon emissions reduction. The European Commission (EC) has set a target of 300 GW of offshore wind energy by 2050[12] as part of its Green Deal strategy.[13] The strategy focuses on creating a legal framework, mobilising funds, and strengthening the supply chain across the European Union (EU).[14]

The legal framework is critical to such efforts. Countries with favourable wind conditions for building offshore wind farms must act quickly and create the necessary framework to attract international investors.[15] The industries' development also leads to the establishment of contractual standards. Major offshore wind industry players (ie, Vestas, Ørsted, Iberdrola, and Siemens Gamesa) have developed tailor-made agreements grounded in international construction standard contracts such as the International Federation of Consulting Engineers (known by its French acronym, FIDIC), Leading Oil and Gas Industry Competitiveness (LOGIC), Baltic and International Maritime Council (BIMCO), or the Norwegian Offshore Standard Contracts.[16] However, applying an international contractual standard verbatim to an offshore wind project presents challenges. A nuanced consideration of various factors, from legal and contractual frameworks to investment incentives and protective mechanisms, is thus necessary.[17]

[6] van Elden, Meeuwig, Hobbs and Hemmi (n 1) 1–2.

[7] Environmental and Energy Study Institute, 'Offshore Wind Energy Factsheet' (October 2010), www.eesi.org/files/offshore_wind_101310.pdf.

[8] M Dolores Esteban, José-Santos López-Gutiérrez and Vicente Negro, 'Offshore Wind Farms' (2020) 8(2) *Journal of Marine Science and Engineering* 120.

[9] Statista, 'Number of offshore wind farms operating worldwide as of January 2023, by country', www.statista.com/statistics/264257/number-of-offshore-wind-farms-worldwide-by-country/.

[10] IEA, 'Offshore wind to become a $1 trillion industry' (25 October 2019), www.iea.org/news/offshore-wind-to-become-a-1-trillion-industry.

[11] ESI Africa, 'What are the long-term prospects for Offshore Wind?' (30 July 2020) www.esi-africa.com/industry-sectors/renewable-energy/what-are-the-long-term-prospects-for-offshore-wind/.

[12] European Commission, 'An EU Strategy to harness the potential of offshore renewable energy for a climate neutral future' ec.europa.eu/energy/sites/ener/files/offshore_renewable_energy_strategy.pdf; Offshore Wind Biz, 'Confirmed: EU Aims for 300+ GW of Offshore Wind by 2050' (19 November 2020), www.offshorewind.biz/2020/11/19/confirmed-eu-aims-for-300-gw-of-offshore-wind-by-2050/.

[13] European Commission, 'A European Green Deal', ec.europa.eu/info/strategy/priorities-2019-2024/european-green-deal_en.

[14] ibid.

[15] Chatham Partners, 'Offshore Wind in High Seas, Unlimited potential beyond national control?' (December 2019), chatham.partners/site/assets/files/1031/chatham-partners-offshore-wind-farms-in-high-seas.pdf.

[16] Cristian Rubanovici, 'The Applicability of FIDIC Contracts in Offshore Wind Projects' (2022) *International Construction Law Review* 210.

[17] ibid.

The next sections of this chapter are organised into two parts. The first provides an overview of the interplay of the international, regional, and domestic governance mechanisms of offshore energy projects, concentrating on pivotal themes of public law, such as resource allocation and environmental protection. The second delves into the policy matters driving offshore energy development, such as regulatory, economic, technological, and contractual incentives, after which the chapter concludes.

The authors wish to acknowledge the inherent limitations of a book chapter, which may not allow for a comprehensive exploration of the topic. As a result, the examples provided are not specific to any region or country. This underscores the universal nature of the concerns and solutions discussed, which are relevant across the globe.

2. Interplay between International, Regional, and Domestic Laws Governing Offshore Energy Projects

A. Resource Allocation

Offshore energy projects often span national boundaries, necessitating cooperation between countries. Although they provide the basis for developing and managing offshore energy projects, international agreements, such as the United Nations Convention on the Law of the Sea (UNCLOS)[18] and International Maritime Organization (IMO) regulations, carry the seed of potential disputes. The principles of public international law allow coastal states to exercise sovereign rights over their territorial waters, exclusive economic zones (EEZs), and continental shelves. These principles can enable neighbouring countries to stake competing claims to the same offshore resources. This section highlights how international, regional, or bilateral agreements may facilitate the joint development and management of shared offshore resources, encouraging collaboration and reducing potential conflicts.[19]

i. Cooperation

Effective coordination among legal frameworks is essential to managing shared resources, avoiding or resolving disputes, fostering collaboration, and protecting investments. The international regime governing offshore natural resource exploitation is based on UNCLOS. This treaty outlines the rights and responsibilities of states in managing and using oceans. It establishes maritime boundaries, EEZs, and continental shelves, which form the basis for allocating and developing offshore energy resources. UNCLOS allows countries to explore and exploit offshore resources within their jurisdictions, providing a degree of control and potential economic benefits. However, UNCLOS gives due regard to the sovereignty of all states, requiring countries

[18] Available at www.un.org/depts/los/convention_agreements/texts/unclos/unclos_e.pdf.

[19] According to Anders Opedal, executive vice-president for Technology, Projects, and Drilling at Equinor, 'good and efficient cross-border cooperation' leads to 'solutions ensuring proper resource management'. See www.offshore-energy.biz/equinor-brings-online-cross-border-north-sea-field/.

to consider the interests of others when using the oceans and seas.[20] The treaty encourages states to collaborate on joint development projects in disputed areas and promotes diplomatic solutions to resource-sharing disputes, fostering regional stability.[21]

Cross-border cooperation is crucial in managing coastal resources, including fish, minerals, and energy. International principles of equitable sharing[22] and responsible resource management influence regional and domestic laws. The UN's International Resource Panel has emphasised the importance of coastal resources, fish, minerals, and energy, which constitute the key focus of the emerging Sustainable Blue Economy agenda.[23] The 2021 Report on Governing Coastal Resources[24] estimates the global ocean-based economy at USD 3 trillion annually, representing approximately 5 per cent of the worldwide gross domestic product. The report highlights the need for blue economic growth to sustain and enhance the natural capital it depends on and generate equitably distributed economic and social benefits.

Cross-border cooperation on hydrocarbon projects ('unitisation') has been a reality in the energy sector for years. In Europe, many of these occurred in the North Sea,[25] including the Orca project on the UK/Dutch North Sea median line, which became operational in 2013,[26] or the Utgard project along the Norwegian-UK border.[27] Collaborative projects are not limited to Europe: in March 2023, Equatorial Guinea and Cameroon signed a bilateral treaty that could result in cross-border cooperation on hydrocarbon developments, including joint development of the Chevron-operated Yoyo (offshore Cameroon) and Yolanda (offshore Equatorial Guinea) gas fields.[28]

Cross-border cooperation has also been expanded to renewable energy projects. For instance, ONE-Dyas started developing the GEMS project at the Dutch/German border in 2021.[29] With its partners Hansa Hydrocarbons and EBN, ONE-Dyas intends to extract natural gas from the German and Dutch North Sea. The offshore platform will be in the Netherlands, approximately 1.5 kilometers from German waters. It will be the first Dutch offshore gas treatment platform in the North Sea running entirely on

[20] UNCLOS, Articles 87(2), 56(2), and 58(3).

[21] UNCLOS, Articles 74(3) and 83(3).

[22] Jorge Cabrera Medaglia and Frederic Perron-Welch, 'The benefit-sharing principle in international law' (2019) 14(1) *Journal of Intellectual Property Law & Practice* 62–76, doi.org/10.1093/jiplp/jpy162; Jorge Cabrera Medaglia and Frederic Perron-Welch, 'Rules and Practices of International Law on Benefit-Sharing for Sustainable Development' in Volker Mauerhofer, Daniela Rupo and Lara Tarquinio (eds), *Sustainability and Law* (Springer Cham, 2020) doi.org/10.1007/978-3-030-42630-9_21.

[23] UNEP, 'Sustainable Blue Economy' www.unep.org/topics/ocean-seas-and-coasts/ecosystem-based-approaches/sustainable-blue-economy.

[24] IRP, 'Governing Coastal Resources: Implications for a Sustainable Blue Economy. Report of the International Resource Panel' (Nairobi, Kenya: United Nations Environment Programme, 2021) 18, www.resourcepanel.org/file/2272/download?token=5qq_lDTm.

[25] Stuart G Archer, Henk Kopbrink, Stefano Patruno, Domenico Chiarella, Christopher A.-L. Jackson and John A Howell, 'Cross-border petroleum geology in the North Sea: An Introduction' (2021) 494 *Geological Society* 1–11, doi.org/10.1144/SP494-2021-182.

[26] Offshore Mag, 'First Gas Flows from North Sea Cross-border Orca Project' (18 December 2013) www.offshore-mag.com/production/article/16772227/first-gas-flows-from-north-sea-crossborder-orca-project.

[27] Offshore Energy, 'Equinor brings online cross-border North Sea field' (17 September 2019) www.offshore-energy.biz/equinor-brings-online-cross-border-north-sea-field/.

[28] Offshore Mag, 'Treaty opens path to cross-border oil and gas projects in Equatorial Guinea, Cameroon' (21 March 2023) www.offshore-mag.com/regional-reports/africa/article/14291287/treaty-opens-path-to-crossborder-oil-and-gas-projects-in-equatorial-guinea-cameroon.

[29] GEMS project, www.gemsnorthsea.co.uk/gems-project/.

wind energy via a cable linked to the nearby German wind farm Riffgat.[30] In 2021, the Danish Kriegers Flak project achieved a significant milestone by connecting offshore wind farms in Denmark and Germany through an offshore power grid as part of the Combined Grid Solution project.[31]

In August 2022, the EC adopted its first renewable energy cross-border (CB RES) projects list[32] under the Connecting Europe Facility (CEF) regulation.[33] One of these is a hybrid offshore wind park between Estonia and Latvia.[34] Cross-border cooperation involves planning, developing, and exploiting renewable energy sources and is established through the mechanism defined in the recast of the Renewable Energy Directive.[35] The mechanism encourages cooperation between EU Member States, third-party countries, or regions within the EU. It aims to help EU Member States reach their renewable energy targets more effectively by developing renewable energy projects and infrastructure together. Cross-border cooperation is expected to decrease the costs of renewable energy projects, improve their efficiency, and promote the use of renewable energy sources across the EU.

International and regional agreements foster cooperation by facilitating technological knowledge exchange and best practices. These agreements allow countries with advanced technology to assist others in developing their offshore energy sectors. Organisations like the Global Wind Energy Council,[36] Wind Europe,[37] and the International Renewable Energy Agency (IRENA)[38] promote and create forums for technology transfer and knowledge sharing between countries and companies. IRENA's Coalition for Action[39] is one such initiative, bringing together over 100 leading renewable energy players worldwide. It facilitates discussions on advancing renewable energy adoption, including offshore wind technology, particularly in emerging markets.

Ultimately, international investment treaties, such as bilateral investment treaties, multilateral investment treaties,[40] or free trade agreements,[41] play a pivotal role in

[30] One North Sea, onenorthsea.com/project-database. See also the project website for GEMS: www.gemsnorthsea.co.uk.

[31] On the Kriegers Flak project, see powerplants.vattenfall.com/kriegers-flak/.

[32] European Commission, 'Commission adopts first list of renewable energy cross-border projects' (30 August 2022) commission.europa.eu/news/commission-adopts-first-list-renewable-energy-cross-border-projects-2022-08-30_en.

[33] Regulation (EU) 2021/1153 of the European Parliament and of the Council of 7 July 2021 establishing the Connecting Europe Facility and repealing Regulations (EU) No 1316/2013 and (EU) No 283/2014, PE/52/2021/INIT, data.europa.eu/eli/reg/2021/1153/oj.

[34] For a wider discussion of cross-border considerations and implications arising from the development of wind farms, see Eirik Finserås et al, 'Gone with the wind? Wind farm-induced wakes and regulatory gaps.' (2024) *Marine Policy* 159.

[35] Directive (EU) 2018/2001 of the European Parliament and of the Council of 11 December 2018 on the promotion of the use of energy from renewable sources (recast), PE/48/2018/REV/1, eur-lex.europa.eu/legal-content/EN/TXT/PDF/?uri=CELEX:32018L2001.

[36] gwec.net.

[37] windeurope.org.

[38] www.irena.org.

[39] IRENA Coalition for Action, gwec.net/irena-coalition-for-action-green-recovery-statement/.

[40] Cyrus Benson, Penny Madden and Nicholas Tomlinson, 'Investment Treaty Considerations for Deal Makers' (2015) www.gibsondunn.com/wp-content/uploads/documents/publications/Benson-Madden-Tomlinson-Investment-Treaty-Considerations-For-Deal-Makers-Law360-11-6-2015.pdf.

[41] One such example is the North American Free Trade Agreement (NAFTA), whose Chapter 6 is dedicated to energy and basic petrochemicals, while Chapter 11 deals with investments. See www.sice.oas.org/trade/nafta/chap-06.asp and www.sice.oas.org/trade/nafta/chap-111.asp.

protecting investors' interests in offshore energy projects. The most important of these remains the Energy Charter Treaty (ECT), which aims to create a common framework to encourage investment and trade in the energy sector.[42]

These treaties establish legal frameworks that offer protection based on internationally recognised standards regarding fair and equitable treatment,[43] expropriation,[44] non-discrimination,[45] full protection and security,[46] and, most importantly, dispute resolution mechanisms.[47]

Dispute resolution mechanisms are critical as they provide neutral forums, confidentiality, enforceability, and expertise. Neutral forums offer a platform for resolving disputes and avoiding the potential biases of national courts in host states. Confidentiality protects sensitive business information and allows parties to maintain their reputation via non-public arbitral proceedings. Enforceability enhances the effectiveness of the dispute resolution process by making arbitration awards generally applicable in multiple jurisdictions through international conventions such as the New York Convention.[48] Finally, arbitration panels often consist of experienced legal professionals with expertise in international law, investment treaties, and related fields, ensuring well-informed decisions.

In addition to international treaties, many countries enact domestic investment laws that provide additional protection to investors in offshore energy projects. These laws can include investment guarantees related to property rights, fair treatment, and legal stability for investors,[49] as well as stabilisation clauses in contracts[50] or laws freezing certain regulatory aspects for a defined period, protecting investors from adverse regulatory changes. However, as we show later on, some argue that investment protection

[42] The Energy Charter Treaty was signed in December 1994 and came into force in April 1998. See the ECT's official website: www.energycharter.org/process/energy-charter-treaty-1994/energy-charter-treaty/.

[43] For instance, the FET standard is mentioned in Article 10(1) of the ECT or Article 1105(1) of NAFTA.

[44] To illustrate, specific protection against expropriation is mentioned in Article 13 of the ECT and Article 1110 of NAFTA.

[45] The principle of non-discrimination appears throughout the text of the ECT: Article 8(1), Article 18(4), and Article 25(5)(ii). Non-discriminatory treatment is mentioned several times in NAFTA as well: Article 1105(2), Article 1110(1)(b) and (8).

[46] Article 10(1) of the ECT requires that 'investments enjoy the most constant protection and security' while Article 1105(1) of NAFTA asks its parties to grant 'full protection and security' to the investments of investors of another party.

[47] Article 26(3) and (4) of the ECT enable an aggrieved investor to submit a dispute to international arbitration with the International Centre for Settlement of Investment Disputes (ICSID), a sole arbitrator or an ad-hoc arbitration tribunal established under the Arbitration Rules of the United Nations Commission on International Trade Law (UNCITRAL) or the Arbitration Institute of the Stockholm Chamber of Commerce. Similarly, Articles 1116–1120 of NAFTA enable investors to bring claims under ICSID or UNCITRAL rules.

[48] United Nations Convention on the Recognition and Enforcement of Foreign Arbitral Awards (New York, 10 June 1958) www.newyorkconvention.org/english.

[49] Details can be found in the OECD's databases, which provide descriptions of current trades in each country covered and examine their foreign direct investment institutional and legal framework: Reviews of Foreign Direct Investment, www.oecd-ilibrary.org/finance-and-investment/oecd-reviews-of-foreign-direct-investment_20743734, and the Investment Policy Reviews database, www.oecd-ilibrary.org/finance-and-investment/oecd-investment-policy-reviews_19900910. However, these are not the only available sources. Brill's Foreign Law guide offers access to foreign investment laws, including the existence of translations and selected references to secondary sources, available at referenceworks.brillonline.com/browse/foreign-law-guide.

[50] For a comprehensive view, see Peter D Cameron, *International Energy Investment Law. The Pursuit of Stability*, 2nd edn (Oxford University Press, 2021) 92–247.

mechanisms grant excessive powers to corporations and can discourage host countries from regulating in the public interest.

ii. Conflicts

Disputes commonly arise when neighbouring countries have conflicting claims to the same offshore hydrocarbon resources. Concurrently, recent studies show that the wind wake effect (or 'wind theft') also carries the potential for conflict between states or operators.[51]

Recent examples of offshore hydrocarbon-related conflicts concern the Eastern Mediterranean region. For instance, Israel and Lebanon postponed their plans to exploit natural gas reserves off their coastlines for a decade due to a maritime border dispute, which was ultimately settled in October 2022.[52] Similarly, the Turkish government's assertive policy on hydrocarbon extraction has put it at odds with the Republic of Cyprus and Greece, leading to further delays or abandonment of plans to supply the EU with offshore natural gas from the region.[53]

Disputes over resource ownership and extraction rights tend to escalate without effective conflict resolution mechanisms. As a response to the growing tensions in the region and to counter the disrupting actions of Turkey, the Eastern Mediterranean Gas Forum was formed. This partnership between Egypt, Israel, Cyprus, Greece, Jordan, Palestine, Italy, and France aims to enhance economic cooperation and regional integration through the region's gas reserves. However, the notable absence of Turkey and Lebanon is a cause for concern as it perpetuates regional divisions and exacerbates existing tensions.[54] The recent war in Gaza has further complicated the situation and made an agreement even less likely.[55]

Importantly, this should not be construed as a failure of 'gas diplomacy', which uses the prospect of gas exports to encourage regional players to make breakthroughs toward conflict resolution in non-energy-related matters. Energy can create relationships that help prevent conflict, and the bilateral deals between Israel and Jordan or Egypt are good examples. Nonetheless, an effective strategy for achieving political reconciliation is also needed.[56]

Political cooperation is also required to efficiently manage wind resources in transboundary regions, especially when dealing with wake effects caused by offshore wind farms. Studies from the North Sea region and the east coast of the US have shown that offshore wind farms reduce wind speed and increase small-scale turbulences, which can disrupt the operation of adjacent wind farms by up to 33 per cent. Without proper bilateral or multilateral cooperation among coastal states, the absence of regulatory

[51] Finserås et al (n 34).
[52] International Crisis Group, 'Rethinking Gas Diplomacy in the Eastern Mediterranean' (26 April 2023), www.crisisgroup.org/middle-east-north-africa/east-mediterranean-mena-turkiye/240-rethinking-gas-diplomacy-eastern.
[53] ibid.
[54] ibid.
[55] 'Israel Gaza war: History of the conflict explained' (*BBC*, 5 April 2024) www.bbc.com/news/newsbeat-44124396.
[56] ibid.

instruments and legal uncertainty concerning existing ones could lead to disputes, ultimately undermining energy transition efforts.[57]

Conflicts may also arise from differences in energy needs and environmental priorities across regions and reactions to international events, such as resource diversification, reduction of import dependency, or the pursuit of green energy. The geopolitical situation created by the Russian invasion of Ukraine in 2022 and the ongoing war in which the EU has assumed a supportive role vis-à-vis Ukraine[58] is a good example. The EU's dependency on fossil fuel imports from Russia and the energy security concerns arising from the war have forced a fundamental rethink of the energy policy.[59] The diversification of the energy mix or energy import partners became necessary,[60] worsening the relationship with Russia[61] and further highlighting the significance of the interconnections between international agreements, regional goals, and domestic interests concerning the management of energy projects.

B. Environmental Protection

Numerous laws in various countries include international standards, which indicates the positive impact of global agreements and organisations on national regulations. One example of international regulatory cooperation is the United States-Mexico-Canada Agreement, which facilitates regulatory cooperation between the parties and ensures environmental protection.[62] This shows the continuous convergence and harmonisation of regulatory frameworks for energy projects. Yet, there can be differences between regional and international environmental regulations and a country's domestic laws or economic objectives, leading to conflicts between national development goals and international environmental commitments.

i. Harmonisation

There are numerous international efforts to harmonise environmental protection standards. UNCLOS requires coastal states to adopt laws and regulations to prevent, reduce,

[57] Finserås et al (n 34).

[58] European Council, 'EU response to Russia's invasion of Ukraine' www.consilium.europa.eu/en/policies/eu-response-ukraine-invasion/.

[59] The EU imposed a series of sanctions against Russia, many of which targeted the energy sector (the second package of 25 February 2022), prohibition on new investments in the Russian energy sector (the fourth package of 15 March 2022), prohibitions on imports of crude oil and refined petroleum products from Russia (with limited exceptions; sixth package of 3 June 2022), a price cap related to maritime transport of Russian oil for third countries (eighth package of 6 October 2022). The REPowerEU strategy was announced in March 2022 with the stated aim of reducing Russian gas imports by two-thirds in the same year; see eur-lex.europa.eu/legal-content/EN/TXT/?uri=COM%3A2022%3A108%3AFIN.

[60] European Commission 'REPowerEU: affordable, secure and sustainable energy for Europe', commission.europa.eu/strategy-and-policy/priorities-2019-2024/european-green-deal/repowereu-affordable-secure-and-sustainable-energy-europe_en#diversifying_our_energy_supply.

[61] Pjotr Sauer, 'Russia will not resume gas supplies to Europe until sanctions lifted, says Moscow' *The Guardian* (5 September 2022) www.theguardian.com/world/2022/sep/05/russia-will-not-resume-gas-supplies-to-europe-until-sanctions-lifted-says-moscow.

[62] OECD (2021), International Regulatory Co-operation, OECD Best Practice Principles for Regulatory Policy, p 27, OECD Publishing, Paris, doi.org/10.1787/5b28b589-en.

and control marine environment pollution caused by 'seabed activities subject to their jurisdiction'[63] from installations, vessels, and other devices flying their flag.[64]

The IMO sets safety and operational standards for maritime activities, including offshore energy operations, such as safety protocols, navigation, and pollution prevention measures. The International Convention on Oil Pollution Preparedness, Response and Cooperation (OPRC)[65] is one example. It requires operators of offshore units to have oil pollution emergency plans or similar arrangements coordinated with national systems for responding promptly and effectively to oil pollution incidents.[66] These help ensure consistent environmental protection and safety measures and foster harmonisation concerning challenging aspects of energy projects, onshore or offshore.

There are also regional standards around the globe,[67] such as:

(i) The Convention for the Protection of the Marine Environment of the North-East Atlantic (OSPAR Convention),[68] which deals with the deliberate disposal of offshore installations or pipelines in the maritime area, excluding disused offshore facilities left wholly or partly in place;[69]
(ii) The Convention on the Protection of the Marine Environment of the Baltic Sea Area (Helsinki Convention),[70] which dedicates an entire section to preventing pollution from hydrocarbon offshore activities;[71]
(iii) The Convention on the Protection of the Black Sea against Pollution (Bucharest Convention)[72] and its Protocol on Cooperation in Combatting Pollution of the Black Sea Marine Environment by Oil and Other Harmful Substances in Emergency Situations,[73] which require contracting states to take appropriate measures to prevent, reduce, and control the pollution of the marine environment of the Black Sea by vessels, including offshore platforms;[74]
(iv) The Convention for the Protection of the Marine Environment and the Coastal Region of the Mediterranean (Barcelona Convention) and its Protocols, which also cover offshore installations and energy facilities.[75]

[63] UNCLOS, Articles 208(1) and (4).
[64] UNCLOS, Article 209.
[65] Available at www.ilo.org/dyn/natlex/docs/ELECTRONIC/93349/109093/F578688552/International%20Convention%20on%20Oil%20Pollution%20Prepare.pdf.
[66] OPRC, Articles 3(2) and (3).
[67] Mariko Kawano, 'Implementation of the Rules of the UNCLOS Through Universal and Regional Organizations' in Marta Chantal da Cunha Machado Ribeiro, Fernando Loureiro Bastos, and Tore Henriksen (eds), *Global Challenges and the Law of the Sea* (Springer Cham, 2020) doi-org.ep.fjernadgang.kb.dk/10.1007/978-3-030-42671-2_2.
[68] Available at www.ospar.org/site/assets/files/1169/ospar_convention.pdf.
[69] See the corroborated provision of OSPAR, Article 1(f) and (g).
[70] Available at helcom.fi/wp-content/uploads/2019/06/Helsinki-Convention_July-2014.pdf.
[71] Helsinki Convention, Annex VI.
[72] Available at cil.nus.edu.sg/wp-content/uploads/2017/08/1992-Bucharest-Convention-for-the-Protection-of-the-Black-Sea-Against-Pollution.pdf.
[73] Available at leap.unep.org/sites/default/files/treaty/TRE-001391.doc.
[74] Bucharest Convention, Articles VIII and II(2)(a).
[75] For instance, Barcelona Convention, Articles 11 and 15 and Protocol on Integrated Coastal Zone Management in the Mediterranean, Article 9(f).

Recent agreements such as the Convention on Biological Diversity[76] and the Paris Agreement[77] set global environmental protection and sustainable development standards. They influence how offshore energy projects are planned, executed, and monitored to minimise their ecological impact and incentivise countries to adopt sustainable energy sources like offshore wind to reduce greenhouse gas emissions and mitigate climate change. For example, the Paris Agreement establishes a framework for financial assistance through mechanisms like the Green Climate Fund,[78] which assists developing countries in implementing renewable energy projects, including offshore wind energy.[79]

Ultimately, regional regulatory harmonisation streamlines operations and lowers compliance costs for energy companies operating in multiple countries. The Renewable Energy Directive sets a binding renewable energy target for the EU to derive at least 32 per cent of its total energy consumption from renewable sources by 2030.[80] This directive helps harmonise renewable energy policies across EU Member States and promotes an environment more conducive to investment in regional offshore wind projects by reducing regulatory discrepancies.

ii. Misalignments

Despite attempts to harmonise environmental protection standards, conflicts exist between international and domestic approaches.

a. General Inconsistency between Climate Policies and Other Areas

In 2015, the Organisation for Economic Cooperation and Development (OECD), the IEA, the International Transport Forum, and the Nuclear Energy Agency published a Report on Aligning Policies for a Low-carbon Economy.[81] It identified inconsistencies between policies and regulations across various areas, such as investment, taxation, innovation, trade, and adaptation. These inconsistencies were found to hinder the achievement of climate change-related objectives. The report also highlighted that climate policy activities, such as electricity, urban mobility, and rural land use, must be implemented more effectively.

A key obstacle identified was the regulatory and policy frameworks outside the climate policy portfolios, which must be aligned with climate objectives. The report recommended that each country systematically identify and address such misalignments to enhance the responsiveness of economic and social systems to the climate change agenda. The report also suggested that a similar approach could aid governments be more ambitious in implementing policies and emissions objectives.[82]

[76] Available at www.cbd.int/doc/legal/cbd-en.pdf.

[77] Available at unfccc.int/files/essential_background/convention/application/pdf/english_paris_agreement.pdf.

[78] Paris Agreement, Articles 9, 10, and 11.

[79] UNFCCC, 'Key aspects of the Paris Agreement', unfccc.int/most-requested/key-aspects-of-the-paris-agreement.

[80] Finserås et al (n 34).

[81] Available at doi.org/10.1787/9789264233294-en.

[82] ibid 24.

In 2022, a report examined how the UN Sustainable Development Goals (SDGs) were incorporated into various recovery and growth strategies, such as the European Semester, the National Recovery and Resilience Plans, and local and regional authority strategies.[83] It identified 'persisting challenges' in implementing the SDGs at the local level, such as 'administrative and financial barriers, lack of support from national governments and coordination across different levels of governance.'[84] The report recommended aligning local, national, and regional strategies to overcome these challenges.[85]

Further, domestic laws may prioritise local economic benefits over global environmental concerns, creating conflicts with international and regional sustainability objectives. To illustrate, the Biden administration's extension of Trump's America First policies aimed to curb Chinese economic power and restore local jobs while reducing the trade deficit.[86] Although the US-Chinese trade war did not target offshore energy, the US policies and incentives for domestic production of windfarms (along with other protectionist measures) created disagreements with other economic partners, such as the EU.[87] Careful negotiation, diplomacy, and cooperation among nations, regional organisations, and stakeholders are necessary to manage these conflicts and overlaps.

b. Inconsistency with Investment Protection Mechanisms

Conflicts can arise when strict environmental regulations clash with investment protection provisions in international treaties. While investment protection focuses on economic and legal aspects, projects must still comply with general environmental and social regulations, which are frequently and rapidly amended because of international agreements. Frequent changes to environmental rules can create uncertainty for investors,[88] mainly when their investments depend on consistent regulatory conditions, such as financial incentives for renewables.[89] The risk of changing laws can cause investors to hesitate to commit resources, affecting the overall pace of offshore energy development.

Investors may also oppose regulatory measures that are detrimental to their investment interests. In 2022, the United Nations Conference on Trade and Development (UNCTAD) identified as a 'major concern' the risk of treaty-based investor-state dispute settlement (ISDS) being used to challenge climate policies.[90] The forum has called for

[83] European Committee of the Regions, Commission for Economic Policy, 'Synergies between Sustainable Development Goals and the National Recovery and Resilience Plans – Best Practices from Local and Regional Authorities' (Brussels: European Committee of the Regions, 2022).

[84] ibid 9.

[85] ibid 69.

[86] Anshu Siripurapu and Noah Berman, 'The Contentious US-China Trade Relationship' (*CFR*, 2 December 2022) www.cfr.org/backgrounder/contentious-us-china-trade-relationship.

[87] Stanley Reed, 'Europe's Wind Industry Is Stumbling When It's Needed Most' *New York Times* (22 November 2022) www.nytimes.com/2022/11/22/business/wind-power-europe.html.

[88] Ming Che, Hongmei Wu and Yujia Li, 'Do Fluctuations in Environmental Regulations Inhibit Investment: Evidence from China' (2023) 20(3) *International Journal of Environmental Research and Public Health*, doi.org/10.3390/ijerph20032021.

[89] Nico Tyabji, 'How to Lose Investors and Alienate People in Renewable Energy' (*Bloomberg*, 10 April 2013), www.iene.eu/how-to-lose-investors-and-alienate-people-in-renewable-energy-p43.html.

[90] UNCTAD, 'Treaty-based Investor–State Dispute Settlement Cases and Climate Action' (2022) 4 *International Investment Agreements Issues Note* 2, investmentpolicy.unctad.org/publications/1270/treaty-based-investor-state-dispute-settlement-cases-and-climate-action.

reform measures to reduce ISDS risks and 'create the necessary policy space for States to take urgent climate action.'[91]

Striking a balance between safeguarding investments and promoting responsible development is one of the main challenges in modernising the ECT.[92] The challenge arises from perceived incompatibility with the EU's Green Deal and the climate goals of the Paris Agreement. Additionally, the ECT offers extensive protection to hydrocarbon investments, and eight EU Member States have withdrawn from it for these reasons.[93] In July 2023, the EC proposed a coordinated withdrawal of the EU, its Member States, and Euratom from the ECT.[94]

While the fate of the ECT remains uncertain, the OECD has started a comprehensive public consultation as part of its multilateral initiative on investment treaties and climate change. The submissions highlight, among other things, the need to rapidly amend all investment instruments, bilateral or multilateral, to support climate goals.[95]

Notably, the possibility of climate-related claims being brought within the international energy investment framework, particularly the ECT, is more than a theoretical concern. In 2017, a British-Italian oil and gas company initiated a case under the auspices of the International Centre for Settlement of Investment Disputes (ICSID) after Italy's decision not to grant a production licence due to the government's ban on offshore oil and gas exploration and production.[96] In 2022, the tribunal ruled in favour of the company and ordered Italy to pay over EUR 190 million in compensation, plus compounded annual interest and arbitration costs.[97] Similarly, in 2021, the Netherlands was summoned before the ICSID for its decision to phase out coal power plants by 2030.[98] The case is pending. The ECT's protection mechanism has also led to 55 ICSID cases in the past decade,[99] forcing state budgets in Spain and Romania to compensate renewable energy investors for non-sustainable financial incentives.

c. Regulatory Chill

Critics argue that investment protection mechanisms and international arbitration proceedings can prevent host countries from enacting stricter ecological or social

[91] ibid 3.

[92] Holly Stebbing, India Furse and Aman Tandon, 'Going green? Modernizing the Energy Charter Treaty' (2022) 18 *Norton Rose Fulbright International Arbitration Report* 14–16.

[93] Johannes Tropper, 'Withdrawing from the Energy Charter Treaty: The End is (not) Near' (*Kluwer Arbitration Blog*, 4 November 2022) arbitrationblog.kluwerarbitration.com/2022/11/04/withdrawing-from-the-energy-charter-treaty-the-end-is-not-near/; Karl Mathiesen, 'Spain pulls out of energy treaty over climate concerns' (*Politico*, 12 October 2022) www.politico.eu/article/spain-pulls-out-of-energy-treaty-over-climate-concerns/.

[94] European Commission 'European Commission proposes a coordinated EU withdrawal from the Energy Charter Treaty' (7 July 2023) energy.ec.europa.eu/news/european-commission-proposes-coordinated-eu-withdrawal-energy-charter-treaty-2023-07-07_en.

[95] OECD, 'OECD Public Consultation, January – March 2022, Investment Treaties and Climate Change' (13 April 2022) www.oecd.org/investment/investment-policy/OECD-investment-treaties-climate-change-consultation-responses.pdf.

[96] *Rockhopper Italia S.p.A., Rockhopper Mediterranean Ltd, and Rockhopper Exploration Plc v Italian Republic* (ICSID Case No. ARB/17/14), icsid.worldbank.org/cases/case-database/case-detail?CaseNo=ARB/17/14.

[97] The award is available at jusmundi.com/en/document/decision/en-rockhopper-exploration-plc-rockhopper-italia-s-p-a-and-rockhopper-mediterranean-ltd-v-italian-republic-final-award-wednesday-24th-august-2022. Italy's attempt to annul the award is currently pending.

[98] *RWE AG and RWE Eemshaven Holding II BV v Kingdom of the Netherlands* (ICSID Case No. ARB/21/4), icsid.worldbank.org/cases/case-database/case-detail?CaseNo=ARB/21/4.

[99] A complete list can be found at icsid.worldbank.org/cases/case-database.

welfare measures due to fear that legal disputes[100] may arise from negative impacts on investors' profitability.[101] This phenomenon is known as 'regulatory chill'.[102] Yet, the available empirical evidence has failed to demonstrate that investment protection mechanisms, including access to ISDS mechanisms, have such a general effect.[103]

d. Balancing Economic Development and Sustainability

Investment protections can create situations where resources are exploited for short-term economic gain without considering long-term sustainability or environmental conservation.[104] This complicates the balancing of economic benefits and ecological sustainability. Careful policy design and decision-making are required to achieve both goals without compromising either.

Balancing investor rights with host state sovereignty and public interests is crucial but can be difficult. Host states may try to attract foreign investment to boost their economy, sometimes leading to less strict enforcement of environmental regulations to make their investment climate more appealing.[105] This approach can create tensions with the need to ensure responsible and sustainable resource extraction, particularly in the case of oil and gas projects that pose potential environmental risks.

Several examples show how some countries fail to ensure that factories, mines, or other facilities do not harm people or the planet. According to the World Resources Institute's 2015 Index of Environmental Democracy, countries like Ethiopia, Nicaragua, Guatemala, Bangladesh, and Thailand have some of the lowest scores.[106] Additionally,

[100] Kyla Tienhaara, 'Regulatory Chill in a Warming World: The Threat to Climate Policy Posed by Investor-State Dispute Settlement' (2018) 7(2) *Transnational Environmental Law* 229–50, doi:10.1017/S2047102517000309.

[101] *Rockhopper Italia S.p.A.* (n 96).

[102] Satwik Shekhar, '"Regulatory Chill": Taking Right to Regulate for a Spin, Centre for WTO Studies, CWS/WP/200/27' (Centre for WTO Studies, September 2016) 14–17, wtocentre.iift.ac.in/workingpaper/%27REGULATORY%20CHILL%E2%80%99%20TAKING%20RIGHT%20TO%20REGULATE%20FOR%20A%20SPIN%20(September%202016).pdf.

[103] Tarald Laudal Berge and Axel Berger, 'Does investor-state dispute settlement lead to regulatory chill? Global evidence from environmental regulation' (2019) *Political Economy of International Organisation* 12, paper 78, www.peio.me/wp-content/uploads/2019/01/PEIO12_Paper_78.pdf. The authors returned with a new study and qualified findings in 2021: Tarald Laudal Berge and Axel Berger, 'Do Investor-State Dispute Settlement Cases Influence Domestic Environmental Regulation? The Role of Respondent State Bureaucratic Capacity' (2021) 12(1) *Journal of International Dispute Settlement* 1–41, doi.org/10.1093/jnlids/idaa027. In the context of the Transatlantic Trade and Investment Partnership, a study prepared for the Dutch Ministers for Foreign Trade and Development Cooperation and of Foreign Affairs in 2014 found 'no conclusive empirical evidence for 'regulatory chill' due to the existence of an investment treaty providing for ISDS.' Christian Tietje and Freya Baetens, 'The Impact of Investor-State-Dispute Settlement (ISDS) in the Transatlantic Trade and Investment Partnership' (24 June 2014) para 283, www.eumonitor.eu/9353000/1/j4nvgs5kjg27kof_j9vvik7m1c3gyxp/vjn8exgvufya/f=/blg378683.pdf.

[104] Ben Purvis, Yong Mao and Darren Robinson, 'Three pillars of sustainability: in search of conceptual origins' (2019) 14 *Sustainability Science* 681–95, doi.org/10.1007/s11625-018-0627-5.

[105] Nick Mabey and Richard McNally, 'Foreign Direct Investment and the Environment: From Pollution Havens to Sustainable Development' (WWF UK) 39–41, www.oecd.org/investment/mne/2089912.pdf. See also OSCE, 'Best-Practice Guide for a Positive Business and Investment Climate' (2006) 134, www.osce.org/files/f/documents/c/f/19768.pdf.

[106] Jesse Worker, 'The Best and Worst Countries for Environmental Democracy' World Resources Institute, www.wri.org/insights/best-and-worst-countries-environmental-democracy#:~:text=National%20governments%20in%20Ethiopia%2C%20Nicaragua,harming%20people%20or%20the%20planet.

the first-ever global report on the environmental rule of law,[107] published in 2019 by researchers from the UN Environment Programme (UNEP), found that weak enforcement of environmental legislation is a worldwide trend. Despite the significant growth in environmental laws and agencies over the past four decades, environmental threats continue to increase because of this.[108]

e. Public Perception and Opposition

Avoiding the perception that foreign investors use investment protections to challenge legitimate environmental regulations is crucial. This perception can lead to public opposition and negative sentiment toward the industry and the legal mechanisms that support it. Such resistance can erode public trust in the industry and the legal framework, hindering efforts to develop sustainable offshore energy projects.

Legal advisers and companies now understand that addressing environmental, social, and governance (ESG) externalities is essential to maintaining their social licence. Despite criticism, current data shows that true ESG is consistent with a well-considered strategy and advances a company's business model.[109]

Existing conflicts must be handled thoughtfully and with much attention to detail. Mechanisms that safeguard investments will continue to be necessary for offshore energy ventures to attract capital. These mechanisms create a stable and predictable atmosphere for investors, giving them the confidence to make long-term commitments while balancing the broader goals of responsible energy development and public interest.

3. Incentives

Much like investments in onshore energy projects, investments in offshore energy infrastructure are long term, capital intensive, and require the state's regulatory powers to be exercised.[110] Various incentives developed through international and regional agreements or national initiatives are needed to attract and encourage investments.[111] Many are common to all energy projects, while some are specific to the offshore sector. These incentives can be grouped into four main categories: regulatory, economic/financial, technological, and contractual. Each is influenced by different national interests, such as promoting local economic development and ensuring energy security.

[107] UNEP, 'Environmental Rule of Law. First Global Report' (2019), wedocs.unep.org/bitstream/handle/20.500.11822/27279/Environmental_rule_of_law.pdf?sequence=1&isAllowed=y.

[108] UNEP, 'Press Release: Dramatic growth in laws to protect environment, but widespread failure to enforce, finds report' (24 January 2019), www.unep.org/news-and-stories/press-release/dramatic-growth-laws-protect-environment-widespread-failure-enforce.

[109] Lucy Pérez, Dame Vivian Hunt, Hamid Samandari, Robin Nuttall and Krysta Biniek, 'Does ESG really matter – and why?' (10 August 2022) www.mckinsey.com/capabilities/sustainability/our-insights/does-esg-really-matter-and-why#/.

[110] Nikolaos Giannopoulos, 'International Protection of Foreign Investments in Offshore Energy Production and Marine Environmental Protection: Birds of a Feather or Frenemies Forever?' (2021) 68 *Netherlands International Law Review* 249–80, doi.org/10.1007/s40802-021-00192-9.

[111] Yelena Shliomenzon, 'Mapping policy and legal framework for the offshore wind energy development' (*S&P Global*, 5 April 2022).

A. Regulatory Incentives

Regulatory incentives[112] increase investor confidence, attracting a wider pool of investors and speeding up project development. Projects that follow efficient regulatory processes tend to move from planning to production more quickly.[113] Nevertheless, regulatory processes that are too lenient can compromise environmental and safety standards.[114] It is crucial to strike a balance between making it easy to do business and maintaining essential regulatory oversight.

i. Streamlined Permitting and Licensing

Efficient and transparent permitting processes can encourage companies to undertake offshore projects[115] by reducing administrative burdens and uncertainties for investors. Simplified procedures can lead to quicker project approvals, enabling faster deployment, as acknowledged by various EU documents, such as the 2022 European Strategy for Offshore Renewable Energy.[116]

To illustrate, Danish offshore renewable energy development has been greatly supported by a clear policy and legal framework anchored in broad political energy agreements in the Danish Parliament. This resulted in a transparent, swift, and coordinated approval system for offshore wind projects, stable energy targets, and reduced risk for investors.[117]

At the EU level, the revised Regulation on Trans-European Energy Networks (TEN-E) aims to simplify and accelerate the scale-up of offshore grids[118] by including permitting provisions. These provisions operationalise the ambitions set in the EU offshore strategy.

ii. Stable Regulatory Environment

Legal frameworks that provide regulatory stability and predictability create an environment where investors can confidently commit resources without fear of abrupt

[112] Regulatory incentives may also include investment protection mechanisms. These are discussed separately in Section 2(A)(i).

[113] Joshua V Berliner, 'US BOEM Proposes Modernized Offshore Wind Regulations' (*Mayer Brown*) www.mayerbrown.com/en/perspectives-events/publications/2023/01/us-boem-proposes-modernized-offshore-wind-regulations.

[114] Report of the US National Commission on the BP Deepwater Horizon oil spill and offshore drilling: Written Ministerial Statement by Charles Hendry, www.gov.uk/government/news/report-of-the-us-national-commission-on-the-bp-deepwater-horizon-oil-spill-and-offshore-drilling-written-ministerial-statement-by-charles-hendry.

[115] IRENA, 'Enabling frameworks for offshore wind scale up: Innovations in permitting', www.irena.org/Publications/2023/Sep/Enabling-frameworks-for-offshore-wind-scale-up.

[116] European Parliament, 'P9_TA (2022)0032 A Strategy for Offshore Renewable Energy' para 44, www.europarl.europa.eu/doceo/document/TA-9-2022-0032_EN.pdf.

[117] Danish Energy Agency, 'De-risking Offshore Wind Power in Denmark' (November 2018), https://ens.dk/sites/ens.dk/files/Globalcooperation/de-risking_offshore_wind_nov2018.pdf.

[118] European Commission, 'Trans-European Networks for Energy', https://energy.ec.europa.eu/topics/infrastructure/trans-european-networks-energy_en.

policy changes. This contributes to investment protection indirectly. Conversely, poor coordination can result in inconsistent policy decisions that may weaken environmental protections or investor confidence. Thus, ensuring coherence between investment protection policies and environmental regulations is complex. Different ministries, departments, and stakeholders influence both domains.

These factors equally affect investments in fossil fuel and renewable energy, as reflected by several guidelines, including the 2015 OECD Policy Guidance for Investment in Clean Energy Infrastructure[119] and the European Investment Bank's Breaking Down Investment Barriers at Ground Level, or regional strategies such as the EU Strategy on Offshore Renewable Energy.[120]

Several good examples have been set at the governmental level. Romania demonstrates the importance of stability for investors within the oil and gas sector. After significant offshore deposits were discovered in its Black Sea EEZ,[121] the government adopted dedicated legislation[122] and reconfirmed the stabilisation principle. The principle is now reflected in the Petroleum Law and reinforced by stabilisation clauses in petroleum agreements.[123] These legal measures ensure that the terms set at the signing of the contract remain unchanged throughout its duration, providing a dependable framework for investors. However, the law also makes room for mutual amendment in the face of unforeseen circumstances, illustrating a balanced approach to regulatory stability and adaptability. This framework not only underscores the importance Romania places on fostering a stable investment environment but also highlights a level of flexibility that could be instrumental in adapting to evolving market conditions or unforeseen scenarios.[124]

Denmark relies on a transparent, swift, and coordinated approval system for offshore wind projects coupled with stable energy targets, which reduce risks for investors.[125] The US Department of Energy and the UK Government have taken similar approaches in their 2022 Offshore Wind Energy Strategies[126] and 2023 Offshore Wind Net Zero Investment Roadmap,[127] respectively.

[119] Available at OECD (2015), Policy Guidance for Investment in Clean Energy Infrastructure: Expanding Access to Clean Energy for Green Growth and Development, OECD Publishing, Paris, doi.org/10.1787/9789264212664-en.

[120] European Commission, 'Boosting Offshore Renewable Energy for a Climate Neutral Europe' (19 November 2020).

[121] 'Black Sea gas potential huge, but regulation needed to speed up development' (*Reuters*, 23 September 2022) www.reuters.com/business/energy/omv-petrom-needs-9-12-months-final-decision-black-sea-gas-project-ceo-2022-09-22/.

[122] Sam Morgan, 'Romania adopts offshore energy law, angers majors' (*Euractiv*, 10 July 2018) https://www.euractiv.com/section/energy/news/romania-adopts-offshore-energy-law-angers-majors/; Adrian Stoica, 'New Offshore Law Adopted by the Romanian Parliament' (*Energy Industry Review*, 24 May 2022) energyindustryreview.com/marketplace/new-offshore-law-adopted-by-the-romanian-parliament/.

[123] Petroleum Law no. 238 of 2004.

[124] Buzescu Ca, 'Romanian Oil and Gas Laws' (*Chambers and Partners*) chambers.com/articles/romanian-oil-and-gas-laws.

[125] See Section 3(A)(i).

[126] Available at www.energy.gov/sites/default/files/2022-01/offshore-wind-energy-strategies-report-january-2022.pdf.

[127] Available at assets.publishing.service.gov.uk/government/uploads/system/uploads/attachment_data/file/1167856/offshore-wind-investment-roadmap.pdf.

iii. Infrastructure Development

In a future with a resilient and decarbonised energy system, offshore renewable sources and grids that can accommodate the increasing amount of renewable capacity will be crucial. Therefore, investment and grid planning are more important than ever. Legal frameworks can encourage the establishment of shared infrastructure, such as offshore transmission networks and upgraded port infrastructure. The former reduces development costs for individual projects and accelerates the deployment of energy resources, while the latter is necessary to support the connection and deployment of offshore energy.

The EU's offshore renewable energy strategy recognises that the rapid and coordinated deployment of offshore renewable energy is key to reducing its dependence on fossil fuel imports from Russia, as outlined in the REPowerEU Plan.[128] Accordingly, the revised TEN-E Regulation includes a new chapter on offshore grids with provisions to support the scale-up of offshore grid development across the EU.[129]

The North Seas Energy Cooperation (NSEC) is an excellent example of how legal frameworks can encourage shared infrastructure. It is a collaborative initiative that links nine countries in the North Sea region through an offshore grid to promote renewable energy and stimulate economic growth.[130] The NSEC develops cross-border offshore wind and grid projects through structured cooperation, significantly lowering costs and space requirements for offshore developments in line with the EU's broader climate and energy goals for 2030 and 2050.

iv. Environmental Impact Assessment Guidelines

Clear guidelines for conducting environmental impact assessments (EIAs) help developers comply with environmental standards and regulations. At the EU level, the EIA Directive 2011/92/EU establishes clear guidelines for assessing the environmental impacts of public and private projects. These assist developers in ensuring that their projects align with the ecological standards set by the directive. The directive mandates that developers identify, describe, and assess their projects' direct and indirect effects on various environmental factors. This legal framework promotes sustainable practices and helps safeguard the environment while facilitating the necessary developmental initiatives.[131]

B. State-Driven Economic Incentives

Financial incentives can attract investment, especially in capital-intensive sectors like offshore energy. They help investors by reducing the financial burden and making

[128] European Commission, 'REPowerEU', commission.europa.eu/strategy-and-policy/priorities-2019-2024/european-green-deal/repowereu-affordable-secure-and-sustainable-energy-europe_en.

[129] European Commission, 'Trans-European Networks for Energy,' energy.ec.europa.eu/topics/infrastructure/trans-european-networks-energy_en.

[130] European Commission, 'The North Seas Energy Cooperation', https://energy.ec.europa.eu/topics/infrastructure/high-level-groups/north-seas-energy-cooperation_en.

[131] Article 4(2) Annex 2, Section 3(i) of the EIA Directive 2011/92/EU, eur-lex.europa.eu/legal-content/EN/TXT/?uri=CELEX%3A32011L0092.

projects more financially viable and attractive. Financial incentives can significantly accelerate the deployment of offshore energy projects, especially in the initial stages of market development. They enable companies to secure funding, develop infrastructure, and achieve economies of scale more quickly.[132] However, over-reliance on financial incentives alone can pose challenges as they might not address non-monetary barriers such as regulatory complexities, social acceptance, and infrastructure availability.[133]

i. Taxes

Various countries offer tax incentives to attract investment in offshore energy projects. These include reduced corporate income tax rates, investment tax credits, or accelerated depreciation for capital expenditures.[134] Waiving these taxes decreases the per-unit electricity cost, making the technology more competitive with other power generation sources, such as gas and oil.

Denmark[135] successfully created a supportive environment for the growth and sustainability of offshore wind energy through financial support and tax incentives during the early development of the offshore industry and now through the CO2 tax.[136] This strategy has set an excellent example for other countries aiming to enhance their renewable energy sector.[137]

The UK has introduced an attractive temporary investment incentive under the 2022 Energy Profits Levy, which offers higher tax depreciation rates for decarbonisation projects than for exploration and production investments until 2028. This is an excellent way to use the tax system to accelerate decarbonisation projects like floating offshore wind. However, there are worries that significant tax increases may cause uncertainty in the long run.

The US provides tax credits to build the offshore wind supply chain. The Inflation Reduction Act expanded existing tax credits for offshore wind projects by up to 40 per cent of the cost of constructing a new wind farm. However, due to local content requirements, projects must use domestically sourced materials to qualify for the full tax credit.[138]

[132] Office of Energy Efficiency & Renewable Energy, 'U.S. Department of Energy's Strategy to Advance Offshore Wind Energy in the United States', www.energy.gov/eere/us-department-energys-strategy-advance-offshore-wind-energy-united-states.

[133] 'Why People Oppose Or Support Offshore Wind: Distilling The Key Factors That Drive Social Acceptance Of Ocean Renewable Energy' (*Energy Innovation*) energyinnovation.org/2022/07/01/why-people-oppose-or-support-offshore-wind-distilling-the-key-factors-that-drive-social-acceptance-of-ocean-renewable-energy/.

[134] PWC, 'Green Taxes and Incentives Tracker', www.pwc.com/gx/en/services/tax/green-tax-and-incentives-tracker.html.

[135] Ministry of Foreign Affairs of Denmark, 'Denmark Expands Renewable Energy and CO2 Tax', investindk.com/insights/denmark-expands-renewable-energy-and-co2-tax.

[136] World Economic Forum, 'Explainer: Which countries have introduced a carbon tax?', www.weforum.org/agenda/2022/07/carbon-tax-emissions-countries/.

[137] Klint Klingberg-Jensen, Malene Harkjaer Frederiksen and Laura Higham Schlüter, 'Renewable Energy in Denmark' (*Poul Schmith/Kammeradvokaten*) media.poulschmith.dk/media/2kilqw0a/renewable-energy-denmark.pdf.

[138] Casey Crownhart, 'What's Next for Offshore Wind. New Projects and Financial Headwinds will Make 2024 a Bumpy Year for the Industry' (*MIT Technology Review*, 10 January 2024) www.technologyreview.com/2024/01/10/1086354/whats-next-for-offshore-wind/.

ii. Subsidies and Grants

Financing has been a significant obstacle to the deployment of renewables in many countries, and policy intervention has been required to provide greater certainty to investors. According to UNCTAD, financing remains a significant challenge in many developing countries.[139]

Governments may offer direct financial support to offset the high upfront costs associated with offshore energy development, such as infrastructure setup or exploration. This support comes through subsidies, grants, or low-interest loans. Support schemes for developing offshore wind play a crucial role because the economics of offshore wind are currently still challenging on a purely commercial basis in many countries.[140]

The EU has 12 funding programmes for offshore renewable energy projects, which offer a wide range of financing instruments. However, one should remain mindful of applicable state aid rules and the impossibility of obtaining double funding.[141]

At the national level, there is still debate on how countries should spend public money to stimulate renewable energy innovation and diffusion, including the offshore sector. One option is to promote the adoption of renewable energy systems by providing financial incentives to companies investing in innovation that could become marketable and adopted. The downside is that it will only bear fruit in the future once a new technology is developed and commercialised.

Another option is subsidising production via green certificates, contracts for difference, or guaranteeing generous prices to sell excess electricity back into the grid (feed-in tariffs). Nonetheless, this option puts pressure on state budgets (rendering them unsustainable) and tends to favour existing technology. Consequently, recent comparative studies into financial incentives encourage countries to adopt a multifaceted approach to renewable energy investments by creating niche markets through demand-based policies and supporting research and development (R&D) to finance both the short-term and long-term growth of the market.[142]

The issue of financing is even more contentious in changing markets. The cost of materials, such as steel for offshore wind turbines, fluctuates rapidly. The price of other materials has also increased due to inflation, while higher interest rates make borrowing money more expensive. Without adequate subsidies or flexible pricing, developers pull out of or attempt to renegotiate offshore projects. One example is Ørsted's cancellation of two offshore wind projects that would have supplied over 2.2 gigawatts to New Jersey because of rising interest rates, high inflation, and supply chain bottlenecks.[143] However, the industry's economic problems are global, with similar issues impacting projects in the UK, Denmark, and Taiwan.[144]

[139] UNCTAD, 'The Role of Science, Technology and Innovation in Promoting Renewable Energy by 2023' (United Nations publication, 2019) 5, unctad.org/system/files/official-document/dtlstict2019d2_en.pdf.

[140] Shliomenzon (n 111).

[141] European Commission, 'EU funding for offshore renewables', energy.ec.europa.eu/topics/renewable-energy/financing/eu-funding-offshore-renewables_en.

[142] Andrea Masini and Sam Aflaki, 'What's the Best Way for Governments to Support Renewable Energy' (*HEC Paris*, 27 January 2022) www.hec.edu/en/knowledge/articles/what-s-best-way-governments-support-renewable-energy.

[143] Crownhart (n 138).

[144] ibid.

Governments also grant significant subsidies to fossil fuels, including those produced offshore. These lower the price paid for fuel by consumers or increase the price energy producers receive. Such measures vary between countries and can be classified into four categories: direct financial transfers, preferential tax treatments, trade restrictions (ie, import duties and tariffs), and regulations (ie, price controls and rate caps). The US and the EU support fossil fuels through tax credits and loan guarantees for production. Starting in 2015, these amounts decreased due to the environmental impact of fossil fuels. Unfortunately, as of 2022, fossil fuel support has soared again because of the war in Ukraine.

iii. Technological Incentives

R&D incentives encourage technological innovation in the energy industry, promoting the adoption of innovative solutions, improving project efficiency, and reducing environmental impact. Technological incentives can catalyse breakthroughs in renewable energy technologies, making offshore energy projects more sustainable and cost effective.[145] They can also contribute to local innovation ecosystems. However, predicting the impact of technological incentives can be challenging as innovation timelines and outcomes are still being determined.[146] It is essential to ensure that incentives target viable and impactful technologies.

The EU offshore renewable energy strategy considers a broad range of technologies, some still in the developmental stage.[147] Therefore, the European Parliament strongly believes that R&D support plays a significant role in the European offshore renewable energy strategy. They urge the EU and its Member States to support R&D of multipurpose interconnectors, especially those that can efficiently integrate the offshore and onshore markets or floating offshore wind, tidal, wave, and current stations that could be adapted to different seabed conditions and minimise environmental impact. At the same time, they urge the private sector to increase R&D investments into circular and nature-inclusive offshore renewable energy design as well as technology for recycling and dismantling offshore stations.[148] Concurrently, the EC announced that Horizon Europe funds will support R&D, particularly in less mature technologies.[149]

Governments can incentivise innovation by offering grants, subsidies, or tax benefits for R&D activities related to offshore energy technologies. These incentives encourage the development of innovative solutions that enhance project efficiency and sustainability.[150]

[145] European Commission, 'Horizon Europe', commission.europa.eu/funding-tenders/find-funding/eu-funding-programmes/horizon-europe_en.

[146] European Commission, 'Horizon Europe – Performance', commission.europa.eu/strategy-and-policy/eu-budget/performance-and-reporting/programme-performance-statements/horizon-europe-performance_en.

[147] European Commission, 'Offshore Renewable Energy Strategy. Key Technologies' (19 November 2020) ec.europa.eu/commission/presscorner/api/files/attachment/866963/Offshore_Renewable_Key%20Technologies.pdf.

[148] European Parliament, 'A European Strategy for offshore renewable energy' paras 30–34.

[149] European Commission, 'Boosting Offshore Renewable Energy for a Climate Neutral Europe'.

[150] George Atalla, Meghan Mills and Julie McQueen, 'Six ways that governments can drive the green transition' (EY) www.ey.com/en_gl/government-public-sector/six-ways-that-governments-can-drive-the-green-transition.

Denmark's venture into wind energy technology began in response to the energy crises of the 1970s and strong public opposition to nuclear power. The Danish government imposed energy taxes on electricity prices in the mid-1970s to support the transition towards renewable energy. The funds from these taxes were then used to support renewable energy R&D. This initiative demonstrated the government's commitment to fostering a sustainable energy sector. Public opposition to nuclear energy and the emergence of alternative energy plans highlighted wind power as a viable alternative.[151] Despite the high costs of wind turbines in the early 1980s, the concept of local wind cooperatives emerged. This allowed for shared investments in wind turbines and propelled the development of the wind energy sector. Denmark's early financial support for renewable energy R&D, combined with a collaborative community-based investment model, significantly contributed to its progress in wind energy technology, paving the way for the country to become a global leader in wind energy.

C. Contractual Incentives

The advancement of offshore wind projects from idea to operation embodies a comprehensive convergence of financial, legal, and regulatory aspects. While robust regulatory frameworks, streamlined permitting processes, and incentivising schemes provide fertile ground for the inception and progression of offshore wind projects, project financing and contracting are decisive factors in developing such projects. Financing significantly impacts offshore wind projects' contracting structure and risk allocation. Therefore, it must be analysed to understand how it can benefit the development of offshore wind projects.

i. Bankability Considerations for Offshore Wind Projects

Most offshore wind industry developers (especially new ones) finance their projects through non-recourse project finance, typically engaging various parties to sponsor the project's development.[152] Generally, non-recourse financing is a way to finance a project where the borrower only has to pay back the loan with the money made from the project, without using any of their own money or other assets. For offshore wind farms, this implies that repayment to the lenders commences once the farm begins generating and selling electricity. To secure such financing, the developer needs to meet the bankability requirements set forth by the lenders.

Bankability refers to the project's financing through non-recourse schemes and risk allocation among the parties involved, predominantly focusing on the 'bankability review' of the contracts crucial for the wind farm's development.[153]

[151] IRENA, '30 Years of Policies for Wind Energy: Lessons from Denmark', www.irena.org/-/media/Files/IRENA/Agency/Publication/2013/GWEC/GWEC_Denmark.pdf?la=en&hash=C14BEEC4FFEEBA20B2B1928582AA23931F092F48.

[152] Jérôme Guillet, 'Financing Offshore Wind – Part 9, World Forum Offshore Wind', wfo-global.org/financing-offshore-wind-part-9/.

[153] Damian McNair, 'Investing in Infrastructure – International Best Legal Practice in Project and Construction Agreements – 2016' (PwC Australia) 263, www.lexology.com/library/detail.aspx?g=61b0822c-5e60-4400-8197-86b1c81fa1ce.

Several characteristics define a bankable project, including: (i) robust contractual structure (which will be further analysed below), (ii) experienced contractors, financing parties and developers, (iii) stable cash flow, and (iv) proven technology.[154]

The bankability of a project holds significant weight as, without it, the project cannot secure financing; if the financing conditions are unattractive, an offshore wind project may stagnate or be abandoned.

However, there needs to be a balance in bankability requirements among various participants. At times, the lenders may impose stringent requirements, exerting undue pressure on parties ill-equipped to manage such risks.[155] These rigorous requirements from lenders can increase the contract price, subsequently driving up the costs of offshore wind projects. The more risks the developer assumes, the lower the contract price for a particular scope, albeit at the expense of lenders' hesitance to accept such risks.[156]

Challenges arise when a negotiated contract sent to lenders for approval faces disagreement on the contracting setup, potentially reigniting discussions. This process can be burdensome as negotiations for critical offshore wind contracts, like wind turbine generators, can stretch up to a year, consuming valuable resources on both sides.[157]

Overall, bankability plays a crucial role in the development of the offshore wind industry. Yet, it can also create bottlenecks.[158] When lenders are satisfied with a project's viability and risk allocation, the path toward development is significantly smoother.

On top of other aspects that contribute to making a bankable offshore wind project (eg, having experienced contractors/subcontractors and proven technology), the contracts are pivotal in this equation as they orchestrate the risk allocation among the parties, making the project more attractive to financial stakeholders. Predetermined contracting frameworks, such as those provided by FIDIC,[159] contribute to a more predictable and structured approach to addressing bankability concerns. They help streamline the risk assessment process, thus enhancing the confidence of financing parties (lenders) in the project. For example, during the assessment of a project's bankability, the financing parties analyse whether the contractor provides any securities such as parent company guarantees or performance and warranty bonds and the value of such securities. This gives them confidence in the project's stability and covers potential scenarios where the contractor fails to perform the work, for instance. Additionally, this involves, among other things, reviewing the clauses related to the liability of the

[154] David Wadham, 'Bankability in offshore wind financing' Ashurst, www.asiawind.org/wp-content/uploads/2019/02/02-ASHURST-WADHAM.pdf.

[155] Jérôme Guillet, 'Financing offshore wind' (Green Giraffe) green-giraffe.com/wp-content/uploads/2021/02/110624_financing_offshore_wind_chapter_14_of_the_principles_of_project_finance.pdf.

[156] Cristian Rubanovici, 'Particularities of International Construction Contracts in the Offshore Wind Industry' Master's thesis (University of Copenhagen, 2021) papers.ssrn.com/sol3/papers.cfm?abstract_id=4125324.

[157] ibid.

[158] Nina Chestney, 'Analysis: Wind power industry drifts off course' (*Reuters*) www.reuters.com/sustainability/climate-energy/wind-power-industry-drifts-off-course-2023-09-28/.

[159] FIDIC, 'About us', www.fidic.org/about-us.

parties, any caps and carveouts to the liability, and the termination of the contract and its consequences.

Although not offshore wind related, the agreement between FIDIC and the World Bank, which endorses the utilisation of FIDIC's standard contracts in infrastructure projects (globally), is a robust example of approval and trust of 'pre-agreed' contractual standards by the financing parties. Through such frameworks, a precise and balanced risk allocation is delineated, effectively reducing contractual uncertainties and significantly enhancing the bankability and allure of projects to financiers. This ease in the risk assessment process directly accelerates the industry's growth.[160]

ii. Contracting

A proven contracting structure can accelerate the development of offshore wind projects, significantly reduce the negotiation period for wind contracts, and ensure a balanced risk allocation and predictability in the contracting setup.[161] An accepted contract standard helps the project's bankability by securing the financing parties' trust in the project. In dealing with the bankability exercise and the contracting, the developers must address various operational aspects, notably the procurement strategy, contracts, and risk allocation.[162]

This section refers only to contractual standards used for, inter alia, the supply, design, construction, and installation of offshore wind farm components. Aspects related to procuring consulting services and performing various environmental assessments are not analysed herein.

An offshore wind farm consists of several main components (packages) that together generate electricity: wind turbine generators, foundations, cables, offshore substations, and an onshore substation.[163] These components may be divided into different scopes based on the technical, commercial, and contractual aspects of the project. Some packages might only involve the supply of a component by a contractor, with installation services procured from another, for example, procuring wind turbine generators from Vestas and engaging DEME for the installation works of the generators. Given the complexities involved, negotiations can be time-consuming and contracts extensive, often exceeding 150 pages without including any commercial and technical schedules.

Opting for standard forms of contract might appear straightforward at first, as many industry players are already familiar with them. However, these standard forms may not always align perfectly with the specific objectives of a project. Given that offshore wind is a relatively new industry, parties must either carefully negotiate a bespoke agreement or select an international contractual standard and tailor it to the

[160] FIDIC, 'World Bank signs five-year agreement to use FIDIC standard contracts', fidic.org/world-bank-signs-five-year-agreement-use-fidic-standard-contracts.

[161] 'What are the advantages and disadvantages of using standard or customized procurement contracts?' (LinkedIn) www.linkedin.com/advice/1/what-advantages-disadvantages-using-standard-1c.

[162] Tim Vipond, 'Due Diligence in Project Finance' (Corporate Finance Institute) corporatefinanceinstitute.com/resources/valuation/due-diligence-project-finance/.

[163] 'Guide to an Offshore Wind Farm' guidetoanoffshorewindfarm.com.

project's needs. Various standard contracts are utilised in the construction of offshore wind farms, some of the most common ones being heavily amended versions of existing forms, notably:[164]

(i) **FIDIC**[165] provides nine contractual standard forms that can be used for different scopes of work depending on, for instance, who is providing the design or whether the works are to be performed 'on key'. In offshore wind, the FIDIC Yellow Book is commonly used. This book is primarily an onshore contract for building and engineering works where the contractor is responsible for the design. However, the Yellow Book – and other FIDIC standards – cannot be directly applied to offshore wind projects; they require modifications to adequately incorporate offshore-specific elements. Such amendments often include clauses addressing the risks associated with adverse weather conditions, installation vessels, the liability regime reflecting the offshore environment, and 'knock-for-knock' indemnities (see below).[166]

(ii) **LOGIC**[167] is a UK organisation that provides standard contracts for offshore oil and gas projects whose scope of work relates to, for instance, pipelaying and offshore hydrocarbon installation on the UK Continental Shelf. Being used for oil and gas, LOGIC contracts operate with the knock-for-knock indemnity principle, which has been adapted to offshore wind projects. A knock-for-knock indemnity means that each contracting party covers its own costs resulting from an incident (eg, damage to property, injury or death of an employee), and the damaged party covers the costs of the incident despite the negligence of the other party.[168] Overall, LOGIC already features built-in offshore provisions, unlike the FIDIC Yellow Book, which makes it usable for offshore wind projects, specifically in set-ups where the contractor would deliver the works 'on key,' assuming the lion's share of the risks. However, the contract is based on English law, and its original design for offshore oil and gas projects makes it less suitable for international offshore wind projects.[169]

(iii) **Norsk Industri NF/NTK**[170] is a set of contracts used in oil and gas projects for supplying and installing significant components to produce hydrocarbons on the Norwegian Continental Shelf. They are known for their balanced risk allocation and the knock-for-knock regime. However, their application to international offshore wind projects may be difficult due to their specific grounding in Norwegian law. Despite these limitations, NF/NTK contracts offer a neutral and balanced framework for risk allocation in offshore wind projects.

[164] Rubanovici (n 16) 210.
[165] FIDIC, 'About us', www.fidic.org/about-us.
[166] Rubanovici (n 16) 217.
[167] OEUK, 'Leading Offshore Energy Industry Competitiveness', oeuk.org.uk/legal-and-regulatory-competition-law/.
[168] Sylvie Cécile Cavaleri, 'The Validity of Knock-for-Knock Clauses in Comparative Perspective' (2018) 1 *European Review of Private Law* 3–30.
[169] Rubanovici (n 156).
[170] Norsk Industri, 'Norwegian Fabrication Contract (NF) and Norwegian Total Contract (NTK)', www.norskindustri.no/dokumenter/leveringsbetingelser/nfntk-standardkontrakter/.

(iv) **BIMCO**[171] is an international shipping industry organisation that develops contracts with amendable (in tracked changes) general terms and conditions to suit specific needs. These contracts generally favour vessel owners, protecting them from various risks, but charterers can adjust the risk balance. A classic unmodified SUPPLYTIME 2005 may be used for hiring transportation vessels for offshore wind farm personnel to perform necessary maintenance work or other activities. However, using the SUPPLYTIME for transporting and installing wind farm components requires specific amendments for jack-up vessels, grillage, and sea fastening. Unlike construction-focused FIDIC/LOGIC/NF/NTK contracts, BIMCO's scope is primarily vessel chartering, with modifications often required for comprehensive coverage in projects like offshore wind farms.[172]

(v) Generally, the advantages of using a standard contract form are closely linked to the fact that insurance companies, financing parties, and suppliers are familiar with the contracting obligations, which facilitates the negotiation process and the contract review by the parties.

It is worth noting that the offshore wind industry has been using a customised approach based on the FIDIC Yellow Book 1999 (Conditions of Contract for Plant and Design-Build) for developing offshore wind projects. This particular contract has been used for the supply and installation of various components of offshore wind farms. However, the standard contract in its original form did not meet the industry's requirements, necessitating significant modifications by the parties involved. This is mainly because the Yellow Book is designed for onshore work.[173] The choice of the FIDIC Yellow Book as a standard for offshore wind is linked to historical circumstances: when DONG Energy (now Ørsted) began working with international contractors, they struggled to convince them to accept a Danish standard contract form. As a result, the parties had to agree on an international standard, and FIDIC was chosen. Some of the main motives include its suitability for project finance and the parties' familiarity with the standard.[174]

Recognising that the onshore contract cannot adequately answer the stakeholders' needs, FIDIC took a proactive step and announced in July 2023 the establishment of Task Group 14, which is dedicated to drafting a specialised offshore wind contract anticipated to be unveiled in late 2025.[175] The industry players have been eagerly awaiting a standard that can offer balanced contracting and speed up the development of offshore wind projects. The future contract is designed to capture and regulate elements related to the offshore environment, such as adverse weather risks and knock-for-knock indemnities. The goal is to draft a standard contract that can be applied to different packages of an offshore wind farm.

[171] Baltic and International Maritime Council, 'About us and our members', www.bimco.org/about-us-and-our-members.

[172] Ralph Busch, 'Construction Contracts for Offshore Wind Farms' (2014) *International Construction Law Review* 426.

[173] Rubanovici (n 156).

[174] ibid.

[175] FIDIC, 'Work starts on new FIDIC contract for offshore wind farm projects', fidic.org/node/41494.

FIDIC is not the only organisation looking to provide a contractual baseline for offshore wind projects. The International Marine Contractors Association (IMCA) has developed a set of contracting principles tailored to renewable energy projects as well as a standard contract for the transportation and installation of offshore wind farm components. IMCA aims to foster long-term relationships among industry stakeholders by encouraging a balanced contractual framework that not only improves operational efficiency but also has the potential to reduce overall project costs.[176]

Creating standardised contracting frameworks is crucial in speeding up the development of offshore wind projects. By learning lessons from offshore oil and gas projects, a more established industry with recognised and globally applied standard contracts, offshore wind can benefit from a contractual foundation that helps overcome bankability challenges and promotes smoother relationships between developers, contractors, and financiers. This also ensures a fair distribution of risk between all parties involved in the project and predictability in addressing potential disputes throughout the project lifecycle.

D. Local Economic Development

Incentives are often coupled with governmental requirements that a certain percentage of project expenses be spent on local goods, services, and labour, promoting local employment and industry development.[177]

i. Local Content Requirements

These requirements aim to boost economic growth, create jobs, and develop local expertise in offshore energy sectors. However, the industry opposes them, believing they will lead to additional burdens and foster corruption.[178] In some instances, these requirements (along with taxation measures) can have a counterproductive effect by discouraging investments and delaying the development of offshore resources. This was seen in Romania after the first version of its offshore operations law was adopted.[179]

The most recent illustration of the local content requirement comes from the United States. The Biden-Harris administration's Inflation Reduction Act plans to fight climate change and accelerate America's clean energy economy.[180] Offshore wind projects will be built with 'good-paying, union jobs and 'Made in America' materials,' ensuring that nationals benefit from the new developments. Financial incentives have been

[176] IMCA, 'IMCA renewables contracting principles', www.imca-int.com/product/imca-renewables-contracting-principles/.

[177] OECD, 'Local content requirements impact the global economy,' www.oecd.org/en/publications/local-content-requirements_5b1c38d5-en.html.

[178] Ted Rhodes, 'Brazil proposes relaxation of local content requirements' (*CMS Law-Now*, 27 February 2017) cms-lawnow.com/en/ealerts/2017/02/brazil-proposes-relaxation-of-local-content-requirements.

[179] Morgan (n 122).

[180] The White House, 'Building a clean energy economy: a guidebook to the inflation reduction act's investments in clean energy and climate action, January 2023, version 2', www.whitehouse.gov/wp-content/uploads/2022/12/Inflation-Reduction-Act-Guidebook.pdf.

implemented to encourage investors to use locally produced wind turbine blades, towers, and cables.[181]

ii. Revenue Sharing

Countries sometimes require a portion of the revenue generated from offshore energy projects to be allocated to local communities or regions. This helps to develop the local economy and gain support from the community.

In the UK, community benefit funds are associated with offshore wind projects. For instance, the Beatrice Offshore Wind Farm established a community fund administered by SSE Renewables. This fund commits £6 million over the wind farm's operational life to projects, community groups, and organisations in the Highland and Moray regions.[182] The primary objective is to encourage sustainable community and economic growth, particularly in areas affected by offshore wind development. Through arrangements like these, revenue generated from offshore wind projects is shared with local communities, fostering support and providing financial resources to promote local development and sustainability.

4. Conclusion

The importance of legal frameworks regarding offshore energy projects cannot be overstated. The complex interplay among international, regional, and domestic laws governing such projects reveals a delicate balance between cooperation and conflicts. While efforts to align resource allocation and environmental protection standards exist, misalignments persist, often driven by domestic economic priorities and geopolitical realities. This evolving landscape necessitates ongoing diplomatic negotiations, regulatory harmonisation, and strategic international cooperation to ensure sustainable development.

A multifaceted approach is necessary to create an environment conducive to accelerating offshore energy project growth. This approach should incorporate regulatory, economic, technological, contractual, and local development incentives. However, achieving the delicate balance between encouraging investment and ensuring environmental sustainability requires thoughtful consideration of diverse national interests. The evolving landscape calls for continuous adaptation of legal frameworks to address challenges, promote innovation, and navigate the complex interplay shaping the offshore energy sector's trajectory.

Safeguarding offshore energy investments necessitates an equilibrium between international treaties and domestic laws, especially regarding environmental

[181] The White House, 'FACT SHEET: Biden-Harris Administration Races to Deploy Clean Energy that Creates Jobs and Lowers Costs' (12 January 2022) www.whitehouse.gov/briefing-room/statements-releases/2022/01/12/fact-sheet-biden-harris-administration-races-to-deploy-clean-energy-that-creates-jobs-and-lowers-costs/.

[182] Beatrice Offshore Wind Farm, 'Community Investment', www.beatricewind.com/funds.

considerations. Investment protection frameworks, crucial for investor confidence, face challenges such as regulatory tensions and public opposition, highlighting the need for nuanced policy design. Achieving harmony between economic development and sustainability requires careful navigation of legal mechanisms, and acknowledging the evolving landscape of environmental consciousness and societal expectations. This balance ensures a robust foundation for the offshore energy sector's growth while upholding responsible development practices.

8

Energy Transition and Tax Considerations for Oil, Gas, Wind Projects, and Carbon Taxation for Offshore Energy – Focus on the Brazilian Experience

DIANA RODRIGUES PRADO DE CASTRO

1. Introduction

Climate change is a leading topic of global discussion and one of the most critical challenges of this century.[1] The issue of greenhouse gas emissions has sparked a massive global shift from an economy heavily reliant on fossil fuels to business models predominantly powered by renewable energy. Although this shift may result in lower demand for oil and gas, fossil fuels will continue to be an important energy source in the coming years.

The energy transition is driven by financial investments intended to benefit both investing firms and the states that host energy production. Tax structures can both promote and hinder investment. Fiscal and incentive policies may encourage the rollout of specific technologies or project profiles. Offshore energy developments are no exception, and states worldwide seek to balance extracting revenue from the exploitation of their offshore natural resources.

Using the Brazilian energy transition as a case study, this chapter examines the importance of tax concerns as well as financial and fiscal incentives. It compares and emphasises the significance of taxes as a political strategy in the rise of renewable energy sources, the decarbonisation of the economy, and the possibility of lower oil and gas consumption in the coming years. The chapter focuses on recent legislative actions in Brazil that demonstrate the country's commitment to attaining energy transition goals, as well as how taxation affects the oil and gas industry, particularly offshore operations.

[1] 'Climate Change' (*United Nations*) www.un.org/en/global-issues/climate-change.

2. Preliminary Aspects Regarding Energy Transition: World Context vis-à-vis the Brazilian Perspective

A. Introduction

Climate change, exacerbated by the extensive burning of fossil fuels, poses the most critical environmental challenge of the twenty-first century.[2] The growing concentration of greenhouse gases (GHGs) in the atmosphere has resulted in rising global temperatures, which has far-reaching effects on ecosystems, human health, and the global economy. This situation has intensified discussions on the global energy transition, a process crucial for decarbonising the environment and reducing our reliance on fossil fuels. The urgency of this transition is underscored by the need to ensure energy security and mitigate the risks associated with fossil fuel dependence.

The global reliance on fossil fuels not only accelerates climate change but also poses significant risks to energy security.[3] The ongoing war between Russia and Ukraine provides a stark example of these risks. Both nations are major exporters of natural gas, and the conflict has led to severe disruptions in energy supply chains. This has resulted in energy shortages in various regions and a sharp increase in the price of natural gas, with oil prices peaking at $130 per barrel and US natural gas prices reaching $13 per million British thermal units (mmbtu).

The conflict has forced European nations, heavily dependent on Russian energy exports, to adopt energy rationing policies and seek alternative energy sources. Countries like Italy, Germany, Austria, and the Netherlands have reactivated coal-fired power plants to address immediate energy shortages,[4] while the United Kingdom has announced plans to construct eight nuclear power plants by 2030. These actions highlight the vulnerability of fossil fuel-dependent energy systems and the need for a diversified and resilient energy matrix.

In response to the challenges posed by climate change and energy insecurity, the global energy transition has emerged as a critical strategy.[5] The energy transition involves a paradigm shift from energy generation and consumption patterns that rely on polluting fossil fuels to those based on clean, renewable sources such as hydroelectric, wind, solar, and biomass. This shift is essential not only for mitigating the impacts of global warming but also for reducing the geopolitical risks associated with fossil fuel dependence.

In parallel to this transition to an economy less dependent on fossil fuels and the emergence of renewable sources of energy, it is worth noting the role of oil and gas

[2] 'Climate Change' (*United Nations*) www.un.org/en/global-issues/climate-change#:~:text=Global%20warming%20of%201.1%C2%B0,on%20nature%20and%20people%20worldwide.

[3] Bernard Njindan Iyke, 'Climate change, energy security risk, and clean energy investment' (2024) 129 *Energy Economics* 107225, doi.org/10.1016/j.eneco.2023.107225 (www.sciencedirect.com/science/article/pii/S0140988323007235).

[4] Available at www.washingtonpost.com/world/2022/06/22/coal-plant-europe-germany-austria-netherlands-russia-gas/.

[5] Fengyun Li, Junxia Zhang and Xingmei Li, 'Energy security dilemma and energy transition policy in the context of climate change: A perspective from China' (2023) 181 Energy Policy 113624, doi.org/10.1016/j.enpol.2023.113624 (www.sciencedirect.com/science/article/pii/S0301421523002094).

sources in achieving energy transition goals, considering that global demand would remain significant in the following years. In this context, according to the World Oil Outlook 2024 issued by the Organization of Petroleum Exporting Countries (OPEC),[6] the share of oil and gas in the energy mix stays above 53 per cent through 2050, with oil retaining the largest share at above 29 per cent. Thus, although big shifts in the energy mix would be verified in the following years, oil and gas are set to remain crucial for energy supply in the period to 2050. Their combined share in the energy mix is expected to stay above 53 per cent throughout the outlook period. Oil retains the largest share at 29.3 per cent in 2050, with gas at 24 per cent.

B. The Energy Transition in Brazil in a Nutshell

Specifically in Brazil, despite the country's dependence on energy sources derived from fossil fuels, it is possible to identify a leading role in projects using renewable energy matrices.[7] It is worth noting that, unlike the rest of the world, which depends primarily on coal, Brazil's electricity matrix corresponds primarily to hydroelectric energy (representing more than 60 per cent of the matrix), while natural gas, solar, and wind power jointly represents around 20 per cent of the matrix.[8]

Regarding the Brazilian energy matrix,[9] unlike the rest of the world, there is no significant dependence on coal as an energy source, while oil and derivatives still represent a substantial share of the matrix, followed by renewable sources such as sugar cane, hydroelectric, wind, and solar.

The relevant share of renewable sources in the energy matrix vis-à-vis the commitment of the country to reduce the emissions of GHGs has been supporting the energy transition in Brazil, which has been followed by several legislative initiatives to regulate this market and enable the increase of investments in these new businesses.

Despite this fact, it is worth noting that oil and derivatives still represent a substantial share of the energy matrix and the Brazilian Gross Domestic Product (GDP). According to data released by the National Confederation of Industry (CNI), based on information from the Brazilian Institute of Geography and Statistics (IBGE), the oil and gas industry represented 17.2 per cent of Brazilian industrial GDP in 2021, marking the highest value in the composition of the indicator in the last decade.[10] It places the sector as a leader in participation within the industry's GDP, highlighting its strategic importance for the national economic panorama. It is worth mentioning

[6] World Oil Outlook 2024, Organization of Petroleum Exporting Countries (OPEC) publications.opec.org/woo.

[7] Daphiny Pottmaier, CR Melo, MN Sartor, S Kuester, TM Amadio, CAH Fernandes, Daniel Marinha and OE Alarcon, 'The Brazilian energy matrix: From a materials science and engineering perspective' (2013) 19 *Renewable and Sustainable Energy Reviews* 678–91, doi.org/10.1016/j.rser.2012.11.063.

[8] Juliana de Almeida Yanaguizawa Lucena and Klayton Ângelo Azevedo Lucena, 'Wind energy in Brazil: an overview and perspectives under the triple bottom line' (2019) 3(2) *Clean Energy* 69–84, doi.org/10.1093/ce/zkz001.

[9] Pottmaier, Melo, Sartor, Kuester, Amadio, Fernandes, Marinha and Alarcon (n 7).

[10] See Brazilian Petroleum Institute (IBP), *Setor de Petróleo e Gás lidera PIB Industrial Brasileiro* (22 May 2024) www.alemdasuperficie.org/ibp/setor-de-petroleo-e-gas-lidera-pib-industrial-brasileiro/.

that Brazil is the ninth largest oil producer in the world,[11] and Brazilian oil has a lower carbon intensity than the global average, an important characteristic in the context of energy transition.[12]

According to a study published by the Institute for Applied Economic Research (INEA),[13] oil and its derivatives represented, in 2023, US$42,611 million, corresponding to the country's second most exported product.

The Brazilian Institute of Petroleum (IBP)[14] states that this segment experienced a substantial expansion, increasing its participation in industrial GDP from 4.4 per cent in 2020 to 11.6 per cent in 2021. Such growth would have been driven by an increase in the international price of oil from around 70 per cent, offsetting the 1.5 per cent drop in national crude oil production in 2021. The derivatives and biofuels segment remained relatively stable during the same period, and its contribution to industrial GDP rose from 5.8 per cent in 2020 to 5.6 per cent in 2021.

In this context, we will analyse how the energy transition is being addressed in Brazil, the relevance of the oil and gas industry and the role played by taxation, whether to encourage investments in projects and new business models using renewable energy sources and decarbonisation in the country or to discourage the use of fossil energy sources, notably oil and natural gas and its derivatives associated to offshore activities.

3. How to Achieve the Energy Transition and the Role of Taxation Policies: Perspectives in Brazil

A. Introduction

Energy transition initiates have been leading the legislative and political debates in recent years and several measures have been adopted in Brazil to reduce GHG emissions while enabling new investments in projects associated with renewable sources of energy.[15] Taxation policies, as well as levies set by the Brazilian government to steer certain investments, have played a key role, as discussed below.

In this section the author addresses the participation of Brazilian states in renewable energy projects, the Brazilian sources of energy, and the main legislative initiatives recently adopted and/or under discussion in the Brazilian Congress.

[11] Brazilian Petroleum Institute, 'O setor de O&G brasileiro' – The Brazilian O&G sector (2022), www.ibp.org.br/personalizado/uploads/2022/09/ibp-the-brazilian-og-sector-en.pdf.

[12] Marco Antonio Montoya, Gabriela Allegretti, Luís Antônio Sleimann Bertussi and Edson Talamini, 'Renewable and Non-renewable in the energy-emissions-climate nexus: Brazilian contributions to climate change via international trade' (2021) 312 Journal of Cleaner Production 127700, doi.org/10.1016/j.jclepro.2021.127700.

[13] Instituto de Pesquisa Econômica Aplicada, Visão Geral da Conjuntura (2024).

[14] Brazilian Petroleum Institute (IBP) (n 10).

[15] Center For Integrated Studies on Climate Change and Environment – COPPE/UFRJ, rep www.climate-transparency.org/wp-content/uploads/2019/04/Brazilian-Policy-Paper-En.pdf.

B. Alternative Energy Sources Used in Brazil

Renewable and alternative energy sources are being promoted throughout Brazil through a combination of governmental initiatives and private capital investment.[16] Some are linked directly to offshore activity, with important offshore wind ambitions, while others are still onshore. These alternative energy forms include hydroelectric, wind, solar, and biogas.

i. Biogas and Biomethane

Biogas, whose production has doubled in the last five years in Brazil, is generated by the anaerobic decomposition of organic waste through the action of bacteria.[17] Biomethane, produced through carbon capture and biogas treatment, removing dust, sulfur, and moisture, increased by 82 per cent in its production compared to production in 2021.

Biomethane can be considered one of the key elements in the energy transition process in Brazil.[18] This is because its chemical composition is similar to that of natural gas, which means that its use does not require equipment to be replaced or adapted to use biomethane. Although partially, this fuel replaces Natural Gas, in several applications, such as in the form of fuel, piped gas, and fertiliser production process for agribusiness.

Biomethane is also considered a cleaner energy source since it releases less CO^2 in the atmosphere compared to fossil fuels. In addition to producing 'clean' fuel, biomethane provides adequate treatment for organic waste, such as Urban Solid Waste (MSW) (ie, landfills), and agricultural and industrial waste.

Bill of Law No. 528/2020, also called the Fuel of the Future Bill, was approved by the Brazilian Senate on 4 September 2024, establishing: (i) the National Sustainable Aviation Fuel Program (ProBioQAV), (ii) the National Green Diesel Program (PNDV), and (iii) the National Program for Decarbonization of Natural Gas Producers and Importers and Incentive to Biomethane.[19]

It changes the maximum and minimum limits of the blend content of anhydrous ethanol in gasoline C and the blend content of biodiesel in diesel, sold to the end consumer. The Bill of Law regulates and provides for the inspection of activities involving carbon dioxide capture and geological storage and the production and sale of synthetic fuels.

[16] Brazil – County Commercial Guide, 'Renewable Energy Infrastructure' (*International Trade Administration | Trade.gov*) www.trade.gov/country-commercial-guides/brazil-renewable-energy-infrastructure-0.

[17] Carlos H Coimbra-Araújo, Leidiane Mariane, Cicero Bley Júnior, Elisandro Pires Frigo, Michelle Sato Frigo, Izabela Regina Costa Araújo and Helton José Alves, 'Brazilian case study for biogas energy: Production of electric power, heat and automotive energy in condominiums of agroenergy' (2014) 40 *Renewable and Sustainable Energy Reviews* 826–39, doi.org/10.1016/j.rser.2014.07.024.

[18] Geraldo de Lemos, Maxiane Frank Oliveira Cardoso and Hirdan Katarina de Medeiros Costa, 'Biogas and Biomethane in Brazil: Overview and Perspectives' (2024) 63 *DMA* 464.

[19] 'Brazil's Ministry of Mines and Energy Advances Sustainable Aviation Fuels' (*Secretaria de Comunicação Social*, 12 September 2024) www.gov.br/secom/en/latest-news/2024/09/brazils-ministry-of-mines-and-energy-advances-sustainable-aviation-fuels.

It also integrates initiatives and measures adopted in the National Biofuel Policy (RenovaBio), Mover Program (both abovementioned), and Brazilian Vehicle Labeling Program (PBEV). It created the National Sustainable Aviation Fuel Program (ProBioQAVb), which aims to encourage research, production, sale, and energy use of sustainable aviation fuel in the Brazilian energy matrix. Under the programme, air operators are required to reduce GHG emissions through SAF, starting in 2027.

The National Green Diesel Program (PNDV) was created to encourage research, production, sale, and energy use of green diesel. The programme establishes, by 2037, the mandatory minimum volumetric participation of green diesel about diesel sold to the end consumer.

The Bill also creates the National Program for Decarbonization of Natural Gas Producers and Importers and Incentives for Biomethane. This programme encourages research, production, sale, and use of biomethane and biogas in the Brazilian energy matrix to decarbonise the natural gas sector.

There is a forecast for defining an annual target for reducing GHG emissions in the market for commercialised natural gas, to be met through the participation of biomethane in natural gas consumption. Furthermore, the targets will be accompanied by a Biomethane Origin Guarantee Certificate (CGOB), which consists of a tradable traceability certificate backed by the volume of biomethane produced and sold by the biofuel producer, which reinforces the characteristics of the production process and which must include, at least, the origin of the input for biomethane production and the location of production.

Finally, the Bill of Law provides for the regulation of the Carbon Dioxide Capture and Storage Industry, through which the activities to be carried out must follow the following guidelines: (i) economic efficiency and sustainability; (ii) adoption of methods, techniques, and processes that consider local and regional specific characteristics and the best practices of the industry; and (iii) integration of infrastructures, services and geological and geophysical information for efficient management of the natural resources involved in the development of the activity.

ii. Low-carbon Hydrogen

Low-carbon hydrogen (ie, primary green hydrogen), produced through the electrolysis of water using renewable energy, represents a pivotal shift in global energy strategies.[20] As a carbon-free fuel, its production process eliminates GHG emissions.

This chapter explores the growing importance of green hydrogen, examining its anticipated global demand, diverse applications, and the strategic initiatives of Brazil – a country with significant potential to become a leading exporter by 2030. The study also delves into the policies and frameworks being developed to support the expansion of the green hydrogen market, particularly through the Brazilian National Hydrogen Program.

[20] 'Green Hydrogen: The Energy of the Future Essential for Decarbonisation' (ACCIONA) www.acciona.com/green-hydrogen/#:~:text=Also%20called%20renewable%20hydrogen%2C%20green,cleanest%20and%20most%20sustainable%20hydrogen.

Hydrogen has long been recognised as a versatile energy carrier, but its production methods have historically been associated with significant carbon emissions.[21] Green hydrogen, however, offers a sustainable alternative, produced from renewable sources through the electrolysis of water.[22] This process not only provides a renewable energy source but also ensures zero emissions across all production phases. The global energy landscape is evolving, with green hydrogen positioned as a critical component in achieving decarbonisation targets.

Recent projections highlight the growing global demand for green hydrogen. In 2019, the demand was recorded at 71 million tons. By 2040, this figure is expected to nearly double, reaching 137 million tons, with a further increase to 519 million tons by 2070. These forecasts underscore green hydrogen's potential to play a central role in the future energy mix.

It is worth noting that green hydrogen's versatility is evident in its wide range of applications. It can be utilised in internal combustion engine vehicles, including cars, motorcycles, and aircraft. Additionally, it is used in electricity generation through turbo generators, powering electric vehicles, and generating heat. Beyond energy, green hydrogen serves as a crucial raw material in the steel and metals industry and the pharmaceutical industry. Furthermore, it is essential for producing green ammonia (NH3), a key component in fertilisers, cleaning products, and plastics.

Brazil is poised to become a major global player in the green hydrogen market. By 2030, the country is expected to be one of the leading exporters, with over $30 billion in hydrogen projects announced. Brazil has the technical potential to produce 1.8 gigatons of hydrogen annually, positioning itself as a crucial supplier in the global market. The country's strategy focuses on accelerating the green hydrogen economy, making the market competitive, and offering solutions for sectors with high emission reduction challenges.

To support the development of a green hydrogen economy, Brazil has implemented the National Hydrogen Program, with a three-year work plan spanning from 2023 to 2025.[23] The programme outlines several key priorities, including the definition of a national legal-regulatory framework, increased investment in research, development, and innovation (R&D&I) aimed at cost reduction, and the expansion of financing options. Additionally, the programme emphasises the importance of strengthening scientific and technological foundations, training human resources, improving the representation and modeling of the hydrogen energy chain, and developing a robust legal and regulatory framework.

Green hydrogen represents a transformative shift in global energy strategies, with the potential to significantly reduce carbon emissions across various sectors. Brazil's proactive approach to developing its green hydrogen economy, supported by

[21] IEA, 'Hydrogen' (*IEA*) www.iea.org/energy-system/low-emission-fuels/hydrogen.

[22] Qusay Hassan, Sameer Algburi, Aws Zuhair Sameen, Hayder M Salman and Marek Jaszczur, 'Green hydrogen: A pathway to a sustainable energy future' (2024) 50(B) *International Journal of Hydrogen Energy* 310–33, doi.org/10.1016/j.ijhydene.2023.08.321.

[23] Serhat Demirkol, 'Brazil's National Hydrogen Program Propels the Nation towards Energy Transition Leadership' (*Brazilian NR*, 20 January 2024) braziliannr.com/2024/01/13/brazils-national-hydrogen-program-propels-the-nation-towards-energy-transition-leadership/#:~:text=The%20triennial%20plan%20sets%20ambitious,carbon%20hydrogen%20hubs%20by%202035.

strategic investments and regulatory frameworks, positions it as a key player in the global market.[24] As the demand for green hydrogen continues to grow, the importance of establishing a competitive and sustainable market will be critical to achieving global decarbonisation goals.

On 11 July 2024, the Brazilian Congress passed Bill of Law No. 2,308/2023, establishing the legal framework for green hydrogen in Brazil. This Bill of Law, as we discuss below, was enacted in August 2024. Together, this legislative milestone outlines key provisions for the regulation, production, and development of low-carbon hydrogen, positioning Brazil as a future leader in the global hydrogen market.

Green hydrogen, recognised as a pivotal element in the transition to a low-carbon economy, has gained significant traction worldwide. In Brazil, the recent passage of Bill of Law No. 2,308/2023 marks a critical step in creating a robust legal and regulatory environment for the production and commercialisation of green hydrogen. This legal framework not only defines the key types of hydrogen – Low-Carbon Hydrogen, Renewable Hydrogen, and Green Hydrogen – but also sets forth a comprehensive strategy to promote its development through regulatory oversight, subsidies, and incentive programmes.

In 2023, with the Bill of Law No. 2,308/2023, the first steps to the development of a comprehensive hydrogen regulation were established in Brazil. On 6 August 2024, the Bill of Law was published as the Law nº 14.948/2024 – or the Low-Carbon Hydrogen Act.[25] The adoption of the Low-Carbon Hydrogen Act marks a significant advancement in Brazil's efforts to develop a sustainable and competitive green hydrogen economy. This comprehensive instrument includes:

(i) Definitions: The law provides clear definitions for Low-Carbon Hydrogen, Renewable Hydrogen, and Green Hydrogen, establishing the basis for regulation and policy-making.
(ii) Regulatory Authority: The Brazilian Agency of Petroleum, Natural Gas, and Biofuels (ANP) is designated as the regulatory authority with jurisdiction over the hydrogen chain. ANP is responsible for regulating hydrogen activities, issuing production authorisations, and overseeing the entire hydrogen lifecycle.
(iii) National Low-Carbon Hydrogen Policy: The establishment of this policy aims to foster the production and use of low-carbon hydrogen within Brazil's energy matrix, encouraging the development of a competitive and sustainable hydrogen industry.
(iv) Subsidies and Incentives: The creation of the Low-Carbon Hydrogen Development Program (PHBC) and the Special Regime of Incentives to Low-Carbon Hydrogen Production (REHIDRO) are designed to provide financial support and promote the competitiveness of hydrogen projects.
(v) Certification System: The Brazilian Hydrogen Certification System (SBH2) will ensure that hydrogen production meets national and international standards for sustainability and carbon reduction.

[24] '12 Insights on Hydrogen – Brazil Edition' (*Agora*) www.agora-industry.org/fileadmin/Projekte/2023/2023-24_IND_H2_Insights_BRA/A-IND_322_12-Insights-H2-Brazil_EN_WEB.pdf.

[25] Brazilian NR, 'ANP Takes Charge of Low-Carbon Hydrogen Regulation in Brazil', braziliannr.com/2024/08/07/anp-takes-charge-of-low-carbon-hydrogen-regulation-in-brazil/.

The National Policy of Low-Carbon Hydrogen, as defined by the new legal framework, serves as a nationwide instrument to guide public policy development on low-carbon hydrogen. This policy identifies 23 objectives aimed at promoting energy transition and supporting the domestic and international markets for low-carbon hydrogen. Key principles include:

- Technological Neutrality: Ensuring that incentives for hydrogen production and use are not biased toward specific technologies.
- Market Integration: Facilitating the inclusion of low-carbon hydrogen within the Brazilian energy matrix.
- Regulatory Predictability: Establishing a stable regulatory environment to encourage market expansion.
- Infrastructure Utilisation: Promoting the efficient use of existing energy infrastructure.
- Research and Development: Encouraging innovation and technological advancements in low-carbon hydrogen production.

The ANP is tasked with regulating and controlling the production of hydrogen, including natural hydrogen (white hydrogen), under the new legal framework. Companies or consortia involved in hydrogen production must obtain authorisation from ANP, which also has the authority to implement a regulatory sandbox to test and refine regulatory approaches. ANP's jurisdiction extends to activities related to the transportation, processing, importation, exportation, storage, and commercialisation of hydrogen and its derivatives.

The framework also amends Law No. 9,427/1996 to include the National Electric Energy Agency (ANEEL) in supporting ANP by contributing to the regulation of low-carbon hydrogen produced via electrolysis. ANEEL is empowered to grant Public Utility Declarations (DUP) for facilities exclusively intended for connecting low-carbon hydrogen projects to the grid.

In addition to the passing of the Low-Carbon Hydrogen Act, on 2 August 2024, Bill No. 2308/2023 was approved by the Brazilian Chamber of Deputies, establishing the legal framework for a special Regime of Incentives for Low-Carbon Hydrogen Production (REHIDRO). REHIDRO is a special programme and state-led incentive established to enhance the competitiveness of the low-carbon hydrogen industry in Brazil.[26] Modelled after successful incentive policies like REIDI, REHIDRO provides tax incentives valid for five years, starting from 1 January 2025. These incentives are available to companies that meet specific criteria, including the use of a minimum percentage of Brazilian goods and services and investment in research, development, and innovation (RD&I).

Eligible participants in REHIDRO include not only hydrogen producers but also those involved in packaging, storage, transportation, renewable electricity generation for hydrogen production, and biofuel production for hydrogen.

[26] ibid.

Furthermore, the Brazilian Federal Government has enacted Law No. 14.990/2024, establishing the Low-Carbon Hydrogen Development Program (PHBC). The PHBC is a financial programme designed to fund low-carbon hydrogen projects, inspired by international initiatives such as the Inflation Reduction Act (IRA) and REPowerEU. PHBC offers 10-year economic subsidies to support the trade of low-carbon hydrogen and its derivatives, with funds sourced from various public and private entities. The allocation of tax credits under PHBC will be determined through a competitive process, prioritising projects that demonstrate the lowest GHG emissions intensity and the highest potential for value chain densification.

By establishing a comprehensive legal framework through the enactment of the Low-Carbon Hydrogen Act and the REHIDRO incentive programme, Brazil is positioning itself as a key player in the global hydrogen market. The coordinated efforts of regulatory bodies, incentive programmes, and policy initiatives under this framework are expected to drive innovation, investment, and the integration of green hydrogen into the national energy matrix, contributing to global decarbonisation goals.

iii. Offshore Wind Promotion

Brazil has a vast offshore wind energy potential. In July 2024, the World Bank published a report focusing on different scenarios to untap such potential, which may reach over '1,200 Gigawatts (GW), including 480 GW of fixed foundation potential (at water depths less than 70 m) and 748 GW of floating foundation potential (at water depths from 70 m to 1,000 m)'.[27] While the report points out at this immense potential, it also discusses whether this is the right economic and policy choice based on the vast array of low-carbon energy options. The report stresses the importance of governance frameworks and policy choices if offshore wind is to be promoted by the Brazilian state. We discuss this regulatory landscape below.

The Federal Decree No. 10,946/2022 constitutes Brazil's first wind power generation legislation. This Decree provides for the assignment of use of the project's area and use of offshore natural resources for power generation in offshore facilities.

The Decree was further regulated by: (i) MME Ordinance No. 52/2022, providing for rules and guidelines for the assignment of use of offshore areas for power generation; and (ii) MME/MMA Joint Ordinance No. 03/2022, instructing the creation of the Unified Portal for Managing the Use of Offshore Areas. Both diplomas became effective simultaneously on 1 November 2022. Additional regulations are still pending.

Major E&P companies are assessing wind offshore opportunities in Brazil. Over 90 projects have been submitted to IBAMA so far. Both the Decree and the Bol No. 11. 247/2018 allows for the construction of offshore wind power facilities for self-generation purposes, which can be used to supply production unit facilities and other offshore infrastructures.

On 17 August 2022, the Brazilian Federal Senate approved Bill No. 576/2021, which in general terms regulates seabed area rights for offshore power generation. The Bill was

[27] World Bank. *Scenarios for Offshore Wind Development in Brazil* (2024) XIII.

initially known as the 'Offshore Wind Farms Bill' (Bill 11247/2018). However, after the presentation of the new wording, it was verified that such new wording contributed to Bill 576/2021, to which it was attached at the time. As a result, Bill 576/2021 began to be processed as the main bill of law related to this matter.

In summary, the Bill of Law foresees using Federal Government assets to generate electrical energy from offshore projects. The purpose is for the offshore areas to be offered to be granted by the Executive Branch through authorisation or concession.

The offer will be through: (i) a permanent offer, in which the granting authority defines the development limits; (ii) a planned offer, in which the granting authority previously defines the development limits.

This bill of law was approved by the House of Representatives, new wording was presented to the reviewing house (Federal Senate), and is currently, awaiting new analysis by the House of Representatives.

C. State Investment Promotion Measures

i. Research and Development Promotion

On 30 December 2023, the Brazilian government passed Provisional Measure No. 1.205/23, converted into Law No. 14.902/2024 in early 2024, creating the Green Mobility and Innovation Program (the 'MOVER Program').[28] The Mover Program establishes a system of incentives for carrying out research and development and technological production activities. Financial credits are granted for: (i) research and development expenses and (ii) investment in technological production carried out in the country.

The financial credit is granted for IRPJ and CSLL levied on the taxable income of the portion corresponding to the export of industrialised products within the scope of the technological development and production project.

Reduction to zero of the Import Tax rate (I.I.) for qualified development projects related to relocation and a 2 per cent rate for non-produced auto parts. There is also a provision for reducing the IPI rate for automobiles and light commercial vehicles that meet requirements such as energy efficiency, structural performance, recyclability, energy source, and propulsion technology.

ii. Corporate Credits and Sustainable Investment

Bill No. 327/2021 was passed by the Brazilian Senate on 15 December 2021, establishing the Energy Transition Acceleration Program (PATEN). The Bill aims to create the Energy Transition Acceleration Program to encourage sustainable development projects with resources from corporate credits towards the Federal Government.

[28] 'Deloitte: Tax@hand' (*Deloitte | tax@hand*) www.taxathand.com/article/34187/Brazil/2024/Green-Mobility-and-Innovation-Program-for-auto-industryintroduced.

The Bill also creates the 'Green Fund', which constitutes a Guarantee Fund administered by BNDES, which has the purpose of guaranteeing, in whole or in part, the risk of financing granted by financial institutions for the development of projects within the scope of PATEN for the development of technology, new facilities and expansion of renewable and low-carbon fuel generation units.

This Fund will be composed of: (i) court orders and credit rights arising from final and binding court decisions against the Federal Government; and (ii) tax credits with electronic requests for refund, reimbursement, or recovery granted by the Special Secretariat of the Brazilian Federal Revenue, related to IPI (Excise Tax), PIS, PIS-Import, COFINS and COFINS-Import (Social Contributions on Imports and Revenues).

A Tax Transaction model can be created for debts owed to the Federal Government and subject to the investment in sustainable development, that is, only legal entities that have sustainable development projects approved within the scope of the Program will be eligible.

This Bill of Law was approved in the House of Representatives and is currently being reviewed by the Federal Senate.

D. Decarbonisation and Carbon Markets

The Brazilian Carbon Emission profile is mainly related to deforestation, while in the rest of the world, the carbon emissions are based on energy production. Although Brazil does not have a legal framework for the taxation of carbon credits, we reproduce below some legislative initiatives adopted in the Country and how the participation of the carbon market is relevant to the energy transition process in Brazil.

First, we would like to clarify that transactions in the carbon market are segregated into two types of markets: the Regulated Market and the Voluntary Market, the main difference of which is the legal requirement to reduce greenhouse gas emissions. In the Regulated Market, companies use credits to meet the obligations imposed by legislation or agreements. In this scenario, companies receive emission rights in decreasing quantities over time: therefore, each year, the company will be entitled to fewer permits. In this market, companies that reduce greenhouse gas emissions beyond their legal obligation can sell their unused permits to other companies that have greater difficulty in decarbonising their production.

In the Voluntary Market, companies or other entities acquire credits to meet climate commitments that are **not** subject to legal obligations to reduce emissions. In this market, companies, or even individuals, acquire verified reductions or removals of emissions for reputational or ethical purposes or as preparation for the future implementation of a regulated market. These credits are not used to calculate countries' target reductions. Brazil does not have a regulated carbon market, and transactions carried out in Brazil are restricted to the voluntary market.

We emphasise that 377.3 MtCO2e* were transacted in 2021 in voluntary carbon markets, of which 45.3 MtCO2e came from Brazil. Brazil has the potential to generate 360 to 1,200 MtCO2e in 2030. In this context, Brazil stands out as a protagonist, as the country concentrates 15 per cent of the global potential for carbon capture by natural means, with the chance of meeting 48.7 per cent of global demand, according to a study carried out by the consultancy firm McKinsey.[29]

i. Voluntary Carbon Market Integrity Initiative (VCMI)

Through VCMI, the Carbon Market Code of Conduct was created in June 2023 in Brazil. This measure aims to guide companies that acquire credits in the Voluntary Market to make climate claims more reliable.

Such context resulted from the drop in the sale of carbon credits and the issuance of bonds for avoided deforestation in 2022, not only due to a crisis of confidence in the market and several greenwashing scandals but also because companies preferred to invest in equipment to offset greenhouse gas emissions. For example, there was a 4 per cent drop in sales in the Voluntary Market compared to 2021.

As mentioned, there is no Carbon Tax in Brazil. However, through the recently approved Tax Reform, the Federal Constitution introduced the possibility for the Federal Government to establish an Excise Tax on the extraction, production, import, and sale of goods and services that are harmful to health or the environment. We analyse the main aspects of the Tax Reform and the Excise Tax.

According to the European model carbon tax model, there is an emissions cap (CAP), that is, there is a quantity of emission allowances distributed to companies in a given sector. Companies that can reduce their emissions at a lower price can sell (Trade) the surplus allowances to other companies that face higher costs.

Brazil's closest proposal to this model is the National Biofuels Policy (RenovaBio) for fuels/biofuels, which is discussed below.

Law No. 13,576, of 26 December 2017, established the National Biofuels Policy (RenovaBio) to expand the production and use of biofuels in the Brazilian energy matrix.[30] This State policy considers the relationship between energy efficiency and the reduction of greenhouse gas emissions to assist in the decarbonisation of the Brazilian transport matrix, contributing to energy security and market predictability.

The main instruments for implementing the Policy can be divided into three strategic axes which will be elaborated in the following order: (i) the definition of targets for reducing greenhouse gas (GHG) emissions, (ii) the certification of biofuel production, and the (iii) Decarbonisation Credit (CBIO).

ii. Axis 1: GHG Emission Reduction

Every year, the National Energy Policy Council (CNPE) establishes national decarbonisation targets for a period of ten years, according to the definitions in Decree No. 9,888/2019.

[29] Valor Económico and B3, *Brasil pode liderar mercado de carbono no mundo; previsão é que setor movimente US$ 50 bi até 2030* (6 March 2024) valor.globo.com/conteudo-de-marca/b3/financas-sustentaveis/noticia/2024/03/06/brasil-pode-liderar-mercado-de-carbono-no-mundo-previsao-e-que-setor-movimente-us-50-bi-ate-2030.ghtml.

[30] 'Law No. 13576 – Provides for the Brazilian Biofuel Policy (RenovaBio)' (*Brazilian NR*, 28 March 2024) braziliannr.com/brazilian-environmental-legislation/law-no-13576-provides-for-the-brazilian-biofuel-policy-renovabio/.

These annual targets are broken down by the National Agency of Petroleum, Natural Gas and Biofuels (ANP) to fuel distributors, the obligated party to the policy, based on their fossil fuel market share.

This Decree No. 9,888/2019, in addition to providing for the definition of targets, established the National Biofuels Policy Committee – the RenovaBio Committee, responsible for the governance of the Program, bringing together across the board the main bodies of the Executive Branch that have, among other powers, the responsibility of recommending decarbonisation targets to the CNPE.

In this regard, the Committee must take into account the reduction of the carbon intensity of the Brazilian fuel matrix for a minimum period of ten years, while protecting consumer interests in terms of price, quality, and supply of fuels. In addition, the Committee also considers the availability of biofuels by producers and importers holding the Efficient Production of Biofuels Certificate, the appreciation of energy resources, the evolution of domestic demand for fuels and imports, and the international commitments to reduce greenhouse gas emissions assumed by Brazil, in addition to sectoral actions within the scope of these commitments and the impact of fuel prices on inflation rates.

The economic modelling of RenovaBio's targets was improved in 2023 based on the preparation and execution of a Regulatory Impact Analysis, which aimed to define the best strategy for proposing decarbonisation targets for the following decades, specifically for the decade 2024–2033, in compliance with the provisions outlined in article 6 of Law No. 13,576/2017. The goal of decarbonising the fuel matrix by 10 per cent from 2018 to 2030 was maintained.

Table 1 below presents the targets for the 2024–2033 cycle, established by CNPE Resolution No. 6/2023, which were based on the trend curve for reducing the intended carbon intensity for the fuel matrix:

Table 1

Year	**2024**	**2025**	**2026**	**2027**	**2028**	**2029**	**2030**	**2031**	**2032**	**2033**
Projected Carbon Intensity	72,77	71,7	69,97	68,74	67,67	66,68	66,02	65,56	65,44	65,22
Target IC Reduction (base 2018)	−0,80%	−2,20%	−4,60%	−6,30%	−7,70%	−9,10%	−10,00%	−10,60%	−10,80%	−11,10%
Annual Target (million CBIOs)	28,78	42,56	48,09	52,37	56,41	61,24	64,08	67,13	68,81	71,29
Tolerance Ranges	–	48,94	55,3	64,87	64,87	70,43	73,7	77,2	79,14	81,98
Upper and Lower Limits	–	36,17	40,88	47,95	47,95	52,05	54,47	57,06	58,49	60,59

iii. Axis 2: Certification of Biofuel Production

Biofuel producers (primary emitters) participate voluntarily in RenovaBio. Producers who certify their production based on Life Cycle Analysis (LCA), in light of ANP Resolution No. 758/2018, receive energy-environmental efficiency scores as a result.

These scores are multiplied by the volume of biofuel sold that meets the programme's eligibility criteria, resulting in the amount of decarbonisation credits (CBIOs) that a specific producer can issue and trade on the market, in compliance with the provisions of Normative Ordinance No. 56/GM/MME, of 21 December 2022.

iv. Axis 3: Decarbonisation Credit (CBIO)

The Decarbonisation Credit (CBIO) was created as an instrument of RenovaBio, which is registered in written form, to prove the individual target of the fuel distributor as outlined in article 7 of Law No. 13,576/2017.[31]

In simple terms, the CBIO is the result of multiplying the energy-environmental efficiency rating (NEEA) assigned to the biofuel producer or importer during the certification process by the volume of biofuel sold that meets the programme's eligibility criteria. Each CBIO issued by biofuel producers and importers corresponds to one ton of carbon that is no longer issued into the atmosphere. Therefore, CBIO is defined as an environmental asset whose trading has been allowed since December 2019 on the Stock Exchange Market (B3).

CBIOs must be purchased by distributors and removed (permanently removed from market circulation) by 31 March of the following year to prove compliance with the target assigned to them by the ANP.

v. Bill Proposal 182/2024: Regulation of the Carbon Market

This proposal seeks to establish the Brazilian Greenhouse Gas Emissions Trading System (Sistema Brasileiro de Comércio de Emissões de Gases de Efeito Estufa – 'SBCE') to limit emissions, sell assets representing emissions, and reduce or remove GHGs. In a nutshell, the system demands companies to buy carbon credits to cover their emissions, requiring entities to report and eventually pay emissions if they emit more than 10,000 metric tons of CO^2.[32]

The SBCE is responsible for, among other things: (i) regulating the asset market; (ii) defining methodologies for monitoring emissions, reducing emissions, and removing GHG; (iii) defining the activities, facilities, and sources to be regulated; (iv) defining the annual GHG emission level to which the operators of the facilities or sources are subject.

[31] www.gov.br/anp/pt-br/assuntos/renovabio/credito-de-descarbonizacao-cbio. For reference, CBIO is equivalent to 1 ton of CO2 not emitted by the use of biofuels. Please refer to: Brazilian Ministry of Mines and Energy, *Painel Dinâmico de Certificações de Biocombustíveis RenovaBio* (2020), www.gov.br/anp/pt-br/centrais-de-conteudo/paineis-dinamicos-da-anp/paineis-dinamicos-do-renovabio/painel-dinamico-de-certificacoes-de-biocombustiveis-renovabio.

[32] Alex Chyzh and Illuminem, *How Brazil is building a framework to promote carbon capture and storage* (13 July 2024) illuminem.com/illuminemvoices/how-brazil-is-building-a-framework-to-promote-carbon-capture-and-storage.

a. Assets that Compose the SBCE

- Brazilian Emissions Quota (CBE): tangible, tradable asset, representing the right to emit 1 tCO_2e free of charge or for a fee (auction or other administrative instrument), for regulated facilities or sources;
- Certificate of Verified Emissions Reduction or Removal (CRVE): tangible, tradable asset, representing the effective reduction of emissions or removal of greenhouse gases of 1 tCO_2e following an accredited methodology and with registry carried out within the scope of the SBCE, under the terms of a specific act of the SBCE management body.

b. Taxation of SBCE Assets

Regarding tax aspects, there is a provision for taxation on the gain resulting from the sale of assets. The cancellation of carbon credits and SBCE assets to offset GHG emissions will allow a deduction from the Corporate Income Tax and Social Contribution on Profits (IPRJ and CSLL) calculation basis.

Furthermore, the sale of assets will not be subject to the Contribution for the Social Integration Program (PIS), and the Contribution for the Financing of Social Security (Cofins), which are both social security contributions that are levied in the revenue recognition.

c. Creation of the National Allocation Plan

The plan will establish the maximum limit for GHG and CRVES emissions. Operators responsible for facilities and sources that emit more than 10,000 tCO_2e per year will be subject to SBCE regulation.

d. Periodic Reconciliation of Obligations

At the end of each commitment period, which corresponds to one year, the operator must have assets forming part of the SBCE in a quantity equivalent to its emissions incurred in the respective period and meet environmental commitments and may suffer several fines.

e. Voluntary Carbon Credit

Generated from projects or programmes that involve reducing emissions or removing GHGs, which do not follow SBCE standards.

They may be voluntarily offered by any carbon credit generator or project developer.

f. Creation of the Environmental Credit Receivables Certificate (CRAM)

A nominative credit title, freely negotiable, represents a promise of payment in cash or delivery of carbon credits, which constitutes an extrajudicial execution title.

Please note that this Bill of Law was approved in the initiating house (House of Representatives) and is currently under revision process in the Brazilian Senate.

E. Brazilian Tax Reform and Impacts on the Energy Transition: The Taxation in Oil and Gas Activities vis-à-vis Incentives in Low Carbon Sources

i. Introduction

After years of discussion, the final wording of Constitutional Amendment No. 132/2023 was enacted on 20 December 2023, also known as the Consumption Tax Reform, which substantially changes the current form of taxation of goods and services, replacing the current indirect taxes with the dual-modal Value Added Tax (VAT) system, composed of the Contribution on Goods and Services (CBS) and the Tax on Goods and Services (IBS), in addition to the creation of an Excise Tax (Imposto Seletivo or IS), the latter with regulatory purposes.

In short, the CBS replaces the Social Security Contribution for the Social Integration Program (PIS), and the Social Security Contribution for the Financing of Social Security (Cofins), while the IS partially replaces the Tax on Manufactured Products (IPI). The IBS will be the result of the merger between the Tax on Circulation of Goods and Provision of Interstate and Intermunicipal Transportation and Communication Services (ICMS or State VAT) and the Municipal Tax on Services of Any Nature (ISS).

These taxes are subject to a broad tax base, non-cumulative, subject to a single rate, are calculated separately, and are collected at the destination (following the destination/consumption principle). The new Excise Tax (IS) will have an extra-fiscal purpose (ie, regulatory) and may be levied on the extraction, production, sale, or import of goods and services considered harmful to health and/or the environment. The changes introduced in the Federal Constitution reflect the legislator's intention to bring legal certainty and establish a less complex and more transparent tax system for the end consumer.

The recent enactment of Constitutional Amendment No. 132/2023, which includes the principle of environmental protection in the third paragraph of Article 145 of the Federal Constitution, marks a historic moment in Brazilian tax legislation. For the first time, the Brazilian tax system is directly supporting environmental protection, aligning the country with global guidelines for sustainability and ecological responsibility.

By prioritising sustainability in various aspects of the tax policy, such an event reflects a movement towards a more sustainable tax system that is cohesive with environmental needs.

Regarding Constitutional Amendment No. 132/2023, the concerns regarding climate change are incorporated into the constitutional wording for the first time, after having been addressed in the National Climate Change Policy Act (Act 12,187/2009).

The amendment provides, for example, that the granting of regional incentives must consider criteria of environmental sustainability and reduction of carbon emissions whenever possible (Article 43, paragraph 4). Likewise, in applying resources from the National Regional Development Fund, priority will be given to projects that include actions aimed at environmental sustainability and reducing carbon emissions (Article 159-A, paragraph 2).

Furthermore, section VIII was added to paragraph 1, Article 225 of the Brazilian Constitution, which determines that, to guarantee the right to the environment, the Government must maintain a favourable tax system for biofuels and low-carbon hydrogen. This system should guarantee lower taxation compared to the one applied to fossil fuels, which would ensure a competitive advantage for these alternative fuels.

In this regard, Article 19 of Constitutional Amendment No. 132/2023 establishes that tax incentives for the production of vehicles will be granted exclusively to those equipped with an electric motor, capable of driving the vehicle using only electric energy. Combinations with an internal burning engine that uses biofuels, alone or in conjunction with petroleum-derived fuels, are permitted.

In addition, Constitutional Amendment No. 132/2023 introduced the possibility of establishing an Excise Tax on activities involving the production, extraction, marketing, or import of oil and derivatives, under Article 153, VIII. According to this article, this tax will not be levied on exports and transactions involving electric energy and will be levied only once on the good or service provision, which rates will be specifically defined by ordinary law, per unit of measurement adopted, or *ad valorem*.

Specifically concerning extraction of minerals/oil and gas, the tax will be charged regardless of the destination, in which case the maximum rate will correspond to one percent (1%) of the market value of the product.[33]

To regulate the Constitution Amendment and provide enforceability to the recently enacted rules, the Executive Branch presented Complementary Bill No. 68/2024 (PLP 68) establishing the general rules related to CBS and IBS. Recently approved by the House of Representatives, PLP 68 is currently being reviewed by the Federal Senate. The conclusion of the voting is expected to occur during the second half of 2024.[34]

The wording of PLP No. 68 introduces several measures aimed at low-carbon emission policies and aligned with the country's energy transition incentive. Among them, we highlight the following aspects.

First, the suspension of payment of CBS and IBS on imports or acquisitions in the domestic market of raw materials, intermediate products, and packaging materials, for supply to companies authorised to operate in the Export Processing Zones (ZPEs). Electric energy acquired by such companies is considered raw material when its supply is intended for the industrial production of clean energy, including in the form of hydrogen and green ammonia. This suspension will be converted to a 0 per cent rate after export. Second, the set up of a favourable tax system for biofuels and low-carbon hydrogen. Third, the inclusion of coal in the list of products that are harmful to the environment and subject to Excise Tax. Fourth, electric vehicles are in principle included in the IS list. However, there is provision for the graduation of IS rates according to the following requirements, among others: vehicle power and category; structural performance and driving supporting technologies; energy efficiency; recyclability of materials

[33] Please note that the last version of PLP 68 approved by the House of Representatives (subject to approval by Brazilian Senate) establishes a threshold of 0.25% on the extraction.

[34] This article was prepared based on the wording of PLP 68 approved by the House of Representatives on 10 July 2024.

and vehicles; carbon footprint; carbon dioxide emissions (energy-environmental efficiency), considered from the well to the wheel cycle.

ii. The Rules Introduced in Constitutional Amendment No. 132/2023 Related to the Oil and Gas Industry: The Paradox between the Tax Incentives and the New Levies in the Sector

According to §5, V, and VI of Article 156-A of Constitutional Amendment No. 132/2023 (EC 132), the Complementary Law would provide for the form of exemption from the acquisition of capital goods by taxpayers, and the hypotheses of deferral and exemption of the tax applicable to special customs regimes and export processing zones. It is also worth noting that EC 132 introduced a broad tax base, which would allow the taxation of asset leasing and vessel chartering operations inherent to the contractual structure used in the Oil and Gas Industry.

Based on the wording of such provisions, it is possible to conclude, in principle, that the legislation has included the special tax and customs regime for the economic use of goods intended for exploration, development, and production of oil and natural gas deposits (Repetro-Sped), a special regime for the industrialisation of goods intended for exploration, development, and production of oil, natural gas and other fluid hydrocarbons (Repetro-Industrialisation), temporary admission with full suspension of tax payments, temporary admission for economic use, temporary admission for active improvement, temporary export and temporary export for passive improvement, among other customs regimes currently used by the Oil and Gas Industry.

Considering the delegation to the Complementary Law provided for in EC 132, there is uncertainty regarding the maintenance of such incentives in the new Brazilian legal tax system. This is because the permanence of the benefits currently granted to the sector depends exclusively on the regulation to be instituted via Complementary Law.

As mentioned above, the Executive Branch presented Complementary Law Bill No. 68/2024 (PLP 68), to regulate the general rules related to the CBS and the IBS. Article 4, §1 of PLP No. 68 provides, among the exemplary hypotheses of levy of the CBS and the IBS, transactions of assignment and leasing of assets belonging to a legal entity domiciled abroad.

Due to the current wording of the legislation, one may conclude that the asset leasing and vessel chartering operations (currently subject to a zero withholding income tax rate, provided that the limits established by law are respected, but currently not subject to PIS, COFINS, ICMS or ISS taxes) used in the exploration and production of oil and natural gas will be taxed by the IBS and CBS.

There is a specific chapter on special customs regimes, which include the most relevant regime for the oil and gas industry: the Repetro-Sped. In Section III, the legislator provided for the cases of temporary admission subject to suspension of the CBS and IBS, granting the regulation the authority to discriminate the types of special customs regimes for temporary stay, including the provision for proportional collection of CBS and IBS obtained by applying the percentage of 0.033 per cent (thirty-three thousandths of a per cent), with each day included in the period of concession of the regime.

Repetro-Sped was introduced in Section V, which provides for the suspension of CBS and IBS on the following transactions: (i) import of goods intended for exploration, development and production of oil, natural gas and other fluid hydrocarbons, as provided for in specific legislation, whose permanence in the country is temporary, as set out in the list specified in the regulation (Repetro-Temporary); (ii) import of goods intended for transportation, movement, transfer, storage or regasification of liquefied natural gas, as set out in the list specified in the regulation (LNG-Temporary); (iii) import of goods, as set out in the list specified in the regulation, whose permanence in the country is definitive and which are intended for oil and gas exploration and production activities (Repetro-Permanent); (iv) import or acquisition in the domestic market of raw materials, intermediate products and packaging materials to be used entirely in the production process of the final product to be supplied to the company that uses it for oil and gas exploration and production activities (Repetro-Industrialisation). The payment of IBS and CBS is also suspended on the import or acquisition of goods in the domestic market by a company designated as an intermediate manufacturer for the industrialisation of an intermediate product to be supplied to a company qualified as a manufacturer of a final good; (v) acquisition of a final product sold under Repetro-Industrialisation (Repetro-Nacional); (vi) import or acquisition in the domestic market of goods, included in the list specified in the regulation, for conversion or construction of other goods in the country, contracted by a company headquartered abroad, the final product of which must be destined for oil and gas exploration and production activities (Repetro-Entreposto).

The benefits introduced above in PLP 68 aim to reproduce the incentives currently in force, notably Repetro-Sped and Repetro-Industrialisation. There is also provision for equating fictitious exports to regular exports, to enjoy such regimes. In this sense, Article 85 of PLP 68 establishes that the IBS and CBS immunity on the export of material goods applies to exports without leaving the national territory, as regulated in the regulation, when the exported goods are: (i) fully incorporated into goods that are temporarily in the country, owned by the foreign buyer, including under a temporary admission regime under the responsibility of a third party; (ii) delivered in Brazil to be incorporated into a vessel or platform under construction or conversion contracted by a company headquartered abroad, or into its modules, with subsequent allocation to exploration, development and production activities of oil, natural gas and other fluid hydrocarbons, as provided for in specific legislation; and (iii) exclusively intended for exploration, development and production activities of oil, natural gas and other fluid hydrocarbons, as provided for in specific legislation, when sold to a company headquartered abroad and as defined in specific legislation, even if sold by a third party headquartered in Brazil.

There is a general provision in Article 105 of PLP 68, providing for the possibility of defining new cases in which imports and acquisitions in the domestic market of capital goods will be carried out with suspension of payment of IBS and CBS, which will be converted to a zero rate after the incorporation of the asset into the purchaser's fixed assets.

If this text remains unchanged in the Federal Senate and is sanctioned in these terms, the benefits currently provided will be reproduced in this new tax framework.

On the other hand, if changes are introduced by the Federal Senate and sanctioned by the head of the Executive Branch (Brazilian President), it is possible that the Oil and Gas Industry will face an increase in the cost of oil and gas production, and, consequently, loss of investments and productivity in the sector.

It is worth noting, therefore, that any change in tax and customs legislation must reproduce the purpose of supporting the Oil and Gas Industry and avoid any measure that harms investments in the sector and, consequently, the national development.

The concern with investments in the oil industry in Brazil was expressly addressed by the Joint Committee of the National Congress of Provisional Measure 795, when it suggested that the term of validity of the benefits for definitive import be granted until 31 December 2040, precisely because it considers the complexity and deadlines in which investments are made and the start of operations in the exploration and production of oil and natural gas, as well as to attribute symmetry in tax treatment between the national and imported product.

At the time, the Joint Committee of the National Congress highlighted the need to adopt such measures given the fall in oil prices, starting in 2014, and, consequently, the decrease in sectoral investments and the prospect of a decrease in production. The importance of improving the Brazilian tax regime was thus recognised to make oil projects viable and increase the attractiveness for foreign investment.

Therefore, any change in the taxation rules with the levy of IBS and CBS on transactions carried out within the scope of Repetro-Industrialisation and Repetro-Sped represents a breach of legitimate expectations and frustration of the trust and planning of taxpayers, who planned their investments considering the total exemption from federal taxes until 31 December 2040.

The non-consideration of special customs and tax regimes related to Industry could make ongoing and future projects unfeasible, as there is a cautious assessment for investments to take place in the short, medium, and long term. For this reason, the evaluation of projects that contemplated the use of these regimes in their execution and that, with their exclusion, once the new regulations are in force, would have to consider an increase in costs related to the planned operations.

This would be a violation of the principles of legitimate trust, acquired rights, good faith, and legal certainty of taxpayers, who, in exchange for the investments made, trusted to receive tax relief from the Public Administration. Therefore, we emphasise the need for taxpayers' expectations and trust to be protected when granting conditional tax benefits subject to specific deadlines, as in the case of Repetro-SPED and Repetro-Industrialisation. In this same sense, tax neutrality must be guaranteed in transactions involving the leasing of goods and chartering of vessels from abroad, since the incidence of CBS and IBS on such economic facts would represent a significant increase in costs for the Industry and could eventually make it impossible for such goods to enter the country.

Finally, most companies operating in this segment have started their investments related to the energy transition. Consequently, the withdrawal of these regimes (or even the consideration of new ones) could also make it impossible for the country to develop alternative energy sources, preventing the evolution towards low-carbon production goals.

iii. Main Aspects of the Excise Tax and its Potential Similarities to a Carbon Tax

As mentioned by the World Bank report 'State and Trends of Carbon Pricing Dashboard' on the carbon pricing dashboard, direct carbon pricing instruments are categorised as 'compliance' instruments or 'carbon crediting'.[35] Under 'compliance' instruments (such as emissions trading systems or carbon taxes), covered entities are obligated to pay for the emissions from covered activities.

By adopting the levy of a carbon tax a government levies a fee on covered entities for their GHG emissions, providing a financial incentive to reduce emissions. Under a carbon tax, the government sets the price of emissions by the tax rate. The resulting volume of emissions reductions achieved by the policy is determined by the response of the emitting entities to the set price.

Although there is no carbon tax in Brazilian tax legislation, the enactment of the Excise Tax in the recently approved Brazilian Tax Reform might potentially play a similar role in the oil and gas sector. However, different from the carbon tax, the Excise Tax has the specific intention to influence the taxpayer's behaviour, inducing them to consume more or less of a certain product to the detriment of others, beyond mere collection.

We will address below the main aspects of the Excise Tax introduced in Brazilian legislation and how it might affect the oil and gas sector in the country.

iv. The Excise Tax and its Levy on Crude Oil Extraction

As mentioned, Brazilian tax legislation does not foresee any carbon taxes. However, with the enactment of the Tax Reform, the intention of the Excise Tax recently created is to increase the taxation of goods and services that could be potentially harmful to the health and environment and thus reduce the consumption of certain goods and services. Although this initiative is following Brazil's commitment to its own decarbonisation goals, this new levy might have a significant impact on the oil and gas sector, as better addressed below.

According to the Bill of Law No. 68/2024, for purposes of levy of the Excise Tax, the following goods should be considered harmful to health or the environment since classified under the NCM/SH codes listed in Annex XVII of the Bill, relating to, among other products, mineral assets (such as hydrocarbons offshore).

The triggering event of the Excise Tax is considered to have occurred in the following hypotheses: (i) the first sale of the good; (ii) auction at public auction; (iii) the non-onerous transfer of mineral/oil assets extracted or produced (ie, free lease of oil between consortium members for logistic purposes); (iv) incorporation of the asset into fixed assets; (v) by the manufacturer; (vi) the export of extracted mineral goods (the legislation includes oil and gas); (vii) consumption of the good by the extractive producer or manufacturer; or (viii) the provision or payment of the service, the whichever occurs first.

[35] Available at carbonpricingdashboard.worldbank.org/about#download-data.

Moreover, the calculation basis for calculating the Excise Tax is, among others: (i) the sales value in the commercialisation; (ii) the auction value in the auction; (iii) the reference value in: (a) non-onerous transaction or consumption of the good (applicable in case of non-onerous transactions with oil); (b) export of extracted mineral good (also applicable to oil and gas transactions); or (c) marketing of tobacco products; (iv) the accounting value of incorporation of the good into fixed assets.

The taxpayer of the Excise Tax is: (i) the manufacturer, in the first commercialisation, in the incorporation of the good into the fixed assets, in the transfer of the good in a non-onerous transaction, and the consumption of the good; (ii) the importer in the entry of the good of foreign origin into the national territory (the hypothesis that could apply to LNG imports); (iii) the successful bidder in the auction; (iv) the extractive producer who carries out the extraction, in the first commercialisation, in the consumption, in the non-onerous transaction or the export of the good (the hypothesis that might apply to oil and gas industry); or (v) the service provider, even if resident or domiciled abroad, in specific situations defined in the legislation.

As mentioned above, the extraction of minerals/oil and gas would be subject to the Excise Tax regardless of its consumption/destination, in which case the maximum rate will correspond to one percent (1%) of the market value of the product.[36] In other words, the fact that the oil would be exported to a non-resident entity is not relevant since IS would levy in the extraction even though the oil extracted would be entirely exported.

The levy of IS on extracted mineral goods (including oil and gas) is expected to have an annual impact of R$7 billion (US$1.5 billion) on the oil and natural gas sector.[37] The calculation was made by the IBP based on the current price of a barrel of oil and the maximum rate of the new tax, which could reach 1 per cent.

If the maximum rate is set, the IBP states that there will be a loss of competitiveness in the sector and also in the Brazilian economy. This is because the tax will end up being passed on to consumers as an increase in the prices of fuel and natural gas. This will impact practically all production segments. As a consequence, it would result in a burden for the consumer, who would pay more for practically all products due to the tax that will be charged at the beginning of the chain.[38] This levy would trigger a cascade effect and affect petrochemicals, the glass industry, civil construction, thermal generation, steel, and even agribusiness, for example.

It is worth mentioning that this extra cost imposed by the Excise Tax might also reduce the competitiveness of Brazilian oil and gas and the goods that are them as inputs in the global market. In the worst scenario, Brazil would face a reduction in exports and an increase in competition with other markets, such as those from Asia, especially China.

[36] Please note that the last version of PLP 68 approved by the House of Representatives (subject to approval by Brazilian Senate) establishes a threshold of 0.25% on the extraction.

[37] Poder 360 and Geraldo Campos Jr, *Imposto Seletivo causará prejuízo de R$ 7 bi ao setor de petróleo* (24 April 2024), www.poder360.com.br/economia/imposto-seletivo-causara-prejuizo-de-r-7-bi-ao-setor-de-petroleo/#:~:text=%E2%80%9CPorque%20o%20Brasil%20n%C3%A3o%20consegue,para%20o%20pa%C3%ADs%20da%20medida.

[38] ibid.

Although the introduction of this tax into the constitutional tax system is indeed in line with the transition of the energy model and the COP 28 agenda, which foresees the gradual reduction of the use of fossil fuels, it is worth mentioning that there are still no viable alternatives on a sufficient scale to replace them in Brazil and, as mentioned, the country is highly dependent on oil and gas sources of energy.

If there is a value judgment in the extra-fiscality inherent to regulatory taxes such as the Excise Tax introduced by the Brazilian Tax Reform, which seeks to inhibit or encourage behaviours, the following question remains unanswered: how can we discourage oil extraction if there is no viable alternative on a sufficient scale to replace it?

4. Conclusions

Given the above considerations, we can conclude that, in addition to the country's commitment to its own decarbonisation goals, Brazil is also placed as a potential global exporter of low-carbon hydrogen and its derivatives, due to its predominant and competitive renewable energy generation matrix.

Furthermore, integrating tax reform with the energy transition offers an opportunity for Brazil to advance its environmental and economic agenda. Through tax incentives, changes in taxation, and the promotion of clean technologies, the reform can catalyse a more sustainable and resilient economy aligned with global goals of reducing emissions and protecting the environment.

However, the transition to a net zero agenda in Brazil should be followed by the gradual replacement of fossil fuel sources with renewable sources of energy. In this context, legislative initiatives such as the levy of the Excise Tax on the extraction of oil and gas may reduce the competitiveness of Brazilian oil and gas and the goods that use them as inputs in the global market. Considering the estimated annual impact of R$7 billion (US$1.5 billion) on the oil and natural gas sector (assuming the maximum rate of the new tax, which could reach 1 per cent), there might be a loss of competitiveness in the sector and also in the Brazilian economy.

Although those incentives and initiatives to reduce the emissions of GHGs in the atmosphere are needed to carry out the energy transition in the country and allow the inflow of investments in Brazil, the country is still highly dependent on oil and gas sources of energy.

The oil sector is responsible for thousands of jobs and billions of reais in investments, having significant relevance for the Brazilian economy.

This is exactly why this sector should continue to be subject to differentiated tax treatment, to make its activities viable and, therefore, playing its main role: developing the national economy and supporting a fair and equable energy transition.

9

Risk vs Rewards of Oil, Gas and Wind Investments: Dealing with Business, Finance and Economic Issues and how to Attract Investment in these Industries

JOÃO OLIVEIRA

1. Introduction

The world has been undergoing a major transformation in terms of its energy consumption. Climate change, consumer pressure, geopolitics, energy efficiency, technology and economy are some of the factors pushing for a change in how the world produces and consumes energy. As per the latest International Energy Agency World Energy Outlook, the share of conventional oil, gas and coal in the energy mix is declining:

> (…) the share of coal, oil and natural gas in global energy supply – stuck for decades around 80% – starts to edge downwards and reaches 73% in the STEPS by 2030. This is an important shift (…).
>
> Against this complex backdrop, the emergence of a new clean energy economy, led by solar PV and electric vehicles (EVs), provides hope for the way forward. Investment in clean energy has risen by 40% since 2020. The push to bring down emissions is a key reason, but not the only one. The economic case for mature clean energy technologies is strong. Energy security is also an important factor, particularly in fuel-importing countries, as are industrial strategies and the desire to create clean energy jobs.[1]

This means there is a world of opportunities for investors ranging from investment in more traditional sources of energy to investing in the new energies shaping the energy mix of the future. These, as with every investment, come with risks which need to be carefully reviewed. In this chapter, we will review some of the incentives and some of the risks surrounding investment in both offshore oil and gas and wind energy with the aim of allowing prospective investors to understand what they should be accounting for and the existing opportunities in the market.

[1] International Energy Agency, *World Energy Outlook 2023*, iea.blob.core.windows.net/assets/86ede39e-4436-42d7-ba2a-edf61467e070/WorldEnergyOutlook2023.pdf.

This chapter will explore the pros and cons of investing in oil and gas and offshore wind. We will examine the possible difficulties and the benefits and returns that can be gained. Our goal is to offer prospective investors a realistic view of what they can expect when they invest in these areas. Finally, the chapter discusses the implications for investors and suggests how countries can attract investment in their markets.

2. Risks of Investing in Oil and Gas

Conventional wisdom has it that if you drill for oil and gas and you find it, you have hit the jackpot. Reality, as is often the case, is far more complex. As an example, Tullow Oil, once an emergent oil and gas powerhouse with a market value of 15bn Pounds Sterling and with several exploration successes, is currently struggling to pay off its debts and find new ways of financing.

Despite huge discoveries in the early 2000s (mostly in Ghana and Uganda), Tullow Oil had a few unsuccessful exploration endeavours which left it scrambling for cash to pay off the debt load which it had amassed to develop its assets (with ever increasing operating costs) and continue exploring for more oil. Nowadays Tullow continues to produce oil from its producing assets (around 62,700 barrels of oil equivalent per day) but it continues to struggle due to a mix of exploration failures, higher production costs, lower oil prices than expected in the last decade and a heavy anchor in its debt levels.[2]

One needs to look no further than to Tullow Oil's tumultuous story to understand the difficulties of navigating the world of oil exploration and production.[3] Fossil fuels have been the mainstays of the world's energy consumption accounting for more than 80 per cent of the global energy consumption.[4] While there is a downward trend in terms of oil and gas consumption, the decline will be steady but slow, as the world will continue to need investments in oil and gas for years to come.[5]

Investing in oil and gas in 2024 is subject to major pressure from stakeholders, governments and environmental associations due to its externalities – environmental and social impacts being the most important.

If we look at projected investment, despite the pressures, oil and gas producers are expected to invest around 857B Euros in new oil and gas fields by 2030 and this number could grow to 1.4T Euros by 2040.[6] These investments are backed up by the predicted fossil fuel demand which is expected to continue expanding during this decade. Some

[2] Alex Hamer, 'Tullow Oil profits down as it chips away at debt mountain' (*Investors' Chronicle*, 6 March 2024) www.investorschronicle.co.uk/news/2024/03/06/tullow-oil-profits-down-as-it-chips-away-at-debt-mountain/.

[3] For a summary of Tullow Oil's trajectory, see 'Tullow Oil: the end of an era for exploration and production' *Financial Times* (27 January 2023) www.ft.com/content/6031d060-cd0a-454b-ac64-406fa4b7a669.

[4] 'Terajoules of energy used this year' (*The World Counts*) www.theworldcounts.com/challenges/climate-change/energy/global-energy-consumption.

[5] According to bp's 2023 Energy Outlook, www.bp.com/content/dam/bp/business-sites/en/global/corporate/pdfs/energy-economics/energy-outlook/bp-energy-outlook-2023.pdf, even in the best case scenario, the world will still consume around 20mb/d by 2050.

[6] Fossil fuel firms set to spend more than €800bn on new oil and gas fields by 2030, see Rosie Frost, 'Fossil fuel firms set to spend more than €800bn on new oil and gas fields by 2030' (*Euronews*, 12 April 2022), www.euronews.com/green/2022/04/12/world-s-biggest-oil-and-gas-companies-projected-to-spend-more-than-800bn-on-new-fields-by-.

of the more reputable forecasters have published that they expect oil consumption to plateau somewhere in the next decade, but it will continue to grow until then. This increase could be explained by GDP growth in some parts of the world, increase in population and increase in the demand for cheap energy.[7]

Despite increase in investment, the climate consensus shows that the world needs to reduce its reliance on carbon-based energy sources. Fossil fuels, such as oil and gas, can harm the climate, the environment, and human health because of the way they are extracted and processed to produce energy. These harms, if not properly managed and prevented, can result in negative environmental effects, damage to the reputation of the companies involved in them, liabilities to the countries and people affected by the fossil fuel extraction, and many other impacts on social and economic activities.

If we look at the wider climate aspect, oil and gas production is a significant contributor to carbon emissions worldwide.[8] If we then consider the potential for pollution coming out of oil spills, we need to add the impact on wildlife and the various ecosystems. This means producing oil and gas has enormous risks that, if not appropriately managed, could lead to long-term damage to the environment.

Oil and gas are crucial for the world economy, but they also have the potential to cause major damage in the event of an accident. Tourism, businesses that rely on clean seawater, supply chains, etc … all of them can be severely affected.

Adding to these risks, it is also important to note that oil and gas producers face mounting pressure to their investments due to regulatory uncertainties as the world becomes more aware of its need to transition to a lower carbon energy mix. If we consider the numerous agreements being signed between nations to curb carbon emissions, it becomes clear that the legal landscape on which the producers rely is rapidly changing. If we take the example of the Paris Agreement, which aims to limit global warming to well below 2°C, its signing has prompted numerous countries to adopt policies and measures to reduce their dependence on fossil fuels and increase their share of renewable energy.

One of the primary instruments to achieving the Paris Agreement Goals is the implementation of Nationally Determined Contributions (NDC), which are the signatory countries' self-defined national climate pledges under the Paris Agreement. In a nutshell, NDCs are a country's plan of how to achieve the commitments made under the Paris Agreement to help lower greenhouse gas emissions. These plans should detail short to medium term targets and should be updated every five years. In addition to agreeing to present NDCs, countries also agreed to a 'ratchet mechanism' which foresees that countries will ramp up their efforts every five years to reflect their 'highest ambition possible'. This means every generation of NDCs will be more ambitious than the previous one and that will, necessarily, bring regulatory change.[9] As an example, according to the United Nations Development Program, African countries have made more robust

[7] Fossil fuel demand to continue expanding this decade, Economist Intelligence Unit, 'Fossil fuel demand to continue expanding this decade' (10 July 2023) www.eiu.com/n/fossil-fuel-demand-to-continue-expanding-this-decade/.

[8] IPIECA, 'Mapping the oil and gas industry to the SDG's: An Atlas', www.undp.org/publications/mapping-oil-and-gas-industry-sdgs-atlas.

[9] UNDP, 'What are NDCs and how do they drive climate action?' (31 May 2022), climatepromise.undp.org/news-and-stories/NDCs-nationally-determined-contributions-climate-change-what-you-need-to-know.

pledges than the global average which means they are being more ambitious in setting their goals to make their economies 'greener' and commit to moving to a lower-carbon economy. This is (and will increasingly) having an impact on the regulatory landscape and it is undeniable that oil and gas producers will have to adapt.

As an example, the European Council has recently given the green light for the EU to withdraw from the Energy Charter Treaty (ECT)[10] on the basis that the ECT is no longer in line with the Paris Agreement and the EU ambitions on energy transition.[11] The ECT has long been criticised for its protection of continued fossil fuel investments by having outdated investment provisions which allow private companies to sue governments in case they pass legislation on climate change and environment that is seen as threatening those investments. The European Council has recognised this criticism as being fair and has allowed the EU to withdraw from the ECT. Some Member States might still elect to continue to be a party to the ECT and if they do, they will be voting for the adoption of a modernised agreement in the upcoming 'Energy Charter Conference' expected to take place by the end of 2024. It is still too soon to say what challenges this will bring to fossil fuel producers it is undeniable that this is further proof of the change in the regulatory landscape that producers will have to deal with.

In addition to this regulatory uncertainty, oil and gas companies are under pressure from the increase in the so called 'climate litigation'. Climate litigation can be described as '(…) any litigation that involves climate as part of the subject matter. But when people talk about climate change lawsuits, they usually mean efforts to use the litigation process to spur climate mitigation actions or receive adaptation funding. Many cases are being brought by environmental advocacy organizations or governments who anticipate massive costs related to adapting to climate change, and they are suing to try to recover money to support those needs.'[12]

According to a recent report from the UN Environment Program, the number of climate change court cases has more than doubled since 2017 and is growing worldwide. Most of these cases have targeted government decisions based on a specific project's inconsistency with the goals of the Paris Agreement or a country's own net-zero commitments. Climate litigation has also targeted corporations seen as not doing enough or actively acting against what is seen as the path to tackle climate change – some examples include attempts to hold fossil fuel companies and other greenhouse gas emitters responsible for climate harm.[13]

There is a growing body of decisions and precedents being set in a number of ground-breaking decisions such as:

[10] The Energy Charter Treaty is a multilateral agreement that entered into force in 1998 and contains provisions on investment protection and trade in the energy sector. See Rafael Leal-Arcas (ed), *Commentary on the Energy Charter Treaty* (Edward Elgar Publishing, 2023); Kaj Hobér, *The Energy Charter Treaty* (Oxford University Press, 2020).

[11] European Union, 'Energy Charter Treaty: Council gives final green light to EU's withdrawal' (*consilium.europa.eu*, 30 May 2024) www.consilium.europa.eu/en/press/press-releases/2024/05/30/energy-charter-treaty-council-gives-final-green-light-to-eu-s-withdrawal/. See also Tibisay Morgandi and Lorand Bartels, 'Exiting the Energy Charter Treaty under the law of treaties' (2023) 34 *King's Law Journal* 145.

[12] 'Yale Experts Explain Climate Lawsuits' (*Yale Sustainability*, 16 August 2023) sustainability.yale.edu/explainers/yale-experts-explain-climate-lawsuits.

[13] United Nations Environment Programme, 'Global Climate Litigation Report 2023 Status Review', wedocs.unep.org/bitstream/handle/20.500.11822/43008/global_climate_litigation_report_2023.pdf?sequence=3.

1. The UN Human Rights Committee concluding for the first time that a country has violated international human rights law through climate policy and climate inaction, finding Australia's government to be in violation of its human rights obligations to Torres Strait Islanders.[14]
2. Brazil's Supreme Court holding that the Paris Agreement is a human rights treaty, which means it enjoys 'supranational' status.[15]
3. A Dutch court ordered Shell to comply with the Paris Agreement and reduce its carbon dioxide emissions by 45 per cent from 2019 levels by 2030. This was the first time a court found a private company to have a duty under the Paris Agreement.[16]
4. Germany's court striking down parts of the Federal Climate Protection Act as incompatible with the rights to life and health.[17]
5. A United Kingdom court finding that the government had failed to comply with its legal duties under its Climate Change Act 2008 when approving its net-zero strategy.[18]

The legal implications for companies, individuals and government alike can be vast and affect not only the execution of new projects but also the reputation and the bottom line of fossil fuels producers. Time will tell how effective climate litigation will be in terms of impacting how energy is produced and how governments structure policy, but this is a trend that is continuing to grow.

One more factor is that because of the fast shift in the world's energy sources and climate issues, getting funds for new oil and gas activities is getting harder.

It is not surprising that the access to capital for developing oil and gas projects is also affected by all of the above. An interesting paper from the International Monetary Fund (2023) authored by Christian Bogmans, Andrea Pescatori and Ervin Prifti showed that global oil and gas investment fell by 12 per cent between 2015 and 2021 due to international climate policy. The study suggests that the divestment could be caused by producers expecting lower future demand for oil and gas and thus they want to avoid the risk of having assets that may be hard to sell.

[14] Sabin Center and Columbia University Law School, 'U.N. Human Rights Committee finds that Australia is violating human rights obligations towards Torres Strait Islanders for climate inaction' (27 September 2022) blogs.law.columbia.edu/climatechange/2022/09/27/u-n-human-rights-committee-finds-that-australia-is-violating-human-rights-obligations-towards-torres-strait-islanders-for-climate-inaction/.

[15] Eoghan MacDonagh, 'Brazilian Supreme Court recognises the Paris Agreement as a "human rights treaty"' (*Clifford Chance*, 10 August 2022) www.cliffordchance.com/insights/resources/blogs/business-and-human-rights-insights/2022/08/brazilian-supreme-court-recognises-the-paris-agreement-as-a-human-rights-treaty.html.

[16] Maurits Dolmans and Michael J Preston, 'Dutch Court Orders Shell to Reduce Emissions in First Climate Change Ruling Against Company' (*Cleary Gottlieb*, 30 June 2021) www.clearygottlieb.com/news-and-insights/publication-listing/dutch-court-orders-shell-to-reduce-emissions-in-first-climate-change-ruling-against-company.

[17] 'Constitutional complaints against the Federal Climate Change Act partially successful' (*Bundesverfassungsgericht*, 29 April 2021) www.bundesverfassungsgericht.de/SharedDocs/Pressemitteilungen/EN/2021/bvg21-031.html.

[18] High Court of Justice King's Bench Division Administrative Court, Friend of the Earth and others vs Secretary-of-State-for-Energy-Security-and-Net-Zero (3 May 2024) www.judiciary.uk/wp-content/uploads/2024/05/Friends-of-the-Earth-v-Secretary-of-State-for-Energy-Security-and-Net-Zero-003.pdf.

The study also points out that apart from the producers divesting due to diminishing economic prospects, access to financing opportunities is also becoming more difficult. It points out that:

> A large and rapidly growing literature has already analyzed the effects of climate transition risks on various dimensions relevant for private firms. More specifically, research shows that risks related to environmental regulation are increasingly driving up the cost of capital for high emitters in corporate loan markets (Delis, De Greiff, and Ongena, 2019), through syndicated loans (Ehlers, Packer, and Greiff, 2022), corporate bonds (Seltzer, Starks, and Zhu, 2022), and higher interest rates charged by banks to dirtier firms (Fard, Javadi, and Kim, 2020). Investors have been shown to increasingly price in climate policy risks in Germany (see Sen and Schickfus (2020)) and in the U.S. (see Bolton and Kacperczyk (2021)).4 It has also been documented that institutional investors are increasingly factoring in environmental policy risks in their investment decisions (e.g., Egli, Schärer, and Steffen (2022) and Krueger, Sautner, and Starks (2019)), and that fossil fuel divestment campaigns have recently gained in importance (Egli, Schärer, and Steffen, 2022). Increasingly, stringent environmental policies have also been shown to lead firms to shift their capital structure (Ginglinger and Moreau, 2019).[19]

Alongside the challenge of procuring funds, producers also have to deal with rising price fluctuations that are influenced by many factors such as supply and demand, technology and geopolitical events. When we look at the last five years we can see that prices have varied widely (from negative values in 2020 to the predicted 88 USD for the first quarter of 2024) for various reasons such as lower consumption forecasts, COVID-19 and Russia's invasion of Ukraine etc.

3. Risks of Investing in Offshore Wind Energy

Wind energy is one of the growth engines for decarbonising the world energy mix. The need to move away from fossil fuels, rapidly falling costs and an increase in the world's electricity demand means that wind energy is well positioned to respond to the world's needs in the coming years.

When analysing the wind energy industry, it is important to differentiate between onshore wind and offshore wind. Onshore wind is a developed and mature technology present in many countries. Offshore wind, on the other hand, is still in its infancy. In 2022, 93 per cent of the total wind capacity installed in the world was onshore. However, deployment of offshore wind is expected to increase in the coming years. As an example, in 2022, 18 per cent of total wind capacity growth of 74 GW was delivered by offshore projects.[20]

[19] Christian Bogmans, Andrea Pescatori and Ervin Prifti, 'The Impact of Climate Policy on Oil and Gas Investment: Evidence from Firm-Level Data' (*International Monetary Fund*, 30 June 2023) www.imf.org/en/Publications/WP/Issues/2023/06/30/The-Impact-of-Climate-Policy-on-Oil-and-Gas-Investment-Evidence-from-Firm-Level-Data-535491.

[20] Data collected in International Energy Agency, Wind, www.iea.org/energy-system/renewables/wind.

Whilst the future of wind energy seems bright, there are risks that need to be accounted for when investing in the wind industry.[21] Let's look at some of the most important issues to be considered.

One of the challenges that an investor should be aware of is that, unlike fossil fuels or nuclear energy (for example) which have a stable and 'predictable' output, wind energy is affected by what is called intermittency and variability. This means that the wind does not always blow with the same force and varies from time to time. It is crucial for the wind project to be located in an area with strong and consistent winds but, due to various natural factors, the force of the wind fluctuates and thus creates problems in terms of maintaining a steady output of electricity. There are some solutions that can be applied such as energy storage, forecasting tools and strategies to manage demand response but intermittency and variability is an issue that the investors will inevitably face.

In addition to intermittency and variability, there is also another less talked about issue which affects the production of electricity from a wind project which is called 'wake loss'.

One of the most important questions when deciding to invest in an offshore wind project is how much energy the windfarm will be able to produce in any given year. There are multiple factors affecting this such as the wind potential in the area where the windfarm is going to be installed, but there are also internal factors like the design and layout of the windfarm.

When analysing the design of a windfarm it is important to understand that each individual turbine will interact with the wind and change its 'characteristics' as soon as it passes through the blades of the turbine. When passing through the turbine, the speed of the wind is reduced because part of its power has been harnessed by that specific turbine (the effect of this on the wind is called a 'wake'). This means that when reaching the other turbines, the wind has lost some of its 'strength' thus affecting the ability of these turbines to generate electricity (this is called the 'wake loss effect').[22]

These wake losses can have a severe impact in a windfarm as one of the consequences is a decrease in the capacity of the windfarm to generate electricity. Another impact is the fact that turbines operating in wake conditions have lower 'life-expectancy' and are more prone to having to be maintained. Thus, it is extremely important for a windfarm project to be designed in a way that can mitigate wake losses.

Intermittency, variability, and wake losses are all factors that could lead to lower energy yields than initially anticipated which, in turn, will have an impact on the economic returns to investors.

Another issue investors in the wind energy will have to account for is the consenting process and grid integration.

The process of obtaining the necessary permissions and approvals to develop, construct, and operate an offshore wind farm is what is commonly called the 'Consenting Process'. This process can include a variety of consents throughout the project lifecycle,

[21] For reasons of economy, we will focus on specific issues affecting the Offshore Wind Industry.

[22] For a good explanation of the effect, see Eirik Finserås et al, 'Gone with the wind? Wind farm-induced wakes and regulatory gaps' (2024) 159 *Marine Policy* 105897; Saurabh Gunecha, 'Exploring Wake Losses in Offshore Wind' (*Empire Engineering*, 11 August 2023) www.empireengineering.co.uk/exploring-wake-losses-in-offshore-wind/.

such as planning permissions, environmental impact assessments, and other regulatory approvals. The aim of the consenting process is to ensure that all necessary permissions and approvals are obtained for the development, construction, and operation of an offshore wind farm with a view to minimising impacts and maximising potential. The consenting process is a cumbersome and challenging one and if a project fails to secure a successful 'consent', the project cannot be implemented.

Moreover, a wind project produces electricity that needs to be transferred to an electricity grid. For this 'transfer' to happen, there will have to be cables, substations and access points that involve significant technical, operational, and regulatory challenges and limitations. This means, there is also the need to account for challenges such as grid capacity, grid access, grid connection, grid stability, grid management and grid regulation. All these challenges can pose a threat to the ability of a project to monetise its output.

To put it simply, grids are essential for the flow of electricity, and they have a limited ability to 'store' and deliver energy. This means that if we want to produce more electricity to meet the global demand for energy, we need to upgrade our grids. The International Energy Agency (IEA) estimates that to follow their Paris Agreement commitments, countries will have to '(…) build or improve a total of over 80 million kilometers of grids by 2040, the same as the entire existing global grid'.[23]

To achieve this, Deloitte, in a recent study, estimated that, for Europe alone, power grids will require an investment of between 375–425 billion euros in 2020–2030 to accommodate for the extra electricity that is forecast to be injected in the grids in that period alone. A recent report from Bloomberg goes even further to say that the world will need at least $21.4 trillion to be invested in the electricity grid by 2050 to support a net-zero trajectory for the world.[24]

To add perspective the IEA estimates that, as of today, at least 3,000 gigawatts (GW) of renewable power projects, of which 1,500 GW are in advanced stages, are waiting in grid connection queues.[25]

It goes without saying that without grids, electricity cannot reach consumers, thus it is of vital importance that investments in the grids are made by the governments.

Another important aspect of an offshore wind project is the sea and land use implications. Building a windfarm and its transmission network can affect the environment, society, and economy. Visual and noise pollution (which are reduced if the project is offshore), wildlife and habitat disturbance, clashes with other sea users, negative effects on land and difficulties in obtaining legal access for its offshore and onshore transmission assets are some of the challenges that the investors will have to address and need careful planning, assessment and forward thinking to ensure they do not interfere with the windfarm's ability to generate electricity.[26]

[23] International Energy Agency, 'Electricity Grids and Secure Energy Transitions', www.iea.org/reports/electricity-grids-and-secure-energy-transitions/executive-summary.

[24] BloombergNEF, 'New Energy Outlook 2024', about.bnef.com/new-energy-outlook/.

[25] ibid.

[26] See, discussing these issues and the role of licensing systems to mitigate conflicts arising from such interactions, Tina Soliman Hunter and Ignacio Herrera Anchustegui, 'Offshore wind licensing trends and observations' in Ignacio Herrera Anchustegui and Tina Soliman Hunter (eds), *Offshore Wind Licensing* (Edward Elgar Publishing, 2024).

Finally, while the scenario might look bright from an innovation and a reduction in costs standpoint (see below), it is undeniable that at the time of writing this chapter in 2024–25, the offshore wind industry is facing a difficult scenario with a trifecta of surging financing costs due to high inflation, increase in prices for materials used in the production of the turbines and a difficulty in achieving higher prices for the power generated. This difficulty in getting better pricing can be explained by governments wanting to keep costs to consumers down and the fact there is still a big gap between when the projects must lock in deals to guarantee revenues and the time the projects actually obtain all the permits and consents for operation.[27]

If we focus on pricing and the difficulties for offshore wind energy, as an example, we can look at a popular mechanism used by the UK Government to incentivise the build of renewable projects, the Contract for Difference (CfD). This mechanism, despite being a good tool to incentivise production, is falling short of its objectives as the current pricing being offered by the UK Government is not in tune with the current costs of the offshore wind industry.

Under a CfD, developers of offshore wind receive a top up if the strike price falls below a set price they agree with the government. If the strike price is above the set price the developers must pay the difference back to the government. The CfDs are granted through a scheme which allocates these contracts following a public auction.[28]

Despite providing certainty of revenues to developers – which is a major factor when attracting investment for their projects – the 2023 CfD round in the UK failed to attract any offshore wind projects. This is because the strike price being offered by the government was considered insufficient in face of the rising costs for offshore wind.[29]

The UK Government has announced it is reviewing the pricing offered and, due to its ambitions in terms of ramping up investment in the offshore wind space, there seems to be a path for the future CfD rounds to attract offshore wind projects. If we assume inflation 'cools down' in the long run, regulatory changes to shorten the consenting periods, and a better pricing mechanism, there is a lot of positivity around the future of offshore wind projects. Nevertheless, this is an issue that investors need to review carefully.

As a final point, the trifecta of issues affecting the offshore wind industry clearly points to the fact that the technology needed for offshore wind production and the costs it carries means that it will only be available, in the short term, to the nations willing (and able) to subsidise its development. It is not all about having the exposure to the wind, it is about whether countries can subsidise a form of energy which, with

[27] Rachel Millard, 'The struggles of the offshore wind industry' *Financial Times* (31 October 2023) www.ft.com/content/00e8af58-f2b4-4d91-9c6e-bd2045c22c20.

[28] For some literature on this topic see 'Contracts for Difference: the Instrument of Choice for the Energy Transition' (*Oxford Institute for Energy Studies*, April 2024); 'Position Paper on Sustainable Contracts for Difference Design' (*ENTSO-E*, 20 February 2024) eepublicdownloads.blob.core.windows.net/public-cdn-container/clean-documents/Publications/Position%20papers%20and%20reports/2024/240220_ENTSO-E_CfDs_Position_Paper.pdf; 'Contracts-for-Difference to support renewable energy technologies: Considerations for design and implementation (*Florence School of Regulation*, March 2024).

[29] Matt Mace, 'Avoidable and botched: Green groups react to offshore wind omission in CfD auctions' (*Edie*, 8 September 2023) www.edie.net/avoidable-and-botched-green-groups-react-to-offshore-wind-omission-in-cfd-auctions/.

the current market prices and cost of supply chain, does not seem to be able to stand on its own without government subsidies. Another factor we should consider is that the installation and maintenance of wind turbines need skilled labour which is scarce in many developing countries. Running and maintaining an offshore wind farm requires a lot of technical expertise and several engineering specialists to make it work well.

When we compare the situation of developing countries that need cheap energy to grow but lack specialised human resources and often have financial difficulties, it is hard to expect a fast growth of offshore wind in these countries. Rather, we might see a slow growth in the next few years and maybe a rise in growth when some of the problems mentioned above are solved.[30]

If we compare it to the more established oil and gas industry, investing in oil and gas might still present a safer bet for cash-struggling nations.

4. Opportunities and Rewards of Investing in Oil and Gas

As mentioned above, oil and gas are the dominant forces of energy in the world. While that scenario might be changing, it is safe to say investments will continue to be made as the world will continue to consume oil and gas for decades to come.

Oil and gas investments require large scale and long-term investments. They are also capital-intensive projects which require thinking ahead in terms of implementing robust supply chains and guaranteeing financing and the ability to build infrastructure. Despite all the risks, there are still a lot of opportunities and rewards in investing in oil and gas.

According to the latest study by the International Energy Agency, the Return on Capital Employed (ROCE) by the oil and gas industry averaged around 6–9 per cent between 2010 and 2022.[31] Also according to the US Energy Information Administration, when reviewing data for the oil and gas industry regarding Q3 2023, distributions to shareholders via dividends and share repurchases averaged around $67 billion over the previous four quarters.[32] This means that the oil and gas industry is still able to generate high returns for its investors. While we cannot discount that these high returns are not across the board and are highly dependent on resources available, portfolio of each individual company, and market conditions, it seems undeniable that the oil and gas industry still generates strong returns on investment for its shareholders.

[30] See on opportunities and hindrances for (offshore) renewable energy in developing countries: Eric Martinot et al, 'Renewable energy markets in developing countries' (2002) 27 *Annual review of energy and the environment* 309; Benjamin K Sovacool, 'Design principles for renewable energy programs in developing countries' (2012) 5 *Energy & Environmental Science* 9157; Ignacio Herrera Anchustegui, 'Epilogue: Changing Latin America Through the Energy Transformation?' in Geoffrey Wood, Juan Felipe Neira-Castro (eds), *From Fossil Fuels to Low Carbon Energy Transition: New Regulatory Trends in Latin America* (Springer, 2022); Ignacio Herrera Anchustegui and Catalina Vallejo Piedrahíta, 'Offshore wind licensing in Colombia: A pioneer in Latin America and the Caribbean' in Anchustegui and Hunter (n 26).

[31] 'The Oil and Gas Industry in Net Zero Transitions' (*International Energy Agency*, February 2024) iea.blob.core.windows.net/assets/f065ae5e-94ed-4fcb-8f17-8ceffde8bdd2/TheOilandGasIndustryinNetZeroTransitions.pdf.

[32] US EnergyReport, 'Global Oil and Gas Industry Review Unveils Financial Trends for 3Q23' (19 December 2023) greentechlead.com/energy-news/us-energy-report-global-oil-and-gas-industry-review-unveils-financial-trends-for-3q23-45240.

Another reward from investing in oil and gas is the access to well established markets and supply chains. Given the oil and gas ubiquitous presence in the energy markets throughout recent decades, there is a well-established network of producers, transporters, traders, consumers and service providers which allow for investments to be made with the certainty of having a robust market at the disposal of the investor.

If we look at the world's commodities, oil and natural gas have historically been at the top of most traded commodities and are constantly among the top 10 of best performing commodities. This not only reflects their unique position as the major sources of energy in the world but also the fact that their distribution network is highly developed and allows for both to be traded in high volumes. This, in turn, means better returns to investors as the commodity they are investing in is highly sought after and easily reaches target consumers.

Like other commodities, oil and gas are subject to the effects of various factors that impact commodity trading, such as wars, conflicts, sanctions, and trade disputes, but in general, the oil and gas industry has been able to overcome these difficulties and maintain its product trading.

A further 'advantage' of investing in oil and gas is the economic and social progress as well as geopolitical power that helps oil and gas producing nations. Oil and gas are often leveraged to increase the power and strategic interests of the countries that have the reserves. It is common for oil and gas to be employed as a means of diplomacy as well as a method of strengthening the partnership between producing and consuming nations.

If we use level of Foreign Direct Investment (FDI) as a measure of how resource rich countries can attract FDI, we see that according to the United Nations Conference on Trade and Development World Investment Report 2022, FDI to African countries hit a record $83 billion in 2021.[33] A large portion of this FDI is going to energy projects, being oil and gas investments at the top of the list.

Besides FDI and the enhancement of its geopolitical influence, oil producing nations also benefit from the development of their local workforce (specially through the implementation of local content legislation) as well as an increase in tax revenues. This all, in theory, helps balance the countries' balance of payments although some countries, due to poor wealth management, end up suffering from what is described in economic terms as a 'Dutch Disease'.[34]

As a final note, producing oil and gas is still heavily linked to energy security which is something that is treated as a priority by almost all nations. Energy security can be described as the access to reliable and affordable energy to meet the needs of the population of any given country. Given the rising levels of energy consumption (especially oil and gas) it is no wonder being an oil producing nation serves the purpose of increasing

[33] United Nations Trade and Development (UNCTAD), 'World Investment Report 2022' unctad.org/publication/world-investment-report-2022.

[34] For an explanation of the phenomenon, International Monetary Fund, 'Dutch Disease: Wealth Managed Unwisely' www.imf.org/en/Publications/fandd/issues/Series/Back-to-Basics/Dutch-Disease. See also Kwasi Dartey-Baah, Kwesi Amponsah-Tawiah and David Aratuo, 'Emerging "Dutch disease" in emerging oil economy: Ghana's perspective' (2012) 7 *Society and business review* 185; Alexander Kemp Nikolaos Vlassis and Eddy Wifa, *Mitigating the Resource Curse: Economic, Governance, and Policy Considerations* (Routledge, 2024).

domestic energy security (by producing enough to cover its energy needs and allowing for easy access to secure reserves) and helps the economy by allowing the country to export its energy to other countries. If we consider recent events such as US President Joe Biden authorising the release of oil form the US Strategic Petroleum Reserve to compensate for a shortfall in oil supply and the Russin invasion to Ukraine which left EU nations looking for alternative supplies of gas, it is clear energy security is a priority and that oil and gas still play a heavy role in providing it.[35] As an example of how energy security helps shape the markets, after Russia's invasion of Ukraine, most EU nations which depended heavily on Russia for its gas imports turned to liquified natural gas (LNG) to compensate for the shortfall in gas after severing ties with Russia. LNG provides an easy way to acquire gas as it does not need transnational pipelines to move the gas and allows for far nations to trade with non-producing countries by shipping their gas in liquified form.

Most of the LNG acquired by EU nations after the invasion came from the US, and EU leaders were quick to encourage other 'friendly' nations to develop their gas reserves with the promise of firm deals in the future. This, in turn, helped make the gas industry even more attractive to investors.[36]

5. Opportunities and Rewards of Investing in Offshore Wind

Wind energy is one of the fastest-growing sources of energy in the world accounting for around one third of the electricity generation from renewables in 2022 and forecast to hugely increase by the end of the decade. This creates several opportunities for both investors and countries looking to develop their own offshore wind industry.

In terms of opportunities, investors benefit from an expanding market – the forecast is for an additional 380GW of offshore wind capacity to be installed across 32 markets in the next 10 years,[37] from ample incentives to invest (both in the forms of subsidies, tax breaks and other financial incentives)[38] and from a regulatory environment which is increasingly 'friendly' to investments in renewable energies.

Given its potential growth and significant returns on investment, offshore wind has become more popular in terms of investors wanting to finance it. Thus, developers now have a range of financing options available for its offshore wind projects.

One of the most common is project financing. What this means is that the project is financed by a group of lenders, usually banks or other institutional lenders, who provide debt financing based on the projected cash flows of the project. This is a common

[35] S&P Global and Daniel Yergin, 'The return of energy security' (29 February 2024) www.spglobal.com/en/research-insights/special-reports/look-forward/the-return-of-energy-security.

[36] ibid.

[37] Global Wind Energy Council, 'Global Offshore Wind Report 2023' gwec.net/gwecs-global-offshore-wind-report-2023/.

[38] As an example, the EU Commission has a number of incentive programmes and fund for offshore renewable. A list of those programmes can be found here: energy.ec.europa.eu/topics/renewable-energy/financing/eu-funding-offshore-renewables_en.

financing structure for large-scale infrastructure projects and that includes offshore wind farms.

Another option is equity financing whereby the developer raises capital by selling shares in the project to investors. Equity can provide significant returns if the project is successful but also means the investor is exposing itself to more risk due to the project's long-term nature.

Developers can also resort to corporate financing, where the project is financed by the balance sheet of the project developer. This could be a good financing option, specially from the standpoint of control and harnessing all the returns, but it requires the project developer to have a strong balance sheet and credit rating.

Public financing, through government grants or subsidies, is also available to support the development of offshore wind projects. It is also possible, for example in the US, to resort to tax equity finance which provides investors with tax credits if they invest in renewable energy projects.

Last, but not least, there are also other financing options such as green bonds, which are fixed-income securities designed to raise capital for environmentally friendly projects, including offshore wind farms.[39]

Another reward of investing in offshore wind projects is the fact that the costs of developing a project are bound to reduce in the mid to long term due to, among other factors, continuous technological innovation, and increased competition in the market.

BloombergNEF, in a recent report, has reported that in the first six months of 2023, the costs of new-build offshore wind projects have fallen by 2 per cent and went even further to state that its analysis indicated that the global benchmark levelised cost of electricity for offshore wind is now on par with coal.[40]

If we look at the last decade, the International Renewable Energy Agency reports that increases in turbine sizes and ultra-low interest rates helped push overall costs of construction and operation down by 60 per cent between 2010 and 2021.

As an example of the technological innovation, the Global Wind Energy Council 2022 Report stated that:

> (…) technology innovation has been a primary driver in the dramatic cost reductions of renewables, allowing wind power, especially offshore wind, to move from the margins of the energy sector to the mainstream.

[39] More information on financing offshore wind projects can be found in PWC, 'Financing offshore wind' (2020) www.pwc.nl/nl/actueel-publicaties/assets/pdfs/pwc-invest-nl-financing-offshore-wind.pdf; Jérôme Guillet, 'Financing offshore wind' (2021) green-giraffe.com/wp-content/uploads/2021/02/110624_financing_offshore_wind_chapter_14_of_the_principles_of_project_finance.pdf; Wind Energy, 'The Facts, Chapter 3: Project Financing' www.wind-energy-the-facts.org/index-45.html, and 'Green Bond Principles (GBP)' (*ICMA*, June 2021) www.icmagroup.org/sustainable-finance/the-principles-guidelines-and-handbooks/green-bond-principles-gbp/. For academic literature see, inter alia, Mak Đukan and Lena Kitzing, 'The impact of auctions on financing conditions and cost of capital for wind energy projects' (2021) 152 *Energy Policy* 112197; Tyler A Hansen et al, 'Five grand challenges of offshore wind financing in the United States' (2024) 107 *Energy Research & Social Science* 103329; Andrew C Levitt et al, 'Pricing offshore wind power' (2011) 39 *Energy Policy* 6408.

[40] 'Cost of Clean Energy Technologies Drop as Expensive Debt Offset by Cooling Commodity Prices' (*BloombergNEF*, 7 June 2023) about.bnef.com/blog/cost-of-clean-energy-technologies-drop-as-expensive-debt-offset-by-cooling-commodity-prices/.

> Since the world's first offshore wind turbine, the Bonus B35-450kW, was installed at the Vindeby site in Denmark in 1991, the power rating of offshore wind turbine has grown significantly. The global average offshore wind turbine size has passed the milestone of 1.5 MW in 2000, 2.5 MW in 2005 and 6.0 MW in 2020. Excluding China and Vietnam where more of the smaller offshore turbine models have been installed, the average turbine rating for new installations reached 8.1 MW in 2021 and expected to pass the 12 MW mark in 2025.[41]

The size of the turbine matters as a bigger turbine can achieve higher power ratings and, due to its longer blade, can increase energy production.

Despite the technological advances, the report further details that '(…) it must be noted that the possibilities and limits for future offshore turbine design will be determined by factors such as the existing supply chain and infrastructure, drivetrain optimization, foundation design, materials constraints, the logistical constraints for both transportation and installation as well as permitting. To further unlock the potential of offshore wind, technology innovation will remain key and advances in this area are expected to continue.'

There are also inherent environmental and social benefits from investing in offshore wind projects. In terms of the environment, offshore wind generates clean, renewable energy which is abundant and does not emit greenhouse gases. The key benefits are clear, offshore wind helps reduce a country's carbon footprint (by replacing fossil fuel based power generation which emits a lot of Co2), reduces the need for energy to be transported long distances (thus reducing its carbon emissions), helps Public Health as it does not pollute the air – thus, potentially, helping reduce public health issues linked to quality of air – and has a higher sustainability factor than its fossil fuels counterpart (oil and gas takes millions of years to form vs wind which is seemingly inexhaustible). Looking at the need of the world for more clean energy and the agreements made by governments under the Paris Agreements, it seems clear that offshore wind energy is a winner.

Also, if we look at the social benefits, a recent study conducted by KPMG concluded that '(…) building of OWFs creates significant employment. Studies of the UK OWS industry estimate that 1,500 FTE jobs are created per GW output during the construction phase. It is also estimated that 350 local FTE jobs are enabled per year per GW output during the life of the equipment (usually around 25 years). Needless to say, local communities and businesses benefit from this employment as it increases spending and consumption in the local economy – a positive ripple effect. Employment goes much wider than the immediate construction and maintenance teams, too – as OSW also supports significant supply chains that feed into the research, design and production of the necessary equipment. In the UK today, there are thought to be around 430,000 jobs in low carbon businesses and their supply chains, employing people in locations right around the country.'[42]

[41] Global Wind Energy Council, 'Global Offshore Wind Report 2022' (29 June 2022) gwec.net/wp-content/uploads/2022/06/GWEC-Global-Offshore-Wind-Report-2022.pdf.

[42] Elisha Sempa, 'Factoring social and community impacts into the offshore wind business case' (*KPMG*, 14 December 2023) kpmg.com/uk/en/blogs/home/posts/2023/12/factoring-social-and-community-impacts-into-the-offshore-wind-business-case.html. See also discussing benefits and compensations to communities in offshore wind: Ignacio Herrera Anchustegui, 'Distributive Justice, Community Benefits and Renewable Energy: Offshore Wind Projects' in Ruven Fleming, Kaisa Huhta and Leonie Reins (eds), *Sustainable Energy*

Also on this point, peer-reviewed studies have shown that investment in renewable energy generates up to three times more jobs than the same amount of spending in fossil fuels. This is due to the fact that despite being less labour intensive when in production, renewables are expanding and the demand for components, supply-chain management, transportation and projects O&M (to name a few) is expanding, thus the potential for job creating is higher than in the oil and gas industry which is much more established.[43]

Investments in offshore wind are bound to increase thus multiplying social benefits and environmental positive impacts.

6. Conclusions

Oil, gas and wind investments have different risks and rewards, and investors need to evaluate them carefully and comprehensively before making any decisions. Oil and gas investments still offer high returns, established markets and geopolitical influence, but also face environmental and social impacts, regulatory uncertainties and price volatility. Wind investments, on the other hand, offer environmental and social benefits, technological innovation and ample opportunities for financing but also face issues with pricing, intermittency and variability, grid integration and land use.

All of these risks and rewards are weighed by investors against the backdrop of the rapidly changing energy markets and help them make a decision on where to invest. Countries looking to diversify their energy mix or boost their energy production will have to increasingly look to their own business environment and decide what changes need to be made to attract more investment.

When considering how to attract investment in these industries, it is important that countries looking for investment in their energy portfolio try to address the risks to investors. This means, among other things: (i) providing clear and consistent policies and regulations which can create a stable and predictable investment environment, reduce the regulatory uncertainties and risks, and align the incentives and objectives of the investors and the policymakers, (ii) enhancing the financial and fiscal support, which can lower the capital and operational costs, increase the cash flows and returns, and improve the access and availability of the financing sources and instruments, as well as (iii) promoting the innovation and collaboration which can foster the development and deployment of new and improved technologies and solutions, enhance the knowledge and experience of sharing and learning, and strengthen partnerships and networks among the investors and other stakeholders.

If a country tackles these issues, it is sure to attract investment.

Democracy and the Law vol 26 (Brill | Nijhoff, 2021); Beñat Landeta-Manzano et al, 'Wind energy and local communities: A manufacturer's efforts to gain acceptance' (2018) 121 *Energy Policy* 314; John Glasson et al, 'The local socio-economic impacts of offshore wind farms' (2022) 95 *Environmental Impact Assessment Review* 106783. Grant Allan et al, 'The economic and environmental impacts of UK offshore wind development: The importance of local content' (2020) 199 *Energy* 117436.

[43] Heidi Garrett-Peltier, 'Green versus brown: Comparing the employment impacts of energy efficiency, renewable energy, and fossil fuels using an input-output model' (2017) 61 *Economic Modelling* 439.

10

Building Local Capacity and Expertise via Local Content Rules and Transferring Skills and Knowledge between Offshore Developments

ELENA I ATHWAL, EDUARDO G PEREIRA, OPEYEMI OMOTUYI AND IGNACIO HERRERA ANCHUSTEGUI*

1. Introduction

In an era where global progress hinges on the seamless exchange of expertise, the strategic implementation of local content rules emerges as a linchpin in cultivating indigenous capacity and transferring vital skills and knowledge across the dynamic landscape of offshore developments. The energy industry stands at the crossroads of transformation and innovation as the world increasingly acknowledges the environmental, social, and economic ramifications of energy production and consumption. Given the increasing focus on skills development and inclusivity for the energy transition, as highlighted by the International Energy Agency (IEA), there is an urgent need to review and enhance Local Content Requirements (LCRs).[1] Within this complex web lies the concept of LCRs, which signifies the strategic integration of local resources, expertise and labour, crucial for developing nations endowed with natural resources, who face challenge in accessing and developing their natural resources,[2] particularly petroleum resources, effectively due to constraints in technology, infrastructure and finance.[3] LCRs are

* This contribution was made possible by the generous funding granted by the Research Council of Norway to the research projects: Norwegian Centre for Hydrogen Research – HyValue (Project: 333151); and ImpactWind Sørvest (Project: 332034).

All websites were last visited on 1 July 2024.

[1] International Energy Agency (IEA), 'Skills Development and Inclusivity for Clean Energy Transitions' (*IEA 50*, September 2022) www.iea.org/reports/skills-development-and-inclusivity-for-clean-energy-transitions.

[2] The term 'natural resources' refers to 'oil, minerals, forests, water, and fertile land that occur in nature and can be exploited for economic gain', United Nations Development Programme peacemaker.un.org/sites/peacemaker.un.org/files/NRCMediation_UNDPAUNEP2015.pdf.

[3] Damilola Olawuyi and Ayobami Olaniyan, 'Local Content and the Sustainable Development of Oil and Gas Resources in Nigeria' in Damilola Olawuyi (ed), *Local Content and Sustainable Development in Global Energy Markets* (Cambridge University Press, 2021) 167–87.

important developments in energy law and policy. LCRs have emerged due to the legal innovations, policies and measures focused on increasing the gains of natural resource production in the energy industry, while aiming to lower the adverse impacts on the social, economic, environmental and geopolitical spheres, along the lines of the United Nations Sustainable Development Goals (UN SDGs).[4]

Local content requirements are relevant to several UN SDGs, particularly those focusing on economic growth, industry innovation and sustainable energy (see Table 1).

Table 1 UN SDG and Relevant Targets to local content requirements and energy law and policy (own elaboration)

SDG	Relevant Targets
SDG 7: Affordable and Clean Energy	– Target 7.1: Ensure universal access to affordable, reliable, and modern energy services.
	– Target 7.2: Increase substantially the share of renewable energy in the global energy mix.
	– Target 7.3: Double the global rate of improvement in energy efficiency.
SDG 8: Decent Work and Economic Growth	– Target 8.2: Achieve higher levels of economic productivity through diversification, technological upgrading, and innovation.
	– Target 8.3: Promote development-oriented policies that support productive activities, decent job creation, entrepreneurship, creativity, and innovation.
	– Target 8.5: Achieve full and productive employment and decent work for all women and men.
SDG 9: Industry, Innovation, and Infrastructure	– Target 9.2: Promote inclusive and sustainable industrialisation and significantly raise industry's share of employment and GDP by 2030.
	– Target 9.4: Upgrade infrastructure and retrofit industries to make them sustainable, with increased resource-use efficiency and greater adoption of clean and environmentally sound technologies.
SDG 12: Responsible Consumption and Production	– Target 12.2: Achieve the sustainable management and efficient use of natural resources by 2030.
	– Target 12.5: Substantially reduce waste generation through prevention, reduction, recycling, and reuse.
SDG 13: Climate Action	– Target 13.2: Integrate climate change measures into national policies, strategies, and planning.
	– Target 13.3: Improve education, awareness-raising, and human and institutional capacity on climate change mitigation, adaptation, impact reduction, and early warning.

Source: Authors' own.[5]

[4] See Damilola Olawuyi, 'International Energy Law and the Gulf Crisis' in Rory Miller (ed), *The Gulf Crisis: The View from Qatar* (HBKU Press, 2018) 127–35.

[5] Derived from the United Nations Sustainable Development Goals, 'The 17 Goals' (*UN SDGs*) sdgs.un.org/goals; and the Sustainable Energy For All (SEforALL) initiative, 'About Us' www.seforall.org.

After a period of declining interest, industrial policy has re-emerged globally, driven by the need to counter market-fundamentalist approaches in developing countries, address economic challenges in advanced economies, and leverage disruptive technologies, with LCRs emerging as prominent tools to ensure benefits in natural resource and renewable energy development while potentially building up manufacturing capabilities, exemplifying the 'rebirth of industrial policy.[6]

Exploiting the planet's energy resources in a sustainable and equitable manner is a challenge that demands a combination of international cooperation, technological prowess, and policy reforms, in order to mitigate and adapt to the associated environmental and social impacts of climate change. Currently, international efforts are increasingly focusing on fostering international cooperation for more sustainable production and green innovation,[7] in order to align trade with the Paris Agreement on climate change.[8] Although there is no single definition of LCRs, they can be understood as the degree to which the extraction of natural resources and the subsequent activities therein contribute to the local economy through the employment of local labour, utilisation of local services, and the stimulation of local industries.[9] By channelling the benefits of resource extraction to local communities, the promise of local content is vast – building indigenous capacity, enhancing the economic value chain, and fostering long-term, sustainable growth.[10]

Traditionally, energy-rich developing countries have often found themselves subject to, to a certain extent, external forces – foreign corporations, fluctuating market prices, and geopolitical dynamics.[11] The paradox of plenty, or the 'resource curse', as it is popularly known, captures this anomaly where countries endowed with abundant natural resources often witness sluggish economic growth, social inequality, and environmental degradation.[12] The strategic implementation of local content rules and regulations aims to redress this imbalance by enhancing the direct and indirect benefits of resource extraction to the local economies.[13] Countries with expansive domestic markets, such as those who possess components used in domestic solar and wind energy products, have

[6] Karl Aiginger and Dani Rodrik, 'Rebirth of Industrial Policy and an Agenda for the Twenty-First Century' (2020) 20 *Journal of Industrial Competition Trade* 189–207, doi.org/10.1007/s10842-019-00322-3.

[7] United Nations Conference on Trade and Development (UNCTAD), 'Technology and Innovation Report 2023: Opening green windows. Technological opportunities for a low-carbon world' (2023) xxiv, 121.

[8] United Nations Framework Convention on Climate Change (UNFCCC) Adoption of the Paris Agreement, 21st Conference of the Parties, Paris: United Nations (2015).

[9] See Chilenye Nwapi, 'Defining the "Local" in Local Content Requirements in the Oil and Gas and Mining Sectors in Developing Countries' (2015) *Law and Development Review* 8; see also Olawuyi and Olaniyan (n 3).

[10] Organisation for Economic Cooperation and Development (OECD), 'Local content requirements impact the global economy'.

[11] OECD, 'Developing countries and development co-operation: What is at stake?' (28 April 2020) read.oecd-ilibrary.org/view/?ref=132_132637-tfn40fwe1w&title=Developing-countries-and-development-co-operation_What-is-at-stake.

[12] For an account of the effects of petroleum revenue on political stability and instability, refer to Macartan Humphries, Jeffrey D Sachs, and Joseph E Stiglitz (eds), *Escaping the Resource Curse* (Columbia University Press, 2007).

[13] See IRENA, 'Renewable energy benefits: Leveraging local capacity for small-scale hydropower, International Renewable Energy Agency' (2023) Abu Dhabi, mc-cd8320d4-36a1-40ac-83cc-3389-cdn-endpoint.azureedge.net/-/media/Files/IRENA/Agency/Publication/2023/Sep/IRENA_Leveraging_small_scale_hydropower_2023.pdf?rev=dc4b48d2741746018bf11eaa439b7040.

the advantage of potentially subsidising these emerging sectors.[14] As such, these countries can initiate production aimed at replacing imports while concurrently bolstering their export capacity. This can be achieved by enhancing trade facilitation measures and maintaining stable and competitive exchange rates, which would have impacts akin to those of export subsidies.[15]

The global energy landscape is undergoing a paradigm shift, driven by a variety of pressures such as finite natural resources and increasing environmental concerns due to climate change. Within this context, local content has taken on significant new dimensions, ranging from sustainable development to economic diversification, energy security and independence, community engagement and development, and technology transfer and capacity building. In particular, offshore developments – oil, gas, and the emerging wind energy sector – command attention due to their potential for creating value in the energy chain while also pivoting to reduce the environmental footprint.[16] The intersection of these sectors offers an intriguing premise – the transfer of skills and knowledge across spaces to catalyse local content development.[17] While the offshore oil and gas sectors have a considerable history and experience to offer, the nascent offshore wind energy sector stands to benefit from this knowledge and skills repository. It also offers an opportunity for these energy sectors to coexist and complement each other, fostering a synergy that may well be the key to sustainable and resilient energy ecosystems.[18]

The transfer of skills and knowledge across spaces to catalyse local content development and to shape local content strategies has been taken up in literature from varying global contexts. Herrera Anchustegui, for example, notes the importance of energy transition to develop local value chains in the case of Latin America along themes of resource abundance, renewable energy investment and energy justice.[19] Ovadia offers an examination of local content strategies within the Sub-Saharan African oil sector, using case studies from Nigeria and Angola, for instance, underscoring the potential of these policies in shaping sustainable development trajectories.[20] In a similar context, Heum, provides an insightful retrospective of Norway's successful integration of local content initiatives in its oil and gas operations, which significantly spurred industrial diversification.[21] Pivoting to renewable energy, Lewis' work delineates the dynamics of technology acquisition in the developing economies of China and India, highlighting

[14] UNCTAD (n 7).
[15] OECD (n 10).
[16] UNCTAD (n 7).
[17] IEA 'Offshore Wind Outlook'.
[18] Global Wind Energy Council (GWEC), 'Global Wind Report 2023' gwec.net/wp-content/uploads/2023/03/GWR-2023_interactive.pdf.
[19] Ignacio Herrera Anchustegui, 'Epilogue: Changing Latin America Through the Energy Transformation?' in Geoffrey Wood and Juan F Neira-Castro (eds), *From Fossil Fuels to Low Carbon Energy Transition. Energy, Climate and the Environment* (Palgrave Macmillan, 2022) link.springer.com/chapter/10.1007/978-3-031-00299-1_14.
[20] Jesse Ovadia, 'Local content policies and petro-development in Sub-Saharan Africa: A comparative analysis' (2016) 49 Resources Policy 20–30 www.sciencedirect.com/science/article/pii/S0301420716300502.
[21] Per Heum, 'Local content development: Experiences from oil and gas activities in Norway' SNF Report No. 02/08, SNF Project No. 1285, (2008) Institute for Research in Economics and Business Administration snf.no/media/41bep0kg/a02_08.pdf.

the critical intersection between local capacity building and innovation, especially in the wind turbine sector.[22] Meanwhile, Aitken delves into the societal aspect, analysing how wind power projects can be orchestrated to optimise community benefits in the UK, an area often fraught with challenges and opportunities.[23] LCRs have generally not led to competitive export sectors in solar and wind technologies, with notable exceptions being China and Spain, due to their existing industrial capabilities in related fields.[24] These studies collectively signify the multifaceted implications of local content policies in the ongoing global energy transition, stressing the need for a balanced approach that accommodates environmental, economic, and social parameters.

Nevertheless, the journey toward effective implementation of local content regulations is fraught with intricate challenges, not least among them the potential conflict with established international trade and investment norms.[25] Beyond the internal hurdles such as technological gaps, skill deficiencies, and financial constraints, local content measures often find themselves at odds with broader economic legal frameworks. For instance, stringent LCRs may clash with World Trade Organization (WTO) stipulations, particularly the principles discouraging discriminatory treatment between domestic and foreign manufacturers and service providers.[26] The WTO legal framework on subsidies and LCRs may at times constrain how Member States can support renewable energy projects, impacting the growth of offshore renewable energy globally.[27] Similarly, these regulations might conflict with provisions in regional trade agreements or bilateral investment treaties that advocate for liberalised trade and investment environments.[28] Such contradictions can create a contentious dynamic where countries must carefully balance the pursuit of indigenous industry growth and the integration into global economic systems. This delicate equilibrium necessitates a sophisticated understanding of both the international legal landscape and the nuanced factors influencing local content policies within the ongoing global energy transition.

This chapter, therefore, aims to delve into the intricate dynamics of local content, particularly in the offshore oil, gas, and wind sectors. It contains five sections, this introduction being the first. Section 2 examines LCRs and why they are important in the energy sector, while revealing some of their key challenges. Section 3 examines oil, gas and wind offshore developments in the context of the energy transition, while attempting

[22] Joanna Lewis, 'Technology acquisition and innovation in the developing world: Wind turbine development in China and India' (2007) 42 *Studies in Comparative International Development* 183 link.springer.com/article/10.1007/s12116-007-9012-6.

[23] Mhairi Aitken, 'Wind power and community benefits: Challenges and opportunities' (2010) 38 *Energy Policy* 6066.

[24] Fabian Scheifele, M Bräuning and B Probst, 'The impact of local content requirements on the development of export competitiveness in solar and wind technologies' (2022) 168 *Renewable and Sustainable Energy Reviews* www.sciencedirect.com/science/article/abs/pii/S1364032122007146#bib4.

[25] See P Roberts and D Olawuyi, 'Local Content and Sustainable Development in Global Energy Markets' (2021) 14(5) *The Journal of World Energy Law & Business* 412–13, doi.org/10.1093/jwelb/jwab026.

[26] See also Jan-Christoph Kuntze and Tom Moerenhout, 'Local Content Requirements and the Renewable Energy Industry – A Good Match?' (12 September 2012).

[27] V Roeben, 'WTO Law on Subsidies and Local Content Rules in the Renewable Energy Sector' (*OGEL 5*, 2022) www.ogel.org/article.asp?key=4060.

[28] Silvana Tordo et al, 'Local Content Policies in the Oil and Gas Sector' (*World Bank Studies*, 13 October 2013) documents1.worldbank.org/curated/zh/549241468326687019/pdf/Local-content-in-the-oil-and-gas-sector.pdf.

to unravel the potential for knowledge and skills transfer between these sectors, in order to illuminate the pathways towards sustainable growth. Section 4 aims to draw insights from practical experiences, notably through case studies from Europe, evaluating the successes and challenges encountered in realising local content development in this region. Section 5 provides some recommendations and concludes, seeking to underscore the pivotal role of local content in building resilient and self-reliant economies in an era of energy transition and environmental consciousness.

2. Conceptualising Local Content

A. Introduction

The concept of local content is about providing local value in a country through the deliberate utilisation of local materials, local manpower, and local manufacturing. It involves the hiring and training of indigenous workforces, promoting local skills, knowledge, and technology transfer in capital projects, and building infrastructure to become integrated with the local economy.[29] Globally, resource-rich countries leverage on their extractive sector to improve their local economy. These countries, through regulatory, contractual, or other requirements, strive to ensure that extractive companies operating within their jurisdictions implement strategic policies such as hiring of local labour, procuring of local goods and services, from the host country. The value created for the local, regional or national economy by an extraction project pursuant to the implementation of such policies, and beyond the revenues generated by the project is referred to as the local content.[30] Local content policies therefore aim to ensure that the citizens of a country are applied to execute certain projects, where they have the requisite skill and expertise.[31] This section provides an overview of LCRs in offshore developments. It discusses the role of LCRs in building capacity and expertise in the offshore industry, and also examines the key challenges they face in this regard.

B. The Importance of Local Content Requirements in an Offshore Setting

From a different perspective, in acknowledging the global scope of local content strategies, it is notable that even developed countries are innovatively pushing for advanced local content approaches within their energy sectors, especially during this critical energy transition. This '2.0 approach' to local content is not confined to developing economies;

[29] Victoria Okoro and Oko Ndukwe, 'Local Content Act Implementation and Its Impact On Nigeria Economy: An Appraisal' (2022) 13(2) *Journal of Policy and Development Studies* 99–105; see also Ukaegbu Onwuka, 'Strategies for Improving Local Content Development in Nigeria Oil and Gas Industry' (2021) scholarworks.waldenu.edu/dissertations/10449/.

[30] Natural Resource Governance Institute, 'Local Content: Strengthening the Local Economy and Workforce' (*NRGI Reader*, March 2015) resourcegovernance.org/sites/default/files/nrgi_Local-Content.pdf.

[31] ibid.

it resonates in the strategic manoeuvres seen in Europe's offshore wind licensing, where stringent measures ensure local content inclusion. Similarly, countries like Norway and the UK integrate local content considerations into quality criteria during oil and gas bid assessments, underlining a commitment to reinforcing local industrial capacity and economic resilience.[32] Such strategies, often more nuanced and tied to stringent regulatory compliance and sustainability goals, reflect a sophisticated understanding of local content's economic multiplier effects, emphasising its role in national competitive advantage and socio-economic development within the energy sector's evolving dynamics.

Local content encapsulates a range of activities including the use of local labour, services, and goods, promotion of local entrepreneurship, development of local skills and technological capabilities, and fostering local value chains.[33] It is a concept that goes beyond the mere act of employing local workforce or sourcing local goods; it represents a holistic approach to harness the extractive sector for socio-economic development, with the ultimate goal of sustainable growth and economic self-reliance.[34] These factors render LCRs crucial as a tool to reduce social gaps and ensure a just transition.

Local content policies may be implemented on a project-by-project basis, as well as through state development agreements, through contractual requirements, or universally through national laws and regulations relevant to the extractive sector. In addition, local content policies vary from one country to another and from project to project; while some local content policies emphasise value creation anywhere within the host-country, others seek to promote value creation in the resource-rich region of the host-country specifically. Also, host-countries may vary on the level of specificity of LCRs. For instance, while some LCRs may expressly mention provisions for local employment, training, or percentage of local share ownership in extractive companies, other LCRs may be silent on these specifics. Likewise, there is the question as to what constitutes a local business within the framework of LCR; is it based on a certain minimum percentage ownership by nationals of a host-country, on the basis of a corporate registration in the host-country, or on the percentage of local workforce employed by the business? While the LCRs in some countries make express provisions regarding these issues, others do not make express reference to this question.[35]

Notwithstanding, host-governments usually express their local content policies through regulatory and/or contractual requirements such as:

- prescription of quotas requiring extractive companies to award a specified percentage of available job opportunities, contracts or share ownership to local companies or professionals;
- training programme requirements by which expatriates in the extractive sector are obliged to build the skills and expertise of the local workforce in the sector and eventually transfer technology;

[32] OECD (n 10).
[33] Nwapi (n 9).
[34] Olawuyi (n 4).
[35] Natural Resource Governance Institute (n 30).

- public education initiatives whereby host-governments set up training centres and programmes, and establish overseas scholarships in order to build a cadre of local expertise in the extractive sector;
- provision of incentives for entrepreneurship including, enhancing access to credit for SMEs in the extractive sector.[36]

Furthermore, LCRs can manifest in various forms, with variations observed among different countries. They may be imposed as a prerequisite for accessing financial support schemes like Feed-in Tariffs (FITs), direct financial transfers, or public tenders.[37] The specific ratio of LCRs can also vary, necessitating a case-by-case analysis to determine their impact. It is estimated that LCRs implemented in the renewable energy sector have a substantial influence on over USD 100 billion worth of trade annually.[38]

Local content plays a critical role in the extractive/energy sector due to multiple reasons. First, it helps mitigate the 'resource curse' phenomenon,[39] wherein resource-rich countries paradoxically face sluggish economic growth, corruption, and socio-economic inequalities.[40] This phenomenon has also become known as the 'paradox of plenty'.[41] By channelling the benefits of resource extraction back into the local economy, local content aims to translate natural resource wealth into sustainable socio-economic development.

Second, local content has the potential to stimulate local industries and entrepreneurship, promoting economic diversification and reducing reliance on the extractive sector. By fostering local capabilities and technology, it can catalyse innovation and competitiveness, creating an economic environment conducive to growth.[42] For example, since roughly 2008, developed nations and emerging economies have increasingly utilised LCRs to support their domestic renewable energy manufacturers. These LCRs are a key component of green industrial policies implemented by national and local governments to foster and stimulate the growth of domestic manufacturing capacity in the renewable energy sector, particularly in solar photovoltaic and wind turbines.[43]

[36] ibid.

[37] Jan-Christoph Kuntze and Tom Moerenhout, 'Local Content Requirements and the Renewable Energy Industry – A Good Match?' *International Centre for Trade and Sustainable Development* (2013) Geneva, Switzerland.

[38] ibid. See also Sherry Stephenson, 'Addressing Local Content Requirements: Current Challenges and Future Opportunities' (2013) 7 *Biores*.

[39] See Alexander Kemp, Nikolaos Vlassis and Eddy Wifa 'Mitigating the Resource Curse: Economic, Governance and Policy Considerations' in Eduardo G Pereira, Thomas L Muinzer and Patrick R Baker (eds), *Energy Law and the Sustainable Development Goals: Host Government Instruments for Sustainability in Oil and Gas Operations* (Routledge, 2024) doi.org/10.4324/9781003245551.

[40] Humphries et al (n 12).

[41] See Eddy Wifa, 'The Paradox of Plenty: An Analysis of The Environmental and Socio-Economic Symptoms of The Resource Curse in The Niger Delta Region of Nigeria' in Sylvester S Popnen (Editor), BM Wifa (Honoree) and Ibibia Lucky Worika (eds), *The Challenge of Justice: Contemporary Legal Essays in Honour of BM Wifa* (Princeton & Associates Publishing, 2017) 576–60.

[42] UNCTAD (n 7).

[43] See M Tang, 'Local Content Measures and the WTO Regime: Addressing Contentions and Trade-offs' in Olawuyi (n 3) 41.

Third, local content can play a significant role in enhancing social equity and reducing conflict.[44] By ensuring that the local communities benefit directly from resource extraction activities, it can help address social grievances, enhance community acceptance, and promote social stability.[45] Further, the implementation of LCRs may enhance the achievement of some target objectives by host-governments particularly those of developing countries including, employment, industrial, and technological development objectives.[46] Since the implementation of LCRs positively impacts on job creation and economic diversification, it enables inclusive growth on the long term especially in developing countries.[47] LCRs also help to foster the sustainable development agenda through investment in skills acquisition and transfer of technology to the local workforce. Such technical skills enhance the international competitiveness of local workforce in the global market place. Thus, LCRs empower local workforce to expand their horizons therefore lowering their exposure to the risk of unemployment. This contributes to the eradication of poverty and hunger, and the achievement of decent work and economic growth.[48]

C. Role of Local Content Requirements in Building Capacity and Expertise between Offshore Developments

LCRs play a crucial role in building capacity and expertise between offshore developments due to multiple reasons. First, it helps mitigate the 'resource curse' phenomenon which has adversely affected local capacity in the offshore sectors of resource-rich developing countries. Several studies have shown that resource-rich countries may not fully benefit from their mineral wealth and can paradoxically face sluggish economic growth, corruption, and socio-economic inequalities.[49] This phenomenon has become known as 'resource curse' or the 'paradox of plenty'. LCRs have proven useful in combating this phenomenon by requiring foreign companies to procure local goods and services and pursue local employment, training, and technology transfer.[50] Nigeria, for example, has recorded gradual improvement in local content following the enactment of the Nigerian Oil and Gas Industry Content Development Act, 2010 (Local Content Act). The primary

[44] See Olivier Maes (Luxembourg) and Laura Marie Olson (Permanent Observer for the International Federation of Red Cross and Red Crescent Societies) of the United Nations Security Council, 'With Climate Crisis Generating Growing Threats to Global Peace, Security Council Must Ramp Up Efforts, Lessen Risk of Conflicts, Speakers Stress in Open Debate'. 9345th Meeting (AM & PM) SC/15318 (13 June 2023).

[45] ibid.

[46] OECD (n 10).

[47] The World Bank, 'Use of Local Content in the Extractive Industries Enables Inclusive Growth' 20 November 2013, www.worldbank.org/en/news/feature/2013/11/20/local-content-in-extractive-industries-enables-inclusive-growth.

[48] AM George, 'Local Content in Extractive Industries: A Tool for Economic Diversification and Sustainable Development' (*World Bank Blogs*, 27 January 2016) blogs.worldbank.org/energy/local-content-extractive-industries-tool-economic-diversification-and-sustainable-development#:~:text=When%20extractives%20companies%20include%20local,productive%20linkages%20with%20other%20sectors.

[49] Humphries et al (n 12).

[50] Djeynaba Ba and Jeffrey B Jacquet, 'Local content policies in West Africa's mining sector: Assessment and roadmap to success' (2022) 9 *The Extractive Industries and Society* 1, 101030.

goal of the Act is to prescribe minimum requirements for the use of local services and materials, as well as for the promotion of technology and skill to the indigenous labour in the oil and gas sector. Research shows that Nigerians are now developing expertise in jobs that were exclusively preserved for oil expatriates, and most of the jobs executed abroad are now being done by Nigerians in Nigeria.[51] This has retained significant oil and gas expenditure within the country and has improved job opportunities. According to the Nigerian Content Development and Monitoring Board (NCDMB), Nigeria's local content level skyrocketed from 5 per cent in 2010 to 28 per cent in 2017, and 31 per cent in 2022.[52] The Board further projects a 70 per cent increase in local content levels by 2027.[53]

Second, local content has the potential to stimulate local industries and entrepreneurship, promote economic diversification and reduce reliance on the offshore sector. By fostering local capabilities and technology, it can catalyse innovation and competitiveness, creating an economic environment conducive to growth.[54] For example, following the 2008 financial crisis, many developing nations and developed economies like the United States, Canada, EU states, India, Brazil, and China sought to address the consequences of the crisis by utilising LCRs to support their domestic renewable energy manufacturers.[55]

In their study of wind manufacturing across the globe, Lewis and Wiser outline three potential benefits of developing a local manufacturing industry for wind and solar projects: local job creation; export of locally manufactured products to international markets; and cost savings. LCRs are therefore a key component of green industrial policies implemented by national and local governments to foster and stimulate the growth of domestic manufacturing capacity in the renewable energy sector, particularly in solar photovoltaic and wind turbines.[56] India, for example, has used LCRs to promote domestic manufacturing of wind power projects, thereby recording the fourth highest wind installed capacity worldwide.[57] There are over 12 different companies that manufacture more than 24 various models of wind turbines locally in India. These companies have achieved about 70 to 80 per cent of domestic production of wind energy, and have placed India as one of the top players in the global renewable energy market.[58]

Third, the implementation of LCRs may enhance the achievement of some target objectives by host-governments particularly those of developing countries including,

[51] Wisdom Enang, 'Nigerian Local Content Policy: Gains, Improvement Opportunities, And Imperatives For The Future' (14 January 2022) www.majorwavesenergyreport.com/nigerian-local-content-policy-gains-improvement-opportunities-and-imperatives-for-the-future/.

[52] Nigerian Content Development and Monitoring Board, 'Local Content Digest H2, 2022' (2022) ncdmb.gov.ng/lcdm/LocalContentDigestH222.pdf.

[53] ibid.

[54] UNCTAD (n 7).

[55] H Aswicahyono et al, 'Economic Impacts of Local Content Requirements in Indonesia' (*Centre for Strategic and International Studies*, 2023).

[56] See Tang (n 43).

[57] CR Kumar and Mohammed Majid, 'Renewable energy for sustainable development in India: current status, future prospects, challenges, employment, and investment opportunities' (2020) 10 *Energy, Sustainability and Society* 2.

[58] ibid.

employment, industrial, and technological development objectives.[59] Since the implementation of LCRs positively impacts on job creation and economic diversification, it enables inclusive growth in the long term especially in developing countries.[60] LCRs also help in achieving a sustainable energy transition in developing countries. According to Tucho,[61] this is possible if developing countries adopt an integrated policy approach involving the availability of sufficient renewable energy resources to meet local demands and efficient technological options to convert these resources to suitable types of energy.

Another benefit of LCRs is that they foster the sustainable development agenda through investment in skills acquisition and transfer of technology to the local workforce. Such technical skills enhance the international competitiveness of local workforce in the global marketplace. Thus, LCRs empower local workforce to expand their horizons therefore lowering their exposure to the risk of unemployment. This contributes to the eradication of poverty and hunger, and the achievement of decent work and economic growth.[62]

D. Challenges of Building Capacity and Expertise Through Local Content Requirements

Despite the potential of local content, resource-rich countries may sometimes find it difficult to build local capacity and expertise in their offshore industry. A major challenge for developing countries is the gap between technology and skills. The nature of several jobs and services in the offshore sector are extremely technical and requires certain level of capacity that may be unavailable in host-countries.[63] Unfortunately, most developing nations lack the technical know-how and skilled labour necessary to participate effectively in offshore developments, thereby limiting their ability to leverage local content.[64]

Institutional and regulatory challenges can also pose significant barriers. The lack of robust and transparent regulatory frameworks can hinder the effective implementation of local content policies which could lead to corruption and poor practices. Additionally, weak governance and corruption can compromise the benefits of local content, perpetuating inequality and economic disparity.[65] Similarly, local content

[59] OECD (n 10).

[60] The World Bank, 'Use of Local Content in the Extractive Industries Enables Inclusive Growth' (20 November 2013) www.worldbank.org/en/news/feature/2013/11/20/local-content-in-extractive-industries-enables-inclusive-growth.

[61] Gudina T Tucho, 'The Impacts of Policy on Energy Justice in Developing Countries' (19 October 2019) *Energy Justice Across Borders* 137–54; See also Iñigo del Guayo et al, *Energy Justice and Energy Law* (Oxford University Press, 2020); See also Rukonge S Muhongo, 'Local Content Policies in the Energy Transition Era in Africa: A Case Study of the East African Oil and Gas Industry' in Victoria R Nalule, (eds) *Energy Transitions and the Future of the African Energy Sector* (Palgrave Macmillan, 2021).

[62] Anita M George, 'Local Content in Extractive Industries: A Tool for Economic Diversification and Sustainable Development' (*World Bank Blogs*, 27 January 2016) blogs.worldbank.org/energy/local-content-extractive-industries-tool-economic-diversification-and-sustainable-development.

[63] Natural Resource Governance Institute (n 30).

[64] Timothy Meyer, 'How Local Discrimination Can Promote Global Public Goods' (1937) 95 *Boston University Law Review* 1937–2001.

[65] Olawuyi and Olaniyan (n 3).

provisions are oftentimes not strict enough thereby giving offshore companies the opportunity to deviate from LCRs whenever they are of the opinion that resources needed for their operations cannot be met locally, or the available local skills or materials are not up to standard. In other words, the laxity of local content provisions gives room for companies to utilise foreign resources under the guise that such resources cannot be met locally. This poses a grave challenge for the effective monitoring of the compliance level with local content requirements or targets.[66]

Financial constraints are another significant challenge. The high capital requirements in the offshore sector, coupled with the lack of local financial capabilities, often restrict the participation of local enterprises.[67] Furthermore, even though the global transition to cleaner energy sources is already costly for consumers and governments in the short-term, LCRs may make renewable energy more expensive than already envisaged. This is because LCRs encourage the substitution of imports with local goods even when such goods may be inferior and more expensive than foreign goods.[68]

Moreover, the global nature of the offshore industry, with its intricate web of international trade laws and practices, can also pose challenges. For instance, local content rules might conflict with international trade agreements, posing legal and operational challenges for countries aiming to increase their local content.[69] Indonesia and Nigeria are good examples of resource-rich developing countries whose LCR policies appear to be inconsistent with WTO regulations and Free Trade Agreements (FTAs). While the LCR policies of both countries are voluntary and applicable to both domestic and foreign companies indiscriminately, some or all of the policies attempt to encourage companies to use local capacity and to confer benefits on LCR-compliant companies through the use of tariff reductions or exemptions.[70] In addition, LCRs are regarded as a localisation barrier to international trade because it imposes local content obligations on foreign companies if such companies are to operate in a host country. According to Stone et al,[71] this occasions a reduction in global imports and exports, and in the long-term, undermines the international competitiveness of the host-economy.

With respect to LCRs in the renewable sector, there are studies to show that LCRs may not be effective in realising economic and environmental objectives. Rivers and Wigle[72] provide a theoretical assessment of the economic impact of connecting support

[66] Natural Resource Governance Institute (n 30).

[67] Olle Östensson, 'Local Content, Supply Chains, and Shared Infrastructure' in Tony Addison, and Alan Roe (eds), *Extractive Industries: The Management of Resources as a Driver of Sustainable Development* (Oxford Academic, 2018).

[68] Megan Hogan, 'Local Content Requirements threaten Renewable Energy Uptake' (*Peterson Institute for International Economics*, 6 December 2021) www.piie.com/blogs/trade-and-investment-policy-watch/local-content-requirements-threaten-renewable-energy-uptake.

[69] OECD, 'OECD Work on Trade and the Environment A Retrospective, 2008–2020' (June 2021) issuu.com/oecd.publishing/docs/oecd-trade-environment-retrospective-2020.

[70] Aswicahyono et al (n 55); Uchenna J Orji, 'Assessing the Conformity of Nigeria's Local Content Act with GATS Obligations' (2017) 23 *International Trade Law and Regulation* 12–24; See also Oscar Fernando and Lili Yan, 'Indonesia's Local Content Requirements: An Assessment on Consistency with Free Trade Agreement Commitments' (2022) *ERIA Discussion Paper Series No. 420*; Michelle Limenta and Lili Yan, 'Indonesia's Local Content Requirements: Assessment with WTO Rules' (2022) *ERIA Discussion Paper Series No. 414*.

[71] Susan Stone et al, *Emerging Policy Issues: Localisation Barriers to Trade* (OECD Publishing, 2015).

[72] Nicholas Rivers and Randy Wigle, *Domestic Content Requirements and Renewable Energy Legislation* (2011).

of renewably generated electricity to LCRs in wind power. According to these scholars, LCRs have the potential to reduce the production of renewable electricity and in short run, affect the overall employment opportunities in the renewable energy sector.[73] Addressing these challenges therefore requires a thoughtful, holistic, and multi-pronged approach, blending policy reforms, institutional strengthening, capacity building, and international cooperation.

3. Case Studies on the Implementation of LCRs in Building Capacity and Expertise between Offshore Development

A. Brazil

Brazil stands out globally for having a relatively high local content due to decades of nationalistic oil policies and regulations. Due to its geological features, oil and gas explorations are usually conducted through offshore drilling, which demands a high level of innovative capacity and technological development.[74] In an attempt to establish a competitive base for local suppliers, the Brazilian government has implemented various local content policies which aim to integrate more local actors in the country's oil and gas production chain.[75] The implementation of these policies involves applying contractual requirements that mandate operators of oil and gas blocks to procure local labour and local goods and services, as a condition of award of exploration and production rights. In Brazil, several resolutions have been adopted to govern LCRs in the offshore industry. The six major resolutions that touch on Brazilian content are:[76]

1. Resolution 19/2013 (R19/2013), which replaced Resolution 36/2007 and established criteria and procedures for the Local Content Certificate.
2. Resolution 20/2016 (R20/2016), which equated local content relative levels as required among different contractual items.
3. Resolution 27/2016 (R27/2016), which replaced Resolution 39/2007 and deals with the report editing format to inform on the local content levels used for oil and gas exploration.
4. Resolution 726/2018 (R726/2018), which establishes criteria and procedures related to the exemption of compliance to the local content requirements.
5. Resolution 799/2019 (R799/2019), which amends the Technical Regulation No. 3 of 2015 to increase the alternatives of Research, Development and Innovation expenses and activities. The resolution encourages partnerships between universities and companies to expand local content capacities and expertise.

[73] ibid.

[74] Edson Filho et al, 'The pre-salt layer and challenges to competitiveness in Brazil: Critical reflections on the local content policy in the oil and gas Sector' (2019) 6 *The Extractive Industries and Society* 4, 1168–73.

[75] ibid; See also Eduardo G Pereira et al, *Local Content and Sustainable Development in Brazil* (Cambridge University Press, 2021).

[76] ibid.

6. Resolution No. 836/2020 (R836/2020), which establishes deadlines for the submission of local content reports and defines the procedures to be followed by companies when carrying out oil and gas exploration and production.

These resolutions are implemented by the Brazilian National Agency for Petroleum, Natural Gas and Biofuels (ANP), which is the regulatory body for all offshore activities in Brazil, including renewable energy.[77] Over the years, the resolutions have been revised across multiple bidding rounds arranged by the ANP. For example, during the first competitive bidding rounds in 1999, operators were free to set their level of commitment in their bids, as there was no minimum level of investment or type of equipment and services which they should acquire. It was not until the fifth bidding round in 2003 that the ANP began to impose minimum mandatory percentages of LCR in operator's bids, ranging from 30 per cent in deep-sea waters to 70 per cent on land blocks.[78]

By increasing the minimum LCR for the oil and gas concession rounds in this year, the Brazilian government was able to successfully encourage operators to purchase goods and services from Brazilian suppliers. However, there were two major loopholes in the LCR that allowed for manipulation. First, it was difficult to determine whether these Brazilian suppliers actually manufactured the products in the country or merely packaged imported goods. Second, since the ANP adopted a general percentage of local content, companies could easily organise their supply chains to purchase basic products and services in the country while importing sophisticated equipment from foreign countries.[79]

Over the years, Brazil's LCRs have been modified to become even more complex, with the government increasing the minimum mandatory percentages for operators of oil and gas. For example, in 2005, Brazil designed a new LCR model that aims to promote job creation and improve the overall development of the country's domestic supply chain. The model established minimum and maximum requirements for various segments and systems in the oil and gas production chain, while also transferring the process of local content certification to private companies approved by the ANP.

While some scholars have argued that these stringent requirements are essential for building a competitive domestic industry, others contend that they can lead to additional costs in oil and gas projects and potential delays due to limited local capabilities.[80] In 2017, the Brazilian government relaxed the LCRs for the 14th bidding round in an effort to address some of the loopholes of the previous oil and gas regime, and improve competitive licensing rounds. The minimum local content levels have therefore been modified to around 50 per cent and less stringent fines are now in place for operators that are unable to meet these new criteria.

[77] The Government of Brazil, 'What is ANP' www.gov.br/anp/en/access-information/what-is-anp/what-is-anp#.

[78] Yuri Kasahara and Antonio Botelho, 'Ideas and Leadership in the Crafting of Alternative Industrial Policies' (2019) 51 *Comparative Politics* 3, 385–405.

[79] ibid.

[80] 'Brazil proposes relaxation of local content requirements' (*CMS*, 27 February 2017) cms-lawnow.com/en/ealerts/2017/02/brazil-proposes-relaxation-of-local-content-requirements.

B. Nigeria

The enactment of the Nigerian Oil and Gas Industry Content Development Act, 2010 ('Local Content Act') is a major milestone for the implementation of LCRs in the Nigerian oil and gas industry. The objective of the Act is to prescribe minimum requirements for the utilisation of local services and materials, as well as for the promotion of technology, expertise and skill to the indigenous workforce in the oil and gas sector. To achieve this objective, section 2 of the Act provides as follows:

> All regulatory authorities, operators, contractors, subcontractors, alliance partners and other entities involved in any project, operation, activity or transaction in the Nigerian oil and gas industry shall consider Nigerian content as an important element of their overall project development and management philosophy for project execution.

In recent times, the Local Content Act is considered one of the most successful economic policies of the Nigerian government, as it considers indigenous operators first in any award of oil blocks, oil field licences, and projects in the oil and gas sector.[81] The Act further grants Nigerian service companies the exclusive right to bid on oil and gas contracts and services, where they demonstrate ownership of local equipment and availability of personnel and capacity to execute such works on land and swampy areas.[82] In addition, the Act stipulates penalties to be awarded against an operator which fails to comply with LCRs in the oil and gas industry. Such operator will be liable on conviction to a fine of 5 per cent of the value of that project or to a cancellation of such project. The Local Content Act also provides a fiscal framework and tax incentives to both foreign and indigenous companies which establish facilities for the local production of goods and services which are being imported into Nigeria.[83] By enacting this provision, the Nigerian government can encourage investment and the development of local capacity in the country.

The Nigerian Content Development and Monitoring Board (NCDMB) is saddled with the responsibility of enforcing the provisions of the Local Content Act, with a view to ensuring a measurable and continuous growth of Nigerian content in all oil and gas projects and operations.[84] Under Section 8 of the Act, the Board is required to review and assess the local content plans of operators, and ensure they comply with the provisions of the Act. To qualify for a Certificate of Authorization, operators must demonstrate in their local content plans that they have acquired goods and services produced in Nigeria, and that Nigerians are given priority for training and employment in their oil and gas projects.[85] In the event where local expertise is lacking for the execution of a project or service, the Act makes provisions for the development of manpower. Section 28(1) of the Nigerian Local Content Act provides thus:

[81] The Nigerian Oil and Gas Industry Content Development Act, 2010 ('Local Content Act'), s 3(1); See Olusola J Jegede, 'Overview of Nigerian Local Content Law In Oil And Gas Industry' (23 December 2020) www.mondaq.com/nigeria/oil-gas--electricity/1019096/overview-of-nigerian-local-content-law-in-oil-and-gas-industry.

[82] Nigerian Local Content Act, s 3(2).

[83] ibid s 48.

[84] ibid s 5.

[85] ibid s 10.

> Subject to section 10(1)(b) of this Act, Nigerians shall be given the first consideration for employment and training in any project executed by any operator or project promoter in the Nigerian oil and gas industry.

From the foregoing, it is clear that the operator must give priority to Nigerians whenever there is need for employment or training of personnel in the oil and gas industry. Similarly, section 30 of the Act provides that where Nigerians are not employed because of their lack of training, the operator shall make every reasonable effort within a reasonable time to supply such training locally and such effort must be contained in the operator's Employment and Training Plan. Obeagu[86] observed that the training provisions of the Act are commendable, as they envisage intellectual development of Nigerians through the provision of scholarship programmes and sponsorship to deserving citizens in all academic institutions in the country.

Another cardinal provision of the Act is section 45, which encourages indigenous companies to enter into a joint venture agreement with a foreign company, subject to the approval of the NCDMB. This partnership with the foreign company provides an opportunity for Nigerians to understudy the expatriates to ensure knowledge and skill transfer.[87] The Shell Scholarship programme was birth out of this partnership, among others, the programme offers the Niger Delta Postgraduate Scholarship for applicants from oil-rich Bayelsa, Delta, Imo and Rivers states in Nigeria. The objective of the scholarship programme is to provide postgraduate study opportunity in courses that are relevant to the oil and gas industry for qualifying students from these Niger Delta states.[88]

It should be noted that despite the prospects of the Local Content Act in stimulating the growth of indigenous capacity of the oil and gas sector, it has some shortcomings. Oguagha[89] conducted a critical assessment of the effectiveness of local content policy implementation in the Nigerian oil and gas sector. The study revealed that Nigeria struggles with effective implementation of the Local Content Act due to mistrust, shortage of resources and manpower, as well as the poor coordination between the regulatory agencies in the industry.[90] In the same vein, Omenikolo and Amadi[91] highlight corruption, lack of access to capital, inadequate infrastructural base, weak institutions, political instability, and bad investment climate as some of the major problems affecting the implementation of the Local Content Act in the oil and gas industry. In addition,

[86] Christian C Obeagu, 'The Local Content Act, 2010 and Manpower Development Policy in Nigeria: How Far so Far?' (2020) *Scholars International Journal of Law, Crime and Justice* 354–61.

[87] See Denton-ACAS, 'Practical aspects of the implementation of the Nigerian Oil and Gas Industry Content Development Act 2010' (20 April 2022) www.dentonsacaslaw.com/en/insights/articles/2022/april/20/implementation-of-the-nigerian-oil-and-gas-industry-content-development-act-2010.

[88] Shell Plc, 'Shell Nigeria Students Scholarship Schemes', www.shell.com.ng/sustainability/communities/education-programmes/scholarships.html.

[89] VI Oguagha, 'The Nigerian Local Content Policy and its Impact on Sustainable Economic Value Creation' in Victoria Okoro and Oko Ndukwe, 'Local Content Act Implementation and its impact on Nigeria Economy: An Appraisal' (2022) 13(2) *Journal of Policy and Development Studies* 99–105.

[90] ibid; also Peter Nwaguru and W Sylva, 'Local Content Strategy Implementation in Nigeria: Challenges and Prospects' (2022) 2(4) *African Journal of Business and Economic Development* 54–42.

[91] JA Omenikolo and RO Amadi, 'Challenges facing Nigeria local content in the oil and gas industry' (2010) *International Journal of Renewable Energy* 15–20; See also Uwern Udok et al, 'Local Content Development in the Oil and Gas Industry in Nigeria: Problems and Prospects' (2020) 7 *European Journal of Training and Development Studies* 1, 64–83.

there is the argument that the provisions of the Act appear to be inconsistent with Nigeria's obligations under the WTO agreement. According to Orji,[92] the Local Content Act favours the use of local products and materials for oil and gas projects and this violates the WTO's national treatment principle, which prohibits WTO members from discriminating against imported products.

C. The North Sea

The North Sea has been a focal point for energy production, with decades of intensive oil and gas exploration shaping the economic and industrial landscape of the region. Notably, the UK and Norway have exemplified how strategic policy-making and regulation can stimulate local content, encourage capacity building, and fuel economic growth. Both nations have actively pursued autonomy in shaping the future of their petroleum resources and associated industries, establishing a shared 'North Sea' regulatory system. This model, originating from Norway's early twentieth-century hydro resources regulation, was subsequently, though to a lesser extent, adopted by the UK for petroleum resource exploitation in the North Sea.[93]

D. The United Kingdom

i. Oil and Gas Sector

In the United Kingdom, local content in the offshore oil and gas sector has been strategically increased through several government initiatives and regulations. The Oil and Gas Authority (OGA), established in 2015,[94] has played a pivotal role in this regard, and was established as an independent regulator, taking the form of a government company, charged with the asset stewardship and regulation of domestic oil and gas recovery. The Secretary of State for Energy and Climate Change's previous regulatory powers on oil and gas were transferred to the OGA at that time.[95] The OGA's Stewardship Expectation 11, for instance, explicitly outlines that operators should maximise the socio-economic impact of their projects by enhancing local capabilities, promoting technology transfer, and boosting local employment.[96] Additionally, the OGA has an expectation that the 'Upstream Oil and Gas Industry ('Industry') will reduce, as far as reasonable in the circumstances, greenhouse gas emissions from all aspects of their upstream operations.

[92] Uchenna J Orji, 'The Nigerian Oil And Gas Local Content Regime And Its (Non-) Compliance With the TRIMS Agreement' (2018) 9 *Journal of Sustainable Development Law and Policy* 2, 152–86.

[93] See also Tina Hunter, 'Legal Regulatory Framework for the Sustainable Extraction of Australian Offshore Petroleum Resources: A Critical Functional Analysis' (2010); Brent F Nelsen, *The State Offshore: Petroleum Politics, and State Intervention on the British and Norwegian Continental Shelves* (Praeger, 1991) 8.

[94] See Government of the United Kingdom, 'The Energy Bill 2015/2016', www.gov.uk/government/publications/the-energy-bill-201516.

[95] ibid.

[96] North Sea Transition Authority (NSTA), 'Net Zero Stewardship Expectation 11' (March 2021) www.nstauthority.co.uk/media/7184/se11_net-zero.pdf.

This includes: the development of new hydrocarbon projects; existing producing assets; the abandonment and decommissioning of fields; and the progression of potential energy integration/net zero solutions to assist the Secretary of State in meeting the Net Zero Target'.[97] Additionally, the OGA expects that during Lifecycle Phases, specifically Exploration and Appraisal Phases, that the Industry 'fully consider acquiring information which could enable future energy projects such as CCS, hydrogen, windfarms'.[98] The OGA's Supply Chain Action Plans (SCAP) have also provided a platform for operators to set out how they will engage with the supply chain and support local businesses in the procurement process.[99]

ii. *Offshore Wind Sector*

The UK has emerged a success in offshore wind, with long-term government support driving innovation, investment, and decarbonisation. Currently, the UK boasts the world's largest installed offshore wind capacity, with 9.8 gigawatts (GW), set to increase to 19.5 GW by the mid-2020s. The Offshore Wind Sector Deal, established in 2019, aims to enhance the productivity and competitiveness of UK companies, ensuring a leading role in the global market's future growth.[100] The Sector Deal is a prime example of government-led initiatives to boost local content in the renewable sphere.[101] Significant progress has been made in fulfilling the commitments outlined in the Sector Deal, with collaborations between the sector and government resulting in major developments, such as the Offshore Wind Growth Partnership (OWGP), the development of regional clusters, and initiatives to improve diversity and skills within the industry.[102] The deal aims to increase the proportion of UK content in homegrown offshore wind projects to 60 per cent by 2030, up from an estimated 48 per cent in 2018, thereby creating thousands of jobs and fostering innovation and skills development in the local economy.[103]

Regarding local content specifically, the recommendation by the Welsh Affairs Committee stated that the UK Government should introduce enforceable local content requirements in future contracts for difference (CfDs) auctions for floating offshore wind, aligned with The Crown Estate's leasing rounds. Additionally, it should reassess the parameters for Allocation Round 5 (AR5) to ensure the strike price considers the rising costs for developers due to global economic pressures.[104] In response, the Government stated that the Government and The Crown Estate are collaborating on future supply

[97] ibid 1.
[98] ibid 2.
[99] ibid 3.
[100] Government of the United Kingdom, 'Offshore wind energy revolution to provide a third of all UK electricity by 2030' (7 March 2019), www.gov.uk/government/news/offshore-wind-energy-revolution-to-provide-a-third-of-all-uk-electricity-by-2030.
[101] Government of the United Kingdom, 'Policy paper: Offshore wind Sector Deal – one year on' (updated 4 March 2020), www.gov.uk/government/publications/offshore-wind-sector-deal/offshore-wind-sector-deal-one-year-on.
[102] Offshore Wind Growth Partnership (OWGP), 'Supporting high growth companies in the UK offshore wind supply chain' owgp.org.uk.
[103] Government of the United Kingdom (n 100).
[104] ibid.

chain approaches, including the potential introduction of non-price factors in CfD auctions. The government aims to develop a robust and sustainable supply chain for Floating Offshore Wind while respecting WTO trade rules that prohibit local content requirements.[105] CfD auction designs consider various factors to balance renewable deployment and value-for-money outcomes. One of such actions is the Administrative Strike Prices (ASPs), which are based on project costs and future revenues, encouraging participation and aligning with government policies. This CfD scheme provides inflation protection through indexing strike prices to the Consumer Price Index (CPI), offering broad protection to generators throughout the contract duration.

In the United Kingdom, on 3 November 2014, the Offshore Wind Industry Council (OWIC) approved the introduction of a UK Content reporting framework. From 1 January 2015, the owners of all UK offshore Wind Farms achieving final investment decision (FID)[106] will report their UK Content to RenewableUK.[107] UK Content is the percentage of the total undiscounted expenditure by the Wind Farm Asset Owner on a Wind Farm that is ultimately spent through Contracts awarded to companies operating in the UK. It excludes the value of Contracts to UK companies that is spent on Subcontracts to companies not operating in the UK. It includes the value of Contracts to non-UK companies that is spent on Subcontracts to companies operating in the UK. This reporting framework is a mechanism to monitor activities of owners of UK offshore Wind Farms in implementing LCR.

It should be noted that despite the potential of the UK's offshore wind projects, the LCRs for these projects have been criticised for being discriminatory. In 2022, the European Union (EU) filed a complaint against the UK at the WTO on the basis that supply chain plans (SCPs) required from companies who bid for CfDs constitute discriminatory trade practices and are in breach of the WTO agreement. The SCPs set out how bidders will ensure local content for all offshore wind projects over 300MW, which would be approved by the UK Department for Business Energy and Industrial Strategy (BEIS). The EU contends that the criteria used by the UK government in awarding subsidies for these projects favour UK content and "violates the WTO's core tenet that imports must be able to compete on an equal footing with domestic products."[108] According to the organisation, this discriminatory practice undermines its €36 billion wind energy sector and places EU suppliers at a disadvantage.

[105] Improperly designed and implemented LCRs can lead to substantial overlap and lack of coordination in the implementation of various international treaties concerning trade, investment, energy, human rights, the environment, and sustainable development. For instance, domestic LCRs can introduce significant inconsistencies and pose risks to the adherence of international trade and investment laws. See: D Olawuyi, 'Local Content and the Sustainable Development Nexus' in Olawuyi (n 3) 9.

[106] FID is the point of a project life cycle at which all consents, agreements and contracts that are required to commence project construction have been signed (or are at or near execution form).

[107] Allan Roberta and Bruce Valpy, 'Methodology for measuring the UK content of UK offshore wind farms' (BVG Associates, 2015) bvgassociates.com/wp-content/uploads/2016/07/BVGA-uk_content_methodology-1505.pdf.

[108] European Commission, 'EU challenges discriminatory practices of UK's green energy subsidy scheme at WTO' (28 March 2022) policy.trade.ec.europa.eu/news/eu-challenges-discriminatory-practices-uks-green-energy-subsidy-scheme-wto-2022-03-28_en.

E. Norway

i. Introduction

Norway is an offshore energy nation. Its success in the oil and gas industry is beyond any doubt, and this industry constitutes, by far, its largest export, consistently representing over 50 per cent of the total value of exports over the last two decades, and reaching 73 per cent in 2022.[109] Even though current Norwegian legislation for the petroleum industry does not include specific LCRs, previous policies, as we discuss below, played a crucial role in the development of a highly competitive Norwegian petroleum sector. While Norway's success is firmly anchored also on other factors, such as a well-developed infrastructure and a transparent, stable governance framework in place,[110] offshore operations expertise,[111] and a solid regulatory system,[112] combined with a skilled workforce,[113] Norwegian experiences in promoting local participation in offshore energy can and have served as inspiration for other countries.[114] LCRs and policies might be adjusted to new regulatory and technological realities through cross-sectoral linkage to achieve economic benefits from petroleum exploitation and transform other sectors of the economy, such as offshore renewable energies.[115]

This is happening in Norway as we write this chapter. This Scandinavian country has been seeking inspiration from and leveraging its expertise from the offshore oil and gas sector to offshore wind. 2023 marks its first-ever offshore wind licensing rounds for two areas, Sørlige Nordsjø II and Utsira Nord, and its commitment to develop 30 GW of installed offshore wind capacity by 2040.[116] Politicians, including the current Støre-led coalition government (2021 to the present), have named it the country's next industrial adventure (the 'havvindeventyret').[117] The ambitions connected to the development of offshore wind projects in Norway prompted discussions related to the topic of local content development and how this new adventure may strengthen Norway's energy security, industrial capability, offshore expertise diversification, and help reach climate targets. In other words, transforming the expected wind wealth, as done with oil and gas,[118] into a broader-based industrial wealth linked to the energy transition and the digital economy.

[109] Norwegian Petroleum, *Exports of Oil and Gas*, www.norskpetroleum.no/en/production-and-exports/exports-of-oil-and-gas/.

[110] Farouk Al-Kasim, *Managing Petroleum Resources: The 'Norwegian Model' in a Broad Perspective* (Alden Press, 2006) 58.

[111] Catherine Banet, 'Local Content and Sustainable Development in Norway' in Olawuyi (n 3) 246.

[112] Heum (n 21).

[113] Banet (n 111) 246.

[114] Jonathan Moses and Bjorn Letnes, *Managing Resource Abundance and Wealth: The Norwegian Experience* (Oxford University Press, 2017) 14.

[115] Tina Hunter, 'Law and Policy Frameworks for Local Content in the Development of Petroleum Resources: Norwegian and Australian Perspectives on Cross-Sectoral Linkages and Economic Diversification' (2014) 27 *Mineral Economics* 115–26 at 116–17.

[116] Norwegian Government, *Ambitious offshore wind initiative* (Press release, 11 May 2022), www.regjeringen.no/en/aktuelt/ambitious-offshore-wind-power-initiative/id2912297/.

[117] E24, 'Venter på havvindeventyret' (16 March 2024) e24.no/energi-og-klima/i/APeevE/venter-paa-havvindeventyret.

[118] Heum (n 21) 7.

In the following sections, we discuss LCRs and local development policies in the offshore petroleum and wind sector in Norway.

ii. Local Content Rules in the Oil and Gas Sector

Discussions related to local content development and local content rules are not new in Norway. This Scandinavian country has had an important history linked to local content rules and requirements dating back to the 1970s.[119] Oil and gas exploration started in the mid-1960s, and the first field came into operation in 1971. Before this time, no offshore energy expertise existed in the country but, crucially, Norway had an important industrial capacity, including offshore activities, such as shipping and fisheries.[120]

During the initial years of Norway's oil and gas endeavours, its energy policy advocated for the consistent development of domestic entities, which included the establishment of national players such as a state-owned oil and gas company, effectively two: Statoil – now known as Equinor (100 per cent state-owned and founded in 1972) and Norsk Hydro (51 per cent state-owned), as well as indirect support for Saga, a privately-owned Norwegian entity. The Norwegian state perceived participation solely by itself or by small local firms as excessively risky and costly.[121] Therefore, Norway adopted an open stance, welcoming and encouraging international investment and the operation of wells, which included mandated collaboration with local oil and gas companies, in contrast to regimes like the North American hydrocarbon model.

However, as early as the 1970s, various measures were implemented to promote local development in the oil and gas sector. These measures were developed concurrently with the '10 Oil Commandments' of 1971.[122] While soft law, they laid the groundwork for Norwegian offshore oil and gas policy and emphasised the importance of fostering local expertise and ensuring benefits for Norwegian society as a whole. The vision for local development and local content, even then, aimed to prepare Norwegian firms to compete internationally and establish a competitive value chain. Several local content measures were firmly enforced until the mid-1980s,[123] only to be set aside in 1994, at least in theory, with Norway's accession to the European Economic Area Agreement (the 'EEA') and the World Trade Organization. As of 2024, no legal requirements for local content exist in the oil and gas sector, and Norwegian oil and gas companies compete internationally as highly specialised and competitive entities. In the following, we will review the key provisions.

Requirements to include local suppliers were triggered early. Already in 1972 with the Second Licensing Round preferences for Norwegian goods and services were required as part of the contingencies for the licence. The 1972 Royal Decree on

[119] Ministry of Petroleum and Energy, 'Report No. 38 to the Storting (2001–2001) – Oil and Gas Activities: Unofficial translation from Norwegian' (2002) 11. See also Taran Thune, Ole A Engen, and Olav Wicken (eds), *Petroleum Industry Transformations: Lessons from Norway and Beyond* (Routledge, 2018).

[120] Heum (n 21).

[121] Jonathon W Moses, 'Norwegian Local Content Policy' in Eduardo G Pereira, Rochelle Spencer and Jonathon W Moses (eds), *Sovereign Wealth Funds, Local Content Policies and CSR: Developments in the Extractives Sector* (Springer, 2021) 428; *St. meld. nr. 11* (1968–9) 7.

[122] Innst. S. nr 294 (1970–71).

[123] Moses (n 121) 423.

Exploration and Exploitation of Undersea Petroleum Deposits set a relatively model local content provision in its §54 which read:

> Licenses shall use Norwegian goods and services in petroleum operations to the extent that these are competitive in terms of quality, service, delivery time and price.[124]

Under this licensing framework, national authorities were empowered to establish joint ventures, effectively compelling different entities to collaborate and determining the joint venture composition, a practice distinct from other jurisdictions globally.[125] This allowed local firms to quickly learn from much more experienced international counterparts.[126] Surveillance over this local content requirement was conducted by the Goods and Services Office at the Ministry of Industry. This provision underwent reform in 1985 with the Petroleum Act. Also, in its §54, applications for a production licence were required to outline how they would collaborate with Norwegian suppliers to provide 'real opportunities' for supplying goods and services.[127] Similar obligations to describe the use of local suppliers were also present in the Plan for Development and Operation of a Petroleum Deposit.[128]

A new local content practice, mandating that Statoil be automatically allocated 50 per cent participation shares in all new licences, was established in 1974, with Statoil sometimes acting as the field operator. This practice ceased in 1996 with the adoption of the Petroleum Act, prompted by the 1994 Directive on Hydrocarbons Licensing opening up the hydrocarbon market in Norway for EEA/EU companies.[129] Clauses allowing Statoil to cover a lesser amount of costs relative to the proportion of its shares within the joint venture, and sliding scale provisions allowing Equinor's participation to increase from 50 per cent to more in the event of significant oil discoveries, were also included.[130]

Research and development, as well as collaboration with national research and education entities, were promoted as forms of local development policies.[131] In the 1978 licensing rounds, a requirement was introduced that 50 per cent of research and development efforts related to field development had to be conducted in Norway. This requirement led to the establishment of technology agreements between Norwegian research and development institutions and international oil and gas firms. Additionally, requirements to train local personnel and even Norwegian staff were common practice as part of the licensing requirements during the mid-1970s and early 1980s.

[124] §54 of a 1972 Royal Decree on Exploration and Exploitation of Undersea Petroleum Deposits, 8 December 1972 (kongelig resolusjon av 8. desember 1972 om undersøkelse etter og utnyttelse av undersjøiske petroleumsforekomster).

[125] Tina Soliman Hunter and Ignacio Herrera Anchustegui, 'Ernst, are you kidding me? Reflections about Norwegian energy law by non-Norwegian energy lawyers' in Berte-Elen Konow, Hans Frederik Marthinussen and Knut Einar Skodvin (eds), *Fakultetsbyggjar, vestlending og verdsborgar* (Cappelen Damm Akademisk, 2023).

[126] Moses (n 121), 431; Banet (n 111).

[127] §54. Bruk av varer og tjenester of the Lov om petroleumsvirksomhet (The 1985 Petroleum Act), 1 July 1985.

[128] Banet (n 112) 254.

[129] Directive 94/22/EC of the European Parliament and of the Council of 30 May 1994 on the conditions for granting and using authorizations for the prospection, exploration and production of hydrocarbons (OJ [1994] L 164/3).

[130] Moses and Letnes (n 114); Moses (n 121) 432.

[131] Heum (n 21) 9-10.

Requirements related to companies operating oil and gas fields having a subsidiary in Norway have existed since 1965. According to the 1996 Petroleum Act, still in place, for survey licences, firms may be domiciled in any EEA Member State.[132] However, production licences may be granted only to a 'body corporate established in conformity with Norwegian legislation and registered in the Norwegian Register of Business Enterprises'.[133] Physical persons may be awarded production licences, but they need to be domiciled in the EEA.

Finally, another practice aimed at local development was the requirement to process oil and gas in Norway. Since 1965, legislation has included mandates stipulating that petroleum products (gas or oil) must be landed in Norway to promote the processing and refinement of oil in the country.[134] The current 1996 Petroleum Act includes a vague (and toned-down) version of this provision, stating in section 4-11 that the 'King decides where and in which way landing of petroleum shall take place'.

Explicit local content requirements, however, came to a halt in the early 1990s. In 1994, Norway joined the European Free Trade Association (EFTA) and the World Trade Organization. Membership allowed Norway further access to the EU single market but required it to update its petroleum law and local content requirements, and repeal some of its non-compliant local content provisions.[135] Additionally, Norway incorporated the European Union Directive on Hydrocarbons Licensing in 1994, which further restricted discretion around the granting of licences, including reserving a share of the licence for state-owned operators like Equinor, which now had to apply under the same conditions as other players.[136] The outcome of these changes, limiting the possibility to protect its local industry through local content provisions, was the 1996 Petroleum Act, which remains in force. However, by and large, the current regulatory framework still allows the state to develop an energy policy where petroleum resource management can contribute to ensuring welfare, employment, an improved environment, and the strengthening of Norwegian trade and industry and industrial development, while also considering regional and local policy considerations and other activities.[137] Additionally, Norway is bound by several international bilateral agreements that restrict its ability to discriminate in favour of its local industry.

These changes, however, must be viewed in light of the predominantly discretion-based approach to licensing in Norway. Authorities assess bids based on quality factors rather than competitive (cash) bidding, as it is common in other offshore hydrocarbon jurisdictions.[138] Through discretion and the utilisation of expertise or quality, the Ministry of Energy can influence decision outcomes in a manner that may benefit local

[132] Petroleum Act 1996, s 2-1.

[133] Petroleum Act 1996, s 3-3. Oddly enough, '(…) Production licence may also be granted to a physical person domiciled in a state of the European Economic Area (EEA)', as per the same provision.

[134] Petroleum Act 1985, s 26.

[135] Mission of Norway to the European Union, 'The EEA Agreement' (26 April 2022) www.norway.no/en/missions/eu/areas-of-cooperation/the-eea-agreement/.

[136] Directive 94/22/EC of the European Parliament and of the Council of 30 May 1994 on the conditions for granting and using authorizations for the prospection, exploration and production of hydrocarbons (OJ [1994] L 164/3). See on this: Soliman Hunter and Herrera Anchustegui (n 125).

[137] Soliman Hunter and Herrera Anchustegui (n 125).

[138] ibid; Government of the United States, '2023 Investment Climate Statements: Norway' www.state.gov/reports/2023-investment-climate-statements/norway/.

firms, and this influence may be difficult to prove or detect, raising concerns about transparency and fairness in licence allocation.

Lastly, amid these changes, though not strictly local content rules or local development policies, the Norwegian state directly participates in petroleum activities on the Norwegian Continental Shelf through the State Direct Financial Interest (SDFI). To oversee the SDFI, a fully state-owned company – Petoro – was established to serve as a licensee on behalf of the Norwegian State with the objective of maximising government revenue from its share in production licences and facilities.[139] Petoro may occasionally be allocated a portion of the joint venture's share, but Petoro never operates the field.

iii. Local Content Policies in the Offshore Wind Sector

A new adventure in offshore wind has set sail in Norway. Despite its excellent wind resources, it was not until the early 2020s that offshore wind ambitions began to take off in the country.[140] As of writing this chapter, the first licensing round for offshore wind in Norway is underway, with areas in Sørlige Norsdjø II and Utsira Nord being tendered for interested parties to develop projects. However, Norway currently has only one offshore wind park in operation: Hywind Tampen, the world's first medium-sized offshore wind floating facility, which is used to partly electrify two oil and gas fields. Hywind Tampen exemplifies the interaction between these two offshore energy sectors and how Norwegian policymakers and companies aim to leverage competencies and advantages from oil and gas to the wind industry.[141]

The offshore wind venture in Norway begins under significantly different premises than its oil and gas counterpart. Norway is bound by much stricter legislation at both regional and global levels limiting rules or industrial policies that actively promote local content and discriminate against non-Norwegian parties, such as the fundamental freedoms in the EEA Agreement and the secondary legislation on energy law adopted through EEA Directives and Regulations incorporated in the EEA pillar. Furthermore, it would be challenging to argue that Norway could implement local content rules as a developing country or that offshore wind requires further state involvement beyond the public incentives it already receives in Norway.

There are no explicit local content rules in the Norwegian offshore wind framework, namely the 2010 Offshore Energy Act and its 2020 Regulation.[142] Similar to petroleum production licences, the Offshore Energy Act mandates that licensees must be legal entities established according to Norwegian law and registered in the Norwegian Registry

[139] Soliman Hunter and Herrera Anchustegui (n 125); See also Diderik Lund, 'State participation and taxation in Norwegian petroleum: Lessons for others?' (2014) 3 *European Strategy Reviews* 49–54.

[140] Eirik Finserås and Sigrid Schütz, 'Offshore wind licensing in Norway' in Ignacio Herrera Anchustegui and Tina Soliman Hunter (eds), *Offshore Wind Licensing* (Edward Elgar Publishing, 2024).

[141] Ignacio Herrera Anchustegui and Rudiger Tscherning, 'Offshore oil and gas infrastructure electrification and offshore wind: a legal exploration' (2024) 17 *The Journal of World Energy Law & Business* 35; Ignacio Herrera Anchustegui and Aleksander Glapiak, 'Wind of change: A Scandinavian perspective on energy transition and the "greenification" of the oil and gas sector' in *Regional Approaches to the Energy Transition: A Multidisciplinary Perspective* (Springer, 2023); Siv Elén Årskog Vedvik, Hurtigløp for elektrifisering av sokkelen med havvind? – Moglegheiter og hindringar i dagens regelverk, Karnov forlag (2024-1).

[142] Offshore Energy Act, LOV-2010-06-04-21; Regulations to the Offshore Energy Act, FOR-2020-06-12-1192.

of Enterprises.[143] However, the provision includes the caveat that this will be the case 'unless otherwise stipulated by international agreements', which would refer to EEA and WTO law, among other trade agreements.

However, local content provisions as part of the licensing criteria to award a specific project area, either as part of bid assessment or to prequalify bidders, have been included for Utsira Nord and, to some extent, through a series of changes, in the case of Sørlige Nordsjø II. This mirrors the practices in petroleum licensing used in the 1970s and 1980s discussed above.

For Utsira Nord, the competition is based on a qualitative criterion in which applicants will be compared regarding their 'technical expertise and financial strength, and comply with relevant health, safety and environmental requirements'.[144] In Annex 4 of the licensing round, a criterion included to determine the bid winner is the extent to which the project generates 'positive local and regional ripple effects' by the development. As we discuss below, region is not defined and can be interpreted in different ways. These 'positive local benefits' would amount to 10 per cent of the award criteria.[145] Tellingly, Annex 4 emphasises the aim of such a requirement.

> The government's goal is for offshore wind to contribute to industrial development (…).
>
> Offshore wind supply chains are under pressure. In order to contribute to reach of the political ambitions for offshore wind, both in Norway and in Europe, it will be necessary to build up new capacity in the supplier industry (…). The **criteria for Positive local benefits will give an advantage to applicants who make a positive contribution to competence development and development in the supply chains**. It is a goal of the authorities that offshore wind projects should create the greatest possible value for society.
>
> The licence decision will stipulate that the licence holder for the offshore wind park must carry out an analysis of the **regional and local benefits of the offshore wind project**, and submit a final report no later than two years after the installation has been put into operation (…).[146]

In assessing the provision, the emphasis on regional effects (rather than solely local effects) indicates that Norwegian authorities have been cautious in wording these requirements. A local-only requirement would have been overly restrictive. Even the use of the word 'regional' might be perceived as limiting since a region could still be relatively narrow and might not include areas of the EEA far from the North Sea, potentially leading to forms of discrimination based on nationality and affecting freedoms such as that of establishment or giving preference to local/regional firms over European firms. Similarly, Finserås and Schütz remark that such wording 'could be implicitly read as protectionist, considering applicants are more likely to satisfy the criteria of facilitating local and regional industrial growth where they rely on local content as opposed to imported goods and services'.[147] We revisit this point below.

[143] §3-5 of the Offshore Energy Act, LOV-2010-06-04-21.

[144] Ministry of Energy, Announcement of competition for project areas in Utsira Nord for offshore renewable energy production (27 October 2023), para 3.III.

[145] Ministry of Energy, Appendix 4 Description of qualitative criteria for Utsira Nord (27 October 2023) 2 and 3.

[146] Ministry of Energy, Appendix 4 Description of qualitative criteria for Utsira Nord (27 October 2023) 18 and 19 (emphasis added).

[147] Finserås and Schütz (n 140) para 8.042.

The licensing round documents for the Sørlige Nordsjø II area include elements of local and regional content. However, regulatory developments have significantly toned down the importance and prominence of these factors. Initially, when the project was announced in March 2023, 'positive local' effects would amount to 20 per cent of the prequalification criteria, including the requirement to demonstrate how bidders and their projects could contribute to the promotion of expertise and the creation of a value chain.[148]

After hearings before the Norwegian Parliament, public participation, and dialogue rounds with various entities and regional authorities, including the EFTA Surveillance Authority, the pre-qualification criteria were adopted with modifications from its original version. In its 17 October 2023 version, which was used for evaluating bids eventually won by Ventyr AS II on 20 March 2024,[149] there is no mention of the 20 per cent criteria among the evaluation elements for the pre-qualification round in Annex 4.[150] However, positive local and regional effects were mentioned in Annex 11 entitled 'Minimum Requirements for Sustainability and Positive Ripple Effects'.[151] Carefully worded, this document stresses that '[t]he government wishes to ensure that there will be positive ripple effects (…) The requirements for positive ripple effects are intended to contribute to a development of the industry by building experience and developing expertise in the supply chains during the construction of the first phase of Sørlige Nordsjø II'.[152] The words local or regional do not appear in the document in either the Norwegian nor English versions.

It is unclear why there are different stances concerning local content-like requirements for Utsira Nord and Sørlige Nordsjø II. From our perspective, mentioning local or regional effects as part of an assessment or pre-qualification criteria is likely to raise risks of incompatibility with EEA and/or WTO law as it might be contrary to the freedom of movement and the principles of non-discrimination. This has been confirmed through the actions of the Norwegian State itself regarding Sørlige Nordsjø II. On 17 October 2023, when the criteria were modified, the Norwegian Government acknowledged that after state aid-related consultations with the EFTA Surveillance Authority, changes to the pre-qualification conditions had to be made (ie, the removal of the local and regional effects requirement). These changes were made '[t]o **clarify that the ripple effects are not limited to Norway**, the headline for the criterion "positive

[148] The original Annex 4 released in March 2023 is no longer available online. However, a summary of the original criteria can be found at: Thommessen, De første områdene for havvind ble utlyst i dag (29 March 2023), De første områdene for havvind ble utlyst i dag | Advokatfirmaet Thommessen, www.thommessen.no/aktuelt/de-forste-omradende-for-havvind-ble-utlyst-i-dag.

[149] Norwegian Government, Ventyr SN II AS won the auction for the allocation of a project area for offshore wind in Sørlige Nordsjø II (Press Release, 20 March 2024), www.regjeringen.no/en/aktuelt/ventyr-nordsjo-ii-har-vunnet-auksjonen-om-tildeling-av-prosjektomrade-for-havvind-i-sorlige-nordsjo-ii/id3030559/.

[150] Ministry of Energy, Vedlegg 4 Beskrivelse av prekvalifiseringskriterium for første fase av Sørlige Nordsjø II (17 October 2023).

[151] Ministry of Energy, Annex 11 Minimum Requirements for Sustainability and Positive Ripple Effects, available at: www.regjeringen.no/contentassets/bd4d260de2c242beb661494550b8d7a3/annex-11-to-the-competition-announcement-document_contractual-minimum-requirements.pdf.

[152] Ministry of Energy, Annex 11 Minimum Requirements for Sustainability and Positive Ripple Effects, 3 and 4.

local ripple effects" is changed to "positive ripple effects".[153] Sørlige Nordsjø II's state aid regime, based on a contract for differences scheme, was declared compatible with the EEA Agreement by the EFTA Surveillance Authority in December 2023.[154] In contrast, Utsira Nord's state aid regime approval has been pending since October 2024, and on 22 March 2024, the Norwegian Government communicated that dialogue around the assessment of the aid with the EFTA Surveillance Authority was underway.[155] We would not be surprised if these provisions on local and regional content are one of the points of contention in the ongoing discussion and will shed light on the legality of local content-like provisions in Norwegian offshore wind.[156]

4. Building Capacity and Expertise Through Local Content Rules: Drawing Lessons for Policy and Practice Recommendations

A. Lessons Learnt

Lessons learned from Brazil, Nigeria, and the North Sea region highlight that local content goals of capacity building, knowledge transfer, job creation, and local procurement of goods and services have achieved mixed success depending on context and implementation.[157] This chapter reveals both positive and negative lessons concerning local content policies in the offshore industry. Brazil, for example, provides an efficient local content system that creates opportunities for impactful interventions in capacity building and knowledge transfer.[158] However, unrealistic demands placed on operators have posed a major barrier to effective implementation. Criticising the Brazilian model, Jesus et al. argue that Brazil has one of the most controversial LCRs in the developing world due to its high-cost methods, inefficient and unrealistic demands, and excessive emphasis on nationalising the offshore supply chain.[159]

In Nigeria, the Local Content Act has led to systematic but steady improvements in local capacity and knowledge transfer in the oil and gas sector. Yet, this law faces several implementation challenges.[160] According to Iledare, local content policies in

[153] Norwegian Government, Updated Announcement for Offshore Wind at Sørlige Nordsjø II and Utsira Nord (Press Release 17 October 2023), www.regjeringen.no/en/aktuelt/oppdatert-utlysning-for-havvind-i-sorlige-nordsjo-ii-og-utsira-nord/id3001301/ (emphasis added).

[154] EFTA Surveillance Authority, Decision No 194/23/COL (19 December 2023).

[155] Norwegian Government, Veien videre for Utsira Nord (22 March 2024), www.regjeringen.no/no/aktuelt/veien-videre-for-utsira-nord/id3031479/.

[156] For a thorough discussion of offshore wind and Norwegian local content policies and possible consequences arising therefrom, see, Ø Østebø, *Positive lokale ringvirkninger: Et krav om lokalt innhold eller et legitimt kriterie innenfor EØS avtalens rammeverk* (Master's thesis, 2024).

[157] See Ba and Jacquet (n 50).

[158] Pereira et al (n 75).

[159] SR Furtado, ED Junior and MFL Almeida, 'Evaluation of Social and Economic Impacts of Local Content Management in Oil & Gas and Shipbuilding Industry in Brazil: An Application of Input-Output Analysis' (October 2017) www.researchgate.net/publication/320460638.

[160] See Pereowei Subai, *Local Content Oil and Gas Law in Africa: Lessons from Nigeria and Beyond* (Routledge, 2021).

Nigeria are set up to fail not because of a lack of local talent or technological expertise, but due to insufficient financial resources.[161] The country lacks adequate training facilities and educational infrastructure to support innovation in higher institutions, thus limiting technical education and research initiatives. Additionally, the Nigerian government has struggled to retain top talent and employ those sponsored on scholarships to apply their acquired knowledge. These challenges, coupled with the discrimination and under-utilisation of indigenous services in oil and gas projects, and the lack of access to capital for local companies, have stifled local capacity building in Nigeria.[162]

In contrast, developed North Sea countries have recorded success in implementing local content policies. In the UK, for example, LCRs have significantly contributed to the success of offshore wind projects. Since 2013, the UK government has required developers of offshore wind projects to demonstrate how they plan to procure products and develop local capacity, skills, and innovation for successful project execution, supported by the CfD scheme. As a result, the UK has incentivised investments from developers while ensuring a robust and sustainable supply chain for offshore wind projects.

In Norway, the temporary nature of the country's LCRs is a key lesson from its petroleum policy.[163] Effective implementation of these LCRs has created a highly competitive Norwegian petroleum sector that continues to compete globally without a local content policy. When foreign companies entered the Norwegian industry in the late 1970s, the government encouraged collaboration with local companies and institutions to improve research and development in the petroleum industry.[164] For example, during the fourth oil licensing round of 1978, the Norwegian government mandated that at least 50 per cent of research and development efforts in any offshore projects be executed in Norway. To further promote local content growth, the Ministry of Petroleum and Energy required foreign operators to establish strategies for technology transfers to qualify for offshore licensing. The local capacities and technological expertise developed through Norway's local content policies have positioned the country as a leading player in the global oil industry.[165]

Effective implementation of LCR provisions and proactive stakeholder engagement are key enablers for successful local content policies, providing insightful lessons for the offshore sector. The ultimate goal should be to leverage these lessons to foster local capacity building, local expertise, technology and knowledge transfer, and local development.

[161] Wumi Iledare, 'Oil and the future of Nigeria: Perspectives and challenges and strategic actions for sustainable economic growth and development' (2007) Paper presented at the International Association for Energy Economics Round Table, Abuja, Nigeria.

[162] Nathan Agu, 'A Review of the Nigerian Local Content Legislation and its Impact on the Nigerian Oil And Gas Sector' (2022) 6 *African Journal of Law and Human Rights* 1, 60–68.

[163] Banet (n 111) 245. See also Moses and Letnes (n 114) 14.

[164] Eduardo Pereira et al, 'Designing Regulatory Governance Models for Managing Hydrocarbon Resources: Lessons Learned from Norway and the UK' (2020) 11 *Journal of Sustainable Development, Law and Policy* 2, 251–99.

[165] ibid.

B. Recommendations

i. Strengthening Policy Implementation

This domain involves formulating a medium- to long-term strategy for implementing a national infrastructure agenda that aligns with capacity-building initiatives in developing countries. A credible and effective local content programme requires robust national infrastructure before embarking on ambitious capacity development endeavours.

Alternatively, National Oil Companies (NOCs) and International Oil Companies (IOCs) should collaborate to institute concurrent national infrastructure rehabilitation or enhancement programmes alongside the local content agenda. These initiatives would facilitate and catalyse economic growth, elevating the operational stature of IOCs within the country. The selection of specific national infrastructure projects should be guided by their relevance to the targeted oil and gas sectors. Encouraging the establishment of smaller, complementary businesses in related fields would foster the development of regional manufacturing precincts or zones. This integrated approach ensures a symbiotic relationship between infrastructure development, capacity building, and economic growth in the oil and gas industry.

ii. Enhanced Skill and Knowledge Transfer Programmes

The efficacy of local workforce development initiatives hinges on transcending conventional, fragmented strategies that yield limited, short-term outcomes. Collaborative efforts between companies and host countries are crucial. This involves identifying and selecting target disciplines and technical competencies. Additionally, establishing a world-class knowledge diffusion and capital management programme is imperative to seamlessly integrate these elements into the national workforce. The approach to workforce development should be comprehensive, incorporating training, development, internships, and placement programmes. This strategy requires coordination and a steadfast commitment to ensuring the enduring success of the local workforce, the company, and the host country in the long run.

iii. Community Engagement and Stakeholder Collaboration

Collaboration between IOCs and NOCs requires establishing or utilising pre-existing collaborative stakeholder networks within the host country. These networks should include suppliers, service providers, operators, and other key industry participants. Such a network serves as a robust model for stakeholder collaboration, offering a participatory framework crucial for steering the local content agenda, facilitating swift and efficient execution. For example, in Brazil, an association of oil- and gas-related suppliers played a pivotal role by providing essential data, aiding the implementation of some of Prominp's industry programmes.[166]

[166] J Fantine and CF Alvim, 'A Model for National Development' (August-September 2006) Economy and Energy, no. 57.

To expedite local capacity-building and supplier development initiatives, companies must understand pertinent global networks. Additionally, access to relevant alliances and relationships with foreign entities is paramount. These connections foster dialogue and collaboration, potentially leading to foreign ownership stakes in local businesses, technology transfer, and support for capacity building and asset enhancement. It is imperative that all collaborative endeavours result in IOCs' willingness to engage with global service providers, equipment manufacturers, and local companies, ensuring the adequate transfer of technologies without compromising established quality standards.

iv. Realistic Targets

Assessing each country's realities is crucial to determine their short-, mid-, and long-term goals. These goals should align with policies, capacity building, and engagement to ensure progress and achieve more ambitious objectives. If the goals are inconsistent with the country's realities, companies may struggle to comply with the requirements, ultimately deterring investments.

v. Financing

Local content is directly related to local sources of goods and services. However, local companies, especially small and mid-size enterprises, might not meet such requirements without financial support. Securing financial support for the local industry is essential; otherwise, local investments will depend mostly on foreign entities incorporating local subsidiaries, which will not meet the full spectrum of desired local content for large, medium, and small enterprises.

5. Conclusion

The assessment of local content rules and the transfer of skills and knowledge in offshore development presents a compelling narrative of progress, challenges, and opportunities. The comparative analysis between the well-established North Sea Region (represented by the UK and Norway) and the burgeoning economies of Brazil and Nigeria sheds light on the intricate dynamics of building local capacity.

As the developed countries in the North Sea Region exemplify, effective local content regulations can catalyse indigenous growth and technological advancement. The intricate web of policies, incentives, and collaborative frameworks has empowered local industries and fostered a culture of innovation and self-reliance. Successfully transferring skills and knowledge from seasoned professionals to the local workforce has played a pivotal role in creating sustainable expertise. However, these local content policies regarding offshore petroleum were developed in a different regulatory scenario where WTO, EEA, and EU limits were more permissible. LCRs and local development policies have been phased out in the industry and timidly (and with some setbacks) tried to be implemented in offshore wind.

Conversely, Brazil and Nigeria's case studies underscore the challenges faced by developing nations in replicating such success stories. While the growth potential is immense, impediments like infrastructure gaps, regulatory uncertainties, and the need for substantial investments in education and training programmes become apparent. However, these challenges should not be viewed as insurmountable roadblocks but as strategic interventions and international cooperation opportunities.

The journey towards building local capacity and expertise is multifaceted and demands a nuanced approach. The experiences of the North Sea Region and the contrasting landscapes of Brazil and Nigeria offer invaluable insights for policymakers, industry stakeholders, and researchers alike. Through collaborative efforts, adaptive policies, and knowledge exchange, the vision of a globally competitive and sustainable offshore industry can be realised. This chapter serves not only as a reflection on the progress made but as a guide for future endeavours in transforming developing regions into thriving hubs of expertise and innovation.

11

The Prospects for Offshore Wind Investment in the Global South – Lessons from the Offshore Oil & Gas Sector?

REG FOWLER

1. Introduction

The purpose of this chapter is to analyse the models used by the offshore oil and gas industry to structure investment and to compare them with current financing practices in the offshore wind energy sector and consider how each addresses the key risks for investment in the Global South. The offshore wind industry is at a watershed moment, with many opportunities and bankable projects ready to be financed and deployed in the Global North, but it faces significant bottlenecks, impeding roll-out of the next phase of investment. By contrast, investing in offshore wind farms in the Global South, leveraging excellent opportunities in Latin America and Africa, is an exceptionally challenging proposition. The difficulties investors face in such regions have some similarities with the problems overcome by oil and gas investors as that industry expanded offshore and into the Global South in the 1950s and 1960s, despite, and in some cases because of, decolonisation and the politicisation of oil.

This chapter will consider whether offshore windfarm projects require some form of state-provided investment protection, reducing the risks borne by developers and their financiers, or whether other factors are at play which are better addressed by different solutions. In reality, it will become obvious that further investment in offshore wind energy in North America, Europe, China and parts of Southeast Asia does not need enhanced investment protection as a priority, and the lack of such protection is not a deal breaker.

However, the form of host government instrument devised by oil and gas and mining investors in the 1950s and 1960s may provide a framework for cooperation between host state and investor in large-scale and expensive offshore wind farm investment, especially in the Global South. This chapter will try to illustrate how such an agreement, properly adapted, may help address the biggest impediments to offshore wind investment in the Global South – the high cost of capital, the need for upgrading the downstream electricity grid and the lack of reliable offtake cash flows.

2. Offshore Oil and Gas Investment Structures

A. The Offshore Oil and Gas Context

Offshore oil and gas investment is exceptionally risky. Considerable sums must be invested in exploration for potential hydrocarbon reserves, which, if identified by seismic data, must be drilled and tested by expensive exploration wells. Very often such wells prove that no hydrocarbons are present where they were expected. Equally often, a discovered reservoir proves to be much more difficult to exploit than the initial seismic and well results indicated, possibly because the reservoir is not porous or because it is divided up into impenetrable compartments between which hydrocarbons cannot flow. Even if an oil company decides to proceed to invest in the development of a new reservoir, a campaign of production wells must be drilled, and new processing and evacuation infrastructure will have to be put in place, offshore and potentially onshore. The industry is heavily regulated and each step in this process requires government approvals which are increasingly more difficult and time-consuming to obtain as environmental scrutiny intensifies. Consequently, the oil and gas investor places a bet that the very significant upfront investment in exploration and development costs will be paid off by oil revenues, with the potential of significant profits, possibly decades after the reservoir was first discovered.[1]

Privately owned oil majors deploy equity capital and/or funds secured from corporate bond releases to finance oil and gas projects.[2,3] Reputational issues now make it increasingly difficult for financial institutions to invest specifically in upstream oil and gas assets, and oil companies may be accused of diversifying their asset portfolios to include green energy investments in order that their corporate bonds remain investable in an increasingly environmentally sensitive bond market.

This reliance on the corporate balance sheet as a funding strategy marks out the oil and gas industry as an exception compared to less capital intense and less risky forms of business. This characteristic of oil and gas financing is likely only to intensify as private capital lenders are increasingly encouraged to apply sustainability criteria to their lending portfolios.[4] Such encouragement only serves to increase the potential role for private capital investing in clean energy projects whose developers often do not have the corporate deep pockets that oil and gas companies have accrued over the last half-century.[5]

[1] For a general summary of exploration risks and costs, see Xiaoyi Mu, 'Exploration, Development and Production' in *The Economics of Oil and Gas* (Agenda Publishing, 2019) 19–54.

[2] For a discussion of the financing of investment by national oil companies and their role in the energy transition, see David Manley and Patrick Heller, 'Risky Bet – National Oil Companies in the Energy Transition' (National Resource Governance Institute, 2021) resourcegovernance.org/publications/risky-bet-national-oil-companies-energy-transition.

[3] For a discussion of third-party lending to the upstream oil and gas sector see Ross McCall and Huw Thomas, 'Financing Upstream Agreements' in Renad Rounes (ed), *Oil and Gas: A Practical Handbook*, 3rd edn (Globe Law and Business, 2018).

[4] The trend towards sustainable loan portfolios is faltering as claims of sustainability are increasingly subject to regulatory challenge. See Tommy Reggiori Wilkes and Isla Binnie, 'loans linked to ESG face overhaul by under pressure banks' (*Reuters*, 10 November 2023) www.reuters.com/sustainability/sustainable-finance-reporting/loans-linked-esg-face-overhaul-by-under-pressure-banks-2023-11-10/.

[5] Financing strategies open to offshore wind farms are helpfully summarised in 'Financing and Investment Trends – the European wind industry in 2022' (*Wind Europe*, 29 March 2023) windeurope.org/intelligence-platform/product/financing-and-investment-trends-2022/#.

> Capital markets are placing higher value on firms that are structurally aligned with the energy transition across sectors such as liquid fuels, power, and equipment manufacturers. By contrast, the major oil and gas companies that are most invested in low-carbon markets have not yet benefited from material uplifts in company valuation.[6]

However, oil and gas shareholders expect to see capital restraint, prudent selection of bankable projects and nevertheless a decent level of reserves replacement. One method of meeting these optimistic expectations despite the upstream risks described above is achieved by spreading available capital across a large number of attractive prospects, by sharing ownership with other state and private oil companies in joint ventures. After all, the prize is a decent level of oil production saleable at the global crude oil price, regardless of the crude oil's point of origin. Simply put, an oil company can place a bet on four projects by taking a 25 per cent stake in each, rather than relying on a single, 100 per cent owned project to meet shareholders' expectations.[7]

Critically, the prospect of that business model paying off depends on sustained oil prices (which are routinely volatile) and the host state's loyalty to the agreed terms of the oil company's concession agreement or licence by which the investor is granted exclusive access to hydrocarbons extracted from the licence area in exchange for taxes and/or a share of production in kind or in cash.

The host state plays a pivotal role in this context, not merely in the conduct of its regulatory role, but in its fundamental capacity as the custodian of the state's mineral resources, having the unique and exclusive sovereign right to exploit, or delegate the exploitation of, hydrocarbon and mining resources within its territory, territorial seas and ultimately its exclusive economic zone. This principle was formally enshrined by United Nations General Assembly Resolution 1803 of 1962 recognising each independent state's sovereign rights to its hydrocarbon resources, which coincided with newly decolonised states' desire to exercise economic sovereignty over such resources and to ensure profits from its exploitation accrued to the state.[8] Nothing similar has been considered with respect to each state's right to exploit its offshore wind resources arguably because the existing provisions of the United Nations Convention on the Law of the Seas adequately enables states to construct offshore energy facilities within their territorial waters and EEZs.[9]

Many host states whose territories include established hydrocarbon provinces have leveraged their position to form their own state oil and gas enterprises. The media portrays the offshore oil and gas industry as dominated by large independent multinational corporates such as Exxon, Chevron, BP and Shell because of their brand

[6] From Clemens Kienzler, Alexandre Lichy, Humayun Tai, and Fransje van der Marel, 'How oil and gas companies can be successful in renewable power' (McKinsey & Company, 27 February 2023) www.mckinsey.com/industries/electric-power-and-natural-gas/our-insights/how-oil-and-gas-companies-can-be-successful-in-renewable-power#/.

[7] This strategy remains popular for oil majors exploring renewable investments, and de-risking frontier technologies. See 'Partnerships in Kingdom Growing on Aramco Deal Activity' (January 2022) jvalchemist.ankura.com/trends/partnerships-in-kingdom-growing-on-aramco-deal-activity/.

[8] The UN General Assembly Resolution is available at undocs.org/Home/Mobile?FinalSymbol=a%2Fres%2F1803(xvii)&Language=E&DeviceType=Desktop&LangRequested=False.

[9] See United Nations Convention on the Law of the Seas, Article 56.1 (A), 'Rights, jurisdiction and duties of the coastal State in the exclusive economic zone', www.un.org/depts/los/convention_agreements/texts/unclos/unclos_e.pdf. See also Maria Madaléna das Neves, 'Offshore Renewable Energy and the Law of the Sea' in Elise Johansen, Signe Veierud Busch and Ingvild Ulrikke Jakobsen (eds), *The Law of the Sea and Climate Change: Solutions and Constraints* (Cambridge University Press, 2020) 206–33. doi:10.1017/9781108907118.010.

presence. In 2022, oil companies in private ownership earned USD1.8 trillion whereas state-owned companies such as Saudi Aramco, Petronas, ADNOC, CNPC and others earned USD2.2 trillion.[10] In reality, many of the largest offshore producing fields are shared between state and private oil companies under the terms of a joint venture, led by one investor as operator. Increasingly, state oil companies use the services of private oil companies and oilfield service companies to operate their assets as a paid contractor earning a fee and not as an investor earning a share of hydrocarbon production.[11]

The financial risk profile of offshore wind projects is similar to oil and gas investment – very high upfront capital commitment and reliance on volatile market prices for offtake sales and cash flow to achieve acceptable returns deferred for a significant period of time. If the state also controls the price of power or refined petroleum product prices and/or requires the project to sell a minimum proportion of production into the domestic market, then project economics are also exposed to political risk as well.

Nevertheless, offshore wind projects have a lesser nexus with the host state in whose territorial waters they are located, because wind is not treated as a sovereign resource access to which is state-controlled and because to date, states have not invested public funds in such projects as project shareholder or investor. This may partly explain why such projects proceed on the basis of regulatory consent only, and without a commercial 'life of project' investor-state agreement, setting out the allocation of risk and reward between investor and state. This chapter goes on to explain why such an agreement could nevertheless play a significant and productive role in managing some of the risks that offshore wind shares with oil and gas investment, and indeed some risks that are unique to it, particularly its needs for third party funding and its exposure to debt market interest rates.

B. Petroleum Licence Regimes and Investor-State Agreements

Broadly speaking, petroleum states have followed one of two different models for granting permits for petroleum exploitation and its subsequent regulation – either a petroleum licence regime or a contractual regime relying on a concession agreement, often taking the form of a profit or production sharing agreement between the state and the investor.[12] For reasons explained below, such 'host government agreements' are more commonly used in emerging market and less developed countries, predominantly those states which supported adoption of United Nations General Assembly Resolution 1803.

A typical petroleum licence regime has some similarities with the permitting procedures which offshore wind investors must tackle. Licences are often granted by auction

[10] *World Energy Investment 2023* IEA. available at https://www.iea.org/reports/world-energy-investment-2023. Accessed October 2023.

[11] See Jubilee Easo, 'Petroleum contracts: licences, concessions, production-sharing agreements and service contracts' in Rounes (n 3). For a wide-ranging and informative discussion of the extractive industries structure and interface with resource policies, see Peter D Cameron and Michael C Stanley, *Oil, Gas, and Mining: A Sourcebook for Understanding the Extractive Industries* (World Bank, 2017). doi:10.1596/978-0-8213-9658-2.

[12] An excellent summary of key terms is Peter Roberts, *A Practical Guide to Upstream Petroleum Granting Instruments* (Qatar University Press, 2021) qspace.qu.edu.qa/handle/10576/15417.

pursuant to licensing rounds when potential petroleum investors compete for access for unallocated offshore acreage, by offering significant bonuses payable on licence award and committing to conducting extensive exploration activities in the licence area awarded. The licence regime must be backed up by hydrocarbon legislation, fixing the obligations of the investor and the role of the state in overseeing licence activities, on terms that create a 'level-playing field' for every bidder. Consequently, the relationship between state and investor is formalised, with specific 'touch points' when the state approves the investor's next steps with respect to hydrocarbon exploitation. The result is not a 'laissez faire' regime, but a purely regulatory one, where the host state acts as gatekeeper, relying upon the investor to take the initiative in planning and proposing the next steps for resource exploitation, and exercising control in the interests of other stakeholders and interests, with a view to maximising local economic benefits and minimising environmental impact.

By contrast, the permitting process for approval of offshore wind is exactly that – a permitting process approving the concept, design and siting of a particular project prior to and a condition of the developer's final investment decision.[13] The state's ongoing regulatory role may be limited to health, safety and environmental compliance verification and inspection; the state does not expect to regulate wind power production, in contrast to oil and gas licences where the licence holder is expected to agree hydrocarbon production targets with the regulator during the term of the licence. As an exception, an ongoing state – project relationship may arise where the wind farm developer participates in an auction for state subsidies such as 'contracts for differences'; yet such subsidies are unlikely to last for the lifetime of the project.

The alternative regime for oil and gas regulation relies upon the host state and investor negotiating and agreeing a very detailed 'life of project' agreement. Such host state granting instruments can take a number of forms – including tax and royalty agreements and risk service agreements.[14] This chapter discusses production-sharing or profit-sharing agreements, particularly because they have attractive terms for the investor in terms of the recovery of its development costs and offer a model for long term investor-state cooperation. As such, it is the better model for addressing the financial risks shared by offshore wind and oil and gas which were discussed in section 2(A).

Routinely, the fiscal terms of a production or profit sharing agreement allow the investor to recover as a priority the past costs of a successful hydrocarbon exploration campaign and the costs of developing the discovered resources up to the point of first production from the proceeds of sale of that production. Only a reduced proportion of income is shared between the state and the investor, until such costs have been

[13] For examples from Japan and Australia, see Kenryo Mizutani and Haruka Tanida; 'The Wind of Change: The Development of the Legal Framework for Japan's Offshore Wind Energy' (*OGEL* 5, 2022) www.ogel.org URL: www.ogel.org/article.asp?key=4051; and Madeleine Taylor and Riley Grant Taylor; 'Planning for Offshore Wind Energy: The Case for Marine Spatial Planning in Australia' (*OGEL* 5, 2022) www.ogel.org/article.asp?key=4050.

[14] The relationship between the host state and investor under each form of host granting instrument is discussed in Peter Roberts and Reg Fowler, *Joint Operating Agreements – a Practical Guide* (Globe Law and Business, 2020). For a helpful discussion of the contrast between production sharing agreements, tax and royalty agreements and risk service agreements, see Christopher Moore, Christopher Moyes and Paul Patterson, 'The Effect of Non-Fiscal Clauses in Host Government Instruments on the Fair Market Value of Upstream Opportunities' (2019) 12 *Journal of World Energy Law and Business* 480–501.

compensated. Necessarily, this means that the investor's budgets and cost control are closely scrutinised by the state and subject to approval through the management committee discussed below. However, when payback is reached, the investor only recovers its ongoing operating costs as a priority, and the state will normally retain more than 50 per cent of the rent from production. Furthermore, the algorithms which define the state and investor shares of production or cash flow are progressive, allowing the state to recover an increased share when petroleum prices are high and/or when the investor has achieved certain benchmark levels of profitability on its investment. Simply put, the fiscal terms routinely grant the lion's share of windfall prices to the state, whilst giving the investor some comfort that successful exploration and development costs will be recovered and an attractive return earned.[15] From the investor's perspective, this is a conservative strategy, but one which also potentially attracts debt capital because it prioritises a steady income available for the repayment of loans for development expenditure in place of a bigger share of excess profit.

This does not necessarily mean subsidisation, because the overall tax rate payable by the project will often exceed the gross tax rate applicable to a non-petroleum business applying general corporate taxation rules. The fiscal terms ideally should recognise two key characteristics unique to the petroleum business – the extreme risk profile of petroleum exploration for the investor, and the sovereign right of the host state to the greatest proportion of profit arising from the project. Exploration risk is particularly high in this context because most agreements do not permit the investor to recover unsuccessful exploration costs from other projects within the same jurisdiction – in contrast to many petroleum licence regimes, which allow exploration losses to be offset against corporation tax. These points in themselves are sufficient justification for adopting a project- and industry-specific fiscal system. Regrettably, sight of this point may be lost later in the project's duration when the discrepancy between the project's effective rate of tax and general fiscal rules, particularly in periods of high oil prices, comes under political and media scrutiny.

Civil society challenges profit-sharing agreements; they are confidential, allow the investor not to comply with prevailing legislation, and in particular may provide the investor with significant tax concessions or disguised subsidies.[16] Progress has been made toward addressing these concerns.[17] In any event, this particular model of petroleum regulation should not be blamed for its misuse by non-democratic states that are controlled by oligarchic governments, taking advantage of their control of a state's resources to siphon off petroleum rents for the benefit of themselves and their supporters. Any such agreement is capable of being abused where the state routinely overrides the rule of law, often to the detriment of both the civilian population and investors.

[15] See Daniel Johnson, 'Upstream Concessions and Contracts' in Peter Roberts (ed), *Oil and Gas Contracts – Principles and Practice* (Oxford University Press, 2022).

[16] See Mary Peters and Manu Kumar 'An Insight into Production Sharing Agreements: How they prevent States from achieving maximum control over their hydrocarbon resources' (Autumn 2011 and Spring 2012) 37 *The Journal of Energy and Development*.

[17] Examples include the work of the Extractive Industries Transparency Initiative, summarised in their 20 year anniversary report available at eiti.org/sites/default/files/2023-06/EITI%2020th%20Anniversary%20 Report-%20web.pdf, the National Resource Governance Institute (www.resourcedata.org/) and the EU Revised Revenue Transparency Directive 2013/34/EU. The revenue transparency components of the Dodd Frank Act were repealed by the Trump administration in 2017.

Properly negotiated, these agreements offered newly independent petroleum states a vehicle through which to strike a balance between sovereign control of their hydrocarbon resources and the attraction of Western capital needed to exploit them.[18]

The vital utility of the production-sharing or profit-sharing contractual model for capital intensive, long term investment projects is that it offers significant flexibility for the state and investor to negotiate and lock down the terms of the agreed allocation of commercial risk and reward between them, uniquely devised for the investment project at hand. It enables the investor and state to negotiate and agree a blend of subsidies, tax holidays and enhanced tax rates adjusted over the lifetime of the project to enhance its financial stability and capacity to generate income.

Offshore wind investors may struggle in developing countries to overcome the welter of permitting requirements which have not been devised with offshore wind farms in mind and have not yet been consolidated into a single body of applicable legislation.[19] Using the analogy of investor state agreements as applied in the oil and gas industry, an investor state agreement for offshore wind could define a specific, albeit preliminary set of governing rules for initial projects at an early stage of the development of the state's offshore wind industry before the host state's legislative procedures have devised a generally applicable set of rules. This may be particularly applicable to developing countries whose downstream power markets do not have the capacity to justify large-scale offshore wind investment for domestic supply but may have an opportunity to attract offshore wind investment in conjunction with other energy intensive industrial activity as discussed in Section 5.[20]

3. The Importance of Contractual Stabilisation and the Role of Investor-State Agreements

Section 2 explained how production sharing agreements provide the framework for a flexible fiscal regime, generous to the investor in terms of cash flow until the initial investment cost has been recovered and a moderate return on investment obtained, and thereafter generous to the state to compensate it for the exhaustion of its sovereign hydrocarbon resources. For such an agreement to attract investment it must be observed by its parties throughout its term, especially in periods when one party receives a greater

[18] For a balanced view, see 'How to Scrutinise a Production Sharing Agreement – a Guide for the Oil and Gas Sector Based on Experience from the Caspian Region' (*IIED*, 2012) www.iied.org/sites/default/files/pdfs/migrate/16031IIED.pdf and Kirsten Bindemann, 'Production Sharing Agreements: an Economic Analysis' (Oxford Institute for Energy Studies, 2016) www.oxfordenergy.org/wpcms/wp-content/uploads/2010/11/WPM25-ProductionSharingAgreementsAnEconomicAnalysis-KBindemann-1999.pdf.

[19] See das Neves (n 9).

[20] Some established hydrocarbon states make use of investor state agreements alongside and as well as a fully developed petroleum licensing regime. The former are used exclusively for more complex, expensive and challenging projects, precisely because such agreements enable the investor and state to document a flexible and cost sensitive fiscal regime especially for the project, when the project would not meet the investors' investment screening values if operated on the standard fiscal model set by the petroleum licensing regime. See Emma Gordon, 'The Politics of Renewable Energy in East Africa' Oxford Institute of Energy Studies Paper EL (29 August 2019) www.oxfordenergy.org/publications/politics-renewable-energy-east-africa/.

share of income and profit than the other, as the parties intended when the agreement was negotiated.

No commercial agreement can be future-proof in the sense that its terms foresee and legislate for any possible change in circumstances affecting the parties during its validity. Production- and profit-sharing agreements routinely allow for the relevant project to be overseen by a management committee made up of state and investor representatives, usually requiring both parties' approval of key decisions. In practice, this gives the state a significantly greater degree of supervision over the day-to-day operations of the relevant project, and gives the parties a mechanism through which the project can respond to changes in circumstances by a negotiated solution approved by the management committee. The alternative would involve negotiating the formal amendment of the agreement or invoking some form of hardship clause or force majeure, frequently involving litigation. In one sense, the agreement has the characteristics of an ordinary sale and purchase transaction, describing the payments and taxes which the investor will pay in consideration for the grant of the concession. It is also the constitution for a form of joint venture between the host state and the investor, providing the forum in which the parties can negotiate commercial solutions which they perceive as consistent with the allocation of commercial risk and reward they anticipated when the agreement was signed.

The agreement therefore establishes a dynamic, by setting in advance the terms on which a project's profitability is shared, enabling both parties to envisage the potential yield from investment provided by investor and approved by the state. Furthermore, it sets up the management committee by which the investor and state can negotiate commercial solutions in contentious situations created by unforeseen economic circumstances. This provides a significant advantage over petroleum licence regimes in terms of investment protection.

In this context, investment protection refers to the legal rules which control the right of the state to make legislative and fiscal changes affecting the investor's financial position to its detriment. In one sense, the investor state agreements sidestep these issues, by disapplying the state's background legislation and replacing it with specific terms. And by creating project specific terms, it enables the state to update its legislation and apply it case-by-case to each project, through a process of negotiation with the affected investor. This contrasts with a petroleum licence regime where any change to local law, in hydrocarbon legislation or other sectors, is likely to have a blanket, if not uniform, impact on the entire hydrocarbon industry in that jurisdiction, making consultation more complex and time-consuming, and making the impact on the investor group far more difficult to predict. If such change triggers an investment dispute, questions then arise is to whether the relevant investor had a 'legitimate expectation' that the state would not change its legislation in the proposed manner which threatens to impact the investor's foreseeable profitability.[21] In an auction process leading to the award of the petroleum licence, the state/investor interactions are formalised and rarely do the parties negotiate and agree their respective fiscal expectations from the specific project. Still less do

[21] For a discussion of the meaning of 'legitimate expectation' under EU law in the context of offshore wind farms, see *Drax Power Ltd & Anor, R (on the application of) v HM Treasury & Ors* [2016] EWHC 228 (Admin) (10 February 2016).

they agree how revenue from the project will be divided between them in different oil price scenarios or how the costs of compliance with new legislation might be allocated between the parties. Professionally drafted, the profit- or production- sharing agreement will address these points, and the management committee will have the authority to implement the agreement's terms through its decision-making. This consensus-based approach to the joint management of the project does not constrain the state's ability to enact legislation for social or environmental purposes, but it provides a forum by which investor and state can agree how the costs of compliance with new legislation and the impact on their respective cash flows from the project may be divided between them.

Consider the example of the investor-state litigation arising from the Spanish government's decision to reduce and ultimately withdraw feed in tariff concessions intended to encourage investment in photovoltaic solar energy production.[22] Key to this litigation was whether the state had made any promises of an enforceable nature to the investor which the investor could demonstrate it had relied upon to its detriment.

By contrast, the investor state agreement categorically sets out the parties' expectations from the start, on terms that make it difficult for one party to contend that some extraneous additional promise was made to them outside of the agreement's terms. In the context of a profit or production sharing agreement, there is no such uncertainty – the agreement captures the deal and the respective expectations are set out comprehensively. The project agreement may specify the share of income (and possibly loss) between state and investor arising in different offtake price and profit (or loss) scenarios. Even if circumstances change dramatically triggering the agreement's force majeure provisions, the operational outcomes can be negotiated and agreed by the project's management committee. Properly negotiated, the agreement captures a balance of risk and reward between state and investor which encourages both sides to view the dispute as an impediment to the respective commercial interests of state and investor which rely upon the project's continued profitable operation. A stand-alone legal claim under an investment treaty for example may have no business context and little by way of shared commercial leverage and options for amicable resolution.[23]

In the context of an offshore wind farm, such an agreement offers three key characteristics – it can set out the terms of a fiscal package unique to the project's expected cost and cash flow profile; it can provide for the state's oversight of the project and the negotiation of adjustments to the fiscal package to address unexpected changes in economic circumstances, including those caused by changes in the state's taxation and social and environmental policies; and it can set out a permitting and approval regime for the wind project in countries where the domestic power market does not yet justify the full deployment of offshore wind permitting legislation.[24]

[22] This litigation is summarised in S Swaroop and P Parker, 'The Paris Agreement, Net Zero Energy Transition, and Investor – State Dispute Settlement: Aligning the Investment Treaty System with Climate Change Law & Policy' (2023) 20(1) *Transnational Dispute Management.*

[23] See William Burke-White, 'Chapter 17. The Argentine Financial Crisis: State Liability under BITs and the Legitimacy of the ICSID System' in Michael Waibel, Asha Kaushal, Kyo-Hwa Chung and Claire Balchin (eds), *The Backlash Against Investment Arbitration. Perceptions and Reality* (Kluwer Law International, 2010). For an analysis of investment treaty protections as applied to the energy sector, see Peter Cameron, *International Energy Investment Law; the Pursuit of Stability*, 2nd edn (Oxford University Press, 2021).

[24] Gordon (n 19).

Before this chapter goes on to consider the potential application of a state investor agreement to offshore windfarm projects, it is important to consider a key difference in the risk profile of oil and gas and offshore wind projects.

4. Merchant or Offtake Risk – The Analogy of Natural Gas

Market or merchant risk in this context means the risks inherent in the marketing and sale of the project's output or production, its ability to deliver production to market, to find a creditworthy buyer and obtain a profitable price in potentially volatile markets.

Windfarm investors are exposed to market or merchant risk as are oil and gas majors. At first glance, that merchant risk is drastically different for hydrocarbon projects compared to offshore wind. Crude oil markets are some of the deepest and most liquid in the world, and crude oil is a global commodity, capable of being traded between producing and refining states on long-term and spot transactions, supported by a sophisticated derivative market.[25] Crude oil is a raw material, capable of being stored, refined and deployed for a wide variety of purposes.[26] As a transportation fuel feedstock for the internal combustion engine, it has as yet little or no competition at scale. On the supply side, offshore wind farms deliver power as a finished commodity for domestic and industrial consumption, in competition with nuclear, renewable and fossil fuel generation sources. On the demand side, offshore wind farms differ from distributed renewable power sources such as solar and onshore wind because the former rely upon high-capacity connection into a national or regional power grid which defines and constrains the downstream electricity market it serves.

Whilst electricity is also a global commodity, its markets are not, being limited by the extent of inter-continental and inter-state trunk cabling.[27] Simply put, an investment in an oil field requires the investor to take a view on global oil prices over the life of the field, whereas an investment in a windfarm is fully focused on the ability of its host grid end users to absorb and pay for its production. This explains why so many windfarm projects are impeded by the lack of investment in the coastal region's grid.[28] In the Global South, this often means that the investor must rely upon the local, often state-owned and monopolistic power distribution companies for offtake and cash flow.[29]

[25] For the general context of crude oil and refined products trading, see Reg Fowler and Simon Ludgate, 'Crude Oil Sales and Trading Contracts' in Roberts (n 14).

[26] For an analysis of downstream crude oil markets, see Eduardo Pereira, Kim Talus and Reg Fowler (eds), *The Encyclopaedia of Midstream and Downstream Oil and Gas*, 2nd edn (Globe Law and Business, 2023).

[27] See Jerome Guillet, 'Financing Offshore Wind' (World Forum Offshore Wind September 2022) in particular section 6.1.2 'Commodity Price (Merchant) Risk'.

[28] 'If you take just one message from this report, it should be the urgent need to upgrade our national grid for a world of high renewables penetration, and widespread electrification of homes and businesses' Tim Pick UK Offshore Wind Champion, May 2022 – March 2023, 'Independent Report of the Offshore Wind Champion – Seizing Opportunities' (March 2023) www.gov.uk/government/publications/accelerating-deployment-of-offshore-wind-farms-uk-offshore-wind-champion-recommendations.

[29] 'Renewable Energy Market Analysis: Africa and its Regions' (International Renewable Energy Agency, 2022). See also Chris Trimble, Masami Kojima, Ines Perez Arroyo and Farah Mohammedzadeh, 'Financial viability of Electricity Sectors in Sub-Saharan Africa – Quasi Fiscal Deficits and Hidden Costs' (World Bank Group Energy and Extractives Global Practice Group, August 2016).

Oil and gas production sharing agreements often contain a provision setting out the investor's obligation compulsorily to sell a proportion of production into the domestic market ('the domestic market obligation' or 'DMO'). The same may also be included in the state's hydrocarbon legislation. In parallel, the agreement often guarantees the investor the right to export the balance of its production and sell it at an international market price. Consequently, the level of domestic market obligation forms part of the fiscal package negotiated specifically for the project by the investor and state. Indeed, the level of domestic market obligation may change over time, possibly set at zero when the investor needs to maximise cash flow to recover its investment costs. Likewise, such deferral of domestic market obligations may recognise the domestic market is simply not ready to absorb the additional supply and/or generate the cash to pay for it.

The agreement often includes special terms to address circumstances where the investor discovers a significant natural gas field or encounters significant natural gas volumes associated with crude oil. As with electrical power, depending on the location of the resource, there may be limited access to global markets for natural gas, which can be achieved only by liquefying and shipping it in the form of LNG, or, in rare cases, accessing international natural gas trunk pipelines. Investor state agreements may recognise this by including terms that require investor and state to collaborate on natural gas market reforms, seeking to establish a reliable and transparent market into which the investor can sell natural gas at a predictable price, sufficient to support a decision to invest in natural gas production and transportation infrastructure. The agreement may allow the investor extra time for submitting its natural gas development proposal for this reason.[30] These agreements may also provide the state with a right of first refusal to purchase natural gas from the investor for a price linked to international gas prices. These agreements recognise the key limitations imposed by the depth and liquidity of the local natural gas market at the point in time when a natural gas development decision is made.[31]

In remote locations, when a natural gas deposit of a commercial scale is discovered, the state and investor need to collaborate on developing the local downstream market, building an evacuation route to a trunk gas pipeline and/or developing an industrial plant or plants capable of absorbing the additional natural gas supply at a price which justifies the investment. The latter course is often preferred by the state because it offers local industrial development, local employment and increased fiscal revenues. Typically, a natural gas discovery may spur the development of a petrochemical plant, a gas-fired power station, or possibly a beneficiation plant for mined mineral ores. It might be combined with an offshore wind farm, in order to provide dispatchable energy and an overall stable power supply. Whatever the solution adopted, ideally it should generate exportable commodities saleable for hard-currency. The chapter returns to this point in Section 6. A prudent oil and gas investor will mitigate this risk by negotiating into its agreement with the state a requirement that the state cooperates with it in developing

[30] Natural gas and crude oil are often found in association, and must be separated before the crude oil stream can be marketed. As a result, profitable crude oil reserves may be stranded until an offtake mechanism for the natural gas can be found.

[31] Examples of the standard production sharing agreements containing such special natural gas provisions include Angola, Egypt, Cameroon, Ethiopia, Gabon, and Trinidad & Tobago. These agreements can be downloaded from the OGEL website.

the downstream market for natural gas resource at the state's cost, coupled with the right for the investor to walk away or be bought out if the relevant reforms do not bear fruit by the time an investment decision is required.

Offshore wind farms face a similar dilemma – permitting may take three to five years even in OECD jurisdictions, and development may take another three years after consents have been granted. As a result, the windfarm investor must predict the status of the power market accessible via the local grid eight or more years hence.[32] Several pieces of a jigsaw must have fallen into place by that time; first of all, the grid operator must have programmed the relevant capital works to connect the offshore source to the electricity grid, possibly also upgrading the capacity of the grid to absorb the additional supply. Such activity is likely to require environmental and land use permits, presenting regulatory challenges which the offshore investment itself is less likely to face. The offshore wind farm developer accordingly takes a risk on the willingness of the grid operator to conduct the work to schedule and to find the finance for its cost. The relevant onshore works may require planning consent and environmental impact assessments.[33] But equally importantly, the downstream market must have evolved sufficiently to absorb that new supply and pay for it reliably at a price that will compensate the investment. An investor-state agreement provides a vehicle for the investor to lock in the commitments it needs from the host state to support a long-term offshore wind project, especially with respect to grid connections and upgrades which required the state's regulatory approval, and may be conducted by the state-owned grid operator. Such agreement can also lay out the support the investor can expect from the state in developing the power market which that grid supplies. Capturing such commitments in a long-term agreement will assist in obtaining private finance for that project to the extent that it gives lenders comfort that the project's power customers will generate sufficient income for the project to pay off its loans.

5. Offshore Windfarm Investment in OECD Countries and China; Warnings for Wind Investment in the Global South

The purpose of this Section is to briefly discuss the present state of offshore windfarm investment in the Global North, considering emerging challenges to its profitability despite such investment having access to developed and transparent downstream power market and despite the stated commitment of OECD states to their Paris Agreement obligations.[34]

[32] 'Fossil-fuel generation is OPEX-based via short-run marginal costs directly linked to fuel prices. Wind and solar are CAPEX-based and operate with low marginal costs. The latter makes their future revenue predictability crucial for reducing investment uncertainty thus their finance cost'. Wind Europe's position paper on the electricity market design targeted reform (Wind Europe, 25 May 2023).

[33] Independent Report of the United Kingdom's Offshore Wind Champion – seizing the opportunities (March 2023), www.gov.uk/government/publications/accelerating-deployment-of-offshore-wind-farms-uk-offshore-wind-champion-recommendations.

[34] For a general overview of offshore wind licensing and investment trends see Ignacio Herrera Anchustegui and Tina Soliman Hunter (eds), *Offshore Wind Licensing* (Edward Elgar Publishing, 2024). See also Tina Soliman Hunter and Ignacio Herrera Anchustegui, 'Offshore wind licensing trends and observations' in Ignacio Herrera Anchustegui and Tina Soliman Hunter (eds), *Offshore Wind Licensing* (Edward Elgar Publishing, 2024).

Suffice it to say there has been a wind change. Despite the COVID-19 epidemic, offshore windfarm investment in north-west Europe and China progressed strongly in the period from 2015 to 2022.[35] At the same time, the development cost of designing, engineering, constructing and installing offshore wind farms generally fell in the same period, though not as steeply as photovoltaic solar panels.[36] Commentators expressed great optimism for a rapid expansion in the industry; for example, the IEA predicted that EU offshore wind capacity would increase from 15 GW in 2018 to more than 120 W by 2040 and that the costs of energy production would fall from about $100 per megawatt-hour in 2018 to $60 per megawatt-hour by 2025.[37] Judging by the debt interest rates offered to investors in the market at that time, offshore windfarm technology was treated as proven and largely de-risked.[38]

In 2023, these optimistic developments partly went into reverse. This is a surprising turn of events, given that European power prices remain linked to natural gas prices which have increased enormously following Russia's invasion of Ukraine in February 2022. European governments considered imposing windfall taxes not only on oil and gas companies profiting from trading natural gas into a supply-depleted market, but also clawing back profits from renewable sources, whose production is sold at rapidly increased prices but whose costs were not linked, at least directly, to natural gas. Nevertheless, Vatenfall cancelled its Boreas project offshore Eastern England in July 2023[39] and contrary to expectations, the UK government received no bids for any offshore windfarm project in its September auction of contracts for differences.[40] Only nine months previously, the UK was considering how to fix a cap on the electricity price that wind farms could charge for generated power as an alternative to imposing a windfall tax which it wished to impose on North Sea oil and gas.[41]

There are several explanations. First, the reduction in manufacturing and installation costs experienced in the previous decade has gone into reverse.[42] Raw material costs, especially steel, have increased, driven by high input energy costs which have

[35] Additional offshore wind capacity jumped by 15.6 GW in 2021 and added a further 9.4GW in 2022, led by mainland China. See Global Offshore Wind Report 2022 (*World Forum Offshore Wind*, February 2023) gwec.net/gwecs-global-offshore-wind-report/.

[36] Capital expenditure per megawatt of constructed wind generation fell from €5.5 million in 2012 to €3.5 million in 2021. This compares positively to onshore capital costs which fluctuated in the same period between €1.6 million and €1.8 million. 'Financing and investment trends – the European wind industry in 2021' (*Wind Europe*, April 2022).

[37] Fatih Birol, 'Offshore Wind Outlook' (*IEA*, 25 October 2019) iea.blob.core.windows.net/assets/2e7ec2d6-7cf1-4636-b92c-046ae16f4448/OffshoreWind-Launch-Presentation1.pdf. See also 'How to Succeed in the Expanding Global Offshore Wind Market' (April 2022) www.mckinsey.com/industries/electric-power-and-natural-gas/our-insights/how-to-succeed-in-the-expanding-global-offshore-wind-market.

[38] See by Jérôme Guillet, 'Financing Offshore Wind – Part 9' (19 April 2022) wfo-global.org/financing-offshore-wind-part-9/.

[39] 'Vatenfall puts brakes on UK wind farm as costs surge 40%' *Financial Times* (20 July 2023) www.ft.com/content/f9d0f4f9-6d95-44a9-924b-d88627fd6485.

[40] 'UK climate goals are seen at risk after offshore wind spurned auction' (*Reuters*, 8 September 23) www.reuters.com/sustainability/climate-energy/uk-climate-goals-seen-risk-after-offshore-wind-spurns-auction-2023-09-08/.

[41] 'How to make a mess of an energy windfall tax – a cap on UK renewables revenues risks being both complex and underwhelming' *Financial Times* (11 October 22) www.ft.com/content/89fd7fa9-ac2a-48b1-89c3-0db6237bb4b6.

[42] 'Soaring costs threaten offshore windfarm projects' Financial Times (8 August 2023) www.ft.com/content/8b8aaa67-0c9c-47a6-949d-09bd79a5241d.

slowly but inevitably hit output prices.[43] But the increase in corporate interest rates in the external debt market has had a much more significant impact on wind farm developers who rely less on balance sheet financing and more on commercial lending. Such rates were on a steady downward trend, as debt markets grew increasingly confident about the technological risk and the commitment of OECD countries to their respective Paris Agreement targets. Inflationary pressures and firmer monetary policy have resulted in a very significant spike in base rates, feeding into increased debt repayment obligations. This change in circumstances casts doubt on the industry's established strategy of bidding low minimum prices for produced electricity, often accepting a price which is consistent only with meeting forecast debt obligations arising from the cost of borrowing for development and installation costs, allowing nothing for ongoing operating costs and little margin for significant increases in debt coverage costs.

Commentators are concerned with several underlying market characteristics that are not capable of rapid resolution.[44] First, wind turbine developments require considerable amounts of copper, steel and rare-earths such as molybdenum. Global metals production is not presently capable of meeting expected demand if the pace of construction and installation of offshore and onshore projects is increased to meet Paris Agreement targets.[45] Second, offshore windfarm investment faces strong competition from other, potentially more efficient renewable sources, and this may lead states not to compromise on their auction terms to give offshore wind preferential terms. Offshore wind is expensive per development unit cost compared to onshore wind and photovoltaic solar. This exposes offshore wind to the risk of 'revenue cannibalisation'; as interruptible sources of renewable energy such as offshore wind increase their market share, they run the risk of delivering more energy only at times when other windfarms and renewable sources are also producing, the local market is well, if not over-supplied and the market prices are depressed. Increasingly grids are programmed to draw upon the cheapest generating source at any time, apparently suiting windfarms with low marginal cost of production – but it risks forcing windfarms to capture only the cheapest periods of power prices.[46] This presents further challenges to windfarms still paying off construction debt during periods of increased lending rates.

In the next section, the chapter considers whether these market -related challenges can in some degree be managed by an investor state agreement governing a windfarm project because that agreement offers a vehicle by which the windfarm project owner and its sponsors may align with the state and other actors (such as key offtakers) on a strategy for market development without which the project would not be viable.

[43] 'Turbine makers "struggling to achieve profitability" as inflation cost bite' (*Energy Voice*, 2 March, 2023) www.energyvoice.com/renewables-energy-transition/wind/486652/turbine-makers-struggling-to-achieve-profitability-as-inflation-costs-bite/.

[44] 'Renewable energy has hidden costs' (*Economist*, 21 September 2023) www.economist.com/finance-and-economics/2023/09/21/renewable-energy-has-hidden-costs.

[45] For a recent overview of critical minerals, see 'Geopolitics of the Energy Transition – Critical Minerals' (*International Renewable Energy Agency*, 2023) www.irena.org/Publications/2023/Jul/Geopolitics-of-the-Energy-Transition-Critical-Materials. For analysis of this issue as it applies to investor protection, see R Fowler and MCNCG Putra, 'Simplifying the Pathway to 2030: The Need for More, not Less, Protection for Climate Change-Related investment' (August 2023) www.transnational-dispute-management.com.

[46] See Eike Blume-Werry, Claus Huber, Gustav Resch, Reinhard Haas and Martin Everts, 'Value Factors, Capture Prices and Cannibalism: nightmares for renewable energy decision-makers' (2021) 14(4) *The Journal of World Energy Law & Business* 231–47, doi.org/10.1093/jwelb/jwab027.

6. Recommendations for Offshore Wind Investment in the Global South

In this section, the chapter tries to bring together the preceding analysis to a tentative recommendation. The prospects for offshore windfarm investment in the Global South seem poor. There is little prospect of such investments of avoiding some of the challenges that already slowing the pace of developments in the Global North.[47] Further, the underdevelopment of electricity grids and the overall ability of the host economy to use and pay for power, in some cases for the first time, make many such projects unrealistic. This is disappointing given first, the evidence for significant offshore wind potential in Africa, Latin America and Southeast Asia,[48] the investment gap in the energy transition between the Global North and the Global South[49] and, most pressing of all, the increase in the number of people presently without access to electricity.[50]

The development phase of a windfarm project is particularly risky because of the uncertainty and risk of delays associated with identifying sites and obtaining permission to exploit them. There is an analogy here with hydrocarbon exploration in frontier countries in the 1960s and 1970s when concession agreements were signed with the host state on bespoke terms precisely because the host state had not evolved a domestic hydrocarbon legal regime which could be relied upon to grant and uphold a concession holder's rights.

A state-investor agreement, along the lines of those applicable for oil and gas discussed before in Section 2(B), for a windfarm project could specify its own bespoke procedure for identifying and permitting a suitable site or sites before the domestic legislation was in place. At a stroke, this would 'leap-frog' the legislation process, accelerate the permitting process and above all, de-risk the development phase of a windfarm project in the interests of attracting capital. There is no reason why this 'leap-frogging' would involve 'side-stepping' proper environmental precautions and consultation with affected communities; the agreement would require the parties to adopt and apply existing international guidelines, pending their adoption into domestic law. If the agreement provided for the state to be represented in a supervisory or management committee governing the project, the state would have the insight and control necessary to perform its regulatory functions even before those functions were incorporated into its legal administration.

As discussed in Section 3, the key to a successful investor-state agreement is the fiscal terms. By crafting such terms to be project specific, they can take into account

[47] 'BP and Equinor scrap New York offshore wind contract as costs rise' *Financial Times* (3 January 2024); contrast 'Ørsted to go ahead with world's largest offshore wind farm in North Sea' *Financial Times* (20 December 2023).

[48] African countries with significant offshore potential include Mozambique, Tanzania, Angola, South Africa and Namibia. See 'Development of Wind Energy in Africa' African Development Bank Group Working Paper Number 170 (March 2013) www.afdb.org/sites/default/files/documents/publications/working_paper_170_-_development_of_wind_energy_in_africa.pdf.

[49] 'The gap is now about $4 trillion per year – up from $2.5 trillion in 2015 when the SDGs were adopted'. UNCTA D, 'World Investment Report 2023', unctad.org/topic/investment/world-investment-report.

[50] '75 million people are likely to lose access to electricity as prices rise' (IEA Energy Outlook, 2022) www.iea.org/reports/world-energy-outlook-2022/key-findings.

the project's risk profile and propose an allocation of risk and reward appropriate for it. Furthermore, such terms can be specifically stabilised under the agreement so that the investor is not subject to new or amended taxation without its consent.[51]

Production- or profit -sharing agreements are built on the principle that the investor is entitled to recover its development costs as a priority and then shares profits with the state on terms that grant the state a greater share of income during periods of high oil prices. By increasing the investor's chances of recovering the cost of development at the earliest possible stage together with a stable share of profit oil, the project becomes more attractive to external finance, particularly after the construction phase. Such a cash flow model should be attractive to wind farm developers and their lenders.

Suitably modified, this model could be applied effectively to offshore wind farms. The state could offer a form of long-term two-way 'contract for differences' within the terms of a state-investor agreement. The state would subsidise the power price obtained by the investor during periods of sustained low prices, compensated by a levy or tax that it would recover during periods of sustained higher prices. Such levy or tax might be suspended until the project's development costs had been paid off. Sensibly, that levy or tax might also be rebated in proportion to payments made by the investor towards the cost of decommissioning the project. The overall objective would be to mitigate as far as possible the risk that the investor would not be able to repay third-party debt service, potentially attracting investment not only post construction, but pre-construction and for the life of the project.[52] By locating such contract for differences or fiscal regime within an investor state agreement, its terms can be modified to coincide with the cash flow cycle over the project's entire duration, so that the state is guaranteed its upside at a point in that cycle when the project can afford to generate it.

7. Generating Cash and Addressing Merchant Risk – Symbiosis of Offshore Wind and Industrial Offtakers

A developing state is unlikely to have funds for subsidising low-power prices through schemes like a contract for differences. Many developing states are already struggling with the removal of fossil fuel subsidies which have underpinned their economies for several decades and progress towards their elimination has reversed somewhat in the wake of the COVID-19 pandemic.[53] OECD states have struggled too with clean energy subsidy mechanisms and often failed to budget for them accurately,

[51] Guillet (n 26).

[52] The United Kingdom's 'contracts for differences' scheme is one such example. The wind farm developer is subsidised by the state-owned counterparty (the Low Carbon Contract Company) when market prices fall below the agreed strike price, and the wind farm developer pays the state entity the difference between the strike price and market price when the latter is higher. These contracts for differences are awarded by auction and are not calibrated to suit the economic circumstances of a particular project and have a fixed duration of 15 years. See www.lowcarboncontracts.uk/resources/guidance-and-publications/contracts-for-difference-generator-guide-1st-edition/.

[53] OECD (2021), 'OECD Companion to the Inventory of Support Measures for Fossil Fuels 2021' (OECD Publishing) doi.org/10.1787/e670c620-en.

leading to subsidy withdrawal and the investment protection disputes discussed in Section 3.[54]

This chapter previously discussed the way in which production sharing agreements may allow for collaboration between investor and state on the development of natural gas markets where this is required to secure profitable evacuation and sales of natural gas discoveries. Natural gas projects have successfully spawned the co-development of industrial hubs in developing countries, where the oil and gas investor has been able to collaborate with the state, and state-owned utilities, to deliver gas and/or gas-fired power to a heavy industry installation, such as an aluminium smelting plant or a petrochemical business. Could such a model be applied to enable developing states to attract investment in offshore wind farms associated with an industrial customer requiring a stable, sustainable and inexpensive source of power?

Pairing an offshore wind farm with a suitable industrial consumer to create an industrial hub powered by clean energy is vital for countries where the existing domestic electricity grid consumers simply do not have the income to pay for the power they might wish to use and the state lacks the budget to subsidise the windfarm on a standalone basis.[55] Necessarily the industrial plant which will consume the power generated by offshore wind must develop and commission in lockstep with the windfarm so that it is off-taking power and generating income to pay for it when the windfarm project is ready to generate it. In this context, ports and offshore wind farms go together – the industrial consumer is likely to want to export the majority of its production, earning hard currency in international markets. An offshore wind farm can be co-located, minimising the merchant grid that will need to be installed to service it.

In reality, this will only succeed if the windfarm developer and the industrial consumer are also party to the same or a parallel long-term agreement. Such agreement would coordinate the two development projects and help de-risk delays in either case. It would contain the terms of the power purchase agreement between the windfarm and consumer. The issue of power pricing would be key – the parties could de-link the pricing mechanism from international power prices entirely because both supply and consumption are mutually dedicated and interdependent. The key variable would be the international price of the industrial consumer's product. If that product was particularly energy intensive, such as cement, fertilisers or aluminium, a source relying on cheaper clean energy might have a significant market advantage. This might allow the parties to set an energy price which would enable the windfarm investor to share some of the profit margin delivered to the industrial consumer by cheaper input energy costs.

This symbiosis between a windfarm and an industrial project would also avoid the 'revenue cannibalisation' discussed in Section 5. If the industrial plant has a low marginal cost of production, excluding energy costs, it could be incentivised to synchronise production with periods when the windfarm is generating. Raw materials could be

[54] For an in-depth study of the Italian government's management of renewable energy subsidisation, see Giuseppe Bellantuono, 'The Misguided Quest for Regulatory Stability in the Renewable Energy Sector' (2017) 10(4) *Journal of World Energy Law and Business* 274–92. doi: 10.1093/jwelb/jwx017.

[55] It is perhaps relevant that difficulties in sourcing energy supplies have held back some of the industrial hub developments initiated by China in countries such as Ethiopia and Nigeria; see Arkebe Oqubay, 'African Industrial Hubs and Industrialization: Diversity, Unevenness and Strategic Approach' (2022) 29(1) *Transnational Corporations Journal*, ssrn.com/abstract=4096706.

stockpiled ready for such opportunities. The economics of the joint project would be driven by the lack of correlation between international power prices and international prices for the industrial product. Simply put, the windfarm would avoid generating power into an oversupplied power market, pushing low prices lower, but would enable the industrial partner to deliver product at lower costs of production into an uncorrelated market, with a high probability of attractive returns. The power purchase agreement would play a key role in a wider agreement, which would have the trappings of the joint venture contract, committing wind farm developer and its industrial customer to potentially several decades of symbiotic relationship, held together by the pricing formula which enables the wind farm developer to take a share in the downstream profit generated for the industrial offtaker by its reliance on a source of inexpensive energy.

Indeed, that approach could be extended to replace the need for the state's subsidisation of lower offtake prices. The industrial consumer might guarantee a minimum power offtake price irrespective of the prevailing market price of its downstream production, provided that the same offtake price left it with the lion's share of profitability when that downstream price recovered. After all, if the offtake power price is linked to the consumer's downstream commodity price, particularly a commodity that is internationally traded on transparent and liquid markets, that offtake price may be more easily hedged by either the windfarm investor or the industrial consumer, and its derivative counterparties may be more creditworthy than the host state.[56]

The state's participation in the joint project would still be necessary – investors would still expect the fiscal regime applying both to the wind farm and industrial partners to be stabilised under the terms of a long-term agreement. That agreement would also establish the permitting regime for the windfarm, if not also the industrial plant. In common with profit-and production sharing agreements, it can also provide the vehicle for mutual understandings with respect to job creation, local procurement practices, and commitments to sell a proportion of production into local markets.[57] The state might expect the windfarm projects to sell a proportion of generated power into the local grid at an agreed point when the local economy develops sufficient capacity to absorb and pay for such power, in the form of a deferred domestic market obligation discussed in Section 4. Setting the parameters for such local distribution in the agreement would protect the investor from being strong-armed into breaking the economic model before the windfarm investor had recovered an adequate return from its initial investment. In short, the agreement becomes the definitive and exhaustive statement of the parties' respective 'legitimate expectations'.

This model may be particularly attractive to emerging market and developing countries because it addresses risk factors that contribute to increased base rates applied by public and private financial investors and lenders.[58] It locks in the state's commitment

[56] The potential for power purchase agreements to replace state subsidies as a key form of credit enhancement for renewable projects has been recognised in OECD countries – see Sven Heiligtag et al, 'Merchant Risk Management: The New Frontier in Renewables' (2018) *McKinsey & Company Electric Power & Natural Gas Practice* 6, www.mckinsey.com/industries/electric-power-and-natural-gas/our-insights/merchant-risk-management-the-new-frontier-in-renewables#/.

[57] Many industrial hubs in Africa fail to meet their full potential for want of persistent and stable government support throughout their development; see Oqubay (n 54).

[58] Heiligtag et al (n 55).

both in the permitting process and in terms of fiscal stabilisation; it protects lenders against the risk of default when power prices are low; it connects the windfarm's profitability to hard currency earnings from a global commodity, and it prioritises the repayment of the windfarm's development costs at an early stage of production.

By providing a solution to the merchant risk associated with global energy price volatility and the creditworthiness of offtakers in developing states, this model is eminently suitable for project financing. This is of critical importance given that developing countries may struggle to source finance from corporate debt markets for the reasons explained by Baker, leaving project financing as the only viable alternative.

> To minimise costs, power generation projects are generally structured as a utility with predictable cash flows, high leverage and modest utility-type equity returns. This is how thermal power has been financed in many countries, and the model is being successfully applied to renewable finance. To date, however, this has primarily occurred in high income countries where lenders can rely on the stability of the contractual or regulatory framework that provides a predictable income stream, and the ability of consumers to pay. In contrast, the additional risks faced by clean energy investments in many MLICs [Medium and Low Income Countries], in particular reliance on local purchasers, currency risk and political stability/rule of law, makes finance excessively expensive if available at all.[59]

The IEA accordingly estimates that in the period 2026–2030, private finance will provide more than 70 per cent of the clean energy finance required by emerging market and developing economies to meet what the IEA describes as its 'sustainable development scenario', and more than 30 per cent of that finance will be provided 'off-balance-sheet', in other words by project financing.[60]

In brief, many developing states will not have the economic capacity to guarantee minimum prices on a scale adequate to justify investment in a new offshore windfarm project. No investor state agreement will replace the need for such guarantee. However, if the host state partners with an offshore wind farm developer and an industrial power offtaker, and offers both investors fiscal and regulatory stability under the terms of that agreement, project finance may be accessible to both investors. The chances of achieving that result are enhanced if the investor state agreement enshrines a fiscal package for both the wind farm developer and the industrial power offtaker which is sensitive to their respective investment and cash flow cycles.

The practical application of this collaborative model is not as fanciful as may first appear. OECD countries, particularly EU, are increasingly looking to relocate energy intensive industries offshore where greenfield sites can be developed using low carbon or zero carbon energy sources.[61] Production of critical energy transition minerals in

[59] Robin Baker, 'How Project Finance Can Advance the Clean Energy Transition in Developing Countries' (Oxford Institute for Energy Studies ET17, September 2022) www.oxfordenergy.org/wpcms/wp-content/uploads/2022/09/How-Project-Finance-Can-Advance-the-Clean-Energy-Transition-in-Developing-Countries-ET17.pdf.

[60] IEA (2021), Financing Clean Energy Transitions in Emerging and Developing Economies.

[61] Agora Energiewende and Wuppertal Institute (2021): Breakthrough Strategies for Climate-Neutral Industry in Europe: Policy and Technology Pathways for Raising EU Climate Ambition.

Africa must increase for reasons explained above. The IEA predict a wide range of potential applications:

> Some countries are eyeing opportunities beyond mining such as the value-added transformation of minerals (e.g. refining and active material production), although strong policy support would be needed to provide incentives for investment, nurture the development of local workforces and ensure reliable electricity supplies. In 2022 DRC and Zambia set up a common governance structure – the DRC-Zambia Battery Council – to create a business environment conducive to the development of a battery value chain. Where governments have the fiscal space to fund downstream projects they can be driven by public finance, although private mining companies can also play a role. [....]
>
> Africa's vast land area coupled with excellent wind and solar resources, particularly in its northern and southern regions, provide opportunities for low-emissions hydrogen production. According to IEA estimates, just from areas within 200 km of its coastline, the continent has the renewable energy potential to produce up to 5 000 Mt of low-emissions hydrogen per year at a cost below USD 2/kg.[62]

Morocco leads the way in Africa in developing and applying power-to-gas, power-to-liquid, power-to-fuel, power-to-chemicals and power-to-heat), leveraging green hydrogen, supported by an agreement with Germany in 2020. South Africa is reported is looking for potential green hydrogen customers in Japan and Germany.[63] Most significantly, Europe is conscious of the difficulties it will encounter in abating carbon emissions from key energy intensive industries such as iron smelting, fertiliser and cement production. In a report for the EU by Agora Energiewende, potential application of renewable energy combined with hydrogen provides a number of very detailed scenarios for green energy and industrial cooperation which may be difficult to implement by retrofitting existing plants and installations in Europe. The energy transition is inventing its own forms of potential industrial hubs.

8. Conclusions

OECD countries and China are likely to overcome their short-term difficulties in deploying offshore windfarm technology[64] but in doing so may divert a considerable amount of investment capital which could be deployed in the Global South to enable de-carbonised industrial development and to offset the growing investment gap between Global North and Global South accentuated by the COVID-19 and energy crises.

The challenge is to attract not only public capital from multilateral development banks to offshore wind projects but also private capital on market terms and for that,

[62] 'Financing Clean Energy in Africa' (*IEA*, 2023) www.iea.org/reports/financing-clean-energy-in-africa, License: CC BY 4.0.

[63] 'Focus on hydrogen – a new energy frontier for Africa' (Clifford Chance, 2021) www.cliffordchance.com/content/dam/cliffordchance/briefings/2021/01/focus-on-hydrogen-a-new-energy-frontier-for-africa.pdf See also 'Green Hydrogen to Fuel Africa's Rise – Hard Truths and Key Questions' United Nations Office of the Special Adviser on Africa (June 2023) www.un.org/osaa/news/green-hydrogen-fuel-africa%E2%80%99s-rise-%E2%80%93-hard-truths-and-key-questions.

[64] 'Ørsted to press ahead with world's largest offshore wind farm in North Sea' *Financial Times* (20 December 2023) www.ft.com/content/4d3cc6d4-f479-4607-9574-63e320af80ff.

the project must be specifically formulated on terms that address the common risks that define the interest base rate, and in particular overcome the base rate premium charged for projects in emerging markets and developing countries.[65]

Simply put, the electricity grids and consumer demand in developing countries will rarely provide the secure cash flow that an offshore wind farm project requires, and for this reason, distributed photovoltaic solar networks and onshore wind farms will be more successful. Adequate demand and cash flow for offshore wind farms must come from outside, possibly leveraging the Global North's appetite for rapid decarbonisation.

In this sense, the Globe is revisiting the 1962 moment, when a compromise was broadly struck between national sovereignty and economic cooperation over mineral resources. In the years that followed the UN General Assembly Resolution, the investor state agreement enabled capital to be deployed in countries before domestic legislation was fully evolved to manage that investment. It enabled specific investment protections to be implemented on an 'as needed' basis. The production sharing agreement went a step further by providing exhaustive terms for the allocation of hydrocarbon risk and reward between investor and state. Importantly, it allowed the state to participate in the governance of the project, approving development programmes and budgets, and auditing the costs of development in order to preserve its share of rent. Now a new deal needs to be struck between private sources of finance and states in the Global South for whom offshore wind investment seems out of reach at current market lending rates.

If the state is going to assist in de-risking an offshore wind project, by carving out a special permitting and fiscal regime for it, it is reasonable for the state to have similar safeguards, so that it can continue to fulfil its regulatory role and to carry accountability for that role viz. a viz. its population. Striking the balance over the lifetime of the project between the investor's desire for adherence to the negotiated fiscal package and the state's right to affect that package by legislative changes is one key function of the investor state agreement – which is as applicable to wind farm investment as it is to oil and gas projects.

To de-risk windfarm projects as far as possible, an industrial offtaker must be attracted to partner in the project by extending concessions and protections to it as well; without such a partner the windfarm will likely not generate sufficient hard currency income to meet debt repayment obligations. Such partnership may generate sufficient confidence in its profitability to replace the need for state subsidies and lower the applicable lending rates.

With a fair wind, such agreement may deliver local development and prosperity to a degree that would enable the windfarm to deliver an increasing proportion of its production to the local grid for domestic and industrial consumption, but on terms which the investor state agreement would have foreseen. Just as production sharing agreements have allowed for state-investor cooperation in the development of regional natural gas markets, an investor-state agreement can set expectations for the staged introduction of domestic market obligations for wind farm projects without jeopardising their profitability.

[65] Reducing country risk factored into the cost of capital is vital to reducing the cost of transferring offshore wind technology to the Global South. See 'Financing Clean Energy in Africa (*IEA*, 2023) www.iea.org/reports/financing-clean-energy-in-africa, License: CC BY 4.0.

Generally, OECD countries have disconnected themselves from energy markets and are now struggling to find the levers and mechanisms to implement decarbonisation and achieve net zero in the context of a market economy. Arguably, emerging market and developing countries can 'leapfrog' those issues as they did in the 1960s, by dealing directly with private investors where the scale of investment and project justifies the time and resources spent on negotiating. The oil and gas investors achieved the level of investment protection they wanted under the terms of a contractual agreement, without needing the non-specific protections of bilateral investment treaties. In this counterintuitive way, the offshore oil and gas experience may recommend a way forward for the next phase in the future history of offshore wind.

12

Offshore Energy Financing: Trends, Opportunities and Hurdles

CAMERON KELLY

1. Introduction

The offshore wind sector has been in existence for really only the past two decades. The European Union (EU) was the first region to support the sector, with a supportive regulatory and policy framework since the early 2000s.[1] The bloc achieved almost 25 GW of capacity in 2021 (corresponding to over 5,000 grid-connected wind turbines across 12 countries).[2] Alongside the EU, countries like China,[3] Taiwan[4] and the US[5] have made significant progress in offshore wind deployments, with offshore wind now being one of the International Energy Agency's (IEA) 'big three' in its annual World Energy Outlook.[6] Together with onshore wind and photovoltaic solar (PV), offshore wind is projected to be one of the most important sources of electricity in the transition to net zero over the coming decades.[7]

[1] European Commission, *Communication from the Commission to the European Parliament, The Council, the European Economic and Social Committee and the Committee of the Regions, An EU Strategy to harness the potential of offshore renewable energy for a climate neutral future.* COM(2020) 741 final (19 November 2020). eur-lex.europa.eu/legal-content/EN/TXT/?uri=COM:2020:741:FIN&qid=1605792629666.

[2] Wind Europe, *Wind energy in Europe, 2022 Statistics and the outlook for 2023–2027.* Windeurope.org. (February 2023).

[3] In 2021, China's offshore wind capacity accounted for 86 per cent of global capacity – see Sun Chi, 'China tops offshore wind power worldwide' *ChinaDaily* (10 August 2023). www.chinadaily.com.cn/a/202308/10/WS64d4533aa31035260b81b58e.html#:~:text=China's%20cumulative%20installed%20capacity%20of,People's%20Daily%20reported%20on%20Thursday.

[4] The Taiwanese Government plans to have an energy mix comprised of 50 per cent natural gas, 30 per cent coal and 20 per cent renewable energy by 2025. To meet the renewable energy target, the Taiwanese Government is seeking to increase offshore wind capacity by 5.7 GW by 2025 – see www.nortonrosefulbright.com/en/knowledge/publications/e50b5c34/global-offshore-wind-taiwan.

[5] As of May 2023, the US offshore wind energy pipeline was estimated to have 52,687 MW of capacity – see www.energy.gov/eere/wind/articles/offshore-wind-market-report-2023-edition.

[6] International Energy Agency, *World Energy Outlook 2022*, www.iea.org/reports/world-energy-outlook-2022.

[7] Ignacio Anchustegui and Tina Hunter (eds), *Offshore Wind Licensing* (Edward Elgar Energy Law and Practice series, March 2024).

In the early 2000s, the offshore wind sector's beginnings provided a real commercial opportunity for experienced and will financed hydrocarbon (oil and gas) contractors seeking to participate in attractively priced offshore wind contracts, with little in the way of competition from sponsors with comparable offshore experience nor familiarity with the areas where projects were being built (such as the North Sea).[8] Credentialed players like KBR[9] and Fluor[10] – each of whom offered significant experience delivering wrapped engineering, procurement, construction (EPC) contracts for oil and gas projects – were amongst the first contractors to enter the offshore wind market. However, it quickly became apparent that developing and financing offshore wind projects was quite a different proposition to developing their hydrocarbon counterparts, both contractually and commercially. In a zero-subsidy environment, offshore wind revenue streams (and hence profitability) will largely depend on the average wholesale electricity price over the lifetime of the project – this constitutes an important difference to the predictable and potentially uncapped cash flows that can be made from a producing oil or gas well.[11]

Like offshore oil and gas rigs, offshore wind projects are capital intensive undertakings, often requiring up to three (or more) years to construct (onshore wind projects can typically be commissioned within two years). A clear majority of asset-life costs can be on upfront capital expenditure, which may run into billions of dollars.[12] Australia's scientific research body – the Commonwealth Scientific and Industrial Research Organisation (CSIRO) – has estimated that the likely capital costs of offshore wind in 2028 to be just over US$2,534/kilowatt (kW) of capacity installed (more than double that of onshore wind at just under US$1,267/kW).[13] For jurisdictions like Australia, South Korea, Vietnam, India, Brazil[14] and Colombia where offshore wind is still in its infancy, development of a viable and long-term offshore wind industry will be, at least in part, dependent upon private-sector access to reliable commercial and institutional debt markets.[15] Sponsors and financiers alike must adopt a long-term view on the market whilst navigating a plethora of commercial, technical, contractual and regulatory issues.

This chapter explores the avenues available for investors to finance offshore energy projects. It provides a comparative analysis of the variety of financing approaches for

[8] Jerome Guillet, *Financing Offshore Wind* (World Forum Offshore Wind e.V. (WFO), September 2022).

[9] KBR was part of an EPC consortium to develop the 90 MW Barrow Offshore Wind project in the Irish Sea in 2005 – see www.power-technology.com/data-insights/power-plant-profile-barrow-uk/?cf-view.

[10] Fluor provided EPC services to Greater Gabbard Offshore Winds Limited for a 500 MW offshore wind farm off the Suffolk coast of the UK, which at the time was the world's largest offshore wind farm – see www.fluor.com/projects/offshore-wind-farm-epc.

[11] Vincent Graré, Florian Kühn, Florian Küster and Andreas Schlosse, *The offshore-wind industry's moment of reckoning* (*McKinsey*, 12 July 2018) www.mckinsey.com/capabilities/sustainability/our-insights/the-offshore-wind-industrys-moment-of-reckoning#/.

[12] ibid.

[13] Paul Graham, Jenny Hayward, James Foster and Lisa Havas, *GenCost 2022-23 – Final report* CSIRO (July 2023).

[14] There are currently no operational offshore wind projects in Brazil, however the country's 2050 National Energy Plan states that the potential installed capacity of offshore wind power generation should reach 16GW by 2050 – see www.nortonrosefulbright.com/en/knowledge/publications/cb3f61d6/global-offshore-wind-brazil.

[15] Rebecca Williams, Feng Zhao and Joyce Lee, *Global Offshore Wind Report 2022* (Global Wind Energy Council, 29 June 2022).

offshore wind and hydrocarbon projects, and discusses the range of financial risks and considerations project developers, sponsors and financiers need to take into consideration. The chapter begins with a discussion of how the critical concept of bankability is assessed for offshore wind projects – this includes an examination of the role of project finance and the range of factors affecting bankability. Section 3 considers support mechanisms and offtake arrangements available to offshore wind projects, followed by an analysis of typical financing structures – including how equity and security may be incorporated into financing packages – in sections 4–6. Section 7 discusses some trends, opportunities and hurdles for financing offshore oil and gas versus offshore wind projects, whilst section 8 concludes.

2. Bankability

'Bankability' is a key concept when looking at approaches to financing all types of energy projects. At its simplest, a bankable contract involves a risk allocation between the contractor (delivering specified goods or services for a project) and the project company (established to deliver the project overall) that satisfies a financier's lending criteria.[16] Financiers will tend to focus on a contractor's capacity (or lack thereof) to claim extensions of time and/or additional costs on a project, as well as the forms of security provided to ensure that the contractor delivers the project in accordance with the underlying contractual arrangements. The less comfortable financiers are with these sorts of provisions, the greater the amount of equity support sponsors will need to contribute to the project. Financiers will also need to be satisfied with the project's technical and commercial risk profile. Whilst price is an obvious additional consideration, it is usually considered separately to an assessment of the bankability of the contract itself as the contract price of the entire project facility is linked to the economic bankability of the project as a whole.[17]

A. The Critical Role of Project Finance

'Project financing' is the most prevalent form of funding for offshore wind as well as oil and gas projects, and refers to financing where security is limited to the assets of the project (project cashflows or revenues must therefore be adequate to support the terms of the financing package). In terms of recourse to project sponsors, project financing is typically referred to as either 'non-recourse' or 'limited recourse' financing. As the name suggests, non-recourse involves no recourse to the project sponsors whilst limited recourse limits both the times and amounts sponsors are required to contribute. In practice, project financing which is truly non-recourse is rare – in most situations, sponsors are required to contribute at least some additional equity in certain prescribed situations.

[16] Damian McNair, *EPC Contracts in the Oil and Gas Sector*. Investing in Infrastructure, International Best Legal Practice in Project and Construction Agreements PWC (January 2016).

[17] ibid.

Offshore wind projects are one of the most capital intensive of all infrastructure projects – the majority of funding is required upfront to construct the wind farm's components which are then relatively inexpensive to operate and maintain.[18] The cost base of offshore wind is essentially a function of two characteristics: fixed from commencement and dependent on the cost of capital.[19] These characteristics derive largely from the source of (renewable) energy powering the facility – unpredictable but avoidable – whereas a fossil fuel plant's cost base is essentially predictable and unavoidable. These characteristics mean that unless prevented for technical reasons, fossil fuel plants are able to decide whether to generate power or not – they therefore consume fuel only if it is profitable to do so.[20]

The opposing characteristics of (expensively powered) fossil fuelled versus (inexpensively powered) renewable plants means that the single biggest cost driver for renewables is the cost of capital. Amortising a high initial upfront investment over future production years becomes easier where finance is cheap.[21] Debt is structurally cheaper (and therefore less risky) than equity – this is due to the fact that (amongst other reasons) payment of interest on debt is typically by way of fixed mandatory amounts, paid in priority to payment of dividends from equity (which are typically discretionary). Project finance is therefore an attractive proposition for the capital-intensive nature of offshore wind.

An energy project's aggregate cost of capital[22] is the weighted average cost of equity (measured over the duration of the project) and the cost of debt (measured over the tenor of repayments). For a project funded entirely on balance sheet,[23] the cost of capital is the weighted average cost of equity for the investor, together with any corporate debt.[24] The cost of equity for investors incorporating limited (or non)-recourse debt into their capital structure is higher than the cost of sponsor – provided pure equity, however this is offset by the lower cost of debt.[25]

Unlike oil and gas projects, offshore wind projects rely on long-term offtake arrangements (preferably in the form of power purchase agreements (PPAs) with creditworthy counterparties) to generate revenues. Given that project financiers are repaid only from such revenues, they will be incentivised to ensure that the project is built on time and on budget, and is at least capable of generating sufficient revenues to service the debt. If lenders are also required to take upfront construction risk, they will be keen to ensure that construction also occurs on time and on budget. Financiers will need the project to operate for at least as long as the tenor of debt and commercially to produce adequate

[18] Some offshore oil rigs nearing the end of their operational life may be repurposed to offshore wind farms – see www.energymonitor.ai/just-transition/can-the-uss-offshore-oil-and-gas-hub-pivot-to-wind-energy/. Oil and gas projects are also capital-intensive undertakings, and may also involve significant ongoing operational expenditure – see Robert Clews, *Project Finance for the International Petroleum Industry*, 1st edn (Elsevier Inc., 2016).

[19] Clews (n 18).

[20] ibid.

[21] This helps to explain why solar has historically been cheaper in Germany than in Spain (despite the weaker solar resource).

[22] Lauren Saalmuller, *Cost of capital: what it is and how to calculate it* (Harvard Business School, 19 May 2022) online.hbs.edu/blog/post/cost-of-capital.

[23] See Section 4(A).

[24] Guillet (n 8).

[25] ibid.

revenues. To accept such risks, financiers will be keen to ensure that the parties' respective rights and obligations are allocated appropriately and in sufficient detail contractually to cater for all foreseeable contingencies – this necessitates extensive 'due diligence' investigations to assess the project's technical, commercial and legal credentials.

In many sectors, investors rely on project finance to address specific risks. For example, oil and gas sponsors may use limited-recourse debt to share political, technical, completion and operational risk with lenders, but generally will not ask for construction risk to be shared in countries which also have political and/or legal risk. In such circumstances, oil and gas contractors may guarantee the repayment of debt as a result of delays or cost overruns during construction, but will ask financiers to assume some level of country – specific expropriation, seat of arbitration, foreign exchange or transfer restriction risk, or an inability of governmental entities to fulfil all of their commitments.[26]

Unlike oil and gas projects, offshore wind is one of the few energy market sectors where financiers were requested from the outset to assume complex construction risk on a non-recourse basis. To some extent, this is a function of the sector's beginnings, where small developers could access potentially suitable offshore sites but lacked sufficient capacity to finance the projects themselves. This tended to make engineering, procurement and construction (as well as operation and maintenance) project financed contracts more expensive than their on balance sheet equivalents, as financiers would expect stronger warranties, financial covenants and contractual commitments.[27]

The first offshore wind projects were financed in the years leading up to the 2008 global financial crisis (GFC) – this corresponded to a point in time when banks were not only becoming increasingly comfortable with financing renewable energy (then still a relatively new asset class) but were also not as constrained by the restrictions and the heightened risk aversion that materialised post-GFC. Early transactions could establish precedent forms of documentation in relatively favourable conditions, with projects post-crisis correspondingly easier. It also helped that the first offshore wind projects were in countries surrounding the North Sea – all highly rated, stable jurisdictions where financiers had an appetite to provide non-recourse lending into this emerging asset class.[28]

The early years of the offshore wind sector meant that financiers were asked to assume considerable construction risk, in addition to the usual non-construction risks of such projects, in a sector where there was very few banked precedent. Apart from extensive due diligence, this necessitated lenders having the ability to have direct contractual involvement in most material contracts. In a project finance context, banks need to ensure that every material contract is bankable and fully executed at the time they commit their funds. As many of these relationships are contingent upon each other, this means that all contracts need to be executed contemporaneously (ie, 'financial close'). For balance sheet projects, contracting is correspondingly less complicated as investors can themselves provide funding to contractors so not all contracts need to be executed on day one (with a final decision to proceed therefore called 'final investment decision').[29]

[26] ibid.
[27] ibid.
[28] ibid.
[29] ibid.

B. Factors Affecting Bankability

Assessing an oil and gas project's bankability involves a consideration of several factors – typically these will preference a lump sum (all inclusive) contract price, prescribed date for practical completion, liquidated damages (for both delays and performance), adequate forms of security (from both the contractor as well as its parent), adequately sized caps on liability and restrictions on the contractor's ability to claim additional costs and extensions of time.[30] A fully 'wrapped' engineering, procurement and construction (EPC) contract encapsulates (and so prices) all of these factors in the one contract – the contract includes a premium for assuming such risks and is a key reason why oil and gas projects have tended to adopt and rely on such forms of contracting. Similar bankability considerations apply to offshore wind projects, however a number of additional factors may need to be taken into account (each of which entail additional risk for financiers) – these include disaggregated contract packages, weather and seabed conditions, new and evolving technology, approaches to commissioning and taking over, and performance and availability warranties. These factors are discussed in the sections below.

i. Disaggregated Contracting

The capital intensity of offshore wind projects, combined with their modular design and reluctance by equipment manufacturers to assume risk on other contractors, has led to an absence of EPC-style wraps with disaggregated or multi-contracting structures the industry norm (this contrasts with most oil and gas projects to be procured by way of aggregated or wrapped EPC arrangements). Packages for offshore wind facilities may involve up to 20 contracts, including turbine supply agreements (TSAs), civil works/foundations contracts, inter – array cabling contracts, electrical works agreements and export cabling contracts.[31]

Apart from avoiding the risk-premium associated with (lump-sum) EPC contracting, a disaggregated approach to procurement has enabled offshore wind developers to minimise price variability and to better schedule and allocate risk in respect of critical long lead items like WTGs. Disaggregation does, however, involve a number of adverse consequences that financiers need to consider – these include lower liability limits and reduced recourse rights as well as increased interface risk.[32] Contractor liability is generally expressed to be a lesser amount than under an EPC arrangement as caps on liability and performance security levels are expressed as percentages of individual contract prices (not overall capital expenditure as would be the case in an EPC wrap). In terms of recourse, disaggregation may result in developers and financiers being exposed to less stringent contractor covenants and greater insolvency risk than they might otherwise have the benefit of under wrapped EPC contractual arrangements.[33]

[30] McNair (n 16).

[31] Some offshore wind projects may reduce the overall number of contracts by utilising a balance of plant (BOP) contract involving the wind farm's foundations as well as electrical and inter-array cable works – see Clifford Chance, *Offshore wind: procurement and construction in a changing market* (January 2017).

[32] Clifford Chance (n 31).

[33] ibid.

Increased interface risk is a key consequence of disaggregated contract package arrangements in offshore wind projects. A large number of critical works packages means that interface risk essentially resides with the project's contractors, including the risk of contractor-on-contractor delay (which may impact project redesign, windows of weather-related availability when relevant work packages can be carried out,[34] vessel/port availability and related storage costs). Lenders will require extensive cooperation and coordination frameworks (in the form of common terms, interface or umbrella agreements) to manage interface risk, and will need to procure detailed due diligence investigations to quantify such risks.[35]

ii. Weather Conditions and Wind Forecasting

Weather condition risk is an important factor that needs to be managed in the construction of offshore wind projects. Construction progress can be severely impacted during poor weather conditions, with associated (and often significant) time and cost impacts (particularly in circumstances involving prolongation in the hire of specialised long lead time equipment such as jack-up barges or sea excavators) or in circumstances where there is limited availability of vessels.[36]

In addition to prevailing weather conditions, wind forecasting is required for the purposes of conducting energy yield assessments – such assessments determine a wind farm's potential electricity generation and so likely revenues. From a bankability perspective, the key factor to be determined is the wind source variability compared to that which has been modelled or forecast. To minimise such risk, energy yield assessments include net yield and probability of output exceedance figures against which financiers will (amongst other matters) determine debt sizing criteria and remedy breaches of debt service cover ratios (DSCRs) as may arise from unexpectedly lower wind yields (see Section 4(C)(i)).[37]

In relation to probability of exceedance levels, P50 and P90 modelling scenarios are the most commonly adopted, where 'P50' equates to the average level of generation where forecasted output is exceeded half (50 per cent) of the time, and 'P90' equal to the level of generation predicted to be exceeded 90 per cent of the time).[38] In this way, project revenues can be recalculated by reference to refreshed wind yield assessments adopting more conservative forecasting models (for example, if a very conservative P90 model evidences compliance with relevant financial covenant levels, the default will be deemed to have been cured).[39]

[34] See Section 2(B)(ii).
[35] ibid.
[36] Julian Berenholtz, Shirleen Kirk and Andrew McNeill, *Planning for fair winds ahead: key risks for disputes in the Australian offshore wind industry* (Allens Linklaters Insight, 29 November 2022) www.allens.com.au/insights-news/insights/2022/11/key-risks-for-disputes-in-the-Australian-offshore-wind-industry.
[37] Melissa Keane, Lisa Zhou and Jamie Guthrie, *Financing the Australian offshore wind industry* (Allens Linklaters Insight, 18 October 2022) www.allens.com.au/insights-news/insights/2022/10/Financing-the-Australian-Offshore-Wind-Industry/.
[38] Cheng-Dar Yue, Che-Chih Liu, Chien-Cheng Tu and Ta-Hui Lin, 'Prediction of Power Generation by Offshore Wind Farms Using Multiple Data Sources' (2019) 12 *Energies*.
[39] Keane, Zhou and Guthrie (n 37).

iii. Seabed Conditions

Offshore WTGs are attached via foundations to the seafloor or via cables (in the form of floating turbines).[40] Like their oil and gas equivalents, financiers will be interested in a detailed geotechnical assessment of both the seabed and associated water depths, as such factors will exert a strong influence on the type (and cost) of piling equipment needed to anchor the WTGs, as well as the form and structure of required foundations.[41] Consequently, the quality and accuracy of information gleaned from due diligence - type investigations concerning the seabed and water depths can have significant ramifications for the duration, cost and ultimate success of the project.[42]

iv. Technology Risk

New technology associated with offshore wind projects may be obvious (such as a new WTG model or floating technology) but may also be more nuanced (such as gearbox componentry, handling equipment on vessels or foundation techniques). Floating turbines entail a higher degree of technology risk than traditional (fixed to seabed) offshore WTGs, yet the technology has the potential to introduce real advantages, including significant time and capex savings associated with an absence of foundation works (other than anchors and moors).[43]

Due diligence must be procured by financiers to ensure that the rationale for using new (or untested) technology is adequate. To address technology risk, financiers will preference conservative financing packages involving a range of contractual protection mechanisms – these may include shorter tenors, front – loaded repayment profiles, enhanced cash sweep mechanisms, lower gearing, oversized contingency and maintenance reserve packages, extended latent defect[44] and serial defect[45] protection, enhanced insurance arrangements[46] and extensions to O&M arrangements.[47] Similar to that which is observed in oil and gas projects, financiers may also seek completion guarantees.[48]

[40] ibid.

[41] Berenholtz, Kirk and McNeill (n 36).

[42] ibid.

[43] The higher cost and smaller size of floating turbine units may somewhat offset such capex savings as the technology evolves – see: Berenholtz, Kirk and McNeill (n 36).

[44] Until recently, WTG suppliers under TSAs would seek to limit defects liability periods (DLPs) to 2–3 years and accept no liability for latent defects (except where required by law); five-year (or longer) DLPs are now common (even with proven technology) – see Clifford Chance (n 31).

[45] WTG suppliers would historically not accept liability for serial defects; the promotion of new WTG models together with the requirements of financiers mean that serial defect protection is now standard – see Clifford Chance (n 31).

[46] Offshore wind developers need to ensure that insurance coverage will be unaffected by the use of new technology. Whilst oil and gas contractors and suppliers have been willing to enhance insurance arrangements in order to deploy new technology, this has not been a feature of the offshore wind market to date – see Clifford Chance (n 31).

[47] It is common with new WTGs for developers to ask for an option to extend the O&M warranties; WTG suppliers in turn usually require 'black box' technology to be escrowed (to be accessed only in very prescribed circumstances).

[48] Jamie Guthrie, *Financing the green hydrogen revolution – key bankability issues* (Allens Linklaters Insight, 31 May 2022) www.allens.com.au/insights-news/insights/2022/05/Financing-the-green-hydrogen-revolution/.

v. *Commissioning and Taking Over*

Commissioning of wind farms typically occurs over a staged or phased period, with individual WTGs becoming operational and generating electricity prior to the facility's commercial operations date (COD).[49] Developers or sponsors may seek to take advantage of this by requesting that COD may occur following a certain number of WTGs becoming operational. Reaching COD is a critical milestone for any energy project – in the context of offshore wind it allows the financial model to be rerun to determine the level of debt the project can support based on the available (lower) generation capacity. Where the revised model shows a shortfall in the project's ability to service its debt, the base case can be resized and a cash sweep of all available distributions is made until project debt is reduced to a level which project revenues can support.[50]

Once COD has been achieved, transfer of legal ownership via the project's 'Taking Over' regime must occur to satisfy key performance – related criteria. In terms of an offshore wind farm's contractual Taking Over requirements, each WTG must be mechanically complete and commissioned, with agreed minimum performance criteria satisfied over an agreed period of time. Taking Over may occur incrementally via individual WTGs, via strings (or groups) of WTGs or even on a whole of facility basis.[51] In terms of bankability, financiers will prefer to see Taking Over contingent upon commencement of actual revenues so that the contractor cannot avoid delay liquidated damages (DLDs) on a specific string, only to then be subject to a delay on another string – unless that is also protected by DLDs.[52] The approach selected will also impact on how early generation (or pre-completion) revenues might be shared between the parties (see section 5).[53]

vi. *Performance and Availability Warranties*

Following Taking Over, WTG power curve tests are conducted over an extended period to allow for seasonal and weather variations – such tests determine (for the benefit of financiers and developers alike) whether the facility's actual power generation satisfies agreed or warranted levels.[54] Traditionally, availability warranties heave measured the outages, or downtime, of the WTGs comprising the wind farm; in more recent years, however, there has been a trend away from this measure of availability to one based on the output yield of the WTGs.[55] If minimum yield levels are not satisfied, the O&M contractor will be liable for availability liquidated damages to compensate such shortfalls.[56] The warranted minimum level of availability will vary from project to project and will be based on a number of factors, such as the owner's wish to ensure sufficient headroom over and above the availability level used in calculating the

[49] Keane, Zhou and Guthrie (n 37).

[50] Again, it remains to be seen whether this feature will be incorporated into the Australian offshore wind market.

[51] Clifford Chance (n 31).

[52] ibid.

[53] ibid.

[54] ibid.

[55] Clifford Chance, *Offshore wind: operation and maintenance (O&M) agreements* (January 2017).

[56] Clifford Chance (n 31).

financial base case, site and climatic conditions and the findings of the owner's wind forecasting studies.[57]

3. Support Mechanisms and Offtake Arrangements

As discussed in section 2, the bankability of offshore wind projects will predominantly rely upon sponsors being able to demonstrate certainty of underlying cashflows and revenue streams – compared to their oil and gas counterparts, this is arguably more difficult for offshore wind projects as energy yield assessments are subject to greater variability. Different types of financial support mechanisms deliver varying levels of exposure to fluctuating wholesale electricity price (merchant) risk, and include feed-in tariffs (FiTs), green certificates and reverse auctions utilising contracts for difference (CfDs) and offtake agreements in the form of PPAs. These forms of support can be instrumental in making an otherwise uneconomic offshore wind project commercially viable and are discussed in greater detail in the paragraphs below.[58]

Under FiT schemes, eligible generators receive a fixed payment for each unit of produced electricity – payments are made regardless of wholesale electricity market prices so there is no 'merchant' exposure to fluctuating electricity prices. At the other end of the spectrum, green certificate schemes (such as that which exists under Australia's Renewable Energy Target (RET))[59] involve the creation of tradable certificates which create an incentive for (additional) generation of electricity from renewable sources, thereby creating tradeable certificates. Participating generators are eligible to create certificates for every unit of power they generate – creating the 'supply' side of the market; wholesale purchasers of electricity buy these certificates to meet their renewable energy obligations – forming the 'demand' side.[60] Such schemes expose developers to pricing risk in both the wholesale electricity and certificate markets.[61]

The most popular support scheme for European offshore wind projects has been the variable (or sliding) feed-in premium or CfD scheme, with the amount of subsidy provided linked to prevailing wholesale electricity prices.[62] CfDs have been widely deployed in the UK and in a number of EU jurisdictions and effectively eliminate exposure to merchant risk, with the level of support received equating to the difference between the 'strike price' ($ per megawatt hour (MWh)) bid by a proponent and the wholesale electricity market 'reference price' (subject to a cap). If the wholesale market price for electricity is lower than the strike price, the developer

[57] Clifford Chance (n 55).

[58] Guillet (n 8).

[59] See Australian Government, Clean Energy Regulator *Renewable Energy Target* cer.gov.au/schemes/renewable-energy-target.

[60] ibid.

[61] Gulbahar Tezel and Robert Hensgens, *Financing offshore wind. A study commissioned by Invest-NL* (PWC, August 2020).

[62] Competitive auctions are recommended by the European Commission – see Official Journal of the European Union *Communication from the Commission – Guidelines on State aid for climate, environmental protection and energy 2022* (2022/C 80/01) (18 February 2022).

is reimbursed, whilst if the market price is higher, the developer must pay back the difference.[63]

As noted above, CfDs have been a key support mechanism in enabling dramatic levelised cost of energy (LCOE)[64] reductions in the UK's offshore wind sector. Between 2015 and 2019, CfDs provided the support necessary to reduce LCOEs by 65 per cent, with clearing prices in 2019 achieving parity with the wholesale market for the first time.[65] Such competition illustrates the value investors and financiers place on a support mechanism's ability to create long term and stable revenue security for renewable generators which in turn facilitates access to low cost finance.[66]

The existence and quality of PPAs constitute a key bankability consideration for financiers. Owing to the significant (gigawatt (GW)) scale of many offshore wind farms, sponsors may enter into PPAs with multiple counterparties (including utilities and retailers, corporates and large energy consumers) which pay a flat (indexed) rate for generation output over a fixed term (typically up to 20 years).[67] Lenders will preference long-term contracts with creditworthy counterparties, and may seek to manage offtake risk (such as market volatility or counterparty downgrade) by requiring additional contractual protections in the form of credit support and performance guarantees.[68]

4. Financing Structures

Typical financing structures deployed internationally in support of large-scale energy projects include on-balance sheet (equity), holding company, traditional (asset level) project financing and multilateral (governmental) financing. Whilst these forms of financing may be common to both oil and gas and offshore wind projects, the different characteristics (and so risk profile) of offshore wind means that different factors are at play – these are discussed in the sections below.

A. On-balance Sheet

Sponsor–contributed equity (via corporate loans and share issuances) from balance sheets is a common form of financing for offshore wind, with sponsors retaining construction risk. Refinancing may occur post-completion (with cheaper debt finance) via sale of a non-controlling interest in the project. Equity providers are compensated by way of dividends for their investment – where expected equity returns exceed required

[63] Tezel and Hensgens (n 61).

[64] LCOE is an economic measure used to compare the lifetime costs of generating electricity across various generation technologies – it includes upfront capital costs, O&M costs and disposition costs – see Santash Raikar, and Seabron Adamson 'Renewable energy finance in the international context' (2020) *Renewable Energy Finance.*

[65] Simon Virley, Bridget Beals and James Dennis, *Blown away – CFD Round 3 delivers record low price for offshore wind* (KPMG, September 2019) assets.kpmg.com/content/dam/kpmg/uk/pdf/2019/09/kpmg-blown-away.pdf.

[66] ibid.

[67] Keane, Zhou and Guthrie (n 37).

[68] ibid.

hurdle rates, investors will be incentivised to invest (as risk adjusted returns will be deemed to be acceptable).[69]

On-balance sheet financing for offshore wind projects may be preferred by well capitalised large utilities (as well as multinational oil and gas participants) with substantial lines of revenue and a desire to retain autonomy during the capital-intensive construction phase. Following construction, capital may be reallocated to other opportunities by financing (or refinancing) with cheaper third party debt.[70] Such operations phase financing may occur before construction is complete, with the benefit of construction guarantees and non-recourse debt (or 'HoldCo' financing, see Section 4(B)). Utilities can then look to schedule final investment decision (FID) without involving external financing.[71]

B. HoldCo Financing

HoldCo financing structures have been increasingly adopted by infrastructure equity investors in recent years, with such investors using HoldCo facilities to fund acquisitions or recycle equity investments.[72] Institutional investors and financiers with higher risk appetites may also provide HoldCo loans to achieve higher returns.[73] For offshore wind projects, HoldCo may be used to refinance post-construction capex, thereby providing sponsors with access to more diversified sources of debt.

The structurally subordinated nature of HoldCo financings means that lenders have no direct recourse to the project's operating asset.[74] Debt service obligations are satisfied from distributions made upstream from the underlying assets, with the HoldCo lender's security package limited to security over shares held in the project company set up for the wind farm (see section 6).[75] Given the limitations of such security, financiers will typically require a 'direct agreement' with the operator utility, whereby the utility agrees to certain obligations concerning its dual role as owner and operator of the project that provides the requisite assurance to lenders that the project will be operated in a commercially acceptable manner.[76]

From a bankability perspective, HoldCo financing an operations-phase offshore wind farm is less challenging as the project is effectively 'de-risked' from a construction perspective, with offtake revenue available to calculate debt serviceability. Strong sponsors can therefore negotiate favourable financing terms, thereby reducing the extent to which tripartite agreements may be required (see section 6 below) with due diligence also less onerous.[77]

[69] Tezel and Hensgens (n 61).

[70] Guillet (n 8).

[71] ibid.

[72] Herbert Smith Freehills, *Part 26A Restructuring Plans and HoldCo Financings* (20 July 2021) www.herbertsmithfreehills.com/latest-thinking/part-26a-restructuring-plans-and-holdco-financings.

[73] ibid.

[74] Keane, Zhou and Guthrie (n 37).

[75] Guillet (n 8).

[76] ibid.

[77] Keane, Zhou and Guthrie (n 37).

C. Project Finance

Whilst HoldCo financing structures are frequently employed in offshore wind projects, traditional (asset level) project financings also remain common. As discussed in Section 2(A), project finance debt is provided pre-construction (so lenders accept construction risk) whilst post-construction finance (via a HoldCo or some other entity) may involve both debt and equity. Project finance debt is serviced from the project's operating cashflows – lenders have security over (and direct recourse) to the project's underlying assets and typically require tripartite agreements with material project counterparties (such as the turbine supply contractor) to enable various step-in and cure rights in the event of a default.

As noted in Section 2(A), project financed offshore wind farms require bankable underlying cash flows – financiers will therefore preference those projects which have long-term offtake arrangements with credible counterparties.[78] The amount of required revenues will largely be a function of debt-to-equity ratios (see Section 4(C)(i)) and the credit strength of sponsors. Offtakes involving 'take or pay' contracts will be preferred, where the offtaker remains always liable to take delivery of the wind farm's generated electricity (or otherwise pays an agreed amount).[79]

i. Debt Sizing and Pricing

Lenders will generally rely on dual criteria to quantify the amount of project finance debt they are willing to provide to an offshore wind project.[80] The first criterion (leverage) links the project's total overall cost with the proportion of finance lenders are willing to provide. Leverage is measured by a project's 'debt-to-equity ratio' (for example, 70:30) and provides the requisite assurance that investors possess sufficient interest (or 'skin in the game') to ensure the project is able to be constructed on time and on budget and operated commercially. Second, lenders analyse the project's expected operating revenues to service the debt. Determining the sizing of debt depends on a number of assumptions. Probabilistic wind studies (to determine potential revenues during a wind farm's operations) involve differing probability levels – as discussed in Section 2(B)(ii), sponsors may preference the central P50 case, while lenders will typically prefer lower (more conservative) P90 levels, measured over one or more years.[81] Revenues are also a factor of WTG availability (and associated performance) guaranteed by the WTG manufacturer. O&M costs can be both planned (anticipated) and unplanned (reactive), and may themselves involve assumptions regarding the frequency and type of intervention required, as well as expected cost.

Once debt sizing assumptions have been agreed, lenders and the project's sponsor need to negotiate and agree on the debt service coverage ratio (DSCR) – this represents the ratio of cash available over a given period (often expressed as earnings before interest, taxes, depreciation and amortization (EBITDA)) to the repayment profile (principal

[78] Guthrie (n 48).
[79] ibid.
[80] Guillet (n 8).
[81] Keane, Zhou and Guthrie (n 37).

plus interest) acceptable to lenders.[82] The pricing of debt (or 'margin') is effectively the sum of two components – an underlying variable interest rate (such as LIBOR[83] or EURIBOR,[84] being the cost banks are charged to borrow money on the relevant inter-bank market) plus the bank's own margin (or remuneration).[85] Unlike their oil and gas equivalents, offshore wind projects involve essentially capped revenue lines – this makes it challenging to accept interest rate variability. Sponsors will therefore try to 'hedge' variable interest rates by 'swapping' them for a fixed long-term number – this is generally executed on financial close and will determine the final amount of debt given to the project as well as the amount of interest to be paid.[86]

D. Multi-sourced Financing from Multilateral Government Agencies

Governments around the world may provide sanctioned export credits through Export Credit Agencies (ECAs) in support of national exporters competing for offshore sale revenues. Support can be in the form of credits to foreign buyers, refinancing or interest-rate support, or as insurance or guarantee cover for credits provided by private financial institutions.[87] ECA support is a common component of the financing structures of offshore wind projects in many jurisdictions around the world. Given the nascency of many of these jurisdictions, sponsors will likely source components and technical expertise from abroad, thereby triggering eligibility for ECAs to participate. Whilst domestic financial institutions may express a strong interest in financing the local offshore wind sector, the capital intensity of these projects means that multi-sourced financings (including commercial debt, ECA support and funding from domestic multilateral government agencies) are required.[88] If ECAs do participate in offshore wind financings, their participation typically takes the form of a separate ECA tranche or credit enhancement through guaranteeing a percentage of the underlying debt.[89]

5. Equity

In structuring financing packages for renewable energy projects, it is common for equity to be funded after debt, with equity – like instruments such as letters of credit

[82] Guillet (n 8).

[83] The London Inter-Bank Offered Rate is an interest rate average calculated from estimates submitted by leading banks in London.

[84] The Euro Interbank Offered Rate is based on the average interest rate at which a panel of European banks borrow funds from one another.

[85] Guillet (n 8).

[86] Given that swap markets are quite liquid, it is at least possible to have a reasonable idea of where the interest rate will be in advance – see Guillet (n 8).

[87] See OECD, *Recommendation of the Council on Common Approaches for Officially Supported Export Credits and Environmental and Social Due Diligence* (The 'Common Approaches'), OECD/LEGAL/0393.

[88] In Australia, these include the Australian Renewable Energy Agency (ARENA), the Clean Energy Finance Corporation (CEFC) and the Northen Australian Infrastructure Facility (NAIF).

[89] Keane, Zhou and Guthrie (n 37).

(from banks) and/or parent company guarantees (from developers) often required in support of such delayed contributions. Compared to other asset classes involving EPC wraps (such as onshore wind or oil and gas projects) the increased complexity and capital intensity of offshore wind farms means that upfront (or at least pro-rated) equity contributions may be mandated by financiers. Subordinated short-term equity bridge loans may further enhance otherwise marginal project economics.[90]

As noted in Section 2(B)(v), offshore WTGs are typically commissioned in stages – sponsors will therefore need to negotiate whether pre-completion revenues (PCRs) are to be excluded from a project's 'cost-to-complete' test until the expiry of a certain period of time (such as after conversion of the construction facility into the O&M facility). Sponsors may be comfortable in excluding PCRs from financial models where they are insignificant and the construction phase is short – offshore wind farms can however involve long construction periods and (in the leadup to commissioning) generate significant PCRs. Such PCRs may be categorised as equity and included within the project's forward-looking cost-to-complete test – this lowers the amount of 'real' equity contributions and improves the economics of the project. The difficulty of reliably forecasting PCRs means that financiers may be prepared to accommodate material PCRs, but only on a very conservative (P90) basis.[91]

A fully constructed offshore wind farm subsidised by a credible long-term support mechanism (such as a CfD) and involving a creditworthy counterparty (such as a major utility) is an essentially derisked financing option, making it an attractive proposition for equity investors against which more riskier opportunities (such as assumption of construction risk or involvement of debt) can be compared.[92] Expected internal rates of return for investing in an operating offshore wind farm have declined over the years, with 2022 rates around the 5–6 per cent range for unlevered (debt free) investments; HoldCo financings can deliver slightly higher returns (of around 7 per cent) whilst acceptance of construction risk can deliver higher returns again (between 8–9 per cent).[93] Investing in fully constructed and approved (debt free) projects may deliver returns of between 12–15 per cent, whilst investing in an already operating offshore wind project may deliver between 20–25 per cent returns.[94] Such consistent returns compare favourably to the inherent volatility of investing in oil and gas investments, with the rate of return in oil projects (between 2010 and 2022) varying between losses of over 45 per cent and gains of 55 per cent (with crude oil returns of almost 7 per cent).[95]

[90] Jill Christie (née Concannon), James Greene, Gilles Teerlinck, Anna Soroka, Callie Wallace and Phil Houten, *The basics of bridge loans*, White & Case (4 July 2022) www.lexology.com/library/detail.aspx?g=f04ccd4f-4a5d-4c0e-aca0-47596ac6402a.

[91] Keane, Zhou and Guthrie (n 37).

[92] Guillet (n 8).

[93] ibid.

[94] Key assumptions that can affect these figures include the duration (lifetime) of the asset, operational performance (availability levels, technical losses), wind resource used (P50, P75, P90), debt terms, long-term power prices, evolution of operating costs and insurance costs – see Guillet (n 8).

[95] Statistica, *Return rate on crude oil investments worldwide from 2010 to 2022* (2023) www.statista.com/statistics/825581/returns-on-crude-oil-investments-worldwide/#:~:text=Crude%20oil%20is%20a%20volatile,returns%20amounted%20to%206.71%20percent.

6. Security

As noted in Section 4(B), HoldCo financings exclude direct recourse to the operational assets of an offshore wind farm, with security typically constrained to a general security over HoldCo and the shares it holds in the project company.[96] In asset level project financings, however, financiers will typically obtain security over the project's assets in the form of an (all asset) general security, which may then be subject to registration depending on the jurisdiction (mortgages may also be effected over any real property).[97] Financiers will generally look to acquire suitable step-in rights via negotiated tripartite or direct agreements with material project counterparties.

It is instructive to briefly compare potential security interest arrangements available to project financiers in two immature offshore wind jurisdictions, Norway and Australia. Under Norwegian law, a security interest may only be created over an asset pursuant to the Liens Act.[98] Financiers may take security in the borrower's shares, over bank account claims and insurances, charges over trade receivables, operating assets and step-in rights via direct agreements with material counterparties parties.[99]

In Norway, floating and fixed bottom wind turbines are treated differently. Floating turbines may be registered individually under the Norwegian ordinary ship register (NOR) as an 'other floating device' under the Maritime Act, and may then be mortgaged under the Liens Act and Maritime Act.[100] The Liens Act currently provides that charges over the operating assets of the project company exclude floating turbines – fixed turbines do not therefore constitute registerable movable property, cannot be mortgaged and form part of the wind farm's operating assets.[101]

Onshore Norwegian WTGs are subject to the financier's charge over the borrower's rights in the real property upon which the wind farm resides – this is not possible for offshore Norwegian WTGs as the seabed is not subject to private property rights.[102] Floating turbines have greater intrinsic market value than their fixed equivalents as floating turbines can be relocated – mortgaging fixed WTGs is therefore less important than creating a security interest in the licence along with the turbines themselves.[103]

The Norwegian Ministry of Petroleum and Energy is actively considering the efficacy of treating floating and fixed bottom offshore wind installations equally, thereby permitting both types of turbines to be registered under NOR.

In Australia, rules and regulations governing the registration and perfection of mortgages over installations located beyond the three nautical mile coastal exclusion limit are also still under development. There are similarities between the legislation governing

[96] Keane, Zhou and Guthrie (n 37).
[97] ibid.
[98] Siren Skalstad, Alendar Severance and Andreas Helle, *Security when financing offshore wind projects in Norway* (DLA Piper, 28 March 2023) norway.dlapiper.com/no/nyhet/security-when-financing-offshore-wind-projects-norway.
[99] ibid.
[100] ibid.
[101] ibid.
[102] ibid.
[103] ibid.

Australian offshore wind projects (being the Offshore Electricity Infrastructure Act 2021 (Cth)) and oil and gas regulatory frameworks. The National Offshore Petroleum Titles Administrator (NOPTA) is the entity proposed to manage the administration of Australian offshore wind licences and registers – mortgages effected over offshore wind projects beyond the three nautical mile limit will likely need to be registered with NOPTA to be perfected.[104]

The extent to which security can be taken over Australian offshore WTGs is presently untested. In contrast to their onshore counterparts (where financiers may obtain a mortgage over the land on which the turbines sit) 'typical' security interest/mortgage perfection procedures over floating or fixed WTGs will not apply.[105] Perfection of security interests through the project company's entry into general security arrangements with subsequent registration under the Personal Property Securities Act 2009 (Cth) (PPSA) may be a viable approach.[106]

7. Financing Offshore Oil and Gas versus Offshore Wind Projects: Trends, Opportunities and Hurdles

Offshore wind's global supply chains, which include leading global turbine manufacturers and marine contractors, have recently suffered significant financial impairments.[107] Rather than an availability of capital, increasing pressure on already strained supply chains (characterised by insufficient specialist installation vessels and experienced marine contractors) may well be the key limiting factor affecting the sector's short to medium term growth prospects,[108] In addition to supply chains, the sector also needs to address the structural problems associated with relying on highly leveraged project finance. Renewable energy developers have historically led the way, however experienced oil and gas super-majors are becoming more involved. Limited recourse leveraged debt deployed to fund the assets and future cashflows of an offshore wind farm places project financiers and developers in a powerful negotiating position in terms of flowing-down risks to the sector's supply chains[109] – weak global supply chains exacerbate this imbalance.

Like oil and gas rigs, the assembly of offshore wind farm componentry is generally well understood by contractors, however the operational risk profile for wind assets has tended to increase through the evolution of ever-larger turbines (from 3MW to over 15MW over the past decade). This drives a corresponding increased scale of foundations, towers, turbine blades and balance of plant, with ever increasing investment

[104] Anchustegui and Hunter (n 7).
[105] Skalstad, Severance and Helle (n 98).
[106] ibid.
[107] Valentina Kretzschmar, *Why Are Oil Majors Investing In Offshore Wind?* (Wood Mackenzie, 6 April 2021) www.forbes.com/sites/woodmackenzie/2021/04/06/why-are-oil-majors-investing-in-offshore-wind/?sh=441687863ffa.
[108] Allen Leatt, *Project Finance International: Unsustainable Offshore Wind*, IMCA (24 May 2023) www.imca-int.com/published-articles/unsustainable-offshore-wind/.
[109] ibid.

requirements.[110] The operational risk profile for oil and gas rigs has also increased over the same time frame, however this has been more a function of increasingly challenging exploration risk profiles rather than pure asset size.

A standard form of contract is yet to be developed for the offshore wind industry. Contractors and developers have tended to use a highly modified form of the well-known International Federation of Consulting Engineers (FIDIC)[111] onshore civil engineering contract model that is quite inappropriate for offshore facilities and essentially unheard of in the oil and gas world – a world where contractors are experienced and competent in successfully delivering fully wrapped large EPC projects (using FIDIC's template form of EPC contract).[112] As discussed in Section 2(A)(i), offshore contracting mechanisms are typically either disaggregated into various transportation, supply and installation services or integrated into all-encompassing engineering, procurement, construction and installation (EPCI) arrangements. Both forms of contracting have served the oil and gas industry for decades and are well understood by market participants, including financiers and insurers. Developers have expected contractors using disaggregated offshore wind contracting models to accept design warranties for equipment that they have neither designed nor procured – this would be normal in wrapped EPCI contractual arrangements but is not appropriate in split contracting models.

In terms of project cost trajectories, poor economics would typically trigger price corrections (and inflation) resulting in reduced demand. This is already occurring in the US, where many developers are looking to renegotiate their PPAs, putting project FIDs at risk.[113] However, simply increasing prices (thereby making the industry less competitive) is not the solution – a better approach involves taking unnecessary costs out of the system. The North Sea oil and gas industry faced similar challenges in the 1990s, with the high cost of money creating an environment ill-suited to development. The introduction of the 'Cost Reduction Initiative In the New Era' (CRINE) changed this paradigm, and created novel ways for developers to collaborate with supply chains to remove unnecessary costs from budgets.[114]

The success of the CRINE programme led to the creation of a suite of standard contracting models under the banner of LOGIC (Leading Oil & Gas Industry Competitiveness) which remains in use by the oil and gas sector today.[115] Analogous to LOGIC, the offshore wind sector could support a 'Leading Offshore Wind Industry Competitiveness' programme.[116] Developers, contractors and suppliers would attempt to align on project cost, schedule and quality objectives, thereby allocating risks and rewards appropriately. The International Marine Contractors' Association (IMCA) has

[110] For example, a high-end foundation installation vessel can cost up to US$1bn, and a wind turbine installation vessel in the order of US$300m–$400m or more depending on specification, see Leatt (n 108).

[111] fidic.org/.

[112] Leatt (n 108).

[113] US Department of Energy *Offshore Wind Market Report: 2023 edition* (24 August 2023).

[114] Paul Spaven, *Cost Reduction: Initiative for the New Era.* Paper presented at the SPE Offshore Europe, Aberdeen, United Kingdom, September 1993. doi.org/10.2118/26728-MS.

[115] See: www.apollo.io/companies/Leading-Oil---Gas-Industry-Competitiveness--LOGIC-/5e573526a8a12d0001761194.

[116] Leatt (n 108).

developed a set of principles designed to 'level-up' the allocation of risk – offshore wind project financiers could also be part of these discussions.[117]

The availability of capital for offshore wind farms will ultimately be a function of perceived bankability, which in turn is predominantly a function of certainty of revenue lines enabled through PPA arrangements. PPAs involving creditworthy offtakers augment the stability and predictability of offshore wind revenues – this is a natural hedge to increased merchant exposure as might be associated with gradual removal of government – sponsored support mechanisms like FiTs, green certificates and CfDs.[118] The replacement of government – sponsored support mechanisms with consequent exposure to wholesale electricity market price uncertainty also increases risk for capital providers. As recent global geopolitical events (such as the wars in Ukraine and the Middle East) have amply demonstrated, global energy and electricity markets are inherently volatile, with revenues from unsubsidised or unsupported offshore wind farms also becoming less predictable. Long-term PPAs with creditworthy offtakers are a natural hedge, however will inevitably take time to fully mature in nascent jurisdictions like Australia, South Korea, Vietnam, India, Brazil and Columbia. All of this delivers a higher cost of capital for offshore wind facilities in immature jurisdictions, with adverse effects for risk-averse equity investors.[119]

Merchant price risk associated with non – contracted (or partially contracted) projects is a key issue for project financiers to consider when assessing an offshore wind project's bankability. Such risks are in some ways analogous to the risks of a proposed or newly commissioned offshore oil or gas facility failing to deliver expected output. Increased volatility of offshore wind revenue streams arising from non-contracted generation increases the risk of project developers defaulting on repayment obligations. Financiers may seek to mitigate such risks via increased interest rates, higher DSCR ratios, additional cash sweeps or reduced repayment tenor profiles, all of which decrease leverage by requiring equity to contribute greater amounts.[120]

Unlike oil and gas projects, the perceived risk of offshore wind has tended to decrease over the past decade due to a number of factors. First, project financing has increased over this period – as awareness and understanding of sector-specific construction and technology risks has increased, project financing has incrementally replaced on-balance sheet financing.[121] Second, project finance leverage (in the form of debt to equity ratios) has increased from its early levels of around 60 per cent to around 80 per cent in more recent years, thereby reducing overall capital costs and a further sign of increasing confidence.[122] Third, interest rate spreads (between the relevant base interbank rate and bank's interest rates) associated with offshore wind debt financing have declined over the same period, providing further evidence of increased financier familiarity.[123]

[117] ibid.
[118] Tezel and Hensgens (n 61).
[119] ibid.
[120] ibid.
[121] ibid.
[122] ibid.
[123] In 2011, spreads were still roughly 325 bps above LIBOR – by 2019 they had moved below 150 bps – see Tezel and Hensgens (n 61).

8. Conclusion

All forms of offshore energy projects – be they oil and gas or wind – involve significant long-term commitments, both financially and operationally. Whilst such projects may rely on well-known and established funding approaches (such as project finance), the unique nature of constructing and operating offshore wind assets – together with increased interface risk associated with disaggregated contracting packages – means financiers need to adopt a different lens when assessing bankability. As seen with other emerging asset classes with significant capex requirements (such as green hydrogen, pumped hydro and energy from waste), the financing terms for offshore wind projects will likely involve strict debt sizing criteria, a range of financial covenants and comprehensive contingency and security packages, particularly in those jurisdictions where the sector remains nascent. Sponsors will likely preference stacked capital structures involving a variety of government-sponsored support mechanisms and offtake arrangements to mitigate risk and enhance internal bankability.

On the demand side, governments can deploy supportive mechanisms to price negative externalities associated with a failure to address greenhouse gas emissions – this can help unlock demand for renewable (green) electricity and reduce merchant price risk. On the supply side, transitioning towards a subsidy-free market with full (merchant) exposure to wholesale electricity prices will nonetheless require facilitative and supportive policy from government. Zero-subsidy environments lead to an increased risk profile for offshore wind, delivering an increased cost (and reduced availability) of capital. This is not necessarily problematic as it reflects normal pricing uncertainty in financial markets, which at least aims to ensure efficient allocation of capital. The potential residual problem is that zero-subsidies might affect the financial viability of future offshore wind projects to such an extent that net zero targets are compromised.

Absent effective and liquid PPA markets, the possibilities for hedging merchant price risk in offshore wind projects are limited. In such environments, it is unclear how many merchant projects offshore wind developers will be able to fund (either via project finance and/or on balance sheet). Whilst there have been successful zero-subsidy tenders in mature jurisdictions like the EU, there may be limited appetite from potential financiers to take on the risks associated with fully merchant projects (and likely no appetite in nascent markets). It would appear that in the sort to medium term, tried and tested support mechanisms and offtake arrangements (such as CfDs and PPAs) will remain key ingredients to financing a commercially viable offshore wind market. Without a change in contracting strategy to reduce the risk premium and economic wastage evident in the offshore wind sector, ambitious net zero – related targets set by governments and championed by investors and developers appear unlikely to be achieved. Contracting initiatives such as that proposed by the IMCA are informed by what has worked for the oil and gas sector and should be encouraged into the future.

PART III

Offshore Energy: Complex Infrastructure and Overarching Conclusions

13

From a Mature Offshore Oil and Gas Sector to an Embryonic Alternative Energy Sector: The US Experience

KEITH B HALL

1. Introduction

The US offshore oil and gas industry is mature. It is one of the most mature, if not the most mature, offshore oil and gas industries in the world.

In contrast to the long history of offshore oil and gas development off the coast of the United States, the US has only recently begun deploying offshore wind projects, and various other countries are further along in developing offshore wind energy. Thus, while the US experience in offshore oil and gas can provide lessons for other jurisdictions considering offshore oil and gas development, the US cannot provide a case study of a mature offshore wind energy industry. However, the energy transition is also ongoing in US waters. Currently, the US is attempting to rapidly expand offshore wind energy facilities. Additionally, the US is only in the very early stages of other offshore energy projects. Some licences have been granted for test projects for hydrokinetic energy production, and a couple of states have granted offshore, subsurface pore space leases for CCS projects, though those projects have not yet received all required permits, much less begun construction or operation. The challenges that that the US has encountered in its attempt at a rapid development for offshore wind and other offshore energy forms may be instructive in other jurisdictions, especially those with a hydrocarbon past that seek to move towards low-carbon energy solutions. These developments are discussed in this chapter which aims to show the complex interplay between different offshore energy forms and the regulatory bridge between technologies.

2. History of US Offshore Energy Production

The United States has been producing energy offshore for more than a century. Offshore oil and gas drilling began as early as 1896, with drilling that was performed off piers that extended from the coast of Summerland, California.[1] In 1921, California enacted legislation that created an offshore leasing programme.[2] By 1929, over 850 wells had been drilled off the coast of California.

Gulf Oil began drilling in Caddo Lake in Louisiana in about 1910.[3] Although these were drilled in inland waters, rather than offshore, these wells are significant to offshore development because the platforms used in this drilling are believed to have been the first over-water, freestanding platforms in the US.[4] Gulf Oil ultimately drilled more than about 278 wells in Caddo Lake, and in doing so the company developed techniques for drilling from wooden piles that would later be used to drill freestanding wells in US coast waters.

Indian Oil Company drilled the first freestanding well off the California coast in 1932.[5] A few years later, companies began drilling freestanding wells in the Gulf of Mexico, primarily off the coast of Louisiana. In 1937, for example, Pure Oil and Superior Oil drilled a well about a mile off Louisiana's coast,[6] and in 1946 Magnolia Petroleum drilled a well six miles off the Louisiana coast.[7]

Since these early forays into offshore development, thousands of wells have been drilled off the coasts of the United States. These wells are typically drilled pursuant to oil and gas 'leases' that are granted to private companies by either the 'federal'[8] government, if the well is drilled in 'federal waters' (generally, an area more than three nautical miles offshore), or by the nearest 'state',[9] if the well is drilled in 'state waters' (generally, an area within three nautical miles of shore).[10] A majority of the wells drilled in federal waters have been drilled off the coast of Louisiana. In addition to the federal leases, there are state leases in the waters nearer shore off the coasts of Louisiana, Texas, Mississippi, Alabama, Alaska, and California.

More recently, the US government has begun granting offshore wind leases for federal waters, and the State of Louisiana has granted leases for offshore wind development in state waters. There also has been interest and some initial activity relating to offshore carbon sequestration and 'hydrokinetic' projects that would generate power from waves or tides.

[1] Ann Scarborough Bull and Milton S Love, 'Worldwide oil and gas platform decommissioning: A review of practices and reefing options' (2019) 168 *Ocean and Coastal Management* 274, 289; William L Leffler et al, *Deepwater Petroleum Exploration and Production: a Nontechnical Guide*, 2nd edn (PennWell, 2011) 6.

[2] Scarborough Bull and Love (n 1). In the United States, the instrument by which the owner of mineral rights grants a company the right to explore for oil and gas is typically an oil and gas 'lease'. Such 'leases' are generally not governed by landlord-tenant law, but nevertheless are typically called 'leases'. In contrast to the circumstances in most other countries, in the United States the right to explore for oil and gas typically belongs to the landowner, rather than the sovereign. However, the individual states (the main subnational unit of government in the US) typically own the bottoms of inland navigable waters, and also effectively own the waters and water bottoms for the first three nautical miles off the coasts, with exceptions being that Texas owns the offshore area for the first marine leagues and that Florida's territory likewise extends three marine leagues into the Gulf of Mexico (but only three nautical miles into the Atlantic Ocean).

[3] Leffler et al (n 1) 3.

[4] Dianne M Lindstedt et al, *History of Oil and Gas Development in Coastal Louisiana* (La. Geological Survey, 1991) 15.

[5] Leffler et al (n 1) 2.

[6] ibid 6.

[7] Ibid 6–7.

[8] In the United States, the national government often is called the 'federal' government.

[9] In the United States, the main subnational units of government are 'states'.

[10] For an explanation of the distinction between federal and state waters, see the section of this chapter that discusses whether federal law or state law applies.

3. Legal Framework and Agencies

The following portion of this chapter discusses the legal framework, beginning with the question of which unit of government will be the primary regulator, and then moving on from there to discuss which level of government controls the area, and which agencies govern.

A. The Relationship between the Federal Government and the States

In the United States the main subnational units of government are 'states'. There are 50 states in the US. Although 'federal' (national) law is supreme, the states retain some degree of sovereignty under principles of federalism, and some matters will be governed by state law, rather than federal law.

Further, as will be discussed in more detail below, the first few miles of offshore waters are 'state waters,' with 'federal waters' starting further seaward. The nearest state is essentially the owner of offshore state waters, and thus will have significant control over whether this area can be used for offshore energy development. Projects located in state waters may be subject to certain federal laws governing maritime matters and navigation, and some generally-applicable federal laws may apply with respect to environmental issues, but the nearest state and its laws will control many questions. Thus, it is important to examine which law applies.

B. Which Level of Government Controls Development

The general rule is that the area located within three nautical miles of US shores constitutes waters of the nearest state. The state effectively owns this area. The area beyond that, to the limit of the US continental shelf, constitutes federal waters. In these areas, federal law and authority is paramount, though the United States Supreme Court has stopped short of stating that the federal government is the 'owner' of that area. But there are exceptions to the three-nautical-mile rule. The two most notable are that Texas waters extend for three marine leagues from its coast,[11] and Florida's waters extend for three marine leagues off its Gulf of Mexico coast (but not off its Atlantic shore, where Florida's waters extend for only three miles).[12] This system of divided authority has an involved history.

The United States Supreme Court has held that, when the US gained its independence from Great Britain, each of the original 13 states separately gained sovereignty over the navigable waters within its borders, and that the states had never ceded that jurisdiction to the federal government.[13] In those states, the state is the owner of the bottoms of

[11] *United States v Louisiana*, 363 US 1, 65, 80 S. Ct. 961, 997 (1960).

[12] *United States v Florida*, 425 US 791, 791-2, 96 S. Ct. 1840 (1976); see also *United States v Louisiana*, 363 US 1, 123, 80 S. Ct. 961, 1027 (1960).

[13] *Martin v Waddell's Lessee*, 41 US 367.

navigable water bottoms. The Court later held that the same rule applied with respect to ownership of water bottoms beneath inland waters within the State of Alabama, even though Alabama was not one of the original 13 states.[14] The Court reached this result based on reasoning that the inland navigable waters of each state must belong to the state because, under the 'Equal Footing' doctrine, states created subsequent to the formation of the United States 'must be admitted into the union on an equal footing with' the original 13 states.[15] Ownership of the bottoms of offshore areas had not yet come into any significant dispute, but, to the extent anyone considered the issue, many legal scholars believed that offshore water bottoms waters would be treated similarly and that those water bottoms would belong to the nearest state.

Eventually, some people would begin to question this rule, and offshore energy production was the catalyst that triggered this reconsideration. By the early 1900s, the states of California, Texas, and Louisiana had each begun granting offshore oil and gas leases, but the amount of offshore activity remained modest, and still virtually no one questioned the individual states' ownership of these offshore areas. Indeed, by some accounts, officials with the US Department of Interior also took the position that the offshore waters were owned by the nearest state. But offshore oil production was growing, and had become very important during World War II. US Secretary of Interior Harold Ickes began lobbying for the federal government to claim ownership of offshore areas.

Ickes' lobbying bore fruit. In September 1945, President Harry S Truman declared that the area beyond the low tide mark was federal territory and subject to management by the United States Department of Interior.[16] At his direction, the US Department of Justice filed lawsuits against California, Texas, and Louisiana, seeking declaratory judgments that the federal government owned and had jurisdiction over the area beyond the low tide mark. This litigation became known as the 'Tidelands litigation.'[17]

In 1947, the United States Supreme Court granted judgment in favour of the federal government in *United States v California*.[18] The court stopped short of stating that the federal government had title to the offshore areas in dispute, but the Court ruled that the federal government had 'paramount' authority over those areas. The Court later issued similar decisions in favour of the federal government in its lawsuits against Texas[19] and Louisiana.[20]

The United States Congress responded with legislation to quitclaim offshore areas to the nearest coastal states, but President Truman vetoed the legislation.[21] Ownership of the offshore areas became an issue in the 1952 US Presidential election, with candidate Dwight D Eisenhower supporting Congressional attempts to quitclaim the offshore area

[14] *Pollard v Hagan*, 44 US 212 (1845).
[15] ibid 216.
[16] Executive Order 9633; see also Proclamation 2667.
[17] For a thorough treatment of the Tidelands litigation and related political disputes, see Ernest R Bartley, *The Tidelands Oil Controversy* (University of Texas Press, 1953).
[18] 333 US 19 (1947).
[19] *United States v Texas*, 70 S. Ct. 918 (1950).
[20] *United States v Louisiana*, 339 US 699, 70 S. Ct. 914 (1950).
[21] Bartley (n 17) 227–28.

to the states, and candidate Adlai Stevenson supporting President Truman's position opposing any quitclaim. Eisenhower won the election in late 1952 and took office in early 1953.

Later in 1953, the Congress passed, and President Eisenhower signed the Submerged Lands Act.[22] It provided that each coastal state could claim as its own territory an area extending for three 'geographic miles' from the shore,[23] and the federal government would recognise such a claim as valid. Further, it provided that states with coasts along the Gulf of Mexico, the federal government would recognise state sovereignty for a greater distance, not to exceed three marine leagues,[24] provided that the state could prove that it claimed such an area as its sovereign territory at the time that the state first was admitted into the union as a state.

Texas and Florida each succeeded in proving they had claimed boundaries at least three marine leagues off their Gulf of Mexico coasts at the time they first became states within the US system. Accordingly, the Supreme Court held that, under the Submerged Lands Act, Texas[25] and Florida were entitled to a border set at three marine leagues from their shores along the Gulf of Mexico.[26] No other states proved that they had claimed borders further than three miles seaward at the time they were admitted into the union. Accordingly, the Supreme Court held that the boundaries of other states may not be set further than three miles seaward from the coast.[27]

In 1953, the Congress also enacted the Outer Continental Shelf Lands Act (OCSLA), which provided a legislative framework for leasing and regulation of oil and gas activities in federal waters of the continental shelf.[28] OCSLA is supplemented with an extensive set of federal regulations promulgated by federal agencies,[29] as well as by guidance documents issued by federal agencies. Later, OCSLA was amended to authorise and control the leasing of federal waters and water bottoms for the development of other sources of energy.[30] Still later, OCSLA was amended to authorise and control the leasing of pore spaces for carbon sequestration beneath federal waters. Thus, OCSLA will control most energy development in federal waters.

In contrast, the individual states are effectively the owner of the offshore areas that constitute state waters. Although some federal laws relating to navigation and other

[22] 43 USC. §§ 1301.

[23] A 'geographic mile' is approximately equal to a nautical mile. Each is about 1.86 kilometers or about 1.15 statutory miles.

[24] A marine league is equal to 3 nautical miles, and each nautical mile is approximately 1.15 geographic miles.

[25] *United States v Louisiana*, 363 US 1, 65 (1960) ('… Texas is entitled to a grant of three leagues from her coast under the Submerged Lands Act.').

[26] *United States v Louisiana*, 363 US 121, 129 (1960) ('We hold that the Submerged Lands Act grants Florida a three-marine-league belt of land under the Gulf, seaward from its coastline, as described in Florida's 1868 Constitution.').

[27] *United States v Louisiana*, 363 US 1, 79 ('We decide now … that Louisiana is entitled to submerged-land rights to a distance no greater than three geographical miles from its coastlines …'), 82 ('We must told that Mississippi is not entitled to rights in submerged lands lying beyond three geographical miles from its coast.'), 82 ('The same reasons applicable to the claims of Louisiana and Mississippi compel us to hold that Alabama is not entitled to rights in submerged lands lying beyond three geographical miles from its coast.').

[28] 43 USC. §§ 1331 et seq.

[29] 30 C.F.R. §§ 550.101 et seq.

[30] The regulations for renewable energy leases in federal waters are found at 30 C.F.R. Part 585.

maritime matters, and some generally applicable federal environmental laws will apply in state waters, state law will govern most issues and the nearest state will determine, in the role of owner, whether it will authorise energy development in state waters, and if so, what the process for authoring offshore projects will be.

C. Which Agencies Regulate?

In most cases, multiple agencies will have some role in regulating any given offshore energy project. Which agencies have a role will depend in part on whether the activity occurs in federal waters or state waters.

i. The Federal Agencies that Regulate Energy Activities in Federal Waters

For many years, the entity that regulated offshore oil and gas activity in federal waters was the Minerals Management Service (MMS), which was part of the US Department of Interior. But MMS was the subject of significant adverse publicity, particularly after the explosion of Transocean's *Deepwater Horizon* drilling rig in April 2010. The rig had been drilling the Macondo well for BP in the Gulf of Mexico. The explosion resulted in the deaths of 11 workers and the largest oil spill in US history. MMS was eventually eliminated and its responsibilities were divided into amongst three new agencies within the Department of Interior. MMS's leasing and lease management duties were delegated to the Bureau of Ocean Energy Management (BOEM). Its duties relating to environmental protection and safety were delegated to the Bureau of Safety and Environmental Enforcement (BSEE).[31] Finally, the collection of payments owed to the federal government with respect to offshore oil and gas leases was delegated to the Office of Natural Resources Revenue, which also collects payments owed to the federal government under leases of onshore federal lands.

Now that OCSLA has been revised to authorise the leasing of federal waters for other types of energy development, as well as for carbon sequestration, BOEM will control the leasing process for those other types of activities, BSEE will govern safety and environmental protection issues relating to those other activities, and ONRR will be the collector of revenue associated with the activities.

ii. Agencies that Regulate Leasing of State Waters

The leasing of state waters for energy development will be controlled by state law and one or more state agencies. For example, the Louisiana State Mineral and Energy Board controls leasing of offshore Louisiana waters for oil and gas activity, carbon

[31] In addition, a new agency within the Department of Interior was formed to collect revenue from the leasing of federal lands – both offshore and onshore. This agency is called the Office of Natural Resources Revenue (ONRR). Prior to the creation of ONRR, BOEMRE had collected revenues for leasing on the federal outer continental shelf.

sequestration, and wind energy projects. The Texas General Land Office controls the leasing of offshore Texas waters. A state-by-state analysis of whether state law authorises offshore energy development, and if so, what state agency would control the leasing process, is beyond the scope of this chapter. Suffice to say, a lawyer advising a client will need to evaluate the law of the relevant state.

4. Offshore Oil and Gas Leasing

Oil and gas activity occurs both in federal waters and in the state waters of various states.

A. Offshore Oil and Gas Leasing in Federal Waters

OCSLA and the regulations promulgated pursuant to OCSLA provide for four distinct stages to offshore oil and gas development in federal waters. These are: (1) the development of a five-year plan by BOEM; (2) lease sales; (3) exploration by the lessee; and (4) development and production of the leased area.[32]

i. Five-year Plans

Pursuant to the US Outer Continental Shelf Land Act, the Bureau of Ocean Energy Management (BOEM) is required to develop successive five-year plans for holding 'lease sales' (bid rounds) covering various offshore areas.[33] OCSLA Typically, one or more lease sales are held each year, with each sale applying to a particular offshore region (for example, the Gulf of Mexico or portion of it, such as the Central Gulf of Mexico, or perhaps an area of the coast of Alaska). In these lease sales, qualifying bidders may submit closed bids for the right to acquire leases covering specific offshore lease 'blocks'. In these lease sales, the federal government typically specifies the language of the lease and a royalty rate in advance of the sale, with bidders competing against one another based on the amount of the signing bonus they offer in their bids.

Under current policy, BOEM does not hold lease sales for federal waters off the nation's Atlantic coast, the portion of the Gulf of Mexico nearest the State of Florida, or the Pacific coast (other than certain Alaskan waters). The 2017–2022 plan, which provides for 11 potential lease sales, with 10 being for the Gulf of Mexico – with one of those scheduled in 2017, two each year during from 2018 through 2021, and one lease sale in 2022 – and one lease sale being scheduled for the Cook Inlet area, off the coast of Alaska, in 2021.

In the past, a new five-year plan was always developed before the prior five-year plan lapsed. In an unprecedented move, however, the President Joseph Biden administration allowed the 2017–2022 five-year plan to lapse without a new plan having been adopted. Later, the administration finalised a 2024–2029 plan calling for just three

[32] *Secretary of the Interior v California*, 464 US 312, 337 (1984).
[33] 43 USC. § 1344(a).

lease sales – one in 2025, one in 2027, and another in 2029.[34] This is the smallest number of lease sales in any prior five-year plan, and the small number of lease sales has been criticised by the oil and gas industry, as well as some others.

ii. Lease Sales

Pursuant to the five-year plan, BOEM will periodically hold 'lease sales'. The dates of lease sales are published in advance, along with a listing of what areas (lease blocks) are being offered for lease. Qualified bidders may submit bids. Typically, BOEM sets a deadline for submitting closed bids. Thus, there is not a live auction with ongoing bidding. Rather, bidders who wish to participate submit a closed bid in advance. On the date of the lease sale, the closed bids are opened, revealing which bid is the highest. Typically, all terms of the lease are set in advance, including a royalty rate that the lessee will owe to the federal on oil and gas production, if any, eventually obtained pursuant to the lease. The bidders compete against each other for who will offer the highest 'bonus' – a flat fee paid in advance for the lease. BOEM is not required to award a lease, but if it does award a lease, it typically must grant the lease to the qualified bidder who bid the highest amount. The award of a lease is not an authorisation to drill, but the lease give the lessee an exclusive right to drill, and generally will be allowed to drill if other requirements are met.

iii. Exploration

Before conducting any exploration pursuant to a lease covering federal waters, the lessee must submit an exploration plan to BOEM and receive approval of that plan.[35] The plan must satisfy various environmental requirements, including being consistent with coastal zone management plan, if any, that the nearest coastal state has developed under the Coastal Zone Management Act and which the federal government has approved.[36]

iv. Development and Production

The fourth stage is development and production. Before developing any hydrocarbon field that has been found during exploration, or producing from that field, the lessee must submit a development and production plan to BOEM and obtain approval for that plan.[37] The plan must be consistent with any applicable state coastal management plans developed and approved pursuant to the Coastal Zone Management Act. In addition, development and production plans cannot be approved without an environmental review pursuant to the National Environmental Policy Act, which is discussed in more detail later in this chapter.

[34] Information regarding the 2024–2029 plan is available on BOEM's website at www.boem.gov/oil-gas-energy/national-program/national-ocs-oil-and-gas-leasing-program.
[35] 43 USC. § 1340.
[36] 43 USC. § 1340(c)(2). The Coastal Zone Management Act is discussed in more detail later in this chapter.
[37] 43 USC. § 1351(a).

B. Offshore Oil and Gas Leasing in State Waters

Lease sales for state waters are conducted by state governments. In recent history, Louisiana and Texas have been the most active in granting offshore oil and gas leases for their state waters, but a thorough discussion of state leasing is beyond the scope of this chapter.

5. Offshore Wind Energy

Offshore wind leasing and development is occurring in federal waters and in the states waters of certain states.

A. Offshore Wind in Federal Waters

Although OCSLA was enacted to govern oil and gas development in federal waters, it has been amended to authorise BOEM to grant leases for other forms of energy development, including offshore wind farms in federal waters. BOEM has a standard form that it now uses for wind leases. The form is available online.[38] Examples of executed leases also are available online.[39]

The United States is behind some other nations in developing offshore wind energy, but the President Joseph Biden administration, which took office in January 2021, has stated goals of constructing 30 gigawatts of offshore wind energy by 2030, and 15 gigawatts of floating offshore wind energy by 2035. The first two commercial scale wind projects in federal waters was approved in 2021.[40] As of July 2024, BOEM had held four offshore lease sales, including lease sales for areas off the coasts of New York, New Jersey, and the Carolinas, as well as offshore in the Pacific and Gulf of Mexico, and had approved eight commercial-scale wind projects for federal waters.[41]

On 24 April 2024, Secretary of the Interior Deb Haaland announced a five-year wind leasing schedule.[42] The schedule anticipates up to 12 potential wind lease sales through 2028, including

- four potential lease sales in 2024 (for areas in the Central Atlantic, Gulf of Maine, Gulf of Mexico, and off the coast of Oregon);

[38] See BOEM-0008, 'Commercial Lease of Submerged Lands for Renewable Energy Development on the Outer Continental Shelf (OCS)', www.boem.gov/BOEM-0008/.

[39] See BOEM, 'Lease and Grant Information' (including a list of leases with links to copies of the leases), www.boem.gov/renewable-energy/lease-and-grant-information.

[40] These were the Vineyard Wind project, an 800-megawatt project approved 11 May 2021, and the South Fork Project, a 130-megawatt project approved 24 November 2021.

[41] US Dept. of Interior, 'Biden-Harris Administration Announces Offshore Wind Lease Sale in Central Atlantic) (June 28, 2024), www.doi.gov/pressreleases/biden-harris-administration-announces-offshore-wind-lease-sale-central-atlantic.

[42] US Dept. of Interior, 'Secretary Haaland Announces New Five-Year Offshore Wind Leasing Schedule' (Apr. 24, 2024). A copy of a statement regarding the announcement is available at https://www.doi.gov/pressreleases/secretary-haaland-announces-new-five-year-offshore-wind-leasing-schedule.

- one in 2015 (in the Gulf of Mexico);
- one in 2026 (in the Central Atlantic);
- two in 2027 (in the Gulf of Mexico and New York Bight); and
- four in 2028 (off the coast of California, off the coast of a US territory, in the Gulf of Mexico, and off the coast of Hawaii).

The Department of Interior followed-up on the plan on 28 June 2024, by announcing a lease sale for the Central Atlantic, which would be held by auction on 14 August 2024.[43] The Department asserted that the lease sale could lead to 6.3 gigawatts of electricity generation and that this would be enough to power 2.2 million homes. The area included in the lease sale includes areas off the coasts of Delaware and Maryland, and an area off the coast of Virginia.

B. Offshore Wind in State Waters

The leasing of state waters for wind energy projects is being done or considered in certain states. For example, California is considering a proposed wind project that would be located in state waters. Further, as of mid-2024, the State of Louisiana has granted two offshore wind leases for state waters.[44]

The State of Louisiana granted the two leases through its State Mineral and Energy Board, based on direct negotiations, rather than a public bidding process.[45] One of the agreements granted by the State of Louisiana was issued to Cajun Wind LLC in December 2023, covering an area in the Gulf of Mexico, just off the coast of Cameron Parish. A copy of the lease is available online.[46] The other offshore wind lease granted by the State of Louisiana was likewise granted in December 2023. This one was granted to DOW LA Gulf Wind LLC, for an area off the coasts of Terrebonne and Lafourche Parishes. A copy is available online.[47]

6. Carbon Sequestration

In the United States, the right to use subsurface pore spaces for storage of fluids generally belongs to the landowner. Thus, for offshore areas seaward of state waters, the

[43] US Dept. of Interior, 'Biden-Harris Administration Announces Offshore Wind Lease Sale in Central Atlantic) (28 June 2024). A press release regarding the announcement is available at www.doi.gov/pressreleases/biden-harris-administration-announces-offshore-wind-lease-sale-central-atlantic.

[44] The agreements are called 'operating agreements', based on the statutory authority on which the Louisiana State Mineral and Energy Board relied when it granted the agreements, but in substance, the agreements are leases.

[45] The Louisiana Mineral and Energy Board generally uses a public bidding process for oil and gas leases, but it is using direct negotiation for the early wind leases. It also used direct negotiation for the early CCS pore space leases.

[46] A copy is available at www.dnr.louisiana.gov/assets/OMR/media/forms_pubs/Cajun_Wind_FINAL_AGMT_SIGNED.pdf.

[47] A copy is available at www.dnr.louisiana.gov/assets/OMR/media/forms_pubs/WE002_Dow_Wind_Energy_Agreement.pdf.

federal government controls the use of pore spaces. The right to control the use of pore spaces beneath the bottoms of offshore waters generally belongs to the nearest state for state waters.

A. Carbon Sequestration in Federal Waters

Section 40307 of the Bipartisan Infrastructure Law enacted in November 2022 amended OCSLA to authorise BOEM to grant leases, easements, or rights-of-way agreements for purposes 'related to the injection of a carbon dioxide stream into sub-seabed geologic formations for the purpose of long-term carbon sequestration' or CCS.[48] So far, BOEM has not conducted any lease sales for CCS or even developed rules and regulations to govern CCS in federal waters. The Bipartisan Infrastructure Law directed the Department of the Interior to promulgate regulations to carry out this amendment by November 2023, but as of summer 2024 the Department of Interior was still working on regulations and had not yet published proposed rules. BOEM has participated in workshops,[49] made several presentations,[50] and published an assessment of carbon storage potential on the US outer continental shelf.[51]

B. Carbon Sequestration in State Waters

At least two states – Louisiana and Texas – have granted leases for use of pore spaces beneath state waters for CCS.[52] As with oil and gas leasing, state law controls whether pore spaces beneath state waters can be leased for CCS, and if so, what the rules governing the leasing process are, though this leasing may be subject to certain federal laws regarding navigation and certain federal environmental statutes.

The Louisiana pore space agreement was granted by the Louisiana State Mineral and Energy Board to Venture Global CCS Cameron, LLC in September 2022, pursuant to the Board's authority under Louisiana Revised Statute 30:209. The agreement covers an area in Louisiana state waters in the Gulf of Mexico, off Cameron Parish. The agreement

[48] This amendment is codified at 43 USC. § 1337(p)(1)(E). 43 USC. § 1337 is sometimes called 'subsection 8' of OCSLA.

[49] An example of a presentation made by BOEM at a workshop in 2022 is available at www.boem.gov/about-boem/regulations-guidance/boem-cs-sseb-reg-workshop-nola.

[50] Links to PDFs of several PowerPoint presentations made by BOEM are available at www.boem.gov/about-boem/regulations-guidance/carbon-sequestration.

[51] See BOEM, 'BOEM Carbon Storage National Assessment Methodology', www.boem.gov/node/35601; BOEM, 'Atlantic CCS Assessment: An Introduction and Status Update' (April 2023), www.boem.gov/about-boem/regulations-guidance/atlantic-secarb-presentation; BOEM, 'Identification of Tier 1 Depleted Reservoirs in the Gulf of Mexico' (March 2022), www.boem.gov/about-boem/regulations-guidance/boem-depleted-reservoir.

[52] The Louisiana pore space agreement was granted by the Louisiana State Mineral and Energy Board to Venture Global CCS Cameron, LLC in September 2022, pursuant to the Board's authority under Louisiana Revised Statute 30:209. The agreement covers an area in Louisiana state waters in the Gulf of Mexico, off Cameron Parish. The agreement is styled an 'operating agreement', based on the statutory authority on which the Board relied to grant the agreement, but the agreement effectively is a lease. A copy is available at www.dnr.louisiana.gov/assets/OMR/media/forms_pubs/CS004.pdf.

is styled an 'operating agreement,' based on the statutory authority on which the Board relied to grant the agreement, but the agreement effectively is a lease. A copy of the agreement is available.[53]

The Texas General Land Office granted a pore space lease to Bayou Bend CCS LLC, pursuant to the Texas Natural Resources Code (Chapters 33 and 51), in March 2022, covering certain areas in Texas waters in the Gulf of Mexico, off the coast near Beaumont and Port Arthur. The lease is available by public records request to the Texas General Land Office.

7. Floating Solar, Tidal, and Wave Energy

OCSLA authorises BOEM to grant leases for the development of energy resources generally in federal waters. This grant is broad enough to cover such sources of energy as floating solar, wave, ocean current, and tidal power. A floating solar energy project could generate energy from solar radiation using solar panels mounted on floating stands. A wave energy project could produce energy from the up-and-down movement of the surface of the water (and any object floating on the top of the water) as a wave passes. An ocean current or tidal power project could use underwater turbines that are turned by water that moves with currents or the tides. Although BOEM discusses these source of energy production on its website, there has been relatively little activity to date in the US regarding use of these sources of energy.[54]

The use of state waters for floating solar, wave, or tidal power would be controlled by state law, though a permit might be needed from the Federal Energy Regulatory Commission (FERC) for the development of wave or tidal energy. Pursuant to the Federal Power Act, FERC approval generally is needed to construct and operate hydroelectric dams – most of which would be on streams or rivers where the state owns the waters and water bottoms[55] – and FERC has asserted that a permit from FERC would be necessary to develop 'hydrokinetic' power, such as ocean wave, current, or tidal energy.[56] FERC has granted a few licences for pilot projects for hydrokinetic power, including both tidal and wave power pilot projects. Information on these permits, as well as pending hydrokinetic energy permit applications, and on the permitting process, can be found on FERC's website.[57] FERC's assertion that hydrokinetic projects require FERC's approval has not yet been tested in the courts.

FERC and BOEM have entered a memorandum of understanding (MOU) regarding the two agencies' roles in the event that a company wishes to lease a portion of federal waters for a hydrokinetic problem. The MOU provides that BOEM would

[53] A copy is available at www.dnr.louisiana.gov/assets/OMR/media/forms_pubs/CS004.pdf.
[54] BOEM, 'Renewable Energy on the Outer Continental Shelf,' www.boem.gov/renewable-energy/renewable-energy-program-overview.
[55] The general rule is that the bottoms of navigable waters are owned by the states in which the waters are found.
[56] FERC, 'Hydrokinetic Projects,' available at www.ferc.gov/licensing/hydrokinetic-projects. See also AquaEnergy Group, Ltd., 102 F.E.R.C. ¶ 61,242 (2202).
[57] FERC, 'Hydrokinetic Projects,' www.ferc.gov/licensing/hydrokinetic-projects.

control the leasing process, but that a hydrokinetic project in federal waters would need a licence from FERC to operate.

8. Ocean Thermal Energy

The Ocean Thermal Energy Conversion Act, 42 USC §§ 9101 through 9168[58] establishes a statutory framework for regulating and licensing of facilities 'designed to use temperature differences in ocean water to produce electricity or another form of energy capable of being used directly to perform work.'[59] Under the Ocean Thermal Energy Conversion Act, no one is allowed to construct or operate 'an ocean thermal energy conversion facility', whether in state or federal waters, without a licence issued pursuant to the Ocean Thermal Energy Conversion Act.[60] The licensing of such facilities is managed by the National Oceanic and Atmospheric Administration (NOAA).[61]

This framework contrasts with other offshore energy development in at least three ways. First, offshore thermal energy conversion is governed by the Ocean Thermal Energy Conversion Act, whereas most forms of offshore energy development in federal waters is primary controlled by OCSLA. Second, NOAA manages the licensing process, whereas BOEM and BSEE are the primary regulators for other offshore development in federal waters.[62] Third, the Ocean Thermal Energy Conversion Act applies in both state and federal waters, as far out as the 'seaward boundary of the territorial sea of the United States', whereas federal control of energy development under OCSLA applies only in federal waters, but extends beyond the territorial sea.

NOAA states that '[t]he technology is viable primarily in equatorial areas of the earth where the year round temperature differential between the deep cold and warm surface ocean waters is greater than 20 °C (36 °F).'[63] So far, there has been very little activity in the US relating to ocean thermal energy conversion other than research.

9. Challenges to Offshore Energy Development

Offshore energy projects face many challenges. Some of these are opposition from people who oppose a particular project. Below, this chapter discusses opposition to offshore projects and the legal and policy tools that opponents can use. Offshore projects can also face economic and technical challenges. To a large extent, those challenges are outside

[58] The Ocean Thermal Energy Conversion Act was enacted as part of the Energy Security Act of 1980.

[59] The quoted language is from the definition of 'ocean thermal energy conversion facility' which is found at 42 USC. § 9102(11).

[60] 42 USC. § 9111(a).

[61] The Act refers to the duties and authority of the 'Administrator' and 'Administrator' is defined by 42 USC. § 9102(2) as meaning the 'Administrator of the National Oceanic and Atmospheric Administration.'

[62] The Ocean Thermal Energy Conversion Act state that it applies from 'between the highwater mark and the seaward boundary of the territorial sea of the United States.' 42 USC. §§ 9101(a)(1) (purpose of legislation), 9111(a) (licence requirement).

[63] NOAA, 'Technology Factsheet', coast.noaa.gov/data/czm/media/technicalfactsheet.pdf.

the scope of this chapter, which focuses on legal and policy issues. However, a couple of challenges that offshore wind projects have faced recently – one economic and the other technical – are briefly discussed below also.

A. Opposition to Offshore Energy Projects

Some people in the United States oppose fossil fuel production, including the production of oil and gas offshore. In part, this is based on concern about climate change, and in part it based on fears of oil spills or other adverse local impacts.

Some people oppose renewable offshore energy projects for a variety of reasons. Those who own beachfront property or depend on tourism in coastal areas believe that wind turbines are unsightly and will adversely affect the view of the ocean from the beach. Others have fears that the electricity transmission lines that would bring power from offshore wind farms to the coast will emit hazardous electromagnetic radiation. Some worry that wind turbines will kill migrating birds. Others worry that the increased vessel traffic needed to construct, maintain, and operate offshore wind turbines, as well as the seismic studies performed to study the ocean floor where a proposed project would be installed, will harm whales or other marine animals. Some commercial fisherman and lobsterman worry that offshore wind farms will physically interfere with their ability to conduct their activities. Other opponents of energy projects may have any number of other bases for their opposition.

The opponents can seek to block projects through the political process – for example, by lobbying local, state, or the federal government to refuse to authorise specific projects and to authorise fewer projects (or no) projects of a particular type or in a particular area. In addition, there are certain laws that opponents can use in an attempt to get courts to block a project. Some of the laws that opponents can use in an attempt to block a project are discussed below.

B. Legal Tools that Project Opponents can Use

There are several legal tools that opponents of energy projects can use.

i. National Environmental Policy Act

The National Environmental Policy Act (NEPA) became law in 1970.[64] It has often been called a 'procedural statute' because it does not create any substantive environmental rules.[65] Instead, NEPA imposes two procedural requirements. First, it imposes on federal agencies 'the obligation to consider every significant aspect of the environmental

[64] NEPA is found at 42 USC. § 4331 et seq. NEPA is sometimes called the 'National Environmental Policy Act of 1969' because it was enacted by the US Congress in 1969, but NEPA was not signed into law until 1 January 1970.

[65] See eg *Dine Citizens Against Ruining Our Environment v Bernhardt* 923 F.3d 831, 839 (10th Cir. 2019).

impact of a proposed action.'[66] Second, it requires the agency to 'inform the public that it has indeed considered environmental concerns in its decision-making process.'[67] NEPA does not require agencies to give environmental protection a higher priority than other policy goals. Rather, it merely requires an agency to take a 'hard look' at the environmental consequences' of a proposed action before taking that action.[68]

To meet these requirements, an agency typically performs a detailed study that is documented in an 'Environmental Impact Statement' (EIS), though in some cases a less-detailed Environmental Assessment may be sufficient if the agency has made a finding that a proposed action will have no significant environmental impact – a so-called 'Finding of No Significant Impact' or 'FONSI'. Often, the EIS takes years to prepare. Typically, it must include not only a consideration of the environmental impacts of a proposed project,[69] but also a consideration of alternative courses of action, such as doing nothing or doing an alternative project.

Although NEPA does not impose substantive environmental rules, it often is a powerful tool for opponents of a project for a few reasons. First, an EIS can take years to complete, thereby causing delays and increasing the costs of a project. Second, if the EIS finds that the proposed project will have an adverse impact on the environment, that finding will provide support to opponents who seek to block a project or require that a project be modified to lessen the environmental impact[70] (though it will not act an absolute prohibition on the project moving forward).

Finally, if opponents of a project convince a court that an agency has failed to consider certain environmental impacts of a project or failed to consider important environmental impacts of considered an important alternative course of action, a court may block the proposed action or project until the agency has re-done the EIS to consider those impacts or alternatives. This can substantially delay a project. Often, the original EIS can take years, the litigation over whether the original EIS was sufficient can take years, and then (in the event that a court requires the agency to consider additional potential environmental impacts or additional alternatives to the proposed project) additional years on supplementing the original EIS. And sometimes, after opponents of a project have created years of delays based on NEPA, they will argue that the original EIS is now out-of-date and requires additional work to bring it up-to-date.

There are numerous examples of energy projects, including offshore energy projects, that have been delayed when opponents brought a lawsuit based on NEPA and then convinced a court that the original EIS was not sufficient. In recent years, there has been much debate regarding the extent to which an EIS must consider not only the

[66] *Baltimore Gas & Elec. Co. v Natural Resources Defense Council, Inc.* 462 US 87, 97 (1983).

[67] *Baltimore Gas & Elec. Co. v Natural Resources Defense Council, Inc.* 462 US 87, 97 (1983). 42 USC. § 4332 requires the agency make a 'detailed statement'.

[68] *Baltimore Gas & Elec. Co. v Natural Resources Defense Council, Inc.* 462 US 87, 97 (1983).

[69] 42 USC. § 4332 requires the EIS include a detailed statement that discusses 'reasonably foreseeable environmental effects of the proposed agency action' (the proposed agency action may consist of granting a permit that authorises a project), as well as 'any reasonably foreseeable adverse environmental effects which cannot be avoided should the proposal be implemented.'

[70] 42 USC. § 4332 requires the EIS to discuss 'a reasonable range of alternatives to the proposed agency action, including an analysis of any negative environmental impacts of not implementing the proposed agency action in the case of a no action alternative, that are technically and economically feasible, and meet the purpose and need of the proposal.'

direct environmental impacts of a project, but also indirect environmental impacts. For example, a proposal to grant a permit to drill an offshore oil and gas well certainly must include consideration of the impacts that drilling will have on the local environment.

But to what extent must the EIS consider the effect of using any oil or gas that the proposed well might produce? This can be difficult to evaluate. Not only is it not known in advance whether a well will produce any oil, but in the event it does produce oil it is not known in advance how much oil it will produce. Further, even if it was known how much oil the well would produce, that does not mean that the world would use that much additional oil, because the oil produced from that well may simply substitute for other oil that would have been produced and used int eh event the proposed well had not been drilled.

ii. Endangered Species Act

In 1973, the US enacted the Endangered Species Act (ESA), 16 USC. §§ 1531 et seq, which is enforced by the National Marine Fisheries Service (NMFS) with respect to marine species and the US. Fish and Wildlife Service (FWS) with respect to other species. The purpose of the ESA is 'to provide a means whereby the ecosystems upon which endangered species and threatened species depend may be conserved, to provide a programme for the conservation of such endangered species and threatened species.'[71] The ESA protects species listed as either 'endangered'[72] or 'threatened'[73] by NMFS or FWS.

The main way that the ESA protects endangered and threatened species is by prohibiting any 'take' of a species within the United States, the territorial seas of the US, or the high seas,[74] with 'take' being defined broadly as meaning 'to harass, harm, pursue, hunt, shoot, wound, kill, trap, capture, or collect, or to attempt to engage in any such conduct.'[75] As interpreted by regulations and courts, an action that harms an endangered or threatened species can constitute a 'take' even if the person committing the action did not intend to harm the species or any member of the species.[76] The ESA provides for both civil and criminal penalties for violations of the ESA, depending on circumstances.[77]

Because some marine species are listed as endangered or threatened, there sometimes will be plausible arguments that a proposed offshore energy project would harm an endangered or threatened species. Opponents of projects can present such arguments to regulatory agencies, arguing that the agencies should not grant permits to authorise

[71] 16 USC. § 1531(b).

[72] The ESA defines 'endangered species' as meaning 'any species which is in danger of extinction throughout all or a significant portion of its range other than a species of the Class Insecta determined by the Secretary to constitute a pest whose protection under the provisions of this chapter would present an overwhelming and overriding risk to man.' 16 USC. § 1532(6).

[73] The ESA defines a 'threatened species' as 'any species which is likely to become an endangered species within the foreseeable future throughout all or a significant portion of its range.' 16 USC. § 1532(20).

[74] 16 USC. § 1538(a).

[75] 16 USC. § 1532(19). Certain limited exceptions to the 'take' prohibition are found in 16 USC. § 1539.

[76] For example, 50 C.F.R. § 17.3 defines 'harm' for purposes of the ESA's prohibition on 'take' as meaning 'an act which actually kills or injures wildlife.'

[77] 16 USC. § 1540.

the offshore projects. Further, the ESA contains a so-called 'citizens suit' provision.[78] Under this provision, 'any person may commence a civil suit on his own behalf' to stop any activity alleged to be in violation of ESA, if the person has given written notice of the alleged violation to the appropriate federal agency and the agency itself has not taken action to stop the alleged violation.[79] Thus, even if an opponent of a project does not convince a regulatory agency to reject a permit application or otherwise block a project, the citizen himself can file an action in court, asking the court to block the proposed project.

The ESA can be a powerful tool for opponents of projects. With respect to both offshore wind and offshore oil and gas activity, some opponents of proposed projects have argued that the projects should be prohibited under the ESA because the projects allegedly would harm endangered or threatened marine species, such as the right whale or other species.

iii. Marine Mammal Protection Act

The Marine Mammal Protection Act (MMPA) of 1972 is found at 16 USC. §§ 1361 et seq. The MMPA is administered by the National Marine Fisheries Service. It is designed to protect marine mammals. Like the ESA, the MMPA has a general prohibition on any activity that will 'take' a marine mammal.[80] The MMPA defines 'take' as meaning 'to harass, hunt, capture, or kill, or attempt to harass, hunt, capture, or kill any marine mammal.'[81] This definition is similar to the ESA's definition of 'take', though the MMPA contains a definition of 'harassment' that seems broader than the concept of harassment under the ESA. The ESA's definition requires a *likelihood* that an activity would harm a species by annoying it to such an extent that the species' behavioural patterns would be disrupted, MMPA's definition only requires the 'potential' for harm by altering the species' behavioural patterns.[82] The MMPA provides another potential legal tool for opponents of offshore energy projects.

iv. Migratory Bird Treaty Act

The Migratory Bird Treaty Act (MBTA) is found at 16 USC. § 703 et seq. It was enacted to implement the United States' obligations under certain multilateral treaties designed to protect migratory birds. The MBTA is another tool that persons could us to oppose offshore energy projects.

v. Coastal Zone Management Act

The Coastal Zone Management Act (CZMA), 16 USC. §§ 1451 et seq was enacted in 1972. Its purpose is 'to preserve, protect, develop, and where possible, to restore or

[78] 16 USC. § 1540(g).
[79] 16 USC. §1540(g).
[80] 16 USC. § 1372.
[81] 16 USC. § 1362(13).
[82] 16 USC. § 1362(18).

enhance, the resources of the Nation's coastal zone for this and succeeding generations.'[83] The CZMA encourages coastal states to development their own programmes to manage coastal areas and submit their proposed programmes to the federal government for approval.[84] If a coastal state does so, and the programme is approved, each federal agency generally must carry out is duties 'in a manner which is consistent to the maximum extent practicable with the enforceable policies of approved State management programs.'[85] This gives states that develop and submit a coastal management plan (assuming the plan is approved by the federal government) significant control over coastal activities. If, for example, a state's plan provided that certain activities are inconsistent with proper use of coastal areas, federal agencies generally would not be allowed to grant permits authorising those sorts of activities. Opponents of certain types of projects can attempt to use the CZMA as a legal tool by lobbying their state to prohibit certain types of activities. Further, if a state's coastal use plan requires that certain types of activities in the coastal area require a permit from a state agency, any opponents of that sort of activity may oppose the granting of permits for that sort of activity.

C. Examples of Local Opposition to Offshore Renewable Energy Projects

Often, local citizens oppose the construction or operation of new industrial facilities. There are various motivations for such opposition – fear of the technology or process involved, concern that the project might negatively impact property values, worry that the project might be unsightly or impair an ocean view or view of the surroundings, and more.

Energy industry projects often face such opposition, whether the project is an oil and gas project, renewable energy project, or carbon sequestration project.

For example, several proposed offshore wind projects for federal waters off the coast of Massachusetts have faced significant local opposition. Some opponents have objected to the fact that wind turbines could be visible from shore, thereby allegedly detracting from the ocean views. Others have expressed fear that powerlines associated with the project would have adverse health impacts on local citizens. Commercial fishermen have opposed the projects, worried that the wind turbines would interfere with fishing in the area. Some conservationists have expressed fears that increased vessel traffic and the use of sonic waves to map the ocean floor and its subsurface would have adverse impacts on whales.

One of the proposed projects was the Cape Wind project, which would have been a 454-MW offshore wind farm. In 2010, the federal government granted Cape Wind Associates, LLC the first commercial offshore wind lease in the United States.[86] However, a group called 'Alliance to Protect Nantucket Sound' filed lawsuits opposing

[83] 16 USC. § 1452.
[84] 16 USC. §§ 1452, 1454.
[85] 16 USC. § 1456(c)(1)(A).
[86] A copy of the lease is available from BOEM's website at www.boem.gov/sites/default/files/uploadedFiles/BOEM/Renewable_Energy_Program/Studies/CapeWind_signed_lease.pdf.

the project[87] and was able to delay it. Because of the delays, it became apparent that Cape Wind was unlikely to meet certain construction deadlines contained in power purchase agreements that the owner of the project had negotiated to sell power that would be generated by the project. The prospective buyers cancelled the power purchase agreements, and in 2018 Cape Winds Associates relinquished its lease.[88] Thus, the opponents succeeded in defeating the project.

Other proposed offshore wind projects in the area are continuing to move forward, but also are facing local opposition that adding to the expenses incurred by the project developers and potentially causing delays. Avangrid is a company that proposed an offshore wind project formerly called 'Commonwealth Wind' but now called 'New England Wind 2', which would involve a 1,200-MW wind farm to be developed in federal waters south of Martha's Vineyard on the Massachusetts coast.[89] The project would bring a transmission cable from the wind farm to the shore at Barnstable, a village in Massachusetts. A citizen group has opposed the company's plans to bring the transmission cable to shore at Barnstable, citing fears about electromagnetic fields created by the transmission line, as well as other concerns, such as a fear that installing the underground cable would contaminate underground sources of drinking water. The citizen opposition group even has a website.[90]

Similarly, a citizen group opposed a proposed offshore wind project by Vinyard 1 Wind, LLC. The Vineyard 1 project would involve a 60-turbine, 800-MW project located in federal waters south of Nantucket and Martha's Vineyard, Massachusetts.[91] This citizen group is called Nantucket Residents Against Turbines. This project has also been opposed by fishing industry participants who believe that the wind farm would interfere with commercial fishing. The citizens group and fishing interests filed separate lawsuits to oppose the project. Those efforts have failed at the district court level, and in April 2024 the United States Court of Appeals, First Circuit affirmed the dismissal of one of those lawsuits.[92]

Proposals for offshore wind projects in other areas also have faced opposition. A proposed floating offshore wind project planned for state waters off the coast of California is the CADEMO Wind Project.[93] The project continues to move forward, but it has faced local opposition. The State of Maine passed legislation in 2021 to prohibit offshore wind energy projects in state waters.[94] The legislation in Maine was supported

[87] See eg *Alliance to Protect Nantucket Sound, Inc. v United States Army* 398 F.3d 105 (1st Cir. 2005).

[88] See BOEM, 'Cape Wind' (providing information on the Cape Wind project and noting Cape Wind Associate's relinquishment of its lease).

[89] Information regarding the project is available on BOEM's website at www.boem.gov/renewable-energy/state-activities/new-england-wind-1-and-2. Information is available on the company's project website at www.commonwealthwind.com/.

[90] The website is found at savedowses.org/.

[91] BOEM's website relating to Vineyard 1 Wind is available at www.boem.gov/renewable-energy/state-activities/vineyard-wind-1. The company website for the project is available here: www.vineyardwind.com/vineyardwind-1.

[92] *Melone v Coit* 100 F.4th 21 (1st 2024).

[93] The company's website for the project is available here: cademo.net/. The California State Lands Commission's website has information about the proposed project here: www.slc.ca.gov/renewable-energy/offshore-wind-applications/.

[94] The prohibition is codified at 35 Maine Rev. Stat. § 3405. A copy of the legislation is available from the Maine Legislature's website at legislature.maine.gov/legis/bills/display_ps.asp?LD=1619&snum=130.

by lobstermen who fear that an offshore wind project would adversely impact lobster fishing. In Maryland, some local officials and business groups have opposed Skipjack Wind, a proposed offshore wind project for federal waters, fearing that the project would ruin the ocean view and discourage tourism.[95]

D. Inflation and Supply Chain Issues

In 2021 and 2022, it appeared that the offshore wind energy was poised for a rapid expansion in the United States. However, the industry has begun to experience significant challenges that have been brought on by inflation and supply chain problems. For decades the United States had experienced relatively little price inflation. But inflation increased significantly in 2021, continued to be high in 2022. The rate of inflation moderated in 2023 and 2024, but remained at levels higher than the rates seen in 2010s.

Many offshore wind projects had been planned, and had entered agreements to sell power, based on estimates of the cost to build the offshore wind farms that were prepared prior to the significant increase in inflation. The projects entered agreements to sell power at prices that were projected to be profitable, based on the initial estimates of construction costs, but the prices in the power purchase agreements were no longer viable after inflation pushed construction costs up. In addition, Russia's invasion of Ukraine has disrupted steel mills in Ukraine, increasing the world price for steel. Moreover, the rapid increase in the number of offshore wind projects has outstripped the availability of vessels specialised for constructing offshore wind farms. This has led to the delays in projects and may ultimately lead to the outright cancellation of some projects.

There are several examples of offshore wind projects encountering such problems. For example, Ørsted announced in January 2024 that it was withdrawing from its agreement to sell power in Maryland from its Skipjack Wind project because the prices approved by the Maryland Public Service Commission orders were no longer commercially viable under new market conditions.[96]

The State of New York had aggressive plans to acquire power from offshore wind, but in April 2024 the State cancelled plans to purchase power from three proposed wind farms after a turbine manufacturer cancelled plans to manufacture the larger-sized turbines that the three proposed wind farms had planned to use. That meant that, to generate the same amount of power, the proposed wind farms would have to install more wind turbines, but that would drive up costs – costs that already had increased because of inflation. These projects – each of which has secured an offshore wind lease from BOEM – are Attentive Energy,[97] the Community

[95] The owner of this project is Ørsted, a Danish company. The company's website for the project is available here: skipjackwind.com/.

[96] Ørsted, 'Skipjack Wind to be repositioned for future offtake opportunities' (25 January 2024 press release) orsted.com/en/media/news/2024/01/skipjack-wind-to-be-repositioned-for-future-offtak-815811.

[97] BOEM's website has a page for this project at www.boem.gov/renewable-energy/state-activities/attentive-energy-ocs-0538. The company's website for the project is available at attentiveenergy.com/.

Offshore Wind[98] and Excelsior Wind.[99] Each of these projects seem to be continuing, but the loss of the power purchase agreements from the State of New York is a setback.

Construction of other offshore wind projects continues, and as of 2024 some offshore wind farms have been put into producing, supplying electricity to the mainland United States. Thus, the economic challenges discussed above are not stopping the development of offshore wind altogether. However, those challenges are making it appear unlikely that President Biden's goals for the deployment of 30 gigawatts of offshore wind projects by 2030 will not be met.

E. A Recent Technical Hurdle to Construction of Offshore Wind Farms

Some offshore wind projects on the US Atlantic coast are encountering glauconite on the ocean seafloor. This mineral has sand-like crystals, but when pile drivers are used to drive supports into the ocean floor, the crystals shatter and form a claylike layer that resists pile driving. Some projects have eliminated turbine positions in specific locations where glauconite has been found, but a reduction in turbine locations can make a wind farm less economical. Wind projects planned for the US Pacific coast are less likely to encounter this problem. Many of the projects planned for the Pacific will involve floating wind farms because the ocean is too deep at those locations to for wind turbines that have a foundation in the ocean floor.

10. Conclusions

Some nations are in the early stages of offshore oil and gas development, and many others are in the early stages of developing other offshore industries relating to the energy sector, such as offshore wind, kinetic energy production, and offshore carbon storage. The United States provides an interesting case study. The US has a mature offshore oil and gas sector that has been producing hydrocarbons in significant quantities for decades. This sector is sufficiently mature that the US has significant experience with decommissioning and associated issues, such as financial assurance. It also has dealt with large oil spills.

On the other hand, the US is only in the early stages of developing offshore wind energy. Thus, the US cannot serve as an example of a mature offshore wind industry. Nevertheless, multiple offshore wind projects are in the construction or planning stages, and some have been cancelled or scaled back. The growth of the offshore energy industry in the US has been slowed by supply chain issues and rising prices for construction

[98] The company's website for the project is available at communityoffshorewind.com/. BOEM's website has a page for the Community Offshore Wind project at www.boem.gov/renewable-energy/state-activities/community-offshore-wind-ocs-0539.

[99] The Excelsior Wind project is owned by Vinyard Offshore. The company's website for the project is available at www.vineyardoffshore.com/excelsiorwind, and BOEM's website's page for the project is available at www.boem.gov/renewable-energy/state-activities/vineyard-mid-atlantic-ocs-0544.

materials. The industry also is seeing some resistance – based on wildlife concerns (such as fear that offshore wind projects will harm endangered whale species, offshore fishing interests (worried that offshore wind infrastructure will interfere with fishing activities or harm fishing populations, and opposition from local residents (worried that wind turbines will mar their ocean views or that transmission lines bringing power onshore will create health or safety issues). Observation and consideration of the challenges faced by the embryonic US offshore wind sector can be instructive for other nations that are considering developing offshore wind energy or other forms of offshore renewable energy.

14

Coupling of Petroleum, Offshore Wind, and CCS: Scopes, Interfaces, and Coordination of Licensing Regimes – The Norwegian Experience

KNUT HØIVIK, HEIDI EIKENES SEGLEM,
SONDRE DYRLAND AND CAMILLA GRYTTEN

1. Introduction

In the current energy transformation, offshore core oil and gas basins like the Norwegian Continental Shelf (NCS) are transforming into broader energy provinces,[1] adding renewable energy production from offshore wind and potential hydrogen production to the energy mix. In addition, industry players and governments are working to decarbonise oil and gas production by electrifying oil and gas installations and developing a carbon capture and storage (CCS) industry that uses geological structures as carbon storage facilities.[2] CCS can potentially contribute to decarbonising oil- and gas production and other industries.

The main reason for the transformation is the call for action to meet international climate ambitions and obligations. Under the Paris Agreement, which entered into force in 2016, each party has submitted its nationally determined contribution (NDC) to reduce emissions to the UN.

As part of the transformation, we have observed increased coupling between traditional oil and gas production, renewable energy production, and CCS. We will

[1] See eg Ignacio Herrera Anchustegui and Aleksander Glapiak, (2023). 'Wind of Change: A Scandinavian Perspective on Energy Transition and the 'Greenification' of the Oil and Gas Sector' in Katarzyna Gromek-Broc (ed), *Regional Approaches to the Energy Transition* (Springer, 2023) doi.org/10.1007/978-3-031-19358-3_6. Equinor ASA, the largest operator on the NCS, has launched an industry plan for Norway, the 'Norway Energy hub', that fits with this picture. The plan consists of four pillars: Decarbonising oil & gas, industrialising offshore wind, providing commercial CCS, and Hydrogen on an industrial scale. See Norway Energy Hub – Equinor, www.equinor.com/energy/norway-energy-hub.

[2] The related concept of Carbon Capture Usage and Storage (CCUS) focuses on reusing the CO_2 by conversion to biofuel, concrete, or other materials. We will focus on CCS in this chapter.

focus on three examples of such coupling: First, offshore wind farms can be used to electrify oil and gas facilities to reduce emissions from petroleum production. Second, oil and gas fields may serve as commercial CO_2 storage facilities for third parties. Third, following the cessation of petroleum activities, petroleum facilities may be used for renewable energy production or CCS.

Petroleum production, CCS and offshore wind are subject to different licensing regimes: the Petroleum Act, the CO_2 Storage Regulations, and the Offshore Energy Act. However, the respective application scopes are not mutually exclusive in all respects. For example, an offshore wind farm supplying power to a petroleum installation may be considered a petroleum activity governed by the Petroleum Act rather than the Offshore Wind Act. Similarly, storage of CO_2 removed from produced natural gas before marketing may be considered a petroleum activity governed by the Petroleum Act rather than the CO_2 Storage Regulations.

Such coupling tests the regulatory interfaces and requires coordination of these regimes. This creates regulatory challenges because neither system is typically designed for such coupling. This article will explore how the coordination of licence regimes is or can be managed based on the Norwegian regulatory framework for petroleum activities, offshore wind, and CCS.

We will start by providing a comparative overview of the Norwegian licensing regime for petroleum activities, offshore wind, and CCS, respectively, see section 2. Then in section 3 we will explore the regulatory challenges when offshore wind farms are wholly or partly used for the electrification of petroleum facilities3. In section 4, we will analyse the application of the licensing regimes for petroleum production and CCS when licensees of a petroleum production licence want to use the production facilities and reservoirs for commercial carbon storage. Finally, in section 5, we will explore the regulatory consequences of reusing decommissioned petroleum facilities for renewable energy production or CCS.

2. Overview of Norwegian Licensing Regimes for Petroleum Activities, CCS and Offshore Wind

A. Introduction

As introduced above, petroleum production, CO_2 storage, and offshore wind production on the NCS are governed by three acts. A common feature of the legal regimes for these natural resources is that the right to the resources rests with the Norwegian state.[3] Thus, a licence under these three acts entails both a transfer from the state to the licensee of a right to utilise natural resources and a right to carry out certain activities – typically to install and operate related facilities.

As renewable and non-renewable resources are different by nature, the character of the state's rights is also different. Whereas the state owns oil and gas resources

[3] This also applies to seabed minerals, see the Seabed Minerals Act (Norwegian: havbunnsmineralloven), s 1-4.

and reservoirs suitable for CO_2 storage, the state only has an exclusive right to use the resources in relation to offshore renewable energy. The legal status is nevertheless the same: the right to exploit the resources belongs to the Norwegian state. Consequently, only the state can produce oil or gas, inject CO_2 into subsea reservoirs, or produce power offshore without a licence.[4]

In addition to a licence that confers a right to utilise the relevant natural resource, all three acts provide a legal basis for granting a supplemental licence to install and operate facilities other than production facilities. The main scope of application of these supplemental licences is for the installation and operation of transport infrastructure – typically pipelines and processing facilities under the Petroleum Act and the CO_2 Storage Regulations, as well as transmission cables, transformers, and converters under the Offshore Energy Act.[5] But except for the Offshore Energy Act, the legal basis is not limited to specific types of facilities, so in principle, a licence under the Petroleum Act and the CO_2 Storage Regulations may be granted to any kind of facility related to an activity under the respective act.

The licensing regimes for petroleum, CO_2 storage, and offshore wind share many similarities. However, they also have significant differences in terms of specifics. Below, we give a brief overview of the main differences.

B. Petroleum Licensing Regime

The Petroleum Act applies to petroleum activities on the Norwegian Continental Shelf (NCS).[6] The term 'petroleum activities' includes all activities related to petroleum deposits, including exploration, production, and pipeline transport. In case of uncertainty, the King may also decide whether the Act comprises a facility or activity.[7]

The essential licence of the Petroleum Act is the production licence, which confers an exclusive right to exploration, drilling of exploration wells, and production of petroleum.[8] The licensee becomes the owner of petroleum as it is being produced. In addition, a specific licence to install and operate facilities may be granted when such a right is not comprised of an approved plan for development and operation (PDO) under a production licence.[9] Typical examples are gas pipelines and processing facilities that are not field-specific and have multiple users other than the owners.

Production licences are awarded in officially announced licensing rounds. They are awarded based on objective and non-discriminatory criteria and the requirements and conditions in the announcement. The main criteria are the applicant's technical competence, financial capacity, and plan for exploration and production in the area applied for. Production licences are awarded to a group of companies decided by the government, which also decides each company's licence interest and appoints one of them as

[4] Petroleum Act, ss 1-1 and 1-3, CO_2 Storage Regulations, ss 1-2 and 1-4 and the Offshore Energy Act, ss 1-3, 3-1- and 3-2.

[5] Petroleum Act, s 4-3, CO_2 Storage Regulations, s 6-1 and the Offshore Energy Act, s 3-2.

[6] Petroleum Act, s 1-4, para 1.

[7] ibid.

[8] Petroleum Act, s 3-3.

[9] Petroleum Act, s 4-3.

operator. A unique feature of the petroleum licensing regime is that the government also determines the terms of cooperation between the licensees by imposing a standard Joint Operating Agreement (JOA) as a licensing condition.[10]

If the licensees decide to develop a field, a PDO must be submitted to and approved by the Ministry of Energy before development can occur. The PDO concerns the economic, technical, safety-related, commercial, and environmental aspects of the development, as well as production and transportation facilities.[11]

C. CO_2 Storage Licensing Regime

The EU CO_2 storage directive has been implemented in Norwegian law through three legislative measures: the CO_2 Storage Regulations, Chapter 4a in the Petroleum Regulations, and Chapter 35 in the Pollution Regulations.[12] The Petroleum Regulations apply to CO_2 storage, where considered petroleum activity and, therefore, falls under the scope of the Petroleum Act. CO_2 storage for other purposes, such as commercial CO_2 storage, for instance the Longship project, is governed by the CO_2 Storage Regulations. In both instances, the provisions of the Pollution Regulations apply.

The CO_2 Storage Regulations have three types of licences concerning the resources: survey, exploration, and exploitation. In addition, similar to the system in the Petroleum Act, a specific permit for installing and operating facilities may be granted.[13] The exploration licence confers an exclusive right to explore and assess the potential of a subsea reservoir for CO_2 storage. In addition to being exclusive, the exploration licence also gives a preferential right to be awarded a subsequent exploitation licence in the area. The exploitation licence confers an exclusive right to use a specific subsea reservoir for CO_2 storage. Compared to the system under the Petroleum Act, the combined exploration and exploitation licences essentially correspond to a petroleum production licence – covering both the exploration, development, and production phases.

Exploration and exploitation licences are awarded based on published objective and non-discriminatory criteria. In practice, areas have primarily been announced ad hoc, based on known interest from the industry, a so-called 'open-door policy.' The main criteria for the award are the applicant's financial strength, technical competence, and reliability, which are considered necessary, including the organisation's competence. If a licence is awarded to a group of companies, the award can be made on the condition that the licensees enter into a cooperation agreement that must be approved by the Ministry. However, contrary to the Petroleum Act, no express provision in the CO_2 Storage Regulations states that the Ministry may impose a standard JOA on the licensees. Similar to the system under the Petroleum Act, a plan for development and

[10] Petroleum Act, s 3-3, para 4. The standard JOA is at view.officeapps.live.com/op/view.aspx?src=https%3A%2F%2Fwww.regjeringen.no%2Fcontentassets%2F133274c0e30f4ad7abd475b6d2d46e63%2Fagreement-concerning-petroleum-activities-incl-attachments-a-and-b-with-state-participation.docx&wdOrigin=BROWSELINK.

[11] Petroleum Act, s 4-2.

[12] Regulations 1 June 2004 No. 1 on limitation of pollution (Pollution Regulations).

[13] CO_2 Storage Regulations, s 6-1.

operation must be submitted to and approved by the Ministry of Energy before development can occur.[14]

D. Offshore Energy Licensing Regime

The Offshore Energy Act applies to the production and transmission of renewable electricity in Norwegian territorial waters outside coastal baselines and on the NCS.[15] In regulations of general applicability or specific cases, the King may decide that all or parts of the act shall not apply to facilities or activities governed by a different act. Thus, it can be decided that offshore wind production, considered part of 'petroleum activity' shall be governed solely by the Petroleum Act.[16]

The Offshore Energy Act is based on a multi-step permitting system, where the first step is to open an area for potential licensing.[17] The Offshore Energy Act formally acknowledges two types of licences: one for energy production facilities – for natural resource utilisation – and one for energy transmission facilities.[18] In addition, there is a mechanism for the award of acreage. The acreage gives the holder an exclusive right to apply for and be awarded a licence for energy production in that area later. In legal substance, the right to a defined acreage – a so-called project area – is, therefore, a licence.[19]

The main rule under the Offshore Energy Act is that opened (project) areas shall be officially announced and awarded using a competitive procedure.[20] The procedure can be either a monetary auction, a qualitative assessment based on objective and non-discriminatory criteria, or a combination of the two, for example, a multi-factor auction. Applicants must satisfactorily demonstrate technical expertise and financial strength and comply with relevant HSE requirements. The Ministry can require potential applicants to submit to a pre-qualification procedure and may limit the number of applicants accepted for pre-qualification.[21] The award of a project area entails a time-limited, exclusive right to mature the applicant's project and apply for a licence.[22]

Facilities for offshore renewable energy production and transmission cannot be constructed, operated, or owned without a licence from the Ministry.[23] The same applies to changes to and expansions of existing facilities. Under the Offshore Energy Act, production facilities and transmission network facilities are subject to separate licences, but the conditions are essentially the same for both types.[24] In addition, once a licence has been obtained, the Ministry must submit and approve a detailed plan for

[14] CO_2 Storage Regulations, s 4-5.
[15] Offshore Energy Act, s 1-2.
[16] See section 3 below.
[17] Offshore Energy Act, s 2-2.
[18] Offshore Energy Act, ss 3-1 and 3-2.
[19] Offshore Energy Act, s 2-3.
[20] ibid.
[21] ibid and Offshore Energy Regulations, s 2c.
[22] Offshore Energy Regulations, s 2d.
[23] Offshore Energy Act, sh 3.
[24] Offshore Energy Act, ss 3-1 and 3-2 respectively.

development and operation.[25] This applies to both production facilities and transmission network facilities. The detailed plan is thus like the PDO under the Petroleum Act and the CO_2 Storage Regulations.

E. Reflections

This brief overview has shown a partial overlap between the scope of application of the Petroleum Act and the Offshore Energy Act and, similarly, between the Petroleum Act and the CO_2 Storage Regulations. However, the regulatory techniques are different. The interface between the Petroleum Act and the CO_2 Storage Regulations is set out in the relevant acts, so it is, in principle, clear which regime applies. The Petroleum Act and the Offshore Energy Act are formally partly overlapping. Thus, to prevent both acts from being used, a decision must be made to limit the application of the Offshore Energy Act.

In all three licensing regimes, one licence gives an exclusive right to utilise the relevant natural resource under the respective act: the production licence under the Petroleum Act, the exploitation licence under the CO_2 Storage Regulations, and the energy production licence under the Offshore Energy Act. Furthermore, all three licensing regimes have a separate, additional licence for the installation and operation of other facilities. The main application would be related to infrastructure, but except for the Offshore Energy Act, there are no legal limitations on the type of facilities. Finally, in all three licensing regimes, a subsequent plan for development and operation must be submitted and approved before project development can begin.

The main difference between the three licensing regimes is the process and intermediate steps before the issue of the exclusive licence to the resources. Whereas the system under the Petroleum Act is that the production licence is the first and only step, the Offshore Energy Act and the CO_2 Storage Regulations have one or more preceding steps with more limited exclusive and preferential rights before the licence conferring the right to utilise the resources as such is granted. The latter two licensing systems are more fragmented and less streamlined than is the case for petroleum.

3. Offshore Wind as Petroleum Activity

A. Introduction and Regulatory Starting Points[26]

Offshore wind parks can be designated for the electrification of oil and gas facilities to reduce GHG emissions stemming from petroleum production. An example of this on the NCS is the Hywind Tampen, an offshore wind farm producing electricity designated

[25] ibid.

[26] For a comparative legal analysis of the existing and planned developments in Norway and Atlantic Canada, see Ignacio Herrera Anchustegui and Rudiger Tscherning, 'Offshore oil and gas infrastructure electrification and offshore wind: a legal exploration' (2024) 17(1) *The Journal of World Energy Law & Business* 35–53, doi.org/10.1093/jwelb/jwad035.

for the oil and gas production at the Gullfaks- and Snorre fields.[27] Another example on NCS was the Trollvind. The project, which aimed to produce electricity for the Troll, Oseberg, and the onshore plant at Kollsnes, has been put on hold.

When offshore wind parks are used in connection with core petroleum activities, the question arises whether the project is or should be subject to the licensing system for *petroleum activities* or whether it should be treated as an offshore wind project and thus be subject to the licensing system for *offshore renewable energy activities*. The choice, which is a matter of law and policy-making, has both practical and legal consequences, which we will explore from a Norwegian perspective in the following.[28]

The regulatory starting point is that the Norwegian Offshore Energy Act applies to all offshore renewable energy production and conversion and transmission of electric power,[29] including offshore wind parks designated for electrification of petroleum activities. The Ministry of Energy has expressed that the Offshore Energy Act is the crucial legislation for developing offshore wind on the NCS. However, the Offshore Energy Act contains a provision that grants the Ministry of Energy the authority to wholly or partly waive the application of the act by regulation or by individual decisions where a facility, an objective, or an activity is also subject to the licensing system of other legislation.[30] This means that if an offshore wind park is subject to the licensing system of the Petroleum Act, the Ministry has the discretionary power to choose between the Offshore Energy Act and the Petroleum Act. If no decision is made, the Offshore Energy Act will prevail.

B. When may an Offshore Wind Park be Subject to the Petroleum Act?[31]

The Petroleum Act applies to 'petroleum activities in connection with subsea petroleum deposits.'[32] The term 'petroleum activities' is defined as 'all activities associated with subsea petroleum deposits, including survey, exploration drilling, production,

[27] See Iben Ringvej Dahl, Bård Wathne Tveiten and Emily Cowan, 'The Case for Policy in Developing Offshore Wind: Lessons from Norway' (2022) 15 *Energies* 1569, doi.org/10.3390/en15041569; Ignacio Herrera Anchustegui, 'Is Hywind Tampen's State Aid Approval a Kickstart for the Norwegian Offshore Wind Industry? Annotation on Decision 017/20/COL of the EFTA Surveillance Authority of 11 March 2020 on the Hywind Tampen Project' (2020) 19(2) *European State Aid Law Quarterly* (ESTAL) 225–31; David McLaurin, Mike Paulin, Cheng Peng and Rama Yadlapati. 'The Use of Offshore Wind to Reduce Greenhouse Gas Emissions in Offshore Hydrocarbon Production – A Case Study' Paper presented at the Offshore Technology Conference, Virtual and Houston, Texas (August 2021) doi.org/10.4043/30993-MS and Bjørn-Tore Tangerås, and Åsmund Sandvik Tveiten, 'Hywind Tampen, project NPV calculation. With and without subsidies' University of Stavanger, TN-ISØP, hdl.handle.net/11250/2587180.

[28] For further analysis, see Ignacio Herrera Anchustegui, *Offshore Wind Licensing* (Edward Elgar Publishing, 2024) 127–48; Eirik Finserås and Sigrid Eskeland Schütz, *Offshore wind licensing in Norway* (Edward Elgar Publishing, 2024) www.elgaronline.com/edcollchap/book/9781800886278/book-part-9781800886278-15.xml.

[29] Offshore Energy Act, s 102, para 1.

[30] Offshore Energy Act, s 1-4, para 6.

[31] For a more detailed analysis, see Maria Koch Haugane, 'Petroleumshavvind – Havenergilovas og petroleumslovens regler om tildeling av konsesjon for kraftleveranser til petroleumsanlegg' in *MarIus* No. 572, Scandinavian Institute of Maritime Law, University of Oslo 2023, ch 5.

[32] Petroleum Act, s 1-4, para 1.

transportation, utilisation and decommissioning, including the planning of such activities, but not including transport of petroleum in bulk by the ship.'[33] This definition covers the development and operation of offshore infrastructure to produce or transmit electricity for petroleum production. For instance, gas turbines on petroleum platforms produce power for petroleum production, or subsea cables and transmitters receive power from the onshore grid to petroleum platforms. Offshore wind farms designated for power production to specific offshore oil and gas production facilities and physically connected to them are clearly within the scope of the Petroleum Act.[34] This was the situation for 'Hywind Tampen.'[35]

Another scenario is where an offshore wind farm is used for power production to offshore petroleum facilities by connecting both the wind farm and the petroleum production facilities to the onshore grid.[36] Such an 'indirect' connection may be beneficial because the petroleum facilities would have a more stable power supply and allow the wind farm to produce power for the onshore grid when power production exceeds demand from the petroleum facilities. This was a key element of the Trollvind project. The Ministry indicated that this project would be subject *not* to the Petroleum Act but to the Offshore Energy Act.[37]

A third scenario is where an offshore wind farm is physically connected to a petroleum facility that already has a power-from-shore solution in place and therefore does not as such need additional power.[38] The Minister of Energy has expressed that he will *not rule out* that the Petroleum Act, under the circumstances, may be applicable in such cases.[39] This will depend on a case-by-case assessment where the wind farm's *importance for and integration with* petroleum production will be critical. Also, matters relating to the construction, ownership, and operation may be relevant elements in such an assessment. In our view, these considerations will always be appropriate when assessing the applicability of the Petroleum Act for an offshore wind farm that has an interphase with petroleum activities.

An example of the latter is the GoliatVIND project.[40] GoliatVIND, like Hywind Tampen, plans to connect directly to petroleum facilities. A key difference, in addition to the fact that the petroleum facilities at Goliat already have a power-from-shore solution in place, is that GoliatVind is also connected to the onshore grid via the existing power cable between the Goliat FPSO and the onshore grid. The Ministry found the project to be outside the scope of the Petroleum Act. The reason is that the offshore wind developer will construct, own, and operate the offshore wind park separate from the petroleum field and directly relate to the onshore system operator and onshore

[33] Petroleum Act, s 1-6(c).

[34] Referred to as the 'island' model by Haugane in *MarIus* 572, ch 1.2.

[35] The 'Hywind Tampen' turbines are not situated within the geographical area of the petroleum production licences of the off-takers. Placing the offshore wind farm outside the licence borders will, therefore, not exclude the applicability of the Petroleum Act.

[36] Referred to as the 'via' model by Haugane in *MarIus* 572, ch 1.2.

[37] Dokument nr. 15:2807 (2021-2022): Skriftlig spørsmål – stortinget.no, www.stortinget.no/no/Saker-og-publikasjoner/Sporsmal/Skriftlige-sporsmal-og-svar/Skriftlig-sporsmal/?qid=90322.

[38] Similar to the model referred to by *Haugane* as the 'exchange' model in ch 1.2.

[39] Dokument nr. 15:1999(2022-2023): www.stortinget.no/no/Saker-og-publikasjoner/Sporsmal/Skriftlige-sporsmal-og-svar/Skriftlig-sporsmal/?qid=93891.

[40] EnergiWatch: energiwatch.no/nyheter/politikk_marked/article16470552.ece.

customers, with no contractual obligation for the petroleum licensees to purchase the power.[41] Hence, more than the physical connection to the petroleum facilities was needed for the project to be covered by the Petroleum Act. The Minister of Energy summarised the legal situation as follows:

> If the wind power plant is built, operated, and connected to a petroleum facility primarily to sell and deliver the power from the wind power plant to the onshore grid, this suggests that wind power production is not regulated by the Petroleum Act (own translation).[42]

C. Consequences of Applying the Licensing Regime of the Petroleum Act to an Offshore Wind Farm

The ordinary licensing process under the Offshore Energy Act is time-consuming. No licences for commercial offshore wind projects have been issued under the Act. The first licensing rounds were initiated in March 2023 by announcing competitions for project area awards at Sørlige Nordsjø II phase 1 (SNII) and Utsira Nord, two areas opened for offshore wind activities in 2020.[43] A project area award at SNII was issued one year after the announcement, in March 2024. We expect the performance of environmental impact assessments (EIA) for SNII to occur from 2024 to 2026 and licence applications to be filed in 2026. On a non-binding basis, the government indicated a licence processing period of 12 to 18 months, in which case the SNII licence award could be expected around 2027/2028. The Utsira Nord process suffers a significant delay. The competition for project area award in Utsira Nord will likely occur in 2025.

There is an expectation that the licensing process will become more streamlined and less time-consuming in future licensing rounds. However, some of the steps of the licensing process are inherently time-consuming, such as the requirements for strategic and project-specific environmental impact assessments, the extensive use of public hearings throughout the process, and the recently added requirement for competitive tendering and project area awards, the latter being a move away from the *open-door* concept that was previously in place. The extensive licensing process is generally a concern for the offshore wind industry but particularly challenging where the purpose is the electrification of petroleum facilities already in operation. This is because the economics of an electrification project is closely connected with the remaining lifetime of such facilities and the volume of in-place oil and gas in the reservoir. The closer to decommissioning, the less attractive a modified power solution is.

For time-critical electrification projects, applying the licensing system in the Petroleum Act is more effective than the ordinary licensing process in the Offshore

[41] Based on information published by EnergyWatch.no on 29 September 2023. energiwatch.no/nyheter/politikk_marked/article16470552.ece.

[42] www.stortinget.no/no/Saker-og-publikasjoner/Sporsmal/Skriftlige-sporsmal-og-svar/Skriftlig-sporsmal/?qid=93891.

[43] Royal Decree 12 June 2020, case no. 20/88, Ministry of Petroleum and Energy: 'Opning av områda Utsira Nord og Sørlige Nordsjø II for konsesjonshandsaming av søknader om fornybar energiproduksjon etter havenergilova'.

Energy Act. Under the Petroleum Act, the offshore wind project can be licensed either by amendment to an existing PDO issued under section 4-2 of the Petroleum Act or by a specific licence to install and operate facilities under section 4-3. Both alternatives are typically more expedient than a complete licensing process under the Offshore Energy Act. For example, it took approximately six months between submitting and approving amended PDOs for the Snorre and Gullfaks fields, whereby the Hywind Tampen wind farm was included under their respective production licences. The wind farm is owned by the licensees of the two fields and operated by Equinor Energy AS, which also is the operator of both fields. It started production on 23 August 2023.[44]

However, there are also opportunities to expedite the licensing process under the Offshore Energy Act by using a 'fast track' process.[45] Also, awarding a licence to construct and operate an offshore wind farm under the Offshore Energy Act may provide possibilities for or even obligations to supply power from the offshore wind farm to nearby petroleum facilities. We will take a closer look at these alternatives in the following.

D. 'Fast Track' under the Offshore Energy Act – The Alternative Licensing Scheme for Time-critical Projects[46]

i. Introduction

By 'fast track', we refer to an expedited licensing process achieved by exemptions from specific steps of the ordinary licensing process. The Offshore Energy Act opens for two such exemptions. The first is an exemption from the requirement to decide upon opening an area for offshore renewable energy production (see section 2-2), and the second is an exemption from the project area award (see section 2-3).

ii. Exemption from Requirement for Opening of an Area

The Ministry of Energy has the discretionary power to exempt from the requirement to decide upon opening an area for offshore renewable production in 'exceptional cases'.[47] The wording indicates that the threshold is high, meaning that the benefits of omitting the opening process would need to outweigh the disadvantages substantially.[48] This is supported by the preparatory works to the Offshore Energy Act, expressing that the

[44] 'The world's largest floating offshore wind farm officially opened' (*Equinor*, 23 August 2023), www.equinor.com/news/20230823-hywind-tampen-officially-opened.

[45] The modifications to be implemented on the petroleum facilities will be handled under the Petroleum Act.

[46] For a more detailed analysis, see Haugane in *MarIus* 572, chs 3 and 4, Siv Elen Årskog Vedvik, 'Hurtigløp for elektrifisering av sokkelen med havvind? Handlerom og hindringar i dagens regelverk' (*Karnov Forlag*, 9 February 2024).

[47] cf Offshore Energy Act, s 2-2, para 4.

[48] We have not assessed any obligations that may follow from the EEA agreement relating to development of offshore wind farms.

exemption rule should be restrictive, mentioning examples such as *limited pilot projects* and *smaller facilities that are supply facilities for petroleum installations*.[49] Exempting from the opening implies, *among other things*, that preparing a strategic EIA and conducting two public hearings will be omitted. Omitting the opening process saves time in the licensing process but also comes with disadvantages. Not only could it give rise to low public legitimacy of the specific project, but it could also prevent relevant information from being brought to the attention of the Ministry and the offshore wind developer. Lack of information should, in any case, be compensated for by corresponding requirements to the scope of the project-specific EIA, which accompanies the licence application.

Although the wording and the preparatory works of section 2-2 implies a high threshold, the term 'special cases' also indicates that the interpretation is intended to be *dynamic*, ie considering changes in society and policies at the time of the assessment. For example, energy security considerations are probably far more important today than when the Offshore Energy Act was prepared. Under the circumstances, this may support a less restrictive exemption practice today than what the preparatory works indicate. However, new arguments are also pulling in the opposite direction, one being the increased spatial conflict and, hence, a political need to prioritise offshore areas due to the emergence of new industries.

Besides considerations relating to energy demand, a critical factor in the Ministry's assessment will be the expected impact of the potential offshore wind development, including the size and impact of the development, whether the area is vulnerable in terms of wildlife and nature, and whether other users of the area may be impacted. It is also important whether the area has been subject to thorough mapping. The less information available, the higher the threshold for omitting the opening process.

iii. Exemption from Requirement of Project Area Award by Competition

The subsequent licensing process step generally involves the Ministry dividing the opened area into project areas and awarding such areas by competition.[50] This step is, however, not applicable where an exemption from opening has been granted pursuant to section 2-2. In such cases, a licence award pursuant to chapter 3 of the Offshore Energy Act will be the first step of the licensing process. Omitting both the opening process and the project area award process represents a significantly shortened licensing timeline.

For areas opened under section 2-2, the Ministry can award a project area directly without competition in 'special cases'.[51] The wording '*special cases*' suggests a high threshold. However, a majority of the members of the parliamentary Standing Committee on Energy and the Environment (the 'Committee') emphasised in the legislative process

[49] Ot.prp. nr. 107 (2008-2009) s 11.4.3.
[50] Offshore Energy Act, s 2-3.
[51] Offshore Energy Act, s 2-3, para 1.

that the exemption is essential for the political objective to electrify the petroleum sector (own translation):[52]

> The Committee's majority […] refers to the exceptions clause […] which concerns granting areas directly in special cases, and states that this provision must be understood such that the government may directly grant licenses to licensees within existing petroleum production licenses where the power production from offshore wind directly or indirectly shall be used for electrification of petroleum facilities. […].
>
> Another majority […] is of the opinion that this will facilitate for the petroleum industry to take greater responsibility for cutting own emissions, and reduce the need for power from shore. If the continental shelf is to be electrified by offshore wind to the greatest extent possible, arrangements should be made fast due to considerations of supply. Then, the licensees on the continental shelf themselves have the opportunity to carry out the electrification in collaboration with their partners and subcontractors, also in combination where there is a power-from-shore solution.

This statement supports that the threshold should be lower for allowing direct awards where the purpose of the wind farm is the electrification of oil and gas installations. However, the purpose of the planned wind farm is not the only relevant factor to be considered. The Ministry needs to make a holistic assessment where other elements are appropriate. The guiding principle should be that the benefits of omitting the competitive process outweigh the disadvantages.

A key question is how close connection is required between the planned offshore wind farm and the relevant petroleum facilities for the offshore electrification purpose to apply. Offshore wind farms are to be connected to petroleum facilities, with no supply to other users, and will typically be governed by the Petroleum Act, not the Offshore Energy Act. This may imply that the exemption practice prescribed by the Committee is aimed at *other* situations, for instance, where the offshore wind farm is not directly connected to the petroleum facilities or where power is supplied to other off-takers than petroleum facilities. Applying the Petroleum Act could be challenging in such situations, depending on how close the wind farm is associated with the petroleum activities. The main object of the Committee's statements, to promote the use of offshore wind to reduce carbon emissions from the petroleum sector by expedited processes under the Offshore Energy Act, seems to imply that the offshore electrification purpose can be deemed present in any situation where the planned offshore wind farm will contribute to reduced use of gas turbines on offshore petroleum facilities.

Besides the physical integration with petroleum activities, the ownership of offshore wind farms is relevant when deciding whether there is a basis for an exemption. The Committee refers in its statement to offshore wind developments by 'licensees within existing petroleum production licenses.' The statement gives rise to several interpretation issues, for instance, whether a planned offshore wind farm to be exempted from section 2-3 will need to be developed by petroleum

[52] Innst. 81 L (2022–2023), www.stortinget.no/no/Saker-og-publikasjoner/Publikasjoner/Innstillinger/Stortinget/2022-2023/inns-202223-081l/?all=true.

licensees only or whether, for example, offshore wind developers may take part in the development.[53]

According to the Committee, a precondition for allowing direct award is that the criteria are objective and verifiable. This could, for instance, be achieved by adopting regulations with criteria for direct award.

iv. Power Supply to Petroleum Facilities as a Licence Condition

One way to facilitate the electrification of petroleum facilities when developing offshore wind under the Offshore Energy Act is to implement possibilities for or even obligations to supply power from the offshore wind farm to nearby petroleum facilities. Several models could be imagined, the most extensive being a model where the required power supply to a specific petroleum facility is included as a licence condition. Another less extensive example is to include as a condition for project area award that the developer shall study the potential for power supply to petroleum facilities. Although the power supply to offshore petroleum facilities could, at least in theory, be seen as an opportunity by offshore wind developers, one should not undermine the fact that several challenges are associated with the power supply to petroleum facilities. One obvious challenge is that supplying power to petroleum facilities could add costs to the project, especially when petroleum facilities cannot offtake the entire power production from the wind farm. In such respect, a petroleum facility's need for power may not always be stable. Another and perhaps more critical issue is the inherent uncertainty associated with petroleum prices, petroleum volumes available for production, and production costs. These factors impact field economics and, thus, the remaining life of the petroleum field. Securing a stable, long-term income from the sale of power is key for developers and others to invest in and finance offshore wind development projects. By including requirements concerning off-take, the project may become less attractive. On the other hand, petroleum licensees may be willing to pay higher power prices than grid users to reduce their CO_2 taxes and emission allowances (EU ETS) costs.

On the NCS, there is only one example that supply to nearby petroleum facilities is catered for in a licensing process under the Offshore Energy Act, namely the Sørlige Nordsjø II process. In connection with the announcement of the prequalification process leading up to the project area award, ConocoPhillips Skandinavia AS, in its capacity as operator of the Ekofisk field, requested the Ministry of Energy to cater for an award process where applicants are urged to investigate an alternative offtake solution, catering for electrification of petroleum facilities. The Ministry reflected the request in pre-qualification criteria, stating that:

> […] if the applicant can demonstrate that the project concept may be adapted to connection to and electrification of Ekofisk, provided that further studies show that this is relevant, this will be weighted positively.[54]

[53] See also Caroline Skaar Landsværk and Elise Johansen, Norsk Lovkommentar: Havenergilova, note (19), Rettsdata.no (read 24 January 2024) min.rettsdata.no/Dokument/gL20100604z2D21?noteid=gN20100604z2D21z2E55,gN20100604z2D21z2E19.

[54] Ministry of Petroleum and Energy, Announcement of competition for a project area in Sørlige Nordsjø II for offshore renewable energy production, Appendix 4, Criterion 1G.

In the project area announcement, the Ministry emphasised that a potential connection to Ekofisk will not alter the permitted maximum capacity in the project area or the right to state aid under the contract for difference.[55] Implicitly, a future power supply to Ekofisk will not affect the legal framework for the Sørlige Nordsjø II licensing process, which the Offshore Energy Act will still govern. The modifications required on the petroleum facilities are expected to be treated under the Petroleum Act as an amendment to the Plan for Development and Operation. After the project area award, the commercial agreement between the offshore wind developer and the Ekofisk licensees must be negotiated.

The Ministry has, in connection with the parliamentary approval process of the Sørlige Nordsjø II contract for difference, expressed an intention to implement provisions regarding third-party access to offshore radials, including an obligation for the owner to connect third-party users as long as there is available capacity and the connection is feasible without a need for upgrade or investments.[56] Based on similar legislation for the onshore grid, we assume that these will be general provisions, ie, not applicable to Sørlige Nordsjø II only, and that the requirements be implemented in or under the Offshore Energy Act.

E. Reflections

Electrification of petroleum facilities on the Norwegian Continental Shelf is key and time critical for Norway to meet its obligations under the Paris Agreement. Whereas offshore wind farms, due to natural limitations, cannot meet the energy demand on petroleum facilities alone, it is generally accepted that offshore wind may contribute to such electrification.

The Ministry has the authority to exempt offshore wind projects that form part of the petroleum activities from the Offshore Energy Act and apply the Petroleum Act instead. Experiences so far suggest that this is a faster and more efficient licensing route.

However, connecting offshore wind farms to the onshore grid in combination with power-from-shore to the offshore petroleum facilities will, under the circumstances, often secure better power stability and more effective offtake of power. The Petroleum Act may not be applicable to these projects. The 'second best' alternative in these cases seems to be to apply a 'fast track' process under the Offshore Energy Act by granting exemptions from fundamental elements of the licensing process. It can be challenging to carry out sufficiently robust assessments of nature protection and co-existence with other industries in such fast-track processes under the Offshore Energy Act. The dilemma is that the alternative, applying the full process under the Offshore Energy Act,

[55] Ministry of Petroleum and Energy, Announcement of competition for a project area in Sørlige Nordsjø II for offshore renewable energy production, Appendix 3.

[56] Prop.93 S (2022-2023) 7, www.regjeringen.no/contentassets/e719f8aef2a844fc9db99a91f315e1dd/nn-no/pdfs/prp202220230093000dddpdfs.pdf.

is too time-consuming to effectively accommodate for the urgent need for electrification of offshore facilities.

4. CCS as Petroleum Activity

A. Background

Storage of CO_2 in an underground storage facility shares many similarities with the production of hydrocarbons; in some instances, it has also been explained as 'gas production in reverse.' Although this statement is inaccurate, there is still some truth to it. As pointed out by IEA,[57] there is a need for carbon capture and storage to be on track for a zero-emissions future. Reducing lead time related to the development of CO_2 storage will be critical to reaching net zero emissions by 2050. EU has also focused on accelerating the capacity to store CO_2, and in the Net Zero Industry Act,[58] CCS is included as a key technology. The regulation also emphasises the need to provide measures to reach a target of 50 million tonnes of annual operational CO_2 injection capacity by 2030. It points to the oil and gas industry as having the assets, skills, and knowledge to explore and develop additional storage sites.[59]

Article 23 of the Net Zero Industry Act imposes an individual obligation on authorised oil- and gas producers to contribute to the union-level objective in Article 20. The contribution obligation will be calculated proportionally based on oil and gas production within the EU territory, economic zones, and continental shelves during 2020–2023.

Historically, the participants in production licences have been front runners in developing CCS on NCS. CO_2 has been used as a measure to increase pressure in the reservoir for enhanced oil/gas recovery, and most of today's operational CCS facilities are 'full chain' projects, whereby the CO_2 is captured and stored as part of petroleum production. Examples include the Sleipner field, where CO_2 from Sleipner's production has been reinjected to the formation since 1996. Also, on the Snøhvit field, the formation has been used for CCS of CO_2 from production since 2002.

However, there is a need for and a development towards offering CO_2 storage capacity to the market. Licensees participating in petroleum activities under a production licence may be interested in providing such a service to the market using the reservoir comprised by the licence, typically after the end of oil and gas production. The question is to what extent a production licence under the Petroleum Act may allow for such activities and when a (new) separate licence under the CO_2 Storage Regulations is required.

[57] IEA Net Zero by 2050 – a roadmap for the global energy sector. The report includes CCUS as one of the key pillars of decarbonisation. iea.blob.core.windows.net/assets/ad0d4830-bd7e-47b6-838c-40d115733c13/NetZeroby2050-ARoadmapfortheGlobalEnergySector.pdf, chapter 2.5.7. and IEA (2023), How new business models are boosting momentum on CCUS, IEA, Paris.

[58] Net Zero Industry Act was approved by the European Parliament on 25 April 2024 and adopted by the European Council on 27 May 2024.

[59] Net Zero Industry Act preamble (15).

B. When are CO_2 Storage Activities Part of the Petroleum Activities?

i. The Regulatory Starting Point

The starting point is that the CO_2 Storage Regulations regulate any CO_2 storage activity in Norway. However, the CO_2 Storage Regulations, section 1-3, third paragraph states that CO_2 storage carried out 'as part of the petroleum activities' is regulated by the Petroleum Act.

The term 'petroleum activities' refers to the definition in section 1-6(c) of the Petroleum Act, as reviewed in Section 2(B) above.[60] This is a broad definition. Regarding the application of the act to CCS activities, the question will typically be if the CCS activity in question is covered by the scope of the JOA under the production licence, which is 'conducting petroleum activities in accordance with the Production Licence,' cf Article 1 of the special provisions. If the CCS activity falls outside the scope of the JOA, the JOA cannot form a basis for cooperation on an application for a separate CO_2 licence under the CO_2 Storage Regulations.

Further, it will not always be evident whether CO_2 storage is undertaken as part of petroleum activities under the production licence. There may typically be a gradual transition from CO_2 storage as part of petroleum activities under a production licence towards storage being a separate stand-alone activity that requires a licence under the CO_2 Storage Regulations.

In the following, we will assess the interface between the CCS licence regime and the petroleum licence regime by reviewing some typical activity scenarios.

C. The Interface Question in Practice

i. The Clear Cases

There are certain cases where there is no doubt about which licence regime applies. Regular commercial CO_2 storage services, where the main activity is to provide CO_2 storage services, require licences under the CO_2 Storage Regulations. One Norwegian example of this is Northern Lights. Northern Lights JV DA is a partnership established between Equinor, TotalEnergies, and Shell to carry out CO_2 transport and storage activities and is part of the Norwegian Government's full-scale carbon capture and storage project, Longship.

On the other hand, the licensees of a production licence under the Petroleum Act can separate CO_2 from the gas as part of the processing of the produced petroleum on the topside installation and, after that, reinject the CO_2 into a reservoir within the geographical boundaries of the licence, either as a disposal of the CO_2 or for enhanced

[60] Whether an activity is part of petroleum activities is also discussed in Section 3(B). The evaluation has the same starting point and must be a case by case evaluation concerning among others the activity's importance for and integration with petroleum production.

oil/gas recovery purposes. This has been done at the Sleipner field since 1996 and is clearly within the scope of the production licence under the Petroleum Act. There are several variations between these clear cases.

ii. Can the Licensees of a Production Licence Offer CO_2 Storage in their Reservoir to Third Parties?

The licensees of a production licence under the Petroleum Act may carry out capture and storage of CO_2 stemming from their petroleum production. However, if the production licence includes a reservoir with sufficient capacity for CO_2 storage service to third parties, the question is to what extent the joint venture can offer such services to third parties within the production licence or if a separate licence under the CO_2 Storage Regulations is required.

The licensing regime under the Petroleum Act includes mechanisms for third-party use of production facilities, typically tie-in and processing services to a joint venture under another production licence.[61] If the joint venture under a production licence (A) already undertakes CO_2 storage as part of its petroleum activities and offers processing services to a third party under another production licence (B), such processing service may also include the storage of CO_2. This service must be considered part of the petroleum activities for the joint venture carrying out the CO_2 storage service and the third party. In our opinion, the same applies even if A does not undertake CO_2 storage activities as part of its petroleum activities, ie, provides CO_2 storage services exclusively for B. Such storage is clearly within B's petroleum activities, and the use of A's production facilities, including the wells and reservoir, for storing B's CO_2 must also be regarded as petroleum activity within A's production licence.

Another scenario is where A offers the use of its facilities for CO_2 storage to a third party that is not undertaking petroleum activities, for example, an onshore cement factory with a CO_2 capture facility installed. If A can use the stored CO_2 for enhanced oil/gas recovery, it would be part of A's petroleum activities and carried out under an existing production licence. For CO_2 storage as a separate independent activity, it is unlikely that it can be considered petroleum activity. Section 4-8(3) of the Petroleum Act explicitly states that the Ministry may decide that others can use petroleum production facilities to treat, transport, and store CO_2. According to the preparatory works, the provision addresses this situation where the third party does not undertake petroleum activities.[62] The objective is to integrate activities that need CO_2 storage with petroleum facilities that can be used for such storage. The Ministry's authority under section 4-8(3) aims to prevent owners or users of petroleum facilities from establishing monopolies and exploiting the market for CO_2 services. However, this authority for the Ministry does not automatically imply that A's CO_2 storage service to such a third party is a petroleum activity within A's production licence. On the contrary, the preparatory works suggest that this service is outside the scope of A's petroleum activities under the

[61] Petroleum Act, s 4-8.

[62] Ot.prp. nr. 48 (2008–2009) 4.

production licence and the JOA.[63] The same authority for the Ministry is also set out in section 5-12 first paragraph of the CO_2 Storage Regulations.

This suggests that A must obtain a separate licence under the CO_2 Storage Regulations to offer such CO_2 Storage services to third parties not undertaking petroleum activities. A consequence is that A's JOA cannot form a basis for storage activities under the separate CO_2 Storage licence. This is because the JOA is limited to petroleum activities under the production licence. This raises some practical and regulatory challenges. The Ministry's authority under section 4-8(3) to decide whether third parties can use the facilities for CO_2 storage purposes does not extend to a rule requiring A to apply for a licence under the CO_2 Storage Regulations. If A decided to obtain such a licence, this would have to be regulated under a separate operating agreement by a separate legal entity in accordance with the CO_2 Storage Regulations and the Company Act. If A already provides CO_2 storage services under its production licence to third parties undertaking petroleum activities, it seems to create unwarranted administrative burdens to have to establish a separate legal entity and apply for a licence under the CO_2 Storage Regulations just to be able to provide the same service to a third party not engaged in petroleum activities. It could also be questioned whether this would even be possible, as the facilities would be owned by the licensees in the production licence, not the new legal entity.

iii. Can the Licensees of a Production Licence Offer CO_2 Storage to Third Parties after the Petroleum Production is Terminated?

Another scenario that may become more relevant in the future as oil and gas fields are reaching the end of life is using a reservoir within a production licence for CO_2 storage purposes after the cessation of petroleum activities. Using the existing facilities for CO_2 injection may be possible and cost-efficient. For example, this was previously considered in the Peterhead CCS project in Northeast Scotland, where re-use was essential.[64] Surveys have demonstrated that infrastructure generally has the potential to be re-used for CO_2 storage purposes.[65] However, this needs to be evaluated on a case-by-case basis and may depend on the infrastructure's technical integrity, material specification, and the life extension option. If this is done at the end of field life in connection with a cessation plan, it can be slightly more straightforward from a licensing perspective.[66]

[63] In this direction, Ulf Hammer, Trond Stang, Sverre B Bjelland, Yngve Bustnesli and Amund Bjøranger Tørum, *Petroleumsloven* (Universitetsforlaget, 2009) 345.

[64] The Peterhead CCS project was cancelled in 2015 but has since been revitalised as a Low Carbon CCGT Power Station Project with use of the Acorn CO_2 storage. For project information, see www.geos.ed.ac.uk/sccs/project-info/32, www.theacornproject.uk/projects and www.ssethermal.com/media/3isawytf/peterhead-a4-1.pdf.

[65] Juan Alcalde et al, 'Acorn: Developing full-chain industrial carbon capture and storage in a resource- and infrastructure-rich hydrocarbon province' (2019) 233 *Journal of Cleaner Production*, doi.org/10.1016/j.jclepro.2019.06.087.

[66] Although it may be slightly more straightforward from a licensing perspective, there may be liability concerns that should be considered. This is discussed under Section 5(C) below. For example, the former licensees risk liability for pollution damages under the Petroleum Act. If the licensees remain the same under the production licence and the new licence under the Storage Regulations this is less of a concern, but the new activity may impact the risk.

Section 5-1 of the Petroleum Act states that licensees must submit a decommissioning plan to the Ministry before the licence expires or the facility's use is terminated. The plan must include proposals for the disposal of the facilities. One alternative in this respect is further use of facilities for purposes other than petroleum activities (cf section 5-1, first paragraph). This includes CO_2 storage.

Using the facilities and reservoirs for CO_2 storage after cessation will require a separate new licence under the CO_2 Storage Regulations. If the licensees of the production licence are interested in such use, they can apply for an exploitation licence under the CO_2 Storage Regulations and include the future use of infrastructure for CO_2 storage activities as part of the decommissioning plan.

However, there are no firm preferential rights for the licensees of the production licence to obtain an exploitation licence for the area and to use the facilities for CO_2 storage following the cessation of petroleum production. Without preferential rights for the licensees, they may not have sufficient incentives to optimise late-life investments to prepare for CO_2 storage after cessation, which may lead to suboptimal economic outcomes for society. The licensees may mitigate the uncertainty by applying for an exploitation licence before cessation and as part of the decommissioning planning. In practice, clarity can also be obtained through dialogue with the authorities.

iv. Gradual Transition from Petroleum Activities to CO_2 Storage Activity

As outlined in Section 4(C)(i) above, the licensees of a production licence under the Petroleum Act may inject and store CO_2 stemming from their petroleum production and third parties' petroleum activities without a separate licence under the CO_2 Storage Regulations. But what if the CO_2 storage activity gradually becomes the main activity under the production licence? Will, at some point, a separate exploitation licence be required?

The Sleipner case could serve as an example. The licensees of Sleipner are currently conducting CO_2 capture, injection, and storage activities as part of their petroleum activities for themselves and for a third party (conducting petroleum activities). As gas production starts to decline, one could envisage that CO_2 storage activities will be the main activity.

If the licencees have not ceased their petroleum production, and the production licence has not expired, it seems clear that no separate CO_2 storage licence is required unless the services are (also) offered to third parties that do not undertake petroleum activities. If the licence expires and/or the end of petroleum production is reached, the licence question to continue the CO_2 storage activity must be solved based on the provisions of cessation of the petroleum activities, cf Section 4(C)(iii) above.

v. Which Licence Regime Applies to CO_2 Storage from Petroleum Production but Outside the Geographical Limits of the Licence?

A joint venture established under a production licence may want to capture and store CO_2 from petroleum production without any CO_2 storage capacity available within the licence boundaries. If the joint venture finds a suitable reservoir for such purposes outside the licence's geographical limits, the question is what licence is required for such storage.

This CO_2 storage is part of the joint venture's petroleum activity within the scope of the Petroleum Act. Hence, the CO_2 Storage Regulations do not apply, cf section 1-3 (3). However, the licence regime under the Petroleum Act does not seem fit for this purpose. A production licence under section 3-3 of the Petroleum Act is intended for extracting petroleum from the licence area and not for 'sole' CO_2 storage stemming from production in another licence. Chapter 4a of the Petroleum Regulations applies to the capture, transport, and storage of CO_2 as part of petroleum activities initiated under an approved plan for development and operation under the Petroleum Act section 4-2. The specific licence to install and operate facilities under section 4-3 of the Petroleum Act is unsuitable.

In our opinion, allowing for an exploitation licence under the CO_2 Storage Regulations in these situations can make sense, even though the literal wording of section 1-3 (3) of the Regulations suggests otherwise. However, there are pitfalls to consider. The Ministry of Energy's primary driver for implementing the CCS-Directive into two separate legislations, ie, chapter 4a in the Petroleum Regulations and the CO_2 Storage Regulations, was that it could cause difficult legal and financial questions if CO_2 storage, which is part of petroleum activities, were licensed under the CO_2 Storage Regulations. Among other things, the Ministry pointed to the challenges related to having integrated activities undertaken by the same group of companies under two different sets of regulatory regimes, hereunder the fact that the Company Act would apply outside the Petroleum Act. There could also be tax consequences that would need to be thoroughly analysed. The same would be the case if a separate legal entity consisting of the same participants were established to apply for the exploitation licence under the CO_2 Storage Regulations with the sole purpose of providing the service to its own production licence.

One alternative to consider is to grant additional acreage to the existing production licence that covers the reservoir for CO_2 storage. This is a practice that the Ministry sometimes applies when a discovery or a prospect straddle beyond the geographical area of a licence. The additional acreage is awarded as a separate licence, but the participants and participating interests are identical in the two licences, and in practice, they will operate as one licence. However, this alternative is not suitable if the reservoir for CO_2 storage is not adjacent to the existing licence. Another solution could be to allow the activity under a PDO pursuant to the Petroleum Act section 4-2 and chapter 4a of the Petroleum Regulations, even though the reservoir is outside the geographical boundaries of the production licence. This could be comparable to Hywind Tampen, as described in footnote 35, where the wind farm is outside the licence borders.

There does not seem to be an obvious solution to the case described here. It could also be relevant to consider whether the CO_2 storage would have sufficient capacity to receive CO_2 from third parties. If it could be regarded as offering storage as a separate service, applying for an exploitation licence under the CO_2 Storage Regulations could make the most sense, even if the initial and primary purpose is to store CO_2 as part of petroleum activities.

D. Reflections

As illustrated above, there can be commercially and technically sound solutions for CO_2 storage either as part of petroleum activities or as a continuation of petroleum activities. Still, there are some cases where it is unclear which licensing regime is applicable, or the change of licensing system from the Petroleum Act to the CO_2 Storage Regulations could lead to a less efficient transition from petroleum activities to CO_2 storage activities. In many cases, this can be solved. Still, it is essential that the regulatory regimes do not hinder the development of commercially sound projects critical to achieving net zero emissions.

5. Repurposing of Decommissioned Petroleum Facilities for Renewable Energy Production or CCS

A. Introduction and Regulatory Starting Points

So far, we have discussed coordinating licence regimes when offshore wind and CCS are used to decarbonise petroleum production. The final topic we want to address is a 'reverse' scenario. The question is how the licence regimes are coordinated to facilitate the use of decommissioned oil and gas facilities to produce renewable energy or CCS.[67]

Under the Petroleum Act, the licensees of a production licence have an obligation to submit a decommissioning plan to the Ministry of Energy when the petroleum activity or the use of a facility approaches the end of a lifetime.[68] The plan needs to include a proposal for the disposal of the facilities. In this respect, the alternatives are not only removal, abandonment, or further use in petroleum activities; the Petroleum Act also allows for 'other use' as an alternative disposal. Such repurposing may include renewable energy production or CCS. For example, depleted reservoirs, wells, and platform topsides can be repurposed for injection of CO_2, pipelines can be repurposed to transport hydrogen, and platform substructures can be converted to facilitate offshore wind infrastructure.

[67] For a comparative introduction to decommissioning framework for oil- and gas facilities and offshore wind facilities, including reuse and repurposing, see for example Ignacio Herrera Anchustegui and Gunnar S Eskeland et al, *Understanding Decommissioning of Offshore Infrastructures: A Legal and Economic Appetizer* (1 July 2021) https://ssrn.com/abstract=3882821 or dx.doi.org/10.2139/ssrn.3882821. Regarding regulating reuse- and repurposing of oil- and gas facilities, see Catherine Banet, 'Regulating the Reuse and Repurposing of Oil and Gas Installations in the Context of Decommissioning: Creating Incentives and Enabling Energy System Integration' in Eduardo G Pereira, Alexandra Wawryk, Heike Trischmann, Catnerine Banet and Keith B Hall (ed.), *The Regulation of Decommissioning, Abandonment and Reuse Initiatives in the Oil and Gas Industry* (Wolters Kluwer, 2022) 361–86.

[68] Petroleum Act, s 5-1. For a general introduction to the regulatory framework for decommissioning in the Petroleum Act, see Yngve Bustnesli, Olav Boye Sivertsen, Hans Petter Nordby and Tore Ulleberg (eds), *Oil and Gas Activities in Norway – Regulatory and contractual framework* (Gyldendal, 2021) 120–33.

The Ministry of Energy makes the decision on disposal and sets a deadline for implementation.[69] So far, the repurposing of facilities for renewable energy production or CCS has not been applied in any decision on disposal in Norway.

The Ministry of Energy's decision that the facilities shall be used for offshore renewable energy production, or CCS, is part of the licensing regime under the Petroleum Act. However, repurposed use is not a petroleum activity and, thus, is not within the scope of the Petroleum Act at the outset. Repurposing oil- and gas facilities for CCS or offshore wind will require new licences as applicable.

However, the Petroleum Act regulates the distribution of liability for future disposal of the facilities and for the potential damage caused by the facility between the former licensees of the production licence and the new users of the facilities. At the same time, decommissioning of facilities repurposed for CO_2 storage will be subject to the decommissioning regulation in the CO_2 Storage Regulations Chapter 7, and facilities repurposed for offshore wind will be subject to decommissioning regulations in the Offshore Energy Act Chapter 6.

B. Allocation of Future Disposal Obligations

The Petroleum Act does not regulate future disposal in detail. It neither regulates the interface with the CO_2 Storage Regulations nor the Offshore Energy Act. Still, section 5-3, fifth paragraph sets out that the former licensees (and, if relevant, the former owner of the facility) and the new users are jointly obliged to ensure that future decisions on disposal are implemented unless the Ministry decides otherwise. Although the regulation may seem fair at the outset, it may disincentivise the repurposing of existing petroleum facilities: By becoming jointly obliged to dispose of the petroleum facility, the new user takes on a substantial financial burden.[70] The benefits of taking over the facilities will not necessarily outweigh such a financial burden.[71]

Further, the continued liability for the former licensees of the production licence implies that they will not be released from the liability of final disposal, even though new users have taken over the facilities.[72] Postponement of removal costs and shared liability with new users may benefit them. However, the liability makes the financial exposure uncertain due to factors such as the future technical condition of the facility, which disposal alternative the Ministry will decide upon, and which environmental requirements will apply in the future. Also, the individual former licensee will have joint and several liabilities for the disposal obligations of the former licence group, meaning that a future payment default by one of the licensees would increase the exposure of the other licensees.

[69] Petroleum Act, s 5-3, para 1.

[70] Anne Ingeborg F Reiestad, 'Erstatningsansvar ved avslutning av petroleumsvirksomhet – med særlig fokus på forurensningsskader' (2015) 447 *MarIus* 97–98.

[71] Hammer et al (n 63) 441 argue that the rule should be interpreted narrowly so that the new user's removal obligations are limited to those parts of the removal that are within the new user's control.

[72] Reiestad in *MarIus* (n 70) 97–98. Any guarantees or other security arrangements that a licensee has provided to the Norwegian state for possible decommissioning liabilities will apply unless the Ministry of Energy has released the former licensees from such security arrangements.

There is also a risk that the relevant facility's condition will be impaired after repurposing. The facility must be adequately maintained to avoid the subsequent removal becoming more risky and costly. Which party should bear the responsibility for maintenance of the facility during the new use is not currently regulated by law.[73]

Although a joint obligation for disposal is the main rule, the Ministry has broad discretionary authority to allocate responsibility for executing the disposal decision. Thus, the Ministry may relieve one or more obligated entities from their disposal obligations or parts thereof. In this regard, the Ministry must also consider regulating liability for disposal obligation under the licence regime for the repurposing in question.[74]

C. Liability for Future Damage

Liability for future damage is particularly relevant concerning pollution damage. Still, other damage may also occur during other use or under decommissioning after the other use is terminated.

Legal predictability and certainty are imperative for developers considering taking over a decommissioned petroleum facility for repurposing. For example, an offshore wind developer is most likely unwilling to risk liability for leaks of chemicals or petroleum originating from former petroleum activities. Although the former licensees have a legitimate interest in being relieved from liability, such liability for the new users may not be reasonable where the damage is wholly or partly caused by circumstances related to the petroleum activities on the facility. On the other hand, the offshore wind activities on the facility could continue for decades, and the former licensees of the petroleum production licence have a legitimate interest in being relieved from liability at some point. If the licensees were to remain liable during the entire period of repurposing, the risk is that they may not have sufficient incentives to facilitate repurposing and prefer to promote a decommissioning plan to bring the facility to shore for final removal instead.

The conflicting interests between the former licensees and the new users warrant a precise distribution of liability, especially liability for pollution damages. However, as of today, this is arguably not the case. With respect to any pollution damages that stem from the previous petroleum activities that materialise during the period of repurposing, the former *licensees* risk liability for pollution damage under Chapter 7 of the Petroleum Act.[75] Since this is a strict liability for the licensees,[76] this puts licensees at risk of being liable for pollution damage regardless of fault for the entire reuse period.

Since repurposed use is not a petroleum activity, the Petroleum Act will not apply to new facilities users.[77] Thus, any compensation claim for damages caused by the new

[73] ibid.

[74] The CO_2 Storage Regulations, ch 7 regulates cessation of injection and storage of CO_2, and the Offshore Energy Act, ch 6 regulates cessation of offshore energy facilities.

[75] Reiestad in *MarIus* (n 70) 93.

[76] Petroleum Act, s 1-4 and s 7-3.

[77] Petroleum Act s 1-4.

user must be submitted on other grounds. In this respect, the new users risk strict liability for pollution damage based on the Norwegian Pollution Act.[78] In principle, this includes pollution originating from previous petroleum activities.[79] Consequently, both the former licensees and the new users risk liability for pollution damage originating from previous petroleum activities. If both the repurposing and the previous petroleum activity have contributed to the damages, the parties risk joint and several liability.[80] If the petroleum facilities are repurposed for CCS, the new user risks strict liability for pollution damage based on Chapter 8 of the CO_2 Storage Regulations.

D. Reflections

In summary, reusing petroleum facilities would entail uncertainty both for the new users and the petroleum licensees.[81] As such, the current legislation may deter the parties from considering new areas of utilisation for petroleum facilities.

If the Norwegian Government wishes to promote the utilisation of petroleum facilities for offshore wind, an alternative could be for the State to use its right to take over fixed installations.[82] Such take-over would relieve the petroleum licensees of their obligation to remove the installation.[83] The terms and conditions for the new use, including the allocation of liability between the State as owner and the new user, can then be separately agreed between the State and the user. Regulating pollution liability will be essential.

[78] Pollution Act, s 55.
[79] Reiestad in *MarIus* (n 70) 96.
[80] Norwegian Pollution Act, s 59.
[81] Reiestad in MarIus (n 70) 97-98.
[82] Petroleum Act, s 5-6.
[83] Bustnesli, Sivertsen, Nordby and Ulleberg (n 68) 131.

15

Three Parts to the New Offshore Economy: Integrating Offshore Wind Energy with Hydrogen Electrolysis on Repurposed Oil and Gas Installations

RÜDIGER TSCHERNING*

1. Introduction and Context

This chapter examines the role of a nascent offshore wind energy industry in Atlantic Canada and its role in the development of a hydrogen economy. It explores the idea of co-locating offshore wind energy generation with hydrogen electrolysis on repurposed offshore oil and gas infrastructure, as part of an 'integrated' new offshore economy. The concept of an integrated offshore economy would, first and foremost, address the challenges of connecting offshore wind energy projects to an onshore electricity network via complex subsea electricity transmission infrastructure. Although some offshore projects have successfully been electrified using HVDC cables with distances of 292 km (such as the Valhall field in Norway),[1] given the geographic distances of existing offshore oil and gas installations to shore in Newfoundland and Labrador, production of hydrogen could capture the generated electricity instead as part of a wider push towards a shift from electrons to (hydrogen) molecules. Moreover, the produced hydrogen could be stored (subject to rigorous safety regimes) on the repurposed installations, and then subsequently exported directly to regional and international offtake markets, without the associated cost of investment in offshore grid infrastructure and the efficiency losses resulting 'from transporting electricity over long distances' to produce the hydrogen onshore.[2]

* This chapter has been made possible thanks to the generous funding to the Norwegian Centre for Hydrogen Value Chain Research (HyValue) by the Research Council of Norway under the project: 333151.

[1] Ignacio Herrera Anchustegui and Aleksander Glapiak, 'Wind of Change: A Scandinavian Perspective on Energy Transition and the "greenification" of the Oil and Gas Sector' in Katarzyna Gromek-Broc (ed), *Regional Approaches to the Energy Transition: A Multidisciplinary Perspective* (Springer, 2023).

[2] Ignacio Herrera Anchustegui and Rudiger Tscherning, 'Offshore oil and gas infrastructure electrification and offshore wind: a legal exploration' (2024) 17(1) *Journal of World Energy Law & Business* 35–53, 39.

What distinguishes the design of the proposed offshore wind energy project from more conventional wind energy generation models is that the renewable electricity would not be transmitted onshore via sub-sea electricity transmission cables for onshore hydrogen electrolysis.[3] Instead, the hydrogen would be produced on repurposed offshore oil and gas installations as part of a co-located and 'integrated system', via electrolysis (powered by offshore wind energy) using desalinated seawater (with desalination also powered by the offshore wind energy).[4] The produced hydrogen would be directly transported by ship from the point of production to regional and international markets. RWE's AquaVentus initiative in the North Sea offers an example of a forward-thinking and integrated offshore wind and hydrogen production project and may act as a helpful point of reference for this chapter.[5] Overall, the concept of integrated offshore wind and hydrogen production, as proposed in this chapter, could therefore serve as a model for future sector coupling and greater alignment of the offshore renewable energy sector with an emerging hydrogen economy as well as with the legacy oil and gas sector.[6] This shift towards a new offshore economy would come at a time of transition, when existing offshore oil and gas projects in Atlantic Canada are experiencing natural declines in production.[7]

Within the context of a changing offshore economy, the chapter discusses the legal challenges to achieving the integration goal using hydrogen production (powered by renewable offshore wind energy) as the lead objective. The chapter proceeds as follows: in Part I, it examines the development of an offshore wind energy sector in Atlantic Canada and introduces the idea of co-locating of offshore wind energy projects in close proximity the hydrogen production, at a time when Canada's legal regime for offshore wind energy generation is slowly emerging. Part II of the chapter then examines the key legal issues arising from the idea of repurposing offshore oil and gas infrastructure for hydrogen production, including the role of repurposing within the waste management hierarchy, potential incentives aimed at encouraging an owner of an offshore installation not to proceed with decommission, as well as introducing the idea of 'displaced' greenhouse gas emissions for climate credits by repurposing instead of building new offshore infrastructure. In Part III of the chapter, the third step of the future offshore economy, the siting of desalination and electrolyser infrastructure on decommissioned

[3] Offshore Energy, 'Repurposing oil & gas infrastructure to harness offshore wind power' (29 May 2023) www.offshore-energy.biz/repurposing-oil-gas-infrastructure-to-harness-offshore-wind-power/; see also GH2 Green Hydrogen Organisation, 'Key considerations for hydrogen offtake agreements' (June 2024) gh2.org/sites/default/files/2024-05/GH2_Considerations%20for%20Hydrogen%20Offtake%20Agreements_2024.pdf.

[4] G Kubilay Karayel and Ibrahim Dincer, 'A study on green hydrogen production potential of Canada with onshore and offshore wind power' (2024) 437 *Journal of Cleaner Production* 140660.

[5] RWE, 'AquaVentus Hydrogen Production Project', www.rwe.com/en/research-and-development/hydrogen-projects/aquaventus/; see also H2 Green Steel Project.

[6] International Renewable Energy Agency (IRENA), 'Renewable Energy Policies in a Time of Transition' (2018) 93.

[7] Canada Energy Regulator, 'Market Snapshot: 25 Years of Atlantic Canada Offshore Oil & Natural Gas Production' (12 October 2017) www.cer-rec.gc.ca/en/data-analysis/energy-markets/market-snapshots/2017/market-snapshot-25-years-atlantic-canada-offshore-oil-natural-gas-production.html.

offshore oil and gas installations, is discussed as part of an examination of the legal issues arising from the idea of 'integrated' offshore hydrogen production. These legal issues include ownership and transfer risks including long-term liabilities and decommissioning costs, commercial risks and their allocation in project-specific contracts as related to water and electricity supplies (for hydrogen electrolysis), and risks arising from the practicalities of directly shipping the hydrogen to offtake markets.

2. Rationale for Integrated Offshore Hydrogen Production

A. Introduction

In the offshore environment, hydrogen can be produced through energy-intensive electrolysis, using desalinated seawater as a feedstock together with renewable electricity as the 'green' energy source to power the electrolyser infrastructure. As a zero-carbon pathway to hydrogen production, electrolysis contrasts with the more prevalent and currently cost-competitive form of production of hydrogen from hydrocarbon feedstock (such as natural gas) through steam methane reforming or pyrolysis. Irrespective of the elected pathway, hydrogen production requires vast amounts of energy. On this basis, using renewable electricity such as onshore or offshore wind energy significantly improves the climate credential of hydrogen, although, as noted, at increased cost due to losses in energy efficiencies to produce so-called 'green hydrogen.'

B. Project Models for Offshore Hydrogen Integration

At its simplest, there are three conceptual project models for offshore wind energy integration with hydrogen production, consisting of direct transmission of the electricity via cables to onshore electrolysers; the use of centralised electrolysers in the offshore environment; or on-turbine electrolysers.[8] Given that direct transmission is not the focus of this chapter and on-turbine electrolyser-led projects would require new infrastructure to collect the produced hydrogen, only the second model will be further examined. As proposed in several feasibility studies,[9] the idea of locating the electrolyser and desalination infrastructure on offshore installations will introduce additional technical and legal complexities arising from the need to decommission and repurpose complex large offshore oil and gas installations, including the criteria and processes to determine when an asset can be transferred in law and when decommissioning obligations are extinguished.

[8] Arthur D Little, 'Offshore Wind & Hydrogen Integration' Report 2023, 9, www.adlittle.com/sites/default/files/reports/ADL_Offshore_wind_and_hydrogen_2023.pdf.

[9] For helpful background to this concept, see Vysus Group, 'Feasibility study on repurpose of oil and gas infrastructure for offshore hydrogen generation' (30 June 2021) 23.

C. Impulses for Developing Hydrogen Offshore in Atlantic Canada

Why is the concept of an integrated hydrogen production value chain in the offshore introduced at a time of heightened interest in transitioning regional electricity grids to renewables, including the build-out of an onshore hydrogen production industry? First and foremost, the grid in Newfoundland and Labrador is already green, generating approximately 96 per cent of its supply from hydroelectricity.[10] Offshore wind integration in the existing energy mix would add little to decarbonise the grid. In Nova Scotia, the share of renewables is approximately 25 per cent, but expected to increase significantly as coal fired electricity generation will be phased-out by 2030 and replaced by renewables both onshore and offshore.[11] Second, complex geographic and technical constrains (as well as socio-environmental constraints) may make it difficult to connect the offshore wind energy to an onshore grid, due to long-distances, sensitive coastal environments, competing uses of the marine environment,[12] and the risk that no existing onshore transmission infrastructure may exist, thereby requiring additional infrastructure investment.

At the same time, Atlantic Canada's oil and gas production has been steadily declining,[13] with the Sable Offshore Energy Project in Nova Scotia decommissioned as recently as November, although new discoveries and planned projects (such as Equinor's Bay du Nord Development project) could reverse this trend.[14] For example, in February 2024, the Canada-Newfoundland and Labrador Offshore Petroleum Board issued a Significant Discovery Licence to Equinor for the Cambriol G-92 discovery with a recoverable oil volume estimated to be 340 million barrels, which is adjacent to the Bay du Nord discovery.[15] Hydrogen production on existing hydrocarbon platforms would, in the first instance, extend the economic life of the installation (assuming that, as examined below, both liability questions and the physical conditions would allow this as a viable prospect). It would also reduce environmental damage which would otherwise have resulted from the construction of new infrastructure, by repurposing (at least to some degree) the existing physical infrastructure.[16]

[10] Canada Energy Regulator, Provincial and Territorial Energy Profile – Newfoundland and Labrador, www.cer-rec.gc.ca/en/data-analysis/energy-markets/provincial-territorial-energy-profiles/provincial-territorial-energy-profiles-newfoundland-labrador.html.

[11] www.canada.ca/en/natural-resources-canada/news/2023/10/governments-of-canada-nova-scotia-and-new-brunswick-show-progress-toward-phasing-out-coal-by-2030-and-expanding-their-clean-reliable-and-affordable.html.

[12] Ignacio Herrera Anchustegui and Tina Soliman Hunter, 'Geographical, technological, and legal perspectives of offshore wind energy' in Ignacio Herrera Anchustegui and Tina Soliman Hunter (eds), *Offshore Wind Licensing* (Edward Elgar Publishing, 2024).

[13] Canada Energy Regulator (n 7).

[14] Equinor Canada, The Bay du Nord project, www.equinor.com/where-we-are/canada-bay-du-nord.

[15] Canada-Newfoundland & Labrador Offshore Petroleum Board, News Release 2024, C-NLOPB ISSUES SIGNIFICANT DISCOVERY LICENCE TO EQUINOR CANADA LTD. AND ANNOUNCES VOLUME ESTIMATE FOR THE CAMBRIOL G-92 DISCOVERY (2 February 2024) www.cnlopb.ca/news/nr02022024/.

[16] Liv Malin Andreasson and Martha Roggenkamp, 'Deliverable 2.2, 2.3 – Regulatory Framework: Legal Challenges and Incentives for Developing Hydrogen Offshore, North Sea Energy' (2020) 11.

3. Part I: Towards Regulatory Certainty to Build-Out an Offshore Wind Energy Industry

A. Early Stages of Offshore Wind Energy Development

The build-out of an offshore wind energy industry in Canada is still at the very early stages of development, let alone any governance for the integration of offshore wind with hydrogen production. Still, the longer-term potential to develop hydrogen based on offshore wind is gaining attention. For example, the Hydrogen Strategy for Canada: Progress Report of April 2024, highlights that 'while developers are getting started with onshore wind, they will look to scale up using the abundant offshore wind resources off Nova Scotia's coast.'[17] This has been also matched by regional authorities; to support the scaling-up of offshore hydrogen production, Nova Scotia has 'set a target to offer seabed leases for 5,000 MW of offshore wind energy by 2030.'[18] The recent Newfoundland and Labrador Hydrogen Development Action Plan 2040 of May 2024 does not, however, include any targets for hydrogen production or the scaling-up of an offshore wind energy industry. Outside of the provinces, Canada's federal government has taken steps through both policy and fiscal incentives, including incentives to expand a domestic hydrogen electrolyser manufacturing industry.[19] In reality, however, Canada's hydrogen economy remains at the early stages even for onshore wind energy generation, let alone for integrated hydrogen production and offshore wind energy.

B. A New Emerging Regime for 'Offshore Renewable Energy Projects'

At the outset, it should be acknowledged that the regulatory regime for offshore wind energy is still at a very early point of development in Canada. The governance of energy in Canada, broadly speaking, is made up of a complex mosaic of federal, provincial/territorial and shared jurisdictional regimes. The Canadian Energy Regulator (CER), as the full lifecycle regulator, has jurisdiction over offshore energy activities outside provincial or territorial waters,[20] including for so-called 'offshore renewable energy projects', by virtue of Part 5 of the Canadian Energy Regulator Act 2019 (CERA). In addition to CER as the lead regulator, several other federal authorities exercise their 'complementary

[17] Natural Resources Canada, Hydrogen Strategy for Canada: Progress Report, May 2024, https://natural-resources.canada.ca/climate-change/canadas-green-future/the-hydrogen-strategy/hydrogen-strategy-for-canada-progress-report/25678#a7a.

[18] ibid 5.

[19] ibid.

[20] Daniel Watt and Lucia Westin, 'The Regulation of Offshore Renewable Energy under the Canadian Energy Regulator Act: Towards Full and Rational Development of ORE in Atlantic Canada' (2022) 10(1) Energy Regulation Quarterly, energyregulationquarterly.ca/articles/the-regulation-of-offshore-renewable-energy-under-the-canadian-energy-regulator-act-towards-full-and-rational-development-of-ore-in-atlantic-canada#sthash.8jH5koco.mDq4zyXN.dpbs.

responsibilities in the offshore', including Transport Canada, Department of Fisheries and Oceans, and Environment and Climate Change Canada.[21]

In Atlantic Canada, there is also a long history of joint management of offshore oil and gas resources between the federal and provincial governments of Nova Scotia and of Newfoundland and Labrador, respectively, administered by two offshore petroleum boards.[22] The Canada-Nova Scotia Offshore Petroleum Board and the Canada-Newfoundland and Labrador Offshore Petroleum Board are currently in the process of modernisation, in large part with a view to exercising their new jurisdiction over renewable energy opportunities.[23] This jurisdictional expansion process is undertaken pursuant to federal Bill C-49 (An Act to amend the Canada – Newfoundland and Labrador Atlantic Accord Implementation Act and the Canada-Nova Scotia Offshore Petroleum Resources Accord Implementation Act and to make consequential amendments to other Acts), which was introduced in the legislative process in May 2023 and which will also see the renaming of the respective boards from oil and gas to 'Offshore Energy Boards.'[24]

At the time of writing, Bill C-49 is awaiting the third (and final) reading before the House of Commons. One of the major consequences of Bill C-49 is that once the expansion and modernisation provisions are implemented in practice, CERA will no longer apply in the two respective joint management areas of Newfoundland and Labrador and of Nova Scotia. This, in turn, will require new or revised regulations respecting the safety, security, and environmental protection of offshore renewable energy projects. Critically, this will mean that the draft offshore renewable energy regulations, examined below, may have to be replaced shortly after their anticipated coming into force. The CERA-regulations will, however, act as the 'basis for these future regulations',[25] meaning that all efforts to prepare them may not be lost.

As noted, Part 5 of CERA came into force in August 2019 and provides the legislative framework to govern an 'offshore renewable energy project', which comprises activities carried on in Canada's federal offshore area related to:

> '…
> (b) exploitation of a renewable resource to produce energy;
> (c) storage of energy produced from a renewable resource; or
> (d) transmission of such energy, other than the transmission of electricity to a province or a place outside Canada.'[26]

As a first observation, the definition of offshore renewable energy project could encompass the idea of a co-located hydrogen production project, provided that such

[21] Natural Resources Canada, Discussion Paper, Canada's Approach to Offshore Renewable Energy Regulations, 2.

[22] Canada-Nova Scotia Offshore Petroleum Resources Accord Implementation Act, SC 1988, c 28; Canada–Newfoundland and Labrador Atlantic Accord Implementation Act, SC 1987, c 3.

[23] *Canada Gazette*, Part I, Vol. 158, No. 8, 458. See also Canada-Nova Scotia Offshore Petroleum Board, Canada-Nova Scotia Offshore Energy Regulator (CNSOER) Updates, www.cnsopb.ns.ca/canada-nova-scotia-offshore-energy-regulator-cnsoer-updates.

[24] Canada, Bill C-49 (An Act to amend the Canada – Newfoundland and Labrador Atlantic Accord Implementation Act and the Canada-Nova Scotia Offshore Petroleum Resources Accord Implementation Act and to make consequential amendments to other Acts, www.parl.ca/legisinfo/en/bill/44-1/c-49.

[25] *Canada Gazette*, Part I, Vol. 158, No. 8, 458.

[26] Canadian Energy Regulator Act, SC 2019, c 28, s 2. See also Watt and Westin (n 20).

integrated projected is electrified by a power line connection to an offshore wind energy project. As Part 5 of CERA provides only an initial framework on offshore renewable energy projects or offshore power lines,[27] the actual details will be set out in accompanying Offshore Renewable Energy Regulations, the first draft of which was released in February 2024 (ORER). Lack of progress of almost five years on these regulations has certainly introduced a degree of uncertainty. It also remains to be seen if there is any scope in the final regulations to include provisions that could be drawn upon for purposes of the proposed integrated offshore wind and hydrogen project, including drawing on the legacy of the offshore oil and gas regulatory regime. One tentative indicator is that the Government of Canada has noted that the regulations were drafted to align with the regulation of existing offshore petroleum activities so as 'to allow for consistency [...] while ensuring that the requirements for [offshore renewable energy] were not unnecessarily burdensome, given the risk profile for [offshore renewable energy] is much lower than that of petroleum.'[28] On the point of risk profiling, Wifa and Hunter have previously investigated and concluded (albeit in the context of the Australian offshore wind energy industry) that 'the two offshore energy industries share remarkably similar characteristics and in turn, share similar health and safety risks.'[29]

As the ORER remain under consultation at the time of writing, this section will introduce the key provisions relevant to an international audience only. Whether the ORER will advance the development of offshore wind energy in the first instance, and potentially act as a longer-term incentive to integrated hydrogen production, remains to be seen. As noted, at this initial stage, there are some indicators to suggest that integrated offshore projects could be included in the offshore governance. For example, as set out in the Regulatory Impact Analysis Statement accompanying the ORER, the regulations are said to 'propose a combination approach of management-based and outcome-based regulatory frameworks, with a strong emphasis on safety management systems.'[30] The objective of this combination approach is to provide 'the flexibility necessary to support the use of innovations in science, technologies, and methodologies that would increase safety, security, and environmental protection while reducing costs and allowing the proposed Regulations to remain evergreen as the [offshore renewable energy] sector evolves over time.'[31]

There is also a strong emphasis on the role of the operator and the operator's responsibility to 'eliminate potential hazards to safety, security, and the environment through various management, planning, and analysis activities.'[32] These core principles of operator-led innovation, regulatory flexibility, and adherence to safety, security, and environmental protection are noticeable throughout the draft ORER and the CERA Part 5 governance and may need to be navigated as part of the proposed co-location

[27] Canadian Energy Regulator Act, s 298(1).

[28] *Canada Gazette*, Part I, Vol. 158, No. 8, 480. www.gazette.gc.ca/rp-pr/p1/2024/2024-02-24/pdf/g1-15808.pdf.

[29] Eddy Wifa and Tina Soliman Hunter, 'Mitigating Occupational Health and Safety Risks in the Proposed Australian Offshore Wind Energy Industry: Lessons from the Safety Case Regime' (2022) 40(1) *Journal of Energy & Natural Resources Law* 83–104.

[30] *Canada Gazette*, Part I, Vol. 158, No. 8, 458.

[31] ibid.

[32] ibid.

of offshore infrastructure. At the same time, this embedded flexibility, as well as the emphasis on the operator as the driver of the regulatory process, could actually advance integration of offshore wind and hydrogen in Canada's offshore environment, if the first step in the hydrogen production project (mirroring the structure of this chapter), is the offshore wind energy project. The regulations are also clear as to the requirements which an operator must meet to obtain an authorisation pursuant to section 298 of CERA, for each of the different phases of the offshore wind energy project and that any work or activity is prohibited unless authorised. Per Canada's offshore renewable energy governance, the key phases consist of the initial site assessment, the construction and operation of the project, and the decommissioning and abandonment phases of the project.[33]

As noted in the *Canada Gazette*, this phased regulatory approach allows for 'one application and related authorization for each major phase of a project, rather than having numerous individual applications and authorizations for each discrete work or activity at each phase.'[34] This is an important provision, given the fact that the ORER and the existing regime for offshore oil and gas infrastructure should be aligned as a key objective, and the fact that it may be possible (in theory at least) that there will be one application, and the grant of one authorisation, for each phase of a project. Here, it could be anticipated that the regulatory application for the offshore wind phase, the electricity power line, and the hydrogen infrastructure (at least as individual components), would consist of no more than three applications. Finally, every application pursuant to CERA is subject to the condition 'that the operator develop and implement' a management system and several detailed plans before the authorised works commence.[35] Section 7 of the draft ORER sets out the detailed provisions on the management system, which 'must establish the overall direction and framework for reducing risks to safety, security, and the environment, including measures for ensuring the reliable operation of the facilities, equipment and systems related to an offshore renewable energy project or offshore power line and appropriate response in case of an emergency.'[36]

4. Part II: Decommissioning and the Idea of Repurposing Existing Offshore Oil and Gas Infrastructure for Offshore Hydrogen Production

A. Repurposing within the International Law Context as Relevant to Atlantic Canada

The international legal framework for decommissioning of offshore infrastructure consists of a complex web of international as well as regional obligations.[37] As

[33] *Canada Gazette*, Part I, Vol. 158, No. 8, 459.

[34] ibid.

[35] Canada, Offshore Renewable Energy Regulations, Draft, (ORER), s 6(1); *Canada Gazette*, Part I, Vol. 158, No. 8, 486.

[36] ORER, s 7, *Canada Gazette*, Part I, Vol. 158, No. 8, 487–90.

[37] For a helpful overview of the international law regime, see Yoshifumi Tanaka, *The International Law of the Sea*, 3rd edn (Cambridge University Press, 2019); see also, Tina Soliman Hunter, 'Best practice for

Andreasson and Roggenkamp note, in contrast to the '1958 Geneva Convention on the Continental Shelf, the current [Article 60 UNCLOS] regime no longer requires a "complete removal" but merely a "removal" of abandoned or disused installations or structures.'[38] Article 60 of the United Nations Convention on the Law of the Sea 1982 is the cornerstone of the international decommissioning regime, together with the International Maritime Organization's 1989 Guidelines and Standards for the Removal of Offshore Installations and Structures on the Continental Shelf and in the Exclusive Economic Zone.[39] The IMO guidelines provide that abandoned or disused installations should be removed, but there are several exceptions to this rule, including 'when the installation or structure will serve a new use' or when 'the installation or structure can be left in place without causing unjustifiable interference with other uses of the sea.'[40] This would suggest that repurposing of the installation, as contemplated in this chapter, would be permitted under the IMO guidelines, subject to the condition that no unjustifiable interference with other ocean users is caused. Although Canada is not a party to the Convention for the Protection of the Marine Environment of the North-East Atlantic (OSPAR Convention)[41] and its governance of marine pollution in the North-East Atlantic, this section would be incomplete without a brief reference to OSPAR Decision 98/3, which sets out several provisions on the treatment of 'disused offshore installations.'[42] Accordingly, the OSPAR regime acts as an important additional point of reference for any discussion on decommissioning and repurposing of offshore installations.

B. Inventory of Existing Offshore Infrastructure in Newfoundland and Labrador

Offshore installations are typically made up of three components, consisting of platforms, substructures and sub-sea production systems. Platforms 'support the structures and equipment necessary to explore for, extract and process oil and gas.'[43] Fixed substructures support the oil and gas platforms. Sub-sea production systems of 'subsea pipelines, subsea wells and the various technologies that connect multiple well heads to pipelines and other transmission and production infrastructure.[44]

dismantling, recycling, and disposal of offshore petroleum structures' (Macquarie University, June 2023) researchers.mq.edu.au/en/publications/best-practice-for-dismantling-recycling-and-disposal-of-offshore-.

[38] UN General Assembly, Convention on the Law of the Sea, 10 December 1982, Article 60; see also Andreasson and Roggenkamp (n 16).

[39] The 1989 Guidelines and Standards for the Removal of Offshore Installations and Structures on the Continental Shelf and in the Exclusive Economic Zone, Resolution A. 672 (16), Adopted by the International Maritime Organization on 19 October 1989.

[40] The 1989 Guidelines and Standards for the Removal of Offshore Installations and Structures on the Continental Shelf and in the Exclusive Economic Zone; see also Andreasson and Roggenkamp (n 16) 20.

[41] Convention for the Protection of the Marine Environment of the North-East Atlantic (OSPAR Convention 1992).

[42] Convention for the Protection of the Marine Environment of the North-East Atlantic 1992, OSPAR Decision 98/3 on the Disposal of Disuse Offshore Installations 1998; see also Andreasson and Roggenkamp (n 16) 20.

[43] McInnes Cooper, 'Offshore Oil and Gas Decommissioning Best Practices' (December 2015) 13.

[44] McInnes Cooper (n 43) 14.

Based on 2020 figures, Newfoundland and Labrador's crude oil production of 282.7 thousand barrels per day amounted to approximately 5 per cent of Canada's overall production and 24 per cent of Canada's light oil production.[45] Production is currently from four offshore developments, consisting of the Hibernia, Terra Nova, White Rose and Hebron projects. A brief review of these projects reveals that the infrastructure for the Hibernia and Hebron projects is the most feasible to explore for potential repurposing to host hydrogen projects, as the Terra Nova and White Rose installations consist of floating production, storage and offloading (FPSO) vessels.[46] All four projects are located a large distance from Newfoundland's shore, with Hibernia located some 300 miles (482 km) from the provincial capital St John's. Although they are relatively modern projects in comparison to the North Sea fields, with the first project, the Hibernia platform, starting production in late 1997.[47]

To provide a sense of the size and scale of the offshore infrastructure in question, the Hibernia project consists of a '550,000 tonne concrete [Gravity Base Structure] that sits on the ocean floor. The structure supports a 37,000-tonne topside deck, featuring drilling and production facilities, and accommodations for up to 185 people. Crude oil extracted by the Hibernia installation is stored in tanks located in the GBS, which have a storage capacity of 1.3 million barrels of oil. Oil recovered by the installation is collected by tankers through an offshore loading system and either shipped internationally or brought to a Newfoundland transhipment facility.'[48] The Hebron installation is also a Gravity Base Structure of 120m in height and with a lower diameter of 130m, supported by a 40m 'topside deck featuring drilling and production facilities and accommodations for up to 220 persons.' The installation also includes an offshore loading system.

Another advantage for the proposal to repurpose some offshore infrastructure in Atlantic Canada is that there is already experience with decommissioning of oil and gas infrastructure. The most recent project to be fully decommissioned is the Sable Offshore Energy Project in Nova Scotia, following permanent shutdown of production in December 2018. This decommissioning project, undertaken between May and November 2020, included the 'Engineering, Preparation, Removal, and Disposal (EPRD) of seven platform topsides, seven jackets, and 22 conductors. A total of five barge loads carrying Sable platform components, weighing approximately 48,000 metric tons, were towed across the Atlantic.'[49]

[45] Canada Energy Regulator, Provincial and Territorial Energy Profiles – Newfoundland and Labrador, www.cer-rec.gc.ca/en/data-analysis/energy-markets/provincial-territorial-energy-profiles/provincial-territorial-energy-profiles-newfoundland-labrador.html#:~:text=In%202020%2C%20Newfoundland%20and%20Labrador's,of%20Canada's%20light%20oil%20production.

[46] McInnes Cooper (n 43) 51–52.

[47] Canada Energy Regulator (n 7).

[48] McInnes Cooper (n 43) 51.

[49] Heerema Marine Contractors, 'Offshore decommissioning, 48,000 metric tons of infrastructure removed with zero recordable HSE cases' (undated) www.heerema.com/heerema-marine-contractors/offshore-decommissioning/sable-project. See also, Canada-Nova Scotia Offshore Petroleum Board, 'Sable Offshore Energy Project' Decommissioning and Abandonment, www.cnsopb.ns.ca/offshore-activity/current-activity/sable-offshore.

C. Decommissioning Methods for Oil and Gas Installations

The decommissioning methods for offshore oil and gas installations included complete removal, partial removal, and (as proposed in this chapter) the repurposing for secondary uses.[50] Complete removal of the physical infrastructure may, depending on the individual context of project, be considered 'the most environmentally sound strategy',[51] but does not automatically have to be, given the experience with so-called rigs-to reefs projects.[52] In any case, complete removal will provide commercial certainty for 'expenses associated with the partial removal of an offshore installation, including ongoing maintenance costs, legal liability and financial responsibility expenses.'[53] Partial removal, as the name suggests, is the deconstruction of offshore installations and the removal of some of their components, 'while leaving others in place.'[54] In this context, there has been extensive discussion around so-called 'rigs to reefs' projects involving partial removal of infrastructure. Alternative secondary uses for repurposed post-production offshore installations 'maximizes its recoverable value and accords with notions of environmental and economic sustainability. In particular, it satisfies the precepts of the waste management hierarchy.'[55] Within this hierarchy, repurposing is considered the reuse of an installation 'for a different purpose than the original one … for example, oil and gas infrastructure can be reused in relation to … hydrogen production and transport.'[56] At the risk of stating the obvious, repurposing does not entail the complete removal of a fixed installation.

D. Repurposing of Existing Offshore Infrastructure

Depending on the project, the viability of repurposing an installation will depend on several factors. Concerns about the physical condition of the infrastructure, as well as regulatory and economic considerations, play a key role in operator's multi-criteria evaluations when they determine the appropriate decommissioning methods. The selection criteria may therefore include the physical characteristics and conditions of the offshore installation and those of the installation site, regulatory requirements, secondary use

[50] For an overview on decommissioning of offshore infrastructure see: Ignacio Herrera Anchustegui, Gunnar S. Eskeland, Frode Skjeret, Mariia Melnychenko, Jonas William Eikenes Lødøen, Henrik Holmen Brown and Lasse Erik Christian Lund, 'Understanding decommissioning of offshore infrastructures: A legal and economic appetizer' (2021).

[51] McInnes Cooper (n 43) 15.

[52] See eg Ann Scarborough Bull and Milton S Love, 'Worldwide oil and gas platform decommissioning: A review of practices and reefing options' (2019) 168 *Ocean & Coastal Management* 274–306.

[53] McInnes Cooper (n 43) 15.

[54] McInnes Cooper (n 43) 16.

[55] McInnes Cooper (n 43) 17.

[56] Catherine Banet, 'Regulating the re-use and re-purposing of oil and gas installations in the context of decommissioning: creating incentives and enabling energy system integration' in Eduardo G Pereira, Alexandra Wawryk, Heike Trischmann, Catherine Banet and Keith B Hall (eds), *The Regulation of Decommissioning, Abandonment and Reuse Initiatives in the Oil and Gas Industry: From Obligation to Opportunities* (Kluwer, 2020) 205–20, 207.

possibilities, health and safety considerations, environmental considerations, socio-economic considerations, and political considerations.[57]

A guide to best practices for offshore decommissioning in Canada has suggested that as part of a technical description of the proposed decommissioning method, 'the issues that flow from the decision to select one method over another' should be clearly identified in any decommissioning process.[58] Further, the decommissioning and abandonment sections of a project's development plan should not include a firm commitment to the removal of all infrastructure given that the decommissioning might not take place for decades and that by then, the decommissioning plan may contemplate alternative uses of the infrastructure. For example, 'the post-production use of an offshore installation, at the top of the hierarchy of waste principles, may well be the most efficient and environmentally sensible alternative in its decommissioning.'[59]

E. The Decommissioning Regime for Atlantic Canada – Is Repurposing Contemplated in Law?

The reality is that the potential reuse of an installation 'is often addressed for the first time when the draft decommissioning plan is elaborated, which leaves a relatively tight window of opportunity to find reuse or repurposing options, if not already envisaged by the licensee and the owners.'[60] The regulatory approvals process for offshore development projects in Atlantic Canada is administered by the Offshore Petroleum Boards (as noted, soon to be renamed) and consists of a two-tier process. First, the board approves a Development Plan and second, grants authorisations to carry out specific works or activities.

Provisions for decommissioning and abandonment must be included in the Development Plan and 'are a precondition for Development plan approval.'[61] Section 42 of the Offshore Petroleum Installations Newfoundland and Labrador Regulations provide further that:

> **42** Where the removal of a fixed production installation is a condition of a development plan approval, the operator shall incorporate in the design of the installation such measures as are necessary to facilitate its removal from the site without causing a significant effect on navigation or the marine environment.

Further, the Development Plan Guideline of the Canada-Newfoundland and Labrador Offshore Petroleum Board requires submission of a 'Decommissioning and Abandonment Programme' as part of the Development Plan. The programme must include details on the design 'to facilitate decommissioning and abandonment of the installation at the end of its production life; a discussion of the feasibility of the proposed procedures; the forecasted costs of decommissioning and abandonment; and a description of the measures that would have to be taken to leave the site in a fishable

[57] McInnes Cooper (n 43) 19.
[58] McInnes Cooper (n 43) ch 5: Decommissioning Best Practices, 87.
[59] McInnes Cooper (n 43) 89.
[60] Banet (n 56) 215.
[61] McInnes Cooper (n 43) 61.

and navigable state.'[62] Given the above regime, complete decommission is not required, especially if this is not a condition of a development plan per section 42. As part of a future decommissioning programme, therefore, repurposing could be contemplated where the programme can assure the regulator that leaving the (repurposed) infrastructure in place would not detract from the site's fishable and navigable state.

By way of a case study, as the Consolidated Hebron Development Plan 2011 notes, 'the actual need for removal of the Hebron Platform will depend on regulatory requirements and analysis conducted when the decision to abandon the field is made.'[63] According to the plan, the Hebron Project Gravity Base Structure was designed to be 'removable at the end of field life … the procedure for platform removal/decommissioning will be developed during front-end engineering and design (FEED).'[64] The Development Plan also contemplates, 'pending further evaluation to determine if the GBS may be re-floated with the Topsides intact' that it may be possible to tow the Hebron platform to an inshore site for decommissioning.[65] These excerpts 'demonstrate the highly anticipatory nature of decommissioning provisions and the extent to which proposed decommissioning procedures are conditional on changes in technology, regulations and other factors, including safety and the environment.'[66] The fact that the decommissioning programme will be determined at such a later point in the project's life may make it difficult to 'lock in' considerations on reuse and repurposing, but it may also permit for new technologies to emerge.

F. Potential Steps to Encouraging the Repurposing of Offshore Installations

What incentives are there to encourage an owner of an offshore installation not to go ahead with its decommissioning and to contemplate the repurposing of the installation instead? In the first instance, an owner would need to be compensated for taking such a step, which, depending on the commercial arrangements between the parties and the national regulatory regime applicable to the installation, may involve the owner taking on a deferred future decommissioning obligation or involve the owner being required to continue to maintain and monitor the installation (possibly in compliance with legal obligations). There may therefore be a need to develop and establish (public or private) transition funding regimes and the need for much clearer assessment criteria to determine how a 'reuse decision' could 'provide a clearer legal framework … [to] better foresee the new legal situation created by transfer of assets through the reuse project.'[67]

[62] Canada-Newfoundland & Labrador Offshore Petroleum Board, 'Development Plan Guideline' (August 2022) 5.8: Decommissioning and Abandonment (n 49) 31. See also McInnes Cooper (n 43) 61.

[63] Canada-Newfoundland & Labrador Offshore Petroleum Board, Development Plans, Hebron Development Application, 12: Decommissioning and Abandonment (n 49) www.cnlopb.ca/information/development/.

[64] Canada-Newfoundland & Labrador Offshore Petroleum Board, Development Plans, Hebron Development Application, 12.2.1.

[65] ibid 12.2.3.

[66] McInnes Cooper (n 43) 72.

[67] Banet (n 56) 224.

How could participants in integrated offshore hydrogen projects benefit from a decision to locate the electrolysers on repurposed installations, instead of building new infrastructure? In an increasingly carbon-constrained economy, what immediately comes to mind is the idea of 'displaced' greenhouse gas emissions. In short, is there a way to receive certain carbon/climate credits for the reuse of existing offshore infrastructure, instead of building new infrastructure? This discussion, in turn, will require mechanisms to calculate the entire life-cycle emissions of a proposed project to allow for greenhouse gas deductions from the repurposed infrastructure such as installations, pipelines and oil and gas collection infrastructure. For example, the concrete and steel in rigs, existing pipelines, the collection infrastructure for oil and gas, the shipping and transportation infrastructure (including onshore) could all, potentially, be included in a full lifecycle calculation for future hydrogen production using installations and offshore wind energy in Atlantic Canada. Such a step, though highly complex both technically and legally, may provide the necessary incentives to make offshore hydrogen projects economically attractive. To achieve the objective, as proposed in this chapter, of generating credits for displaced greenhouse gases, at the very minimum, a much more rigorous climate regime both domestically and, ideally, internationally would have to be established. It would also require inclusion in emerging 'green' hydrogen certification and guarantee schemes and as part of these, verifiable methodologies to calculate how many greenhouse gas emissions have been 'displaced' because of repurposing the offshore infrastructure. As part of these discussions, the treatment of embedded carbon, the role of hydrogen production pathways and hydrogen imports into Member States of the European Union under the EU's Carbon Border Adjustment Mechanism (CBAM) regime may be a necessary step to explore further.[68]

5. Part III: Aligning the Complexities from Integrating Offshore Wind with Hydrogen Electrolysis on Repurposed Offshore Oil and Gas Installations

A. Recap of Part I and Part II

Complex legal risks and regulatory uncertainties, emerging from the discussions in Part I and in Part II, will have to be coordinated and aligned between different project parties and interests in order to achieve the successful delivery of integrated hydrogen projects. Given the focus on repurposing existing oil and gas platform infrastructure, the idea of a centralised offshore infrastructure hosting the offshore wind conversion and electrolyser infrastructure would appear to be a plausible evolution of the existing offshore installation. This is the core of the repurposing discussion in Part II. From the repurposed oil and gas platform, just as with oil and gas, the hydrogen would be

[68] SES Hydrogen, 'CBAM-from October 1, companies are obliged to report the volume of imports and related emissions' (23 October 2023) seshydrogen.com/en/cbam-from-october-1-companies-are-obliged-to-report-the-volume-of-imports-and-related-emissions/.

transported for storage on shore, either by ship or a network of repurposed sub-sea pipelines,[69] or shipped directly from the installation to points of offtake and demand. In Atlantic Canada, sub-sea pipelines are not practical or economically feasible, unless they are for short distances to connect to offshore loading systems as, for example, for the Hebron Project.

B. Key Legal Risks and Challenges Arising from Integration of Offshore Hydrogen Production

The idea of converting offshore oil and gas infrastructure to hydrogen-production infrastructure raises several legal issues, which for purposes of this chapter, can be organised into several themes. First, the critical ownership and transfer of ownership question, as discussed below, is closely related to the allocation and responsibility of long-term liability and decommissioning costs. Second, as projects dependent on water-intensive electrolysis to produce hydrogen from offshore wind energy, how can risks related to supplies of water, connection of the renewable electricity to the installation, and production of hydrogen from the electricity be addressed and adequately integrated between the parties in law? Third, to address geographic constraints due to lack of pipelines onshore, it is highly lightly that that produced hydrogen on the repurposed installations would be shipped directly to offtake in regional and export-oriented markets. How can the legal regime for the offshore environment support this growth of hydrogen markets?

Throughout these themes, the questions relate to how the different project participants may be arranged and how ownership questions are addressed between them and how, as novel projects in a challenging offshore environment, integrated hydrogen producing projects can overcome the 'misalignment' challenge, where real risks related to integration of Part I and Part II of the proposed project arise. These are, by far, not the only legal and economic challenges, but their brief discussion here serves to illustrate the sheer complexities of the task, all at a time of fluctuating economic conditions and shifting energy and climate policy environments. Within these themes, without any doubt, the key question relates to the potential transfer of ultimate decommissioning liabilities arising from repurposing and hydrogen production on a former oil and gas installation. How is liability of a previous owner, who (depending on the national offshore oil and gas regime) may be held 'liable on a secondary basis towards the State and the other licensees for financial obligations arising from the disposal [of the installation]',[70] resolved between the parties? Some commentators have noted that there may also be a risk that if secondary liability for former licensees is included in the domestic legal system, this may be 'applied to reuse and repurposing of installations, [meaning that] the seller/previous licensee may decide not to engage in the reuse project, as the risk of additional decommissioning costs are too high.'[71]

[69] Little (n 8).
[70] Banet (n 56) 225.
[71] ibid.

C. Practical and Legal Risks Arising from Access to Water for Industrial-Scale Electrolysis

In order to produce hydrogen on offshore installations, the project will require access to both electricity and to seawater (for subsequent desalination). To meet the need of electricity access, both the offshore wind energy project and the platform would require to be directly connected via sub-sea cables.[72] Part I has set out to identify some of the challenges related to this issue considering the emerging offshore renewable energy project governance in Canada. It is clear, however, that this legal regime cannot also be expected to contemplate (and provide for in law) a licensing regime for the taking of water and its desalination on a repurposes oil and gas installation. Certainly, here potential analogies could be drawn with seawater intake for cooling of nuclear power plants or other power plant infrastructure onshore, but how is the water question resolved offshore? Potential guidance may be found in the regulation of the discharge of wastewater and by-products because of desalination processes for oil and gas activities. For example, the Canada-Nova Scotia Offshore Petroleum Board Offshore Waste Treatment Guidelines of 2010 provide that 'desalination brine recovered from the production of potable water may be discharged without treatment.'[73] But this provision is more suggestive of day-to-day operations on an installation and not industrial scale production of hydrogen. In any case, it is clear that this issue must be resolve in law, so as to permit a licensed hydrogen producer to undertake desalination and production at commercial volume.

D. Connecting Part I and Part II in Law: Electricity Supply for Hydrogen Conversion Offshore

How will the offshore wind energy project be connected to the platform hosting the hydrogen electrolyser infrastructure? The first question is to ask if the applicable national law facilitates the construction of electricity cables and the transmission of the wind energy to a platform?[74] Related to this question is the critical issue of responsibility for the financing, construction, and operation of the cable. Is it the operator of the wind energy project or the operator of the electrolyser project, or is it a shared responsibility? These questions are inherently commercial and will need to be addressed in contracts between the parties on a project-to-project basis.

Comparing the legal regimes pertaining to hydrogen activities offshore of the Netherlands, Denmark and the UK, Andreasson and Roggenkamp have identified several legal obstacles and challenges. The first is, how, in law, the generated offshore wind energy will be transported to the platform for hydrogen production. For example, the offshore electricity networks developed in the Netherlands and in Denmark

[72] Andreasson and Roggenkamp (n 16) 10.

[73] Canada-Nova Scotia Offshore Petroleum Board Offshore Waste Treatment Guidelines, 2010, 2.12 Desalination Brine.

[74] Andreasson and Roggenkamp (n 16) 56.

are 'only intended for the transport of electricity from one or more wind farms to the onshore transmission network in each respective country' and in the United Kingdom, it is 'explicitly stated … that all wind farm projects are required to connect through the national transmission network onshore.'[75] The purpose of these offshore electricity networks is thus not to facilitate offshore electricity supply and offshore consumption but to transmit the electricity onshore.[76] There is thus a clear lack of dedicated legislation governing the connection of a wind energy project with an offshore platform via electricity cable. Examining the three legal regimes, Andreasson and Roggenkamp identify that 'in order to facilitate hydrogen conversion on offshore platforms, it should be clarified whether an offshore electricity cable connecting an offshore wind farm and an offshore platform is to be defined as a 'direct line', meaning that it would not be considered part of the transmission network. If not, a definition, and possibly a separate legal regime governing such cables, must be adopted.'[77]

E. Offshore Electrolysis: Converting Offshore Electricity to Hydrogen

If, as anticipated, a platform is no longer producing oil and gas, then the question arises if the existing infrastructure will still be licensed under a permit for these activities or if a new (and as yet to be developed) regulatory regime will apply to govern the construction and installation, and operation of, the electrolyser infrastructure? A required change in licence regimes from offshore oil and gas to offshore electricity consumption and hydrogen production would seem inevitable.

Having review the emerging regimes in the Netherlands, Denmark and the United Kingdom, Andreasson and Roggenkamp concluded that 'there is no specific legislation regulating the installation of an electrolyser and the subsequent production of hydrogen from an existing hydrocarbon platform.'[78] Further, their analysis concluded that it is 'extremely unlikely' that a natural gas production licence would cover the construction and subsequent operation of an electrolyser on a platform as this 'falls outside the scope of legislation governing specific offshore activities, such as *inter alia* legislation governing extraction of hydrocarbons and the generation of electricity.'[79] Absent specific legislation as part of a wider framework for offshore hydrogen production, it remains unclear what rules would apply.

In contrast to emerging hydrogen economies where the hydrogen will be transported by pipeline, for the proposed projects in Atlantic Canada, the hydrogen would have to be transported by ship, akin to oil and gas shipments via an offshore loading system (as is the case for the Hebron Project). This provides another incentive to explore offshore hydrogen production, given that the transmission of via sub-sea electricity cables to the coast (as feasible in other markets such as in the North Sea) will be near impossible

[75] ibid 78.
[76] ibid 78.
[77] ibid 79.
[78] ibid.
[79] ibid.

given the long distances and challenging geography. There may also not be an existing onshore electricity grid into which to connect the offshore capacity. On this basis, the idea to directly transport the hydrogen via offshore loading to points of demand by ship is potentially a very attractive one. At the very minimum, it would thereby avoid the necessary investment in either electricity transmission infrastructure or new pipeline transportation infrastructure (if technically feasible and economically viable).

F. Keeping Hydrogen at Sea: Production for Direct Supply and Offtake in Regional and Export-Oriented Markets

There may be significant obstacles to the growth of an offshore wind energy industry in Atlantic Canada if the focus is limited to the supply of renewable electricity through grid connection to onshore electricity markets (even if distances and geographic constraints are addressed). As noted in the Introduction, another incentive to the production of hydrogen from offshore wind energy is in large part due to competition from onshore renewable energy sources (not least, hydroelectricity) as well as onshore grid connection constraints. For example, the March 2024 Interim Report on Offshore Wind Development in Nova Scotia, notes that:

> The limited capacity of the existing Nova Scotia electrical grid means that development of offshore renewable energy at any large scale will depend on development of alternate markets for the energy. Such markets could be through direct electricity export and/or conversion of electricity to hydrogen and other green energy forms.[80]

One potential tool to support the expansion of the offshore wind energy and hydrogen sectors in Atlantic Canada is to explore the growth of regional and export-oriented hydrogen offtake markets such as the coastal communities and the natural resources sector in Northern Canada, where diesel imports could be replaced in the long-term by hydrogen exports. Northern Canada's remote communities, including Indigenous communities, depend on the import of diesel by land and sea, and diesel generators, to meet their energy needs at great economic, public health, and environmental costs. Energy-intensive natural resources projects, such as mining projects in Northern Canada, import significant quantities of diesel to generate electricity, power, and heat at their operations, which could be displaced (even in part) by hydrogen. To date, most progress on offtake market development has been made for internationally focused hydrogen exports, including as part of so-called 'green shipping corridors', primarily between Atlantic Canada and Germany's largest port, the Port of Hamburg (as recently as March 2024).[81] This may be an area of future hydrogen market development, supported by strategic hydrogen shipping, bunkering and transportation infrastructure.

[80] Canada, Impact Assessment Agency, Regional Assessment of Offshore Wind Development in Nova Scotia, Interim Report, iaac-aeic.gc.ca/050/documents/p83514/156045E.pdf.

[81] 'Port of Hamburg and Germany forge closer ties on hydrogen' *Hamburg News* (21 March 2024) hamburg-business.com/en/news/hpa-and-port-of-argentia-decide-to-increase-hydrogen-transports.

6. Conclusions

Integrating offshore wind energy with hydrogen electrolysis on repurposed oil and gas installations cannot be achieved if each of these three parts is not closely aligned and focused on the concept of integrated project development. Integration starts with the build-out of an offshore wind energy industry in Atlantic Canada that is co-located with the production of hydrogen. By siting the hydrogen production on repurposed oil and gas installations, two objectives are achieved. One, it provides the offshore wind industry with an immediate offtake of the electricity, thus creating strong incentives to build-out the technology. Two, it provides the oil and gas industry with new opportunities in the offshore economy transition, through repurposing of existing installations to site hydrogen electrolysers. Focusing on offshore wind and hydrogen integration, and the repurposing of oil and gas infrastructure, should therefore be at the core of any ambitious offshore energy transition strategy.

Thinking longer term and as argued in this chapter, offshore wind energy and hydrogen integration could contribute to energy security and to meet decarbonisation objectives, for example by introducing an alternative energy source to communities in Northern Canada and to heavy-industrial mining and oil and gas projects, including through hydrogen-driven electrification.[82] All of this will require a concerted build-out of infrastructure and the development of hydrogen markets, where much work remains to be done on alignment of codes and contracts, and the standardisation of hydrogen to facilitate exports.[83]

In conclusion, the emerging regime for offshore renewable energy projects, as currently developing for Atlantic Canada, should be drafted in careful alignment with the established governance for the offshore oil and gas sector, something that the draft offshore renewable regulations clearly contemplate. This is certainly encouraging from a public governance perspective. At the same time, key legal risks and challenges arising from the integration of offshore hydrogen production, in particular on the transfer of ownership of offshore oil and gas installations and with it, the critical question of decommissioning, are yet to be resolved through private law mechanisms. Much works remains to be done on these pieces to build a future offshore economy around the integration of offshore wind energy with hydrogen production.

[82] Canada, Impact Assessment Agency, Regional Assessment of Offshore Wind Development in Newfoundland and Labrador, Interim Report: Preliminary Offshore Wind Licencing Area Recommendations, 22 March 2024, Annex I – Summary of Feedback Received, 195; see also Anchustegui and Tscherning (n 2) 35–53.

[83] See, for example, Canada Hydrogen Strategy 2020, Chapter 7: Remaining Challenges, 97; see also, Kim Talus, Francisca Gallegos & Jaqueline Pinto, 'Importing US-produced hydrogen and its derivatives into the EU – examples of unnecessary complications, barriers and distinctions', 2024 Journal of Energy & Natural Resources Law, 1–23.

16

Circular Economy in the Decommissioning of Oil and Gas Platforms: Costs, Legislation, and Importance for Energy Transition

EDUARDO G PEREIRA, ANA CAROLINA MARINS DE CARVALHO AND AURELIA REID

1. Introduction

The thousands[1] of offshore oil and gas platforms installed around the world will ultimately face decommissioning due to resource depletion, outdated infrastructure and irrelevancy as countries transition to renewable energy. This scenario presents complex legal and regulatory challenges which are the result of the cessation of activities, cleaning, structure removal, and environmental recovery of the site associated with decommissioning. This process is called abandonment or decommissioning and represents the final phase of a platform's production, during which the facilities are deactivated, wells are plugged, equipment is dismantled, and removal takes place.[2] These operations come with high costs and significant potential for generating environmental impacts. This stage can have negative impacts on marine biota due to possible oil spills and toxic waste releases, loss of habitat for artificial reefs, and the use of explosives, which can also directly affect fishing and navigation activities.[3]

Decommissioning in the oil and gas industry is an area of significant importance due to the aging of offshore platforms and the need for replacement with more modern and efficient facilities. According to estimates from Rystad Energy consultancy, it is expected that by 2030 approximately 2,500 oil and gas platforms will need to be

[1] Norton Rose Fulbright (2023), 'Sustainable offshore platform decommissioning', www.nortonrosefulbright.com/en/knowledge/publications/dde54462/sustainable-offshore-platform-decommissioning.

[2] Samuel Dike, 'Decommissioning and Abandonment of Oil and Gas Facilities Legal Regime in Nigeria: Any Lesson from Norway, the UK and Brazilian Legal Frameworks?' (2017) papers.ssrn.com/sol3/papers.cfm?abstract_id=3771074.

[3] Francois Ars and Renato Rios, 'Decommissioning: A Call for a New Approach,' Day 3 Wed, May 03, 2017 (OTC, 2017) dx.doi.org/10.4043/27717-ms.

decommissioned solely in the North Sea, and 10,000 by 2050, totaling an estimated cost of $100 billion.[4] Despite the existence of various guidelines for countries to follow when establishing their regulatory frameworks regarding decommissioning, some countries still lack a developed legislative framework. Further, there are countries that experience difficulty in transparency and enforcement of regulations that do exist. One example of a country experiencing these challenges is Russia, which is a major producer of oil and gas. Although Russia has some regulations for the decommissioning of oil and gas facilities, these regulations are insufficient as technical regulations in that they do not provide consistent rules and standards for setting up abandonment funds and for the decommissioning of offshore oil rigs.[5] Further, some criticisms have been raised regarding the lack of transparency and effective enforcement of the regulations that they do have. Additionally, Russia faces challenges concerning the proper removal and treatment of hazardous waste and materials during the decommissioning process.[6] Another example is Brazil which faces significant regulatory challenges in its decommissioning efforts, including gaps in legal frameworks, coordination issues among authorities, complexities in securing financial guarantees, and limited experience in handling decommissioning projects. Brazil's legal framework for decommissioning is still developing. Although there have been efforts to establish clear guidelines, such as the ANP Resolution No. 817/2020, significant gaps remain. These regulations do not comprehensively address all aspects of decommissioning, such as the dismantling and recycling of materials, which poses challenges for compliance and implementation.[7] Petrobras, as one of the main operators, is called to play a more active role in this process, as the country grapples with challenges in defining responsibilities, technical standards, and social dialogue, despite substantial planned investments.[8]

The decommissioning of petroleum structures becomes necessary when their lifespan comes to an end and extending their use or replacing them is no longer feasible from a technical or economic standpoint.[9] Further, the sheer number of oil and gas platforms worldwide, makes it imperative to recognise that the imminent need for decommissioning can be connected to the ongoing global energy transition.[10] Recognition of the pressing need to address climate change, combined with the growing use of renewable

[4] Rystad Energy, 'Global offshore wind capital expenditure to more than double, top $100 billion in 2030'. www.rystadenergy.com/news/global-offshore-wind-capital-expenditure-to-more-than-double-top-100-billion-in-2.

[5] Ibragim Khalidov, Konstantin Milovidov and Anzor Soltakhanov, 'Decommissioning of Oil and Gas Assets: Industrial and Environmental Security Management, International Experience and Russian Practice' (2021) www.researchgate.net/publication/353407721_Decommissioning_of_oil_and_gas_assets_industrial_and_environmental_security_management_international_experience_and_Russian_practice#fullTextFileContent.

[6] ibid.

[7] Barbara Eiroa Leite and Bruno Belchior, 'New Frontiers for Decommissioning in Brazil' (2023) 14(1) *Journal of Sustainable Development Law and Policy* 117 www.ajol.info/index.php/jsdlp/article/view/253129.

[8] 'Descomissionamento de Campos de Petróleo e Gás Natural Avança no Brasil' (*PetroleoHoje*, 2023) petroleohoje.editorabrasilenergia.com.br/descomissionamento-de-campos-de-petroleo-e-gas-natural-avanca-no-brasil/.

[9] Shahriar Shams, DM Reddy Prasad, Monzur Alam Imteaz, Md Munir Hayet Khan, Amimul Ahsan and Md Rezaul Karim, 'An Assessment of Environmental Impact on Offshore Decommissioning of Oil and Gas Pipelines' (2023) 10 *Environments* 104, doi.org/10.3390/environments10060104.

[10] IRENA (2020), 'Energy transition outlook' www.irena.org/Energy-Transition/Outlook.

energy and energy-efficient technologies, could render thousands of offshore oil and gas installations obsolete worldwide.[11] As nations increasingly pivot toward cleaner and more sustainable energy sources, the role and future of these offshore platforms have come under scrutiny. These platforms, once instrumental in the extraction of hydrocarbon resources, are now reaching the end of their productive lifespans. This convergence of factors demands a profound shift in the way we approach decommissioning activities.

Decommissioning is viewed as the termination of a platform's operational life. However, in the contemporary landscape of energy transition, this phase takes on added significance. It serves as a pivotal juncture where the legacy of fossil fuel exploitation meets the dawn of renewable and sustainable energy solutions. Decommissioning offshore installations carries significant risks, including high costs, potential environmental damage, and safety hazards to personnel.

The potential environmental impact of decommissioning offshore oil platforms is substantial, particularly concerning infrastructure left in situ. For example, wells are sealed using cement barriers, however, the long-term integrity of these seals is uncertain.[12] However, it also offers rewards such as reduced long-term environmental impact, opportunities for material recycling and reuse, and alignment with sustainability and circular economy principles. The urgency of this transformation cannot be overstated, as it carries profound economic, environmental, and social implications.[13] The immediacy of this challenge can be addressed by adopting sustainable practices that follow a circular approach in decommissioning projects which presents a pivotal opportunity to manage resources while respecting the Earth's limitations. One example of this is the use of offshore oil rig platforms as artificial reefs which can enhance marine biodiversity by providing habitats for various marine species, leading to increased fish populations and improved ecosystem health.[14] Additionally, they can boost local economies through enhanced fishing and tourism opportunities.[15]

Decommissioning synergies, circularity, and sustainable developments between oil, gas, wind, and hydrogen can play a crucial role in transitioning towards a more sustainable energy future.

For example, the expertise and infrastructure developed in the oil and gas industry can be utilised for the decommissioning of offshore wind farms. This can lead to cost savings, knowledge sharing, and efficient utilisation of resources.

A circular economy can be defined as 'an economy in which stakeholders collaborate to maximise the value of products and materials, and as such contribute to minimising the depletion of natural resources and create positive societal and environmental

[11] M Lockman et al, 'Decommissioning Liability at the End of Offshore Oil and Gas: A Review of International Obligations, National Laws, and Contractual Approaches in Ten Jurisdictions' [2023] *SSRN Electronic Journal*.

[12] Luc Van Nuffel et al, 'Study on Decommissioning of Offshore Oil and Gas Installations: A Technical, Legal and Political Analysis' (European Commission, 2021).

[13] UNDP, 'What are the socio-economic impacts of an energy transition?' (2021) www.undp.org/eurasia/blog/what-are-socio-economic-impacts-energy-transition.

[14] Higgins E, Metaxas A, and Scheibling RE, 'A Systematic Review of Artificial Reefs as Platforms for Coral Reef Research and Conservation' (2022) 17 PLoS One e0261964.

[15] J Walter Milon, *The Economic Benefits of Artificial Reefs: An Analysis of the Dade County, Florida Reef System* (Florida Sea Grant College, 1987) repository.library.noaa.gov/view/noaa/39699.

impact'.[16] Another definition connects the circular economy concept to the goal of sustainable development in all three dimensions (society, economy, and environment):

> An economic system that replaces the 'end-of-life' concept with reducing, alternatively reusing, recycling and recovering materials in production/distribution and consumption processes. It operates at the micro-level (products, companies, consumers), meso level (eco-industrial parks) and macro-level (city, region, nation and beyond), to accomplish sustainable development, thus simultaneously creating environmental quality, economic prosperity, and social equity to the benefit of current and future generations. It is enabled by novel business models and responsible consumers.[17]

Adopting a circular economy approach in decommissioning can promote resource efficiency and minimise waste. This involves considering the reuse, recycling, and repurposing of materials and equipment from decommissioned infrastructure. For instance, components from oil and gas platforms can be repurposed for wind turbine foundations or used in hydrogen production facilities. As a foundation for wind turbines, a completely dismantled jacket platform can be repurposed to hold a single horizontal-axis wind turbine or a group of vertical-axis wind turbines. These platforms are connected by underwater electric cables, and the electricity they produce can be used to make hydrogen.[18] To be used as a Hydrogen production facility, an offshore production platform with an unused gas pipeline can be converted to produce hydrogen. The old oil and gas processing equipment can be swapped out for a hydrogen production plant, and the hydrogen sent to shore through the upgraded gas pipeline. These platforms can also be adapted for capturing and storing carbon.[19] This approach reduces the need for new materials and contributes to a more sustainable and circular energy system.

The European Union's Circular Economy Action Plan is instructive as a guide to integrating circular economies into the decommissioning process related to offshore platforms. This action plan aims to enable a sustainable, resource-efficient economy, by focusing on reducing the environmental impact of decommissioning, guiding the transformation of production, consumption, waste management, and resource use to create a more circular economy. The European Commission through this plan advocates for products that are durable, reusable and repairable; enhancing waste prevention and the reuse of secondary raw materials; targeting economic sectors which have high resource use as well as potential for circularity; creating legislative frameworks which include sustainable product initiatives, promotion of longer lifespans in electronics through a circular electronics initiative and setting new targets for waste reduction and recycling. The plan also supports innovation and aims to attract and promote investment

[16] Christiaan Kraijenhagen, Cecile Van Oppen and Nancy Bocken, 'Circular business: collaborate and circulate' Amersfoort: Circular Collaboration (2016) 175.

[17] Julian Kirchherr Denise Reike and MP Hekkert, 'Conceptualizing the circular economy: An analysis of 114 definitions' (2017) 127 *Resources, conservation and recycling* 221–32.

[18] Russell McKenna, Matteo D'Andrea and Mario Garzón González, 'Analysing Long-Term Opportunities for Offshore Energy System Integration in the Danish North Sea' (2021) 4 *Advances in Applied Energy* 100067 doi.org/10.1016/j.adapen.2021.100067.

[19] Seyed Mojtaba Alirahmi et al, 'Renewable-Integrated Flexible Production of Energy and Methane via Re-Using Existing Offshore Oil and Gas Infrastructure' (2023) 426 *Journal of Cleaner Production* 139125 doi.org/10.1016/j.jclepro.2023.139125.

in sustainable business models and technology. It also seeks to establish a monitoring framework so as to track progress and modify policies as needed.[20]

With the advent of synergistic plans such like the one put forward by the European Commission, decommissioning, often associated with substantial financial investments and intricate logistical challenges,[21] now emerges not only as a closure process but as a catalyst for innovation and sustainability.[22] It prompts us to rethink the purpose and potential of these aging platforms in a rapidly evolving energy landscape. Consequently, the core question arises: Can decommissioning go beyond being a mere financial burden to become an opportunity for repurposing these structures in ways that align with the goals of the energy transition through the use of circular economy?

To answer this question and navigate the complex interplay of economics, ecology, and energy policy, this chapter explores whether circular economy can be used by governments and companies during the decommissioning of oil and gas facilities. Global and national regulations, and costs related to decommissioning, are considered. Through a discussion on circular economies as it relates to decommissioning, the chapter explores whether current global and national regulations support or hinder the integration of circular economy principles in the decommissioning of offshore oil and gas facilities, and what legal frameworks are needed to ensure that facility reuse aligns with environmental stewardship and sustainable energy goals. This, in turn, will pave the way for understanding the pivotal role that offshore facility reuse plays in shaping the future of energy production and environmental stewardship. The chapter culminates in a set of recommendations aimed at harnessing the opportunities presented by decommissioning to accelerate the shift toward a more sustainable energy future.

2. Where Do We Stand in Petroleum Decommissioning: Jurisdiction, Numbers, Costs and Experiences?

The decommissioning process involves significant costs due to the complexity of operations and the requirements for safety and environmental protection. Several factors contribute to the high costs of decommissioning, including the dismantling and removal of structures, proper treatment of hazardous waste and materials, and the restoration of the affected environment. One of the main factors influencing decommissioning costs is the size and complexity of offshore platforms. Larger and older platforms often require more resources and time to be dismantled and removed. Additionally, the location of

[20] European Commission, 'A New Circular Economy Action Plan For a Cleaner and More Competitive Europe' (Communication) COM (2020) 98 final, 11 March 2020, eur-lex.europa.eu/legal-content/EN/TXT/?qid=1583933814386&uri=COM:2020:98:FIN.

[21] OGV Energy. Oil & Gas Decommissioning – Challenges & Opportunities (2021). See www.ogv.energy/news-item/oil-gas-decommissioning-challenges-opportunities.

[22] Nunzia Capobianco, Vincenzo Basile, Francesca Loia and Roberto Vona, 'Toward a Sustainable Decommissioning of Offshore Platforms in the Oil and Gas Industry: A PESTLE Analysis' (2021) 13 *Sustainability* 6266, doi.org/10.3390/su13116266.

the platforms can also impact costs, especially when they are situated in remote areas or deep waters.

Within the decommissioning process, some of the most expensive processes include the dismantling and removal of structures, the treatment of hazardous waste and materials, and the restoration of the marine environment. The dismantling and removal of structures involve the use of specialised vessels, lifting and cutting equipment, as well as skilled labour. The treatment of hazardous waste and materials requires specific processes to ensure safety and environmental protection, which can escalate costs. The restoration of the marine environment is also a complex process, involving the removal of contaminated sediments and the recovery of affected marine life.

In summary, the most common decommissioning options are as follows: (a) Onshore disposal (bringing the installation to land, cleaning it, dismantling it into scrap for recycling in the steel industry or disposal in licensed sites); (b) In-place burial (cleaning the installation, placing or burying the cut section on the seafloor); (c) Deepwater deposition (cleaning the installation and subsequently towing and placing it in deep waters); (d) Leave in place (making the installation safe and leaving it in its current location); (e) Artificial reef (cleaning the installation and using it to form an artificial reef to enhance local marine life); (f) Reuse at another location (cleaning the installation, conducting non-destructive tests, removing and transporting it to another location suitable for the platform's characteristics, and subsequently installing it at the new location); and (g) Repurposing for another scope (making the installation safe and transferring its use, purpose, and potential ownership).

Companies in the oil and gas sector have been bearing the costs of decommissioning their own facilities even though they might recover such costs through taxes or cost recovery. Typically, these companies establish decommissioning funds and/or collaterals to ensure that the necessary financial resources are available when the time comes to dismantle and remove the platforms. These funds are gradually built over the facilities' lifespan through regular contributions, so decommissioning costs are spread out over time. Furthermore, in some cases, companies may choose to share the decommissioning costs with other companies operating in the same area and they might share part of the costs with the government, depending on regulations and established agreements. Even though this approach can help to reduce individual costs and promote cooperation among the involved parties, the use of circular economies can further reduce costs, wastage and environmental impact of these post-production oil facilities.

Decommissioning is an activity regulated by different jurisdictions worldwide. While most oil-producing countries are signatories to international treaties governing decommissioning such as the United Nations Convention on the Law of the Sea (UNCLOS), each country establishes its own regulations and guidelines for the decommissioning of oil and gas platforms, aiming to ensure safety, environmental protection, and compliance with local laws. Jurisdictions vary in terms of regulatory approach and specific decommissioning requirements. Some countries have stricter and more detailed regulations, while others may have fewer specific requirements. These differences in regulation can cause challenges with the legalities of implementing circular economy in decommissioning. However, there is a growing trend to enhance regulations and establish clearer guidelines for decommissioning as awareness of environmental impacts and safety considerations increases.[23]

For example, in the United Kingdom (UK), all decommissioning activities must be preceded by a detailed programme presented and discussed with different stakeholders impacted by the activity.[24] Once the discussion about the appropriate decommissioning programme is sufficiently mature, a proposal is submitted for approval by the Department for Business, Energy & Industrial Strategy (BEIS), which is responsible for the effective regulation of decommissioning, according to the Petroleum Act of 1998.[25] Additionally, the Oil and Gas Authority (OGA)[26] oversees the decommissioning of offshore facilities. The OGA works closely with industry companies to ensure compliance with regulations and promote the adoption of best practices. The UK is even considered a global leader in decommissioning regulation, with extensive experience in decommissioning offshore platforms in the North Sea.[27] Of note UK legislation states that the owners of an offshore installation or pipeline at the time it is decommissioned will continue to own any leftover materials and debris, and they will retain responsibility for any remaining liabilities indefinitely.[28] It also leaves space for the implementation of circular economies by stating that reuse of facilities is prioritised if it is pragmatic and economical.[29]

In Norway, the Norwegian Petroleum Safety Authority (PSA)[30] is the authority responsible for offshore facility decommissioning. The PSA establishes regulations and guidelines to ensure safety and environmental protection during decommissioning. Furthermore, the PSA conducts inspections and audits to verify companies' compliance with regulations and promote continuous improvement of decommissioning practices. Norway has a long history of decommissioning offshore platforms and is also recognised for its advanced regulation in this area. Additionally, Norway's Petroleum Act 29 November 1996 No. 72 relating to petroleum activities requires a decommissioning plan from licensees.[31] The ministry makes the decision related to decommissioning which the licensee is obliged to carry out even if the licence is expired.[32] The licensee is also responsible for damage or inconvenience caused intentionally or by negligence

[23] GUIDANCE NOTES: Decommissioning of Offshore Oil and Gas Installations and Pipelines, Offshore Petroleum Regulator for Environment and Decommissioning 72 (November 2018), assets.publishing.service.gov.uk/government/uploads/system/uploads/attachment_data/file/760560/Decom_Guidance_Notes_November_2018.pdf.

[24] Climate and Pollution Agency, Decommissioning of Offshore Installations (TA 2761 2011) www.miljodirektoratet.no/globalassets/publikasjoner/klif2/publikasjoner/2761/ta2761.pdf.

[25] United Kingdom. Scotland Act 1998, www.legislation.gov.uk/ukpga/1998/17/contents.

[26] United Kingdom. Decommissioning Strategy. www.nstauthority.co.uk/media/7538/decommissioning-strategy-may-2021.pdf.

[27] United Kingdom. Strengthening UK Offshore Oil & Gas Decommissioning Industry. assets.publishing.service.gov.uk/government/uploads/system/uploads/attachment_data/file/943745/strengthening-uk-offshore-oil-gas-decommissioning-industry-cfe-.pdf.

[28] Guidance Notes on the Decommissioning of Offshore Oil and Gas Installations and Pipelines (n 23).

[29] ibid.

[30] Thommessen Advokatfirma AS (2022), 'Legal Framework of Petroleum Activity on the Norwegian Continental Shelf' www.thommessen.no/en/news/legal-framework-of-petroleum-activity-on-the-norwegian-continental-shelf.

[31] Petroleum Act, s 5-1.

[32] Petroleum Act, s 5-3.

during the decommissioning process.[33] What is however lacking in both the regulations of the PSA and the Petroleum Act are concrete steps to reduce cost, encourage sustainability and innovation. Nevertheless, the Act does allow for the government to take over the facilities of the licensee after the licence has expired.[34] This leaves an avenue for circular economy to be introduced as the government can repurpose these facilities for more sustainable use. As decommissioning offshore platforms involves the dismantling and removal of complex structures, along with proper treatment of hazardous waste and materials. Circular economies may help alleviate some of this cost by maintaining existing infrastructure in operational condition on site can reduce the expenses related to constructing and commissioning new facilities; buildings, structures, and spaces can be repurposed for new functions, thereby decreasing the necessity for fresh investments and avoiding demolition expenses.[35]

The numbers associated with decommissioning in the oil and gas industry are substantial and present a significant challenge for the sector.[36] The aging of offshore platforms and the need for replacement with more modern and efficient facilities demand substantial investments and the adoption of appropriate dismantling and disposal practices. By becoming signatories to treaties such as UNCLOS, states agree on decommissioning terms. This imposes an international obligation on each state to be the main authority overseeing offshore oil and gas exploration and production activities inclusive of decommissioning within its territorial waters.[37] As such states are often seen as 'decommissioner of last resort', it is thus crucial for companies in the sector and regulatory authorities to collaborate in developing efficient and sustainable decommissioning solutions, ensuring safety and environmental protection. It is noteworthy that even though legislation may mandate that private companies granted licences pay for the decommissioning process,[38] these do not guarantee that the finances would be available at the time decommissioning becomes necessary.[39] It is therefore imperative for governments and companies to engage in sustainable an innovative decommissioning. Some examples of approaches to decommissioning that countries and the international community have taken are below.

The United Kingdom is one of the countries with a significant number of decommissioning cases. So far, over 100 offshore platforms have been decommissioned in the North Sea, with the majority belonging to the oil and gas industry.[40] Norway, a pioneer in this field, has invested in research and development of advanced decommissioning technologies to reduce costs and minimise environmental impacts. Additionally,

[33] Petroleum Act, s 5-4.

[34] Petroleum Act, s 5-6.

[35] 'CIRCL-E: From Decommissioning to Regeneration Circular Strategies for Energy Power Plants' (January 2019) www.arup.com/insights/circl-e-from-decommissioning-to-regeneration/.

[36] Demolition & Recycling International, 'Cost of Decommissioning Oil Platforms to Rise', www.demolitionandrecycling.media/news/cost-of-decommissioning-oil-platforms-to-rise/8025076.article.

[37] Lockman et al (n 11).

[38] Annie Leeks, Steven Smith, Sylvia Tonova and David Wallach, 'Offshore Oil and Gas Field Decommissioning: Disputes And Other Challenges' (*MONDAQ*, 23 October 2021) www.mondaq.com/unitedstates/oil-gas-electricity/1123876/offshore-oil-and-gas-field-decommissioning-disputes-and-other-challenges.

[39] Lockman et al (n 11).

[40] Ministério de Minas e Energia (2020), 'Challenges Decommissioning Offshore', www.gov.br/anp/pt-br/assuntos/exploracao-e-producao-de-oleo-e-gas/seguranca-operacional/arq/challengesdecommissioningoffshore.pdf.

other countries such as the United States,[41] the Netherlands,[42] and Denmark[43] have also been carrying out decommissioning of oil and gas platforms in their respective offshore areas. While the exact number of decommissioned platforms in each country is not known, these nations have gained valuable experience in this field.

The United States has comprehensive regulations for the decommissioning of oil and gas facilities. The Bureau of Safety and Environmental Enforcement (BSEE),[44] under the Department of the Interior, is responsible for regulating offshore decommissioning. The country has specific guidelines for the dismantling and removal of structures, treatment of hazardous waste and materials, and restoration of the marine environment. Additionally, the United States maintains a rigorous approach to compliance and oversight of decommissioning operations. The United States also practices rig to reefs as a means of sustainable decommissioning whereby the top portion of the rig is removed and the bottom portion is left in the ocean as a habitat for wildlife.[45] This leaves space for legislation related to circular economies and reuse of post-production offshore oil facilities to be implemented. Canada also has advanced regulation for the decommissioning of oil and gas facilities. The Canada Energy Regulator (CER)[46] is the authority responsible for offshore decommissioning regulation. The country establishes specific guidelines and requirements to ensure safety, environmental protection, and compliance with local laws. Notably, the United Kingdom, The United States of America and Norway have all implemented trailing liability whereby former owners of an offshore rig installation can be ordered to pay for decommissioning expenses where the current owners cannot pay.[47] Implementing circular economy can reduce financial risks to companies which may have to take on the high costs of decommissioning.

The international collective approach to managing offshore oil installations post-production consists of agreements and conventions such as: The 1958 United Nations Convention on the Continental Shelf (Geneva Convention)[48] which was the first international treaty addressing the deactivation of offshore oil and gas installations and continues to serve as a reference for regulations and other international treaties. The Convention stipulates that any abandoned or deactivated installation must be fully removed and establishes guidelines urging signatory countries to take appropriate

[41] Keith Hall, 'Decommissioning of Offshore Oil and Gas Facilities in the United States' (2020) digitalcommons.law.lsu.edu/cgi/viewcontent.cgi?article=1442&context=faculty_scholarship.

[42] EBN, 'Netherlands masterplan for decommissioning and re-use', www.ebn.nl/wp-content/uploads/2016/12/EBN-Masterplan-for-decommissioning.pdf.

[43] Mordor Intelligence, 'Denmark Offshore Oil and Gas Decommissioning Market Size & Share Analysis – Growth Trends & Forecasts (2023–2028)', www.mordorintelligence.com/industry-reports/denmark-offshore-oil-and-gas-decommissioning-market#:~:text=Denmark%20Offshore%20Oil%20And%20Gas%20Decommissioning%20Market%20Trends&text=It%20is%20also%20expected%20that,the%20decommissioning%20market%20a%20lot.

[44] Bureau of Safety and Environmental Enforcement – BSEE. Decommissioning, www.bsee.gov/decommissioning.

[45] Rigs to Reefs, Bureau of Safety and Environmental Enforcement, available at www.bsee.gov/what-we-do/environmental-compliance/environmental-programs/rigs-to-reefs#:~:text=What%20is%20Rigs%2Dto%2DReefs,reef%20development%20by%20coastal%20states.

[46] Canada Energy Regulator – CER Home page, www.cer-rec.gc.ca/en/.

[47] Lockman et al (n 11).

[48] United Nations, Convention on the Continental Shelf, legal.un.org/ilc/texts/instruments/english/conventions/8_1_1958_continental_shelf.pdf.

measures to protect the biota that may be affected by such operations, including setting safety zones of about 500 meters around all platforms. It also specifies that exploration of the continental shelf and exploitation of its natural resources must not result in unjustifiable interference with navigation, fishing, or the conservation of living resources of the sea.

The 1972 London Convention,[49] covering the Northeast Atlantic, the North Sea, and portions of the Arctic Ocean, was held with the goal of preventing indiscriminate dumping at sea of waste that may pose risks to human health, harm living resources and marine life, or interfere with other legitimate uses of the sea. In 1996, through a special meeting, the Protocol to the Convention on the Prevention of Marine Pollution by Dumping of Wastes and Other Matter was adopted, clarifying the treaty's position on the decommissioning of oil equipment and installations, starting from 2006.

The International Convention for the Prevention of Pollution from Ships (MARPOL),[50] established in 1973 and amended in 1978, aimed to minimise pollution of the seas, including oil discharge and any pollution from emissions. In 1982, the United Nations Convention on the Law of the Sea (UNCLOS III, 1982)[51] determined that any abandoned or deactivated installation or structure must be removed to ensure navigation safety, taking into account generally accepted international standards established by the relevant international organisation. This removal must also consider fishing, the protection of the marine environment, and the rights and duties of other states. Adequate notice of the depth, position, and dimensions of any partially removed installations or structures must also be provided.

The 1992 Oslo-Paris Convention[52] further established, for 15 countries, that 'no out-of-use offshore installation or out-of-use offshore pipeline shall be dumped and no out-of-use offshore installation shall be wholly or partly left in place in the maritime area without authorization from the competent authority of the Contracting Party concerned on a case-by-case basis.'[53] This convention does not explicitly mention circularity, yet it represents a notable departure from previous international laws focused mainly on mandatory removal and the prohibition of dumping. Instead, it emphasises collaboration among its Member States and adopts a more comprehensive regulatory framework. These fundamental aspects create a foundation for potentially integrating circularity in the future. Circular approaches in decommissioning rely on cooperative efforts and a holistic approach, contrasting with earlier international laws that adopted narrower perspectives.

Finally, the 1989 International Maritime Organization (IMO) established global minimum standards for the removal of offshore installations and structures, referred to as 'Guidelines and Standards for the Removal of Offshore Installations and Structures on

[49] International Maritime Organization (IMO) (1958), 'London Convention and Protocol' www.imo.org/en/OurWork/Environment/Pages/London-Convention-Protocol.aspx.

[50] IMO (1973), 'International Convention for the Prevention of Pollution from Ships' (MARPOL), www.imo.org/en/about/Conventions/Pages/International-Convention-for-the-Prevention-of-Pollution-from-Ships-(MARPOL).aspx.

[51] United Nations (UN) (1982), 'United Nations Convention on the Law of the Sea' (UNCLOS), www.un.org/depts/los/convention_agreements/texts/unclos/unclos_e.pdf.

[52] OSPAR Commission (1992), 'Convention for the Protection of the Marine Environment of the North-East Atlantic' (OSPAR Convention), www.ospar.org/convention.

[53] OSPAR Convention, Article 5(1).

the Continental Shelf and in the Exclusive Economic Zone' (EEZ).[54] These Guidelines allow for exemptions from the general obligation to remove. Some of these exceptions are outlined in the IMO Guidelines Article 3.4, which specify that a coastal State may decide that an installation or structure can remain wholly or partly in place on the seabed under certain conditions, those conditions being; if it serves a new purpose, such as enhancing a living resource; and if its presence does not unjustifiably interfere with other sea uses.[55] This opens a pathway for circular economy to be used in decommissioning plans.

While these agreements are generally seen as recommendations, countries that have ratified UNCLOS III 1982 (which determines that abandoned or out-of-use facilities must be removed, considering generally accepted standards) are obligated to follow these guidelines. These obligations mean that the costs associated with decommissioning cannot be avoided or at the very least, failure to comply and or inadequate compliance may lead to diplomatic pressure, international scrutiny and or reputational damage. One example of this is the Brent Spar incident where the Shell UK, supported by the UK government proposed to dispose of a floating oil storage facility in deep Atlantic waters. There was swift international backlash causing these plans to be abandoned.[56]

3. Synergies

The global attention has become increasingly fixated on environmental concerns that reverberate across the planet.[57] Amidst these concerns, the decommissioning of offshore platforms has gained prominence as a challenge that spans multiple disciplines. The industry has found the need to assess the ecological ramifications of decommissioning activities while simultaneously amplifying their consideration of public consciousness about this matter.[58] Additionally, it has been recognised that legal and regulatory harmony is necessary to manage the complexities and environmental risks associated with decommissioning offshore oil and gas installations.[59] Furthermore, the enforcement of international and regional (environmental) conventions poses challenges. Although many of these instruments are legally binding and frequently contain enforcement provisions, it ultimately falls to the discretion of sovereign states to decide whether

[54] IMO. Assembly Resolution A.672(16). wwwcdn.imo.org/localresources/en/KnowledgeCentre/IndexofIMOResolutions/AssemblyDocuments/A.672(16).pdf.

[55] IMO Guidelines, Article 3.4.

[56] Ngozi Ole and Hernen Philip Faga, 'Assessing the Impact of the Brent Spar Incident on the Decommissioning Regime in the North East Atlantic' (2017) 3 *Hasanuddin Law Review* 141 pasca.unhas.ac.id/ojs/index.php/halrev/article/view/1075BrentConventionDecommissioningFacilityInternational.

[57] 'The World's Energy System Must Be Transformed Completely' (*The Economist*, 2020) www.economist.com/schools-brief/2020/05/23/the-worlds-energy-system-must-be-transformed-completely?utm_medium=cpc.adword.pd&utm_source=google&ppccampaignID=19495686130&ppcadID=&utm_campaign=a.22brand_pmax&utm_content=conversion.direct-response.anonymous&gclid=CjwKCAjw38SoBhB6EiwA8EQVLiYXF_nI4eejUfybr5t8ThOtjBkuyjIn3v3-C4EpXJ-XvXi5v0yXAhoCTrwQAvD_BwE&gclsrc=aw.ds.

[58] Ann Scarborough Bull and Milton S Love, 'Worldwide Oil and Gas Platform Decommissioning: A Review of Practices and Reefing Options' (2019) 168 *Ocean & Coastal Management* 274 doi.org/10.1016/j.ocecoaman.2018.10.024.

[59] Van Nuffel et al (n 12).

they will become signatories to these agreements and ratify specific provisions within them.[60] Moreover, one of the main issues is determining liabilities and managing default risks, particularly when operators fail to meet their decommissioning obligations. This necessitates a robust legal framework to ensure that financial responsibility does not fall on the state or taxpayers, especially when dealing with smaller companies that may lack sufficient financial resources. Another challenge arises from regulatory inconsistencies and gaps across different regions.[61] Additionally, ensuring that operators have adequate financial security, such as guarantees, insurance, and reserved funds, is critical to covering decommissioning costs and preventing defaults. Environmental considerations also play a significant role, as decommissioning activities must be conducted in a way that minimises environmental impact and restores the seabed to its natural state.[62] Addressing these challenges requires comprehensive regulatory frameworks that include clear guidelines for decommissioning obligations, financial securities, and environmental protections.

The UK sought to address this in their decommissioning of offshore installations guidelines.[63] These guidelines recognise that decommissioning decisions must consider environmental impacts, with a strong emphasis on the waste hierarchy, which prioritises waste prevention, followed by reuse, recycling, and disposal as a last resort. It states that environmental appraisals are required to assess the impact of decommissioning options on the environment. The guidelines outline various pathways to decommissioning these installations including full removal, partial removal, and in-situ decommissioning. The choice of pathway is based on environmental, safety, and technical considerations, and is subject to a comparative assessment.[64] Operators must engage in extensive consultation with stakeholders, including government departments, environmental agencies, and the public. The consultation process is highlighted as integral to ensuring transparency and public trust in the decommissioning process. The guidelines focus on minimising waste and maximising the recovery of valuable materials supports the transition to a circular economy by reducing the environmental impact of decommissioning activities and conserving natural resources.

Norway has also recognised the challenges faced in decommissioning offshore oil platforms and has emphasised the need for robust regulatory frameworks to manage the environmental impacts of decommissioning offshore petroleum structures.[65] These frameworks must ensure that dismantling, recycling, and disposal activities are conducted in ways that minimise harm to the environment. For example, in Norway, the Pollution Control Act mandates that decommissioning facilities must hold permits that regulate releases to air, water, and soil, with strict requirements based on best available techniques (BAT). The challenges of managing hazardous materials, such as heavy metals, asbestos, and low-specific activity (LSA) radioactive materials. Safe handling and disposal of these materials are crucial to preventing environmental contamination.

[60] ibid.

[61] Anchustegui et al, 'Understanding Decommissioning of Offshore Infrastructures: A Legal and Economic Appetizer' (n.d.) ssrn.com/abstract=3882821.

[62] ibid.

[63] Guidance Notes on the Decommissioning of Offshore Oil and Gas Installations and Pipelines (n 23).

[64] ibid.

[65] Decommissioning of Offshore Installations (n 24).

Facilities must be designed with impermeable surfaces and effective treatment plants to manage contaminated water and prevent runoff or infiltration into the soil.[66]

In 2021 the European Union conducted a study on decommissioning of offshore oil and gas installations which focused on the technical, legal, and environmental aspects of decommissioning these installations in the EU, UK, and Norway. The study highlights how decommissioning aligns with circular economy principles and emphasises that the decommissioning should aim to leave a clean seabed where technically possible and environmentally beneficial.[67] It highlights that EU legislation, such as the Offshore Safety Directive, Environmental Liability Directive, and Marine Strategy Framework Directive, governs the environmental impact of decommissioning activities. However, these frameworks do not fully address long-term environmental impacts when infrastructure is left in place.[68] Standardising decommissioning processes globally by adopting best practices from established regions can further mitigate these challenges and ensure safer and more effective decommissioning practices.[69]

Remarkably, decommissioning isn't merely a procedural task; it stands as a pivotal pillar within the complex framework of the worldwide energy system, holding the reins of economic and societal progress. In the midst of this landscape, embracing sustainable methodologies that adhere to a circular approach within decommissioning initiatives emerges as a transformative opening to oversee resource management within the confines of our planet's limitations.[70] Actions embarked upon in the realm of oil and gas decommissioning, through the prism of a circular economy framework, wield the potential to dovetail with the pursuit of sustainable development goals (SDGs).[71] Grasping the nuances of circularity within products and services, or their contribution to the circular economy becomes instrumental in shaping policies and business strategies within the oil and gas sector. This perspective encompasses holistic thinking and the eradication of wasteful practices.

As recent as 2021,[72] initiatives have sprouted that reorient the trajectory of obsolete installations towards marine research, aquaculture, renewable energy solutions, and leisure – a commendable stride towards recycling materials from these structures. By mitigating the adverse effects linked with the decommissioning of offshore oil and gas platforms, a gateway is opened to craft fresh economic prospects while simultaneously fostering environmental enhancements. Where once the ecological implications of decommissioning remained somewhat concealed, the current era has ushered in heightened awareness, sparking the engagement of stakeholders.

One example of this can be found in Brazil which has faced challenges with the decommissioning of offshore oil and gas platforms.[73] As a major oil-producing nation,

[66] ibid.

[67] Van Nuffel et al (n 12).

[68] ibid.

[69] Anchustegui et al (n 61).

[70] Capobianco et al (n 22).

[71] ibid.

[72] Krista Laktuka, Antra Kalnbalkite, Liga Sniega, Kalvis Logins and Dace Lauka, 'Towards the Sustainable Intensification of Aquaculture: Exploring Possible Ways Forward' (2023) 15(24) *Sustainability* 16952 doi.org/10.3390/su152416952.

[73] Fernanda Delgado et al, *Offshore Decommissioning in Brazil – Opportunities, Challenges & Solutions* (FGV Energia, 2021).

Brazil has many offshore platforms that are approaching or have reached the end of their productive life. The regulations established by Brazilian government and regulatory bodies, focus on ensuring that the removal of offshore structures is carried out in a way that minimises environmental impact, promotes safety, and considers the potential for repurposing platforms, such as using them for artificial reefs or other sustainable purposes.[74] However, the high costs associated with decommissioning, along with the technical and environmental challenges, have led Brazil to explore more sustainable and economically viable solutions. This includes looking into circular economy practices, such as reusing materials and repurposing platforms for alternative uses, which aligns with global trends in offshore platform decommissioning.[75]

Traditionally, decommissioning takes place through the removal and recycling of structures, restoring the environment to its natural state. However, alternatives exist, such as repurposing for a new use, particularly in the offshore wind energy sector. The UK's Oil and Gas Authority (OGA) created a strategy which lists as one of its obligations to ensure the maximum value of economically recoverable petroleum is secured from UK waters in a manner that assists the Secretary of State in meeting the net-zero carbon emissions target. One of its mandates is to ensure that, all options for continued use or repurposing of infrastructure must be explored to ensure cost-effective decommissioning which supports petroleum recovery and net-zero targets before decommissioning is undertaken.[76] The OGA Strategy aligns with circular economy principles by focusing on minimising waste, maximising resource efficiency, and ensuring that products and materials are reused, recycled, or repurposed rather than disposed of. Emphasis is put on the importance of securing the maximum value of economically recoverable petroleum from UK waters, which reflects the circular economy's goal of fully utilising resources before decommissioning or disposal.[77] Additionally, the strategy encourages the exploration of all viable options for the continued use or repurposing of infrastructure before decommissioning, such as using it for carbon capture and storage (CCS) projects. This approach aligns with the circular economy's emphasis on extending the life of assets, reducing waste, and turning waste into new resources.

Aligning with the principles of environmental conservation, the OGA Strategy supports reducing environmental impact by promoting the reduction of greenhouse gas emissions and the deployment of technologies that can minimise environmental harm,[78] consistent with the circular economy's goal of reducing the ecological footprint of industrial activities. The strategy also stresses the importance of managing lifecycle costs, including decommissioning and reuse, which reflects the circular economy's focus on considering the full lifecycle of products and materials to ensure efficient resource use and minimise costs associated with waste and disposal. Additionally, this strategy encourages collaboration among industry participants, particularly in carbon

[74] ibid.

[75] ibid.

[76] Oil and Gas Authority, 'The OGA Strategy' (Presented to Parliament pursuant to Section 9G of the Petroleum Act 1998, 2021) www.ogauthority.co.uk.

[77] ibid.

[78] ibid.

capture and storage, which mirrors the circular economy's emphasis on systems thinking and stakeholders working together to create closed-loop systems that reduce waste and enhance resource efficiency.[79]

Notably, this strategy ensures that investments and activities are sustainable and do not undermine investor confidence, supporting the circular economy principle of creating sustainable business models that prioritise long-term environmental and economic benefits over short-term gains.[80] Overall, the OGA Strategy's focus on maximising resource recovery, promoting the reuse and repurposing of infrastructure, reducing environmental impact, and managing lifecycle costs closely aligns with the principles of a circular economy. By integrating these practices, this strategy contributes to a more sustainable and efficient use of resources in the oil and gas sector, supporting the broader transition to a circular economy.

Repurposing offshore infrastructure can aid energy transition in several ways. It allows existing oil and gas infrastructure to be utilised by other industries such as carbon capture and storage, preventing the wastage of resources and material.[81] By repurposing offshore infrastructure, the transition to cleaner energy sources like hydrogen projects can be expedited, contributing to a more sustainable energy landscape. As such, time and cost efficiencies are offered to new users who can leverage existing infrastructure rather than building from scratch, making the transition to cleaner energy more economically viable.[82] However, the process of repurposing would involve collaboration between the authorities and industry stakeholders to identify suitable infrastructure, overcome barriers, and ensure a smooth transition towards cleaner energy sources. Repurposing offshore oil structures allows for the safeguarding of assets for potential future use by other industries, ensuring that valuable resources are not left unused but contribute to the energy transition.[83]

It is estimated that approximately one-third of the total lifetime costs (operation, maintenance, and service costs) of an offshore wind project can be positively impacted by significant synergies with the Oil and Gas (O&G) supply chain.[84] This synergy makes it feasible to electrify offshore O&G operations by installing wind farms nearby or through floating turbines. This reduces the need for operating diesel or gas generators on the platform, cutting greenhouse gas emissions and air pollutants. Additionally, it facilitates the energy transition, with platforms serving as bases for wind farms.

Considering all scenarios in an integrated manner is essential to ensure that the best actions are taken regarding the decommissioning of oil and gas platforms, in order to achieve optimal outcomes in economic, social, political, and environmental terms.

With due attention, studies, and procedures, it is possible to assign diverse purposes to these facilities, other than simply removing them entirely from their sites, contributing to the decarbonisation of energy matrices. Below are examples of the reuse of such facilities.

[79] ibid.
[80] ibid.
[81] North Sea Transition Authority, Repurposing Offshore Oil and Gas Infrastructure (North Sea Transition Authority, 2024).
[82] ibid.
[83] ibid.
[84] IEA, Offshore Energy Outlook 2018, www.iea.org/reports/offshore-energy-outlook-2018.

A. Platforms for Photovoltaic Farms

Converting decommissioned offshore platforms into photovoltaic farms offers a multifaceted solution with numerous advantages.[85] This innovative approach harnesses the existing infrastructure, such as the robust steel framework of the platform and its offshore location, to create a highly efficient solar power generation system. It optimises the platform's extensive surface area, which would otherwise go unused after decommissioning, making efficient land use a primary advantage. Furthermore, repurposing offshore platforms for photovoltaic farms significantly reduces the environmental impact compared to traditional land-based solar farm development, as it eliminates the need for extensive land clearing, thus preserving habitats and biodiversity.

Moreover, the transformation process is quicker and more cost-effective than building entirely new solar installations from scratch, owing to the platform's pre-existing structural framework. This expedites the transition to renewable energy sources. Additionally, many offshore platforms are already grid-connected, simplifying the integration of photovoltaic farm-generated electricity into the existing energy infrastructure and ensuring efficient distribution to consumers. The proximity of offshore platforms to coastal populations further reduces energy losses during transmission, enhancing the overall efficiency of the energy supply chain and contributing to energy diversification and security.

Another advantage lies in lower operating costs, as offshore platforms are designed to withstand harsh marine conditions, translating to reduced maintenance and repair expenses. Furthermore, platforms can be equipped with energy storage systems, such as batteries, to store excess solar energy for use during periods of low sunlight or high demand, enhancing the reliability and consistency of renewable energy supply.

B. Offshore Wind Energy Projects and Offshore Wind Hydrogen Projects

The utilisation of oil and gas platforms for hydrogen production is gaining prominence as a means to decarbonise challenging sectors.[86] A converted jack-up rig from Borr Drilling illustrates this potential, as it was intended for green hydrogen production in Project Haldane. This project, a collaboration between Aquaterra Energy, Borr Drilling, and Lhyfe, aimed to develop an industrial-scale offshore green hydrogen production concept by deploying an electrolyzer system on the converted rig. This approach provides an alternative deployment option to traditional oil and gas assets, such as jack-up drilling rigs, potentially enhancing the commercial viability of remote offshore wind projects.

[85] Gardenio Diogo Pimentel Da Silva and David Alves Castelo Branco, (2018), 'Is floating photovoltaic better than conventional photovoltaic? Assessing environmental impacts' (2018) 36(5) *Impact Assessment and Project Appraisal* 390–400.

[86] Mariella Leporini, Barbara Marchetti, Francesco Covaro and Fabio Polonara, (2019), 'Reconversion of offshore oil and gas platforms into renewable energy sites production: Assessment of different scenarios' (2019) 135 *Renewable Energy* 1121–32.

Research findings indicate a considerable CapEx discount rate for wind power projects that offset decommissioning costs. Moreover, delaying decommissioning offers benefits such as reduced carbon emissions and increased local employment rates through the repurposing of offshore oil and gas facilities. With the global push for a low-carbon energy matrix, repurposing oil and gas infrastructure for offshore wind and hydrogen usage appears to align with environmental objectives while supporting decarbonisation efforts and local socio-economic development.

Furthermore, the potential application of solar energy and wind farms to old offshore oil and gas fields and infrastructure introduces a new dialogue between the fossil fuel and renewable energy sectors. This dialogue promotes the advancement of offshore renewable energy in line with the ongoing energy transition aimed at mitigating greenhouse gas emissions within the energy sector. The recognition of offshore wind energy as a solution for offshore rigs is exemplified by Transocean's recent memorandum of understanding with Eneti. This signifies their intent to establish a joint venture focused on offshore wind foundation installation activities, converting drilling vessels into floating offshore wind foundation platforms, equipped with substantial cranes capable of transporting multiple monopile foundations.[87]

C. Liquefied Natural Gas (LNG) Terminals

Besides the benefits of cost savings, the offshore location of these platforms is strategically advantageous for LNG operations.[88] Offshore terminals can tap into nearby natural gas reserves, simplifying the transportation of natural gas to the terminal for liquefaction. This proximity streamlines the supply chain, minimising the energy and resources needed for long-distance gas transportation.

Moreover, the offshore environment offers a solution to the space constraints often associated with onshore LNG terminals. Offshore platforms provide ample space for the construction of LNG liquefaction and regasification facilities, as well as storage tanks, without encroaching on valuable coastal land or disrupting local communities.

The integration of LNG terminals into decommissioned platforms also aligns with sustainability goals. LNG is considered a cleaner-burning fossil fuel compared to coal and oil, resulting in reduced greenhouse gas emissions when used for power generation or transportation. By facilitating the efficient import and export of LNG, these platforms contribute to cleaner energy matrices and support the transition to lower-carbon energy sources.

Furthermore, the adaptability of these platforms extends to their ability to accommodate advanced safety and environmental measures. The existing infrastructure can be retrofitted with state-of-the-art technologies for natural gas processing, ensuring safe and environmentally responsible LNG operations. This includes systems for vapor control, leak detection, and emergency shutdown, which help minimise environmental risks.

[87] Offshore Energy, 'Repurposing Oil & Gas Infrastructure to Harness Offshore Wind Power' www.offshore-energy.biz/repurposing-oil-gas-infrastructure-to-harness-offshore-wind-power/.

[88] Irfan Ahmad Gondal, 'Offshore renewable energy resources and their potential in a green hydrogen supply chain through power-to-gas' (2019) 3(6) *Sustainable Energy and Fuels* 1468–89.

D. Marine Farming that Includes Farming Finfish, Shellfish and Aquatic Plants

At the conclusion of a platform's life cycle, diverse marine species inhabit the subaqueous structure, their presence influenced by water conditions and depth.[89] The exploration of potential endeavors aimed at repurposing decommissioned offshore oil and gas platforms for aquaculture has attracted considerable attention. In the context of the widespread decommissioning of numerous oil rigs globally, with a specific focus on Brazil's mature fields, the overarching goal is to optimise the conversion of these rigs for alternative uses. One of the most promising alternatives involves transforming these platforms into focal points for various aquaculture activities, encompassing the cultivation of finfish, oysters, and algae, thereby offering a biologically sound and sustainable solution.

Minimising the adverse effects associated with the decommissioning of offshore oil and gas platforms offers the opportunity to create new economic prospects and environmental enhancements. Among the promising sectors for prolonging the platforms' usefulness, aquaculture stands out. In the United States, there are existing regulations allowing for diverse uses of Gulf of Mexico platforms beyond oil and gas production, including aquaculture, as permitted by previously granted Right of Use and Servitude (RUE) licences.

These platforms, known for their stable placement in open ocean waters, often in deep locations, feature substantial deck areas that appeal to various facets of the aquaculture industry. These sectors include commercial net pen aquaculture, on-platform hatcheries for habitat restoration projects, the production of commercial shellfish, and the harvesting of shellfish from the platform's structural elements, particularly its support legs.[90]

E. Marine Protected Areas or Artificial Reefs, either Left in Place or Relocated to a Designated Reefing Location (Rigs-to-Reefs)

Offshore platform operators noticed a phenomenon – over the productive years of rigs, substantial marine life had congregated on and around their structures.[91] It is important to note that the areas surrounding offshore platforms are typically off-limits to commercial fishing vessels due to safety considerations. As a result, marine life in these regions flourished, leading to an increase in biomass and the proliferation of various species.

[89] Bela H Buck and Richard Langan, *Aquaculture Perspective of Multi-Use Sites in the Open Ocean: The Untapped Potential for Marine Resources in the Anthropocene* (Springer Nature, 2017).

[90] The Fish Site, 'From Shell to shellfish: can aquaculture offer new lease of life to offshore oil platforms?' (2022) thefishsite.com/articles/from-shell-to-shellfish-can-aquaculture-offer-new-lease-of-life-to-offshore-oil-platforms-imta.

[91] Erika Techera and John Chandler, 'Offshore installations, decommissioning and artificial reefs: Do current legal frameworks best serve the marine environment?' (2015) 59 *Marine Policy* 53–60.

In essence, these areas transformed into de facto marine protected areas, contributing to biodiversity and ecological richness. Recognising this opportunity, marine scientists proposed preserving this marine ecosystem and promoting its natural productivity.

From an operational perspective, this approach was also advantageous as it allowed operators to circumvent the considerable removal costs associated with decommissioned rigs. Simultaneously, it created a sanctuary for marine species seeking refuge and habitat around these structures. These compelling discoveries resonated with a diverse group of stakeholders, including recreational fishermen, divers, offshore oil and gas operators, and aquaculturists, all of whom stood to gain from the enhanced marine biodiversity in these areas.

In response to these insights, the 'Rigs-to-Reefs' programme was established in American and European Seas. This innovative initiative saw decommissioned offshore oil and gas rigs being repurposed into artificial reefs. Subsequent studies by numerous scientists confirmed the positive impact of these artificial reefs, demonstrating an increase in both the number and diversity of marine organisms in close proximity to these sites. Importantly, these reefs attracted commercially important fish, shellfish, and crustaceans, further underscoring the ecological and economic benefits of this transformative approach.

F. Offshore Structures for Tourism, Leisure, and Sports Activities

The idea of using decommissioned oil and gas platforms for tourism has already been put into practice.[92] In Texas, in Galveston, Ocean Star rig-turned-museum has demonstrated the feasibility of such projects, offering tourism and educational opportunities. Aberdeen is also studying the possibility of repurposing a decommissioned oil platform, like Shell's Brent Alpha, into a premier tourist attraction for the city, capitalising on its status as Europe's oil hub. They envision various tourism activities, including walking, boat, and helicopter tours, with the possibility of serving meals in the rig's mess hall. While Aberdeen City Council has acknowledged tourism proposals related to decommissioned oil platforms, it has not evaluated this specific idea. Decom North Sea sees merit in the concept, estimating that the costs for a static display would be relatively low compared to recycling the steel.[93]

Furthermore, if these structures are maintained in an environmentally respectful manner, they can become a hub for sports and leisure activities such as diving and fishing. As mentioned earlier, they can provide a conducive environment for the development of various species of fauna and flora. This biodiversity, including the growth of

[92] B Sommer, AM Fowler, PI Macreadie, DA Palandro, AC Aziz and DJ Booth, (2019), 'Decommissioning of offshore oil and gas structures-Environmental opportunities and challenges' (2019) 658 *Science of the total environment* 973–81.

[93] Energy Voice, 'Aberdeen should use decommissioned oil platform as tourist attraction' (2023) www.energyvoice.com/oilandgas/north-sea/253433/aberdeen-should-use-decommissioned-oil-platform-as-tourist-attraction/.

rare fish species, as seen in the Gulf of Mexico[94] makes the environment appealing to both fishermen and divers. This also contributes to the reuse of these facilities, without the need for structure removal, avoiding exorbitant expenses.

Adopting circular economies for decommissioning offshore oil facilities can pose several legal challenges. Guaranteeing regulatory compliance by ensuring that all decommissioning activities comply with environmental, safety, and other regulatory requirements can be complex and may require adapting existing regulations to fit circular economy principles. Additionally, determining ownership of materials and liabilities associated with decommissioned assets can be challenging, especially when materials are repurposed or reused in new ways. Also, offshore facilities often operate in international waters or across different jurisdictions, leading to complexities in applying consistent circular economy practices across borders.

Existing contracts and agreements may not anticipate circular economy approaches, requiring renegotiation or clarification to accommodate reuse, recycling, or repurposing of materials. Additionally, circular economy practices may impact the financial models and economics of decommissioning, requiring new financial instruments or incentives to encourage circularity. Developing standards for decommissioning processes that align with circular economy principles may require collaboration across industries and regulatory bodies. Even though these obstacles may exist, the international agreements and guidelines leave space for circular economies to be implemented in the decommissioning process. Industry stakeholders, policymakers, and legal experts may need to collaborate to develop frameworks that support sustainable decommissioning practices while ensuring compliance with legal and regulatory requirements.

4. Recommendations and Conclusion

It is evident that the decommissioning of oil and gas facilities is a significant topic in the global context of energy transition and the approaching end of many platforms' operational lifespans. Beyond the need to ensure environmental preservation and prevent any harm resulting from fossil resource exploitation, it is intriguing that this process takes into account the global movement towards developing new energies, such as offshore wind and hydrogen.

Despite many countries not yet having a comprehensive and consolidated legal framework regarding the use of circular economy in decommissioning, lacking significant incentives for facility reuse, and having no mandatory requirements for this form of recycling, legislative progress can be observed in some countries such as the United States. With the imminent end of platform lifespans, countries are in an urgent position to address any regulatory gaps in this matter.

Furthermore, it is important to conduct case studies considering already decommissioned platforms to evaluate procedures, costs, and challenges. This will enable the development of a more suitable and efficient method to fulfil all decommissioning

[94] Bureau of Safety and Environmental Enforcement (BSEE). (s.d.). 'Gulf's Rigs and Platforms Attract Offshore Anglers', www.bsee.gov/newsroom/feature-stories/gulfs-rigs-and-platforms-attract-offshore-anglers.

functions and requirements. It is worth highlighting the importance of collaborative action among stakeholders for sharing experiences, technologies, and guidelines. This collaborative approach will facilitate the promotion of the most appropriate repurposing of these facilities among the various possibilities mentioned above.

Finally, it would be beneficial for countries to consider circularity as an alternative for decommissioning and to introduce or adapt, as the case may be, their legislative and regulatory frameworks to ensure that circularity options are not only facilitated but also incentivised. For this purpose, countries should study which alternatives would make the most sense within their respective contexts and characteristics.

17

Joint Development in the Energy Transition: From Joint Petroleum Zones to Joint CO_2 Storage Zones

CONSTANTINOS YIALLOURIDES

1. Introduction

Through joint development, coastal States can agree to jointly explore, exploit, and manage seabed energy resources in areas under overlapping maritime claims.[1] Where States fail to agree on a maritime boundary and there is no appetite for litigation, Articles 74(4) and 83(3) of the UN Convention on the Law of the Sea (UNCLOS) call for States to avoid unilateral actions and to seek to reach 'provisional arrangements of a practical nature'.[2] These provisional arrangements are without prejudice to the final delimitation agreement. The obligation to make every effort to conclude provisional arrangements of a practical nature, including joint development, derives from the general principles of good faith and peaceful settlement of disputes.[3] International jurisprudence, from the *North Sea* cases,[4] *Eritrea/Yemen*,[5] *Guyana/Suriname*,[6] and *Ghana/Côte d'Ivoire*,[7] emphasises that the parties to a maritime boundary dispute can

[1] Masahiro Miyoshi, 'The Basic Concept of Joint Development of Hydrocarbon Resources on the Continental Shelf' (1988) 3 *International Journal of Estuarine and Coastal Law* 1, 5; Ibrahim F Shihata and William Onorato, 'Joint Development of International Petroleum Resources in Undefined and Disputed Areas' in Gerald Blake et al (eds), *Boundaries and Energy: Problems and Prospects* (Kluwer Law, 1998) 433.

[2] United Convention on the Law of the Sea (adopted 10 December 1982; entered into force 16 November 1994) 1833 UNTS 39 (UNCLOS), Articles 83(4) and 74(3); for an analysis see Constantinos Yiallourides, 'Oil and Gas Development in Disputed Waters' (2016) 5(1) *UCL Journal of Law and Jurisprudence* 59–86; BIICL, 'Report on the Obligations of States under Articles 74(3) and 83(3) of UNCLOS in respect of Undelimited Maritime Areas' (30 June 2016).

[3] BIICL Report, ibid.

[4] *North Sea Continental Shelf Cases (Germany v Denmark; Germany v Netherlands)* [1969] ICJ Rep 3, para 19.

[5] Eritrea/Yemen Arbitration (Award, Phase II: Maritime Delimitation), para 86.

[6] Arbitration Between Guyana and Suriname (Annex VII Tribunal) (2007) 139 *International Legal Materials* 566, paras 460–64.

[7] Dispute Concerning Delimitation of the Maritime Boundary in the Atlantic Ocean (Ghana/Côte d'Ivoire) ITLOS Case No 23 (Judgment) (Merits), paras 626–28.

draw mutual economic benefits by cooperating over natural resources in a disputed maritime area.

Historically, joint development agreements (JDAs) have played a crucial role in the oil-rich Middle East and resource-promising regions of East Asia, South-East Asia, the Asia Pacific and in the African continent.[8] While unique to their political and geographical contexts, past JDAs have primarily been driven by States' desire to develop untapped offshore hydrocarbon resources in areas of overlapping maritime claims.[9] However, with the shift towards a low-carbon future, fossil fuel use is being increasingly challenged and deep carbon dioxide (CO_2) emissions reductions are urgently needed. One should reconsider the traditional narrative of 'petroleum development'in joint development zones (JDZs), ie, the geographic area in which the cooperative joint development regime applies. States might now consider adopting a post-fossil joint development approach to leverage these zones for joint CO_2 storage as part of carbon capture and storage (CCS) operations.

Joint CCS operations introduce issues not necessarily present with traditional hydrocarbon operations. These issues include injection site selection, sequestration, and post-injection monitoring and liability.[10] Increased risks from CCS revolve around both the sheer volume of injected CO_2 and the specific properties of CO_2.[11] Mistakes with CO_2 sequestration and storage could result in serious environmental harm, including transboundary harm, in the short and long term.[12] Environmental harm could include groundwater contamination, geologic hazards, injuries to marine ecosystems, harm to human health, and other damages resulting from hydrocarbons where CO_2 injection is combined with enhanced oil recovery operations.[13] For instance, in shared geological reservoirs, where CO_2 storage occurs across an international boundary, one State's CO_2 sequestration operations on one side of the boundary could nullify a neighbouring State's ability to store CO_2 on the other side of the boundary.[14] This could reignite disputes among States seeking to transition from joint petroleum development to joint CO_2 storage operations.

Existing JDAs may not necessarily cover joint CCS operations.[15] To ensure proper management of joint CCS operations, additional provisions should ensure harmonised standards of due diligence and monitoring for CO_2 capture and storage activities in

[8] Constantinos Yiallourides, 'Joint Development of Seabed Resources in Areas of Overlapping Maritime Claims: An Analysis of Precedents in State Practice' (2019) 31(2) *University of San Francisco Maritime Law Journal* 129–74; Anna Khalfaoui and Constantinos Yiallourides, 'Maritime Disputes and Disputed Seabed Resources in the African Continent' in Penelope Crossley et al (eds), *Routledge Handbook of Energy Law* (Routledge, 2020) 526–46.

[9] ibid.

[10] For a complete analysis, Mark Anthony de Figueiredo, 'The Liability of Carbon Dioxide Storage' (2007) (PhD Dissertation, MIT) sequestration.mit.edu/research/liability.html.

[11] Alexandra B Klass and Elizabeth J Wilson, 'Climate Change and Carbon Sequestration: Assessing a Liability Regime for the Long-term Storage of Carbon Dioxide' (2008) 58 *Emory Law Journal* 103, 119.

[12] Michael Faure, 'Liability and Compensation for Damage Resulting from CO_2 Storage Sites' (2016) 40 *William & Mary Environmental Law and Policy Review* 287.

[13] Klass and Wilson (n 11) 103, 119.

[14] Jens T Birkholzer, Curtis M Oldenburg, and Quanlin Zhou, 'CO_2 migration and Pressure Evolution in Deep Saline Aquifers' (2015) 40 *International Journal of Greenhouse Gas Control* 203, 209.

[15] Nigel Bankes, 'The Use of Sub-Seabed Transboundary Geological Formations for the Disposal of Carbon Dioxide' in Catherine Banet (ed), *The Law of the Seabed Access, Uses, and Protection of Seabed Resources* (Brill, 2020) 397, 413–16.

the joint development regime. These provisions would not necessarily alter the States' existing obligations in the JDZs, but they would detail the implementation of existing legal obligations in the context of joint CCS operations. For example, they would clarify the roles and responsibilities of parties involved in the transboundary movement of CO_2, including managing risks and liabilities associated with potential leakage after geological storage.

Against this background, the present chapter, first, underscores the critical role of offshore CCS in the energy transition. Second, it outlines key joint development characteristics as evidenced in past State practice, with a focus on the governance of joint seabed energy operations in JDZs. Third, it provides preliminary thoughts on the potential for joint CO_2 storage in disputed maritime areas and identifies relevant legal and technical requirements when transitioning from 'joint petroleum development zones' to 'joint CO_2 storage zones'.

This chapter focuses on the use of JDZs for joint CO_2 storage operations in areas of overlapping maritime claims. It does not review the general international frameworks dealing with seabed CO_2 injection and disposal, except to the extent that these frameworks specifically touch on the joint use of geological seabed structures.[16]

2. Offshore Carbon Capture and Storage and the Energy Transition

Anthropogenic emissions of CO_2 are the largest driver of climate change.[17] The main source of emitted CO_2 globally is the combustion of fossil fuels for energy production, such as coal, crude oil, and natural gas.[18] Global energy demand is forecast to increase by 66 per cent by 2030, with fossil fuels accounting for a staggering 80 per cent of the energy mix in 2022.[19] Scientific scenarios suggest that, even with substantial increases in energy derived from other sources, fossil fuels will remain a major energy source in the twenty-first century.[20] The consequences – global temperature rise exceeding 2°C in the next decades – could prove disastrous for future generations.[21] As concerns about

[16] Such as, for instance, the UN Law of the Sea Convention, the 1972 London Convention on the Prevention of Marine Pollution by Dumping of Wastes and Other Matter (London Convention), and the 1996 Protocol to the London Convention; for a discussion, see Constantinos Yiallourides and Tina S Hunter, 'Maritime Boundaries in the Energy Transition: Sub-Seabed Carbon Dioxide (CO_2) Storage in Transboundary Geological Formations' Journal of Energy & Natural Resources Law (forthcoming 2024) – on file with the author.

[17] IPCC Report, 'Climate Change 2022: Mitigation of Climate Change' (IPCC, 2022) (Summary for Policymakers) www.ipcc.ch/report/ar6/wg3/; IPCC, 'Special Report: Global Warming of 1.5 °C' (IPCC, 2018) Ch 2, www.ipcc.ch/sr15/chapter/chapter-2/.

[18] A Shahbazi and BR Nasa, 'Carbon Capture and Storage (CCS) and its Impacts on Climate Change and Global Warming' (2016) 7 *J Pet Environ Biotechnol* 291.

[19] BP Energy Outlook 2023, www.bp.com/content/dam/bp/business-sites/en/global/corporate/pdfs/energy-economics/energy-outlook/bp-energy-outlook-2023.pdf; IEA, 'CO2 Emissions in 2022', www.iea.org/reports/co2-emissions-in-2022.

[20] Anissa Nurdiawati and Frauke Urban, 'Towards Deep Decarbonisation of Energy-Intensive Industries: A Review of Current Status, Technologies and Policies' (2021) 14 *Energies* 2408.

[21] IPCC, 'Climate change widespread, rapid, and intensifying' (9 August 2022) www.ipcc.ch/2021/08/09/ar6-wg1-20210809-pr/.

human-induced climate change intensify, the need to decarbonise energy systems and 'avoid a climate disaster' becomes increasingly salient.[22]

Ensuring large CO_2 emission reductions requires a fundamental shift in how we generate, transport, and use energy. Energy-hungry nations must meet their commitments under the Paris Agreement to reduce substantially CO_2 emissions and keep global temperature rise below 2°C.[23] At the same time, nations must safeguard their energy security, namely the 'uninterrupted availability of energy sources at an affordable price'.[24] Recent events have highlighted the urgent need for new pathways to low-carbon energy transition. The COVID-19 pandemic and the war in Ukraine, in particular, have disrupted energy markets, leading to price instability, energy shortages, and heightened energy security concerns worldwide.[25] Losing just a fraction of the world's fossil fuels amidst the war in Ukraine caused significant economic and social disruptions. The scale of these disruptions has also highlighted the need for a just and orderly transition away from fossil fuels to avoid future energy shortages and higher prices.[26] Renewable power is fast increasing, but it remains insufficient to meet significant energy demands, particularly in developing economies.[27] Thus, these events have reminded us that any successful and enduring low-carbon energy transition must address both energy security and sustainability objectives.

In this context, CCS has emerged as a potentially crucial tool which could be deployed at scale to reduce the impact of CO_2 emissions on global temperatures.[28] CCS involves capturing CO_2 emissions at their source, including power generation or industrial facilities that use either fossil fuels or biomass for fuel, and securely storing them deep underground, usually in depleted or nearly depleted hydrocarbon reservoirs.[29] Such reservoirs are often comprised of layers within hydrocarbon fields which do not contain hydrocarbon themselves but have the necessary characteristics for storing CO_2, such as cap rock, base rock, permeability, and containment fractures.[30] These fields have proven to be effective hydrocarbon storage reservoirs for millions of years. Depending on porosity, permeability and geological seals, these sites could be utilised for CO_2 injection and long-term storage.[31]

[22] UNEP, Emissions Gap Report 2022, www.unep.org/resources/emissions-gap-report-2022.

[23] Daniel Bodansky, 'The Paris Climate Change Agreement: A New Hope?' (2016) 110(2) *American Journal of International Law* 288–319.

[24] IEA, 'Energy Security' www.iea.org/topics/energy-security.

[25] IEA, World Energy Outlook 2022, https://www.iea.org/reports/world-energy-outlook-2022/executive-summary; Jinfang Tian, 'Global low-carbon energy transition in the post-COVID-19 era' (2022) 307 *Applied Energy* 1.

[26] BP Energy Outlook 2023; Klaus Hubacek et al, 'Russia–Ukraine war has nearly doubled household energy costs worldwide – new study' (*The Conversation*, 17 February 2023) theconversation.com/russia-ukraine-war-has-nearly-doubled-household-energy-costs-worldwide-new-study-200104.

[27] Ofélia Araújo and José Luiz de Medeiros, 'How is the Transition Away from Fossil Fuels Doing, and How Will the Low-Carbon Future Unfold?' (2021) 23 *Clean Techn Environ Policy* 1385–88; Philip Ringrose, *How to Store CO2 Underground: Insights from Early-Mover CCS Projects* (Springer, 2020) 6.

[28] Tiina Koljonena et al, 'The role of CCS and Renewables in Tackling Climate Change' (2009) 1 *Energy Propedia* 4323–30.

[29] Sarah Hannis et al, 'CO2 Storage in Depleted or Depleting Oil and Gas Fields: What can We Learn from Existing Projects?' (2017) 114 *Energy Procedia* 5680–90.

[30] ibid.

[31] K Michael et al, 'CO_2 Storage in Saline Aquifers II – Experience from Existing Storage Operations' (2009) 1 *Energy Propedia* 1973–80, 1973.

The 2005 Special Report on CCS of the Intergovernmental Panel on Climate Change (IPCC) served as a catalyst for CCS to enter the low-carbon energy transition arena. Most international prospective scenarios have since depicted CCS as a crucial tool in low-carbon energy transition.[32] The potential role of CCS in low-carbon energy transitions has been acknowledged by the International Energy Agency (IEA), the International Renewable Energy Agency, and the IPCC.[33] In a 2020 report, the IEA estimated that achieving the net-zero emissions goal by 2050 would require 50 per cent more CCS deployment, alongside other serious decarbonisation targets.[34]

The IEA also estimated in its Sustainable Development Scenario, where global CO_2 emissions from the energy sector fall to zero on a net basis by 2070, that CCS would account for 15 per cent of the cumulative reduction in emissions.[35] CCS appears to offer a technically feasible and policy-desirable pathway for reducing the carbon footprint of fossil fuel-based energy production while also ensuring sustainability.[36] Indeed, the IEA has noted that 'a faster transition requires more CCS' and highlighted four essential roles of CCS in the low-carbon energy transition: (a) addressing emissions from established energy infrastructure; (b) serving as a solution for sectors with emissions that are challenging to mitigate; (c) acting as a foundation for low-carbon hydrogen production; and (d) enabling the removal of carbon from the atmosphere.[37]

Over 3,000 projects would be required by 2050 to reach the net zero goal which is 'a major technical, financial and logistical challenge' as well as 'a significant regulatory challenge'.[38] The Global CCS Institute has noted that CCS demands substantial investment in capital-intensive assets like capture plants, CO_2 transport pipelines, many of which offshore, and geological storage assets.[39] Despite the maturity of CCS technologies, their adoption in most major industries remains limited, which increases perceived risk.[40] Widespread scepticism about CCS is also fuelled by environmental and safety concerns in the event of faulty implementation.[41] While there is strong scientific evidence that CO_2 can be securely stored in underground reservoirs for very long periods of time, it is also clear that, under certain circumstances, accidents resulting from errors in CO_2 storage could result in serious environmental harm, liabilities and compensation claims.[42] Thus, while the potential benefits of sub-seabed CO_2 storage are

[32] For an overview, see Ringrose (n 27) 126–28.

[33] IPCC, 'Special Report on Carbon Dioxide Capture and Storage' (Cambridge University Press, 2005); IEA, 'Carbon Capture and Storage: The Solution for Deep Emissions Reductions' (EIA Report, 2015); IEA and IRENA, 'Perspectives for the Energy Transition: Investment needs for Low-Carbon Energy System' (2017).

[34] IEA 2020, ibid 14.

[35] IEA, 'Special Report on Carbon Capture Utilisation and Storage: CCUS in Clean Energy' (EIA, 2020) 44–54 www.iea.org/reports/ccus-in-clean-energy-transitions.

[36] IEA, 'Special Report on Carbon Capture Utilisation and Storage' (2020) 13–29.

[37] ibid Ch 2.

[38] IEA, 'Carbon Capture and Storage and the London Protocol Options for Enabling Transboundary CO2 Transfer' (IEA, 2011) 6.

[39] CCS Global Institute, 'Carbon Capture and Storage: Challenges, Enablers and Opportunities for Deployment' (30 July 2020) www.globalccsinstitute.com/news-media/insights/carbon-capture-and-storage-challenges-enablers-and-opportunities-for-deployment/.

[40] ibid.

[41] Bert Metz et al, 'IPCC Special Report on Carbon Dioxide Capture and Storage' (Cambridge University Press, 2010).

[42] Michael Faure and Roy A Partain, *Carbon Capture and Storage: Efficient Legal Policies for Risk Governance and Compensation* (MIT Press, 2016); Faure (n 12) 28.

seemingly numerous, the international regulatory landscape for such activities will play a crucial role in facilitating, or otherwise inhibiting, large-scale CO_2 storage deployment across states.

3. Joint (Petroleum) Development in State Practice

While CO_2 storage in the sub-seabed could support the energy transition, the concept of joint development remains a product of its own time. Joint development emerged during the 1950s as States began claiming sovereign rights over the greater part of the continental shelf, where oil and gas deposits were thought to be found, and thus swiftly entered into the necessary agreement to exploit these deposits.[43]

Legally, joint development has broadly been described as a 'cooperative regime' between two States to develop and share jointly in agreed proportions offshore seabed deposits 'in an area of overlapping claims'.[44] Indeed, a review of State practice indicates that past joint development agreements have focused primarily on offshore hydrocarbon resources.[45] States with overlapping claims have often placed those resources under a cooperative regime, in conjunction with partial delimitation (such as the Iceland–Norway Delimitation Agreement),[46] or instead of a maritime boundary delimitation (such as the Nigeria– São Tomé Joint Development Treaty).[47]

Joint development should be distinguished from the closely related concept of transboundary unitisation. Joint development is relevant to hydrocarbon deposits within overlapping maritime claims, while transboundary unitisation deals with hydrocarbon deposits straddling established maritime boundaries.[48] Transboundary unitisation, akin to domestic oil and gas unitisation, involves two or more States or concession holders cooperating over the modalities of exploration and exploration of a continuous hydrocarbon deposit across their respective licensing areas, treating it as a single unit to avoid competitive drilling and property disputes. An early and much cited example is the Anglo-Norwegian Treaty of 1965, which provided for the transboundary unitisation of any 'single geological structure or petroleum field extending across the agreed international maritime boundary line'.[49] Despite their distinct objectives and characteristics, joint development and unitisation agreements may well coexist, especially when an oil

[43] Hazel Fox et al (eds), *Joint Development of Offshore Oil and Gas*, 1st edn (BIICL, 1989) 54.

[44] Fox et al (ibid) 45, citing R Lagoni, 'Oil and Gas Deposits across National Frontiers' (1979) 73(2) *American Journal of International Law* 215; see also Arbitration between Guyana and Suriname (Annex VII Tribunal) (2007) 139 *ILR* 566; (2008) 47 *International Legal Materials* 166, para 462; Vasco Becker-Weinberg, *Joint Development of Hydrocarbon Deposits in the Law of the Sea* (Springer, 2014) 5–6.

[45] Constantinos Yiallourides, *Maritime Disputes and International Law: Disputed Waters and Seabed Resources in Asia and Europe* (Routledge, 2019) 173–210.

[46] Agreement on the Continental Shelf (Iceland/Norway) (signed 22 October 1981, entered into force 2 June 1982) (1982) 21 International Legal Materials 1222.

[47] Treaty on the Joint Development of Petroleum and Other Resources in Respect of Areas of the Exclusive Economic Zone of the two States (Nigeria/São Tomé and Principe) (signed 21 February 2001, entered into force 16 January 2003) [Nigeria/São Tomé Treaty].

[48] Yiallourides, 'Joint Development' (n 8) 129, 133–37.

[49] Agreement Relating to the Delimitation of the Continental Shelf between the two Countries (United Kingdom/Norway) (adopted 10 March 1965, entered into force 29 June 1965), Article 4.

and gas deposit in a joint development area extends into a jurisdictional zone of one or more States. For instance, Article 31 of the Nigeria– São Tomé Joint Development Treaty provides for three different unitisation scenarios: (a) when a petroleum field extends across the dividing line between the joint development zone and an exclusive maritime area of one of the States; (b) when a petroleum field extends across the dividing line between any contract areas within the joint development zone and (c) when a petroleum field extends across the dividing line between the joint development and an exclusive maritime area of a third State.[50] Thus, in such cases, unitisation procedures complement the joint development framework.[51]

The two prevailing aspects of joint development, as developed in State practice, are: (a) the creation of a zone of cooperation (the JDZ); and (b) the creation of a mutually agreed regulatory system applicable to hydrocarbon operations in that zone.[52]

On the first element, States have discretion in defining the precise zone to which the joint cooperative regime will apply. However, in practice, the zone's exact location will often be determined, if not defined, by the parties' overlapping claims on maritime delimitation. This is a negotiation that takes place against the background of international legal principles. Each State will often emphasise early in the joint development negotiations where it considers that the maritime boundary should be located, and it will often stick to that position. Therefore, the JDZ will typically consist of primarily the maritime area claimed by all parties.[53]

On the second element, namely establishing a common regulatory system, like any domestic petroleum regulatory regime, having in place a composite legal framework helps determining, among others, ownership over the hydrocarbon resources in the JDZ (ie, ownership of hydrocarbons *in situ*) and the system for granting rights to interested investors (eg, licences or contracts of work).[54] By clarifying the regulatory regime in the JDZ, States confer greater jurisdictional clarity and legal certainty to an area which would otherwise have been governed by political instability and legal uncertainty.[55] Clarity and certainty can attract international investors with the requisite funds and technical expertise to develop the resources in disputed areas.[56]

There are three basic variations for the governance structure of the JDZ.[57] First, one State can manage the JDZ on both States' behalf subject to an agreed payment to the non-managing State. For instance, in the Bahrain–Saudi Arabia Agreement, the parties agreed that Saudi Arabia would develop the resources in JDZ on a sole basis, as though it was managing its own resources, subject to paying half the proceeds to Bahrain.[58]

[50] ibid.

[51] Nigeria/São Tomé Treaty (2001).

[52] Becker-Weinberg (n 44) 8–9.

[53] Jianjun Gao, 'Joint Development in the East China Sea: Not an Easier Challenge than Delimitation' (2008) 23 *International Journal of Marine and Coastal Law* 39.

[54] Bernard Taverne, *An Introduction to the Regulation of the Petroleum Industry: Laws, Contracts and Conventions* (Martinus Nijhoff, 1994) 7–29.

[55] Becker-Weinberg (n 44) 8–9.

[56] ibid 163.

[57] Yiallourides, 'Joint Development' (n 8) 129–74.

[58] Agreement Concerning the Delimitation of the Continental Shelf in the Persian Gulf(Bahrain/Saudi Arabia) (adopted 22 February 1958, entered into force 22 February 1958).

Second, the States can promote joint ventures between companies incorporated in their respective legal systems.[59] For instance, in the Japan–South Korea JDZ regime, petroleum companies appointed by one State as the concession holders are entitled, and obliged to, explore for and exploit any hydrocarbon resources in the defined subzones, in collaboration with petroleum companies appointed by the other State. Concession holders must designate a single operator amongst the companies.[60] The designated operator receives exclusive control of all petroleum operations in the relevant subzone. The duties of the operator and the rights of the other concession holders (ie, the non-operators) are detailed in a joint operating agreement (JOA). Thus, the State-granted concession sets out the 'vertical' relationship between the States (as the joint grantors of the concession) and the petroleum companies (in their capacity as the concession holders). The JOA defines the 'horizontal' relationship between concession holders and provides for the sharing of rights and liabilities connected to the concession between the petroleum companies.

Third, States can designate a supranational committee or joint authority tasked with the management of the JDZ. As an example, the Mauritius–Seychelles Joint Management/Joint Exercise Treaty stipulates that 'Parties shall exercise sovereign rights jointly for the purpose of exploring the continental shelf and exploiting its natural resources in the area [defined as Joint Zone]'.[61] It establishes a three-tier joint administrative set-up with a ministerial council, a joint commission, and a designated authority. The designated authority has juridical personality under the law of the contracting parties and is responsible for the day-to-day regulation and management of natural resource activities in the joint management area. This includes the right to contract, to acquire and dispose of movable and immovable property, and to institute and be party to legal proceedings.[62] Several other JDAs offer useful examples of the joint authority model in practice. These include Australia–Timor-Leste,[63] Colombia–Jamaica,[64] Guinea-Bissau–Senegal,[65] and Nigeria–São Tomé and Principe.[66]

Past analysis of State practice on joint development indicates that while there are at least three basic governance variations, these are not mutually exclusive: choosing a compulsory joint venture model does not necessarily preclude the establishment of a joint authority with supervisory or administrative duties.[67] A supranational joint

[59] Agreement Concerning Joint Development of the Southern Part of the Continental Shelf Adjacent to the Two Countries (South Korea/Japan) (signed 30 January 1974, entered into force 22 June 1978) 1225 United Nations Treaty Series 113.

[60] South Korea/Japan 1974 Agreement, Article V(1)(b).

[61] Treaty Concerning the Joint Exercise of Sovereign Rights over the Continental Shelf in the Mascarene Plateau Region (Mauritius/Seychelles) (adopted 13 March 2012, entered into force 18 June 2012), Article 23; Treaty Concerning the Joint Management of the Continental Shelf in the Mascarene Plateau Region (Mauritius/Seychelles) (adopted 13 March 2012, entered into force 18 June 2012), Article 1.

[62] Mauritius/Seychelles Joint Management Treaty (2012), Article 4(d).

[63] Timor Sea Treaty (Timor-Leste/Australia) (signed 20 May 2002, entered into force 2 April 2003) 2258 United Nations Treaty Series 3, Article 6(b)(iv) and Annex C.

[64] Maritime Delimitation Treaty (Jamaica/Colombia) (adopted 12 November 1993, entered into force 14 March 1994) (1994) 26 LOS Bulletin 50.

[65] Management and Cooperation Agreement (Senegal/Guinea-Bissau) (adopted 14 October 1993, entered into force 21 December 1995); Protocol to the Senegal/Guinea-Bissau 1993 Agreement (adopted 12 June 1995, entered into force 21 December 1995).

[66] Nigeria/São Tomé Treaty (2001).

[67] Yiallourides, 'Joint Development' (n 8) 129, 173.

authority can be created as the main policy and decision-making body, but its functions may be under the overall control of the respective states' governments. Additionally, interested states are not barred from dividing the joint development zone into distinct sections, with different administrative structures applicable within each. Ultimately, the choice of the cooperation model and the associated administrative arrangements rests with the interested states and 'each agreement is naturally shaped and tailored to the political, economic and geographical peculiarities which it seeks to address'.[68]

Overall, joint development, as a legal concept, has offered a pragmatic and functional way forward for coastal States wishing to explore hydrocarbon resources in overlapping maritime areas, which would otherwise have remained locked by entrenched or inflexible delimitation positions.[69] Agreeing on the applicable rules for the joint development of such deposits 'helps to provide a secure basis for the necessary commercial arrangements and contributes to certainty of investment'.[70] Thus, past JDZs have primarily been driven by States' desire to explore for, and eventually develop, offshore hydrocarbon resources. No such agreement has covered CCS so far.

4. From Joint Petroleum Zones to Joint CO_2 Storage Zones

Much like typical seabed hydrocarbon reservoirs, sub-seabed CO_2 storage reservoirs can lie across international maritime boundaries or within joint management areas, such as JDZs. When hydrocarbon reservoirs are within a JDZ, or potentially straddle the JDZ, inter-state disputes may arise due to unilateral exploration and exploitation activities and the volume of extracted hydrocarbons. For instance, an oil and gas deposit could be discovered straddling the boundary of a JDZ and an area where one of the State parties, or even a third state, exercises jurisdiction.[71] In the case of CO_2 storage reservoirs, inter-state disputes will arise in relation not of hydrocarbon extraction, but instead of the unilateral injection, movement, and sequestration of CO_2 into the reservoir's pore space. Without a clear definition of rights and access arrangements for every phase of a CO_2 injection and storage project, States and their CCS operators will face legal uncertainty.

Establishing a new JDZ, or repurposing an existing JDZ, for joint CO_2 sequestration operations is not straightforward. Where the applicable delimitation approaches are hotly disputed, each claimant State will seek to ensure that any seabed energy arrangement, even provisional arrangements, will not prejudice its long-term maritime positions on delimitation. For each claimant State, agreeing to develop seabed resources

[68] ibid 155.

[69] Ian Townsend-Gault, 'Maritime Cooperation in a Functional Perspective' in Clive Schofield (ed), *Maritime Energy Resources in Asia: Legal Regimes and Cooperation* (National Bureau of Asian Research, 2012) 17.

[70] Nigel Bankes, 'The Regime for Transboundary Hydrocarbon Deposits in the Maritime Delimitation Treaties and Other Related Agreements of Arctic Coastal States' (2016) 47(2) *Ocean Development & International Law* 141, 142.

[71] Bastida et al (2007) 355, 359.

jointly means sharing with the other claimant State sub-seabed geological assets to which it believes it is exclusively entitled under international law.[72]

For this reason, should States wish to pursue a joint regime with CCS elements, they must be prepared to incorporate specific key provisions guiding their cooperation to govern the joint CCS regime within, or across, the JDZ. Such key provisions include establishing the pro-cooperation nature of the agreement; defining the meaning of natural resources; deciding on the mode of joint operations and benefit-sharing arrangements; establishing a legal and regulatory structure, including environmental provisions; and setting the duration of the agreement and continuity arrangements. These key provisions are discussed in turn below.

A. Principle of Cooperation

The first key issue is to record the pro-cooperation nature of the JDZ. An agreement to establish a JDZ regime is an agreement to cooperate between States. Thus, the JDZ should exclude unilateralism from the outset. The agreement should contain specific provisions setting out the objectives of the cooperation. It should make clear that the 'joint development' of the specified zone, and resources therein, may take place only according to the terms of the agreement. Neither State will be entitled to act unilaterally with respect to seabed activities in the specified zone and its resources. This is the position under both UNCLOS and general international law.[73]

International law recognises a general legal obligation to cooperate on shared resources.[74] A geological structure which could be used for CO_2 injection and storage by multiple States would arguably constitute a shared resource.[75] The common sub-seabed geological 'container' forms the shared resource in relation to which a duty of cooperation applies. States must 'co- operate in the … harmonious utilisation of natural resources shared by two or more States', as recognised in resolutions by the UN Environment Programme[76] and later the UN General Assembly.[77] These resolutions are not legally binding. However, they have been widely implemented in State practice and serve as evidence of customary international law on shared resources, including straddling hydrocarbon deposits.[78] Indeed, under international customary law, no State may unilaterally exploit a common natural resource deposit before negotiating the matter with neighbouring States in good faith with a view to concluding an agreement.[79]

[72] Gao (n 53) 39.

[73] Report on the Obligations of States under Articles 74(3) and 83(3) of UNCLOS in Respect of Undelimited Maritime Areas' (British Institute of International and Comparative Law, 2016) (BIICL 2016 Report).

[74] Neil Craik, 'The Duty to Cooperate in International Environmental Law: Constraining State Discretion through Due Respect' (2019) 30(1) *Yearbook of International Environmental Law* 22, 32–37.

[75] International Law Commission, 'Draft Articles on the Law of Transboundary Aquifers, with commentaries' Adopted at the ILC 60th Session (2008).

[76] Decision 6/14 of the Governing Council of UNEP (19 May 1978).

[77] GA Res 34/186 (1979) undocs.org/en/A/RES/34/186.

[78] David Ong, 'Joint Development of Common Offshore Oil and Gas Deposits: "Mere" State Practice or Customary International Law?' (1999) 93(4) *American Journal of International Law* 771–804.

[79] James Crawford, *Chance, Order, Change: The Course of International Law (Hague Academy of International Law* (Martinus Nijhoff, 2014) 504.

The parallel duties under Articles 83(3) and 74(3) of UNCLOS to: (a) make every good faith effort to enter into provisional arrangements; and (b) refrain from taking any actions that might jeopardise or hamper reaching a final agreement apply to CCS operations just as they apply to conventional hydrocarbon operations.

The first duty would require the State proposing to authorise CCS evaluation activities in the JDZ area to notify the other State(s) concerned; provide relevant information; seek cooperation; and commit to sharing any information obtainedto achieve the optimum use of storage sites, without causing damage to the resource and the legitimate interests of the other participating State(s).[80]

The second duty would require the proposing State not to authorise drilling activities for any CCS-related purposes, such as for taking core samples from target formations to assess porosity, permeability, and injectivity and for assessing the characteristics of sealing formations.[81] Existing oil and gas JDAs already include common principles providing for inter alia notification, exchange of information, effective exploitation, and unitisation of common resources.

Unitisation is typically achieved by agreement between the commercial parties which have an interest as a licensee (ie, as a working interest owner) from either State over a geographical area forming part of the shared deposit.[82] The unitisation agreement will provide for the apportionment of production and expenses in accordance with the best scientific understanding on the distribution of reserves and each of the different licence areas (or tracts). Thus, each tract will be assigned a tract participation factor. The agreement will also make provisions on future operations. Unitisation agreements are only necessary where there are multiple tracts and multiple parties. If there is only a single tract, or a single owner of the different tracts forming the reservoir (or storage unit), unitisation is arguably unnecessary. This would be unusual in an oil and gas production context. However, it could be more likely in the CO_2 disposal context where operations would likely be less competitive and more coordinated from the outset. Indeed, regulatory coordination between national authorities would likely seek to ensure unified exploitation and development of a target CO_2 storage and disposal complex by coordinating CO_2 storage acreage.

B. Defining Natural Resources

Specifying the type of common natural resources which will be subject to the JDA is crucial. Experience shows that past JDAs were concluded specifically to search for and exploit natural resources like hydrocarbons.[83] Typical resource clauses refer only

[80] Peter D Cameron, 'The Rules of Engagement: Developing Cross-Border Petroleum Deposits in the North Sea and the Caribbean' (2006) 55(3) *International and Comparative Law Quarterly* 559, 560–61.

[81] Bankes (n 15) 397, 413–16.

[82] Eduardo G Pereira and Giulia Carloni, 'Unitisation and Unit Operating Agreements' in Eduardo G Pereira (ed), Understanding Joint Operating Agreements (Intersentia, 2016) 43–60; Bernard Taverne, *Co-operative Agreements in the Extractive Petroleum Industry* (Kluwer Law International, 1996) 79.

[83] Moritaka Hayashi, 'Recent Developments in the Law of the Sea and China' in Myron Nordquist, John Norton Moore, and Kuen-Chen Fu (eds), *Recent Developments in the Law of the Sea and China* (Brill, 2016) 219–37.

to hydrocarbon reservoirs and exploiting hydrocarbons. For instance, the Australia–Timor-Leste Maritime Boundary Treaty established the Greater Sunrise Special Regime for the joint development, exploitation, and management of the Sunrise and Troubadour (Greater Sunrise) petroleum deposits. The Australia–Timor-Leste Treatydefines 'Petroleum Activities' as '[a]ll activities undertaken to produce Petroleum and includes exploration, development, initial processing, production, transportation and marketing.' The majority of JDZ agreements concluded to date include almost identical definitions. As mentioned before, they have focused primarily on the economic development of common petroleum resources. These agreements do not expressly mention CO_2 sub-seabed injection for permanent storage. Similarly, agreements such as those between Indonesia–Malaysia,[84] Colombia–Honduras,[85] and the Norway–UK Frigg Agreement are explicitly confined to oil and natural gas.[86]

Other agreements have defined natural resources using more general language which does not specifically refer to hydrocarbon resources or petroleum reservoirs. For example, the France–Spain delimitation agreement, which also creates a JDZ, refers to the exploitation of a 'deposit of a natural resource'.[87] Another example is the Nigeria–São Tomé Treaty which establishes a JDZ in an area of overlapping maritime claims for the orderly exploration and exploitation of 'petroleum and other resources'.[88] This agreement defines 'petroleum' as 'any hydrocarbon or mixture of hydrocarbons, whether in a gaseous, liquid or solid state, naturally occurring beneath the seabed' and covers among others 'any petroleum … that has been returned to a reservoir'.[89] This provision likely alludes to enhanced oil recovery, where hydrocarbons are injected ('returned') into the sub-seabed to mobilise hydrocarbons through pore spaces. Such methods can boost the recovery of residual hydrocarbons from mature wells with declining oil and gas production.[90]

There are arguments going both ways as to whether this and similar enhanced oil recovery provisions could embrace CO_2 injection and storage operations. On the one hand, it is not unreasonable for CO_2 injection into a common reservoir to qualify as the exploitation of that shared resource. Equally, many similar clauses are explicitly confined to petroleum and natural gas or exploiting mineral resources deposits, ruling out application to joint CO_2 activities in sub-seabed reservoirs. One could also argue that CO_2 sequestration and storage is only the continued exploitation of a transboundary seabed formation. On the other hand, unlike conventional hydrocarbon resource activities, CO_2 injection for permanent storage was not intended in previous JDZ agreements. This creates legal uncertainty. Many States across the world may wish to exploit

[84] Agreement on the Delimitation of the Continental Shelves between the Two Countries (Malaysia/Indonesia) (signed 27 October 1969; entered into force 7 November 1969), Article 4.

[85] Maritime Delimitation Treaty (Colombia/Honduras) (signed 2 August 1986; entered into force 20 December 1999), Article 3.

[86] Agreement relating to the exploitation of the Frigg Field Reservoirs and the transmission of gas therefrom to the United Kingdom (10 May 1976) 1098 UNTS 3.

[87] Convention on the Delimitation of the Continental Shelves of the two States in the Bay of Biscay (France/Spain) (signed 29 January 1974; entered into force 5 April 1975).

[88] Nigeria/São Tomé Treaty (2001).

[89] ibid.

[90] Arnold W Reitze, 'Carbon Capture and Storage (Sequestration)' (2013) 43 *Environmental Law Reporter* 10414.

depleting petroleum reservoirs for CO_2 storage, including in areas of joint jurisdiction. Therefore, this legal uncertainty is problematic and could foster disputes over shared deposits, their CO_2 storage potentials, and possible transboundary implications.[91] Thus, States would be well advised to specify that natural resources, and any exploitation activities thereof, include sub-seabed geological assets and geological CO_2 storage sites.

C. Joint Operations and Benefit-Sharing Arrangements

Several options exist for joint CO_2 operations in, or in respect of, the JDZ.[92] For instance, CO_2 capture could occur in both State A and State B, with transportation through pipelines from both States and final sequestration into a common sub-seabed storage site within the JDZ. In this scenario, both States have the right to inject into to the common sub-seabed storage. Thus, close collaboration is required to achieve uniformity on a range of regulatory issues and procedures for the safe and ecologically sound sub-seabed storage of CO_2. This would include inter alia provisions for site selection; environmental impact assessments; monitoring; reporting; and granting authorisations for CO_2 transport, injection, and storage operations.[93]

Another scenario could involve State A injecting into a sub-seabed storage site within the JDZ, subject to an agreed payment to State B. As mentioned above, Saudi Arabia and Bahrain agreed to place the disputed yet resource-rich Fasht bu Saafa Hexagon area under Saudi Arabia's control and jurisdiction on the condition that a monetary payment be given to Bahrain.[94] Similarly, Abu Dhabi and Qatar agreed to place the disputed Al-Bunduq field under Abu Dhabi's control and jurisdiction subject to a monetary payment to Qatar.[95] Analogous benefit-sharing arrangements could be made where only one party injects CO_2 into the JDZ formation. In this situation, the injecting State would likely have more responsibilities over issues such as waste management and waste pollution prevention audits; characterisation of the waste stream; screening for determining acceptability for seabed injection; site selection and assessment; risk management and pre- and post-injection monitoring; and licensing requirements and conditions.

For instance, to regulate the environmental risks inherent in the transboundary sub-seabed sequestration and storage of CO_2, the State parties to the Convention on the Prevention of Marine Pollution by Dumping of Wastes and Other Matter (London

[91] Hannis et al (n 29) 5680; Martha M Roggenkamp, 'Re-using (Nearly) Depleted Oil and Gas Fields in the North Sea for CO2 Storage: Seizing or Missing a Window of Opportunity?' in Banet (n 15) 454–80.

[92] Moonsook Park, 'Study on Legal Systems for Transboundary CCS Implementation and Transboundary Environmental Liability Regarding CCS' (2020) 16(1) *Loyola University Chicago International Law Review* 45.

[93] For a comprehensive study, see Martha M Roggenkamp and Edwin Woerdman (eds), *Legal Design of Carbon Capture and Storage, Developments in the Netherlands from an International and EU Perspective* (Intersentia, 2009).

[94] Bahrain/Saudi Arabia 1958 Agreement, Article 2(7).

[95] Abu Dhabi/Qatar 1969 Agreement, Articles 6 and 7.

Convention) and its Protocol,[96] agreed to a set of guidelines in 2012 specifically addressing the transboundary sub-seabed storage and sequestration of CO_2 (Specific Guidelines).[97] Article 1(10) of the Specific Guidelines under the London Protocol enshrines that the State where the migration or injection occurs has operational responsibility over the activities.[98] Article 1(10) also underscores that the injecting State should seek consent from all other Stateswith jurisdiction over the shared sub-seabed geological formation.

D. Without Prejudice Clause

Furthermore, the JDA should typically include a robust provision preserving the two States' legal positions on maritime delimitation. This is commonly known as a 'without prejudice' clause.[99] The parties typically seek to ensure that their agreement on joint development, even if provisional, will not nullify or weaken their long-standing maritime positions and their respective sovereign rights in the relevant area.[100] For instance, the Mauritius–Seychelles Treaty stipulates that 'Parties shall exercise sovereign rights jointly for the purpose of exploring the continental shelf and exploiting its natural resources in the area [defined as Joint Zone]',[101] without prejudicing or affecting their legal positions concerning any future delimitation of the continental shelf between them in the Mascarene Plateau region.[102]

Not all JDAs address the sovereign rights of participating States in a uniform way. For example, the Saudi Arabia–Sudan Agreement provides that both States have 'equal sovereign rights in all the natural resources' in the JDZ and that these rights are exclusive to them.[103] By contrast, in the Bahrain–Saudi Arabia Agreement, the parties agreed that Saudi Arabia would develop the resources in the joint development area as though it was managing its own resources subject to a monetary payment to Bahrain.[104] Bahrain conferred, in effect, the exercise of its sovereign rights to Saudi Arabia. Saudi

[96] Convention on the Prevention of Marine Pollution by Dumping of Wastes and Other Matter (London Convention) (Adopted 29 December 1972; Entered into force 30 August 1975) (1972) 11 International Legal Materials 1294; Protocol to the Convention on the Prevention of Marine Pollution by Dumping of Wastes and Other Matter (London Protocol) (Adopted 7 November 1996; Entered into force 24 March 2006) (1997) 36 International Legal Materials 1.

[97] Specific Guidelines for the Assessment of Carbon Dioxide for Disposal into Sub-seabed Geological Formations' (IMO, 2012).

[98] ibid.

[99] Paul M Blyschak, 'Offshore Oil and Gas Projects amid Maritime Border Disputes: Applicable Law' (2013) 6(3) *Journal of World Energy Law and Business* 210, 217.

[100] Gavin Maclaren and Rebecca James, 'Negotiating Joint Development Agreements' in Robert Beckman et al (eds), *Beyond Territorial Disputes in the South China Sea: Legal Framework for the Joint Development of Hydrocarbon Resources* (Edward Elgar Publishing, 2013) 139–44.

[101] Mauritius/Seychelles Joint Exercise Treaty (2012), Article 1.

[102] ibid Article 3.

[103] Agreement Relating to the Joint Exploitation of the Natural Resources of the Sea-bed and Subsoil of the Red Sea in the Common Zone (Sudan/Saudi Arabia) (adopted 16 May 1974, entered into force 26 August 1974), Article 4.

[104] Agreement Concerning the Delimitation of the Continental Shelf in the Persian Gulf (Bahrain/Saudi Arabia) (adopted 22 February 1958, entered into force 22 February 1958).

Arabia, thus, acts as the agent of Bahrain with respect to exercising the sovereign rights in question.

The Malaysia–Thailand Agreement set up a supra-national Joint Authority to which the States granted all their rights and responsibilities for exploring and exploiting the non-living natural resources of the seabed and subsoil.[105] Pursuant to this agreement, the Joint Authority assumes the administration, on behalf of the participating States, of their sovereign rights in the JDZ. Furthermore, the Malaysia–Vietnam Agreement provides for a joint venture between the parties' respective national oil companies, Petronas and Petrovietnam. This joint venture is granted the right to undertake, on behalf of the participating States, the exploration for and exploitation of petroleum in the overlapping maritime areas.[106] Last but not least, the Japan–South Korea Agreement does not make any reference to the States' sovereign rights in the zone of cooperation, but it considers the natural resources extracted from specified blocks in the JDZ as if they were extracted from the continental shelf of the State whose appointed concession holder operates the specified block.[107] Consequently, Japan and South Korea delegated the exploration of the JDZ to private sector investors without prejudice or hampering their sovereign rights in the area.

E. Regulatory Structure

Another central issue when negotiating a joint development regime is to agree on a mutually acceptable management arrangement through which participating States may conduct coordinated seabed activities in the JDZ.[108] A key challenge is for the States to agree on the legal rules and regulations that would apply to CCS operations in the JDZ. If one State alone is responsible for managing the JDZ, the issue of applicable law is much more straightforward. However, where two States opt to share the management and regulation of CCS activities, they would also have to agree on the applicable law in the area. The applicable law may be that of one or other of the States, a combination of these, or even a sui generis regime designed especially for this JDZ.[109] As mentioned earlier, several different regimes are possible within a joint area. Each model can be tailored to the specific context at hand.

The IEA has created a Model Regulatory Framework for CCS activities.[110] Its principal purpose is to offer advice on the design of a domestic regulatory framework. However, the Model also emphasises various international legal issues, including the

[105] Memorandum of Understanding on the Establishment of the Resources of the Sea-bed in a Defined Area of the Continental Shelf of the Two Countries in the Gulf of Thailand (Malaysia/Thailand) (adopted 21 February 1979, entered into force 24 October 1979) (Malaysia/Thailand 1979 Agreement), Article 3(2).

[106] Memorandum of Understanding for the Exploration and Exploitation of Petroleum in a Defined Area of the Continental Shelf Involving the Two Countries (Malaysia/Vietnam) (adopted 5 June 1992, entered into force 4 June 1993) (Malaysia/Vietnam 1992 Agreement), Article 3.

[107] Japan/Korea 1974 Agreement, Articles XVI and IX.

[108] Yiallourides (n 45) 173.

[109] ibid 193–210.

[110] IEA, 'Carbon Capture & Storage Model Regulatory Framework' (November 2010) www.iea.org/reports/carbon-capture-and-storage-model-regulatory-framework.

monitoring and verification protocol for CO_2 storage in a transboundary context.[111] This encompasses not only CO_2 export and transit matters, but also other topics outlined in this chapter, which the report lists as:

(i) Unintended migration or leakage of injected CO_2 in the sub-surface across jurisdictional boundaries;
(ii) Use of storage complexes spanning jurisdictional borders (such as JDZs); and
(iii) Secondary effects from storage activities occurring across jurisdictional borders (eg, due to a sub-surface pressure front or displacement of subsurface fluids across borders).

In addressing these issues, the IEA Model Framework highlights the need for regulatory coordination and harmonisation and either the choice of a single competent authority for a CCS project or 'joint regulatory responsibility'.[112] This harmonisation and coordination could encompass coordinated bidding rounds for CO_2 storage exploration and efforts to optimise the use of pipelines and other infrastructure; application of market rules for access to storage; and agreement on liability and greenhouse gas emissions accounting rules.[113] Thus, the IEA Model Framework offers valuable guidance to States wishing to establish a regulatory framework for carrying out joint CCS activities in a JDZ.

Another helpful resource is the Technical Paper by the UN Framework Convention on Climate Change (UNFCC) Secretariat regarding qualifying CCS projects as Clean Development Mechanism eligible under the UNFCCC.[114] The Technical Paper advises to draw from experience with shared aquifers and shared oil and gas resources and briefly surveys a range of relevant international agreements.[115] It notes that international agreements on shared resources already embody common principles which could guide States' decisions on joint CCS (including within joint development regimes). These include the exchange of information; joint management structures; equitable sharing of the resources; appointment of contractors and operators; financial provisions; and environmental protection.[116]

The Technical Paper suggests that States contemplating joint CO_2 storage may adopt any of the joint petroleum management approaches developed in State practice. Experience in the oil and gas sector appears to indicate that there is no preference for a single management approach. Choosing between establishing Joint Authorities, private-sector joint ventures, or relying on cooperation between existing regulators will depend on the circumstances in each case.[117]

[111] ibid 30–33.
[112] ibid 31.
[113] ibid.
[114] UNFCCC Secretariat, Transboundary Carbon Capture and Storage Project Activities, Technical Paper (1 November 2012) UNFCCC/TP2012/9 (UNFCCC, Transboundary CCS Technical Paper) unfccc.int/resource/docs/2012/tp/09.pdf.
[115] ibid paras 63–76.
[116] ibid paras 156–61.
[117] ibid.

F. Environmental Protection

Marine environmental protection was not at the forefront of States which negotiated and adopted early JDAs.[118] However, more recent JDAs have incorporated a higher level of environmental cooperation, thereby denoting the 'raised level of environmental consciousness' between the parties which negotiated, adopted, and are charged with implementing more recent JDAs.[119] For instance, Article 10(a) of the 2002 Timor Sea Arrangement between Timor Leste and Australia established an obligation to cooperate 'to prevent and minimise pollution *and other environmental harm*'(emphasis added) in the designated JDZ.[120] According to Ong, this provision acknowledges that environmental damage can occur from a range of sources, and not necessarily only as a result of marine pollution caused by petroleum exploration activities. Additionally, Article 10(a) requires the parties to consult as to the best means to protect the marine environment in the JDZ from the harmful consequences (ie, not merely pollution) of petroleum activities. Article 10(a) specifies that special efforts must be made to protect marine wildlife, including marine mammals, seabirds, fish, and coral. In respect of these endeavours, the designated Joint Authority shall issue regulations to protect the JDZ marine environment.[121] Should pollution nevertheless occur, the parties shall cooperate in mitigating and eliminating such pollution.[122] Moreover, companies shall be liable for damage as a result of pollution within the JDZ marine environment, and claims can be brought in either party's jurisdiction.[123] Similar environmental protection provisions have been included in the agreements between, among others, Guinea-Bissau–Senegal,[124] Colombia–Jamaica,[125] and Nigeria–São Tomé.[126]

For joint CCS operations, the purpose of environmentally safe geological storage of CO_2 is to permanently contain the CO_2 so as to prevent and, where this is not possible, eliminate as far as possible negative effects and any risk to the integrity of surface and sub-surface geological assets, benthic ecologies, the marine environment more broadly, and human health.[127] Current seabed injection practices for enhanced oil recovery in a

[118] Patricia Birnie, 'Protection of the Marine Environment' in Hazel Fox et al, *Joint Development of Offshore Oil and Gas*, Vol 2 (BIICL, 1990)202; see also AD Read, 'Protection of the Marine Environment: A View from Industry' in Fox et al, ibid 223.

[119] David M Ong, 'The Progressive Integration of Environmental Protection within Offshore Joint Development Agreements' in M Fitzmaurice and M Szuniewicz (eds), *Exploitation of Natural Resources in the 21st Century* (Kluwer, 2003) 116–40.

[120] Timor Sea Treaty (2002), Article 10(a).

[121] ibid Article 10(c).

[122] ibid Article 10(b).

[123] ibid Article 10(d).

[124] Senegal/Guinea-Bissau Protocol to the Agreement of 14 October 1993, concerning the organization and operation of the Management and Cooperation Agency (entered into force 10 January 1996), Articles 10.5, 11.4(k).

[125] Jamaica/Colombia (1993), Article 3(2).

[126] Nigeria/São Tomé Treaty (2001), Articles 9, 38; see also Biang J Tanga, 'The Joint Development Zone between Nigeria and Sao Tome and Principe' (United Nations Publications, 2009) 50–52.

[127] Leonard Jan Müller, 'A Guideline for Life Cycle Assessment of Carbon Capture and Utilization' (2020) 8 (15) *Frontiers in Energy Research* 1–20; UK Environmental Agency, Scoping guidelines on the Environmental Impact Assessment (EIA) of Carbon Capture, Transport and Storage Projects (2011) assets.publishing.service.gov.uk/media/5a7564f940f0b6360e473c6b/geho0811bucq-e-e.pdf.

shared hydrocarbon reservoir of the continental shelf do not necessarily require long-term monitoring or verification regimes. However, sub-seabed sequestration of CO_2 for permanent storage in shared geological formations poses marine environmental risks. Many of these risks are not present when developing conventional offshore hydrocarbons. The 'sub-surface elements of CO_2 projects … may present new issues in relation to environmental impact assessment (EIA) practice'.[128] Therefore, the parties would have to scrutinise carefully environmental provisions which would govern large-scale CO_2 storage operations in a JDZ.

A good example of environmental regulation of inter-state CCS activities is the European Union (EU) Directive 2009/31/EC (EU CCS Directive).[129] This Directive sets out a uniform framework of legal requirements for the safe and ecologically sound sub-seabed storage of CO_2. This includes provisions for monitoring and reporting and for granting authorisations for CO_2 transport, sequestration, and storage projects in geological sites straddling the boundaries of two or more EU Member States.[130] The EU CCS Directive is 'the first comprehensive legal framework for the management of environmental risks related to CCS.'[131] It requires, among others, that CCS storage be rock-based and not water-column-based and that the sequestered CO_2 volumes be contained. The examination of potential CO_2 storage sites must be rigorous, 'to ensure that the stored CO_2 will be completely and permanently contained', taking account of their geological characteristics, for example seismicity, 'in the most objective and effective way possible'.[132] Per Article 4(4) of the CCS Directive, a 'geological formation shall only be selected as a storage site, if under the proposed conditions of use there is no significant risk of leakage, and if no significant environmental or health risks exist.'[133]

Additional rules prevent environmental harm. For example, EU Member States must cooperate to prevent transboundary injuries. In alignment with the Aarhus Convention, Article 26 requires EU Member States to make available 'public environmental information relating to the geological storage of CO_2'.[134] Article 28 also mandates that EU Member States ensure 'effective, proportionate and dissuasive' penalties for operators operating within and across EU borders. It should be noted, however, that the EU CCS Directive is based on the 'principle of minimum harmonisation'.[135] Member States have a degree of discretion when implementing the EU CCS Directive.[136]

[128] OECD/IEA, 'Carbon Capture and Storage Model Regulatory Framework (Information Paper, November 2010).

[129] Directive 2009/31/EC on Capture and Storage Technology in Europe (2013/2079 (INI)).

[130] For a comprehensive study, see Roggenkamp and Woerdman (n 93).

[131] 'UNFCCC, 'Transboundary Carbon Capture and Storage Project Activities' (Technical Paper, 1 November 2012) Doc FCCC/TP/2012/9.

[132] Directive 2009/31/EC of the European Parliament and the Capture and Storage Technology in Europe (2013/2079(INI)), para 19.

[133] For a discussion, see also David Langlet, 'Transboundary Dimensions of CCS: EU Law Problems and Prospects' (2014) 8(3) *Carbon & Climate Law Review* 198–207.

[134] Convention on Access to Information, Public Participation in Decision-Making and Access to Justice in Environmental Matters (adopted 25 June 1998; entered into force 30 October 2001) UNTS 2161, p 447.

[135] Consolidated versions of the Treaty on European Union and the Treaty on the Functioning of the European Union, Article 193; for a discussion, see Avelien Haan-Kamminga, Martha Roggenkamp and Edwin Woerdman, 'Legal Uncertainties of Carbon Capture and Storage in the EU: The Netherlands as an Example' (2010) 4(3) *Carbon and Climate Law Review* 240–49; Scott Brockett, 'The EU Enabling Legal Framework for CCS' (2009) 1 *Energy Procedia* 4433, 4441.

[136] Haan-Kamminga et al (ibid) 240, 242–44.

G. Duration and Continuity Arrangements

Another key element is the duration of the JDA. If the agreement is intended to be provisional, this should be clearly stated in its text. The duration of a typical petroleum JDA is normally 30–50 years. This provides some certainty to potential petroleum investors on the continued existence of the JDZ and its petroleum regulatory system. However, the distinctive characteristic separating offshore CCS from other seabed activities is that CCS is designed to store CO_2 for a very long time, amounting to hundreds or thousands of years.[137] States may consider establishing arrangements to ensure the continuity of rights and obligations for CCS operators in the zone. This should include monitoring responsibilities during closure and post-closure, especially if the agreement is terminated.

For instance, in the case of a CO_2 leakage incident occurring after the termination of the agreement, safeguard mechanisms must remain in place where States disagree on the origin of the leakage or the form of redress in the case of transboundary environmental harm. The JDA would establish a framework regulating leakage, storage permanence in geological formations, and post-closure liabilities.[138] At the domestic level, the duration of this post-closure liability may vary from State to State. For example, in the United States, the State of Wyoming assume liability 20 years after a CO_2 project closure.[139] The EU CCS Directive also requires a minimum post-closure period of 20 years.[140] Thus, if the parties wish to terminate the JDA, they should consider making additional arrangements to clarify post-closure liabilities associated with CO_2 streams stored in, or across, the JDZ.

5. Conclusion

The chapter has shown that JDZs have historically been designed to explore, exploit, and manage seabed hydrocarbon resources in areas of overlapping maritime claims. However, the global shift towards a low-carbon future necessitates re-evaluating the role and operation of JDZs. With the emerging emphasis on offshore CCS in depleted or nearly depleted oil and gas reservoirs, JDZs could be transitioned away from their traditional role in hydrocarbon development and instead leveraged for joint CO_2 storage.

This transition is not devoid of challenges. The preceding analysis has shown that joint CO_2 storage operations in JDZs bring forth novel legal and technical issues, not necessarily present with conventional hydrocarbons. Potential environmental harms and the risk of nullifying neighbouring States' CO_2 storage capabilities in the shared

[137] See de Figueiredo (n 10) 387; Park (n 92) 45, 48.

[138] See for instance, CCS Directive concerning Closure and post-closure obligations and financial security, Articles 1719.

[139] Peter Fitch et al, 'Australia's Carbon Sequestration Potential' (CSIRO, November 2022) 149, CCA-Report-Australias-Potential-Sequestration-Final-28-November-2022.pdf.

[140] See CCS Directive, Article 18.

formation underscore the complexity of this transition. To manage these challenges, States interested to undertake a joint development regime with CCS elements must be prepared to incorporate specific key provisions in the JDZ regime. These include specifying the principle of cooperation; the natural resources; the mode of joint operations and benefit-sharing; the CCS legal and regulatory structure; environmental protection; and the duration and continuity arrangements.

18

On the Future of Offshore Energy

IGNACIO HERRERA ANCHUSTEGUI, EDUARDO G PEREIRA, EDDY WIFA AND MADELINE TAYLOR*

1. Introduction

Offshore spaces and their resources will play a pivotal role in the future of energy and its transition. Through the three thematic pillars of our book: Offshore Energy: Fostering Environmental Stewardship and Community Collaboration; Offshore Energy: Business and Financing; and Offshore Energy: Complex Infrastructure, our authors have offered a detailed analysis of the current regulatory challenges surrounding the exploitation of energy at sea. Although offshore petroleum exploration has provided decades of valuable lessons as stressed throughout this book, the fast-evolving nature of emerging energy systems and technologies at sea pushes regulatory frontiers.

The contributions to this volume highlight both the potential of marine spaces and offshore resources to support the energy transition. Our collection highlights the complex balance linked to marine protection, the needs of other sea users, and technological complexity. Our book contributors emphasise that while there are commonalities with onshore energy regulation, offshore energy activities present different and sometimes novel regulatory challenges for State and non-State actors alike, with States and regulators often struggling to adapt to the pace of emerging technological solutions. The chapters also share two underlying themes. First, offshore energy is expanding rapidly and represents, in a way, the final frontier on the planet for energy harvesting and exploitation. Energy development is currently being undertaken in national waters, but it is foreseeable that future offshore energy activity will be done in spaces beyond national jurisdictions. Much of the regulatory effort has been made, so far, to grant access and regulate this rapid offshore expansion to increase access to energy and balance interests between different stakeholders. Second, sea spaces and offshore energy exploitation are, at the same time, affected by and an answer to climate change.

* The research for this chapter has benefited from the generous funding granted by the Research Council of Norway to the research projects: Norwegian Centre for Hydrogen Research – HyValue (Project: 333151); and ImpactWind Sørvest (Project: 332034), and the Transforming Energy Markets Research Centre, Macquarie University.

All websites were last accessed on 10 October 2024.

Governance frameworks aim to accommodate and balance environmental protection with infrastructure project development designed to mitigate and adapt to climate change. This is the complex framework in which ocean energy governance will play out in the years to come.

In this final contribution to *Offshore Energy Law*, we focus on the *future* of offshore energy. We aim to help develop an offshore energy research and policy agenda based on the different contributions of the authors featured in our collection. It is our aspiration that these reflections will spark further work and debate in academic, legal practice, and regulatory circles.

2. Part I – Offshore Energy: Fostering Environmental Stewardship and Community Collaboration

Part I of *Offshore Energy Law* provides an intricate analysis of the role of legal instruments in ensuring the environmentally sustainable development of offshore energy resources and in integrating the interests of offshore energy workers and energy communities.

In the case of environmental protection and the interaction between marine spaces and the rapid development of energy infrastructure, several chapters in Part I emphasise the importance of protecting the marine environment while also highlighting the suite of regulatory options to ensure the sustainability of our oceans. Additionally, Part I raises questions about the climate compatibility and greenhouse gas emissions associated with future offshore energy licences, both for hydrocarbons and renewable projects.

The Blue Economy[1] is intricately linked to the broader goals of sustainable development, which integrate not only economic but also environmental and social considerations, both of which are discussed in Part I of this book.[2] Its development and promotion, including the offshore energy expansion, bring about challenges that in our view require further research to develop better practices and balancing tools between economic, social, and environmental considerations, as we discuss below.

The Blue Economy reflects an attempt to align economic pursuits with ecological limits, a key theme of the United Nations Sustainable Development Goals (SDGs), particularly SDG 14, which seeks to 'conserve and sustainably use the oceans, seas, and marine resources'.[3] Energy exploitation is one of its pillars. Nonetheless, the tension

[1] World Bank, 'What is the Blue Economy' (2017), www.worldbank.org/en/news/infographic/2017/06/06/blue-economy. This concept has been understood as supporting the harnessing of ocean resources to drive economic growth, enhance livelihoods, and foster ocean health. It encompasses activities such as fisheries, marine transport, offshore renewable energy, and tourism, with a growing emphasis on sustainability. At the heart of the Blue Economy is the dual objective of promoting economic development whilst ensuring the long-term health of ocean ecosystems. For some general discussions on the topic, see: Simone Smith-Godfrey, 'Defining the blue economy' (2016) 12(1) *Maritime Affairs: Journal of the National Maritime Foundation of India* 58–64; Gunter A Pauli, *The blue economy: 10 years, 100 innovations, 100 million jobs* (Paradigm Publications, 2010).

[2] See United Nations Environment Programme (UNEP), Blue Economy Concept Paper (2016) www.unep.org.

[3] United Nations, Sustainable Development Goal 14: Life Below Water (United Nations, 2024) sdgs.un.org/goals/goal14.

between maximising economic output from marine sectors and safeguarding marine biodiversity often complicates offshore energy policymaking.[4] The complex balance between maximising the utilisation of ocean resources and environmental preservation is largely influenced by various issues, including political and economic pressures. This challenge is particularly acute in developing countries where economic needs are pressing, and the regulatory capacity to enforce environmental protections is limited.[5] Offshore energy developments are no exception, as discussed in this part of the *Offshore Energy Law*.

Part I probes the Blue Energy Economy within the context of the energy transition, analysing both renewables and hydrocarbon activities. This discussion is particularly relevant because it debunks the false assumption that the ocean has unlimited space for offshore energy development, and demonstrates the complex interaction with other sea uses.[6] This complexity serves as a formidable testing ground for the role of law and regulatory institutions. The chapters within Part I are theoretically framed within the confines of both the energy trilemma and the quadrilemma,[7] thus seeking the balance of economic, environmental, and social dimensions in developing and maximising offshore energy resources. For example, offshore renewable energy, particularly wind and tidal energy, is often cited as a critical pillar of the Blue Energy Economy, providing a sustainable alternative to fossil fuels.[8] Offshore wind farms have the potential to significantly reduce greenhouse gas emissions and contribute to energy security.[9] However, the installation and operation of these facilities can also disrupt marine habitats, specifically if sited in ecologically sensitive areas.

Closely linked with a need to develop further research and policy strategies in relation to the Blue Energy Economy, we observed how important environmental and industrial policy tools have been developed and evolved. A notable example are maritime or marine spatial planning frameworks (MSP), seeking to find ex ante solutions for spatial and user-related conflicts at sea.[10] MSP aims to allocate ocean space to various activities and users based on an ecosystem-based approach to minimise environmental impacts and reduce stakeholder conflicts.[11] An example is the co-location of activities, as discussed in this book, or requiring nature-positive solutions – a concept yet to be fully developed – when new offshore projects are licensed.[12] However, effective

[4] ibid.

[5] World Bank, The Potential of the Blue Economy (2017), https://openknowledge.worldbank.org.

[6] See also the following discussion of this issue of 'fight for ocean space' in light of energy and non-energy-related activities: Abdullah Al Arif and Ignacio Herrera Anchustegui, 'Regulatory and Policy Frameworks for Offshore Wind Projects: Spatial and Temporal Considerations in Light of Fisheries Sustainability amid Climate Change' (2022) 20(5) *Oil, Gas & Energy Law*.

[7] Abdul Ghani Olabi, 'Energy quadrilemma and the future of renewable energy' (2016) 108 *Energy* 1–6.

[8] World Bank (n 5) 25.

[9] World Bank (n 5) 27.

[10] See United Nations Educational, Scientific and Cultural Organization (UNESCO), 'Marine Spatial Planning: A Step-by-Step Approach toward Ecosystem-Based Management' (2009); Madeline Taylor and Riley Taylor, 'Planning for Offshore Wind Energy: The Case for Marine Spatial Planning in Australia' (2022) *Oil, Gas & Energy Law* 1– 23; Madeline Taylor, 'Marine Spatial Planning and Offshore Wind: Preliminary Principles for Australia' (2023) 11 *Renewable Energy Law and Policy Review* 48.

[11] Helsinki Convention, 'Towards an Ecosystem Approach to the Management of Human Activities' (26 June 2003).

[12] Norsk institutt for vannforskning (NIVA), 'We need a better definition of nature positivity' (5 January 2024) www.niva.no/en/news/we-need-a-better-definition-of-nature-positivity.

implementation of MSP requires robust scientific data, transparent governance, and the active involvement of all stakeholders, which remains a challenge in many parts of the world.

A new trend that we expect to see more of in the future is the expansion of offshore energy and mining activities in areas beyond national jurisdiction (ABNJ), that is, the High Seas.[13] These are true uncharted waters and areas of the seabed where both the exploitation of natural resources and the protection of the marine environment remain relatively less regulated. The focus of these legal discussions has been placed on ideas such as the principle of freedom of the seas or that these resources belong to mankind,[14] rather than on developing robust and well-balanced regulatory frameworks related to energy and mining-related activities.

The tides are turning. Developments regarding the regulatory framework in public international law are happening to protect the marine environment and allow for the exploration and exploitation of minerals in the Area. In the case of environmental protection, the adoption on 19 June 2023 of the Agreement under the United Nations Convention on the Law of the Sea on the Conservation and Sustainable Use of Marine Biological Diversity of Areas beyond National Jurisdiction (BBNJ Agreement) represents a pivotal development.[15] The BBNJ Agreement creates a framework that addresses the sustainable use of marine biological diversity in ABNJs, with a particular focus on the conservation of marine genetic resources, area-based management tools (including marine protected areas), environmental impact assessments, and capacity-building for developing states. A central component of the BBNJ Agreement is the establishment of marine protected areas (MPAs) in ABNJs, which would create legally binding conservation zones where human activities are restricted or prohibited in order to protect vulnerable ecosystems. While the objective is to ensure that conservational measures are effectively implemented across different marine sectors, the extent to which the BBNJ will affect the development of offshore energy resources remains unclear.[16]

In the case of deep seabed mining, offshore oil and gas, or even offshore wind activity in ABNJ or extended continental shelves, the discussion is focused on the role of the International Seabed Authority (ISA). The ISA is established under UNCLOS and is responsible for regulating mineral-related activities in the deep seabed, ensuring that such activities are carried out in a way that minimises harm to the marine environment.[17] In particular, controversy exists concerning deep seabed mining and the approval of rules for the commercial exploitation of marine minerals in the Area. In August 2024,

[13] Paul Elsner and Suzette Suarez, 'Renewable energy from the high seas: Geo-spatial modelling of resource potential and legal implications for developing offshore wind projects beyond the national jurisdiction of coastal States' (2019) 128 *Energy Policy* 919–29; Ignacio Herrera Anchustegui and Violeta S Radovich, 'Wind energy on the high seas: Regulatory challenges for a science fiction future' (2022) 15(23) *Energies* 9157; Anna Zalik, 'World-making and the deep seabed: mining the Area beyond national jurisdiction' in Matthew Himley, Elizabeth Havice and Gabriela Valdivia (eds), *The Routledge Handbook of Critical Resource Geography* (Routledge, 2022) 412–24.

[14] International Maritime Organization (IMO), 'IMO and the Law of the Sea' (2018).

[15] In October 2024, the BBNJ has 104 signatory states but only 13 parties: treaties.un.org/Pages/ViewDetails.aspx?src=TREATY&mtdsg_no=XXI-10&chapter=21&clang=_en.

[16] See International Seabed Authority (ISA), Regulations on Prospecting and Exploration for Polymetallic Nodules in the Area.

[17] ibid.

at its Assembly meeting, it was concluded that there was no consensus for the approval of rules for the exploitation of marine minerals, with 32 States calling for a precautionary pause or moratorium for exploitation activities.[18] We anticipate developments and tension in ABNJ as technology advances and the race for rare minerals needed for the energy transition, inserting further ashore the energy discussion in Public International Law and Law of the Sea circles.

Shifting to offshore energy and community collaboration, contributions in *Offshore Energy Law* examine varied socio-legal pathways across multiple jurisdictions in the three key industries at the heart of offshore decarbonisation: oil and gas, offshore wind, and critical minerals. In doing so, this book has made significant contributions to the literature and the growing corpus of research, such as mapping socio-legal approaches across multiple offshore sectors by crafting a tripartite of future-focused solutions moving beyond the contested goal of a Social Licence to Operate, and towards the more nuanced multifaceted concept of striking a Social Contract. A Social Contract requires sustained relationships, not only between energy proponents and communities, but between regulators, energy developers, and communities striving for co-beneficial collaboration.

Concerning these socio-legal considerations, the contributions introduce a renewed multidimensional application of social gap assessments for offshore wind development. Second, it surveys the increasing need to recognise seabed rights for communities in the context of offshore critical minerals mining. Finally, it presents new conceptualisations of strategic local content provisions for traditional and renewable offshore energy operations. In sum, this 'Triple S' framework of inquiry (social gaps, seabed rights, strategic local content requirements) featured in Part I may serve as a foundation for innovative legal reform, nuanced collaboration, and a sustained social contractual nexus between developers, the State, and communities. Each pillar of the 'Triple S' social framework is examined in turn.

Mapping social gaps as a key measure to first understanding social risks and requirements of a community prior to proposed project consultation and relevant impact assessments, for example, within Environmental Impact Assessments, is proposed in Part I of the book. Several chapters within the *Offshore Energy Law* book project examine project-level Environmental Impact Assessments often entailing community economic incentives. The traditional Environmental Impact Assessment 'catch all' approach to authorising offshore energy activities without effective engagement with social issues may create distinct litigation risks.

For example, in the USA, litigation against the state of New Jersey to overturn a recent approval for the South Fork Wind and Revolution Wind projects rests on social impact arguments of the 'severe and long-lasting effects on the character, community, and heritage-tourism-driven economy'.[19] In Ireland, an emerging offshore wind

[18] International Seabed Authority, 'The 29th Session of the International Seabed Authority – Daily Journals of the Assembly' (29 July to 2 August 2024), www.isa.org.jm/sessions/29th-session-2024/. See also Deep Sea Conservation Coalition, 'Pivotal shift at the ISA: Nations rally for deep-sea mining moratorium' (3 August 2024), deep-sea-conservation.org/pivotal-shift-at-the-isa-nations-rally-for-deep-sea-mining-moratorium/.

[19] Cultural Heritage Partners, Southeast Lighthouse Foundation vs US Department of the Interior and Bureau of Ocean Energy Management (2023), www.culturalheritagepartners.com/wp-content/uploads/2023/11/South-Fork-SELF-Filed.pdf.

jurisdiction, judicial reviews were launched by fishers challenging the 834 MW Dublin Array Offshore Wind project.[20] Evidence increasingly suggests that the lack of effective community engagement creates commercial litigation vulnerabilities. To address these rising social impact risks, social gaps offer the opportunity to develop more robust Social Impact Assessments of both mature and emerging offshore petroleum and renewable energy developments.[21]

In our view, the social gaps method produces a social baseline study of subject communities to address democratic deficits, legal conditions, and place protections. A crucial aspect of any public resource and energy system is minimising competition and conflict with communities while recognising place-based impacts and allocating and developing resources in the public interest. Despite this, there is currently no global or country-level social gaps policy for offshore wind. We envisage social gap policies as a key social risk mitigation tool, drawing on the traditional petroleum risk regulatory principle of reducing social risks As Far As Reasonably Practicable.

Seabed rights are a critical 'hotbed' of policy and regulatory analysis within Part I of *Offshore Energy Law*.[22] Inverting the state-based principle of Natural Resource Sovereignty,[23] an evident trend is emerging for people-based community sovereignty over natural resources, particularly in the context of First Nations communities.[24] People-based community sovereignty advances a challenge to the doctrine of permanent sovereignty to enable more explicit dissemination of rights to derive income from the sale of access to natural resources.

As previously discussed, marine minerals within and outside ABNJ will play a critical role in the energy transition. However, an aspect often overlooked in the seabed mining discussion is the interaction with coastal communities. In our view, frontier offshore minerals development will require critical engagement with communities, and potentially usher in a new era of community engagement.[25] While research on coastal communities' participation and/or benefits, or compensation awarded to different affected sea users or coastal neighbours by offshore developments exists,[26] less attention is paid to Indigenous rights and their interaction with offshore energy. In this

[20] Breaking News, 'Court asked to quash licence for investigating offshore site for proposed wind farm' (2023), www.breakingnews.ie/ireland/court-asked-to-quash-licence-for-investigating-offshore-site-for-proposed-wind-farm-1474967.html.

[21] As examined in ch 6 of this volume, Madeline Taylor, 'Beyond Social Licence to Operate: Charting "Social Gaps" and the Social Contract in the Emerging Australian Offshore Wind Sector'.

[22] As examined in ch 4 of this volume, Solomon Obulor, Joy Debski and Nnenaya Nwali, 'Avoiding (Offshore) Renewable and Critical Mineral-Based Resource Curse in Africa: The Role of Continent-wide Legal Regime'.

[23] United Nations General Assembly, resolution 1803 (XVII), 'Permanent sovereignty over natural resources' (14 December 1962).

[24] Temitope Tunbi Onifade, 'Peoples-Based Permanent Sovereignty over Natural Resources: Toward Functional Distributive Justice?' (2015) 16 *Human Rights Review* 343–68.

[25] Becky Hitchin et al, 'Thresholds in deep-seabed mining: A primer for their development' (2023) 149 *Marine Policy* 105505.

[26] See eg David Rudolph, Claire Haggett, and Mhairi Aitken, 'Community benefits from offshore renewables: The relationship between different understandings of impact, community, and benefit' (2018) 36(1) *Environment and Planning C: Politics and Space* 92–117; Ignacio Herrera Anchustegui, 'Distributive Justice, Community Benefits and Renewable Energy: Offshore Wind Projects' in Ruven Fleming, Kaisa Huhta and Leonie Reins (eds), *Sustainable Energy Democracy and the Law* (Brill Nijhoff, 2021) 214–39; Michelle Voyer and Judith van Leeuwen, '"Social license to operate" in the Blue Economy' (2019) 62 *Resources Policy* 102–13.

sense, the understanding of seabed rights forming a part of First Nations arguments for non-exclusive control and elevated compensation will likely emerge as a fundamental challenge to Westphalian notions of renewable and non-renewable offshore energy and minerals development.[27] Such arguments are emerging in Norway, the US, Canada, and Australia amongst others, steeped in the duty to respect the rights of Indigenous peoples and Free, Prior, and Informed Consent of First Nations communities.[28]

Regulators are facing increasing claims over Sea Country and Indigenous rights, where First Nations communities in Commonwealth legal states assert rights over sea spaces subject to offshore energy exploitation. For example, The Humchitt Nation in British Columbia, Canada, sought direction from the International Maritime Organization to advocate for a reform of Canada's Marine Liability Act to recognise cultural losses following the Nathan E Stewart oil spill in 2016.[29] The trend of Indigenous recognition, economic compensation, and social benefits – such as local content and community-ownership vehicles – are likely to increase, particularly in emerging offshore wind jurisdictions such as Australia, Norway, New Zealand, and Canada. Earning a Cultural Licence to Operate is forecasted to be a critical enabler or hindrance to the offshore energy transition.[30]

Another important element of the socio-legal discussion that is gaining traction is connected to the health and safety of offshore energy workers. While offshore wind energy is largely an environmentally friendly alternative to fossil fuels, the construction, maintenance, and decommissioning of wind parks and turbines raise health and safety issues.[31] These risks are linked to the remoteness of the offshore environment and the shortage of skilled workers. With an expected increase in workers owing to the industry's growth, these health and safety concerns are likely to remain and could potentially increase. The role of law will increasingly be tested as lives are at stake. Regulatory strategies for mitigating these risks will need to be evaluated, and there is justification for drawing on experience from highly developed and analogous industries such as offshore oil and gas,[32] as discussed in Part I of *Offshore Energy Law*. For example, the safety case regime used in the United Kingdom is adjudged as the most sophisticated health and safety regulatory strategy for mitigating risks in the offshore oil and gas industry.[33] Such a regime was adopted in the aftermath of the Piper Alpha disaster, which saw the death of 167 men, and created enhanced risk assessment measures.[34]

[27] Chris Armstrong, 'Against "permanent sovereignty" over natural resources (2015) 15(2) *Politics, Philosophy, and Economics* 129–51.

[28] United Nations General Assembly, United Nations Declaration on the Rights of Indigenous Peoples, G.A. Res. 61/295, U.N. Doc. A/RES/61/295 (13 September 2007), Article 19.

[29] 'Frustrated with Canada's spill response, Heiltsuk leaders take their fight international' (*The Narwhal*, 2024) thenarwhal.ca/heiltsuk-nation-international-marine-organization/.

[30] Blue Economy CRC, Cultural Licence to Operate in the Blue Economy (2024) blueeconomycrc.com.au/wp-content/uploads/2024/05/BECRC_CLTO-Report_A4_S_e290524.pdf.

[31] David Rowell, David McMillan and James Carroll, 'Offshore Wind H&S: A Review and Analysis' (2024) 189 *Renewable and Sustainable Energy Reviews* 113928.

[32] Eddy Wifa and Tina Soliman Hunter, 'Mitigating Occupational Health and Safety Risks in the Proposed Australian Offshore Wind Energy Industry: Lessons from the Safety Case Regime' (2021) 40(1) *Journal of Energy and Natural Resources Law* 83.

[33] Eddy Wifa, 'The Offshore Oil and Gas Safety Case Regulatory Model: Is it Worth the Hype?' (2018) 36(6) *International Energy Law Review* 206.

[34] ibid 206.

Will offshore wind adopt similar health and safety standards or will the development move towards a lighter and less stringent regime that sees the industry as implying minor risks?

To finalise these reflections connected to *Offshore Energy: Fostering Environmental Stewardship and Community Collaboration*, we would like to stress that the challenge of offshore decarbonisation involves market institutions, marine spaces and their protection, regulators, energy proponents, and communities. The dilemma ahead is how to embed justice principles within socio-legal frameworks and physical energy assets across the supply chain. The Social Licence to Operate, once focused on voluntary commitments by energy proponents, is evolving to integrate legal principles steeped in the Social Contract that support communities as active participants and resources.[35] These community resources are crucial in shaping the design, development, and operation of energy projects.

The Triple S framework principles – social gaps, seabed rights, and local content provisioning – proposed in *Offshore Energy Law* are central for connecting community participation through holistic impact assessments, ownership opportunities, and local content provisions. Key questions for future research include: In which way will environmental protection tools be adopted and applied by States and non-State actors amidst the rapid surge of offshore energy developments? Is Public International Law prepared for the challenge of offshore energy exploitation in ABNJ? How should participatory processes for social gap mapping be designed? How can a rapid yet justice-driven offshore energy transition be crafted, inclusive of seabed rights? Lastly, how can energy policy and regulation better safeguard and promote the co-design of strategic local content provisioning with communities? Part I of *Offshore Energy Law* starts to address these crucial challenges, offering timely and inclusive perspectives on the future of offshore energy development.

3. Part II – Offshore Energy: Business and Financing

The offshore energy sector is undergoing a significant transformation, driven by the global shift towards cleaner energy sources and the need to balance economic development with environmental sustainability. Exploring the complex interplay between international, regional, and domestic governance frameworks, financing trends, and innovative financial and tax-project structures provides valuable insights into the challenges and opportunities that traditional hydrocarbon and emerging renewable offshore energy projects face. The intricate balance between global climate and environmental commitments of both State and non-state actors and national economic priorities emerge as a central theme, underscoring the need for ongoing diplomatic negotiation, regulatory harmonisation, and strategic international cooperation when developing

[35] Madeline Taylor, 'The Power of Energy Justice for Rural Communities' in Raphael Heffron and Louis de Fontenelle (eds), *The Power of Energy Justice and the Social Contract* (Palgrave Macmillan, 2024) 129–35. Tomas Moe Skjølsvold et al, 'Conditions for just offshore wind energy: Addressing the societal challenges of the North Sea wind industry' (2024) 107 *Energy Research and Social Science* 103334.

financial frameworks and market conditions. The contributions to Part II of *Offshore Energy Law* emphasise the need for adaptive governance structures that can keep pace with the rapid evolution of offshore energy technologies and market dynamics to develop financially secure and commercially robust projects. Flexibility in regulatory approaches, combined with clear, long-term policy signals, will be crucial for creating an environment conducive to investment and sustainable development.

The offshore energy sector represents one of the most capital-intensive industries in the world, comprising both traditional hydrocarbons and emerging renewable energy sources, such as offshore wind.[36] As governments and businesses shift towards a cleaner energy future, substantial investments are needed to maintain and upgrade infrastructure while simultaneously developing innovative financing mechanisms that support both fossil fuel and renewable energy projects.[37] The transition to a low-carbon economy, reinforced by international climate goals, demands a multi-faceted approach to financing and business development in offshore energy.[38]

This financing challenge is compounded by geopolitical and market volatility, regulatory developments, and technological advancements.[39] For instance, the global energy demand is projected to rise by 25 per cent by 2040, requiring substantial investments in offshore energy infrastructure.[40] Estimates suggest that the energy transition could require $4.6 trillion in annual investments by 2030 to achieve global climate goals. At the same time, the offshore energy sector must adapt to risks and uncertainties related to commodity prices, regulatory changes, and environmental concerns.[41]

Part II of this book underscores the critical role of innovative financing mechanisms, financial and tax incentives, and risk mitigation strategies in unlocking the full potential of offshore energy. In the case of hydrocarbons, there are decades of experience concerning various business models and financial arrangements all over the world. Offshore oil and gas remain a critical component of the global energy mix, particularly for countries with significant reserves in deep and ultra-deep waters, such as Brazil, Norway, and the United States.[42] Historically, the financing of offshore hydrocarbon projects has relied heavily on a combination of equity, debt financing, and government subsidies.[43] Oil and gas companies often utilise project financing, a method where loans are secured by the future cash flows of the project itself rather than the currently existing assets of the company. This allows for risk mitigation and limits the financial exposure of the parent company.[44] Large multinational oil and gas companies typically secure financing through syndicated loans from a consortium of banks and financial institutions.[45] This model reduces the financial risks associated with the high upfront exploration

[36] International Energy Agency (IEA), World Energy Investment 2021 (2021) 14.
[37] ibid.
[38] David L McCallum, 'Financing Offshore Oil Projects: Trends and Challenges' (2020) 45 *Oil & Gas Financial Review* 89, 93.
[39] International Energy Agency (IEA), World Energy Investment 2021 (2021) 25.
[40] ibid 29.
[41] Paris Agreement to the United Nations Framework Convention on Climate Change, opened for signature Apr. 22 April, 2016, T.I.A.S. No. 16-1104.
[42] McCallum (n 38) 89.
[43] ibid.
[44] ibid.
[45] International Energy Agency (IEA), World Energy Investment 2021 (2021) 37.

and production costs. However, project delays, cost overruns, and fluctuating oil prices pose ongoing risks to profitability, which financial institutions consider when structuring loans.[46] As decarbonisation efforts gain momentum by state and non-state actors, a financial shift towards offshore energy markets is increasingly evident. This shift has accelerated as traditional lenders, such as banks and institutional investors, face growing pressure to divest from fossil fuel projects in favour of green financing.

Technological development and the reduction of costs in offshore energy renewables due to economies of scale, technological development, and experience create the foundation for large-scale deployment of offshore wind projects worldwide.[47] Like offshore oil and gas, offshore renewable energy projects have the potential to act as a catalyst for wider economic development, particularly in coastal regions of developing countries. By fostering local industry, creating skilled jobs, and providing clean, reliable energy, offshore wind projects can contribute to sustainable economic growth and improved energy access. However, realising these benefits requires careful planning, stakeholder engagement, and a long-term commitment to capacity building and infrastructure development.

Enhancing local content provisions is a prevailing theme related to both oil and gas and renewable offshore energy policies.[48] As discussed in Part II, workforce development is emerging as an essential regulatory component to secure financing and for the grant of licences and leases for both offshore petroleum and renewables.[49] Developing value chains through local content strategies for offshore oil and gas, such as employment quotas or training programmes, are or were found in Northern Europe, China, India, Nigeria, Angola, and Latin America, to name a few.[50] The IEA recently emphasised the importance of governments forming strategic partnerships, such as those between the US and Japan, the EU and the Democratic Republic of Congo, and the UK and Zambia.[51]

However, commercial tensions constituting potentially discriminatory trade practices and providing a just transition for existing exiting carbon-intensive offshore energy labour forces will remain a complex legal balance to strike. The EU has brought a WTO dispute settlement request for consultation[52] against Taiwan's offshore wind local content[53] requirement of at least 60 per cent of offshore wind farm components

[46] ibid.

[47] Ignacio Herrera Anchustegui and Tina Soliman Hunter, 'Geographical, technological, and legal perspectives of offshore wind energy' in Ignacio Herrera Anchustegui and Tina Soliman Hunter (eds), *Offshore Wind Licensing* (Edward Elgar Publishing, 2024).

[48] As examined in ch 10 of this volume, Elena I Athwal, Eduardo G Pereira, Opeyemi Omotuyi and Ignacio Herrera Anchustegui, 'Building Local Capacity and Expertise via Local Content Rules and Transferring Skills and Knowledge between Offshore Developments'.

[49] Tyler Hansen, 'Five grand challenges of offshore wind financing in the United States' (2024) 107 *Energy Research and Social Science* 103329.

[50] As examined in ch 10 of this volume (n 48).

[51] International Energy Agency (IEA), Can government partnerships support responsible and reliable critical mineral supply chains? (2024) www.iea.org/commentaries/can-government-partnerships-support-responsible-and-reliable-critical-mineral-supply-chains.

[52] World Trade Organization, General Agreement on Tariffs and Trade (GATT), Agreement on Trade-Related Investment Measures (TRIMs) and General Agreement on Trade in Services (GATS).

[53] World Trade Organization, Chinese Taipei Measure Relating to Investments in Offshore Wind Installations (2024), docs.wto.org/dol2fe/Pages/SS/directdoc.aspx?filename=q:/WT/DS/625-1.pdf&Open=True.

to be procured locally to participate in offshore wind auctions.[54] Such a move signals a new era in balancing international commercial obligations, trade agreements, and local content mechanisms in offshore decarbonisation projects.

While still novel, the financing of offshore wind projects has evolved significantly in recent years.[55] Whereas early projects were often financed by utilities or government support schemes, the growing commercial viability of offshore wind has attracted a diverse range of investors.[56] Debt financing, green bonds, and public-private partnerships have become critical tools in mobilising the necessary capital for these large-scale projects. Additionally, project financing, similar to that used in the oil and gas sector, is often employed in offshore wind to mitigate risks for developers and investors.[57]

Contributions to Part II of the *Offshore Energy Law* stress synergies and lessons to be learned from the oil and gas industry to these new renewable energy projects. By adapting and tailoring successful models concerning project financing, symbiotic partnership structures, state-led financial incentives, taxation mechanisms, and licensing schemes, the offshore renewable sector may overcome the significant capital barriers and operational challenges it faces. This financial evolution and learning process is crucial for accelerating the deployment of offshore energy technology and achieving the scale necessary to make a meaningful impact on global energy systems and help promote decarbonisation.

One area for further research is the implications and effects of responsible or impact investing principles, also known as Environmental, Social, and Governance (ESG) investment considerations.[58] Green bonds, which are financial instruments issued to raise capital for projects supporting environmental objectives, have gained traction as a tool to finance offshore wind, solar, and other renewable energy projects. In 2021 alone, global green bond issuance reached over $500 billion, marking a significant shift in how energy projects are financed.[59]

Offshore energy companies are increasingly turning to green bonds to attract ESG-focused investors who prioritise sustainability and social responsibility.[60] For instance, Ørsted, a global leader in offshore wind development, issued $1.4 billion in green bonds to finance the construction of new wind farms in Europe. Similarly, TotalEnergies has leveraged green bonds to finance its transition from being an oil major to a broader energy company with a growing renewable portfolio.[61]

The growth of ESG investments is also shaping the strategies of traditional oil and gas companies, many of which are diversifying their energy portfolios.[62] Companies like BP, Equinor, and Shell have announced significant investments in renewable energy

[54] European Commission, 'EU challenges Taiwan's discriminatory rules on offshore wind projects' (2024), policy.trade.ec.europa.eu/news/eu-challenges-taiwans-discriminatory-rules-offshore-wind-projects-2024-07-26_en.

[55] International Renewable Energy Agency (IRENA), Offshore Wind Outlook (2020) 27.

[56] ibid 29.

[57] International Renewable Energy Agency (IRENA), Offshore Wind Outlook (2020) 30.

[58] Climate Bonds Initiative, 2021 Green Bond Market Summary (2022), www.climatebonds.net.

[59] ibid.

[60] Ørsted, Annual Report 2020 (2020) 34.

[61] TotalEnergies, 2020 Sustainability Report (2020) 15.

[62] BP, Annual Report and Form 20-F 2020, (2020) 12.

supported, in part, by green bond issuances and ESG-linked loans. These financial tools allow companies to raise capital while demonstrating their commitment to sustainability goals.[63]

Another area ripe for further research to further develop offshore energy financial governance frameworks is that of private equity and venture capital. These financial avenues have also played a critical role in developing offshore energy projects, particularly in the offshore renewable energy sector.[64] With their ability to provide large amounts of capital and take on higher risks, private equity firms have increasingly invested in offshore wind projects. For instance, Blackstone and Global Infrastructure Partners have invested billions in offshore wind farms in Europe and the United States.[65] Conversely, venture capital has been instrumental in driving innovation within the offshore energy sector, particularly in developing new technologies.[66] Emerging start-ups in offshore wind, wave, and tidal energy are receiving significant venture capital funding, which is essential for scaling up innovative solutions and bringing them to the market.

In the interaction between offshore hydrocarbons and offshore renewable projects, one of the most promising avenues for financing the offshore energy transition is the strategic use of revenues derived from oil and gas activities. As discussed above, major oil and gas companies have started allocating a portion of their capital expenditure towards offshore wind, solar, hydrogen production, and carbon capture, utilisation, and storage (CCUS) technologies.[67] More often than not, this is voluntary. However, European Union legislators are requiring companies involved in the extraction of hydrocarbons to contribute to the European Union-wide target for available CO_2 injection capacity as part of the EU Net Zero Industry Act.[68]

By redirecting revenues from oil and gas operations, these companies can finance renewable projects that support global decarbonisation goals while mitigating the financial risks associated with the long-term decline in demand for fossil fuels. This also permits offshore petroleum proponents to lower their respective carbon footprints and develop coupled energy solutions, such as offshore wind parks that power offshore oil and gas exploitation.[69] Lowering their carbon footprint is critical for climate mitigation and reporting requirements but also in connection to financial incentives. For example, the rise of carbon pricing schemes, also applicable to the offshore energy industry, incentivises operators to adopt cleaner technologies and reduce their carbon footprints. As nations and regions work towards achieving their carbon neutrality targets, carbon pricing mechanisms will continue to play a pivotal role in accelerating the offshore energy transition. Another key driver for these 'greener' investments by large offshore

[63] ibid.

[64] Blackstone, Annual Investment Report 2020 (2020) 22.

[65] Global Infrastructure Partners, Infrastructure Investment Strategy: Renewable Energy (2020) 7.

[66] International Energy Agency (IEA), World Energy Outlook 2021 (2021) 32.

[67] International Energy Agency (IEA), The Oil and Gas Industry in Energy Transitions – Analysis (20 January 2020).

[68] Regulation (EU) 2024/1735 on establishing a framework of measures for strengthening Europe's net-zero technology manufacturing ecosystem and amending Regulation (EU) 2018/1724 (2024), Article 23.

[69] The Hywind Tampen project in Norway, which has been operational since 2023, and the Green Volt wind park to be built in Scottish waters, licensed in 2024, are examples.

energy companies is the need to secure a 'licence to operate' in a world, as discussed above in Part I, where investors increasingly focus on ESG metrics.[70]

Government policies and subsidies are essential in incentivising offshore energy investments.[71] In the European Union, for example, the Renewable Energy Directive sets binding targets for renewable energy production, providing a stable regulatory framework encouraging private investments. Similarly, in the United States, tax credits, such as the Investment Tax Credit (ITC) and the Production Tax Credit (PTC), have been instrumental in catalyzing offshore wind development.[72] Although there are plenty of examples of national subsidies and policies to accelerate the offshore energy transition, setting up these incentives and fiscal schemes in a rapidly changing geopolitical world still presents challenges.

Ultimately, the future of offshore energy will depend on the ability of all stakeholders to collaborate in creating robust, flexible, and sustainable frameworks that can adapt to technological advancements, changing market dynamics, and evolving environmental imperatives. By addressing these challenges head-on and leveraging the opportunities presented by the offshore energy transition, there is significant potential to drive the global energy transition while fostering economic growth and energy security.

4. Part III – Offshore Energy: Complex Infrastructure and Overarching Conclusions

Part III of *Offshore Energy Law* delves into various infrastructural aspects, exploring how technological advancements, the combination of different energy solutions in the same project, and the concurrent utilisation of marine spaces challenge established regulatory frameworks. The contributions in this book showcase how the extensive deployment of new offshore infrastructure will be at the center of offshore energy law discussions. Most projects will involve some form of energy sector coupling and interact with and affect other sea uses and users. Co-existence, planning, and collaboration will be important variables in addition to the business and financial complexities covered in Part III of this book for a successful infrastructure rollout.

Size and volume are the main characteristics of energy infrastructure trends. The expansion of offshore energy is well underway, with a significant surge in the scale and number of infrastructure projects. According to DNV, offshore wind capacity alone is projected to reach a staggering 2,000 GW by 2050, a remarkable leap from the current 70 GW installed in 2024.[73] While much of this growth will occur in regions with existing activity and regulation (such as China, Europe, and North America), offshore wind is expected to become a global phenomenon. Other offshore renewable technologies are still at a nascent stage, as not all developments are only about bottom-fixed offshore

[70] Becca Hunziker, The role of oil and gas companies in the energy transition (Atlantic Council, 9 January 2020) www.atlanticcouncil.org/in-depth-research-reports/report/the-role-of-oil-and-gas-companies-in-the-energy-transition/.

[71] US Department of Energy, Offshore Wind Market Report 2021 Edition (2021) 16.

[72] US Department of Energy, Offshore Wind Market Report 2021 Edition (2021).

[73] DNV, Energy Transition Outlook (2023). 72.

wind. New technologies are being rolled out at different speeds. While hydrogen is expected to expand rapidly, other renewable offshore sources like floating solar panels, and tidal and power plants may enter the scene more slowly. Simultaneously, even if offshore oil and gas activities are expected to decline, this will not be until 2030.[74] Mature offshore energy provinces, like Norway and the UK, are adopting offshore energy transition strategies from oil and gas extraction to renewables deployment but show no sign of stopping new oil and gas licensing rounds. In contrast, new offshore oil and gas jurisdictions, like Guyana or Suriname, are just starting their offshore oil and gas adventure to develop their economy.[75] This massive expansion of offshore infrastructure in order to meet the world's energy demand will impact offshore and onshore spaces and stakeholders as electricity cables and pipelines transport energy to end consumers. Such substantial infrastructure developments necessitate robust regulatory frameworks. In the following paragraphs, we discuss several infrastructural trends that will delineate offshore energy regulatory developments and governance schemes.

As stressed by several chapters in *Offshore Energy Law*, offshore infrastructure is being planned and initiated by the energy transition, with the intention of maximising synergies between existing and future projects. This includes both coupling between hydrocarbons and renewables, such as electrifying oil and gas operations by cables onshore or wind parks offshore, as well as renewables-to-renewables integration, such as offshore green hydrogen production. The integration of different energy technologies into a single project is legally challenging as regulators grapple with defining the project's nature and identifying the applicable regime,[76] to name some unclear aspects. We foresee a need to develop integrated regulatory and governance approaches to integrated energy projects, in opposition to the current 'industrial silo' style of regulation that often deals with individual technologies.

Connected to this trend of combined energy solutions is an emphasis on optimising sea spaces to maximise the co-existence and co-location of different sea uses and activities, including nature-positive or nature-based solutions.[77] This trend is reversing as the legislative focus has been on preventing and minimising conflicts by separating activities or adopting compensation mechanisms for industries affected by energy developments, such as fisheries, maritime shipping, or tourism-related activities. For instance, Denmark and Norway have developed compensatory schemes for fishermen affected or displaced by offshore oil, gas, and wind activity.[78] Policies fostering co-location and coexistence between offshore industries are gaining momentum. In 2024, the Dutch Government organised a tender procedure to award licences for the IJmuiden Ver Wind Farm Sites Alpha and Beta, where one of the award criteria was

[74] ibid 87.

[75] IL Griffith, *Oil and Climate Change in the Guyana-Suriname Basin* (Taylor & Francis, 2024).

[76] Ignacio Herrera Anchustegui and Rudiger Tscherning, 'Offshore oil and gas infrastructure electrification and offshore wind: a legal exploration' (2024) 17 *The Journal of World Energy Law & Business* 35.

[77] JCF Pardo et al, 'A synthesis review of nature positive approaches and coexistence in the offshore wind industry' (2023) *ICES Journal of Marine Science*; EJ Rendle, EL Hunt and AWJ Bicknell, 'A three-step approach for co-locating nature-based solutions within offshore wind farms' (2023) 11 *Frontiers in Ecology and Evolution* 690382; S Fluharty et al, 'Opportunity between the turbines: Willingness-to-pay for co-location activities with an offshore wind farm' (2024) 28 *Aquaculture Economics & Management* 281.

[78] Herrera Anchustegui (n 26); Eirik Finserås and Sigrid Eskeland Schütz, 'Offshore wind licensing in Norway' in Herrera Anchustegui and Soliman Hunter (n 47); Birgitte E Olsen and Bent Ole G Mortensen, 'Offshore Wind Licensing in Denmark' in Herrera Anchustegui and Soliman Hunter (n 47).

to assess to which extent the project contributed to the 'ecosystem of the Dutch North Sea'.[79] In Norway, applicants for a licence for the offshore wind area Sørlige Nordsjø II must have a plan that facilitates good co-use and coexistence within the project area and with affected stakeholders.[80] However, most jurisdictions still lack developed regulatory schemes in this regard, with only a few examples being tested.[81] In the future, regulatory practices and instruments will be developed and also put to the test regarding the promotion of optimal space utilisation.

New and existing infrastructure projects will be subject to states' circularity, sustainability, and carbon intensity requirements.[82] In the case of offshore oil and gas, we anticipate that most future developments will be conditioned and subject to requirements related to reducing the project's carbon footprint. This could mean, for example, that new licences will be granted only if the project addresses Scope 1 and Scope 2 emissions, and may extend to requiring Scope 3 greenhouse gas emissions reporting. Examples could be requiring the project to be developed along with carbon capture or electrification solutions, and/or having the operator mitigate emissions occurring downstream in the value chain but associated with the oil and gas development. Judicial decisions, such as the two 2024 cases: *Finch v Surrey County Council and others* before the UK Supreme Court,[83] and *Greenpeace Nordic v The State of Norway* before the Oslo District Court, clearly point in this direction.[84]

In addition, decommissioning will become a central issue for existing and planned infrastructure. As offshore energy projects mature and reach the end of their life, the question arises of what to do with these structures and how to maximise their utility based on the waste hierarchy principle and policy objectives related to the repurposing and reutilising of materials. For example, Norway's 2024 tender requirements for Sørlige Nordsjø II and offshore wind areas stipulate that applicants must ensure that the

[79] This was explicitly mentioned in the Site Alpha licensing rounds, see: Regeling van de Minister voor Klimaat en Energie van 12 december 2023, nr. WJZ/ 41336172, houdende regels inzake de vergunningverlening kavel Alpha in windenergiegebied IJmuiden Ver, and Netherlands Enterprise Agency, Permits for wind farms at IJmuiden Ver Alpha and Beta (last reviewed 26 June 2024), english.rvo.nl/subsidies-financing/offshore-wind-energy/ijmuiden-ver.

[80] Norwegian Ministry of Energy, Annex 11 – Minimum requirements for sustainability and positive ripple effects for Sørlige Nordsjø II (17 October 2023) 2, www.regjeringen.no/no/tema/energi/landingssider/havvind/sorlige-nordsjo-ii/id2967231/.

[81] For example, see highlighting the legal gaps and different practices regarding fisheries activities in offshore wind areas in the North Sea, inter alia, PO Bonsu and others, 'Co-location of fisheries and offshore wind farms: Current practices and enabling conditions in the North Sea' (2024) 159 *Marine Policy* 105941; Al Arif and Herrera Anchustegui (n 6); H-S Tseng and S-M Kao, 'Conflicts between Fisheries and Offshore Wind Power in Taiwan: Legal and Administrative Prospects' (2022) 10 *Journal of Marine Science and Engineering* 1745.

[82] See the circularity and value retention requirements set by the Dutch Government in 2024 for the Site Alpha and Site Beta offshore wind areas. See Netherlands Enterprise Agency, Permits for wind farms at IJmuiden Ver Alpha and Beta (last reviewed 26 June 2024), english.rvo.nl/subsidies-financing/offshore-wind-energy/ijmuiden-ver. In Norway, requirements connected to the sustainability of the project such as climate footprint or a focus on recycling have been utilised for a competition to award project areas in Sørlige Nordsjø II and Utsira Nord as either minimum requirements to tender or part of the qualitative award criteria, respectively. On 20 March 2024, the consortium Ventyr SN II AS was awarded a project area to develop a project application and ultimately obtain a licence to operate the wind park. For more, see Norwegian Government, Announces the first competitions for offshore wind (29 March 2023), www.regjeringen.no/en/aktuelt/announces-the-first-competitions-for-offshore-wind/id2969473/.

[83] *R (on the application of Finch on behalf of the Weald Action Group) (Appellant) v Surrey County Council and others* [2024] UKSC 20.

[84] *Greenpeace Nordic v The State of Norway (represented by the Ministry of Petroleum and Energy)* Oslo District Court, Case No 23-099330TVI-TOSL/05, 18 January 2024.

'project contributes to a well-functioning waste management, with particular focus on recycling', especially regarding turbine blades, towers, foundations, cables, and substations, as well as the reuse of other elements or infrastructure belonging to the wind park.[85] More regulatory research should be conducted to promote better practices and a life-cycle approach to offshore decommissioning.

The construction of offshore energy facilities will have a significant onshore impact. As offshore renewable electricity generation increases, so will the expansion of the grid, both onshore and offshore, as well as the associated onshore infrastructure. The rapid development of port facilities, coastal infrastructure, onshore-offshore expertise, and downstream value chain providers will be necessary to meet the increased demand for constructing and servicing offshore projects. Land-sea interactions and governance frameworks related to land planning will be tested. Additionally, this onshore expansion is likely to trigger conflicts over property rights, as states may need to expropriate land or companies may acquire it to extend associated energy infrastructure.[86] This is already evident with the current onshore expansions and conflicts, for example, between agricultural landowners and renewable energy developers,[87] or the well-studied Not-In-My-Backyard effect. Furthermore, internal disputes between different state organs regarding decision-making powers are likely to arise. For example, while municipalities often have authority over onshore coastal areas or land planning, they tend to lack power over offshore developments or marina areas. At the same time, they will have different incentives, policy goals, and regulatory tools compared to national governments. Yet, both entities will likely have to approve different elements of a project that have implications both onshore and- offshore, creating a complex regulatory patchwork and approvals process.

Finally, the scale of offshore energy development will also create both opportunities and friction related to cross-border interactions, especially concerning new renewable energy projects. Offshore international collaboration is needed to coordinate and optimise international projects, as it is likely to, for instance, reduce project costs, facilitate permitting processes, and/or ensure several interconnections to more than one country to address intermittency issues. While there is existing experience with international oil and gas pipelines, we now see more ambitious collaboration projects regarding offshore renewables. Examples include the multi-state offshore wind farms Kriegers Flak in Denmark and Germany,[88] the proposed Latvian and Estonian Elwind,[89] and prospects for international offshore carbon capture between Norway and several Northern European states.[90] Offshore collaboration and coordination by coastal states related to

[85] Norwegian Ministry of Energy (n 80).

[86] Sandy Kerr, Kate Johnson and Jonathan Charles Side, 'Planning at the edge: Integrating across the land sea divide' (2014) 47 *Marine Policy* 118–25; Alberto Innocenti and Francesco Musco, 'Land–Sea Interactions: A Spatial Planning Perspective' (2023) 15(12) *Sustainability* 9446.

[87] Madeline Taylor, 'Planning the energy transition: a comparative examination of large-scale solar energy siting on agricultural land in Australia' (2022) 18(2) *Utrecht Law Review* 70–86.

[88] Vatenfall, Kriegers Flak, powerplants.vattenfall.com/kriegers-flak/.

[89] Elwind, Bring Baltic's wind together, elwindoffshore.eu/.

[90] Norwegian Government, 'Five northern European countries conclude international arrangements on transport and storage of carbon across borders' (18 April 2024) www.regjeringen.no/no/aktuelt/five-northern-european-countries-conclude-international-arrange-ments-on-transport-and-storage-of-carbon-across-borders/id3035286/.

infrastructure development in their marine-controlled environments, and even in areas beyond national jurisdictions, will be crucial to avoid duplication of efforts, reduce project costs, and mitigate adverse cross-border effects such as wind wakes.[91]

5. Final Words

Offshore Energy Law is a book about complex regulatory decisions with no easy shortcuts. As this book illustrates, the regulation of offshore energy matters stands at a critical juncture, given the important role that the marine environment and its resources have to play. Offshore energy will be paramount in the decades to come to help satisfy the world's energy needs as energy consumption increases, land spaces and land-based resources become scarce, and climate change challenges threaten our way of life. However, while clean energy technologies promise a bright and blue future, new and old offshore regulatory challenges must be tackled.

Rapid technological advancements have unlocked new offshore energy possibilities. Offshore wind turbines, hydrogen electrolysers, and, on a minor scale, pilot projects linked to tidal and wave convertors, and floating offshore solar technologies are being installed at lightning speed across the seas. However, the regulation of these new energy forms is sometimes non-existent, or if it does exist, it is much influenced by our experiences regarding oil and gas exploitation. Contributions to this book emphasise the need to adopt integrated, or at least compatible, regulatory schemes for offshore energy regulation covering renewable and non-renewable energy sources, as sector integration and technological interplay will be the norm rather than the exception.

An expansion in offshore energy activities will trigger new conflicts between energy stakeholders, other maritime and marine industries, citizens living on the coast, environmental organisations, and marine life. While this is already happening regarding offshore hydrocarbons, we expect the same to take place concerning offshore renewable energy sources. While these energy forms are perceived as more benign than offshore hydrocarbons, they have lower energy density and may occupy more extensive areas of marine space. As such, the competition for location and availability of marine resources will increase. This will likely lead to legal tensions and therefore increases the need to make policy choices when determining priorities related to sea use spaces, obligations related to protecting and conserving marine environments, and energy availability and affordability. Energy policy will be more closely linked to Maritime Spatial Planning as States seek to promote synergies between sea users and develop *ex-ante* rules to prevent or minimise conflicts between stakeholders. This offshore expansion of energy matters will give prominence to new energy justice discussions with a marine perspective.

Finally, the influence of climate change on the regulatory schemes and obligations of both states and companies will likely have the largest impact on delineating the future of offshore energy. With States committed to reaching climate targets, including carbon neutrality and carbon negative pledges, more robust requirements related

[91] Eirik Finserås et al, 'Gone with the wind? Wind farm-induced wakes and regulatory gaps' (2024) 159 *Marine Policy* 105897.

to sustainability, circularity, and climate mitigation and adaptation strategy will be imposed in offshore energy companies. Some of these will bring about opportunities for new business models associated with the energy transition, like carbon capture and deep seabed mining projects. At the same time, other regulatory interventions may mean the end of activities, in particular hydrocarbon exploitation. Along with already established litigation against states and companies related to climate obligation breaches, we expect to see a trend of litigation against states related to expropriation and compensation measures prompted by state climate policies that affect acquired commercial rights.

The challenges ahead will test the limits of regulation. While regulation does and will continue to play a significant role in mitigating offshore energy risks and balancing various interests, regulation is not without its limitations. Much reliance will be placed on a consensus amongst stakeholders at all levels to adopt a more collaborative approach. With the twin crisis of energy security and climate change, the pressures exerted by the political economy of speed must be minimised. Decisions on the development of offshore energy resources must be evidence-based and guided by robust regulatory approaches.

We hope that the contributions and insights presented in *Offshore Energy Law* will guide energy stakeholders in navigating the most effective regulatory and policy pathways for a sustainable and just offshore energy future.

INDEX

www.ingramcontent.com/pod-product-compliance
Ingram Content Group UK Ltd.
Pitfield, Milton Keynes, MK11 3LW, UK
UKHW020229290926
15470UKWH00002B/443

9 781509 964390